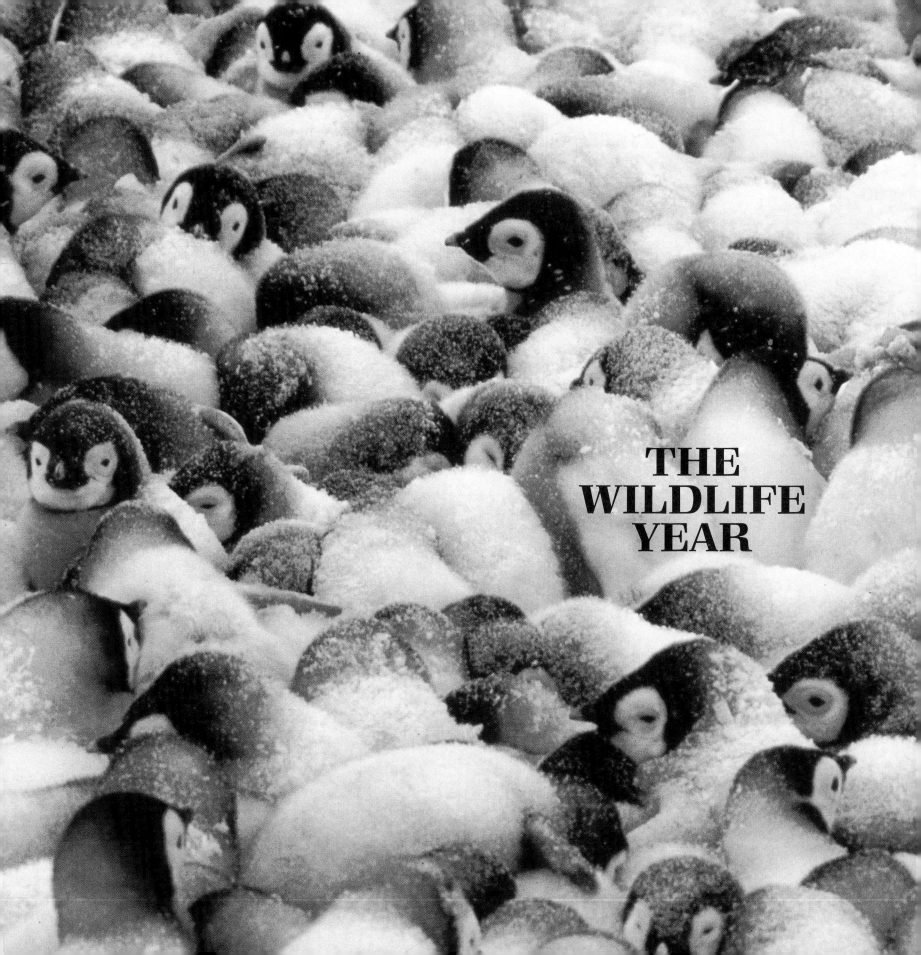

THE
WILDLIFE
YEAR

THE WILDLIFE YEAR was edited and designed by
The Reader's Digest Association Limited, London.

The credits and acknowledgments that appear on page 360 are hereby made a part of this copyright page.

ISBN 0-276-42012-8

Printed in the United States of America
1993

Wildebeests wait for the rains to
bring fresh grass to a dusty African plain.
Previous page: Emperor penguin chicks huddle together
for warmth in Antarctica.

READER'S DIGEST

THE WILDLIFE YEAR

Reader's
Digest

Published by The Reader's Digest Association Limited
LONDON · NEW YORK · SYDNEY · CAPE TOWN · MONTREAL

CONTENTS OF THE WILDLIFE YEAR

REGIONAL MAP: PAGES 8 AND 9

Peacock's feather

Bison grazing

Lioness and cubs

Emperor penguin and chick

Queen butterfly

Giant panda

Black-browed albatross

African elephants

THE WILDLIFE REGIONS

NINE VAST AREAS OF THE LAND AND OCEANS, EACH WITH A
FASCINATING RANGE OF ANIMALS AND PLANTS

Most stories in *The Wildlife Year* highlight an event in the yearly life cycle of an animal or plant – the birth of a whale, the mating of a dragonfly, young tigers on their first hunt – and each event is set in its appropriate month. Others tell of animals and plants such as desert flowers whose life cycles break the pattern of the seasons and do not fit into a yearly cycle.

Each story is also set in one of nine regions, with **The Arctic** and **Antarctica** – earth's great wastes of snow and ice – at the extremes. In the New World, **North America** stretches from the mossy tundra and vast coniferous forests of the frozen north to Mexico's arid, tropical, southern border. Between, the Rockies form a backbone, with prairies and forests to the east and the Pacific coast to the west. **Central and South America** is a region of superlatives – rolling, grassy plains, the rugged Andes mountains, the cold and wind-swept plateaus of Patagonia, and the Amazon basin with the world's largest tropical rain forest.

The Atlantic divides the New World from the Old World, where **Europe and North Asia** ranges from the coniferous forests of Scandinavia and Siberia in the north to the woods and mountains of southern Europe, and from the British Isles in the west to the islands of Japan in the far east. It includes Central Asia's mountains and steppes. **South Asia** takes in the Himalayas, the Tibetan Plateau, and the monsoon lands of India and South-east Asia. And splitting away along the cleft of the Red Sea is **Africa**, dominated in the north by the harsh Sahara. The eastern and southern grasslands, teeming with wildlife, include the Serengeti, and West and Central Africa have rain forests. Hawaii, in the **Pacific Islands**, has some unusual plant life. **Australasia**, a world apart, consists of Australia (with its unique pouched animals), New Zealand and New Guinea.

Polar bear

Bison

White-tip reef shark

NORTH AMERICA

CENTRAL AND SOUTH AMERICA

PACIFIC ISLANDS

Golden toad

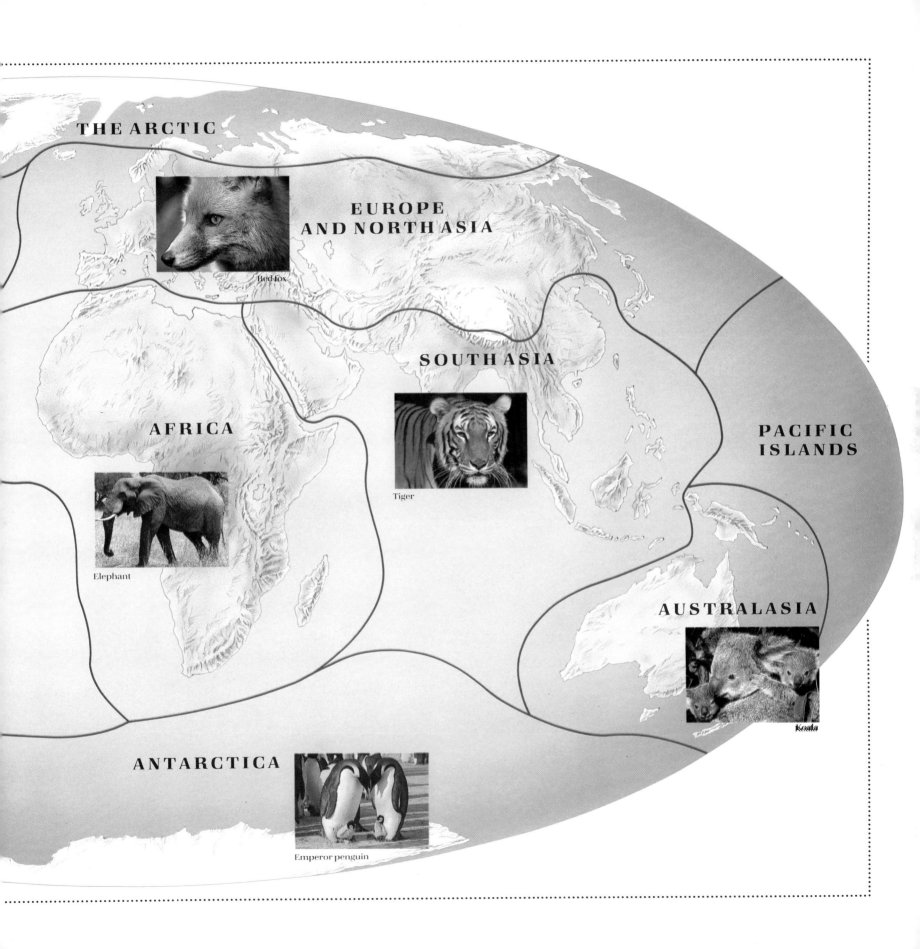

THE ARCTIC

EUROPE
AND NORTH ASIA

Red fox

SOUTH ASIA

AFRICA

Tiger

PACIFIC
ISLANDS

Elephant

AUSTRALASIA

Koala

ANTARCTICA

Emperor penguin

A lion cub naps at midday

....

CONTRIBUTORS

Consultant editor
Michael Bright, BSc

Contributors
Mark A Brazil, BA, PhD · Nicola Davies, MA
Robin Dunbar, BA, PhD · Jessica Holm, BSc, PhD
Tess Lemmon, BA, MPhil
Michael M Scott, BSc · Gerald L Wood

Consultants
E N Arnold, PhD · Brian Cogan, MSc
J J M Flegg, PhD · David George, PhD · J H W Gipps, PhD
Gordon Howes, BSc · Anthony R Martin, PhD
Chris Mead · Nigel Merrett, MSc
Peter D Moore, PhD · D J Siebert, PhD

Artists
Richard Bonson
Malcolm McGregor · Sandra Pond
Malcolm Porter

....

JANUARY

WHILE WINTER HOLDS THE NORTHERN HEMISPHERE IN ITS GRIP,
THE SOUTH BASKS IN THE HEAT OF SUMMER. THE ANTARCTIC'S BRIEF
BREEDING SEASON IS IN FULL SWING, AFRICAN WEAVER BIRDS ARE
KNOTTING THEIR NESTS AND AMAZON BUTTERFLIES SIP SALT AT LOW WATER

Africa: A hyena among the flamingos

Frozen wilderness *In the snow-covered Yellowstone National Park, a herd of stocky North American bison is drawn to the warmth of the hot springs.*

Where bison keep warm at steaming geysers

Few visitors see Yellowstone National Park on its Rocky Mountain plateau during January. This Wyoming wonderland the size of Corsica is closed from mid-November, when a blanket of snow about 18ft (5.5m) deep makes roads impassable. Only animals that can survive the icy, cruel winter are here now. Some have come from higher terrain to eke out a meagre existence. Others are avoiding the sub-zero temperatures by hibernating. The magnificent North American bison is an astute survivor, for it has learned to head for the year-round warmth of Yellowstone's unique Geyser Basin.

Life in the basin is sustained by the heat from molten matter deep down in the earth, below land that was once a vast and violent volcano with a crater 40 miles (64km) across. Now the energy bursts out at the surface through 200 geysers and 10,000 steaming hot-water springs and bubbling hot mud pools – one of the most spectacular sights in the world. The basin is like a gigantic hothouse, with a carpet of green sedges and grasses that provide sustenance for bison, moose and other grazers. Here, the air reeks of the rotten-egg odour of hydrogen sulphide, and of slowly cooking bison dung. When the vegetation in the basin is used up, the

unusual in the depths of winter, are swarms of tiny insects called brine flies. They live in a tight-rope world, having to balance precariously between the cold air that could freeze them and the hot water that could boil them alive. During their brief two-week adult life, they mate on cooler patches of algae and lay their conspicuous salmon-pink eggs there. Few nest robbers are at large in this place of extremes, save a tiny red mite that has exploited a vacant niche in the community, and feeds on the brine-fly eggs.

Away from the thermal springs, the January temperatures can drop to $-32°C$ $(-25°F)$. By this

Natural freezer *Coyotes find a constant supply of frozen meat from the casualties of winter, killed by the low temperatures and the scarcity of food.*

Winter refuge *Where there are hot springs, the bushes protrude above the blanket of snow, and moose come down from the mountains to browse.*

time, animals are hungry and exhausted, with their fat reserves and food stores getting low. It is the start of the 'winter-kill'. For the weak, the elderly and the infirm, death is not far away. But for coyotes this can be a time of plenty. Guided to dead or dying grazing animals by the noisy attentions of ravens, the coyotes put aside their constant territorial disputes and cooperate in hunting down weakened animals, or feed together on frozen carcasses.

Steam from the geysers coats the snow-laden trees with an icy glaze, but they do not freeze or die. Yellowstone's lodge-pole pines are resistant to cold. In the autumn, they produced their own natural antifreeze by reducing the water content of the pine needles and increasing the concentration of sugars in the sap.

Since the November freeze, Yellowstone's two species of bear, the grizzly and the black bear, have retreated from the world for about three or four months of hibernation in their dens, often under tangled tree roots on the higher slopes. Unlike other hibernating animals, a black bear does not lower its body temperature to match the surrounding air temperature, but maintains it to within a degree or two of normal.

Grizzly and black bear males and young females who are not pregnant simply go to sleep, but a pregnant female gives birth to her young and suckles them without leaving the den for food or drink until about April. While the bears hibernate, their bodies break down stored fats and proteins, and the water left over from the process partly replaces what goes out from the lungs or evaporates from the skin.

The bears do not urinate – another adaptation to conserve water during hibernation. Wastes that would normally be carried out by the urine are converted into amino acids that form new proteins for the body to re-absorb. So a build-up of life-threatening urea in the blood (as happens during kidney failure) is avoided.

While the bears hibernate, the more active animals such as coyotes and snowshoe hares move between patches of warm ground along regular highways bulldozed through the snow by the bison. As they move in single file, each animal steps in the tracks of its predecessor, forming a belly-deep trench.

Yellowstone's winter is cold, harsh and long. It begins to loosen its grip in April, but mid-June will arrive before the last of the snow melts.

....

Uninterrupted sleep *A black bear is snug in its winter den among tree roots. It sleeps there from about November to late March without feeding or drinking.*

bison are forced to forage farther afield. They shovel through the snow with their broad noses, sometimes pushing down through drifts the height of a man before they reach the growth below. There are some brief thaws when the sun melts the surface snow, but at night the slush freezes so hard that it can cut the legs and muzzles of grazers such as bison and elk.

The temperature of the hot-water springs can be 75°C (167°F) – too hot to bathe in, but a perfect home for mats of blue-green algae. They colour the pools red, orange, blue and green. Here too,

The big sleep *The fur of this hibernating pipistrelle bat is spangled with droplets of condensation.*

How pipistrelle bats beat the icy winter

Icy winter grips the countryside of America's northern states east of the Rocky Mountains. Although the January snow carpets the ground outside, in a silent hillside cave the air temperature remains at a steady 2°C (36°F).

Clinging to the cave roof is a colony of several dozen eastern pipistrelle bats. Their fur-covered bodies are beaded with silvery droplets of water that has condensed from a slight air current blowing through the cave. Little except their wings and ears are visible, looking like scraps of polished leather.

These bats are in deep hibernation, balanced on the very edge of existence. They cling to the roof of the cave with curved claws that lock to provide a constant grip without the need for any muscular effort. Their thumb-length bodies are only a degree or so warmer than the air in the cave, they are hardly breathing and their hearts are slowed almost to a stop. Even the thread-like blood vessels in the thin skin of their ears, wings and feet are shrunken, to reduce heat loss from the blood moving slowly through their bodies. With every bodily system shut down, the tiny bats can survive the winter without feeding. They exist on their stored fat – just a speck-sized amount each day.

Their ability to hibernate is the bats' lifeline. In winter their usual prey, insects, have perished, leaving only eggs or larvae hidden away until the spring. This means that the bats must either move to a warmer climate where insects fly throughout the winter, or hibernate. Some eastern pipistrelle bats do migrate south to Mexico, but most hibernate.

Successful hibernation is a gamble – the bats' preparations have to be just right for the uncertain demands of the coming winter. In autumn, after the night's hunting, each bat sinks during the day into a deep, short-term sleep called torpor, thus saving energy that is stored as fat. However, the bats still have to fly at night, so cannot afford to get too heavy. Only those that lay down just enough fat to last them until spring will survive through winter. Females tend to be slightly fatter than males, and can hibernate for about four months. Their mates will run out of fat about three weeks earlier.

Hibernating bats do not sleep all the time. If the air in their cave warms up, or cools to a dangerously low level, they may wake up. On exceptionally warm nights they may even fly from the cave for a few hours to hunt. Even if the temperature remains constant, the bats may still wake up from time to time to have a drink, to urinate, to groom or just to stretch their wings.

It is during the hibernation period that males and females mate. However, the females do not waste any of their precious winter fat reserves on pregnancy. Instead they store the male's sperm, and fertilisation is delayed until the spring, when the nights are warmer and food is plentiful again.

Finding a good place in which to hibernate is crucial. It is usually a cave, or perhaps a crevice in an old unheated roof or a hollow tree – somewhere dark and undisturbed and humid enough to prevent the bats from drying out. Most important, this 'hibernaculum' must be constantly cool but not likely to freeze. If it is too warm the bats will waken constantly and use up valuable energy. If it is too cool the bats may freeze to death. Eastern pipistrelles select caves where the temperature is 10-15°C (50-60°F) in the autumn, with January temperatures stabilising at 0-5°C (32-40°F).

Mother and child *Female pipistrelle bats that survive hibernation bear a single baby in June. Even a half-grown baby is very small. A mother and youngster can fit onto a house brick with room to spare.*

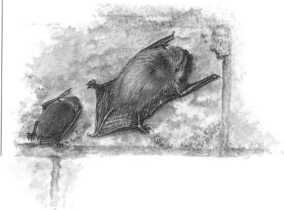

An abrupt awakening for the ground squirrel

Deep in a dark, draught-proof burrow, a Californian ground squirrel lies curled up in a snug nest of dried grass. It is late January, and the ground squirrel is about to wake up after hibernating for three months through the lean days of winter.

As the warm days of last summer drew to an end, the ground squirrel devoted all its time to the task of getting fat. Flower heads, fresh vegetation and seeds provided the fuel for it to develop a fatty envelope as a protection against the imminent cold. It also stored food in its chosen burrow to ensure that a meal would be waiting if it woke up before spring arrived.

During the long hibernation, the squirrel's life-support systems slowed almost to a standstill. The fuel it needed for survival came from the fat under its skin and round its vital organs. If that fat had run out, the squirrel would have died. To survive, it used as little energy as possible. So it allowed its body temperature to plummet, its heartbeat to drop to only four or five times a minute and its breathing rate to slow down so that it used only the equivalent of an egg-cupful of oxygen during all its long sleep.

One-third of adult ground squirrels, and two-thirds of young ones, do not survive hibernation – most either freeze to death when their fat supply runs out, or are discovered and eaten by predators such as weasels.

SQUIRRELS ASTIR

Male Californian ground squirrels are the first to stir from their winter sleep. Females waken a week or two later. What follows must be a tremendous shock to the animal's system – being jerked from an almost death-like sleep into wakeful alertness. As the squirrel rouses, its heart and breathing rates accelerate and its muscles twitch to raise its body temperature.

Within 20 minutes of waking, the animal's heart, after months of beating only a few times a minute, is racing at a rate of up to 400 beats a minute. In the first half-hour of wakefulness, the squirrel uses 2000 times as much oxygen as it used during the whole period of sleep. It breakfasts on the remaining seeds stored in a

The long sleep When ground squirrels hibernate, all their life-support systems slow down almost to a standstill. Only a vital layer of body fat prevents them from freezing to death in an icy grave.

corner of the burrow, and within minutes the fully wakened squirrel is digging its way out of the burrow to reach the surface. By the time it sees daylight it will have used nine times the amount of energy it needed to keep it alive for several months of hibernation.

This instant awakening is a crucial necessity for an animal that lives its life under constant threat from predators such as foxes and hawks. The ground squirrel cannot afford to feel groggy, for its hunters have had a lean and hungry winter too. As soon as it emerges, it must be ready to run fast and hide at the first sign of a marauder. Once released from their hibernation, ground squirrels are quick to make the most of the warmer days. Abundant food ensures a quick recovery from the lean winter.

They will mate not long after they emerge and the females will return to the safety of their underground burrows to give birth. From late May, the males go into aestivation – a process similar to hibernation – to escape the summer droughts. But the females continue feeding and caring for their offspring. When autumn arrives, the males emerge again to fatten up for their long winter sleep, and in November males and females move back into their food-stocked nests to sleep through the winter.

Spring again After three months hibernating in an underground burrow, a Californian ground squirrel emerges into the welcome sunshine.

Food and warmth As it forages in the warmth of an early spring day, the ground squirrel is always alert for danger such as a hunting hawk.

Forest family Crossbills usually rear one brood a year, sometime between August and May. Even after they can fly, the young rely on their parents for weeks.

A winter larder for the nesting crossbill

In the bleak January weather of Europe's northern spruce forests, some crossbills are already raising a family of three or four chicks, long before other seed-eating birds return from wintering in the south. The crossbill has plenty of food at hand – seeds from spruce cones, which ripen on the tree throughout winter ready to open and drop their seeds in spring.

The crossbill uses the two halves of its crossed beak to force apart the cone scales while it plucks out the seed with its tongue. Spruce seeds are the favourites, although a Scottish race of crossbill with a heavier beak relies mainly on Scots pine. With crops varying from year to year and birds moving as seeds ripen, different areas may have periodic invasions of crossbills.

To get at the seeds, a crossbill, which is rather bigger than a sparrow, may hang upside down on a large cone, on a spruce for example. But it breaks off small cones and carries them back to a convenient perch, where it holds the cone in a claw while breaking it open with its beak. Cones are discarded with seeds still in them, but these make many a meal for later in the year.

The bird's powerful crossed beak is useful as a third limb for gripping tree branches, but its shape makes picking up food from the ground difficult. Crossbills occasionally eat other seeds, berries and sometimes insects. Their dry diet makes them drink a lot, and they often gather in family groups at a pool or puddle.

Screaming red foxes find their mates

The eerie wail of a vixen echoes across the frost-bound landscape of a chill January night in Britain. Only a flitting shadow marks her passage as she trots across a patch of open ground or down a lane. She calls intermittently as she goes, pausing to throw her whole body into the scream. In the distance, a dog fox answers and the vixen heads towards him.

Winter is the mating season for red foxes, a time when they are noisier and more active than usual. The vixen pairs with a male who has established a territory and both will scrap to defend it from intruders. The male and female pair for a season (sometimes for longer), but are lone hunters so they are often apart. Other dog foxes may approach the vixen, but she resists them with throaty clicks and her mate will see them off more fiercely. The vixen greets her mate with a high-pitched whine of submission, but she may rebuff him several times before mating.

Between seven and eight weeks after mating, four or five dark-coated cubs are born, and the vixen stays with them in the den – a cavity under tree roots, for example – for the first three or four weeks. The male brings back food for her. Later, when the cubs are being weaned, both parents will regurgitate food for them. When the weaning is completed, both parents hunt at night to bring the cubs earthworms, small mammals and birds to eat. The cubs leave the den at about five weeks old, and stay with the pair until autumn, when they are usually driven off the territory – although one or two may stay on for a year and help with next season's young.

Life for the growing cubs is hazardous. Many lose their lives, often to motorists or hunters, before they are old enough to breed. The survivors often have to travel widely to find a territory and a mate of their own.

Once a fox has established itself in a suitable territory, it will spend several years there. The size of the territory depends on how much food is available. In food-rich European woodlands, a territory is usually about ½ mile square (65ha), but in the food-sparse pine forests of northern Sweden it may be ten times as big. During the last few decades, foxes have invaded towns, where the small size of territories shows how much food is available there.

Faithful mate While the vixen stays in the den to nurse the newborn cubs, the dog fox brings her food. The cubs are usually born in March or April.

Courtship clash In the winter breeding season the vixen may fight off the dog fox before they eventually mate.

How the treecreeper makes its own shelter

For insect-eating birds, January is a lean time in the woodlands of Europe because insects are scarce and the short midwinter days allow little time to search for them. The treecreeper survives by probing tree bark for insects overwintering beneath it as eggs, grubs, chrysalises or adults.

Sparrow-like and sparrow-sized, the bird is related to wrens and nuthatches, and spends its life creeping inconspicuously up tree trunks. It hops up two-legged on its large, curved claws, and uses its stiff tail feathers as a brace while it prises off flakes of bark with its long, down-curving beak, or probes into crevices in the bark.

The treecreeper shelters from the rigours of winter weather under loose strips of bark or in natural cavities in the tree trunk, and can squeeze itself into a surprisingly small space. In Britain, its possibilities for finding shelter improved with the introduction of Wellingtonia trees from America in 1853 to adorn large estates or add to tree collections. By the 1920s, the bird had begun to use these tall conifers – some reaching 150ft (46m) – by digging out hollows in the soft bark. It was a completely new habit in European treecreepers although the closely related American treecreepers did it. Wellingtonias were the first trees in Britain to be suitable for gouging out cavities.

Although it prefers broadleaved rather than coniferous woodland, the treecreeper is found anywhere that offers trees with bark rich in insects and crevices. It is so secretive that it is not often seen, and is more easily detected by its high-pitched calls. Treecreepers rarely stray far from the trees, except to visit stone walls with crevices that shelter insects. They usually have two broods of five or six youngsters a year, in nests built under loose bark.

In southern Europe, the bird is limited mostly to the wooded upper reaches of mountain chains and is rarely seen below 3300ft (1000m). At lower altitudes it is replaced throughout much of southern Europe and the Mediterranean region by the short-toed treecreeper, which has shorter claws, a less distinct white stripe over its eye and lighter-brown flanks.

....

Snug hideaway *A treecreeper sleeps in a hollow in the trunk of a Wellingtonia tree, well protected against a cold winter's night. It scraped out the cavity itself by chiselling into the soft bark with its long, curving beak.*

Where cave swiftlets nest in dark and danger

Imagine a gigantic cave, the size of a cathedral, where tens of thousands of bats roost in the roof and the floor is covered with thick layers of their droppings, called guano. Summon up the noxious smell of ammonia, line the walls with green slime, and you have pictured one of a number of caves in Borneo and Thailand.

Caves like these are not only home to one of the most extraordinary collections of creeping and crawling creatures, but also provide the ingredient for a multi-million dollar food industry. The delicacy is bird's nest soup, and the bird with the valuable nest is the cave swiftlet.

In January, the caves are alive with breeding swiftlets. There are several species. The most numerous ones find their way in the dark by echolocation and nest in the roof of the inner caverns. They navigate like bats by making clicking sounds and listening for the echoes from the cave walls. Species lacking that skill nest in the cave entrances. The cave swiftlets share the huge galleries with roosting bats.

The birds' nests are built at the top of cave walls as high as a 40-storey building. Most are attached to slight overhangs to prevent predators such as snakes and cave crickets from crawling in. A swiftlet starts its nest by clinging precariously to the cave wall and secreting a U-shaped layer of saliva which quickly hardens to form the 'hinge'. Then the nest is built up gradually with layer upon layer of saliva.

The nests, although much the same shape for all species, have different textures. Some have moss and feathers mixed with the saliva, others are pure saliva. It is the white nests made from pure saliva that are favoured by nest collectors, who are allowed to take nests for six weeks from the beginning of February. A bird that has lost its nest early in the season will then build another.

The chicks stay in the nest for about six weeks, fed on insects caught by their parents on daily excursions out of the caves and over the surrounding rain forest. Each morning there is chaos at the cave entrances as the swiftlets leave for the day and the bats return from their night's hunting. Hawks and falcons take advantage of

Collecting nests for soup *Local nest collectors build a fragile scaffolding of bamboo to reach the swiftlet nests that are so prized in soup by oriental gourmets.*

Night fliers *Tens of thousands of wrinkle-lipped bats fly out from the caves to hunt at dusk.*

Cave-floor crab *The freshwater guano crab feeds on any corpses it can get its claws on, such as bats or swiftlets that drop accidentally to the cave floor.*

Death in the dark *A cave centipede overpowers and eats a cave cricket. Many of the cave animals have exaggerated limbs to 'feel' their way in the dark.*

Cave interceptor *A cave snake has snatched a cave swiftlet from midair. How it detects its prey in pitch darkness is not fully understood.*

Peering into the abyss *Newly hatched cave swiftlets sit in their cup-shaped nest, made of moss and hardened saliva, high up on the cave wall.*

the confusion and swoop in to grab a meal. Huge swarms of bats and flocks of swiftlets fly through the air jigging this way and that to avoid being caught. At dusk the flow is reversed as swiftlets return and bats fly out.

At fledging time, a swiftlet chick is in great danger. On its maiden flight it must launch itself into the dark void and navigate its way safely to the cave entrance without making any mistakes. A whole host of hungry creatures is lying in wait

to snap up the unwary or clumsy cave swiftlet.

Cave racer snakes hang from the cave walls ready to intercept swiftlets and bats in flight. They wait at narrow passages, and when they detect a moving object, strike out to catch it in midair. Giant crickets, with muscular legs and formidable jaws, scale the cave walls. They can even reach the nests, where they will break into an egg or tear a swiftlet chick apart.

A chick that loses its way in the dark and

eventually falls exhausted to the ground is doomed. Blind hunting spiders will seek it out with the help of long front legs that probe the way ahead like huge 'feelers'. The bat guano heaps ripple with a seething mass of golden cockroaches. Guano 'mires' are homes for colourless, long-legged guano crabs that fight over the swiftlet corpses. Catfish live in the streams that flow across the cave floor. Dinner-plate-sized toads lie motionless, waiting to gulp down anything that moves.

The entire cave community is dependent on the swiftlets and bats, which can leave the cave and collect food from the forest. The food brought back to the caves, in the form of dead bodies or waste products, gives life to the myriad creatures that spend their whole existence in the dark.

A close call A hyena plunges into a freshwater inlet in a soda lake in pursuit of flamingos. But this time all the birds manage to escape the attack.

Rich pickings for the spotted hyena

Feeding with heads down in the shallows of the lake, or resting peacefully balanced on one of their long, thin, red legs, the flamingos are unaware of being watched. By the edge of the lake – a soda lake with freshwater inlets in Tanzania's Ngorongoro Crater – a creature lies motionless, his yellow-brown coat blending into the surrounding muddy grassland. Slowly he gets to his feet. Ears cocked, tail erect, hair bristling, the hyena makes his move. Suddenly the calm of the lake is shattered by 11 stone (70kg) of carnivore crashing into the water. A goose-like cackling fills the air. In panic, a pink cloud of birds rises from the lake.

With its powerful jaws and bone-crushing teeth, the hyena can finish off a flamingo in seconds. But today the birds get away. After snapping at dangling legs and beating wings, the hyena gives up and lopes off. The flamingos resume feeding or resting.

Luckily for the birds, the hyena is not very hungry. In the crater's flat, open grassland there is plenty of food available at the moment. The floor of the crater stretches across 120sq miles (310sq km) and teems with vast numbers of wildebeests, zebras and gazelles – all grazing animals high on the hyena's list of prey. Other meat-eaters like lions and jackals share this living larder, but in January there is plenty of food to go round, for the November and December rains have transformed the dry grassland into a lush green carpet.

Because of the abundant grass, January and February are the months in which the wildebeests have their calves, and these provide rich pickings for meat-eaters such as the hyena. With

Getting a tree frog's tadpoles to water

High in a tree in a patch of sparse woodland on a grassy South African plain, a frog searches for insects to eat. It seems an odd place for a frog. Ponds, creeks and damp patches are more likely homes for a creature that needs to keep cool and wet.

The grey tree frog has ways of keeping itself moist where water is often scarce, but at spawning time its eggs would shrivel and its tadpoles would die without immersion in water. In January enough rain is falling for ponds and puddles to form, so it is a good time for the tree frogs to breed.

Frogs, being amphibians, live both on land and in water, and breathe not only with lungs but also through their skin, as long as it is moist. Without regular drenching most frogs dry up and die, but the grey tree frog survives by conserving as much water as it can.

Instead of getting rid of its waste matter in a watery solution, as most frogs do, the tree frog excretes a semi-solid paste. Any water that does come its way is sopped up quickly, and in the rainy season tree frogs get themselves as drenched as possible.

But where the tree frog lives, months can go by with little or no rain. All amphibians have glands that produce a slime to moisten the skin, but the grey tree frog goes a step farther and manufactures a waxy substance to seal its skin and prevent water loss. It survives by smearing this waterproof coating over its whole body with its hind legs.

Grey tree frogs gather to mate on a branch overhanging some water. Before laying her eggs, a female excretes a liquid which she and her mate whip into a lather with their back legs. As many as 40 frogs get together to build one frothy ball, and the eggs are laid inside it. Pairs sit clasped together so that the male can fertilise the female's 100 or more eggs as they are laid.

Soon, the outer surface of the foam nest dries in the sun, forming a crust. Moisture is sealed inside and after 3-4 days the eggs develop safely into tadpoles in their suspended capsule.

After a day or two, the movement of the tadpoles breaks the crust open, and they drop into the water below and develop into frogs. Once they are fully grown, the young tree frogs will clamber out of their underwater nursery and take to the trees. They will never be immersed in water again.

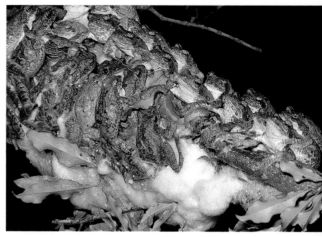

A cluster of foam-makers *About 40 grey tree frogs cluster on a branch in dry grassland, and work together to whip up foam in which they lay their eggs.*

The tadpoles reach water *Inside the foam (above), the developing tadpoles break the crust and fall into the pool under the tree (below) to complete their growth.*

only speed to save itself, a newborn wildebeest on its wobbly legs is no match for a hyena, and its mother is not always successful in driving off an attacker.

As they are able to digest skin and bone that other carnivores leave untouched, hyenas are master scavengers. But they are also formidable hunters – as many as 15 will gang up on an adult zebra. In the Ngorongoro Crater they kill more meals than they steal.

Given the chance, a hyena eats an average of 6lb (2.7kg) of meat a day. Chase, kill and meal are over in a matter of minutes, and at this time of the year the hyena can get away with being active only four hours out of 24.

High-rise homestead *Hundreds of carmine bee-eaters nest in burrows hollowed out in a steep bank, where the eggs and nestlings are out of the reach of most hunters.*

Bee-eaters return to their tower-block nests

On a steep, sandy bank in central Cameroon, crowds of carmine bee-eaters are moving back into their nest holes during the hot, dry weather of late January. They are getting ready for nesting in late March, at the onset of the rainy season. The bank is riddled with neat entrance holes excavated by up to 1000 pairs of thrush-sized birds in previous years and now being cleaned out and spruced up. High on this bank the eggs and young will be safe from most marauders, but not always from snakes and rats.

Young birds in their first breeding season are courting – greeting each other noisily with wings fanning and tails twitching. Males are offering females gifts of insects, or squabbling with other males. Some newly paired couples have already begun work on excavating new burrows in the bank, digging with beaks and leaning on their wings as they shovel the earth out behind them with their short legs.

The bee-eaters stop work on their nests to make regular hunting trips. Flocks of the bright birds swoop low over the tree-scattered grassland on pointed wings, their tail streamers trailing behind them. These carmine bee-eaters belong to the northern race, which has a blue-green throat. A southern race living south of the Equator is similar but with a pink throat.

Locusts, grasshoppers, beetles, flies and other insects, as well as bees are all favourite foods of carmine bee-eaters. Many insects are caught and eaten in flight. Some carmine bee-eaters have been seen in flight knocking the stings off bees or squeezing out their poison before swallowing them. The birds often ride on the backs of large animals such as giraffes, antelopes or farm stock, ready to swoop on any insects stirred up from the ground. They will also fly behind cars to snap up the insects they disturb.

Mating takes place just outside – and occasionally inside – the nest, and the female lays three to five white, oval eggs at two-day intervals in the unlined chamber at the end of the burrow. The young hatch after about three weeks of incubation, and are fed insects not only by their parents, but also by helpers who are not breeding. These are probably brothers and sisters from the previous year. Nestlings can fly after about a month, and the birds leave the nesting site in June.

Why weaver birds are a threat to crops

Sweeping across an African grassland like a living wave, more than a million red-billed queleas, a type of weaver bird, scour the ground for grass or grain seeds. Those at the back of the huge flock keep flying to the front to find an untouched patch of ground, and the air is filled with their restless, murmuring chatter.

It is January, the height of summer in southern Namibia, and the birds have come to feast on the ripening seeds. They follow the rains from area to area, and gather in immense numbers where seeds become plentiful, such as a farmer's millet field ripening ready to harvest, or sometimes grass seeds in the soil revealed by a natural fire. Their survival hangs on a knife-edge, for these small, finch-sized birds must eat half their own weight in seeds every day to be able to survive through the night.

Probably the most numerous bird in the world – the total population is estimated at 10,000 million – the red-billed quelea is also one of the world's most destructive agricultural pests, rivalling the locust as one of the scourges of Africa. The birds are found throughout Africa's grasslands from Sudan to the Cape and from West Africa to the Indian Ocean coast. Farmers often lose half, or even all, their grain crops to these ravenous, teeming birds.

Queleas can breed whenever a good food supply becomes available, so breeding is triggered by the rains. They usually build their woven, globular nests in tall grass or reeds, each

A cooling dip In the heat of the southern summer, queleas bathe in a Namibian water hole.

nest attached to three or four stems. But some nest in thorny bushes or trees – a single tree may house several hundred nests. Making the nest is the job of the male, who collects grass and other suitable material and weaves it together. A well-built nest will attract a female to mate with him. Together, they line the nest to provide a snug home for their clutch of two or three pale blue eggs with dark brown markings.

The largest breeding colonies can cover 1sq mile (2.6sq km) and may contain 10 million nests. Although predators such as snakes and hawks invade nests, the birds are so numerous

that most youngsters are safely fledged. Man is the greatest enemy, destroying whole colonies because of their threat to crops.

Gigantic quelea colonies seem to function as centres for the exchange of information on where to find food. Birds that have fared poorly during the day return late and will hang back the following morning. They then seem to follow birds that are returning to rich feeding sites found on the previous day. Because they eat a dry diet in a hot climate, queleas need to drink regularly. They gather round permanent water holes in their thousands.

THE WEAVER'S ART

A red-billed quelea uses its beak and feet to weave and knot grass and other vegetation into an enclosed nest with an entrance at the base. The bird starts from a central loop, and the internal diameter of the nest is determined by its reach from the loop.

Three-stage nest building *From a grass loop knotted to a twig, the bird builds up a central ring (left). This is the support for building the nest cup (centre). The entrance is built last (right).*

Life at low water in the Amazon forest

By January, some parts of South America's mighty Amazon river system are reduced to a mere trickle. The flood waters have receded, and in the upper Amazon have become so low that small tributaries have broken up into strings of ponds and stagnant lagoons that are low in life-giving oxygen. In such tough conditions, only the fittest and best adapted of the creatures confined to the rapidly shrinking waters will survive.

For some inhabitants of the Amazon forest, the low-water season has advantages. As fish, reptiles and amphibians congregate in huge numbers in the isolated patches of water remaining, fish-eating birds – ospreys, egrets, cormorants, vultures, kingfishers – gather in the trees for the coming bonanza of stranded fish.

TURTLES AND SKIMMERS

As sand and mud are exposed along the water's edge, hundreds of giant river turtles – up to 3ft (1m) long – take the opportunity to lay their 60-100 eggs there, which must hatch in six or seven weeks before the water rises again. Birds gather to raid the shallow turtle nests and swoop on the hatchlings as they scurry across the sand to the comparative safety of the water.

Some sandbanks provide nesting places for black skimmers, relatives of gulls and terns, in crowded colonies with nests sometimes only 3ft (1m) apart. Before sitting on the nest, the parents wet their feet and plumage to keep the eggs cool in the sultry heat. Like the turtles, the skimmers must rear their young before the rivers swell and the sandbanks are submerged once again.

A black skimmer has a long, scissor-like beak with the lower part a third longer than the upper part. The bird feeds on fish, which it 'skims' from the water by flying low over a still lagoon with the lower part of its beak slicing through the water. When the trailing beak touches a small fish, the bird drops its head and closes its beak, trapping the prey inside.

Many small creatures live in the banks of leaf litter that accumulate at river bends as the water

A precarious ride In the shrinking waters and crowded conditions of the Amazon's low-water season, a river turtle mistakes the head of a spectacled cayman for a rock, and finds itself taking an unusual ride.

Race against time A pair of black skimmers bring up their chicks on the sand before the river rises again.

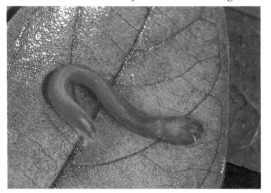

Fish out of water This worm-like catfish, as long as a fingernail, lives in leaf litter on the river's edge.

Living confetti As the water level goes down in the upper Amazon, male butterflies congregate on the wet sand. Each is sucking up water and sodium salts through its straw-like proboscis.

goes down. The heaps of debris offer them shelter and food, for the plant material is broken down, releasing its nutrients, by the activities of fungi and bacteria. The softened tissues are then torn by the claws of freshwater prawns.

Wet or damp leaves provide a home for some of the smallest fish in the world. A single bank can be hiding up to 40 species of tiny fish, some living in submerged leaves, others in damp areas bathed in a film of water.

Elongated knife fish, which can swim backwards as well as forwards, find their way through the tiniest cracks between leaves and twigs by means of electro-location. They emit a weak electric current from modified muscles, and are able to detect distortions in the electric field caused by objects up to 4in (100mm) away.

The fins of some fish have become modified so that they can use them like legs to 'walk' through the debris. Predatory fish and crabs sit with their heads protruding from the leaves and pounce on them as they walk by. Other fish

merge with the leaf litter and can change colour to suit their surroundings. And just below the water surface next to the bank of leaves, there are fish that wait for insects or seeds to fall in.

In the banks of leaf litter along one of the tributaries of the Rio Negro, there lives a creature called a tarumazinho, which looks like

REFUELLING BUTTERFLIES
Millions of butterflies gather on the exposed sandbanks of the Amazon in the low-water season – all males searching for sodium salts. Sodium is vital for the working of nerves and muscles, but a male butterfly transfers much of his body sodium to the female in a sperm package during mating. She needs the supply to replace the sodium taken up in producing eggs. So the males replenish their supply from the mud surface, where evaporation has concentrated sodium salts.

a red worm but is in fact a tiny catfish only recently discovered by scientists. The tarumazinho's only known relatives are blind catfish that lurk in the darkness of caves. The tarumazinho is also blind. It lives about 6in (150mm) down in litter lying some 2ft (600mm) above the river level. Curiously, if the catfish is immersed in water it does a most unfish-like thing – it climbs out, using its whiskers to feel the way. What happens to it when the flood waters return in the wet season, nobody knows.

Dead leaves may be an asset to smaller fish, but can be fatal for bigger ones. As leaves decay in the water they use up oxygen, so fish with normal gills are unable to breathe. Some fish have therefore developed other ways to breathe and survive the low-water season.

The electric eel, for example, which can knock out a person with a single powerful discharge, rises to the surface to absorb oxygen through the lining in its mouth. One fish swallows air and absorbs it through the gut, and many others

Feast for a village *The pirarucu, one of the world's biggest freshwater fish, can grow to 10ft (3m) long and weigh 30 stone (200kg). Local fishermen catch it with nets.*

breathe through modified swim bladders, normally used to keep the fish buoyant.

At the end of the Amazon's many-linked food chain are the monster predators such as the caymans (South American crocodiles) – 20ft (6m) long black caymans and 8ft (2.4m) long spectacled caymans. There are also 30ft (9m) long anacondas (constricting snakes which can eat young caymans), the occasional jaguar (a spotted big cat) and giant fishes.

The biggest of the fish is the giant, pike-like pirarucu (meaning red fish). Up to 10ft (3m) long,

it is one of the largest freshwater fish in the world and a voracious predator. It has teeth not only in its jaws but also on its tongue, which it uses like a second lower jaw.

The pirarucu can survive in ponds and lakes that are poor in oxygen because it, too, has become an air breather. Every 10-15 minutes it surfaces to breathe air, which is absorbed into its blood through its modified swim bladder that works like a lung.

The local Caboclos Indians consider the pirarucu a valuable prize. Fishing for it with

modern nets, especially when the rivers are low and the fish are concentrated in small areas, has resulted in this enormous fish, with few natural enemies, becoming increasingly rare.

The pirarucu is not alone in being under threat. So is the entire Amazon river system. With the removal of vast tracts of tropical hardwood trees for timber, the clearing of forest for agriculture and plans for damming rivers, it is likely that many of the remarkable creatures living in and around the Amazon – some only just being discovered – could disappear for ever.

27

Colour change *Nassau groupers can flash different colour patterns, perhaps to impress a female, deter a territorial rival, or determine the sexual balance.*

Nuptial groupers *Hundreds of Nassau groupers gather at the reef edge to spawn by moonlight.*

Groupers go courting beneath a full moon

As the first full moon of the year shines down on a Caribbean coral reef off Belize, 10,000 brown and white fish congregate 100ft (30m) beneath the water surface, where the reef drops down into the sea depths. They are Nassau groupers that have come to spawn.

On arrival, the 5-20lb (2.3-9kg) groupers form themselves into small groups and flash their coloured body patterns at each other. This, it is thought, is probably the way males impress the females and see off rivals, and could also be a way of determining the balance of males and females in the group. Nassau groupers can change sex from female to male, so if during one spawning season there are too many females, some older females can change sex for the next.

The eggs carried by the females begin to ripen before the mating season starts, and are usually ready to be released on the third night after the full moon. Just before spawning, the shoal of courting fish descends to 120ft (37m). Then, at sunset exactly, they rush to the surface in groups of 30-40, the females releasing their eggs at a depth of 80ft (24m) and the males shedding their milt (sperm). For the next few nights other groups follow the same ritual. By the time of the new moon, all the fish have returned to their respective territories around the West Indian reefs and resumed their solitary way of life.

Groupers spawn in these particular spots because the reef itself is a dangerous place to deposit eggs. Seldom is anything – particularly nutritious eggs – left uneaten for long, for the waters of tropical coral reefs, unlike the nutrient-rich waters of temperate seas, are barren. So many reef creatures protect their eggs. Damselfish guard them until they hatch. Jawfish incubate their eggs in their mouths.

The strategy of the Nassau groupers is to spawn on the edge of the reef so that the tide will carry the eggs well away from the reef to develop where they have a better chance of survival. The groupers all time their spawning by the full moon, as the chances of some eggs surviving is better where there is a large number. The fish also favour sites around underwater projections, where water turbulence creates movement that will help to carry away the eggs and larvae.

The green turtles that are master navigators

For most of the year, the green turtles of Brazil spend their time in protected bays along the Atlantic coast. They feed on underwater fields of sea grass, chomping with their horny, serrated, beak-like jaws, or bolting down seaweed fronds without chewing them.

Along the same stretches of coast there are beaches free from predators that would be ideal places for the turtles to lay their eggs. Instead, in January, many turtles head out to sea against the powerful South Equatorial Current and swim 1250 miles (2000km) to lay their eggs on the beaches of Ascension Island. They mate at sea before they go ashore. Ascension, 34sq miles (88sq km) in extent, is a tiny dot in the Atlantic midway between Africa and South America. Yet the turtles, about 3ft (1m) long, find their way back to the same beach from which they had scuttled as hatchlings years before.

Not all Brazilian green turtles make this journey – only those that hatched on Ascension Island. It takes them six or seven weeks to reach their destination, swimming at a rate of about 30 miles (48km) a day. And all this without food. Scientists can only speculate on how the turtles find their way and why they go so far.

Any guidance system must keep the turtles on a direct course – difficult if, when the turtle is swimming, it pushes harder with one flipper than the other, or if it is dragged to one side by barnacles growing on its shell. There are several navigational techniques a turtle could use. It could swim *against* the westward-flowing South Equatorial Current, or *with* the eastward-flowing counter current 350ft (105m) down.

Alternatively it could taste the water and climb an 'odour ladder', the smell of Ascension strengthening as it swims eastwards. Or it could continually pinpoint its position against the earth's magnetic field. Then there is celestial guidance. A turtle must go to the surface regularly to breathe, so each time it could take a bearing from the sun (in front at dawn) or from the moon and stars. The most intriguing aspect of the turtles' behaviour, however, is why they go to Ascension at all. One explanation offered involves earth's constantly changing geology.

Ancestors of today's green turtles were living at the time of the dinosaurs, more than 100 million years ago. When small mammals began to appear on the scene, some were very partial to turtles' eggs, so sea turtles sought out remote,

Weary traveller *A green turtle completes her marathon swim and hauls herself onto the beach to lay her eggs.*

robber-free, island beaches to lay their eggs. At that time, Africa and South America were close together, with the Atlantic just a narrow strip between. But as volcanic lava was thrust out along the length of the Mid Atlantic Ridge halfway between the two continents, Africa was pushed eastwards and South America westwards, separating by about 1in (25mm) a year.

The theory suggests that, as volcanic islands along the ridge were pushed above the sea, their exposed beaches became ideal turtle nesting

Extended journey The main map shows the turtles' route to Ascension Island. The inset shows the continents as they were about 80 million years ago.

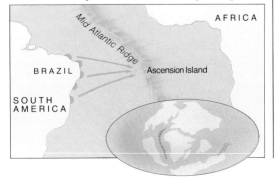

sites, away from the predatory mammals of the continents. And as at first Brazil's north-east coast was close to the ridge, the turtles swam to the islands regularly to lay their eggs. But as the sea floor widened, Brazil moved gradually farther away, and another string of volcanic islands was formed between Brazil and the Mid Atlantic Ridge. At egg-laying time the Brazilian turtles swam to the nearest volcanic island.

As volcanoes became extinct and were slowly washed away to become underwater seamounts, the turtles swam to the next available island. And as the islands disappeared, Ascension was left the nearest to the Brazilian coast. Over millions of years the journey became steadily longer, until the turtles had to travel the extraordinary distance they swim today.

But if this theory is correct, it is likely that populations breeding on Ascension would have developed separately as the Atlantic widened, yet they are more or less identical with other Atlantic turtles. As turtles always return to lay eggs on the beach where they hatched, it is possible that, at some time, some female turtles got to Ascension by accident and laid their eggs there, so their descendants continue to return.

Rare chicks *Two chicks of the endangered orange-bellied parrot peer from their eucalyptus nest.*

Parrots that cross the sea to find gum trees

If the distinctive shape of the trees does not identify them, the smell of their leaves will. Tall trunks stand in graceful ranks. Narrow, evergreen leaves grow at the tips of branches. Their scent floats on the warm air: eucalyptus. In summer in south-west Tasmania, the remote forests of eucalyptus trees provide homes for one of the rarest parrots in the world – the budgerigar-sized orange-bellied parrot.

In spring, the birds behaved in an unparrot-like way. They migrated from south-east Australia to their southern breeding grounds, crossing the sea over the Bass Strait, to take up residence in the hollows of Tasmanian eucalyptus trees.

Now it is early January, and a vivid blue and green female parrot has been incubating her eggs for nearly three weeks, brought meals by her mate. Soon her five chicks will be begging for food. They will remain in their secluded home for about four weeks before they learn to fly.

Then in March the weather will turn. Tasmania's cool, wet winter is too harsh for the parrots, so they will return to the coastal grasslands and salt marshes of south-eastern Australia, where they feed on seeds. They spend most of the time on the ground, tucking themselves behind tussocks. When disturbed, they fly high into the air, revealing the bright orange patch on their underparts.

The parrots' seasonal cycle could soon end forever. So endangered are these birds by land development that fewer than 300 remain.

A tammar wallaby keeps a baby in reserve

It is a long and amazing journey for the tiny tammar wallaby. Expelled from its mother's birth canal on a January day on Kangaroo Island, off the South Australia coast, it begins hauling itself upwards on her fur, unable to see and with no hind legs or tail to help it climb. Yet it manages to scramble into her pouch, where it attaches itself to one of her nipples. The baby's featherweight body is almost transparent, and it is unable to suck the teat its mouth is clinging to. Its mother uses her muscles to squirt her milk into it to feed it. In two months' time the tiny creature will still be blind and naked, but the appearance of its legs and tail will make it just recognisable as a wallaby.

Meanwhile its mother, unlike most mammals, can become pregnant again – within days of giving birth. However, the second embryo grows only until it contains about 100 cells, and then rests inside her body.

Rabbit-sized tammar wallabies live in the coastal mallee thickets – spreading eucalyptus bushes – and scrublands of southern Australia and its offshore islands. They can exist for eight or nine months without fresh water, getting the moisture they need from the juices of the plants they eat, and even by drinking sea water.

In spring (September) the first baby is 'born' a second time, leaving its mother's pouch to stand on its own feet. Even then, until it is too big to do so, it will dive back into her pouch for refuge if danger threatens.

Not until late December will the second, quiescent embryo start to grow again, triggered into action by the shortening of the days. The baby is then expelled from the birth canal a month later, in January or February.

Kangaroos and wallabies vary in size from tiny rat kangaroos to giant red ones, but all have strong hind legs, big feet and a tail that acts as a balance and prop, and all carry their young in pouches. If the infant in the pouch should die, the quiescent embryo can take its place and be born within weeks – a useful device for animals at risk of losing their offspring in the harsh, dry conditions of the Australian scrub.

Having a baby in reserve is common to all 54 types of kangaroo and wallaby. Mothers often have a joey at their heels, a young one in the pouch and an embryo in storage.

Two in one *This tammar wallaby carries a baby in her pouch and an embryo in suspended animation in her body.*

A tree python guards her eggs from harm

Alert to the slightest sign of danger, a green tree python keeps watch high in a tree in New Guinea, coiled round her eggs. It is January, and she has been there since she laid them two months ago. The tree reaches a height of some 180ft (55m), and its canopy of leaves block out the light. Creepers curl up its massive trunk, and bamboo grows thick all round it.

This damp, dark, tangle of forest is one of the world's richest rain forests, spreading its thick cloak across New Guinea and the north-east tip of Australia. It is home to 12,000 species of plant, 700 species of bird and 180 mammal species. At least 60in (1524mm) of rain falls yearly, and January is one of the wettest months.

The green tree python has wrapped herself round her eggs to protect them. Although she has no poison, she has a good set of teeth, and any egg-eating marauders could suffer a nasty bite. But her vigil is almost over. The soft-shelled eggs against her body are now lumpy with life. Two beady eyes and one blunt snout have already emerged from an egg, soon to be followed by 12in (300mm) of slender body. In other eggs, the youngsters have their egg teeth hard at work slicing at the leathery shells.

Before long, 15 bright orange babies will have hatched. Then they will be on their own. It is unusual for snakes to show any interest in their offspring after seeing them into the world. Not all take as much trouble as the python – many just lay their eggs and leave them.

IN PURSUIT OF PREY

The newborn pythons do not need to feed straightaway, but their mother has not eaten since laying her eggs, and she is hungry. When night falls, she goes in search of food – a sleeping bird or lizard, or one of the many forest rodents. Although only 6ft (1.8m) long, she is an extremely effective predator, a relative of the boas and ground-dwelling pythons of Asia, one of which measures up to 30ft (9m) and eats goats and antelopes. The python will pounce on her prey unseen and unheard. On her upper lip she has heat-sensitive pits that she can use to locate warm-blooded prey, even in the dark.

With her head held still, the hungry female fixes her gaze on a mouse, and flows silently over a branch towards it. Then she waits. A mistake could cost her dearly. The animals she eats are equipped with their own weapons and

Tree-top vigil *Guard duty is almost over for this tree python. Her first hatchling peers out at its rain-forest world.*

if she is to avoid having her thin, soft scales torn by teeth and claws, she must time her attack on the mouse precisely.

In a flash, she sinks her teeth into the mouse's back and whips her body round it. Tight in her coils, the animal dies from suffocation within seconds. The python keeps a firm grip on her food with her backward-pointing teeth. Then she stretches her jaw wide and pulls the mouse

into her mouth by working the two sides of her lower jaw, which are joined by an elastic ligament, independently – like two arms hauling on a rope.

The python swallows the mouse whole, and lies low for several days while it is digested. Strong gastric juices break down its flesh, bones and teeth, and a ball of matted fur in her droppings will be all that remains.

Fearsome hunter Adélie penguins watch from their ice-floe refuge as a leopard seal thrashes the sea surface with one of their number, seized when it dived for food.

The leopard seal goes hunting for penguins

Hungry penguins advance to the edge of an ice floe off Antarctica, then lose their nerve and draw back. Each is unwilling to be the first to enter the water. It is January – high summer – and these Adélie penguins have come from their inland rookery to feed on krill and gather food to take back for their growing chicks.

Their feeding trip is a dangerous undertaking,

for there could be a predator lurking in the water below. The penguins' caution is justified, for some distance below the surface, a female leopard seal is gliding up and down with powerful sideways movements of her stream-lined body, awaiting them. She can stay there for up to 15 minutes before surfacing for air, so need not betray her presence to the wary penguins.

The 10ft (3m) long leopard seal lives up to her name, for she is patterned with spots over her dark grey back and paler underside. Like the land leopard, she lives by hunting and her diet regularly includes warm-blooded prey such as penguins, or other seals. She usually hunts

alone, and fears no predators herself, except perhaps killer whales.

About a month ago, this four-year-old leopard seal gave birth to her first pup on the ice. Now it is weaned and she has left it. She is very thin and hungry, and needs to get back to her 56 stone (355kg) weight, putting on enough fat to keep out the cold, for even in midsummer the water is only just above freezing point.

Suddenly, a few penguins launch themselves into the chilly water. If the whole group had dived at once, their numbers might have confused the leopard seal, but instead most of the birds back away yet again and the first birds

scooped up by scavenging petrels circling above.

On their ice floe, the rest of the Adélie penguins look on. All that is left of the kill is a small slick of blubber oil on the rippling water. Although far from satisfied with a meal of one penguin, the leopard seal has barely finished swallowing it, so there may be a brief spell of safety for the rest of the penguins to enter the water and feed. They peel suddenly from the ice as if responding to a starter's gun. But they can never be safe for long with leopard seals about.

But this time the leopard seal has gone to look for larger prey. Even in summer, much of the sea surface in the Antarctic is covered by ice 3ft (1m) thick. Perhaps the pickings will be better under the ice. Weddell seals use blowholes both for leaving the water to rest on the ice and to breathe between dives, and she may be able to pounce on a seal at its hole. The female leopard seal cuts through a veil of silvery bubbles towards a shaft of light spilling down through a hole in the surface. She rolls over on her side and glides just beneath the ice, her whiskers brushing against the hard, frozen mass as she feels for the rim of a blowhole. In winter the Weddell seal – a smaller relative of the leopard seal – maintains the hole by scraping the ice away with its teeth. In summer there is less danger of the hole freezing over.

As the leopard seal patrols below the blowhole, the Weddell seal gingerly tests the water lapping the sides of the hole, submerging first its nose, then its head. Uncertain, it backs away. Hunger has driven the leopard seal to try for the Weddell seal, but she more often hunts for crabeater seals at the edge of the ice-cap and is more successful in catching them. She arcs her body in a graceful curve and makes one more effortless pass beneath the blowhole, then gives up the seal hunt and returns to the penguins.

....

Powerless predator On land, the leopard seal is slow and clumsy. Its presence offers no threat to the nearby penguins, which would be at its mercy in the water.

enter the water alone. They are at their most vulnerable during the few seconds it takes them to gain speed. They swim superbly – at around 17mph (27km/h) – and although they are no match for a determined leopard seal, at full tilt they have some chance of escape.

The leopard seal strikes from below and seizes the last penguin to enter the water in her sharp teeth. As she reaches the surface, she flicks her head violently to one side and thrashes the penguin's body against the water. It goes limp. Diving again, she transfers her grip to the bird's skin and when she next surfaces, deftly skins the bird. She eats the blubber and meat, leaving the head, flippers and feet to be

Sitting it out Undeterred by a flurry of summer snow, a giant petrel continues to warm its single white egg while its mate scavenges for food at sea or on the shore.
....

Where giant petrels are hatched in the snow

As the howling wind ceaselessly batters a bare cliff top on the barren island of South Georgia in the southern Atlantic, a giant petrel crouches on its one white egg. The bird is one of a breeding colony of about 100 pairs, and one bird of each pair is sitting tight on their egg while the other searches for food. January is midsummer in this part of the world, but it is snowing, so the sitting birds are blanketed with white flakes. But they will not stir, or the eggs warmed by their belly feathers might be chilled.

Bleak as it may be, the cliff-top nursery suits the giant petrel well. The bird has a wingspan of up to 6ft (1.8m), and to take off it simply unfolds its huge wings and floats away. Once airborne, the petrel has an extraordinary, stiff-winged flight, seldom flapping its wings. It cruises on updraughts from huge ocean waves, body tilted sideways and wingtips skimming the water.

Giant petrels are scavengers. They quickly sight any seal pups or seabirds that have been caught by killer whales, for example, and cruise in to feast on the scraps. But they are also predators – partial to such meals as penguin chicks, gulls, and shearwaters. Like all petrels, they spit foul-smelling stomach oil if threatened. Their scavenging and spitting habits may be the reason why they are known as 'stinkers'.

With a full crop, each petrel returns to feed its waiting mate or hungry chick – hatched after just over eight weeks of incubation. These large seabirds spend most of their lives on the wing and may return to land to breed only once in two or three years. The chicks take about four months to develop and fly off.

Threat to a crèche *On Ross Island in Antarctica, a south-polar skua harasses Adélie penguin chicks, huddled together in a crèche with a few adult guardians while their parents go to sea to fish.*

Scavenging skuas make a meal of penguins

Standing in front of an Adélie penguin colony on an Antarctic ridge, the skuas look positively menacing. Large, gull-like birds with brown plumage and thick, grey beaks, they wait patiently to swoop down on any penguin chick temporarily unguarded by its parents. By January, the chicks are big enough to make a good-sized meal.

As the snow receded in October, the Adélie penguins returned to their rookeries (breeding grounds) around the Antarctic continent in huge numbers, providing the skuas with a rich food supply – not only eggs and chicks but also the carcasses of dead birds. Sometimes the skuas hunt in pairs, one bird attracting the attention of the parent penguin while the other creeps up to steal an egg. Deaths at the rookery as a result of disease or inexperienced parents are inevitable, and the skuas serve a useful role in removing the carcasses. Their attacks on

chicks and eggs may also help to ensure that the young penguins that survive to go to sea in late January or February are the fittest.

Other skuas gather at seal breeding beaches to scavenge pups that are stillborn or crushed to death in the hurly-burly of the colony. Skuas are supreme opportunists, adept at survival in the harsh Antarctic environment.

As this brief summer period provides rich pickings for the skuas, their own breeding is

timed to coincide with the food bonanza. They nest in November and December, usually close to penguin colonies, laying two olive-brown eggs in a shallow scrape of sand or gravel. Usually only one chick is reared, the other dying of starvation or from attacks by its nest-mate.

At their breeding sites, skuas are strongly territorial. They guard not just their nest but also part of the penguin rookery as a private larder. Human intruders suffer repeated aerial attack, designed to intimidate rather than injure.

South-polar skuas have been recorded (along with Antarctic and snow petrels) breeding farther south than any other bird – in mountains less than 800 miles (1280km) from the South Pole. Occasional birds have been recorded at the Pole itself, where the average summer temperature is −32°C (−26°F), and also at Russia's Vostock research station – close to the Pole at an altitude of 11,500ft (3500m).

WHEN FOOD BECOMES SCARCE

After the penguins leave their rookeries, survival becomes hard for skuas. They scavenge at sea on dead seabirds, or catch fish and shrimp-like krill. Some follow southern Atlantic fishing boats to eat offal thrown overboard, or chase other seabirds and force them to disgorge food.

Even at penguin rookeries, the supply of food limits the number of skuas. At the French Antarctic research base at Pointe Géologie in 1965, the 80-90 pairs of skuas breeding there relied for food on the local Adélie rookery. When the French established a rubbish dump beside their base, the skuas switched to it as an easy and regular food supply, and in 12 years the colony increased to 320 pairs before levelling off at a size the extra food could support. This swift expansion occurred because the abundant food allowed most pairs to rear two chicks.

Other species of skua also prey on penguin rookeries. Brown skuas on the sub-Antarctic island of South Georgia take the eggs and chicks of macaroni, gentoo and king penguins, and the Tristan skuas prey on rockhopper penguins on Gough Island. Skuas in the Northern Hemisphere prey on penguin-like auks – such as puffins, guillemots and razorbills – and gulls in a similar way. But these birds breed on cliffs, so the northern skuas have a difficult time compared to the southern skuas, with their easy supply of penguin food in the brief Antarctic summer.

Aerial attacker *A brown skua swoops on a colony of macaroni penguins in South Georgia, on the lookout for eggs or weakling chicks.*

FEBRUARY

IN THE NORTHERN SEAS THE COD ARE MATING AND THE GREAT
GREY WHALES ARE MIGRATING. NILE CROCODILES TEND THEIR HATCHLINGS,
PEACOCKS FLAUNT IN THE SRI LANKAN SUN, GALÁPAGOS GIANT
TORTOISES MATE IN THE MUD AND PATAGONIAN PENGUINS HATCH THEIR EGGS

Cod cacophony The ocean resounds to the grunts of a shoal of courting cod off the Lofoten Islands, Norway.

The grunting song of the courting cod

Huge shoals of cod gather around Norway's Lofoten Islands, off the north-west coast, in late February, ready for their annual courtship and mating. This is not a quiet affair, for the mating call made by a male cod is a noisy grunt – delivered singly or in short bursts of four at a time. The sounds are made by rapidly contracting muscles round the fish's swim bladder, which acts as a resonator.

Cod spend most of their life feeding and growing in cold seas, as far as 2000ft (610m) below the surface. But in autumn they begin to migrate to shallower waters, and those living in the Barents Sea (north of Norway and the USSR) swim south to the Lofotens. There they spawn in comparative warmth 250ft (76m) down where the cool coastal water meets the deeper but warmer water of the North Atlantic Drift. The water temperature is around 4°C (40°F).

The grunting calls are just one part of the display a male cod puts on to encourage a female to release her eggs. He postures and grunts in a courting dance, presenting his flanks, flicking his fins up and down and changing colour from uniform silver to darkly blotched. If the female is impressed, she will shed her pinhead-sized eggs – up to five million, depending on her size. Only two of the eggs need to survive to keep population numbers stable. Then the male curls round the female in a mating embrace, and becomes silent as he sheds his milt (sperm) to fertilise the eggs.

For two, three or four weeks, depending on the temperature, the eggs float about in the surface waters. Then they hatch as tiny fry, each about the size of a grain of rice. The fry remain at the surface for from three to five months, feeding on tiny sea animals such as shrimps and crab

Mini-cod Tiny cod fry are the size of a rice grain when they hatch from transparent eggs to float about in the sea. As they grow larger, the fish drop to the sea floor.

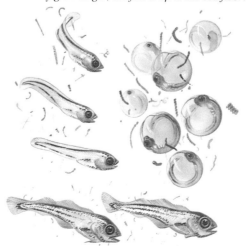

larvae. Then they gradually drift slowly north and into the Barents Sea. Some fry hide beneath the bells of mushroom-shaped jellyfish, somehow protected from the jellyfish's hanging curtain of deadly tentacles – perhaps by slimy mucus on the outside of the body.

When they reach about 2in (50mm) long, the young cod descend to the depths to feed on bottom-dwelling creatures such as slow-moving worms and small shellfish. As they grow larger they begin to catch other fish. Some cod follow the migrations of herring and a small fish called capelin. The immature cod of the Barents Sea are known as 'capelin cod', and in April vast numbers of them arrive off the coast of Finnmark, in the far north of Norway, to feed.

Cod do not reach sexual maturity until 6-15 years of age, depending on the water temperature, the shoal size and the amount of food they get to eat. The Barents Sea fish then make their spawning migration to the Lofoten Islands every year until they are about 20 years old. By this time they can be giants about 4ft (1.2m) long and 2 stone (13kg) in weight. Some old-timers that hunt fish shoals far out to sea are around 5ft (1.5m) long and 7 stone (45kg) in weight. In the 17th century, fish as heavy as 14 stone (89kg) were reputedly caught.

The cod and its relatives – the haddock, whiting and hake – have been popular eating fish for centuries. Their habit of gathering in large shoals to feed and spawn makes them easy to net in commercial quantities.

THE MATING HADDOCK

Male haddocks duel in the North Sea for the right to mate about a month later than the cod. Two males swim side by side, making curious knocking sounds as they try to warn each other off. The more aggressive the encounter, the higher the rate of knocking. The contest may end with the dominant fish butting his opponent.

The winner then courts his intended mate with a combination of sounds, postures and colours. He approaches the silent female, making a sound like a motorcycle starting up, and swims round her in a tight circle. His fins become darker and are spread out in full display, and his skin turns blotchy. As the moment of spawning approaches, he becomes silent.

The mating pair swim towards the surface, the female laying 10,000 eggs and the male shedding his milt to fertilise them.

A night of frenzy for the mating squid

On moonless nights in February, squid congregate in their millions in the Pacific Ocean to breed. For three nights these finger-length squid, known as opalescent squid, shoot about like tiny jet-propelled torpedoes in the shallow waters off Santa Catalina Island, south of Los Angeles, in a frenzied search for a mate.

A mating pair interlock arms (each has eight) and the male may change colour from silver to purple and then to rippling red. So obsessed are the squid that they are an easy target for predators. Blue sharks, with mouths agape, cut a swathe through the mating mass. And as the night passes, sea lions and pilot whales join in.

The surviving female squid sink slowly to the bottom. There each attaches 10-20 gelatinous egg cylinders to rocks or seaweed, which look as if they are sprouting dahlias. Their work done, the exhausted parents die, and large rays arrive to 'vacuum' up the dead and dying squid, and some of the egg cylinders. About three weeks later, the 100-200 eggs in each cylinder hatch, but so many of the hatchlings are snapped up by predators that fewer than one young squid from each capsule will be mating at Santa Catalina Island next February.

Squid hatchery *A milling throng of squid, some still mating, dart above the mass of egg capsules on the sea floor.*

Hot plants *Each skunk cabbage has a fleshy, leaf-like spathe curled round a heated flower stem beginning to push its way through the cold earth.*

Built-in winter warmth for the skunk cabbage

While most other flowering plants are waiting for the warmth of spring to waken them from their winter sleep, the robust skunk cabbage of eastern North America is stirring in the snow. This marsh plant can melt its way through the snow by generating enough heat to maintain a constant temperature of 22°C (72°F) for two weeks or more while the surrounding temperature may be only −13°C (9°F).

The heat is produced by the skunk cabbage's rapid respiration – the process in which plants take in oxygen to break down sugars and release energy as heat. It uses oxygen trapped in the soil, and on cold days takes in more, and burns up more nutrients, than on warm days. Although it seems inactive, the plant is using energy as fast as a busy hummingbird or shrew. The heat evaporates the oils in the tiny flowers clustered on a fleshy club called a spadix, and fills the air with scent. This brings out insects at temperatures well below their normal operating range, and they pollinate the plant while they forage in its warmth.

It is not this scent that gives the skunk cabbage its name, but the putrid skunk odour it releases if one of its parts is damaged.

Dreaded rattlesnakes as round-up victims

Each November in Texas, as winter draws in, western diamond-back rattlesnakes seek refuge from the cold. They crawl into any draught-free hollows below ground, such as small caves and chambers beneath fallen rocks. More and more gather in the best places, until several hundred entwined bodies – the largest about 7ft (2m) long – lie quietly in the dark, moving very little and not eating or drinking.

But now it is late February and the sun is warming the rocks above the rattlesnakes' sleeping place. They begin to respond to the warmth of spring, and emerge from their winter quarters eager to bask in the sun and then to hunt for their first meal in months – a small rodent such as a mouse. Soon they will mate and produce their young, born live ten or more at a time, in late summer.

The western diamond-back, one of the largest rattlesnakes, is greatly feared because its highly venomous bite can kill a man. But few people are actually bitten, and most encounters end with the snake raising its tail and loudly rattling the loosely connected horny segments at the tail tip – a sign of its own fear. Given the chance the rattlesnake will retreat, but if it is trodden on or tormented it will strike.

Annual 'rattlesnake round-ups' are held in spring in Texas, New Mexico and several other states to rid the countryside of the rattler. Ironically, the snake's hibernation helps the hunters. Many rattlesnakes never waken from their winter hibernation because even before the round-ups begin some hunters pour petrol into the caves and hollows to flush the animals out, often ruining the caves for other creatures as well. Captured snakes are put in large corrals, often without food, water or shelter from the cold – sometimes for months – to await slaughter. At round-up time, prizes are given for the most snakes brought in, and local residents and tourists alike are encouraged to behead the snakes before they are barbecued.

With the numbers of western diamond-backs declining from commercial exploitation, conservationists are keen to stop round-ups. Public dislike of round-ups is mounting, and the snakes may soon be able to hibernate in peace.

....

Rattlers awakening *As the late February sunshine begins to warm the rocks, western diamond-back rattlesnakes emerge from their winter hiding places – if not given a ruder awakening by Texan snake hunters.*

Where manatees keep warm in winter

Ripples spread across an inlet near Crystal River, Florida, blue under the February sunshine, as a blunt, bristly, grey nose emerges from the water and puffs a fine mist of breath into the air. Three more follow. They belong to a group of gentle, 60 stone (380kg) giants – West Indian manatees – that have returned to their traditional winter waters. Manatees, like the related dugongs of the Pacific and Indian oceans, are also called sea cows because they live by grazing on the leaves and roots of water plants. Food is digested slowly in a very long digestive canal, and this makes them prone to flatulence. One of the best ways to spot manatees is to look for trails of gas bubbles!

For much of the year, these West Indian manatees feed in the sea grass meadows in the Gulf of Mexico. But last October, as the water temperature in the Gulf began to fall, the manatees began their annual migration to the lagoons and estuaries of Florida's west coast. They come to luxuriate in warm springs and the warm-water outlets from numerous power stations. They can tolerate the change from salt to fresh water with ease, and switch their diet from sea grasses to the abundant freshwater plants that thrive in the Florida streams.

What they cannot tolerate is cold. Although they build up a thick layer of fat under the skin, they burn energy very slowly and find it difficult to keep warm if the water temperature drops. Had they stayed in the cooling waters of the Gulf, their body temperatures would have plummeted, and they would certainly have died.

Many of the females have been pregnant since leaving the Florida coast as the previous winter ended. Now, a year later, they have given birth to their single calves. Although young manatees can graze just a few weeks after they are born, their mothers suckle them for 12-18 months from teats under the front flippers. With the young staying close to mother for so long, they learn the migration routes to and from their winter refuges. Manatees have fairly poor eyesight and regularly bump into things in murky water. They call to one another constantly, using a series of short squeaks and squeals.

It is normally two years after the birth of a calf when the female mates again. Up to 15 males may gather round a female in season, pushing and shoving one another in gentle, lumbering battles for her attention. Eventually many will

A warm bath Manatee mothers and their well-grown calves avoid the winter cold in west Florida's warm water.

withdraw to seek other females and she will mate with the two or three winners.

The mother's long pregnancy and suckling period mean that she produces a calf only once every three years – occasionally every two years. This makes it difficult for manatees to recover from any drop in their numbers. In the past, local hunters killed them for food and oil, but the sale of manatee meat is now banned, so hunting has almost stopped. But another threat to their numbers is the enormous amount of boat traffic along the Florida coast. Many manatees bear scars left by deep wounds from propellers.

A further threat in recent years has been cyclically low water temperatures round Florida. Although the manatees huddle for warmth round warm-water outlets, they soon become chilled and stranded when they venture out to feed in the colder water. Many have been rescued, but others have died.

Marathon to Mexico for rugged grey whales

No migrating mammal travels farther than the rugged grey whale of the Pacific Ocean. Every year, hosts of them travel for three months each way on a 12,500 mile (20,000km) round trip from their summer feeding grounds in the seas around Alaska to spend the winter at the Baja California peninsula of Mexico. February finds the 35 ton, 45ft (14m) long whales courting, mating, or nursing newborn calves in the peninsula's warm lagoons.

The whales left the Arctic before the sea froze over in late October, and journeyed south close to the coast. Pregnant females led the way, followed by immature females and then adult males, with the immature males bringing up the rear. The first females arrived off Mexico in December. As females are pregnant for 13½ months, those who had mated the previous December gave birth in the shallows soon after arrival. Females who calved last winter either mated on the journey south, or are courting now at the lagoon mouths. Newly mature eight-year-olds are mating for the first time.

The baby whales, 15ft (4.5m) long at birth, could not coordinate breathing and swimming at first, and had to be nudged to the surface to 'blow' (breathe) by their mothers. Now they are well on the way to completing the thick layer of insulating blubber they will need in the icy north. They are suckled for seven months, and in August, in the food-rich Arctic Ocean, will learn to dive to suck up mussels and other molluscs, worms and shrimp-like creatures living on the sea bottom.

The first mothers and babies leave Mexico in March, swimming close to the shore where they can hide from groups of marauding killer whales in the thick coastal kelp forests. They arrive in the Bering Sea in late May.

About 500 whales die each year along the migration route, often of old age at about 40. Their bodies fall to the seabed, where they become islands of food for deep-sea organisms that depend for life not on the sun but on heat from the centre of the earth. Seabed cracks in the earth's crust are outlets for underwater geysers that spew out hot water containing sulphur. The bacteria that live on the sulphur are food for creatures such as giant clams and deep-sea crabs, and their larvae use whale carcasses as resting places as they drift in the sea between vents.

Giant baby *A baby grey whale is nudged to the surface by its mother to learn how to blow – breathe in and out several times. Grey whales blow every 3-4 minutes.*

Deep-sea stopover *Young deep-sea mussels nestle in the honeycomb of a decomposing whale rib (left). They are normally found at hot vents on the seabed (bottom left), but use whale carcasses to settle on between vents. The map below shows the migration route of the grey whales in the eastern Pacific in red. The positions of known hot vents, underwater volcanoes and the whale carcass pictured are also marked.*

Chukchi Sea

RUSSIA

Alaska (USA)

Bering Sea

CANADA

Gulf of Alaska

Pacific Ocean

Seattle

Summer feeding grounds
Winter breeding grounds
Migration routes
△ Hot vent (underwater volcano)

USA

Whale carcass

Baja California

Gulf of California

MEXICO

Courting cranes Two Japanese cranes dance their graceful courtship dance on the northern island of Hokkaido.

EUROPE AND NORTH ASIA
The spectacular dance of the Japanese cranes

A February dawn offers little warmth to the wild creatures of Japan's northern island, Hokkaido. Snow blankets the land and hoar frost coats the trees, yet for Japanese (or red-crowned) cranes, this month is the start of their courting season. The frosty dawn light reveals the stately cranes – each at least as tall as a man – standing stock-still on one leg in the shallows of the mist-shrouded river.

Not until the sun warms them will they stir, raising their slender necks, extending their cramped legs and stretching their wings. Then, after restless calling and strolling back and forth, they all suddenly bugle and take flight. Deep, slow, wing beats carry them effortlessly towards their feeding ground on farmland near the town of Kushiro where, in flocks of up to 100, they begin their snow dance – the courtship ritual that binds pairs together throughout the year.

Adult couples dance and display to each other and then to other pairs as they arrive. The dancing is infectious, spreading among the flock until dozens of birds are cavorting in the snow. Courting pairs pirouette, leap, bow gracefully, and turn, each movement related to the next, and each with a set response. While the adults are dancing, youngsters too immature to breed also leap and dance. A twig, a leaf or an old corn cob will attract their attention and excite them to bob, curtsy and climb slowly skywards as if mounting stairs, all the while tossing and catching the object over and over again.

The crane has been revered in Japan since ancient times. To the Ainu peoples of Hokkaido it is the god of the marsh, and to the Japanese the bird has come to represent long life, health, happiness and married union. Generations of Japanese artists and poets have been inspired by the crane, and its image can be found on anything from saké bottle labels to aircraft logos, from family crests to wedding kimonos.

Not long ago, however, it seemed that the symbol would outlive the bird itself. Although it once occurred widely throughout Japan, the crane became a prized target for hunters once feudal firearm restrictions were lifted, and was wiped out almost everywhere. By the end of the 19th century only a small population survived on eastern Hokkaido. The cranes were given legal protection as a 'Natural Monument' in 1935, and since the 1950s food provided for them during winter has encouraged a slow recovery of numbers to 400-450 birds. But land development is now destroying their habitat and limiting their numbers.

From mid-March, pairs of cranes fly to reed beds and marshes to breed. As the snow melts, they select raised areas to build their nests of reed stems. The female lays two eggs during late March or April, and the chicks hatch from late April to late May. The youngsters, in their tawny-brown juvenile plumage, stay with their parents – dependent on them at first for food and for knowledge about life in the marshes. In autumn the families move to cultivated fields, particularly maize stubble, before going to sites where they are fed in winter. When their parents leave again for the breeding grounds the following March, the young cranes are left to fend for themselves.

While Japanese cranes court in the snow on Hokkaido, at Arasaki on the island of Kyushu in southern Japan, up to 9000 cranes are mustering in the fields. Most are diminutive hooded cranes and beautiful, subtly shaded white-naped cranes. Also drawn to this migratory flock are the odd rarities – one or more sandhill cranes, a common crane and every few winters a Japanese crane, a Siberian white crane or a demoiselle crane. This huge gathering flies in to roost and feed during winter before returning north to breeding grounds in China and Russia.

Winter muster Every year, a huge gathering of about 9000 cranes, mostly hooded and white-naped cranes, assembles to winter on the Japanese island of Kyushu.

Macaques find warmth in the winter snow

Filing cautiously across a snow-covered hillside in northern Honshu, Japan's main island, on a day in February, the Japanese macaque monkeys step carefully, each in the footprints of the one in front. The group picks its way towards an area near the head of the valley where steam rises invitingly from some hot springs tucked into the hillside.

With evident relief, the macaques slide gently into the water. As the heat bubbling up from deep within the earth's mantle warms their chilled bodies, they gradually begin to relax.

Living farther north than any other monkey or ape, the Japanese macaque – the only monkey found in Japan – encounters climates that range from the pleasant warmth of Japan's southern islands to the frozen mountains of the north. Braving the winter snows is no easy matter, even when wrapped in the warmth of a macaque's thick fur coat. But the hot springs have provided the ideal solution for some of the mountain population. By sitting it out in the warmth of a thermal pool, the animals are able to stay in the mountains throughout the winter, living on bark. Other northern groups are forced to move to the lowlands for the winter.

Macaques are natural swimmers. Using a dog-paddle stroke, they can swim across the sea channels that separate Japan's many islands. In this way, they have colonised most of Japan. Even the young macaques soon learn to dive and paddle, playing exuberant games of catch-me-if-you-can.

One of 16 species of macaque monkey, the Japanese macaques are renowned for their inventiveness. One day in 1957, a young juvenile female (who was named Imo by the scientists

Dozing in a hot bath *In the snowy mountains of north Japan during winter, Japanese macaques keep warm by relaxing in hot springs.*

studying her group) took a sweet potato down to the shallows by the seashore and washed off the sand that coated it.

Her friends and family soon began to copy her, and the habit of potato-washing spread through the group. Later, the animals adapted this behaviour to other foods like wheat grains that had been put out on the sand for them. Now, years after Imo's death, group members still wash potatoes and wheat regularly – the first documented example of animals other than humans passing on newly acquired behaviour to others of their kind.

Macaques live in groups of 30-40 animals, which typically include five or six mature males and up to a dozen breeding females, together with their dependent young. Each group occupies its own territory, some 3-4sq miles (8-10sq km) of forest. Macaques are largely vegetarians, feeding on the fruits and flowers, leaves and roots of forest plants. They wander in search of food by day, and sleep in the trees wherever dusk finds them.

Studies of individual groups have revealed that all the females in a group are related to one another – descendants of a single matriarch long since dead. A female may ask another to groom her by approaching and presenting her shoulder. Acknowledging the request with a quiet 'coo' call, the other macaque begins to groom the shoulder – methodically combing

Snow monkeys *A young macaque takes to the warm water for the first time with its mother.*

SETTING THE CLOCK
Nature's rhythms – day and night, the moon's phases, high and low tide – help animals to regulate activities such as moulting, mating and migrating. The rhythms affect the creatures' nervous systems, which in turn stimulate glands that bring about changes in bodily functions.

Animals such as monkeys and birds react to changes in day length. The amount of light received by eye and brain activates the glands that organise their yearly timetable, even on the Equator, where, although day length is constant, light varies in intensity. Sea-living creatures such as grunion and coral respond to the phases of the moon, which affect their reproductive activities. Seashore creatures such as crabs have their timetable set by the twice-daily ebb and flow of the tide. Insect swarms for mating are induced by a combination of light intensity and humidity, and tend to occur at dawn and dusk.

through the fur with alternate hand movements and occasionally pausing to pick at a matted clump of hair or to remove debris. Macaques forming such friendships are often allies when quarrels erupt within the group, or will stand together for mutual defence against a common enemy. Female allies may even overpower a larger male when the need arises – if he muscles in on a good feeding patch that a female has found, for instance. Macaques are highly vocal and use a variety of simple calls to communicate with each other. And just as humans have different accents, so macaque populations from different parts of Japan have been found to pronounce the same natural call in noticeably different ways.

In the far north, the timing of mating is crucial. If it is too early the baby will be born before winter has given way to spring and brought a new growth of vegetation. Then the mother may be too ill-nourished to provide enough milk for her newborn infant. Mating too late leaves the baby to face its first winter before it has acquired a fully waterproof coat.

With the severe winters testing the animals' ability to survive, mating takes place as late as December-February, but in Japan's warmer southern parts, the mating season is from September to March. Babies are born five to six months after mating.

A female usually gives birth to a single infant. As with all young monkeys and apes, a baby macaque can cling onto its mother's fur almost from the moment it is born. Gripping tightly with hands and feet, it rides under its mother's belly wherever she needs to go on her daily search for food. Normally, a female gives birth only in alternate years, but where food is ample she may give birth every year.

In some parts of Japan, macaque groups have taken to living in or near temples. With plenty of food provided by the monks and the visitors, such groups may be much larger than those normally found in the wild. Some temple groups consist of a thousand or more animals. In such crowded conditions, the macaques are more aggressive and their relationships with each other are less stable. They will squabble irritably over minor infringements of their personal space, and are often bad tempered.

Shelter from a storm *Floating in the warm spring water, a macaque patiently awaits the end of a snowstorm, secure from the icy temperatures.*

February fisherman *Spurred on by hunger, a robin carries off a small fish it has caught in a stream. Such ingenuity may save the bird from starvation.*

The robin that learned to go fishing in winter

A flash of colour lights up the stream for a brief moment on a bleak February day, and a small bird carries off a slippery meal. The flash is not the electric blue of a kingfisher this time, but the red flush of a robin's breast.

Most of the insects, spiders, woodlice and worms that the robin normally feeds on are hidden away for winter, and in the few hours of daylight, food is hard to find. This robin has learned to fish. Perhaps it picked up the idea from a neighbouring kingfisher, for its first attempts were to pluck fish from the shallows where they fled after the kingfisher dived.

Now it has discovered that it can drive the fish into the shallows by hovering above the water. Then it stands breast high in the shallows and plucks fish from the water like a heron. Robins find their prey by seeing movement, and this one has learned to allow for the fish's position being distorted by the water. It catches small fish such as minnows and carries away those it can keep hold of, beating them senseless before swallowing them whole, head first.

Any robin that can, like this one, find a new food supply will increase its chances of survival through winter. But probably too few live where they have the opportunity to fish. Other song birds sometimes fish – wrens have been known to take troutlets from hatcheries, and blackbirds take tadpoles from garden ponds.

The mass mating habits of the common frog

Emerging from beneath a moss-covered, rotting log, a female frog takes in the damp air of a February night in huge gulps. She has spent the winter in a hollow under the log, protected from both predators and the worst of the weather. Bulging with the eggs that had developed mainly in autumn, before she began her hibernation, she must now make her way to her breeding pond – the place where she will find a mate to fertilise her eggs. It is also the place where her offspring, which live completely in the water at first, will remain while they undergo one of the most extraordinary changes in nature – from black, swimming tadpoles to tiny froglets that will take up life on land.

MIGRATING TO MATE

The damp grass moistens the frog's soft, black-mottled skin, which has dried out a little during the months spent waiting for spring. A frog's skin helps it to breathe, but needs to be moist so that oxygen can be absorbed from the air. Despite her winter without food, the frog does not stop to eat any snails or slugs among the grass as she passes. Her only aim is to reach the familiar waters and find a mate.

The night is perfect for her migration. If there had been snow or frost on the ground she would have returned to her winter hideaway, but light rain and the cool night air spur her on. How she knows the way to the breeding pond is uncertain, but she may be partly drawn by the smell of algae – minute water plants. When they hatch, her offspring will feed on the algae.

To reach the pond of her choice she may cross all sorts of terrain, even other ponds. Generally she heads for the pond where she herself was hatched. Female frogs are known to use the same pond at spawning time year after year. For some unknown reason, females almost always spend the winter on land. Although some male frogs spend the winter in nooks and crannies on land, many do not have to migrate to the breeding ponds at all. They will have spent the winter in the pond, often under a sheet of ice, buried in the mud at the bottom. All frogs can breathe through their skin under-water, and may survive for weeks in winter without coming to the surface for air.

As February progresses, more and more females make the journey to the breeding pond, and as they plop into the water, the males are alerted to their arrival. The males' breeding urge is just as strong as the females', and they swim about frantically in search of a mate.

When a male bumps into a female, he clambers on her back and holds her tight in a mating embrace known as 'amplexus'. The male, who is smaller than the female, reaches round her distended body and grips the slippery skin under her arms with the horny pads on his thumbs. Clasped like this, the pair will remain locked together until it is time to spawn. Once a male has captured a mate, he stays with her, maybe for weeks, and constantly fends off other males who might push him off her back and claim her for themselves.

Nobody knows exactly what triggers the frogs to spawn. The inhabitants of one pond may spread out their spawning over a few weeks, but more often there is a mass gathering and most of the eggs are laid in just a few nights.

In the hours before midnight, the embracing pairs rise from the murky depths of the pond and congregate just beneath the surface. As they gather, the males begin a chorus of feeble

Frogs embrace *Her body bulging with eggs, a female frog is clasped by her mate. He may hold her like this for several weeks before the pair rise to the surface of the pond in the dead of night to spawn.*

croaking, probably to warn off other males and maybe also as a courtship song that encourages the females to spawn.

Spawning begins suddenly. Each female lays between 1500 and 3000 eggs within a few seconds. Her mate reacts quickly, and sheds his sperm over the eggs with lightning speed. The eggs will not be fertilised unless the sperm reaches them before the thick, protective jelly that surrounds each egg reacts with the pond water and swells round it to form a transparent package about ¼ in (6mm) across. If the male were not clasped so close to his mate, he would probably not be able to fertilise any of the eggs before they became securely enclosed.

In a large colony, the clasped pairs of mating frogs are soon floating in a raft of shed spawn that grows larger as the night goes on. Once each female has laid her eggs, the male releases her and swims away quickly to find or steal another mate. The female, thin now that her belly has been emptied of its eggs, leaves the pond in search of food. Neither parent will take any further interest in the offspring.

FROM SPAWN TO FROGLET

The following morning, a few pairs of frogs are still adding to the raft of spawn, but most have abandoned it. The thick jelly surrounding each round black egg makes it unattractive to predators. As it grows, each egg elongates, revealing the shape of the tadpole inside. Eventually, each of the tiny tadpoles struggles free of its jelly, yet continues to grip onto it for a while longer.

Within a few days the tadpoles can swim freely in search of algae to eat. Now without the protection of the jelly, they are hunted by all kinds of fish, insects and other amphibians, and provide a spring bounty for the pond's stirring life. But the vast numbers of the wriggling tadpoles are an insurance for the future of the frog population. Some tadpoles will always be lucky enough to survive. After seven weeks they develop hind legs, and by about three months after hatching have developed all four legs and are ready to leave the pond.

Once on land, the tiny froglets will hunt insects and other small prey abundant in the warmth of summer. Not until they are two or three years old will they feel the urge to return to the pond to spawn.

....

New life launched *Spawning completed, frogs float in a forest pond amid a mass of eggs they will leave there to hatch into tadpoles. In three months time, the surviving tadpoles will have developed into froglets.*

Feeding platform *Two Steller's sea eagles and a smaller white-tailed sea eagle (right) share an ice floe.*

Giant eagles that flock to fish in icy seas

As the February sunrise spreads an orange wash over ice and snow at the north-eastern tip of Hokkaido, Japan, the Steller's sea eagles are there to greet it. These spectacular birds have moved south from their breeding grounds in north-east Siberia to winter around the Shiretoko Peninsula, a wild, mountainous finger of land projecting into the Sea of Okhotsk.

One of the world's biggest congregations of Steller's sea eagles has gathered here. At night the birds roost in the oak and birch woods in the steep, snowy river valleys where there is shelter from the wind. By day more than 2000 – almost one-third of the world population – gather to hunt for fish offshore, some using the ice floes as floating observation platforms.

The handsome eagles have a wingspan of over 8ft (2.4m), and huge, sharply hooked, bright orange beaks. Their plumage is blackish-brown with a white rump and diamond-shaped tail, and they are also white on the shoulders and the leading edges of the wings. Older birds have white foreheads and grey-streaked heads. Young birds are blotched with brown and white, and have creamy-white beaks. As they mature they get progressively darker. They are believed to take up to five years to attain full plumage.

Steller's sea eagles are named in honour of the 18th-century German naturalist Georg Wilhelm Steller, who explored their home range with Vitus Bering (after whom the Bering Sea is named). To the Japanese, the eagle is known as 'O-washi' – the great eagle. The total world population of the birds is estimated to be 6000-7000, and more than 4000 of them are thought to be breeding adults.

DAWN GATHERING

Unlike most eagles, which start the day when the sun is warm, Steller's sea eagles are up and about well before dawn, when the temperature is still as low as −15°C (5°F). The eastern horizon is paling only slightly when the first shadowy shapes float into the dark sky. The eagles rise gradually in twos and threes, and then by the dozen until they fly in hordes, like giant rooks swarming from their roost.

First the birds are picked out in silhouette as the light increases, but then the various stages of adult and immature plumage show up. The light also reveals the presence of some white-tailed sea eagles among the throng; smaller and with no white on the wings, thighs or rump, they are surpassed in size and looks by the stunning Steller's sea eagles.

The eagles range out across the water, some quartering the skies and others perching on ice floes. Sometimes 40 or more eagles gather overhead at once as they choose a direction for the day's hunting, while below them 400 or more have each taken a stance on the offshore ice. These great birds are quite vocal, and their gruff barking calls – a dog-like 'kyow, kyow, kyow' or strong, deep 'kra, kra, kra, kra' – echo among the wooded coastal crags. They call frequently when squabbling over food or roosts.

Although Steller's sea eagles are known to eat large and medium-sized birds, those wintering in Japan feed almost exclusively on fish and carrion. They may be seen gathered on the carcass of a dead seal or sometimes a dead whooper swan, but it is far more usual to see them taking Alaskan pollock from the sea

POWERFUL WEAPONS

The claws of a bird of prey are razor-sharp talons with which they can catch and kill their prey by crushing and piercing. Not all of them have talons of the same type.

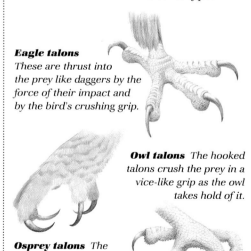

Eagle talons
These are thrust into the prey like daggers by the force of their impact and by the bird's crushing grip.

Owl talons *The hooked talons crush the prey in a vice-like grip as the owl takes hold of it.*

Osprey talons *The bird's toe pads are covered with tiny spines to help it grasp and carry slippery fish.*

Blizzard bound *When heavily falling snow curtails their hunting, the eagles shelter in a tree, looking like huge shadows in the grey, snow-filtered light.*

surface. Often these are injured fish that have escaped from the nets of local fishing fleets, or that have been trapped in the shallows by the drifting ice.

When an eagle hunting from the air spots a fish, it spirals down to the water with feet lowered and tail and wings raised to lose height. Then it swoops in, tail fanned, and swings its legs forward with precision to snatch the fish from the water surface in its talons. A nearby ice floe, preferably with part of it forming a raised block, serves as a dining table. Alternatively, the hunter may return to the safety of a tree branch on the coast.

By three o'clock in the afternoon the light has begun to fade, and the eagles forsake their vantage points on the ice floes and return to their roosts for the long winter night.

On mornings when heavily falling snow obscures their vision, the eagles delay hunting, or sometimes do not leave the roost at all. If snow falls during the day, they give up hunting and roost together in hundreds on the wooded slopes, or anywhere they can escape the wind. They crowd together until the blizzard ends.

Although the great eagles spend most of the winter hunting, on sunny, spring-like days when the temperature climbs to almost freezing point, they may occasionally begin courting. Males and females soar in pairs, chasing each other with remarkably agile close-formation aerobatics and uttering frequent calls. The eagles dive, swoop, turn, and grapple each other with their talons. Sometimes a courting pair of eagles lock their talons together and spin over and over in the air like a living cartwheel.

By March, the numbers will have dwindled considerably as the great birds fly north again to Russia to breed. The eggs (from one to three) are laid in massive nests built high in the trees of the Siberian forests, and the young birds start to hatch from early June. During November or early December, as the Sea of Okhotsk ices over, the birds will begin to fly south once again to spend the rest of the winter in Japan.

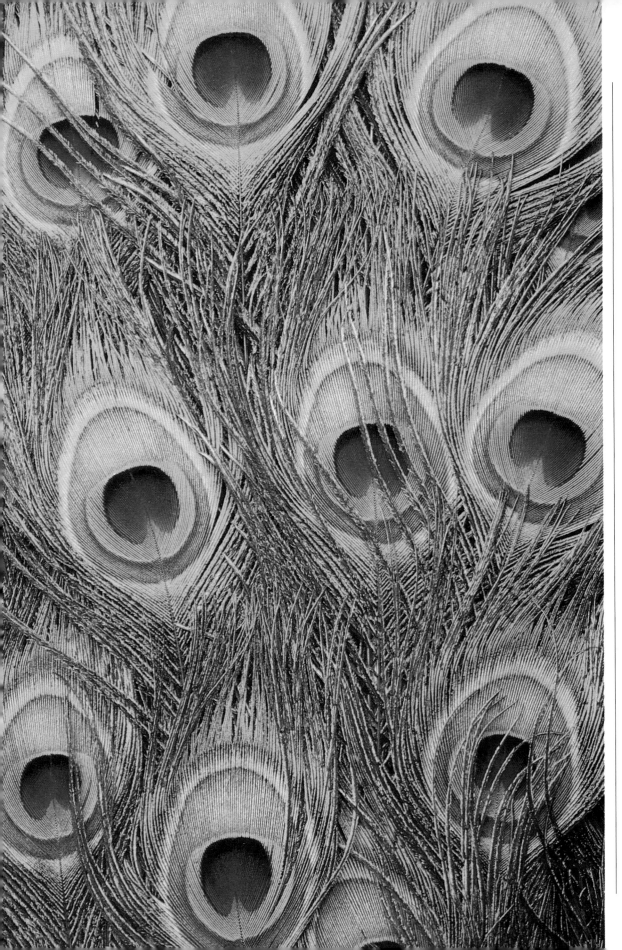

The peacock's hypnotic tail of many eyes

With a coronet of feathers standing proud on its head and its sumptuous train flowing behind, a large bird lands in the forest clearing and struts majestically back and forth. The Sri Lankan sun, filtering through the trees, catches his brilliant blue chest and lights his train, suddenly raised and spread, into a shimmering green fan spangled with 'eyes' that flash out discs of black and purple, blue and gold, as shivers pass through the long feathers.

Suddenly the graceful illusion is shattered as the peacock closes his fanned tail and utters a harsh scream. It is a warning to another peacock stepping into the clearing, and the intruder hurries off. This is February, the mating season, and the peacock (the male peafowl) is defending his territory, the clearing. Not all intruders leave so quickly; sometimes claws and spurs are used and skirmishes go on sporadically for hours.

The territory has two or three secluded spots where the peacock parades to lure in a female. It takes a dazzling display to make the dowdy, brownish peahen show any interest in mating. Time and again she walks away as the cock backs towards her with raised fan rustling and chestnut wings flashing. Then he swivels as if to transfix her with his fan's huge spread of eyes.

Eventually the cock gathers a harem of about four hens. Each hen lays from four to six eggs in a scrape in the ground. She incubates them for four weeks before the chicks emerge fully feathered and leave the unprotected nest within hours. The peahen teaches them to find seeds to eat. She scratches at the ground by the seeds and points with her head down and tail up. The whole courtship display seems to have grown from this teaching, for when the courting cock does this, the hen is drawn to him to look for food. His raised tail fan emphasises the display.

It is not actually the peacock's tail that forms the train, but his tail coverts – the layer of feathers that covers the base of a bird's tail. Each of the peacock's covert feathers has an eye at the tip. If a peacock feather is held up to lamplight sideways on, it will appear black. It is not

The gleam in the eyes The striking beauty of the peacock's train of feathers is flaunted before hen birds. Its shimmering 'eyes' get their colour from the way the feather barbs split up and reflect light.

pigments that give it colour. The tiny filaments, or barbules, fringing the parallel fronds of the feather have surfaces that split the light into its separate, rainbow colours. The colour reflected back depends on the angle of the light.

Not only the fastidious peahen is attracted by the shimmering male. The grounds of princely palaces in India – and the gardens of ancient Greece and Rome – were graced by the birds. They still strut about the lawns of country houses in Europe and North America. But in one sphere peacocks have lost popularity – they are rarely served as a delicacy at table as they once were at English medieval banquets. Even on those occasions the train added glamour. It was fanned out around the turkey-sized cooked bird before the dish went to the guests.

Alluring vibrations *With his back turned, the courting cock flashes his wings and raises and quivers his fan of feathers so that they rattle lightly to attract passing hens.*

Shimmering display *The cock gently waves his finery at an interested hen and captivates her with the array of some 200 eyes.*

Under one cloak *Impressed by the display, the hen crouches to receive the male. The peacock spreads his gorgeous train over her as they mate.*

Sharing the caring *A mother has leisure to clean her feet while her baby is tended by another female langur.*

Langur aunts take part in the baby-minding

The blistering heat of noon in southern India is only partly screened out by the forest canopy, and even in their shady perch the common langurs are content to laze. Snuggling among them are one or two babies, the first of the season, born in January and now a month old. They are being held and groomed by 'aunts' while their mothers look placidly on. Langur mothers, who produce a baby every other year, frequently let others 'borrow' their infants. Adolescent females are particularly common aunts, but adult females also borrow, and may even suckle, another mother's infant.

Sharing the tending of the babies allows young females to practise mothering and frees the mother from constant care. Its aim may also be to bond the females more closely. Females that have cared for youngsters will fight for them, and fighting may occasionally be necessary. When a male outsider ousts the group's sole breeding male perhaps once every few years, the new group leader usually tries to kill the small infants because, with their young wiped out, the females are soon ready to breed again. Then the new leader can father his own young. Mothers and aunts, who make up most of the group of 18 or so, will fiercely resist the killing, sometimes successfully, although the male's larger size makes it difficult.

Apart from such battles, langurs live in peace, whooping to one another as they swoop gracefully through the trees to feed on fruits, flowers, shoots and leaves. In the heat of the day they rest and groom, and at night they sleep on branches that will not bear the weight of their chief enemies, tigers and leopards.

In Hindu legend the monkey-god Hanuman, with a troop of common langurs, helped the god Rama to rescue his wife from a demon. Because of this the langurs are often called Hanuman monkeys, and are treated as sacred. People who offer them food earn merit for their next life. The long-legged monkeys, knee-high to a man, roam freely in villages and fields.

Freshwater bathing Lesser flamingos drink and bathe in a freshwater inlet on Lake Nakuru, in the Rift Valley.

How flamingos survive in the soda lakes

In a string of lakes cupped between the precipitous sides of the East African Rift Valley, the water is almost hidden by the pink glow from a vast flock of lesser flamingos. But amid the pink there are paler patches where crèches of chicks are gathered. Each chick's parents will find it among the thousands and feed it a mush of partly digested algae – minute water plants. In February the chicks are around two months old and almost ready to fly. Soon they will join their parents in nightly journeys

A specialised life Lesser and greater flamingos are among the world's most specialised birds. They alone can find all their food in the Rift Valley soda lakes.

up and down the valley in search of the richest feeding grounds.

The lakes where the flamingos are nesting in the valley bottom are shallow but have no outflow. Rivers and streams gush down into them from the surrounding mountains, and the water they deliver contains minerals leached from the volcanic rocks. The searing equatorial heat evaporates the water, leaving behind an alkaline soup called a soda lake.

Only the most specialised of animals and plants are able to tolerate such an inhospitable environment. Soda lakes have no large plants growing in them and very few fish. Instead there are legions of blue-green algae and many tiny creatures that feed in the rich mud – and the supreme soda-lake specialists, flamingos.

Flamingos are the only birds in the world that prefer soda lakes to any other habitat. Although other birds, including cormorants, fish eagles, herons and great white pelicans, may gather on the African soda lakes to feed, only flamingos breed there and live out their whole lives wading in the salty water. Lesser flamingos are the most abundant. Flocks of more than a million often cover the shores of lakes Nakuru, Natron and Magadi in Tanzania and Kenya. Greater flamingos, although less common, have a wider range and may be found as far north as the salty lagoons of Spain and southern France, and as far east as India.

The flamingo's body is perfectly adapted to its way of life. Long slender legs, webbed feet and a

Taking a bath in steam Hot geysers may be another source of fresh water for lesser and greater flamingos to drink and to wash the thick soda from their feathers.

long neck enable it to wade through the salty shallows and soft mud. Flamingos feed with their necks and heads bent so that their curved beaks are upside-down in the water. They pump water through their beaks with their tongues, expelling it at intervals of a few seconds. Inside the beak, fine filters catch the minute algae, shrimps and water fleas, which the birds then swallow. Most of their feeding is done at night

because during the day the winds stir up small waves that swamp their beaks.

Greater and lesser flamingos have filter systems designed to catch different organisms, so they avoid competing with each other for food. Greater flamingos have relatively coarse filters for catching shrimps and other small creatures living on the lake floor, so concentrate round the banks where the water is shallow. Lesser flamingos have much finer filters for trapping algae, with special anti-clogging structures to keep them free of larger creatures. They do not need to reach the lake bottom, so can feed in deeper water. The two species feed together in vast numbers on the same lakes.

Both types share an environment where fresh water is scarce. They cannot drink the soda lake's alkaline water and must wash the soda from their feathers to keep their plumage waterproof. So every day the rivers and streams that feed the soda lakes are bustling with flamingos. Standing shoulder to shoulder, they drink the welcome fresh water, and splash their feathers to wash away the salt. Some flamingos fly to the many freshwater springs in the hills around, and some use relatively fresh hot-water geysers nearby. *Continued overleaf*

The main lesser flamingo breeding season begins with courting displays in October or November. Each nest is a cylinder of mud crowned with a cup in which the female lays a single white egg. Both parents take turns to incubate the egg; which hatches after about 30 days. The youngster is covered with grey down and has long pink legs and a partly formed pink beak. When it fledges after 9-13 weeks, its feathers are a paler pink than those of its parents, and it does not achieve full pink colouring, which comes from pigments in the diet, until it is three or four years old.

Flamingo chicks are at first completely dependent upon their parents. They cannot feed themselves until the complex filters inside their beaks have fully developed. In their crèches on Lake Natron, their main breeding lake, the youngsters are well protected because most predators find it impossible to walk through the alkaline surroundings without getting burnt. As the water evaporates from a lake, the high concentration of soda causes crystals to form, and they ring the lake in white ridges.

But heavy rains can destroy the mud-tower nests and drown eggs and small chicks. Falling water levels can also be dangerous. In 1962, with more than a million pairs of flamingos nesting on Lake Magadi in Kenya, many chicks died when crystals formed by the rapid evaporation encrusted their legs with heavy anklets of soda crystals. The chicks were unable to fly or even to walk to the water to feed.

....

Newly hatched *A greater flamingo examines its newly hatched, downy grey chick. It will be about ten weeks before the chick can fly, during which time it is completely dependent on its parents.*

Mother's friends *Sable antelope females spend their lives in the same group, joined in February by the calves.*

Sable antelopes look after their calves

Their dark brown flanks glistening in the February sunlight, a small group of female sable antelopes is grazing among the trees. Most of them have given birth to their calves, and as conscientious mothers they will stay near enough to the youngsters to visit them twice a day for feeding. So for now they restrict their usual wanderings through the open woodlands of southern central Africa.

Like the young of many other antelopes and deer, a newborn sable antelope is kept hidden in a clump of tall grass or dense brush. Safe from the prying eyes of passing predators such as lions and leopards, it waits motionless for its mother to come every 12 hours to suckle it. Once it has been fed, the calf snuggles into a new hiding place and will not move an eyelid, even if a predator comes within a short distance of the spot where it is curled up.

By the end of February or in March, the youngsters are strong enough to join the group of from five to ten females as it continues its seasonal circuit round the home range of up to perhaps ½ sq mile (1.3sq km). The animals always make their way to the best grazing and browsing. Favourite spots are woodlands near permanent water, where the grass, leaves and tree shoots are always juicier and more plentiful.

The calves need good feeding for they will grow up to be some of the largest among the antelope family – up to 4ft 6in (1.4m) tall at the shoulder and reaching weights of 35-40 stone (223-255kg). Aggression comes naturally to them and they certainly have the weapons for a fight – their formidable curved horns are up to 5ft (1.5m) long.

Without hesitation, both male and female sable antelopes will lash out with their horns at any predators incautious enough to attack them. Even lions tend to steer clear of them. When battling among themselves for dominance, male antelopes avoid the risk of serious injury by kneeling on their forelegs, locking horns with each other and pushing and twisting heads in a trial of strength.

GROWING UP

The female calves will stay in the same group as their mothers for the rest of their lives, but the bull calves will be driven out when they are about a year old. Then they join the bachelor herds that roam the fringes of the female ranges. They gradually darken as they mature until their backs, flanks and legs have developed the velvety black coat that gives the animals their name.

At five or six years old, a bachelor begins to set up a territory of his own, driving out other males until he is the undisputed master of it. During the April-May mating season, he will try to keep within his territory any adult females that wander into it to feed, so that he can mate with them as they become receptive.

A mature bull will stay in his territory from year to year until a stronger male can oust him.

Protective mother *A female crowned eagle stands guard over her fluffy white chick as it dozes in the treetop nest after a meal brought by its father.*

Monkey-eating eagle of the African forest

Imperious on its lofty nest, a crowned eagle scans the top storey of an East African forest. The February of alternate years is a busy time for the eagles – the month when their one or two eggs hatch and downy white nestlings clamour continuously for fresh meat. For two months it is the father who brings their food. The mother stays on guard at the nest – but will not interfere when the stronger chick inevitably kills the weaker one. Soon both the parents will be cruising close to the treetops on the hunt, and the task of feeding the eaglet will go on for about 11 months while it learns to hunt for itself.

Largest and most fearsome of the African eagles, the powerful crowned eagle has no difficulty in carrying off monkeys in its talons, but prey such as small antelopes are eaten on the ground or torn into pieces for lifting. Despite its heavy build it has superb agility in flight and can weave its way through the tangled branches to swoop without warning on its prey.

If its coming should be spotted, a chorus of alarm rises from the small mammals in the trees. But once the eagle is upon them, the only hope lies in hurried flight to a lower storey of the trees. Dropping like stones, a troop of monkeys will plummet pell-mell, risking injury to escape the cruel grip of the eagle's talons.

Heavyweight buffaloes battle for mates

Surly and suspicious, a veteran Cape buffalo grazes amid the tree-fringed grassland of southern Africa. Defeated in a mating contest, he has joined a bachelor herd and returned to his habitual cud-chewing.

February and March are the peak mating months for buffaloes, a season when the males repeatedly batter their rock-hard heads against equally hard-headed challengers, all of them avid to win the right to mate with a group of cows. At every challenge, the veteran bull and the rival, who are each more than half a ton in weight and around 5ft (1.5m) high at the shoulder, charge at each other head on and meet with a colossal clash of the heavy horn bosses that protect them like helmets. Grunts and hoarse bellows add to the ferocious dramas.

The cows, meanwhile, continue their daily round, alternately munching grass and chewing cud in an endless struggle to nourish their huge bodies. They need to drink every day and cannot stray far from water. Muddy pools also allow them to take cooling dips; if it gets very hot, they will spend the day dozing in deep shade, coming out to eat only at night.

Cows are pregnant for 11 months. Many give birth in January as the rains bring a flush of new grass to the parched plains. With food abundant, the cows will be well nourished and able to provide enough milk for the newborn calves. Despite their size – they weigh in at some 6 stone (38kg), about ten times heavier than a human baby – the calves are vulnerable to predators such as lions. The mothers seek safety in numbers. Banded together in herds of up to 2000, they make a daunting, beefy display.

Dangerous foe *Although a buffalo's quiet life is devoted mainly to feeding, if alarmed it will charge even a lion.*

The tender early life of a Nile crocodile

Gently does it *The mother crocodile delicately digs up her hatching eggs and scoops them, up to 20 at a time, into a pouch in the floor of her mouth.*

February hatchling *A young crocodile greets the world after using the tooth on its snout to split the leathery shell where it has developed for three months.*

When the pelting February rain sweeps away as suddenly as it arrived, a female Nile crocodile lying just a few strides from an East African lake shifts her 14ft (4.2m) length and reveals the flattened patch of dry sand she has so carefully protected from the rain. Buried about two hand-lengths below it, in a constant temperature and humidity, lies her nest of some 60 eggs, each about 3½in (90mm) long. She retreats into the shady undergrowth, but not far away. For the past three months she has barely left her nest – never eating and rarely going to the water to drink. Unguarded nests are often pillaged by large monitor lizards, or the eggs rot through exposure to the rain.

As the crocodile dozes, she is roused by a high-pitched yelping from the direction of her nest. Homing in on the piping calls, she clears away the sand covering the nest, using her powerful front legs carefully so that none of the eggs is crushed. Within minutes, the first baby splits its leathery eggshell with the sharp egg tooth on the tip of its snout. Soon a squirming heap of youngsters, each 10in (250mm) long, is unfolding into tiny, glistening dragons.

The mother stoops into the nest, turns her head to the side, and scoops up a mouthful of dirty white eggs and wriggling babies. As she rights her head, the load falls into the bottom of her mouth, pushing down her tongue and forming a pouch that can hold 20 eggs and young. The mother holds her jaws open in a gaping smile, one or two shiny heads and tails poking out from between her sharp teeth, and makes for a quiet pool with shady, overgrown banks. There she sinks under the water and sways her opened jaws from side to side to flush the hatchlings out. She squeezes open any unhatched eggs to free the babies. It takes several trips to empty the nest, hurried trips in case the youngsters' cries should attract predators. Even when the babies are all in the water, they need constant protection for they make a perfect meal for a hawk or a monitor lizard.

The new crocodile family is soon joined by the father. Absent during the incubation period, he has been attracted by the youngsters' yelps. About September, male Nile crocodiles mate

A perfect mother *With jaws carefully apart, the crocodile transports her wriggling babies and hatching eggs. She takes them to a secluded nursery pool.*

with several females to increase their chances of fathering young, but could not possibly help to raise them all if they hatched at the same time. This seldom happens. Males are drawn to the nearest and first of their broods to hatch, and may then move on to help with others.

Both parents stay in the pool with their brood for a few weeks, coming to the rescue every time a piping alarm is raised. The young crocodiles bask on their parents' knobbly backs, float on the surface stalking water insects, or creep into the undergrowth hunting spiders or tiny frogs. Their short, barking calls keep them in touch with one another, and if there is an alarm, they plunge under the water until their mother gives the all clear. She can fend off most predators with a snap of her huge jaws, and rushes at any intruder who is still not scared away.

After a week or two, the babies start to venture farther afield and as time passes, the parents lose interest and drift away, leaving the youngsters to fend for themselves. This is the most vulnerable time for small crocodiles; only one or two from a nest are likely to survive the attacks of herons, fish eagles, genet cats and numerous other predators. When they are first on their own the young crocodiles stay together in a loose group, basking together on a favourite rock or fallen tree trunk by day, dispersing in the relative safety of evening to feed, and returning to the group at daybreak.

Freed of her maternal responsibilities by March, the thin and hungry mother returns to the lake to feed and grow fat again. It will be about November before she returns to her nesting ground to lay another clutch of eggs and take up her three-month vigil again.

GROWING AND EATING

Nile crocodiles grow by about 12in (300mm) a year during their first three or four years, then slower growth continues for the rest of their lives. By ten years old they are some 5ft (1.5m) long and sexually mature. As they grow, their diet changes from the water insects and spiders of babyhood to frogs and reptiles and, by the age of ten, to fish.

At about 8ft (2.4m) long, crocodiles also eat water birds and animals drinking at the water's edge, such as antelopes. A crocodile lurks underwater to seize prey in its strong jaws, or rushes ashore to take a victim, sometimes felling it with a blow of head or tail. The biggest Nile crocodiles are 18ft (5.5m) long – nobody is sure of their age.

Man's long-fingered relative, the aye-aye

Moving slowly through the high branches of an ancient forest in the dead of a Madagascan night is one of the world's rarest animals – an aye-aye. It is about the size of a large rabbit but resembles a squirrel, with big eyes, big ears, a long, bushy tail and dark fur flecked with white. The aye-aye's strange name is said to imitate its peculiar cry. It belongs to the same group of animals as man, the primates, and is closely related to bush babies and lemurs.

On this February night, a female aye-aye has left her high tree nest of interwoven branches and leaves to forage. As she scrambles through the branches, her tiny baby, just a few days old, clings to her fur. Aye-ayes are solitary animals, and although a male visits a female's territory to court and mate, the one youngster is tended only by its mother. The sharp claws on her feet help her to grip the tree bark and hang precariously to reach food, but on each big toe she has a nail, not a claw. And on each hand she has a long, exceptionally thin third digit.

Suddenly the aye-aye cocks her head and her naked, bat-like ears twitch. With her acute hearing she has pinpointed where beetle grubs are tunnelling in the wood. Stretching forward, she tears off a piece of bark with her 1in (25mm) long incisor teeth to expose the tiny entrance hole, and winkles out the grub with her very thin finger, specially adapted for the job. As the young aye-aye grows, it will learn to do the same, but for now it wants only mother's milk.

After several hours of searching out grubs, the aye-aye descends to the forest floor to look for her other main source of food, fruit and seeds. She walks clumsily on her palms with fingers and toes pointing upwards, and the clinging youngster makes progress particularly slow. But in the dark, she is safe from her most dangerous predators – domestic cats and dogs, and even humans. The Malagasy think these harmless animals bring ill-luck, and often kill them. Once among the leaf litter, the aye-aye sniffs out ripe fruits such as coconuts. Her sharp incisors make a small hole in the nut's hard shell, then she squats on her haunches and scoops out the ripe pulp with her long middle finger.

The only place in the world where the aye-aye is found is the rain forest of Madagascar. Sadly, the forest is fast disappearing.

Rare relative In the forest night, a foraging aye-aye listens intently for grubs tunnelling in tree wood.

Rare occasion Galápagos giant tortoises are noisy suitors, but successful ·mating is rare among these cumbersome creatures. Different forms of the giant tortoise live on the slopes of each of Isla Isabela's five volcanoes.

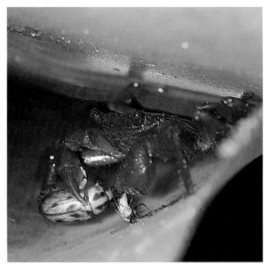

High tea A bromeliad crab hauls a captured beetle into her treetop pool as a feast.

The courting hazards facing a giant tortoise

Long, guttural groans rise and fall in the sulphurous air of a volcanic crater in the Galápagos Islands. They come from a Galápagos giant tortoise in his efforts to mate. February rains have filled the crater's mud wallows, making them a magnet for the tortoises, the largest in the world. Males are more than 4ft (1.2m) long and can be heavier than 35 stone (223kg), but females are smaller.

The crater is on Isla Isabela, largest of the Galápagos Islands that straddle the Equator about 600 miles (960km) off Ecuador. To reach the crater, the tortoises have had to clamber up from the volcano's higher slopes, where they spend most of the year. For creatures that sleep 16 hours a day and normally move very little, such a climb takes considerable effort. On arrival the male sniffed out a female ready for mating, rammed her repeatedly with the front of his shell and nipped at her legs until she drew them beneath her. Now, unable to move, she puts up with his prolonged scramble to mount her. His concave underparts make the task a little easier. But if she does not want to mate, she can still thwart him by lowering her back end to the ground and he will have to try another female.

After mating the female goes down to the dry, sunny lowlands where in June she will dig a hole, moisten it with urine and mould it into a nest. There she will lay about ten eggs and cover them with about 6in (150mm) of damp soil that bakes into a hard lid. When the eggs hatch some six months later, the youngsters will have to hack their way out of the nest.

Domed shell Tortoises have shells suited to their feeding habits. Those that graze plants near the ground have low-slung shells fitted snugly behind the neck.

Saddle-shaped shell Where there is taller vegetation, tortoises have long necks so that they can feed on it. The shell arches behind the neck to let the head reach up.

High life in Jamaica for caring crabs

A reddish-brown crab about the length of a thumbnail is feeding in a tiny pool. Around her the air is filled with the sounds of insects and birds – not shorebirds or sand flies but the animals of the rain forest. This crab's pool, which she has newly cleaned and spruced for the January-February breeding season, is held in a rosette of bromeliad leaves perched on a tree branch in the steep limestone hills of the Cockpit Country, which is just over 12 miles (20km) from Jamaica's north coast.

The pineapple-like rosettes, growing on host trees or on the rain-forest floor, offer ideal homes for Jamaica bromeliad crabs. The rainwater that collects in them is the only permanent standing water for miles around – most rain is almost immediately taken up by the trees or else disappears into the limestone rocks.

For most of the year, male and female bromeliad crabs live in different plants, but at breeding time each male leaves his own pool and heads for a female's. She releases her 100 or so eggs into the clean pool, and the visiting male fertilises the eggs and, duty done, returns home.

The tiny crabs that develop from the eggs by April are protected for three months by their diligent mother, who wards off large spiders, anolis lizards and other predators. She feeds the youngsters too, catching cockroaches, beetles and millipedes for them. Bromeliad crabs are the only crabs known to care for their young.

Half dressed Non-breeding Magellanic penguins crowd together hungrily while they moult. Until their plumage is waterproof again they cannot go to sea to feed.

Patagonian penguins moult on the beach

Traffic jams, fighting neighbours, noise pollution and thieves are not usually associated with life in the wilderness. But at Punta Tombo on Argentina's Patagonian coast, that is what happens for half the year. The culprits are not people but 300,000 Magellanic penguins.

In February thousands of these penguins stand close-packed on the chilly, surf-pounded south Atlantic beach, scoured by ceaseless high winds. The usually immaculate birds are moulting, and have a seedy, unkempt air. Most of the squawking, squabbling mass are immature birds (hatched last season) and young adults. Some breeding birds are still tending late chicks.

The penguins started to arrive at Punta Tombo from the north at the end of August to prepare for the spring and summer breeding time. First the males rode in on the waves and waddled to the land behind the beach, where the earth was just right for digging burrows. There were quarrels over prime sites, with losers forced to nest in open scrapes more exposed to predators such as gulls, skuas and foxes.

When the females arrived in mid-September, some reunited with mates of the previous season in noisy courtship displays, but many new pairings were also made. Each pair took turns in incubating their two eggs for five to six weeks. Once the eggs hatched, the beach traffic became chaotic as birds bustled between nest and sea to feed their fluffy brown chicks.

By April the youngsters will be ready for sea and the moult will be over. The penguin horde will head north for the winter, tailing the pilchards, anchovies and squid they feed on. Some will get as far as Rio de Janeiro, about 1800 miles (2900km) away, but will rarely touch land again until they return to Punta Tombo next spring.

Change of suit Parents of the new generation moult later than the non-breeding birds. They have to wait until they have finished caring for their young.

Turtles for tea Fledgling Nankeen night herons in low, stick-built nests make a meal of baby green turtles, caught for them by their parents.

Nankeen night herons feast on turtles

As night falls on Raine Island on the Great Barrier Reef, Nankeen night herons emerge from their daytime roosts in thick foliage among the low, scrubby vegetation and fly off to hunt. It is February and the breeding season is nearly over. Within the heron colony, many fledglings are clamouring for food. Soon there will be abundant food at hand, however, and a faint stirring in the sand on the shore is the first sign for the herons of a feast to come.

About six weeks earlier, thousands of massive green turtles – up to 45 stone (285kg) in weight and about 3ft (1m) long – hauled themselves up the beach and each laid 50-100 eggs in holes they dug in the sand. The Great Barrier Reef, which lies off the north-east coast of Australia, is a major breeding site for green turtles. More than 10,000 female turtles have been known to lay eggs on Raine Island in one night. Now the eggs have hatched, and the drop in temperature as night falls is the signal for the hatchlings to

emerge from the sand. They struggle to the surface, each one no bigger than a biscuit and much the same weight, and crawl towards the brightest horizon – the sea.

Raine Island herons time their October-March breeding season (spring and summer in Australia) to fit in with the turtle bonanza. Just as the young herons are getting ready to leave the nest and are at their hungriest, the parent birds exploit the rich pickings offered as the turtles hatch. They are easy prey as they crawl towards

the sea. The red-eyed crabs and ghost crabs that congregate on the shore also feast on the tiny turtles, and when day comes, those hatchlings still straggling seawards fall prey to silver gulls, frigate birds, banded land rails and other birds.

The Nankeen night heron, widespread in Australia, is named for the buff colour of its back and wings, which match the colour of the nankeen cloth of Nanjing (Nanking), China. The birds are found where there are swamps or pools for at least some of the year, with tree thickets to roost in close by. They also inhabit offshore islets with only stunted ground cover (such as Raine Island) as well as urban parks and streets. One large winter roost is in Melbourne.

Breeding times vary in different areas, because the herons tend to breed when food is abundant locally. They usually breed in colonies, sometimes with as many as 250 untidy stick nests built on branches overhanging open water. Their food includes small fish, shrimps, prawns, frogs, sea snails and water insects – the young turtles of Raine Island are a special treat.

Running the gauntlet Under cover of darkness, thousands of newly hatched green turtles make a dash for the sea. They provide a rich feast for predators.

MARCH

POLAR BEARS STIR IN THE CANADIAN SNOW AS PRAIRIE DOGS
PEER FROM THEIR BURROWS ON THE NORTH AMERICAN PLAINS. ADDERS DANCE
AND BROWN HARES BOX ON EUROPEAN HEATHS, AND IN THE
INDIAN OCEAN MASSIVE SPERM WHALES ARE MATING OR GIVING BIRTH

Australia: Migrating time for dugongs

Polar bear cubs in the kingdom of ice

In March, life in the Arctic begins anew. Those animals in hibernation, protected in their hideaways against the fierceness of the winter weather, are stirred by the warmth of spring and prepare to emerge. Early sandpipers – the first of the bird migrants – arrive from the south. Seals move to their breeding sites. The southern edge of the pack ice breaks apart and melts again into sea water. Each day lasts three minutes longer than the previous one – more daylight to find food, attract a partner, mate and bring up a new generation of Arctic life.

MOVEMENT IN THE SNOW

On one of the Norwegian Arctic islands of the Svalbard group, on the leeward slope of a snow-covered hillside, something moves below the snow. A moist, black snout pokes a small hole and sniffs the air. Detecting no danger, the animal pushes through, and in a flurry of powdery snow, a large female polar bear breaks out of her self-imposed winter internment.

Other polar bears – young females and males – spent the very short days and long dark nights of winter wandering to and fro across the thick, constantly moving ice of the permanently frozen Arctic Ocean, searching for the scant supplies of food. During the worst of the blizzards, they made temporary dens and slept out the storm. At its passing, they stretched, yawned, shook off the snow and ambled away on their hairy-soled feet (good for gripping ice) with the pigeon-toed gait that earned the polar bear the name of 'the farmer' from early Arctic explorers.

But last November this female bear dug herself a more permanent den in which to sit out the entire winter, for she was pregnant. Her den, dug initially into the frozen ground, became covered by snow – which is a good insulator – and stayed at a temperature up to 21°C (37°F) higher than the air outside. Only a narrow air tunnel linked it to the outside world.

On this March morning, three small white heads appear at the breach in the den wall. The cubs were born in the *Continued on p. 62*

Continued on p. 62

Vulnerable in March *The mother polar bear sniffs the air for danger as she takes her three-month-old cubs on a hunting trip. The greatest threat comes from adult male bears – even, perhaps, their own father.*

Appealing in May These two cubs, bright and appealing at five months old, will grow up to be large, fierce carnivores. A male polar bear may be three times the weight of a lion or tiger.

Playful in July A romp in the snow looks like sheer fun, but it has a serious purpose too. A growing polar bear needs to develop the lightning reflexes that it will one day need when it has to hunt for itself.

Purposeful in August At eight months, the cubs are almost as menacing as their mother. Polar bears endure the biting Arctic winds with the help of a fur coat that looks white but is in fact made up of transparent hollow cylinders. The hairs trap and concentrate the sun's energy like miniature greenhouses.

snow den in December, blind, naked and helpless, and each weighing about 1lb (450g). Polar bears usually have one or two cubs – triplets are highly unusual. Their mother encourages the three-month-old 25lb (11kg) cubs out into the crisp morning air for their first sight of the icy kingdom where they must learn to wrest a living, but for several months will depend on their mother for everything. She will continue to suckle them for a month or so, and then they will gradually share her meals of seals and fish.

As they leave their winter home, the mother sets out to look for food, followed by the cubs. Since last autumn she has lived solely off her body fat, put on the previous summer, and suckling the triplets with her fat-rich milk since December has severely depleted her reserves. In the past six months, she has lost at least half of her summer body weight.

The triplets tumble down the slope, wrestling together. Their mother checks that there is no danger close by, then leads them towards the sea ice. Seals, especially ringed seals, are a favourite food, and during March these seals are having pups in dens on the ice. The mother catches the scent of seals below the snow, and leaps onto the roof of the seal den, shattering it with the weight of her body to reveal the chamber below. With a lightning swipe of her enormous forepaw, the bear scoops out a

The hunter strikes
A polar bear waits on the ice beside a seal's breathing hole, ready to stun the seal with a lightning strike of its massive forepaw and seize it in its jaws.

white-coated seal pup, her first meal of the year.

For the rest of the spring and summer, mother and cubs will travel as Arctic nomads. Life for the cubs will not be easy. Nearly three-quarters of all polar bear cubs do not survive to be two years old, the age at which they leave their mother and fend for themselves. By the time they are adult they will measure 8-10ft (2.4-3m) from nose to tail and weigh on average around 70 stone (445kg). Males vie with their Alaskan cousins, the Kodiak grizzly bears, for the title of the world's largest living land carnivore.

Female polar bears take their first partner when they are four or five years old, and have

cubs every three years, commonly twins. A female may have only eight cubs during perhaps 30 years of life. A mother bear is wary of other polar bears, because a hungry adult bear will readily eat helpless cubs.

Mating takes place in April or May. Several bears gather at a temporary meeting place, often a site close to a large congregation of seals. The normally solitary bears are intolerant of each other, and the males have to fight for the right to mate. Competition is fierce, for each spring there are more males than females ready to breed. The size of the males is significant. The bigger and more powerful the male, the better his chances of winning a female. A triumphant, dominant male chases his chosen partner away from the fray in order to mate without interference. Afterwards, they part and travel their separate ways. The male takes no further paternal interest in his offspring – indeed, he may even kill them.

There are several distinct polar bear populations confined to particular areas of the polar lands and frozen sea. Apart from Svalbard, populations are found in Alaska, northern Canada, Greenland and Siberian islands such as Zemlya Frantsa-Iosifa (Franz Josef Land).

Polar bears do not guard a home range as other carnivores do. The shifting pack ice and ice floes make it too difficult. But their wanderings are not indiscriminate, as was once thought. Each bear rarely moves more than 100 miles (160km) from its population centre, although occasionally Svalbard bears have been known to travel long distances from their normal range, ending up near the North Pole or off the coast of Greenland. Some of these bears were fitted with radio transmitters and tracked by satellites as they travelled up to 25 miles (40km) a day over the pack ice. Alaskan bears have been known to go 50 miles (80km) in a day.

Polar bears endure the biting polar winds and the icy water with the help of a thick fur coat. Although the hairs of the coat look solid and white, they are in fact hollow and colourless, but reflected light gives them the appearance of fine white fur. Some bears are stained yellow from the fats and oils of their seal prey. Polar bears in the San Diego Zoo in the USA once even turned green because algae began to grow in the hollows of their hairs.

Alone in the Arctic *A polar bear wades through ice at Ellesmere Island in the Canadian Arctic. Adult bears are solitary and usually avoid each other – except during the spring mating season.*

NORTH AMERICA

Grunion come ashore with the tide to spawn

As the spring tide is about to ebb on a March night at Cabrillo Beach near Los Angeles, a single, silvery, pencil-length fish – usually a male – rides ashore on a wave. He is the spearhead for a run of tens of thousands of female fish, all closely following him to be deposited on the sandy beach.

Thousands of people come every year to see this extraordinary spectacle. It marks the start of an event that takes place with every night-time spring tide – the extra high tide about the time of a new or full moon – until September. On these nights the grunion spawn on particular Pacific beaches stretching from Los Angeles in the USA to the centre of Mexico's Baja California peninsula. Why the grunion choose some beaches and not others is not clear – perhaps sand texture or water temperature is crucial.

As each female emerges from the sea just above the high-tide mark, she curves her body and drills into the sand with her tail end. Here she lays her eggs. She squeaks as she wriggles, and this squeaking is thought to have given rise to the name grunion – from the Spanish word *gruñon*, meaning 'grunter'.

Perhaps it is this sound that attracts the males to come in on the waves behind the females. Each male curves his body round a laying female and quickly releases his milt (sperm), which trickles down to the eggs in the sand below. The males stay for a few seconds and are swept back out to sea on the next wave, but the females may remain on the beach for as long as 20 minutes. Three hours after the first fish came ashore, the spawning is over for the night.

As the tide recedes, the fertilised eggs, safe in the sand, begin to develop. By emerging to lay them at the highest tide, the female has ensured that they cannot be washed out to sea and gobbled up by predators. After about eight days the eggs are ready to hatch, but the tiny embryos will not break out of their egg cases for another six days – with the next spring tide, which occurs about 14 days after the fish spawned and the eggs were deposited in the sand.

Beached eggs *Grunion eggs are deposited about a finger-depth below the sand surface and left to hatch.*

When the sea water eventually reaches the buried eggs, the tiny fish burst out and are washed away by the waves. Immediately after their release they start to eat ocean plants and animals not much smaller than themselves. They live in shallow coastal waters not far from the shore.

The young grunion feed and grow for several months until the following spring. Then they stop growing and begin to produce the eggs and milt for reproduction. Females start their spawning runs when they are about a year old. By the time a female is in her third year and fully mature, she will spawn regularly for a period of six months, and deposit more than 3000 eggs in the sand at each emergence.

Fish out of water *A mass of wriggling grunion, each 4-6in (100-150mm) long, spawn on a Californian beach by moonlight. The hatchlings from the fertilised eggs leave two weeks later on the next spring tide.*

Sand dance *A female grunion wriggles in the sand as she lays her eggs. A male releases his milt (sperm) as he curves round her. Both are out of the water.*

Social outing Black-tailed prairie dogs emerge from their burrows to sunbathe, feed and socialise. Nibbling at one another's fur to groom it fosters group harmony.

The communal life of city-living prairie dogs

Spring sunshine coaxes fresh shoots from the many herbs and grasses clothing the plains of the central USA. Few of the shoots grow tall, for the March sun also tempts out the black-tailed prairie dogs, which have spent much of the winter below ground. They quickly crop the growth with their chisel-like front teeth.

Despite its name, earned by its bark, the prairie dog is a stout, short-legged type of squirrel. The bark alerts its fellows to the approach of predators such as hawks and coyotes, and sends them scurrying into their burrows, where much of their organised communal life goes on unseen.

Burrow entrances are marked by crater-shaped mounds of earth dotted across the prairie, and some holes with slightly sunken surrounds. The mounds prevent rain from pouring into the burrows, and lower air pressure in the craters causes air to be sucked in through the sunken holes as ventilation. The burrows form a widespread maze of tunnels and dens covering perhaps ¼ sq mile (65ha) and reaching about 10ft (3m) deep. Thousands of prairie dogs occupy this underground city, living in separate groups, or coteries, of eight or nine within neighbourhoods known as wards.

Although each inhabitant occupies its own patch, coterie members are close and familiar. They touch noses in greeting, groom one another and feed and sunbathe together. During the spring breeding season, each coterie defends its territory staunchly, chasing off any intruders and jumping up and down whistling at the burrow entrance to display ownership.

An adult male establishes himself with several females, each of which has one litter a year averaging four pups. The new pups, born after a one-month pregnancy, are naked and helpless. They make their first appearance above ground within five weeks, by which time they are small replicas of their parents. The youngsters are weaned at four to six weeks old and join the nibbling social groups on the prairie above the city. At 11 months they will be fully grown. Adults of both sexes tolerate the antics of playful youngsters. When a growing family overcrowds the coterie, the parents as well as the young males leave, and the young females stay on. So the older, more experienced animals break new ground on the city boundaries.

Prairie-dog city Webs of tunnels and burrows form a vast city, home for thousands of animals. Each one has its own space and its own close group within the city.

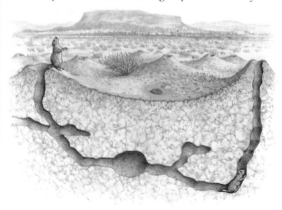

Temporary pools for Californian 'tigers'

For most of the year, the grasslands of the wide Central Valley of California are dull and dry. But for just a few months early in the year, this flat landscape north-east of San Francisco, behind the Coast Range, is transformed. As the winter ends, shallow dips and hollows in the ground fill with rain and melting snow from the mountains, and the broad plain becomes a patchwork of pools, thousands of them. Some reach 1200sq yds (1000sq m) in size, and some are 40 times larger. They provide temporary homes for many plants and animals, among them the tiger salamander, named for its bold yellow and black markings.

Great numbers of these sturdy, broad-headed amphibians, up to about 9in (220mm) long, come here in March to breed. After mating in the water, the females lay eggs in masses that – like fish eggs – are coated in protective jelly that sticks to submerged plants.

On hatching, the larvae look like miniature adults but for their tail fins and feathery gills. The gills allow them to breathe and live underwater, where they hunt a variety of small creatures. There is an ample supply of bugs and beetles, slugs and worms, some of them – such as the delta green ground beetle and several kinds of flatworm – found only here. The young salamanders are themselves the prey for insects – voracious diving bugs known as tiger beetles. The beetles have jaws powerful enough to pierce human skin, and make short work of young tiger salamanders. The salamanders that escape and reach maturity even the score by including tiger beetles in their diet as well as worms and insects.

California's springtime pools have appeared every year for at least 50,000 years and support a range of specially adapted life. They are oases in a dry environment, and attract many visiting animals. Bats and swallows come to feast on flying insects; geese and ducks join avocets and curlews to gorge on shrimps, which by early spring easily outnumber all other pond inhabitants and feed many migrating waterfowl.

The waterfowl add their voices to the resonant chorus of Pacific tree frogs which feed on gnats and midges, but the salamanders stay silent – and despite their bold markings often manage to remain unseen among the profusion of white, yellow and blue flowers. These plants thrive in water, so must grow, bloom and set their seeds in a much shorter time than most plants. By May the pools will have shrunk or dried up. To survive then, the mature salamanders must either stay near whatever ponds are left, seek water elsewhere or go underground – for though they live on land, they cannot survive if they become dry. They need to be in water or in damp earth to stay moist.

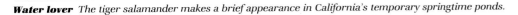

Water lover The tiger salamander makes a brief appearance in California's temporary springtime ponds.

In-flight drink A hovering Costa's hummingbird sips nectar at a cactus flower. As it flits from bloom to bloom, it transfers pollen that fertilises the plants.

Sweet desert spring for busy hummingbirds

Brilliant colours flood California's Colorado Desert as spring reaches the south-western USA. Flowers bloom in the March sun, and darting among them are Costa's hummingbirds, their iridescent plumage gleaming like shot silk.

The tiny birds, about as long as a little finger and weighing less than a tenth of an ounce (2g), hover beside cactus flowers with their bodies held almost upright and wings whirring at 80 beats a second. They thrust their long, slender beaks into the flowers and suck up nectar. Flowers such as those of the giant saguaro cactus are clustered at the ends of stems, making it easy for the hummingbird to visit in mid-flight. In return, the visitor unwittingly brushes against pollen in one bloom and delivers it to the next.

Dependent upon nectar, the bird migrates north some 600 miles (966km) from Mexico each spring and spends summer in the baking desert where temperatures soar above 38°C (100°F). One of the smallest of about 320 species of hummingbird, Costa's is the only one known to be able to survive without water. Sipping nectar sustains it, but this high-energy food – virtually a sugar solution – takes a lot of effort to collect and is quickly used up as energy. Each bird needs the nectar from 1000 flowers a day. Minute insects, some drawn up with the nectar, provide it with body-building protein. At night the bird 'switches off' and goes into a state of torpor, so reducing the drain on its energy.

Wailing for mother *With a cry like a human baby, a week-old harp seal anxiously watches its mother return to their ice-floe home. She recognises her pup by its cry and scent.*

Ice floes cradle harp seal pups in wintry seas

Huddled on a sheet of floating ice behind any hump or hollow that offers shelter from the biting March wind, a female harp seal gives birth to a sturdy 26lb (12kg) pup. She is not alone. All round her, crowds of other harp seals are also giving birth after hauling themselves onto ice floes in the Gulf of St Lawrence in eastern Canada, one of their traditional whelping grounds.

The seals suckle their pups up to three times a day on milk that, with a 43 per cent fat content, is among the richest produced by any mammal. On this, the pups grow at the rate of just over 3lb (1.4kg) a day to around 5 stone (32kg) two weeks later, when they are weaned. This is one of the fastest weaning rates among large animals. Even so, it is not a record – the pups of the slightly larger hooded seals of the northern Atlantic are weaned in only seven days.

When the harp seal pups are about two weeks old, they shed the camouflaging white coats they were born with to reveal short grey fur. At this point, their mothers abandon them and head out to sea. They have eaten very little while suckling their pups, and each one is anxious to make up the fat reserves she has lost. She joins the herds of males and females hunting fish and shrimp-like crustaceans. There she mates and conceives the pup that will be born next March. However, the fertilised egg floats free in her womb for some four months before it attaches itself to the wall and pregnancy begins. Seven and half months after that, in the following March, she will give birth again in the Gulf.

Meanwhile, the pups take to the water near the ice floes, testing out their hunting skills. Their first attempts often fail, and they commonly lose as much as 1 stone (6kg) in weight. To begin with, they feed only near the surface

where they catch crustaceans and small fish. Later, as adults, they will be able to dive as deep as 650ft (200m) and remain submerged for up to ten minutes. At these depths, they will catch larger fish such as herring and cod.

In April, the adults climb back onto the ice floes to moult, then in May, as summer approaches, they head north to their feeding grounds around the Arctic coasts of northern Canada, Greenland and Russia. It is thought that they may find their way partly by navigating along coastal shelves and partly by using the direction of the wind and ocean currents. The pups follow later, finding their own way by some instinct of navigation not yet understood. Fewer than ten per cent lose their way and end up in the wrong feeding grounds. Later, as the sea begins to freeze over, they will all return to the breeding grounds where they were born.

Young harp seals develop the adult coat with its dark saddle mark, or harp, when they are between four and six years old. They begin to breed when they are nearly six. By then, they will have doubled in length to around 6ft (1.8m) and will weigh around 21 stone (135kg). In more than 20 years of adult life, each female seal will produce a pup almost every year.

Bundle of fat *Camouflaged against the snow by its white coat, a newborn harp seal must develop a thick layer of body fat for warmth and survival.*

Otters that fish, feed and sleep at sea

Floating belly-up on the sea near the Californian shore, a mother sea otter cradles her pup on her chest. The pup, born last May, is now about nine or ten months old. Completely helpless and unable to swim at birth, the pup was totally dependent on its mother. Now it can swim, but where food is scarce it will need its mother's help in foraging until it is a year old. The youngster still enjoys nestling under its mother's chin as she sculls along on her back. When it was first born – in the sea – it spent all its time there, except when its mother dived to the seabed for food. Then she simply left it at the surface, kept safely afloat by the air trapped among the hairs of its thick fur.

Being a close relative of the land otter rather than sea mammals such as seals, the sea otter lacks a thick blubber coat to keep it warm. But it has a dense fur coat (with up to 800 million hairs), and relies on trapped air for insulation. As unkempt fur is less insulating, otters often groom their coats.

Food as well as fur helps them to keep warm. An adult eats roughly 18lb (8kg) of food each day, about a quarter of its own weight. It needs a large liver to deal with so much food and, compared to its body size, the sea otter's liver is more than twice as large as that of any other sea mammal. Yet sea otters are the smallest sea-living mammals – adults are about 4ft 6in (1.4m) long – excluding their 10in (250mm) long tails.

Here, near the Californian shore, sea otters

SKILLED TOOL-USER

Sea otters are one of an elite group of animals that use tools. Such skill was once thought to be an exclusively human activity, but now it is known that a small number of other animals use them. The Egyptian vulture, for example, picks up a stone in its bill and drops it on a large egg to break it. And the chimpanzee uses a twig to poke ants from crevices.

When a sea otter collects a hard shellfish from the seabed, it usually picks up a small rock or stone at the same time, and carries both to the surface. The otter rests the stone on its belly while it floats on its back, and then bangs the shell against the stone. As soon as the shell cracks, the otter winkles out the occupant with its teeth.

Shell breaker *Sea otters have devised their own way of opening hard shellfish with rocks – and joined the small group of animals that use tools.*

feed entirely on shellfish – sea urchins, crabs, mussels and clams from the sea floor, and abalones prised off underwater rocks with their strong forepaws or with a small piece of rock. Their diet of seabed shellfish means that sea otters live mostly where the sea is 10-30ft (3-9m) deep, although dives of up to 318ft (97m) have been recorded. They can stay submerged for about four minutes.

When a sea otter picks up a shellfish from the sea floor, it tucks the morsel under its arm to

A bundle of love *Even an eight-month-old sea otter pup, well able to swim, still enjoys nestling on its mother as she swims along on her back.*

carry to the surface. There, the animal turns onto its back to eat. Crabs and sea urchins, which have soft shells, are eaten whole but hard-shelled creatures such as clams and mussels have to be broken open first with the back teeth or some sharp bangs against a rock.

Although they usually go foraging alone, sea otters can be surprisingly social. Where there are few people about, groups of up to 50 otters may gather to rest in kelp beds in the middle of the day. To avoid drifting away on the current they anchor themselves in long strands of seaweed, and doze for hours.

Once sea otters were abundant in the coastal waters of the Pacific rim from northern Japan to Mexico's Baja California peninsula. But fur traders hunted them close to extinction for their thick pelts, and in 1911 they were given legal protection. Since then numbers have increased to about 150,000. Commercial fisheries dislike sea otters because they eat shellfish, yet they also eat lots of sea urchins, which can damage kelp beds supporting many kinds of fish.

The cubs' first outing In the mountains of northern Spain, a female brown bear leads her twin cubs through the dew-soaked meadow grass as she searches for a meal.

As spring arrives the brown bears stir

It is spring in the Cordillera Cantabrica in northern Spain. The high mountain peaks are still capped with snow, but March sunshine has begun to warm the alpine meadows on the lower slopes. In a cave in the hillside, a female Eurasian brown bear begins to stir.

She has spent the winter months sleeping in the cave. Last autumn she grew fat on the beech mast and acorns down in the valleys. As the weather grew colder, she retreated to the cave and sprawled out on its dusty floor to spend the winter alternating between slumber and wakefulness. Although a bear's winter sleep is often called hibernation, it does not drop its body temperature and become torpid like some hibernators. It just slows its heart rate slightly, but if disturbed will rouse immediately.

During her winter in the cave, the bear gave birth to twin cubs. Bears have cubs only once every two or three years, and the male plays no part in rearing his offspring. The newborn cubs are helpless and weigh less than 14oz (400g), but their mother's milk is rich and they grow fast. By March they are ready to leave the warm, dark cave and make their first explorations into the outside world.

The mother bear steps out of the cave and into the sunshine, and stands alert for a few minutes sampling the smells on the spring breeze. Although her eyesight is poor, she has sharp hearing and an acute sense of smell. She stands up on her hind feet and rocks gently as she takes in the view.

Turning towards the mouth of the cave, she utters a low grumble. There is a second's pause before two fluffy brown bundles bounce out of

Where brown bears are found in Europe

Brown bear country *Brown bears are found in many countries in Europe. The total population in 1988 was estimated to be up to 40,000 bears, 35 per cent more than in 1979. They are protected by law.*

the cave onto the grass. Unused to exercising their stumpy legs, they tumble over and clamber towards their mother for reassurance. She rolls over to lie on her back and, scoops them onto her belly to suckle them.

Once the cubs are fed, it is time for the mother to lead them on their first foray. She ambles off down the slope with her offspring cantering beside her. Every few minutes she has to stop and wait for them to catch up. They are preoccupied with constant games of tag and prolonged mock battles accompanied by sharp little squeals and growls.

The mother is content to adopt their slow pace, and is ready to defend them against any threat from another bear or a human. If necessary she can run at a speed of 28mph (45km/h) over a short distance, and stands 6-7ft (1.8-2m) tall on her hind legs. The brown bear is one of Europe's biggest wild animals, weighing around 40 stone (250kg). Although it is the same species as the American grizzly bear, the Eurasian bear is generally smaller.

After a winter in the cave suckling her cubs without eating any food herself, the mother bear is hungry. She soon reaches a favourite meadow verdant with new growth and begins to scrape the soil with her huge paws to unearth some pignut tubers, relatives of the wild carrot.

Over the next few weeks, the mother will suckle her cubs daily while travelling the mountains and valleys in search of food. Bears eat a varied diet, but in the early spring they are almost totally vegetarian, feeding on large quantities of roots, leaves and stems out in the

meadows. In the autumn, they will climb into the trees to shake out seeds, fruit and nuts on which to grow fat before hibernation. And their large paws and massive finger-length claws are perfect tools for breaking into ants' nests or stealing honey from wild bee nests. The bears' thick hide protects them from bee stings. Occasionally they will kill a deer or a wild boar if other food is short.

In spring, the cubs still have a lot to learn but can do so at leisure. They will stay with their mother during summer and through next winter, sleeping together in the cave. The half-grown cubs may even stay with their mother until she mates again the following season. Then they will leave to begin their adult lives alone.

Food and play *Lying on her back, a mother bear keeps a lookout for danger while her cubs lie on her belly to suck her milk. For the first few months of their lives, food and play (below) occupy most of their time.*

Leaving home Driven from the familiar territory of home as the mating season begins, young brown rats move from the security of barns into the hedgerows.

Brown rats leave home to start new colonies

With the arrival of the European spring, young brown rats from last year's litters are driven out of rural barns and outhouses by mating adults. They move to nearby sites and establish new colonies. The rats thrive in hedgerows, rubbish tips and sewers, and where food is plentiful may have five litters a year.

Brown rats are among the most successful migrants in the animal kingdom, and have spread all over the world in the wake of humans. The brown rat, about 10in (250mm) long, originated on the grassy steppes of eastern and central Asia, and first appeared in eastern Europe in the 1730s, when vast hordes were encountered migrating westwards.

In populated areas of Europe, rats found food in houses and barns, so they nested there and bred rapidly. They quickly spread across Europe, and by 1770 reached Britain. Some fifteen years earlier, they crossed the Atlantic in ships sailing to North America from Europe and then got to the Pacific coast by rail in the late 1800s. Sailing aboard convict ships, they arrived in Australia from Britain in 1788.

Within 130 years of their arrival in eastern Europe, the rats had colonised almost every part of the world where human beings had set foot.

Historians believe that rats – both the brown and black species – have caused more human deaths through the spread of diseases during the last 1000 years than all wars put together.

The boxing bouts of the 'mad' March hare

According to country lore, hares go mad in spring, and leap about, chase each other and spar in pairs like boxers. For long it was thought that the boxing hares were males fighting for a mate, but many zoologists are now of the opinion that a sparring pair is almost always a female repelling the advances of a male – who is smaller and lighter.

Boxing bouts between males and females can occur at any time of year; they are not confined to spring. But they are most frequent during the hares' long breeding season from January to August, when they are less solitary than usual. During a bout, a female lashes out with her forepaws and kicks with her hind legs, and can inflict severe claw and bite wounds.

Hares are active mainly in the early evening. Perhaps the myth of their 'madness' in March arose because, with lighter evenings and more countryfolk out and about, they were more likely to be seen than in winter. Also, the hares would be more visible before the vegetation had grown to the luxuriance of later months.

Young hares (called leverets) are born six weeks after their parents have mated. A litter may contain as many as seven, born in the open rather than in the protection of a burrow. The youngsters are born well furred and with their eyes open, and can move about soon after birth. The nest – called a form – is a hollow flattened out amid long grass or other plants. Each leveret is hidden in a separate form. When the mother goes to suckle a youngster, she makes a special 'milk' call, to which the leveret replies.

Leverets are suckled for about a month and then leave the form to fend for themselves, feeding on green plants. When they are a year old, they can breed for the first time. A female hare is capable of bearing three or four litters a year, so could produce around 100 offspring in three or four years. Because of their breeding rate, hares came to be regarded as a symbol of fertility in some parts of Europe.

The brown (or common) hare, which is slightly bigger than a rabbit, is found throughout much of Europe and across to eastern Asia. In the far north of Europe it is replaced by the closely related blue hare. In any area, the number of hares fluctuates considerably in fairly regular cycles of about ten years, and there are corresponding cycles, usually lagging several years behind, in the populations of the hares' main predators, such as foxes and birds of prey.

Hares rest by day, crouched low against the ground. To escape from predators, a hare relies on its stamina and speed – up to 45mph (72 km/h) – and often runs a zigzag course to confuse the pursuer. The animal's speed comes from its large, strong hind legs and also its large nostrils and nasal passages, which allow more oxygen to reach hard-working muscles. Hares are also good swimmers and will often take to water. One was once observed swimming across a bay that was more than 1 mile (1.6km) wide.

Unwanted attentions A female hare will often savagely fight off a male who tries to mate with her.

New eyes on the world Emerging from the underground den where they were born, badger cubs explore the unfamiliar world above ground for the first time.

Badgers at home in an underground palace

Snuffling uncertainly, the two badger cubs emerge from the narrow entrance to their home, or sett, in a European wood on a March night. It is their first time above ground since they were born about ten weeks ago. With noses twitching, the cubs explore the unfamiliar smells and sounds of the night air. Near them their mother, ever watchful, is alert for danger.

For the first six weeks of their lives, the cubs stayed in the cosy warmth of the nest chamber deep underground, where the adults' body heat maintains a comfortable temperature of 18-20°C (64-68°F) even with winter snows outside. They were also well insulated by their nest of dry bedding such as bracken. Badgers regularly take fresh bundles of bedding back to their setts.

When newborn, the cubs had silky white fur and fused eyelids, and were very vulnerable to cold. At six weeks old their eyes opened and they began to develop the familiar dark fur and white-striped face of the badger. By then they were also mobile enough to start exploring the complex tunnel system of their home.

March is the busiest time of the year for the mother badger. Her cubs are at their most demanding for her milk, but there is little food yet available for her to eat. She and the other adults of the group – maybe three breeding sows and one or two boars – must also repair the tunnels of the sett damaged by the winter weather. The cubs will continue to depend on their mother's milk until they are about three months old. Then the late spring weather will make more food available for them and they will be able to fend entirely for themselves.

Badgers feed on insects, worms and small animals such as mice, voles, hedgehogs, rabbits and birds, but earthworms make up the bulk of their diet in winter and spring. Earthworms come to the surface and pull leaves under-ground to eat on damp, mild nights – nights when badgers are particularly active. A single badger can eat up to 200 worms a night. During late summer and autumn they also eat a lot of cereals and fruit. By autumn, the cubs will have reached the adult weight of 26lb (12kg), but they will not be sexually mature until next spring.

The badgers' home, laboriously dug over long

Network of tunnels A badger's sett consists of an interconnecting system of tunnels, providing sleeping and nesting chambers as well as passing places.

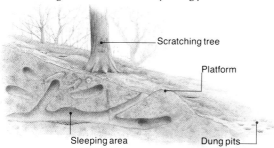

Scratching tree

Platform

Sleeping area

Dung pits

periods of time, is a system of tunnels and nesting and sleeping chambers. Badgers are remarkably efficient at digging. Their wedge-shaped body allows them to shovel earth and rubble out behind them very effectively. A large tunnel system may involve the removal of as much as 25 tons of soil, which is piled up outside the entrance and forms a distinctive platform. A large sett can cover nearly 2000sq yds (1670sq m) and contain 95 tunnels totalling 340yds (310m) in length. Many setts are dug into banks or hill slopes. A sett on flatter ground may be dug at several levels – one examined was found to contain at least four levels, the deepest more than 13ft (4m) below ground.

Most setts have from three to ten entrances, but large ones can have up to 50, many of them hidden beneath bushes, trees or rocks. All badger setts have dung pits about 6in (150mm) deep outside, usually 16ft-32ft (5-10m) from sett entrances. As each pit is filled with dung, a new one is dug close by. One sett in England is known to have been in continuous use for more than 200 years. However, the tunnel systems often change over periods of 30-40 years, the badgers excavating new tunnels as old ones collapse, or when they need more room.

To ensure they have enough food throughout the year, badgers need large territories. In central Europe, a group of five or six animals typically lives in a territory about 800yds square (50ha). Farther north, where the climate is harsher, territories are larger. Cubs are also born later in the north, often in March or April.

....

Night hunter Active mostly at night, badgers have distinctive black-and-white-striped faces and stout bodies. Males are about 2ft 6in (760mm) long.

Explosion of white A male great bustard almost vanishes in an eruption of white feathers while a female looks on.
....

When a great bustard seems to turn inside out

March is the mating season for great bustards, the largest and most impressive birds to roam the wide, open grasslands of southern Europe and central Asia. At this time, bustards gather on large communal display grounds where the males perform extraordinary shows for the females.

First the turkey-sized male struts around with his tail held upright, showing off a flurry of bright white feathers on his rump. Then as the females, who are smaller, draw in to watch, he transforms himself from a mainly brown bird into a shimmering explosion of white. He seems almost to turn himself inside out.

To achieve this astonishing effect, he gulps air noisily and inflates a massive sac in his throat. As the sac balloons out, white feathers along its sides appear to separate and stand out, exposing two greyish stripes of bare skin down his neck. Once fully inflated, the sac forces the bird's head right back so that it seems to disappear in a shroud of white feathers.

At the same time, he lays his tail flat along his back so that it almost touches his head, raising the rump feathers even farther. His wings are stretched down and backwards and the white feathers are twisted and fanned out. The whole effect is finished off by the bird stamping and wheeling about, looking rather like a huge, animated, feather cushion that has burst.

The bustard holds this spectacular posture for a minute or two, then with a reverse flurry once again becomes brown. Then he repeats the whole display until he has won himself a mate.

Female birds watch each male's display, and eventually signal their readiness to mate with the one of their choice by standing very close to the excited bird and sometimes pecking at his show of white feathers.

Each dominant male mates with up to five females. Each will have to raise her family alone, but will do so in the vicinity of the breeding ground. The female's nest is just a shallow scrape in the ground in which she lays two or three speckled, olive or buff-coloured eggs.

The chicks hatch after three or four weeks and the female is then occupied with caring for them. They immediately leave the nest and follow their mother as she walks across the plain, learning to peck at food such as green shoots, seeds and berries. Bustards also eat small creatures such as beetles and frogs.

Although the youngsters can watch their parents' magnificent display, it will be at least four or five years before any young males will be able to take part themselves, and probably very much longer before they number among the dominant performers.

Duels in the sun for the dancing adders

On sunny March days in Europe's heaths and scrubland, the warmth stirs adders (or vipers) to leave the deep, cool burrows where they have spent about five months hibernating. The males emerge first and lie basking in sunny spots, sometimes as many as 800 together with their 2ft (610mm) bodies entwined in a 'snake ball'. They emerge about two weeks before the females to absorb enough heat to mature their sperm, and do not feed but rely on last summer's stored fat. Their old skins are shed, giving their zigzag pattern a new brightness.

As the males become increasingly active, they spread out over a territory around 42yds square (1500sq m) and compete to attract one of the breeding females – a female breeds in alternate years. Sometimes rival males chase each other and wrestle, heads and bodies raised while they sway and jostle until the weaker of the two retires exhausted.

Once a male has a female to himself, he first basks with her for several days. Then he becomes excited and his body twitches as he tries to persuade his mate to uncoil. He tests her readiness by lying close and tapping her with his lower jaw while flicking his tongue over her skin, for she emits scent that excites him. The pair sway and dance in a long and graceful courtship until the female is ready to mate. She slowly uncoils and the mating pair remain entwined for several hours. The male generally stays with the female for a few days longer, then both leave for their separate summer feeding grounds, perhaps a mile (1.6km) away – several days' journey for an adder. The snakes spend the summer basking and feeding on frogs, small mammals such as mice, fledgling birds, and even insects – but do not feed every day.

By August, the female is heavy and slow-moving with 5-12 eggs inside her ready for hatching. She returns to the hibernation site to give birth, each thin egg sac breaking as it is squeezed from her body. Before long, the pencil-length young adders slither away into the undergrowth to fend for themselves. About half will survive till next spring, and if they can keep clear of their chief enemy, man, they will start to breed in their fourth year.

....

Combat dance *When male adders pursue a mate in March, rivals wrestle to establish dominance, and sway like dancers as they push and shove each other.*

A mugger crocodile meets its match

Sambar deer and their fawns are grazing peacefully, though alert, beside a small lake in north-west India. The creaks and cackles of crickets and partridges fill the air of the March evening, and as the deer nose through the shallows for succulent plants, the adults turn often to the long grass behind them to sniff for the scent of a skulking tiger.

A more immediate danger lurks in the water, however – a 13ft (4m) long mugger crocodile, whose log-like knobbled back is gliding towards the herd. Too late the deer cry in alarm and retreat from the reeds. Although the adults can fend off a mugger with a few sharp kicks, they are anxious about their offspring waiting nervously at the water's edge. Hampered by the confusion and the trampled slope, one young fawn is unable to escape in time and is dragged back into the water, its muzzle pinned within the crocodile's jaws. The fawn can offer little resistance, and the crocodile sinks beneath the surface with its prize.

But in the cover of the trees other eyes have been watching the killing. With a loud snarl a large tigress rushes into the water amid an explosion of spray. The sambar panic, but the tigress is after an easier meal. Slapping her forepaw on the water to frighten the crocodile, she dips her head below the surface and grabs the limp fawn. Hauling it ashore, she disappears into the long grass to eat at her leisure. Tonight, even the bellicose crocodile is a loser.

Fortunately for its survival, the mugger makes no attempt to fight back. On the Chambal River not far away, a 10ft (3m) long crocodile was once found floating on its back, its stomach cut open as if by a knife. But the fatal wound had been made by the sabre-sharp claws of an angry tiger.

Sambar deer are particularly vulnerable to crocodile attacks in March, when hot weather dries up rivers and ponds and forces them to congregate at crocodile-infested lakes. For the mugger crocodile, though, the dry season is a boon because shrinking pools become packed with fish, its staple food. To reach such feasts, the muggers will amble across land for several

Second-hand prey Scattering deer before it, a tiger is about to seize a young sambar deer just pulled below the water by a mugger crocodile.

hours – unusual behaviour for crocodiles, which walk awkwardly with legs extended and body raised high. Once in the pools, the largest muggers – about 16ft (5m) long – exert their fishing rights with a gurgling growl, and if necessary chase smaller crocodiles away. A less powerful crocodile holds its snout high in the air and grunts to indicate its inferior status.

Although muggers love fish, they are opportunists, as are all crocodiles, and will snap up anything that comes their way, including frogs and wading birds. Only the large muggers take mammals as big as a wild ox or sambar deer.

To tackle such a wide range of prey, the mugger is equipped with broad and powerful jaws and pointed, interlocking teeth that are regularly replaced. To eat a large meal such as a sambar fawn requires a special technique. After drowning its prey, the crocodile grasps the animal's leg and tears it off by spinning itself rapidly round lengthwise in the water. Then the killer rises to the surface to eat the leg, otherwise it would swallow mouthfuls of water with the meat. It twists off further portions in the same way, and so gradually disposes of the prey.

Really thick-skinned carcasses such as dead cattle are left to putrefy and soften before the mugger attempts to eat them. In the cool season, when decomposition is slow, such booty is guarded from other scavengers for several days before the meal is ready. Crocodiles prefer fresh meat, but will drag away the carcasses of any deer that die beside the lake from wounds, disease or old age. The large, dominant crocodiles always take the choicest carcasses.

Death in the shallows A mugger crocodile drags a young sambar deer to its death by grasping its muzzle. Once in the water, the deer is flipped over and drowned.

A dragon dines A Komodo dragon, the largest lizard in the world, digs in the sand for mallee fowl eggs.

A feast of birds' eggs for Komodo dragons

Pushing through the low scrub of an Indonesian island, what appears to be a prehistoric monster flicks its yellow forked tongue in and out as it tracks down a meal. Close by, a mallee hen and her mate are just completing the mound of earth that covers their eggs. Suddenly the grey monster lunges forward and begins digging furiously at the mound with powerful claws. This is a Komodo dragon, the largest lizard in the world, growing to some 10ft (3m) long and weighing about 26 stone (166kg). The dragons are named after Komodo Island, one of six neighbouring islands on which they live.

In March, mallee fowl eggs are a welcome extra in their diet. For the rest of the year diet varies with size. Young dragons eat insects and small lizards, clambering into the trees to catch them. Half-grown dragons hunt rats and birds; older dragons hide in the bushes and ambush goats, deer and pigs. Occasionally, big dragons eat little ones. They may even follow a pregnant she-goat, waiting to eat her kid. The dragons have fairly poor eyesight and hunt by scent, which they sense partly by sampling the air with the tongue and the roof of the mouth. Surprise is their best chance of a kill. They rip prey apart in their jaws with powerful backward jerks of the head, and swallow the chunks whole.

The dragons probably arrived on Komodo and its neighbouring islands in prehistory, when sea levels were much lower than today. At that time the six islands were joined together and there were many other islands strung out towards Australia, where the lizards' ancestors may have originated. When increases in the population caused overcrowding, the dragons, being good swimmers, began island hopping and eventually reached Komodo. Other carnivores – such as Tasmanian wolves – that could not swim long distances remained in Australia.

Before humans arrived on Komodo 5000 years ago, bringing goats, deer and pigs, the dragons may have hunted pygmy elephants and had this food supply to themselves, for there were no other carnivores competing for it. Today the pygmy elephant is gone, killed by humans, and the dragons feed on the animals that escaped from the human invaders. With this reduced food supply they no longer reach the 20ft (6m) length of their prehistoric relatives.

A sperm whale nursery in the deep blue sea

Launched tail-first into the world, a young sperm whale at birth is about as long as a saloon car. Its mother nudges the 1 ton baby to the sea surface to take its first vital breath.

Sperm whales take their name from the milky fluid found in their heads. They are also known as cachalot whales, from an old French word meaning 'toothed'. The whales are abundant in the Indian Ocean off Sri Lanka in March, their breeding time. The 36ft (11m) long, 20 ton females swim in groups of up to 20 – occasionally with a 50ft (15m) long, 45 ton mature male tagging along as harem master.

Female sperm whales have the longest-known pregnancy of any whale, carrying their babies for about 15 months. They generally suckle the youngsters for two or three years, although some have been seen taking milk at 13 years old.

When a mother submerges to feed – on large squid at 1000-2000ft (300-600m) below the surface – another female in the group acts as babysitter for the youngster. As soon as the mother returns to the surface, the baby takes up its normal position swimming beneath her tail, where it can reach her teats to feed. Occasionally it surfaces, takes a breath, then returns to swim below her tail.

If threatened by sharks or killer whales, the group forms a defensive phalanx round the babies, and the entire group remains silent. Even marauding killer whales think twice about facing the massive jaws of adult sperm whales.

After breeding time, the group splits up. Adult males usually stay with the group for only a few days – long enough to mate with several receptive females. After mating, the adult males go off alone, some ranging as far as the polar seas in search of a good food supply. Younger males swim and feed in small bachelor groups.

Because of her long pregnancy and nursing, a female mates and produces a baby only every 4-6 years. Young males and females are about the same size at birth, but males shoot ahead at three years of age. Females become sexually mature at about 10 years old, males are not fully mature until they are about 20 years old.

Foraging sperm whales can stay underwater for over an hour without coming up for air. The milky fluid – the wax-like oil in the spermaceti organ above the whale's upper jaw – may regulate its buoyancy. It is thought that as the oil cools and becomes denser, the whale sinks.

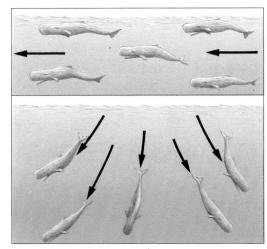

Fan dive *Travelling groups of sperm whales fan out as they dive to hunt for food. The whales use clicking noises to find each other when they surface.*

To surface again, the whale diverts warm blood round the organ, the oil becomes less dense and the whale rises with little effort. The spermaceti organ may also help hunting whales by focusing the high-frequency clicking noises used to locate prey into intense bursts of sound resembling gunfire that can kill or disable prey.

Swimming with mother *Born in warm tropical seas, a baby sperm whale keeps pace with its mother, positioned beneath her tail where it can easily reach her milk.*

Sea lion pups are seized by beach raiders

As the six-week-old South American sea lion pups play among the adults at the water's edge, a line of tall, black dorsal fins suddenly appears off the Punta Norte beach in Argentina. The fins belong to a family of marauding killer whales, and they are hunting baby sea lions.

Panic grips the sea lion colony as the killer whales charge into the shallows and seize a number of the pups. Some of the whales shoot right out of the water and beach themselves in an attempt to reach their prey. They wriggle their way back into the sea. Killer whales do not always kill and eat their prey immediately. Sometimes they 'play' with it, like a cat playing with a mouse. Using their powerful tails the whales toss sea lion pups – and even adults weighing 20 stone (130kg) or more – high into the air to land with a great splash in the water.

Although sea lion pups can grow into for-

....

Mother and baby South American sea lion pups are born black but become dark grey after their first moult. Eventually they will be reddish-brown like their mother.

midable adults, the death rate in their first year of life is high. Some die of starvation after getting separated from their mothers. Others are crushed by huge bull sea lions charging across the beach to drive off other bulls trespassing on their territory. And if a pup gets through all that, various infections account for still more deaths.

The few pups that do survive are suckled for several months, sometimes until the mother produces her next pup. Mothers leave their pups on the beach for up to three or four days at a time while they feed on fish and squid in the open sea, away from the killer whales lurking close to shore. When they return, the mothers spend a day or two suckling their pups. While their mothers are away, the pups gather in groups at the water's edge but do not yet venture into the sea. Eventually they will go for their first swim riding on mother's back.

The sea lion colony began to assemble on the beach at the Peninsula Valdés in December. The adult males arrived first to take the best positions on the foreshore, anticipating where the cows would come ashore. Often they had to fight for their plot and the right to hold a harem of about nine cows. The bulls are huge – almost 8ft (2.4m) long and weighing 39 stone (250kg). Each has a stout neck, thick mane and upturned

Threat from the sea *Killer whales sometimes launch themselves out of the water and come right up onto the beach to seize a sea lion pup. They wriggle back to the water.*

nose. The females are less than 6ft (1.8m) long and only half the weight of the males. Shortly after the females arrived, each gave birth to a pup, conceived last season. A week later mating took place to produce next year's offspring. In mid-January, the height of the breeding season at Punta Norte beach, there were 140 males, 350 females and 430 pups crowded into a stretch of shingle just above the high-tide line.

Groups (or harems) of female sea lions are often so close together that it is hard to tell one group from another. But the harem bulls know the boundaries, and are quick to attack any

trespassers on their patch. Gathered round the edge of the colony are the young pretenders – young bulls who failed to topple a harem bull during the pre-season contests. They are waiting for other opportunities for mating to arise.

At Punta Norte, the young, solitary bulls make sorties into the colony about 25 times a week, and attempt to take possession of a female or a pup. Most of these hijack attempts are thwarted by the resident males, but sometimes the solitary males work together as a group. The rush of one young male into the colony triggers a ten-strong group to charge into the same

breach, all at the same time. In this way, the raiders stand a better chance of stealing and mating with one of the cows than they would if they worked alone. In the melee caused by the intrusion, the entire population gets mixed up. Pups are separated from their mothers, females move from one bull's territory to another's, some harem leaders are deposed, and a few raiders gain a slice of territory and some females.

Adolescent males – younger than three years old – often raid the breeding colony as well, but they seize pups – holding them for several hours and treating them as they would females.

Dugongs – sea-cows mistaken for mermaids

When European sailors first encountered dugongs in the Indian Ocean in the 18th century, they thought they had found the mermaids of legend. In fact, they had chanced upon a vegetarian sea mammal – a sea-cow that grazes on underwater grasses growing on the sandbanks round the rim of the Indian Ocean and the western Pacific.

Shark Bay in Western Australia is one of the remaining strongholds of the now rare dugong, which can be up to 13ft (4m) long and weigh around 47 stone (300kg). In March, as the autumn temperature falls, dugongs travel about 100 miles (160km) from their summer feeding grounds on the eastern side of the bay to spend the winter on the warmer western side. They never go ashore, and even breed in the water.

Dugongs give birth at any time of the year, following a 13-month pregnancy. Although a female can become pregnant again within a month of giving birth, there is usually a gap of 3-7 years between her young. The calf remains totally dependent on its mother's milk for its first four months and continues to be suckled for 18 months. It stays with her for its first two years at least, swimming close to her as she drifts among the beds of marine grass or bobs gently on the water surface in the morning sun.

Like all sea mammals, the dugong rises to the surface to breathe at intervals, but exposes only its nostrils, which are on top of its broad snout, and the top of its head. A dugong can stay submerged for about eight minutes, helped by the weight of its heavy bones, but usually dives for only about a minute. It lives in the shallows and rarely has to dive deeper than about 24ft (7.3m). While grazing on seabed vegetation, dugongs often use their paddle-like front limbs to 'walk' along the sea floor.

Once dugongs were found in herds of thousands or more. Today it is rare for more than one or two to be seen. Although they can live for 50 years or longer, their gentle character and leisurely lifestyle have made dugongs easy to catch. They have been killed not only for their meat, but also for the oil produced from their blubber; a 47 stone (300kg) adult dugong yields 12-13 gallons (56 litres) of oil. Steller's sea-cow, the dugong's sister-species, was slaughtered to extinction within 30 years of its discovery in 1741 in the Bering Sea off Alaska.

Ocean grazer *Accompanied by her calf, which still relies on her milk, a dugong feeds on the ocean floor. She uses bristles on her snout to rake food back into her mouth.*

APRIL

AS TIGER CUBS SPORT IN INDIAN FORESTS, WOMBATS EMERGE
INTO THE COOL AUSTRALIAN AUTUMN. WHITE STORKS FLY IN FROM AFRICA TO
NEST ON EUROPEAN CHIMNEYS, WHILE IN NORTH AMERICA
BEAVERS REPAIR THEIR LODGES AND THE GARTER SNAKES COME OUT TO MATE

India: A sparring match for young tigers

Hooded seals blow up balloons on the ice

When male hooded seals square up to each other at breeding time in April, the result is not bloody noses but balloon noses. A male attempting to see off competitors blows a brilliant red balloon from the elastic membrane that separates his nostrils. He closes off one nostril and blows out hard through the other. The bigger the male, the bigger the balloon – it can be the size of a rugby ball.

A wise male gauges his chances in combat by assessing his rival's strength according to the size of his balloon, and so decides whether to fight or withdraw. Hooded seals are named for the dark hood of skin on top of each male's nose. This, too, can be inflated to warn off rivals.

The females are pregnant when they arrive in March at their breeding grounds on the pack ice off the west Greenland coast, and give birth soon after. Each female is guarded by an 8ft (2.4m) male from the moment she hauls herself onto an ice floe, because two weeks after giving birth she will be ready to mate again and the male wants to have staked his claim. Other males wanting to challenge her guardian gather round the floe. Similar scenes are taking place at other breeding grounds off Jan Mayen island, north-east of Iceland, and off the Gulf of St Lawrence and the Newfoundland and Labrador coasts.

Each mother suckles her pup two or three times a day, sometimes for only three or four days – the fastest weaning rate among large mammals – but sometimes for up to 12 days. A pup receives some 3-10 pints (2-6 litres) of milk a day while it is being suckled, and throughout the nursing period the youngster's anus is plugged so that it can make use of every last drop of nourishment in the milk. The plug is formed naturally from the fur that the pup moults immediately after birth. This concentrated feeding results in rapid growth and the development of a thick layer of insulating blubber. So efficient is the blubber that a seven-day-old pup will have a steady body temperature of 36°C (96.8°F) even when it is lying out in a strong wind with the air temperature around −9°C (16°F). Humans and polar bears are its chief enemies, not the cold.

Within two weeks of birth, the blue-grey seal pups are in the water fending for themselves and are already adept at diving in search of fish. They can dive with ease to about 240ft (73m). Adults can dive four times as deep, but first have to expel most of the air from their lungs, or changes in water pressure would successively compress and rapidly expand the air, perhaps resulting in a fatal air bubble entering the bloodstream. To store oxygen for deep dives the hooded seal, like all other seals, and whales and dolphins, breathes it in at a higher rate than other mammals when resting. This allows them to store enough oxygen for dives lasting about five minutes. During really deep dives lasting up to 18 minutes, the seal will also reduce its rate of oxygen use by slowing its heart rate tenfold to as low as ten beats a minute.

By June, the three-month-old pups are ready to take part in the migration to the hooded-seal moulting grounds off Greenland's south-east coast. Hooded seals from both the western and eastern Atlantic all gather there to spend July and August shedding their summer coats and growing new fur for the winter ahead.

Although the seals mated in April, the fertilised egg remains suspended in each female's womb until the summer moult is over. Then the egg embeds itself in the womb lining to begin the pregnancy that will lead to the birth of a pup the following March, when every hooded seal will have returned to its own breeding ground.

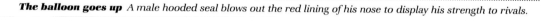

The balloon goes up A male hooded seal blows out the red lining of his nose to display his strength to rivals.

Keep away The dark-coloured balloon that this male hooded seal is blowing is formed from the hood of skin above his nose. He is warning off a rival.

Sky divers Brown pelicans dive in formation to catch a shoal of fish spotted just below the sea surface. Unlike other pelicans, they do not generally fish in fresh water.

Brown pelicans fly and fish in formation

Off the Florida coast, nine swan-sized brown pelicans fly fast and low in single file across the waves beating shorewards in the late afternoon of an April day. They alternate strong, slow wing beats and stiff-winged glides, each bird in the group meticulously following the actions of the leader. Suddenly, they all stretch out their necks, pull in their wings and dive into the sea. A few moments later they surface one by one to bob on the waves, beaks tilted down while they force out the water taken into their voluminous beak pouches along with fish during the dive. Then they tilt back their heads and swallow the fish.

The fishing flock has come from a nearby coastal breeding colony and is busily diving onto a shoal of menhaden, small fish of the coastal shallows. Seagulls harass the pelicans, trying to get them to drop fish so that they can steal it. Some gulls even land on pelicans' heads. A few pelicans lose some of their catch, but the rest take to the air to shake off their tormentors.

The peak period for brown pelicans to lay eggs in much of the USA is in March and April. At the breeding colonies, the nests may be in trees, built of twigs, or scraped out on the ground and perhaps lined with handy local material such as pebbles. Ground nests may be packed close, only just far enough apart to stop neighbouring incubating birds from pecking one other.

Male and female brown pelicans take turns to incubate the eggs and to fish. A bird returning from feeding approaches the nest with beak held high and head waving from side to side. The incubating bird pushes its beak down into the nest and utters low husky gasps while twitching its half-spread wings. Then the two birds preen before changing over. The three eggs (or sometimes two) hatch after 4-5 weeks, and the parents feed the chicks on regurgitated fish. At first they dribble it from their beaks and later the youngsters thrust their heads down the parent's gullet to get fish. At nine or ten weeks old the young can fly, but remain dependent on their parents for several more weeks.

Homeward bound *A beaver tows home a large bough of fresh willow cut from the margin of the lake. Branches and logs are constantly needed to repair the dam or lodge.*

Life and work around a beaver homestead

In April, the streams gushing down from North America's Rocky Mountains begin to swell with the spring thaw, flooding marshes and quickening river currents. In a small lake, formed behind an untidy dam of sticks, stones and mud rising nearly 10ft (3m) high from the lake bed, the surging water breaches the barrier and spills into the stream below.

Within moments, a wide V-shaped wake spreads across the lake behind a furry brown body – a North American beaver. The heavy, thickset beaver, about 3ft (1m) long, has heard the escaping water. Through the evening gloom, he locates the breach and dives to inspect the dam, propelling himself with his webbed hind feet and large, flat, scaly tail. As he dives, his nostrils and ears close tight to keep out the water, and translucent inner eyelids flick over his open eyes to shield them.

The winter weather has weakened the dam, which raises the water level about 3ft (1m) to form a 'moat' round the beavers' lodge, and there is work to be done. The beaver surfaces and slaps his tail on the water to summon his family – his mate and the four surviving offspring from the previous season. All swim to the shore and cut fresh wood with their sharp, chisel-edged teeth, choosing slender shoots of aspen, willow or birch. The beavers' teeth grow throughout life, otherwise their constant gnawing would soon make them toothless.

Beavers can cut through trees up to 20in (500mm) across. They gnaw the trunk as high as they can reach, trim off the smaller branches and drag the logs to the water. As suitable trees round the bank are used up, the beavers have to journey farther afield. They often convert their trails through the marshes into miniature canals along which they float logs to the lake.

For the present repair, the beavers collect thinner sticks, place them over the breach and plaster them on with mud dug from the lake bottom. Small holes are filled with stones, pond weed and more mud, until after a few hours'

work, the beaver family have managed to secure the dam. Their protective moat keeps away predators such as coyotes, bears and lynxes.

The spring flush of fresh vegetation around the lake gives the beavers a welcome change of diet. All winter they have been feeding on tough stems of aspen stored in piles under the water last autumn. Down there in the cold, the stems stay fresh for months, and the beavers had no need to leave their ice-covered lake. Under the ice and in the lodge, temperatures stayed just above freezing, however cold it was outside.

Water baby *Young beavers can swim almost as soon as they are born, but do not leave the safety of the lodge until they are several weeks old.*

Timber store *Beavers have used their sharp teeth to gnaw through these birches, needed for their dam.*

The lodge in the lake *A beaver dam, typically about 30yds (27m) long, interrupts the flow of a small river to create a lake that surrounds the beaver lodge and keeps away predators such as coyotes.*

Beavers are mostly active at night, and since their repair work has brought them all out into the evening air, the family disperses to find food. They fan out round the lake shore and along the canals to find new aspen shoots, waterside herbs and grasses, roots, tubers and algae. Now that winter is over, the canals will be cleared and repaired so that the family can go as far afield as possible by water. Beavers can carry or chew food underwater without choking because they can close a watertight skin flap behind their teeth, and another to seal the gullet. They can stay submerged for four or five minutes, and swim underwater for some 300yds (270m).

After feeding this evening, the female beaver returns to the lodge, using one of its underwater entrance tunnels. This untidy pile of sticks is about 36ft (11m) across at the base and protrudes more than 4ft (1.2m) above the water surface. It has been built up from the bottom of the lake and hollowed out inside to provide a sleeping chamber that is above water level and about 6ft (1.8m) across and 2ft (600mm) high.

Back in the sleeping chamber, the female shakes the water from her lustrous fur and begins to groom. Beavers groom themselves and each other frequently, using the divided claws of the first and second toes on each hind foot to comb the fur. This female and her partner of many years mated in January, and now have a litter of six two-day-old kits safe and warm inside the lodge. They were born with their eyes open and fully furred, and can move about in the lodge and even swim in the water lapping

round the entrance hole. But their small size – about 15in (380mm) including the tail – and dense fur, which traps air between the hairs, makes them too buoyant to dive down the tunnel out of the safety of the lodge.

As yet, they rely for food on their mother's rich milk. They will not be fully weaned until they are 3-4 months old, but when they are about a month old, they will start nibbling solid food, and all the family will help to bring it to them. By

Family home *About 12-15 members of the family live in the lodge. They add a new layer of sticks and mud to the outside every autumn to ensure winter protection.*

June, they will be able to swim well enough to leave the lodge and forage with the family.

The young beavers' education begins almost immediately. Even tiny beaver kits gnaw at sticks and carry building material when the family makes a repair. Their parents will let them stay with the family until the November when they are almost two years old; then they leave to find mates and start their own families, the first in a lifespan of 15-21 years.

Hunted for their pelts for centuries, beavers have become scarce in North America, but their numbers are rising now that hunting is controlled. Beaver dams are an asset to the countryside because they regulate the flow of streams, which reduces drought, flooding and soil erosion. Also, when beavers dig up the bottom mud, they disperse water-plant seeds, and this helps to increase the fish population.

Safe quarters *The lodge, a hollow pile of mud-plastered branches resting on the lake bottom, has an underwater entrance leading to a dry sleeping chamber above water level. The nearby dam maintains a moat round the lodge.*

The seething courtship of the garter snake

As the late April sunshine warms a tumble of limestone rocks in Manitoba in southern Canada, every crack and crevice is soon swarming with snakes. They are red-sided garter snakes that have been hibernating in the hollows below, away from the frosts, in communal dens containing up to 15,000. Now they have sensed the warmth of spring and are moving towards the light.

It is six months or more since the snakes, up to 4ft (1.2m) long, have eaten, but it is their sexual urge rather than hunger that drives them to this mass emergence. During the breeding season, which lasts for the next month or so, appetite will be totally suppressed. The short Manitoba summer allows little time for their eggs to develop, and if the snakes dispersed in search of food, there would not be enough time to search for a mate.

The males emerge first, and lurk at the entrance to the hibernation site eager to seize any opportunity to mate. The females are more cautious. Late frosts could damage their eggs after mating, so they hang back and slither into the sunlight in ones and twos. This means that every female has as many as 50 potential suitors at the den entrance.

The males' urge to mate is so strong that they will even woo sticks. But what particularly excites them is a pheromone – a chemical advertising her fertility – that oozes from the thin skin between the scales on a female's back. Males scent the pheromone with flicking tongues, then rub against her and drape themselves along her back. Each female is soon surrounded by a writhing ball of 30 or more urgent males competing to inseminate her.

After a 20-minute copulation, the successful male wriggles off to find another female. His urge to mate will last until late May, when he will feel hungry and go in search of food such as frogs and mice.

Once mated, the female no longer attracts the males. She can slip away to spend the early summer feeding and basking to incubate the eggs inside her body. They hatch inside her and the fully formed, pencil-length offspring are born about three months after mating.

Successful couple *A male and a female red-sided garter snake rise above a writhing mass of her other suitors as they mate on a warm spring day.*

Why a Fowler's toad wants a deep voice

It is three o'clock in the morning on a warm, wet April night, but the countryside around an Ohio pond is far from peaceful. The night is filled with the croaks of thousands of Fowler's toads. Each toad inflates the sac of skin beneath its chin until it is translucent and almost at bursting point. This sac is the resonating chamber that makes its call carry farther. As the toads call, their bodies stiffen. Croaking is hard work, and they have been croaking since dusk.

All these croaking toads are males, and the females they are serenading are slipping quietly into the water at the pond's edge. Attracted by the male voices, they have come to pick a mate.

When she arrives at the pond, each female is bulging with eggs – she has produced as many as she can and wants to ensure they are all fertilised successfully. Male Fowler's toads are slightly smaller than females, and she must find the biggest possible mate so that he will have enough sperm to fertilise all her eggs. A large male is also likely to be long-lived and successful and so father strong progeny.

As she has to choose between myriad males all calling in the dark, she bases her choice on the sound of their voices. The biggest males have the deepest and slowest voices, so each female swims towards the deepest baritone she can hear. Producing a deep sound from a small body is difficult, but there is one way for a smaller male to deceive a female into choosing him – a cooler body temperature lowers the tone and the calling rate. In April the deeper water away from the pond's edge is cooler, so by calling from the middle of the pond small toads can sound bigger.

Unfortunately for would-be cheaters, big toads know this too. They try to keep the calling sites in the pond centre for themselves so that they can sound even bigger. Tiny tenor toads are pushed to the edge of the pond, where the warmer water makes their calls higher-pitched and faster than ever. However, they still stand a chance of fertilising some eggs and fathering offspring because females must pass through the pond edges on the way to the centre. So a small male may be able to jump on a female's back and hang on tight.

When a female has chosen a male, he grips her behind the forelegs and rides on her back for many hours, waiting for her to lay her eggs. Then he will fertilise them as they leave her body. By morning, the night's activity has left the pond adorned with necklaces of toad spawn, the black eggs poised to become tadpoles and wriggle into life as spring blends into summer.

When a voice really counts A male Fowler's toad inflates his resonating chamber as he croaks for a mate.

An amorous moment A richly coloured male wood duck caresses a sombre brown female during their ballet-like mating display on a New England pool.

A wood duck ballet on a backwoods lake

Mist still lingers around a New England woodland pool early in an April morning. A shaft of sunlight through the treetops lights up the dark surface of the water like a spotlight, and two ducks move like dancers into the beam, heads stretched forwards and wings slightly raised. Now and again they gently nibble at each other's head and throat feathers.

These two North American wood ducks are engrossed in a display that will cement their breeding partnership. His colouring is a riot of metallic green, purple and burnished rust, with white lines dividing his head and body into geometric shapes. She is mottled brown with white throat and eye patches.

He wheels and turns about her in the water, every movement meant to give her the best view of his shimmering plumage. He 'mock preens', reaching far behind his wing like a dandy pulling out a huge silk handkerchief. He swims away from her, flattening and splaying his crest to show an arc of shining green edged in perfect white, and turning his tail so that she sees a patch of violet bounded by an arc of orange.

Soon they will mate, and then he will escort her as she feeds eagerly on water plants to produce her clutch of 8-14 eggs. Together they will search for a nest hole in a tree trunk, but once the eggs are laid, the female alone will incubate them for 4-5 weeks. Within a day of hatching, the young ducks will drop from the tree into the water.

How the arum gains new life from decay

The scent of myrtle and other aromatic shrubs usually fills the April air in Sardinia, but on a rocky cliff top there is an overpowering stench of rotten flesh. Surprisingly, it is coming from a cup-shaped plant the size of a dinner plate – a hairy dragon arum. The smell, so enticing to insects, builds up and fades with the rise and fall of the daily temperature. The cup is a modified leaf (or spathe) rather than a petal, and its purple colour and its texture – as well as its smell – are like rotting meat.

So strong is the dragon arum's attraction that blowflies scavenging nearby on a dead gull leave it and land on the cup. Guided by hairs on its surface, the flies crawl to the bottom, where a small opening leads to a long, narrow chamber housing the plant's male and female flowers massed at the base of a spike. Downward-pointing hairs prevent the flies from climbing out. As they rub against the female flowers, they deposit any pollen picked up in other cups.

Once the female flowers are pollinated, the cup provides nectar and moisture to keep the flies alive until the male flowers, higher on the spike, open three days later. Their shower of pollen coats the trapped flies. Then the grid of hairs withers and the flies return to brief liberty before the irresistible odour of decay lures them into the next trap to be unwitting pollinators.

Welcome guests Flies are tempted to the arum cup by the smell of rotting flesh. Once trapped inside they pollinate the plant, then carry its pollen to the next.

Seduction A male wasp tries to mate with an orchid disguised as a female. In doing so, he pollinates the flower.

Orchids that reproduce by seducing wasps

In the hills of southern Spain a hairy wasp buzzes restlessly in a patch of short grass. The dawn is still cool in early April, and to warm its flight muscles the wasp must vibrate its wings. This is a male hairy wasp, with a dark body covered in reddish-gold hairs. It has just emerged from a hole in a sandy bank, where it has developed from an egg laid by a female hairy wasp last winter, before she died. Now the young male wasp is ready to take off into the early morning in search of a mate.

Sure enough, the scent of a female hairy wasp wafts towards him on the gentle breeze, and he flies towards the scent. Soon he picks out her distinctive dark form with its halo of reddish hairs, resting on an orchid petal. He lands on her back and attempts to mate with her. Unsatisfied, he flies farther afield and finds many more females resting on similar flowers all around for him to mate with.

But the wasp has been duped. These are not female hairy wasps at all, but flowers of the mirror orchid. One of the orchid's petals is fringed with a brush of red and shaped like a wasp. The orchid also mimics the scent that the female wasp gives out to draw the male to her. Its deceptions ensure that it will attract pollinators to fertilise its flowers.

When the male wasp lands on the orchid petal, his weight pushes up two sticky pads that become glued to his head as he brushes against them. Attached to the pads are two thick stalks, loaded with sticky pollen. When the wasp leaves the flower, he pulls the stalks free and flies off with them stuck to his head.

As the wasp lands on another sham female, the stalks, which bend forwards under the weight of pollen, are perfectly positioned to rub against the orchid's sticky, protruding stigma (the part that collects pollen). At the same time, another load of pollen is pressed onto the wasp's head to be carried to the next plant.

The success of the mirror orchid's deception depends on careful timing. In early April, the female hairy wasps have not yet emerged from their holes. When they do, the flowers will not be able to seduce the male wasps so easily. So the orchid flowers late enough to catch emerging young male hairy wasps, but too early for new females to have emerged.

Swallows herald the coming of summer

Just six weeks ago the swallows now swooping around a group of sleepy Friesian cattle in a British meadow were snapping up flies above herds of zebra and wildebeest in southern Africa. On this clear blue April day, these graceful birds with long forked tails are newly arrived from their African wintering grounds and eager to feed and replenish the reserves that the long migration has used up. Each summer they come north for the breeding season, returning to nest at the same place every year.

Their flight north – more than 5000 miles (8000km) – was taken in several stages. They travelled quickly across Africa, rested and refuelled on the North African coast and then crossed the Mediterranean. Cold spells delayed them in Europe and forced them to turn south again for a time to seek food and shelter. Now, the large flies that buzz about the cattle are providing a welcome feast.

Swallows are among the first summer visitors to arrive in Europe. As the weather gets warmer, the males will begin to sing their mating songs, twittering enthusiastically in the early morning sunshine from perches such as telephone wires.

Once paired, the swallows begin nesting. Their cup-shaped mud nests were once built only on cave walls, cliffs and in tree holes. Now most of them are built in spots that humans conveniently provide. Beams and walls in barns and stables are favourite locations because they are warm, and the insects that pester the farm animals provide a ready food supply. But some caves are still used. In Nottinghamshire, in the centre of England, there are limestone caves that look out over rich dairy pastures where insects swarm round the cattle. Here the swallows get the best of both worlds – a natural nest site as well as a good food supply.

Behind the swallows flock vast numbers of other birds, migrating from south of the Sahara. In good weather, the mass movements are picked up on air-traffic-control radar screens. By the end of April, European woodlands and hedgerows are filled with the melodic songs of summer migrants such as willow, wood and garden warblers, adding to the richness of the dawn chorus of resident thrushes, blackbirds and robins. And on still, warm nights, as April gives way to May, the intense, throbbing songs of visiting nightingales ripple from thickets of hazel and bramble.

Creature comforts *A swallow lines its nest on a cave wall with a warm layer of feathers. Nests are mostly built in barns or under the eaves of buildings.*

Flight paths *Millions of birds migrate from southern Africa to Europe each spring. Some of the small birds use islands such as the Balearics as staging posts.*

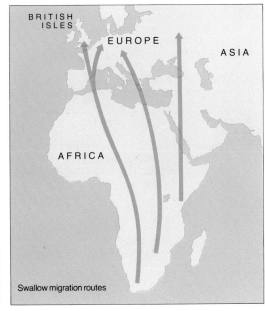

Swallow migration routes

First the eggs *Bumble bee eggs, the size of rice grains, are laid in the nest by the queen bee. The eggs usually take from four to six days to hatch.*

Then the larvae *The helpless, blind larvae feed on pollen for between 10 and 19 days. They are also fed with honey by the queen or worker bees.*

Finally the bee *Each larva then spins a silk cocoon around itself and changes shape inside. An adult bee emerges from each cocoon from 10 to 18 days later.*

A queen bumble bee starts to rear a family

The April sunshine brings a promise of summer, and the spring flowers brighten a European hedgerow where, in front of a sweet violet, a large bee hovers, its wings worn and tattered. The bee is a queen bumble bee, the size of a thumb-joint and covered in stiff yellow and black hairs. She is the lone member of her clan to have survived winter, buried among leaf mould. The sun's warmth has roused her to action, to begin a new bumble bee season.

As she hovers, her rapid wingbeat produces a lazy humming – the origin of the name bumble (or humble) bee. With her tongue she reaches into the flower for its sugary nectar, which gives her valuable energy, and she also eats the protein-rich pollen. This helps her ovary develop into a fully formed organ in which her first eggs now appear, fertilised by sperm stored in her body since she mated last autumn.

She begins to search for a suitable nest site, such as the nest of a field mouse or vole, although nest sites vary among the many species of bumble bee found in most temperate areas of the world. Once she has found a nest, she lines it with grass and moss. Wax begins to ooze from glands between the plates of her abdomen, and she uses it to build her first egg-cell, a neat cup on the nest floor. She stocks the egg-cell with pollen, and into it lays her first batch of about a dozen eggs, each the size of a grain of rice. The bee seals off the cell with wax and begins her next construction – a store at the nest entrance for honey (concentrated nectar).

The eggs hatch into tiny white larvae, which feed on the stored pollen and on honey the queen provides through a hole in the cell wall. The larvae change their skins at intervals as they grow, and the queen has to extend the cell to allow for their growth. She spends long periods stretched across her brood like an incubating bird, using the honey store for food.

When the larvae are fully grown, they stop eating, spin a silken cocoon and turn into pupae. By late April the pupae have changed into adult bees, and chew their way out of the cocoons. These first hatchlings are all female workers, and are much smaller than later offspring. Their vacated cocoons serve as more honey stores for the growing colony.

The queen, meanwhile, has been building more egg-cells on top of the cocoons, and the newly hatched workers must now gather food, provision the cells and maintain the honey store. Throughout the summer, the colony continues expanding until there are several hundred workers. Their body warmth maintains the nest at a steady 30°C (86°F). When the temperature drops outside, more bees cluster into the nest, and if it gets too hot some of the workers fan the nest with their wings.

Towards the end of the summer, the queen lays a batch of eggs which she does not fertilise from her sperm store, and these develop into male bees. The males, which have no stings, are recognisable by their long antennae or feelers, used to 'tune in' to receptive females. By now, late in the season, the colony is well established and food is so abundant that some larvae, living in extra-large egg-cells, can be fed especially freely. The extra food stimulates them to develop into the next generation of queens.

The males leave the nest and wait, hovering near the entrance of their own or a neighbouring nest, to mate with the new queens as they emerge. Afterwards the males die. Back in the nest the old queen has stopped laying. She and her colony will soon die from the autumnal cold. By this time, however, the mated queens will have burrowed into a bank or found a sheltered nook to hibernate through the winter, ready to begin the cycle again next April.

....

Inside the nest *The queen rears her first brood of workers, which then run the hive. The queen can lay eggs every day, but absorbs excess eggs in her body to keep the brood to a size the workers can cope with.*

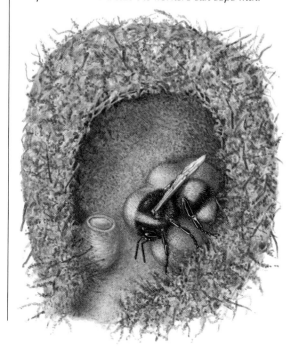

New-world mink taste wild life in Britain

Sleek and sinuous, a weasel-like shape slinks from the late April sunshine into a dark crevice beneath the tangled roots of a riverside tree in Britain. It is a chocolate-brown mink, about the size of a cat, and the descendant of introduced North American mink that escaped from fur farms established in the 1920s. Safely secreted in the crevice are the mink's five newborn kits. They are little bigger than mice, and already have razor-sharp teeth.

The female mated about seven weeks ago. Her partner immediately moved on in search of other mates, taking advantage of the short period of March and April when female mink are in heat. He may remain with his last mate, however, and help rear the kits.

Mink kits grow quickly through the summer on their mother's milk and first venture from the den in June, to play on the riverbank. By July they will be weaned and will hunt with their mother, taking birds, fish, voles and rabbits. In midsummer moorhen and coot nestlings fall easy prey; indeed, mink have almost wiped out these birds as breeding species in some areas.

About September, when the young mink are fully grown, they will seek their own territories beside rivers, lakes or marshes. Several will die during their first winter, but by March the survivors will be ready to breed, ensuring that this immigrant is in Britain to stay.

Furry bundles Peacefully asleep in their den, these young mink will soon grow into voracious hunters that prey on small birds, small mammals and fish.

Elegant courtship Storks mate on their nests, built from huge piles of twigs and lined with grass, rags and paper.

White storks return to the chimney tops

From the chimney stack comes a loud clattering. It is April, and the white storks have returned to their chimney-top nests. Despite the noise the birds make, householders across much of Europe welcome them because they are regarded as symbols of fertility and good luck. Storks nest naturally in trees or on cliffs, but have found that church towers, tall buildings and chimneys also offer suitable sites for massive nests the size of a kitchen table.

These debonair birds stand over 3ft (1m) tall, are white with some black wing feathers and have red beaks and legs. They mate for life and usually return to the same nest. The male is generally first. When the female joins him, they perform a graceful courting display, then mate on the nest. About a week later the first white egg is laid, and another follows every two days, usually until there are three or four.

The female incubates them, occasionally relieved by her mate. The eggs hatch after about four weeks, and one parent shelters the chicks from the weather for a week or so while the other brings back food and regurgitates it for them. As the chicks grow, both parents feed them with frogs, tadpoles, worms, small fish, large insects and lizards. They leave the nest after 8-9 weeks but return to be fed by their parents and to roost at night. By early August they have left for southern Africa, and by mid-August their parents, too, have left.

Good omen Storks, said to bring good luck, often nest on chimneys, which may have a nesting platform fitted.

Tender moment *The start of the weaning period is a stressful time for the four-month-old cubs. They need the security and reassurance of their mother's affection.*

Growing up to survive in a tiger's world

In the warmth of an April morning, the tigress breaks cover and pads effortlessly across the open grassland between two patches of dense Indian forest. Her three cubs tumble playfully in her wake. Born the previous December, they are now four months old and still dependent on her milk for much of their nourishment.

Their progress is marked by the sharp barks of a sambar deer, and then by the hysterical alarm calls of langur monkeys from the forest on the far side. The tigress ignores the cacophony. She is not hunting and makes no attempt to conceal herself. She is more concerned with reaching a set of pools that lie hidden in a ravine on the far side of the forest. Within a few hours, the temperature will rise above 38°C (100°F) and before it does she is anxious for both herself and her cubs to be secluded in the cool of the ravine.

This is the tigress's second set of cubs and she is now an experienced mother. Soon she will have to teach them how to hunt for themselves. Hunting skills are not entirely inborn and have to be learned through repeated practice. But before that, the cubs must be weaned. Their persistent demands for milk are now beginning to irritate her and their sharp new teeth are beginning to make their presence felt on her teats when she suckles them.

Half an hour later, the family arrives at the pools in the ravine. The tigress sinks down against the base of the ravine's rock wall. The cubs scamper about, playing tag among the bushes, batting at each other with their over-sized paws or rolling over each other in mock attacks. In the stifling heat, the tigress dozes fitfully. Eventually, even the cubs retreat into the shade. The awesome stillness of the Indian midday descends. Even the insects are silenced by the energy-draining heat.

By mid-afternoon, the temperature has reached a searing 42°C (108°F). One of the cubs emerges from its hideaway under a bush and walks down towards the nearest pool. It laps quietly at the water and then rolls into the shallows at the edge. The tigress moves down to join it. She slips gracefully into the cooling water, lying fully stretched out with only her head in view.

As the afternoon wears on, the temperature gradually drops to a more tolerable level. The tigress emerges glistening from the pool where she has been lying. With the cubs at her heels, she sets off down the ravine to hunt for food.

LEARNING HOW TO HUNT

After about half a mile (800m) she stops suddenly. Instinctively, the cubs freeze behind her. Heads cocked to one side, they peer quizzically about them, ears twitching. They recognise that mother has suddenly become very alert, but they do not understand why. In fact, the tigress has spotted a sambar deer feeding on the far side of a small clearing. It is facing away from her and does not realise its danger. The tigress crouches and begins to creep forward using small clumps of bushes for cover. She must approach unseen to within 20yds (18m) of the prey if it is not to out-run her.

Then, hurling herself across the ground that separates her from the deer, the tigress catches the animal completely by surprise. In a moment, she has it on the ground, her mouth round its throat, the canines gripping deeper in response to the animal's struggles as it suffocates. The cubs appear out of the bushes and stand beside her. They look on impassively. One of the cubs reaches out a paw uncertainly to touch the deer. A spasm passes down the deer's body, causing a hindleg to kick out. The cub gives a startled cough and backs away.

Tearing at the sambar's belly, the tigress begins to eat. The cubs crowd round her, peering excitedly at the deer. This is the first time they have been present at a kill. Their mother normally leaves them asleep when she goes off to hunt.

A chance encounter has provided the cubs

with a preview of what they will have to learn. Later, the tigress will give them the opportunity to kill an animal for themselves under her guidance. In a few more months, the youngsters will begin to coordinate their behaviour with their mother's when she is hunting, and will work both to scare game in her direction and to prevent it from escaping. Later, they will rush in to attack the hapless prey once their mother has caught it.

A female's ability to rear her cubs depends on her success at hunting. If game is scarce or she is prevented from hunting by injury, her cubs will starve. While raising her young, she has to kill an animal every five or six days. It will usually be a deer or a wild pig, but occasionally the tiger may tackle a rhinoceros, a water buffalo or an elephant calf.

Cubs practise on small game, rodents and birds, but will not make their first solo kills until they are about 18 months old. Even then, they will not be proficient enough at hunting to

Rare occasion It is unusual to see the male tiger join the mother and cubs in a family outing. As the summer temperature approaches 42°C (108°F), the tigers attempt to cool off in a pool.

Hunting lesson *Tiger cubs watch their mother kill a sambar deer she has taken by the throat.*

Rest and play *A mother tigress sleeps after gorging on a kill, while her three 17-month-old youngsters relax above her. The two female cubs (above left) bat at each other in play and their brother (right) flops on the ledge.*

survive on their own for at least another six months beyond that.

In the meantime, the relaxed family atmosphere will gradually disintegrate. The cubs will begin to challenge each other with increasing frequency, for only the most powerful animals will be able to acquire territories once they reach full adulthood.

They will begin to challenge their mother, too, squabbling with her over her kills, sometimes stealing them from her. She, in her turn, will leave them increasingly on their own, abandoning them to their own devices for several days at a time. The cubs will also begin to be less playful when they are together. Although their greetings on meeting after a separation will be intense and friendly, they will continue to grow apart until they are about three years old, when they move out of their mother's territory altogether in search of their own.

The tigress and her cubs live in the Ranthambhore Tiger Sanctuary in northern India. Set in an ancient hunting forest surrounding a now-ruined palace, the sanctuary is home to about 30 tigers. They survive there only because the forest is also a sanctuary for several thousand deer and antelopes, as well as wild boars, langur monkeys and 150 sloth bears. Without the deer and antelopes as food, the tigers would long since have died out.

When they leave their mother, the cubs will be exposed to great risks. If they are forced to search for unoccupied territories beyond the confines of the sanctuary, they will inadvertently come into conflict with their human neighbours. The killing of farm animals will provoke the inevitable response – poisoned bait.

Some of the cubs will die. Others will eventually find territories of their own and settle down to adult life, with its daily round of sleeping and killing, interspersed at intervals with mating and the birth of cubs.

Weighing as much as 43 stone (274kg) and measuring 8-10ft (2.4-3m) from head to tail-tip, the tiger is the largest member of the cat family. Like all large predators, it needs a great deal of room. The females occupy their own territories, each about 3sq miles (8sq km) in area. This area provides each female with her own exclusive walking larder in which she should be able to find enough food for herself and her cubs.

Superimposed over the females' territories are the territories of a smaller number of males. A male's territory is roughly three times larger than a female's and covers the ranges of several females. He alone mates with each of them.

A tiger marks the boundary of its territory in various ways to ensure that other tigers of the same sex know that it is occupied, and will not intrude. The chief form of marking is the

PROJECT TIGER

At the turn of the century, there were some 40,000 tigers in India. Within 70 years, big-game hunting and loss of habitat to a growing human population had reduced the total to 1800. By 1973, alarmed at the prospect of the tiger's imminent disappearance, the World Wide Fund for Nature, the International Union for the Conservation of Nature and the Indian government had launched a rescue operation known as 'Project Tiger'.

A small number of India's 450 wildlife parks and reserves were earmarked as tiger sanctuaries. Ranthambhore, with its 155sq miles (400sq km) of rolling hills, open grassland and ancient forests, is one of the smallest of these. To provide the tigers that live there with sufficient room and enough prey, 16 villages inhabited by 1500 people and more than 3000 of their domestic livestock had to be moved out of the reserve and resettled elsewhere.

Despite the scale of the problem, Project Tiger has been successful. By the mid-1980s it was estimated that there might be perhaps 3000 tigers in India. But tiger habitats are being drastically reduced by deforestation and illegal cattle grazing, and tigers are often too hemmed in by increasing human populations to be able to move to new territories. Inevitably, domestic livestock has been attacked. However, the Ranthambhore Foundation, a local environmental development group, is now working with villagers to improve the living conditions on the arid, drought-ridden fringes of the sanctuary so that the wildlife and the local communities can live in harmony.

Test of strength *The serious life of an adult looms nearer. The two female cubs engage in harmless sparring to settle a minor difference of opinion, but eventually such disputes will result in one being dominant over the other.*

Nineteen months old *Now almost full grown, the cubs cool themselves at a water hole, with their mother.*

spraying of urine on tree trunks or other vegetation, much as domestic cats do. The marks are typically about 3ft (1m) off the ground, and often on the underside of a leaning tree trunk where they are protected from the rain. In such places, the odour may still be detectable as long as three weeks after spraying.

In addition, the tigers claw the bark of trees and the hard-packed earth to provide visual signs of their presence. These scrapes may also be sprayed with urine or rubbed with scent from scent glands along the side of the jaw.

A tiger that intrudes into another's territory risks a fight. With their sharp fangs and massive claws, tigers are formidable opponents capable of inflicting mortal wounds. Marking territory boundaries helps to prevent unnecessary fights.

THE MALE PAYS A VISIT

Having gorged herself on the sambar, the tigress withdraws and lies down a short way off. The cubs begin to nibble at the carcass. The sun is sinking fast, and a flock of greylag geese straggles in to land on one of the lakes in the valley below the forest. The birds are heading north to their summer breeding grounds in Siberia.

Suddenly the tigress stiffens, then rises quickly and moves protectively towards her cubs as they feed on the carcass. A shadow

Lending a helping hand *Aided by her cubs, a tigress hauls the carcass of a sambar deer from the shallows of the lake at Ranthambhore. It was killed by crocodiles, but she has been able to drive them away.*

moves in the forest behind. She turns to face it. A large tiger emerges from the cover of the trees. It is the resident male of the area in which the tigress has her territory.

His reaction towards the cubs is unpredictable. Tiger males commonly kill cubs that they have not fathered in order to bring the female back into heat so that she will breed again. He approaches the remains of the carcass and settles to eat. Although he is the father of the cubs, they back away uncertainly, and the tigress remains wary.

When he has finished the last scraps, the male moves across to the tigress and sniffs her

tentatively. She stands, tense and uncertain. But the male is in a friendly mood. He gives a low-pitched growl, then walks off a short distance to lie down and rest in the grass.

As night falls, the tigress settles down again, her watchful eyes fixed on the male. The cubs join her. Seeking out their favourite teats, they begin to suck her milk noisily. Not until her cubs are nearly three years old and able to fend for themselves will their mother breed again. A tigress usually bears three or four cubs in one litter, but some may die within a week or two of birth. Rarely do more than three survive the first hazardous year of life.

Golden toads of the mountain cloud forest

Streaks of gold begin to brighten the forest floor in the high, damp, cloud-enveloped forests of north-west Costa Rica's Monteverde Mountains. It is late April, and the early rains have stirred the golden toads from their hiding places under the moss and fallen leaves, where they spend most of the year.

The brilliantly coloured males converge on the rainwater pools and sit patiently round the edges waiting for the females who will come there to spawn. Barely 1in (25mm) long, the male toads look like tiny golden statues in a water garden. As the females approach, the waiting males grab hold of them and hang on, and are carried to the spawning site. In the scramble, the males will catch hold of anything that moves, including other males. A male that is grasped by another male gives out a rapid vibration that signals 'Let go – I am male.'

A female rapidly accumulates a horde of males, each holding on to some part of her in a desperate attempt to be able to fertilise her spawn. Sometimes a female is buried for hours beneath a heaving mass of males, unable to move until the stronger individuals have managed to dislodge some of their rivals. Once she can move again, the female heads for the pool and there releases her 200 or so eggs. The males still clinging to her fertilise them.

Within a week, the entire female population has spawned, and the toads retire once more to their solitary lives among the leaf litter on the floor of the forest. The eggs left in the pool hatch as tadpoles a few days after being laid, and they remain in the water feeding on small plants such as algae as they develop into toadlets.

But even a few days without a thunder shower will be enough to dry up the shallow breeding pools. If this happens, many tadpoles and toadlets will die, unable to cope with the heat and lack of water.

About five weeks after hatching the tadpoles will have developed into tiny versions of their parents, and will leave the pool.

Golden toads are found nowhere else in the world, and even here their survival is uncertain.

Breeding display In late April, male golden toads gather at a pond in Costa Rica's Monteverde Cloud Forest Reserve, awaiting the arrival of the females.

Armour-plated comforter A young nine-banded armadillo snuggles up to its mother in her den. Armadillos are among the few mammals to have scales.

Armadillos dig to survive both heat and cold

In her den deep beneath the dry grassland of Central America, scorched by the daytime heat of April, a female nine-banded armadillo suckles her four scaly, month-old babies. Armadillo babies are unique – they are always sets of identical quadruplets, produced from a single fertilised egg cell that splits into four equal parts.

The nine-banded armadillo is one of the few South American mammals to have successfully invaded the North American continent. Its success is due to its ability to burrow deep below the ground. There it can escape the burning heat of the day and the intense cold of the night in the dry grasslands of Mexico and Texas. Its burrows are up to 25ft (7.6m) long and many of them go as deep as 11ft (3.4m) beneath the surface.

An armadillo digging is a remarkable sight. It scrapes with its forelegs at the hard-packed earth while its hind legs kick the loosened soil backwards out of the burrow entrance. Its tail is braced against the floor of the burrow to bear its weight, allowing its hind legs to swing free.

Armadillos feed mostly at night on creatures such as insects, spiders and occasional lizards dug out from the soil. If it detects a predator such as a coyote, an armadillo can bury itself in seconds, or roll into a ball and rely on its bony plates as a shield. Despite the heaviness of these bony plates, armadillos can swim well when water is available, but to avoid sinking must first gulp in air to give themselves buoyancy.

Unlucky frog A large marsh spider carries off a harlequin-patterned tree frog caught during a breeding party in a Costa Rican rain forest. The spider will feast on the frog in its lair among the marsh grasses.

Dangerous embraces for harlequin tree frogs

Costa Rica is home to the beautiful blue-and-yellow-blotched harlequin-patterned tree frog, which for most of the year hides among the dense marsh vegetation of the rain forest. But during the April rains, hundreds of the frogs congregate in the open to court and mate. They are very sensitive to weather changes and when conditions are right for producing flooded areas that tadpoles can develop in, the entire local population emerges to seek a frog of the opposite sex. The air is filled with the noise of croaking males, sitting on leaves and calling to prospective mates.

But if the frogs can be switched on by a change in the weather, so can their predators. Mating parties of harlequin-patterned tree frogs attract particularly dangerous hunters – marsh spiders. Distracted by the urgency of mating, or simply exhausted from the sudden burst of activity, the frogs are easy prey. A spider seizes a frog in its jaws, pumps in its lethal venom and then takes the limp carcass off into the saw-edged marsh grasses to a place where it will not be disturbed while it sucks the tree frog dry.

The frogs, which are up to 1½in (38mm) long,

seek partners about their own size – large males couple with large females and smaller males with smaller females. The ratio of males to females is about the same so there will be a mate for most of them.

A male has more chance of mating successfully with a partner of his own size; he can get a firmer hold on her and is less likely to be dislodged during the mating melée, when males are fighting and kicking vigorously in their attempts to mount and clasp a partner.

A male approaches a female from behind, grasps her beneath her forelimbs and hangs on tight. Small roughened pads, known as nuptial pads, on the inner sides of his front limbs help him maintain a firm grip. He clings on and fertilises the female's eggs as she lays them on a marsh plant leaf. The eggs hatch as tadpoles, which fall into the water, still encased in jelly, then swim away to grow into tiny frogs.

Most of a male tree frog's energy goes into calling for a mate and less into producing the sperm. He calls to outdo rivals and ensure that females are attracted to him rather than another male, for his overriding urge is to pass on his genes. This explosion of activity is over in about two days. Then those frogs that have not ended up as meals for marsh spiders return once more to the undergrowth.

Diving from the nest saves hoatzin chicks

In the Amazon rain forest, in places where the banks of the Negro river are permanently flooded, groups of hoatzins are squabbling over nesting places. All are vying for the best sites – those above the water, which is essential to the survival of their nestlings. April brings the rainy season, when foraging flocks of 20-30 birds split up into family breeding groups, each group defending a 50yd (46m) stretch of river bank.

A most unusual bird, the hoatzin has naked, electric-blue skin round the eyes, a spiky crest and bright red eyes. It feeds on the green leaves of marsh plants, using its scissor-like beak to snip them off. Its enlarged crop has bacteria that, as in a cow's rumen, slowly break down a plant's cellulose and release the nutrients.

Hoatzins do not fly well because of their slow digestion and low-energy food, and also because their flying muscles are small to make way for their large crops. But they can flap along for about 150yds (140m) at a time to search the river bank for the choicest leaves. When a hoatzin lands, it tends to topple forward because of its large crop, and also because it cannot grasp well

Top heavy With its large crop full, the pheasant-sized hoatzin topples forward onto its breast when it perches on a branch. A thick skin pad protects the breast.

with its feet. A bird returning with a full crop perches with its breast bone resting on the branch, cushioned by a specially thickened patch of skin.

The nest is a simple platform made from a loose assemblage of twigs, sited about 15ft (4.6m) above the water. The female lays 2-4 eggs. The breeding group consists of up to seven birds – the two parents and their 'helpers'. These helpers are relatives, sometimes youngsters from last season, who help to incubate the eggs as well as bring back food for the current brood and defend the nesting territory. It is as if they are practising for the time when they will have their own nests. And it is also one way that they can ensure the continuation of their genes (a prime aim in all animals), as their young relatives carry many of the same genes.

If danger threatens in the form of a hungry snake or monkey – particularly black-capped capuchin monkeys, which can smell the nests from some distance away – the hoatzin chicks have a unique escape strategy. They cannot fly yet, so they leap out of the nest into the water and swim under the surface for a short distance.

When the danger has passed, the chicks clamber out of the water onto an overhanging branch. They have developed a couple of claws halfway along the top edge of each wing, which gives them a resemblance to ancient primitive birds. With these wing claws, they are furnished with two more climbing limbs to help them up through the foliage to get back safely to the nest. When hoatzins become adult, the claws are lost and the bird flaps away from danger rather than taking to the water.

Four-footed bird A hoatzin chick dives into the river to escape predators. It clambers back to its nest in the tree with the aid of primitive claws on its wings.

Late call A fringe-lipped bat swoops to grab a male mudpuddle frog in its mouth after tuning in on its call.

A love-call gamble for the mudpuddle frog

In the dark, damp rain forest of Panama's Barro Colorado island, April's seasonal rains bring out tiny frogs about 1¼ in (32mm) long. Known as mudpuddle, or tungara, frogs, they live in and around small patches of water.

Mudpuddle males are noisy creatures. A solitary frog calling to attract a mate may give its *aow-aow* call more than 7000 times in a few hours. If, as is usual, other males are close by, the male changes his call to *aow-chuck-chuck* to make him sound more attractive. Unlike the *aow*, the *chuck* contains sound frequencies that indicate the size of the calling frog. Females prefer large frogs – which are likely to produce stronger offspring.

Unfortunately for the male frog, the *chuck* call not only makes him easier for female frogs to locate, but also gives him away to predators, especially the fringe-lipped bat. Bats usually find their prey by echolocation, sending out high-frequency sound pulses and judging the position and distance of objects from the echoes bouncing back. But when a fringe-lipped bat comes across a chorus of frogs, it stops sending out sound pulses and instead 'tunes in' on the frogs' calls – which are well below the sound frequencies a bat normally hears.

Although the mudpuddle frogs find some safety in numbers, their only real defence is to stop calling when bats are about. On moonlit nights the frogs can spot a bat flying over the pond, and do just that. But on moonless nights the frogs cannot see the danger, so the bats are likely to have good hunting.

Hostel burrows for wayfaring wombats

Snuffling and mumbling, a rounded hump emerges from a burrow under a gum tree and waits for April's autumn sunshine to warm it through. As the common wombat edges into the forest clearing in New South Wales, Australia, a small, paler hump separates from it and mother and youngster nuzzle into the bare earth vainly seeking a root or a fungus before settling for the everyday fare of tough grass. The youngster has been foraging with its mother for just over six months. Before that it spent six months developing in its mother's pouch. Now the pouch, opening at the back so that dirt cannot get in during digging, holds another baby, born this month. By the time it emerges, the present youngster will be independent.

In the cooler April weather the pair have begun to feed in broad daylight. They spent the summer days in their deep burrow and fed at night. They roam a large area – perhaps more than 10sq miles (25sq km) – which overlaps the feeding areas of other wombats. In one night they may trundle about 2 miles (3km), and will rest in any nearby burrow. Wombats have no communal life, but their burrows are like hostels with shifting populations – elaborate hostels with many passages and chambers; some have been in constant use for more than 100 years.

Autumn outing A wombat and her youngster warm themselves in the gentle sun before looking for food. They use regular pathways radiating from their burrow.

Waiting to leave Once the other eggs hatch, the black swans will teach their cygnets to feed in the shallow water.

Black swans seize their chance in the rains

Indifferent to the tempting morsel brought by its mother, the downy grey cygnet stands close to the nest mound in Australia's northern outback as April arrives. Perhaps it is drawn by the cheeps from the other three or four eggs hatching beneath the male black swan, who is taking his turn at sitting on them.

When the summer rains poured onto the outback in January and February, what had been dry beds became lush waterways. Wasting no time – for the water will be here for only a few brief weeks – these black swans, mates for life, put together their nest, choosing a spot near the shallow water of a temporary lake. Once they had mated and the eggs were laid, they embarked on six weeks of incubating.

When all the cygnets have hatched, their parents will lead them down to the water to learn by trial and error what foods are best to eat. Young swans have a natural inclination to peck at anything green and yellow that comes within striking distance, whether it is floating vegetation or an insect. To speed the learning, the adults often put suitable food within the cygnets' reach. By two weeks old, the little cygnets will have learned to feed themselves adequately, success ensured by the shallow water chosen by the parents, which allows the cygnets to reach the plants on the bottom.

It will be some time yet before they can feed as effectively as their parents. That comes only with the development of the long, sinuous neck, which, as with all swan species, has extra vertebrae – usually 24 compared to the 18-19 of geese or the seven of humans. In water less than 18in (460mm) deep, adult swans can lay their heads flat along the bottom and nibble underwater vegetation. In water 3ft (1m) deep, they can touch bottom by up-ending themselves.

Black swans, unlike other swans, are not territorial when breeding. Their nests are in large colonies, sometimes only 3ft (1m) apart. The shallow waters become crammed with feeding swans and cygnets. Such tolerance is necessary for raising a brood during the short time that feeding conditions are right for the cygnets. It will be October before the cygnets can fly and are fully independent. They are still smaller and browner than their parents and will not have full adult plumage until two years old.

By October, the swans will have moved to their summer feeding grounds on more permanent waters in coastal lagoons. There they also crowd together, living in large flocks with as many as 50,000 birds congregating on the more sheltered bays and lakes.

MAY

Antarctica: A nursery of fluffy king penguin chicks

THE ARCTIC

Arctic terns fly the world from pole to pole

When Arctic terns arrive at their northern breeding grounds in May, they have just flown across almost half the world from the Antarctic. This test of stamina, a journey of at least 8000 miles (13,000km), demands great skill in navigation, for each bird returns to the spot it left the previous autumn. Those breeding in Greenland will have made a round trip of some 22,000 miles (35,400km), flying virtually from pole to pole to enjoy perpetual summer. Not surprisingly, the streamlined, 14in (360mm) long terns have exceptionally efficient flight muscles.

The tern – known as a sea swallow because of its forked tail – lives in large noisy colonies. As terns mate for life, many of the returning birds find their partners among the numerous survivors of the long flight. Birds returning to breed for the first time have to seek a mate. Courting terns glide or fly high, or circle round each other on the ground bending and twisting their heads.

Their bond is continually cemented by the male presenting the female with fish – a habit which puts her in prime condition for laying.

The male usually starts scraping out the shallow nest, which the pair line with bits of plant and pebbles. The female usually lays two or three eggs that take three weeks to hatch. Intruders such as gulls, hedgehogs or foxes are noisily mobbed by a throng of birds. Occasionally, the birds panic for no apparent reason – behaviour known as a 'dread'. The harsh *kee-yar* screeches reach a crescendo, then stop, and the entire colony sweeps silently

....

Aerial defence Arctic terns mob a fox intruding into their colony. They swoop so close that their sharp beaks strike the fox on the head and draw blood.

seaward only to return a few minutes later and carry on as if nothing had happened.

The fluffy, mottled, well-camouflaged chicks can move about when two or three days old, and leave the scrape if threatened. The hard-working parents feed them about 25 times a day. Ready to fly at about 28 days old, the youngsters first learn the geography close by, then gradually farther afield, gaining valuable information for finding the spot again to breed. It is thought they may also learn the star patterns at night.

In the autumn all the birds fly south. Terns from Canada and Greenland ride on the winds across the Atlantic to Europe and West Africa before heading south. At the western bulge of Africa, some terns cross to South America, taking advantage of easterly winds. At many resting stops on the West African route, local people trap the birds for food or sport. The survivors fly on beyond South Africa and South America to the sub-Antarctic islands and some stay there. Others fly on and spread round the icy shores and islands of the Antarctic seas, wherever open water offers them a rich food supply. The birds moult at the end of their journey.

About February, adult terns begin their journey back to the Arctic. Only a few birds in their first summer follow the adults north; the rest stay in the southern hemisphere. In their second year they may fly part of the way north, stopping to feed in the food-rich Benguela Current along the coast of southern Africa or back at the dangerous beaches of West Africa, before returning south. By their third spring, they are ready to fly back to the Arctic to seek out a mate. They will spend the rest of their lives – perhaps 20 or even 30 years – flying from one end of the world to the other.

....

Courting gift An Arctic tern presents fish to his mate – an indication that he will feed her and the chicks.

FLY AND DIVE

A hunting tern hovers several feet above the water until it spots a small fish near the surface, then plunges headfirst and grabs it in its beak, sometimes going underwater.

The food the terns eat and give to their young depends on where they are. Around the northern Norwegian islands of Svalbard, many feed crustaceans such as shrimps to the young. In Novaya Zemlya in the Soviet Arctic the young get small fish and large insects. Canadian tern chicks are fed fish, but the adult terns eat sandhoppers and small squid. Icelandic birds will take flies from lake surfaces, and in Scotland they will follow the plough for earthworms.

The victim A newborn reindeer calf can walk within an hour of its birth. It may fall prey to a lynx, although adult reindeer will try to defend it.

Reindeer victims of an Arctic 'who dunnit'

May is the time when the reindeer give birth in Lappland, in northern Scandinavia. The Lapp herdsmen who tend the semi-wild herds had long blamed golden eagles for the disappearance of valuable calves. The birds, they said, swooped in, grabbed the calves and carried them back to their eyries for their chicks. How else, they asked, could you explain the lack of any carcass or remains on the ground?

Many eagles were killed by herdsmen, and conservationists became worried, for golden eagles are rare in many places, and anyway seemed unlikely culprits. Radio collars were attached to some of the reindeer calves. If a tagged calf stayed still for too long, implying that it was dead, the transmitter would be triggered. The scientists would use direction-finding equipment to locate the carcass and then hope to identify the killer. After being alerted to a killing, the scientists allowed time for the killer to take the carcass to its final destination, then set off to find it. But several attempts left them

The killer For a female lynx with kittens to suckle, a reindeer fawn provides a substantial meal – more than she can eat in one sitting. She abandons the rest.

mystified, because the transmitters stopped working and no carcasses were discovered.

Eventually, quite by accident, a carcass was found. The transmitter had not worked because the remains had been buried, and the signals could not penetrate a covering of earth. Tooth puncture marks on the calf's neck showed the killer to be not an eagle but a lynx, a large cat with a short tail and tufted ears. The lynx did not eat all the calf, and did not bury it, as lynxes often do. The leftovers were dragged away and

The undertakers Young wolverines find no difficulty in pulling the abandoned carcass of a reindeer calf. After eating their fill, they may bury the rest for later.

buried, to be eaten later, by a wolverine. So the wolverine (also called a glutton), a fierce, badger-sized member of the weasel family, had thwarted the scientists. Once the truth was known, the eagles were left unmolested.

Although most Lappland reindeer are now domesticated, there are still almost a million wild reindeer in the Russian tundra and its fringe of coniferous forests. There are also wild herds in eastern Russia and southern Norway. Those in North America are called caribou.

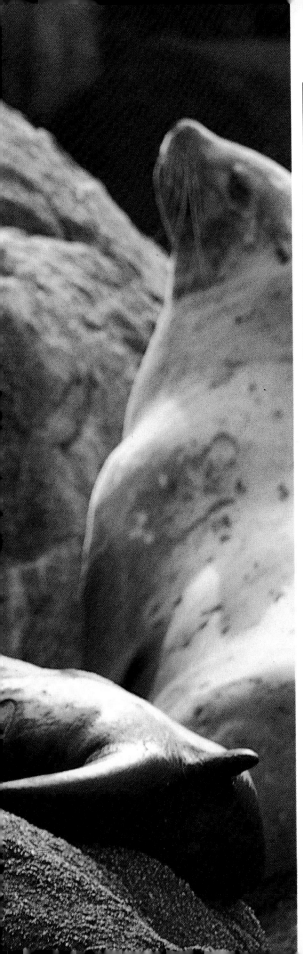

The bumpy birth of a Steller's sea lion pup

Around the shores of the northern Pacific Ocean from California to Japan, small colonies of reddish-brown Steller's sea lions spend May preparing to give birth or looking after their newborn young. The females come ashore at traditional 'hauling out' beaches, and jostle with each other to secure the best places for giving birth. These are located just above the high-water mark, where the pups will be protected from high waves and can shelter among the rocks to avoid too much sun.

As soon as her dark brown pup has been born, the mother lifts it in her mouth and drops it to the ground. This makes the pup cry and helps it to cough up mucus and start breathing. The pups become active very quickly – they begin to crawl within two or three minutes of being born. Mother and pup engage in a great deal of whickering and whimpering, mutual nuzzling and nose-rubbing before the pup takes the nipple for the first time at about half an hour old.

The female never goes far from the beach during the first week. But about nine days after the birth she begins to go on longer fishing trips, staying away for up to three days at a time. While she is away, she leaves her pup in a crèche – in a gathering with other pups in a more secluded part of the beach where it will not be trampled by adults. The pups spend most of their time playing with each other or frolicking among the strands of seaweed. When the mother returns, she takes her pup out of the crèche to join her on the beach. A female recognises her own youngster by its call, and is intolerant of strange pups. Some mothers may still be suckling youngsters that are 12 months old.

Adult sea lions mate again in June and July, and then begin to move north to spend the summer in the coastal waters around the Bering Strait between eastern Siberia and Alaska. Diving to depths of 580ft (180m), they feed on bottom-dwelling flatfish and flounders, octopus, squid and shellfish.

As the northern summer draws to its close, they will move south again, each animal returning to its own traditional breeding area.

Mother and pup A young Steller's sea lion with its mother. Sea lions, or eared seals, are generally bigger than true seals and, unlike seals, have an ear flap.

An elegant courtship Treading water like a pair of aquatic dancers, two western grebes perform an elaborate courtship dance before mating.

Western grebes: ballet stars of the lakes

As summer approaches, the western lakes of central North America echo to the 'c-r-ree, c-r-ree' calls of the western grebe. Arriving from their wintering grounds to the south, these exquisitely graceful birds begin the elegant rituals of their courtship dances. Male and female woo each other by posturing together in a series of coordinated movements that culminate in the remarkable feat of running across the water surface with necks curved and beaks pointing skywards.

Their partnership established, the birds build a nest in which the female lays three or four pale blue or buff eggs. The nest is built from water-plant leaves and stems anchored to reeds, and the nests of a colony of 100 or more pairs form a floating island. Here they are secure from the land predators that steal eggs from shore nests, so the grebes often leave the eggs unguarded for hours while they feed, but cover them from the eyes of scavenging birds.

Grebes are renowned for their agility in swimming underwater while diving in search of fish or small water creatures. On the surface, their long necks give them a stately, swan-like appearance as they drift slowly on the water. Like all diving birds, they spend a lot of time preening to keep their feathers well oiled and waterproof. Preening birds often lie on one side in the water, the sunlight flashing on their glistening breast feathers as if from a mirror.

Crab invasion *Enormous numbers of horseshoe crabs arrive on the beaches of Delaware Bay in the USA. They have emerged from the sea to breed.*

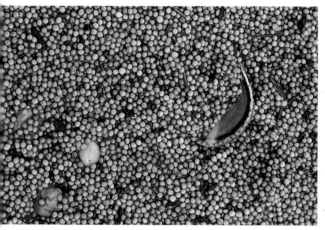

Crab 'caviar' *Female horseshoe crabs each lay up to 80,000 caviar-like eggs in a hole scraped in the sand. The eggs provide food for millions of migrating birds.*

Horseshoe crabs give waders a 'caviar' feast

As the spring tide surges into Delaware Bay on the USA's north-east coast in early May, hundreds of thousands of horseshoe crabs swarm ashore to breed. The first arrivals are the male horseshoe crabs. They form a line along the water's edge that can stretch uninterrupted as far as the eye can see.

Then the females arrive to lay their eggs in the damp sand as the tide ebbs. The waiting males break ranks, and several cluster round each female. One male clamps himself on top of her with his pincers and is dragged to the site the female selects for laying her eggs, where she digs a hole 8in (200mm) deep. In it she lays tens of thousands of eggs and the male releases his sperm, which trickles down to fertilise them. Then the female mixes the sand and eggs together. So many crabs are laying their eggs at the same time that there may be as many as 50 'nests' in 1sq yd (0.8sq m) of sand.

When egg-laying is complete, the horseshoe crabs return to sea. Their exodus is the cue for a new invasion – this time millions of wading birds migrating from their wintering areas in South and Central America to breeding sites in the Canadian Arctic. Delaware Bay is a 'refuelling stop' on the main east-coast flyway. The birds' arrival coincides with the breeding of the horseshoe crabs, and they drop in for a banquet of tiny spherical crabs' eggs resembling caviar.

For some species of birds, the Delaware Bay staging post is vital for survival. About four-fifths

Well-fed birds *After gorging on crabs' eggs, ruddy turnstones rest before continuing their journey north.*

of North America's red knots depend on the crabs' eggs to sustain them on their long flight north. The Arctic breeding season is short, and the quicker they get there the better their chances of rearing a healthy brood.

The red knots probe the sand with their beaks for eggs that are not buried too deep. Flocks of ruddy turnstones also dig to uncover the eggs, then jostle each other for the best positions from which to pluck them. Sanderlings squabble among themselves at the turnstone excavations, and numbers of semipalmated sandpipers and laughing gulls also join in the feast.

There is so much food available that most migrants double their weight during the stopover. During a fortnight of frantic feeding, it is estimated that 50,000 sanderlings eat six billion eggs weighing a total of 27 tons. Yet some eggs escape the onslaught and hatch several weeks later to maintain the horseshoe crab population.

THE CRAB THAT IS A LIVING FOSSIL

Horseshoe crabs all have a hinged, horseshoe-shaped shell that protects them on the topside. Underneath, the hard-bodied creatures have a pair of small pincers and five pairs of legs. They are just like horseshoe crab fossils found in rocks 300 million years old.

Although the horseshoe crab looks like a crab, it is really related to scorpions and spiders. Its shell armour makes it resemble a trilobite – a prehistoric fossil that looked rather like a woodlouse and lived 225-530 million years ago. The horseshoe crab is not as ancient as the trilobite, but is sufficiently primitive to be considered a 'living fossil'.

The moment of birth In a lagoon in the Bahamas, a newborn 2ft (610mm) long lemon shark wriggles free of its mother as tiny fishes swim by.

Baby lemon sharks live amid the mangroves

For just two weeks in May, pregnant lemon sharks enter the great horseshoe-shaped lagoon of the Bimini atoll in the Bahamas to give birth to their pups. Sleek and streamlined, a lemon shark gets its name from the yellow tinge to its light brown or grey body. The largest adults grow to more than 10ft (3m) long.

Lemon sharks do not lay eggs, as some types of shark do, but give birth to babies that look like miniature adults. There are 11 pups in a litter, on average, but sometimes as many as 19. At birth, each 2ft (610mm) long pup swims immediately to the safety of the mangrove trees that fringe the lagoon, where it can shelter among the tangle of underwater roots and stems. Here the youngsters establish long, narrow territories for themselves. Each territory is about 400yds (365m) long and extends about 40yds (37m) from shore. The youngsters stay there for more than a year, feeding mostly on small bony fish such as snappers and grunts, but also on shrimps and crabs. As it grows bigger, a young shark will eat an octopus if it can catch one.

The sharks' teeth are on a kind of conveyor belt and are constantly replaced. The newly emerging teeth move slowly forwards in the jaw and replace the teeth that have dropped out during feeding. By the time it is about two years old and 3ft (1m) long, a lemon shark replaces the front teeth in its lower jaw every eight days.

In their second year the lemon sharks enlarge their range. Sharks of particular sizes tend to gather in different parts of the enormous lagoon. At eight or nine years old, they move outside the lagoon to more open reefs, swimming down to depths of 150ft (46m). They spend the day in deeper water, but at night hunt inshore for bony fish, rays, crabs, other sharks and even seabirds.

Lemon sharks are found only in American coastal waters, from New Jersey to Brazil in the western Atlantic and from the Gulf of California to Ecuador in the eastern Pacific. They do not reach sexual maturity until they are at least 12 years old. In early spring, males and females are believed to congregate on traditional mating grounds that have yet to be found, although Florida Bay is a likely site. Courtship is a rough affair, the male grabbing the female by the pectoral (chest) fin while they mate. Embryos take a year to develop.

Nest village A house martin squeezes out of the narrow entrance to its mud and saliva nest, which took two weeks to build. It is one of a cluster beneath the eaves of a house.

House martins that build like bricklayers

On a bright May morning, house martins are flashing like black and white arrows across a cloudless European sky. The martins have flown all the way from their African wintering grounds to take advantage of the insects that hatch in the northern spring and summer. Before the birds begin a nest-building marathon, they spend their first days in Europe feeding themselves up, hunting for food on the wing with their wide beaks agape for a catch. They twist and dive into clouds of small insects like aerial acrobats.

Towards the end of the month, the birds pair off and begin to prepare a nest for their first brood. A house martin's nest is a superb feat of engineering, originally designed to hug an overhanging cliff ledge. Now nests are more likely to be found under the eaves of a building. House martins are among the few animals that have benefited from man's enthusiasm for building, and now seem to prefer buildings to the natural cliffs. The nest is built almost entirely from mud and saliva, with a few feathers or some plant material to bind it together. The inside is lined with moss or feathers.

Both the male and female martins do the building work, which usually takes them about two weeks. They begin by flying to the nearest sources of soft mud – puddles, ponds or other wet ground. When a martin lands to scoop up the mud, it is vulnerable to attack by cats or other predators. It shuffles towards the edge of a puddle and quickly gathers up a beakful of mud before launching into the air again as quickly as possible. Although masters of the air, house martins are clumsy on the ground, for their short, weak legs and feet, feathered down to the toes, are designed to stay tucked up beneath the belly feathers, presenting the least possible wind resistance in flight.

The pair often collect mud from several sources, possibly to provide added bonding strength when pieces of different consistency are stuck together. At the nest site, the mud is stuck firmly to the wall just below the overhang to form the base platform of the nest. The building is carried out much as a human bricklayer builds a house. More mud is added in courses, which are gradually built up to form a cup-shaped nest. The courses are usually thickest at the base of the nest, which will take the weight of the sitting parent and the eggs or chicks, and decrease in thickness near the rim stuck to the overhanging eave.

The birds' last job is to make the entrance. A shallow scoop of mud is removed from the upper lip of the nest to leave an opening just big enough for an adult bird to squeeze through.

Within a few days of its completion a nest will normally contain four or five white eggs. The female sits on them, fed by her mate for two or three weeks. When her chicks hatch, she joins the male in his constant comings and goings to feed the hungry brood.

The chicks will be ready to fly about three weeks later, becoming increasingly restless then eventually squeezing through the nest entrance to take flight for the first time. They have no opportunity for practice. Failure in the first take-off means a fall to the death, but usually the fledglings spread their wings and within seconds join their parents aloft, swelling the flocks wheeling around the rooftops.

Gathering mud Both male and female martins gather mud from the edges of ponds and puddles. They mix it with saliva and plant fibres to build their nest.

Damselflies mate in a heart-shaped embrace

Perched on a leaf, a male damselfly suns himself at the edge of a stream. He emerged from his larval skin a few days ago, and has spent the time feeding on small insects. Now he prepares himself for mating.

Bending his rear end forwards underneath himself in a loop, he transfers sperm from his genitalia, which are at the rear of the abdomen, to a second set, known as accessory genitalia, under the abdomen just behind the legs. All male damselflies – like their larger relatives the dragonflies – have accessory genitalia.

Then the damselfly launches his gauzy-winged blue body into the air in search of a receptive female. When he finds one, he grabs her behind the head in mid-flight with the pair of claspers at the tip of his abdomen.

The pair alight on a water plant, with the female locked in the male's embrace. Slowly she bends her abdomen underneath him until her genitalia are clasped by his accessory genitalia. In this way the two bodies form a circle known as the 'wheel' or the 'heart-shaped' position.

They remain like this for maybe just a few seconds or for several hours, while his sperm is transferred. After mating, the female releases her abdomen but the male still clasps her firmly behind the head as she pushes her egg-laying tube into a water plant and then lays her eggs in the plant tissue. When this is done, their mating embrace is at last unlocked.

*****The mating moment** These red-eyed damselflies are mating, their bodies locked into a 'heart-shaped' position. They may stay joined for several hours.*

Silent death With wings spread like a parasol, a barn owl swoops on a mouse raiding an open sack of grain.

Ghostly barn owls feed their chicks at night

A pale shape flies silently through the darkness of a May night towards an old barn on a British farm. Like a white ghost, the barn owl swoops effortlessly through the narrow window, despite a wingspan the length of a man's arm. Inside the barn, five chicks perk up as they see the returning bird, which lands on the nest – the bare floor of the old loft, littered with disgorged pellets of indigestible bones, feathers and fur. The owl has caught a mouse, which it holds in its talons and tears apart with its beak to feed to the hungry chicks. They vary in size – the biggest chick is ten days older than the youngest, for the eggs were incubated as soon as they were laid.

As silently as it came, the 14in (360mm) long parent bird leaves the barn to hunt once more. It flies low over the fields with lazy wing strokes, eyes and ears finely tuned to spot mice, voles, small birds, frogs or large insects. So acute is the owl's hearing that it can swoop on a mouse in total darkness, guided only by the soft rustle of dry leaves disturbed by the mouse's movement.

The elegant barn owl, with its white chest and face-mask and its delicately mottled buff and grey back, is found in most parts of the world except in places where there are no small mammals, such as high mountain ranges. But it is not found in Antarctica or the northernmost parts of Europe and Asia, where prolonged snow cover in winter denies it food, nor in places where continuous rain stops the bird flying and so reduces its hunting time.

Most barn owls nest in agricultural buildings, some in the attics of old houses and a few in castles and church towers. They prefer to hunt where there are open fields that have a damp margin of undisturbed grassland in which their prey can flourish. Before humans provided the owl with nest sites and fields surrounded by hedges or fences, the birds nested in caves or hollow trees, and hunted in woodland clearings or on open moorland.

Now their man-made nest sites and agricultural habitats are disappearing. Old trees and ruined farm buildings are not tolerated on modern farms, and large fields suitable for the use of combine harvesters have few grassy margins to shelter small mammals. Modern pesticides also kill the barn owl's prey and reduce its chances of breeding successfully. In some parts of Europe, barn owls have vanished completely and projects are now underway to re-establish them. Some farmers leave old barns standing to encourage the owls, as they are useful in controlling mice and voles.

Most barn owl chicks hatch in May from eggs laid about a month earlier. Both parents feed the chicks for two months, and by the time the youngsters are ready to fly, their appetites will be prodigious. Through the lengthening July nights the parents will be kept busy finding enough food for them. By August, the chicks will have left the nest. Some leave at once to establish territories of their own, others stay with their parents for another month or so. A few lucky young birds will find an unoccupied barn or church tower in which to shelter from the winter cold, and there, next spring, will rear a new generation. Some youngsters, however, will die because they cannot find a suitable site, and others will not find enough food to bring them into breeding condition next season.

Feeding time A barn owl feeds her chicks in an unusually comfortable nest in a bale of straw. Eggs are laid mostly in April, and the chicks hatch after a month.

The great grey shrike stocks its larder

On a hawthorn bush growing in European scrubland, the remains of a dead mouse are skewered on a thorn. This is the larder of a great grey shrike, which will return there later. Shrikes store food most often in May and June, the breeding season, so they can feed their chicks and the male can feed the incubating female. A bird usually returns to its cache within a day or so, although sometimes the larder is abandoned – perhaps because the food has either rotted or dried up.

Starling-sized songbirds that have become highly adapted as hunters, shrikes have even evolved the strong hooked beak of a true bird of prey. They hunt small birds, mammals, frogs and insects, and with their sharp eyesight can spot a bumble bee 100yds (91m) away. Often seen perched on tree tops or telegraph wires watching for prey, shrikes swoop down from the perch onto their victim. Sometimes they then have to pursue it through the air, like a hawk. The prey is killed almost instantaneously by a sharp bite to the back of the neck. Like falcons, shrikes have a small tooth near the beak tip that may penetrate the prey's spinal cord and so speed its death.

A shrike holds its prey in its powerful claws while it dismembers it with its strong beak. To get extra grip, the bird sometimes impales the victim on a thorn or on barbed wire, or wedges it in a crevice. This may be how the habit of keeping a larder originated. Shrikes are noisy and aggressive, scolding intruders with a harsh shriek – possibly the origin of the name shrike – but the bird's gory habits have earned it the name of 'butcher bird' in many countries.

The great grey shrike has a grey back, white breast, black and white wings and tail, and a black bandit's mask across its eyes. It is found at forest edges, in open woodland and open, shrubby country, and in most areas it stays all year round, but in northern Europe it migrates south to milder areas in winter. A shrike builds a bulky, untidy nest of twigs and grass, often in a thorn bush. The female lays from five to seven pale eggs with brownish spots or blotches, and they hatch after two weeks. The youngsters leave the nest after about three weeks.

....

Butcher at work *A great grey shrike finds it easier to dismember its prey, a mouse, when it has impaled it on a thorn. Sometimes prey is left on a thorn as a larder.*

Eating greens The immature speckled bush cricket is a hearty feeder on European shrubs in May. It looks like a vivid greenfly that has been sprinkled with pepper.

The greenfly lookalike that is really a cricket

The tiny, spotted insect walking and hopping along the rose stem as May sunshine warms a European garden looks like a greenfly, but it is not behaving like one. Instead of piercing the plant to drink the sweep sap, it is chewing the leaves. The little creature is an immature speckled bush cricket, newly hatched from a matchhead-sized oval egg, one of a cluster laid on the rose stem last autumn before the frosts. Between May and August it will feed and grow, and mature in six different stages (called instars), moulting its speckled skin at the end of each stage. It finally emerges as a speckled adult little more than ½ in (13mm) long.

The cricket cannot fly, and continues living on low-growing shrubs and bushes. It will chew most garden plants, but bramble leaves are its favourite; it also eats soft-bodied insects. To avoid predators such as birds, the bush cricket either hops out of harm's way or drops to the ground where it may escape among the tangled undergrowth. It can hop about 50 times its own length. Like most crickets, males scrape their forewings together to make a chirping song. This is so weak it can be heard by humans only if they are standing close by, but is loud enough to attract a female or warn off a rival male. Adults live for two or three months before the frosts kill them – ample time to court, mate and lay eggs to provide next year's generation.

Following their leader Pine processionary moth caterpillars leave their web nest in a pine wood and walk nose-to-tail to feed on the needles of nearby trees.

Moth caterpillars go out to feed in Indian file

The small, brown, night-flying, pine processionary moth that lives in southern Europe's warm woodlands gets its name from its caterpillars. These hairy, orange larvae hatch in May and together spin a flask-shaped web nest between the pine twigs. Each night they go out to feed in a long procession that can number well over 100. They ripple along nose-to-tail, and lay down a silk thread to guide them back.

The procession may provide safety in numbers, cutting losses to predators. Birds such as hoopoes pick off caterpillars from a column. The survivors pupate (change to adults) underground or in the nest, emerging in late summer. Each female moth spins a cocoon to protect her eggs, which hatch next May. The cocoon and caterpillars can irritate the skin if touched.

Black grouse gather for a marriage market

In a grassy glade near the edge of a European pine forest, half a dozen black grouse cocks are showing off in the May dawn to a group of sombre-coloured hens. The glade is the traditional site – known as a lek – where the grouse gather to mate. The cocks, similar in size to farmyard fowls, may have been there since autumn, all defending their own space and squabbling constantly over boundaries. Now the hens have joined them, and strut among the excited, leaping cocks to view likely mates.

Two cocks vying to attract hens approach each other stiff-legged, necks outstretched and red wattles prominent. Both cocks hold their wings open and low, and fan out their glossy black, lyre-shaped tails. The contest is usually decided without a fight when the less impressive cock turns away, showing his white rump feathers. Then both utter a loud hiss that may excite the whole lek so much that all the cocks display at once. After a while, a hen approaches the victor and crouches in invitation. He bills and coos, and struts around her before mating.

The hen will lay 6-11 speckled buff eggs in a nearby hollow in the ground. She raises the brood alone, incubating the eggs for almost a month, tending the fast-growing chicks for their first few weeks, and leading them to the shrub shoots and buds they eat. The lek enables hens to choose the superior cocks so that sound genes are passed on to the next generation. Some leks are dominated by one cock or by a group, who do almost all the mating.

Cock of the walk With his bright red wattles erect and his tail fanned out, a glossy black grouse cock displays himself to impress visiting hens and win them as mates.

Beautiful kingfishers nest in foul burrows

Like a bright blue bolt of lightning, a female kingfisher, her short wings folded back, dives headlong into the water from an overhanging willow branch to seize a fish. She is hungry on this May afternoon after spending several hours sitting on the eggs in her nearby nest. Now her mate is incubating the eggs while she fishes. From her perch, she has spotted a shoal of minnows darting in the slow, clear stream.

With a fish in her long beak, the kingfisher surfaces, buoyant from the air trapped in her feathers. A thrust of her wings gets her airborne again to return to her perch. She kills the fish by striking it against the branch, then deftly flicks it round and swallows it head first.

For almost three weeks, she and her mate have been incubating their six glossy white, rounded eggs. The chaffinch-sized pair took about two weeks to dig a nest burrow with their beaks, kicking the earth out backwards. The burrow, a little wider than a golf ball and about as long as a man's arm, slopes slightly uphill. At the end, a chamber about 6in (150mm) across contains the eggs. In a few days they will hatch.

Both parents will take turns to warm the bald, blind and helpless chicks at first, but after about a week both will have to fish all day to feed them. At first each of the six chicks will need one small fish every hour, so each parent bird will have to supply three fish an hour. Each fish is presented to a chick head first so that the fin bones do not stick in its throat when it swallows. By the time the chicks are three or four weeks old and ready to leave the nest, the parents will be delivering up to four fish an hour to each one, so between them will have to catch a fish every two-and-a-half minutes. This is a demanding task, but few chicks starve. The burrow soon becomes fouled with trampled droppings and regurgitated fish

On target *A kingfisher can dive as deep as 3ft (1m) below the surface to seize a fish it has spotted from its perch.*

Bolt hole *Shy and rarely seen, kingfishers lay their eggs at the end of a long burrow in a waterside bank. It is handy for bringing in fish to their hungry brood.*

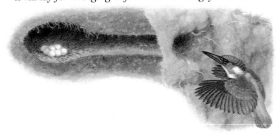

bones, and the parent birds, usually filthy when they emerge, frequently bathe before hunting.

By the time the kingfisher brood leave the nest, their parents have usually mated again, and soon the female will be incubating the next brood in another nest. The male is left to feed the fledglings while they learn to catch fish, insect larvae and tadpoles. He brings them fish less and less frequently, and about two months later the young birds are fully independent.

Predators rarely bother kingfishers because they have an unpleasant taste, but many youngsters die during their first winter when the streams freeze over and cut off their food supply. Perhaps that is why the parents work so hard to raise as many as three broods a season, on average managing to feed and rear four-fifths of their offspring. Kingfishers may survive a harsh winter by moving to the coast and feeding in unfrozen creeks and rock pools.

Mayflies take wing for one night of life

On a warm May evening, the sweet-scented air beside a river or stream is often filled with the tiny, dancing forms of a million insects. Many of them will be mayflies, emerging from the water for their brief adult lives. By morning, they will have mated and laid their eggs, and most of them will have died.

A mayfly larva (or nymph) hatches from an egg and lives underwater for one or two years or more, depending on the species. About 1in (25mm) long and with usually three wispy tails, it feeds mainly on microscopic plants, especially algae. To avoid being swept away it conceals its body in crevices, or clings to pebbles or plants. Many nymphs fall prey to fish, newts, frogs, birds or other water insects – particularly dragonfly nymphs. Mayflies thrive only in clear, unpolluted water, and biologists look for them when assessing the purity of streams and rivers.

When they are ready to become adults, the nymphs find their way to the water's edge and climb out along the stems of water plants. Once out of the water, they moult to become immature (sub-adult) flies. These are dull grey and still have their three long wispy tails, as well as large fore wings and small hind wings folded upright. Within a short time, maybe minutes, they moult again, and in the late evening the newly emerged adult crawls free of its shed skin.

Now the mayfly's body is shiny gold and black, but otherwise it looks the same. For a while the insect sits in the last rays of the sun until its new wings are dry. Then for the first and last time, it takes flight. Males and females all rise into the air in clouds, flying so weakly that thousands dip too close to the water and are snapped up by trout and other fish. Others fall prey to swallows and martins, and as night falls, bats come and dip and twist over the river as they devour mayfly after mayfly.

Although most of the mayflies are eaten, many live long enough to mate on the wing. Then the females shed thousands of eggs either into the air above the water or directly into the water. In the water, the eggs uncoil sticky-tipped threads that anchor them to the bottom. They hatch almost at once and set off the cycle for the next generation of mayflies.

....

One night in May *A newly emerged mayfly dries its wings in the evening sunshine before taking flight. For most mayflies, life lasts just one night.*

Young mountaineer   Within a few hours, this newborn chamois kid will be nimble enough to leap rocks.

The mountain life of a sure-footed chamois

On the high slopes of a southern European mountain, a female chamois has just given birth after being pregnant for five and a half months. She has left the flock and found a secluded spot on an alpine ledge that is all but inaccessible. The May sun warms the grey rocks around her, which are dotted with coarse grass and lichens and a patchwork of scrubby bushes. Her newborn kid nibbles at the greenery almost at once, although she will continue to suckle it for several months.

Stocky chamois are goat-antelopes about the size of roe deer, with pelts the colour of polished teak. All have distinctive black cheek stripes and close-set horns that curve back at the tips. They are fantastically agile, with powerful haunches and soft cloven hooves that will grip the most precarious ledges. A chamois can leap up and down cliffs twice the height of a man, and spring 20ft (6m) from rock to rock.

Before its first day of life is over, the youngster will be strong enough to keep up with its mother. Such fleetness of foot is vital for avoiding the clutches of a hungry lynx, wolf, bear or eagle. Within a day or two, the female has rejoined the flock with the kid at her side. The summer flocks of 10-20 animals are mostly females and youngsters. Males are nomadic, and join flocks only occasionally.

Summer is brief in the lush meadows more than 7000ft (2100m) above sea level, and the youngsters make the most of it, energetically butting and charging one another in play fights. They attack with lowered heads, ready to strike upwards with their horns at an opponent's throat or belly. The weaker animal submits by lying flat on the ground, neck and head outstretched. In two or three years' time, when the young males are old enough to breed, they will battle seriously with rival males every autumn for a chance to mate. At eight years old, most are tough enough to win a harem.

Chamois spend the long, harsh winter in the steep woodland lower down the slopes, feeding on buds, lichens and grasses that they have to dig through the snow to find. Their long, thick winter pelts of brown, black and white hairs keep them warm. Most forage alone and get very thin, and many of the young, inexperienced animals die. So do some of the older males, worn out by fierce fighting and often badly gored. But most old males will have mated successfully with 12 or so females in autumn, and as spring arrives and food becomes more plentiful, the flocks move once more to the meadows above the tree line, where the next generation is born.

What decides the sex of a Greek tortoise

On a bright May morning, the undergrowth rustles as a male Greek tortoise searches for a mate. With the air temperature around 27°C (80°F), his body has been warmed into activity and he hurries at about ¼ mph (0.4km/h) up to a tortoise feeding on leaves and grass close by. He butts his domed, 8in (200mm) shell against the other's and takes a nip at its legs. A female ready for mating will stand still for him, but an unwilling female – or another male – will simply walk away. Mating is a difficult business for a tortoise, because the female's shell is slippery and very rounded. Success is generally marked by high-pitched calls from the male.

The female lays about 12 hard-shelled eggs in a nest dug in the dusty soil. The white, oval eggs, about 1in (25mm) across, take about three months to hatch, but the exact time depends on the soil temperature. A warmer temperature speeds up development, a cooler temperature slows it down, and extremes of temperature can kill the developing embryos altogether.

The soil temperature governs more than hatching time. It determines sex. Eggs laid and buried in a temperature above 30°C (86°F) produce a higher proportion of females. Cooler temperatures favour males. Whatever their sex, the tiny, rounded babies tumble from the nest and scuttle off into the undergrowth, independent from the moment they hatch until they die – which may be more than 100 years later.

Successful courtship   While the male tortoise balances precariously during mating with the high-domed female, he squeals like a crying puppy.

Foraging family A wild boar sow and her daughter unearth roots to eat, while the latest litter of piglets watches.

The ritual parade of the graceful avocets

In a sheltered Baltic bay, long-legged avocets are striding to and fro in pairs, their heads stretched out in front of them. The elegant, 17in (430mm) long birds are scything repeatedly through the water with long, up-curved beaks.

On this early morning in May, the peak time for the avocets' courting displays, a pair begin their ritual. Each bird keeps dipping its beak in the water and preening its neck and breast. Gradually the preening becomes more exaggerated, then the male begins to walk from side to side behind the female. She shows her interest by stretching her beak down into the water.

The pace quickens. The male walks in ever-decreasing half circles behind the female until he has to stoop to duck under her tail as he passes. When she stretches her head down again and splashes the water repeatedly, he raises his wings straight upwards and hops onto her back. She swings her head from side to side as they mate, both birds stretching their heads up to cross their beaks.

In a few days, the pair will make a shallow scrape in the ground above the high tide line. There the female will lay three or four eggs, which the pair take turns to incubate for about 24 days. The hatchlings do not have to be fed – they follow their parents out onto the mud flats and feed themselves. In another five weeks or so they will be able to fly, and about September, as the days get shorter and colder, they will follow their parents south to France, Spain, or even to Africa for the winter.

Courting couple Near the water's edge, a male avocet prepares to mate as his partner signals her readiness by dipping her head forwards into the water.

Lessons in the woods for wild boar piglets

Deep in the heart of a French oak wood in May, a rustling of bushes disturbs the stillness, then explodes into a crescendo of grunts, chirrups and squeals as a party of wild boars tumbles into a clearing. The dark, bristly sow, as big as a small farmyard pig, lifts her head to sniff the wind, her pointed ears pricked. All is clear, so she resumes her feeding while her striped, month-old piglets gather round her.

Two or three weeks before they were born, the sow left the family group of several daughters from previous litters and some of their offspring. She made a rough nest of grass and leaves on the ground in a thicket, where she gave birth to the six piglets she had conceived in January. After ten days in the nest, they were strong enough to follow their mother back to her family group.

The sow will continue to suckle her babies for three months while they learn how to find their own food. As the family wanders through the forest, the piglets pounce with squeals of delight on the roots, worms, grubs or frogs that their elders unearth with snouts and occasionally with their short tusks. If danger looms – perhaps a hungry fox or human hunters – the dominant sow stamps her feet, raises her head and tail and gives a loud squeal or single grunt and the piglets scamper into the undergrowth.

After weaning, the piglets gradually become dark haired. Some females remain with the family group permanently but the males leave when their mother is ready to give birth again next year. They may join a bachelor group for a while, but when they mature at about four years of age, they patrol the forest alone. In autumn and winter they go in search of mates.

Geometrical nesting *With near-perfect precision, sooty terns on Bird Island in the Seychelles space their nests just far enough apart to be out of reach of one another's beaks.*

Sooty terns nest where the fish are teeming

Watchful in their small territories, sooty terns are spread evenly as far as the eye can see on the flat, open ground of Bird Island in the Seychelles. They have gathered here in May, at the start of the monsoon season, with the temperatures and currents in the Indian Ocean promising a surge in fish numbers. For the sooty terns, this plentiful food supply will enable them to breed successfully, so they are busy nesting.

Like all the birds that are ocean wanderers, sooty terns have difficulty in finding safe nesting sites. They protect themselves by crowding into close-packed colonies of hundreds of thousands of birds with just enough distance between nests to prevent a sitting bird from pecking its neighbour. No heron or frigate bird dares to go raiding among them.

The nest where the female lays a single egg is a mere scrape in the ground. Both parents take turns to sit on the egg for up to a month until it hatches. For a hectic and deafeningly noisy eight weeks the parents feed the chick. With so many birds nesting in one place, some may travel up to 60 miles (100km) from the breeding colony to outstrip the competition and bring back fish. Sooty terns returning to the colony give a call that sounds rather like 'wideawake' – appropriate for a bird that never seems to sleep.

Once the breeding season is over, the sooty terns, youngsters included, rapidly disperse. A ringed juvenile seen on Bird Island one September was recorded 5000 miles (8000km) away in Australia only 14 weeks later. Young sooty terns from Florida, in the USA, are regularly found in Africa, 7000 miles (11,250km) away, within a few months of learning to fly. The youngsters do not normally return to the colony where they were hatched until they are at least three years old, and rarely breed before they are six years old.

Between breeding seasons, the terns wander endlessly over the ocean, riding the air currents or hovering at will without ever coming in to land. Neither do they normally roost on the water or on floating vegetation, because they cannot tolerate waterlogged feathers. They fly night and day, and feed by swooping on fish driven to the water surface by enemies below.

A time of strife for the elegant impalas

As the impala breeding season draws to its close in May, the exhausted male impalas can look forward to seven months of rest and recuperation, grazing southern Africa's lightly wooded grasslands after five months of constantly fighting off rivals.

One of the most elegant of antelopes, the lightly built impala is rusty fawn with black-tipped ears and a black tuft at the back of each ankle on the hind legs. It has a black tail-stripe, matched by a black stripe on each buttock. The male also has graceful lyre-shaped horns about 20in (500mm) long, fearsome weapons in the battles that break out at breeding time.

The 11 stone (70kg) animals engage each other with horns interlocked and attempt to throw each other off balance. Bouts are accompanied by much roaring and snorting.

Each male strives to establish a territory that will attract passing females – a large area of light woodland that is free of dense thickets but not too open, where the young will be safe and thrive. The competition among males for such territories is intense. A herd of up to 100 or so females and young animals generally covers an area overlapping the territories of a number of males, each of whom gathers together a harem of females in season.

Most territories are roughly 500yds square (20 hectares), and are acquired by ousting the former holder. Challenges from rivals may be so frequent that defenders have little time for feeding. Such males grow thin and weak, so are easily defeated. On average, a male holds his territory for around 80 days, although some hold on for only about five days. Defeated males

*****Natural athletes** A herd of impalas move with ease over bushy terrain, leaping long and high in giant bounds. Their tail and buttock stripes probably act as alarm signals and guides to other herd members.*

usually move away to join a bachelor herd to graze or to browse on acacia leaves and regain the strength to try for a territory once again.

Injury from a rival's sharp horns is not the only hazard a territorial male has to face. He spends a lot of time on his own in his territory, so lacks the advantages of herd life, with danger warnings from other animals in the group. He is far more likely to be caught unawares by a predator such as a lion or cheetah.

About seven months after mating, female impalas bear their one youngster. In southern Africa this is in early summer, at the start of the rains, so the vegetation will be at its richest for the nursing mothers. The 11lb (5kg) babies are hidden in the grass, discreetly watched over by their mothers, until they are strong enough to join the herd. But many are taken by lions, cheetahs, jackals or hyenas. Young males start to grow horns at about two months old, and stay with the female herd until they are about six months old. Then they join a bachelor herd until they are two and a half years old.

Impalas on the move are a splendid sight, leaping as high as 10ft (3m) in the air and covering almost four times that length in one bound. When alarmed by a predator, the impalas all leap in different directions – a form of defence because the attacker has difficulty in deciding which one to pursue.

Sparring rivals *Two male impalas lock horns and try to wrestle each other off balance as one challenges the other for possession of a territory and harem.*

Well held *An African fish eagle flies off with its catch, plucked from the lake surface. It has chicks to feed in its nest.*

High and mighty *Courting eagles sometimes whirl spectacularly in the air with talons locked and wings spread, plummeting almost to earth before separating.*

Fish eagles feed a family on an African lake

Perched high on a tree branch beside a lake in Malawi, a fish eagle throws back its head and gives a gull-like, laughing call. This haunting cry that carries far across the water is one of the most characteristic sounds of Africa's lakes and rivers. It not only keeps the bird in contact with its mate, it also tells other fish eagles that the pair are at home on their territory.

No time is busier for this fish eagle and his mate than late May, with their two downy white chicks growing larger by the day. The nest of sticks lined with grass and leaves is high in the dead branches of an acacia tree beside open water. So hearty are the chicks' appetites that the father has to make repeated hunting trips.

A fish eagle spotting fish from a waterside perch is a stunning sight, with its black wings and white head and back offset by reddish-brown belly feathers. Many birds that dive for fish are white underneath because fish cannot easily see the white directly overhead. Adult African fish eagles make sweeping low-level attacks on their prey, so the lack of camouflage is no disadvantage.

Occasionally, instead of spotting from on high, a fish eagle will course up and down a stretch of water to search for fish. Upon spotting its prey the eagle swoops low over the water to snatch it up in powerful talons, and can pluck a fish half as long as a man's arm from the water and carry it to its nest with effortless ease.

Fish eagles feed mainly on freshwater fish but coastal birds have been known to fish in the sea occasionally. Sometimes they will take young from colonies of water birds such as flamingos, herons and cormorants. They are inveterate pirates too, stealing fish from each other, as well as from birds such as storks and herons.

Of all the hawks that hunt fish, the African eagle and the osprey are the only species that will sometimes dive right into the water after a fish. They may submerge completely, but do not swim underwater. The powerful downstrokes of their wings, with a span of some 7ft (2m), get them back to the surface and airborne again.

The two chicks, survivors from the three eggs laid early in April, hatched in the second half of May. Their mother spends most of her time with the chicks at the moment, but when they are about six weeks old she will leave them while she goes hunting with her mate to bring back food for them. The youngsters will be fully feathered at seven weeks old, will begin to fly at ten weeks and then stay near the nest site for two or three weeks more. They will not have full adult plumage until they are four years old.

A superb lyrebird flaunts his tail in the forest

Loud and clear, a kookaburra's raucous laughter breaks the eerie silence of a dank, dark world where eucalyptus trees and giant tree ferns screen out most of the light. Soon other calls ring out from the same deep gully – first the harsh croak of a black cockatoo, then a whipbird's sharp crack, quickly followed by a robin's sweet melody.

There is no strange gathering of birds here, deep in the undergrowth of the coastal forest of eastern Australia. All the songs are performed by one of the world's greatest mimics, the male superb lyrebird. His bizarre medley, made up of the calls of many local birds, is part of his elaborate May courtship ritual.

First the lyrebird makes himself a stage, scratching together a mound of earth with the long claws he normally uses to dig up a meal of insects. When he has cleared the mound of leaf litter, the rather dowdy brown and grey bird mounts the stage and transforms himself. He spreads his long tail feathers and throws them forward over his head so that his pheasant-sized body is veiled by a delicate silver canopy. The shimmering cascade is bordered by bold, lyre-shaped feathers that are golden in colour with crescent markings of brown.

Slowly the resplendent bird pivots, flaunting his fanned tail as he sings his borrowed repertoire – which may occasionally include such surprise items as the sounds of barking dogs, car horns and trains. The purpose of the striking song and dance is to attract females to mate with – and to keep other males at bay. The bird has several mounds scattered throughout his territory, and displays at each in turn.

When a female is attracted by the show, the male quivers his fan, utters a clicking call and dances round her. Once the pair have mated, on or near the mound, their brief liaison is over and the female is left with sole responsibility for building a nest – in a bank, on a rocky ledge, or even on a tree stump – and for incubating the single egg and rearing the chick. During the breeding season the male mates with several females, and each female too may visit more than one male before settling down to lay and sit on her egg.

Turning tail Cascading tail feathers, tossed over his head, allow only a glimpse of the courting superb lyrebird.

Welcome break *A gang-gang cockatoo is adept at cracking nuts in its powerful beak, and can balance on one sturdy foot while gripping food in the other.*

Cockatoos get cracking in the city suburbs

Autumn comes to the south-east corner of Australia in May, with the weather turning wetter and the native eucalyptus trees, acacias and cypress pines setting their seeds. In suburban gardens and parks, introduced plants such as hawthorn bushes hang heavy with berries. Yet some trees and bushes are stripped bare within days of becoming laden with ripe berries, nuts and seeds.

The culprits are not hard to find. Feasting parties of pigeon-sized gang-gang cockatoos cluster round the tempting fare, their grey bodies decorated with white scalloped patterns and the males among them identified by fiery red heads. Unperturbed by the nearness of people, up to 100 of the birds feed together, cracking nuts with their strong, hooked beaks, or holding bunches of berries in their dexterous feet. The gardens of Melbourne and Canberra will see them until winter has passed, then they return to the forested mountains inland.

ANTARCTICA

A winter gamble for young king penguins

In May, the end of the southern autumn, most birds in sub-Antarctic islands such as South Georgia have raised their chicks before the onset of winter. But for 3ft (1m) tall king penguins, raising a chick takes nearly a year and continues throughout the winter. By May or June, early chicks – from eggs laid in spring (late November) – are nearly full grown and stand a good chance of survival. They hatched in December or January and, fed on the midsummer bounty of fish and squid, have built up enough fat reserves to face the winter. Late chicks – from eggs laid between February and early April – are poorly equipped to survive the winter.

Both parents incubate their one egg, the male taking first turn while the female has two weeks off after laying the egg. For the next six weeks, each parent spends about five days at a time incubating while the other goes to feed. The parent on duty holds the egg on its large webbed feet and engulfs it in a fold of belly skin. At change-over time, the two birds carefully roll the egg from one pair of feet to the other.

During July and August, the worst of winter, the parents leave the chicks hungry for most of the time; they are too busy finding food for themselves. The chicks huddle together for warmth and may lose nearly half their body weight. Many of the late-hatched chicks die.

In late August or early September, the parents start regularly feeding the survivors again. In November and December, the early chicks have moulted their brown down for adult plumage and are ready to fend for themselves. Any late starters that survived the winter are ready for independence by January or February.

The early breeding parents fatten-up and then moult once their chick is independent. They lay the next egg in February or later, so their next chick will be late and at risk. The late-breeding parents will not lay again until the next spring, and so become early layers. This alternate early and late egg-laying means that many parents lose half their chicks in their 20 or so years of life. It also means that for much of the year, a king penguin colony has birds in various stages of growth and moult, and that eggs are being incubated all summer and autumn.

Penguins galore *Although a king penguin colony looks like a confused crowd, each pair of black-and-white adults knows which large brown chick is theirs.*

JUNE

BARNACLE GOSLINGS PLUNGE INTO LIFE IN THE ARCTIC
SUMMER AS LIONS SUFFER THIRST ON THE AFRICAN PLAINS. IN EUROPE
HONEY BEES SWARM AND FALLOW DEER REAR THEIR YOUNG.
IN AUSTRALIAN SCRUBLANDS MALLEE FOWL PREPARE THEIR HUGE NESTS

Africa: A lioness tends a playful cub

High born Barnacle geese nest high on an Arctic cliff ledge, well out of the reach of hunting Arctic foxes. Before the hatchlings can fly, they must leap off the cliff to find food.

Young barnacle geese step into space

Sitting in her nest on a high cliff ledge in the Arctic, the barnacle goose feels the first stirrings as the eggs beneath her begin to hatch. It is a welcome moment, for she is hungry. She has been incubating the eggs for 24 days – eating little and taking only short breaks to stretch her wings. Her staunch mate has stayed close by to ward off gulls and ravens eager to eat the eggs.

Now it is June, but the pair arrived in eastern Greenland from Scotland's Western Isles in late May, returning to their nest site of previous years. The ledge, as high as a 20-storey building, is safe from Arctic foxes, which would relish both eggs and adults. The female lined a hollow with lichen and down plucked from her breast, then laid four white eggs and covered them with more down. Before long, broken shells litter the nest and the female is itching to leave.

Within a few hours of hatching, the four fluffy goslings – small enough to fit in the palm of a hand – must throw themselves off the ledge to reach the feeding grounds on the plains below. As the snow thaws, sedges and mosses are released for the geese to feed on, but after just a few weeks snow will cover the plain again, so they must start feeding at once.

Calling frantically, the mother takes to the air, followed by her mate. After several false starts the goslings step off and free-fall, to bounce onto the tufty grass below only slightly winded, but many goslings are injured on the rocks. The survivors may well fall prey to foxes, or come to grief on the rock scree as they scrabble to reach their parents.

Once reunited, families march through the mossy tundra, mothers leading and fathers bringing up the rear. In the long summer daylight the geese eat for hours on end. They need to. By September the family will join the migration to western Scotland or Ireland, and the goslings, barely two months old, must fly some 1300 miles (2100km) to their winter home.

The willow ptarmigan's survival strategies

In a shallow dip in the ground at the edge of a birchwood in north Alaska, a willow ptarmigan is incubating her clutch of about nine eggs. It is June, and her plumage blends with the browns, greens and whites – the remaining traces of snow – of her surroundings. These ground-dwelling birds (known as willow grouse in Europe) moult from white in winter to speckled brown in summer, a camouflage against predators such as foxes and goshawks.

But when a fox trots by, it is not only camouflage that saves her. The fox relies more on smell than sight to find prey, so the bird shuts down her system – her heart rate slows from 150 to 20 beats a minute, she scarcely breathes and her temperature drops – to minimise her scent. Yet if the predator threatens and quick flight is needed, she can raise her pulse to 600 beats a minute within a second.

Her unhatched offspring owe their survival to their mother's swift regulation of her body systems. It saves them not only from being eaten, but also from freezing. When the hen returns from foraging for leaves, buds and insects, the eggs may be chilled, but she can quickly warm them. She pumps more blood round her body to heat up the patch of bare skin on her belly in contact with the eggs.

Colour change The plumage of a willow ptarmigan changes from white in winter to brown in summer. This camouflages the ground-dwelling bird from predators.

Crossed swords Two male narwhals fence with their long, straight tusks, perhaps testing each other's strength.

Narwhals, the whales with unicorn 'horns'

The clash of rapiers rises from the water between floating sheets of ice in Baffin Bay as two mottled grey creatures tussle playfully together. They are male narwhals, small whales named for their pale colouring (in Old Norse *nahvalr* means 'corpse whale'). Their swords are tusks. Each male has one – an extended upper left tooth probably used in displays to threaten rivals or impress females and win a mate. Serious contests take place underwater.

Each narwhal is about 15ft (4.6m) long and weighs a ton or more. His spirally grooved tusk reaches straight out 10ft (3m) through the top lip. This tusk was the origin of myths about unicorns, and was prized by Eskimos and Norsemen who traded it as ivory – worth more than its weight in gold and believed to work miracles. Females do not usually have tusks.

It is June and the jagged edge of the Arctic ice is retreating northward. The narwhals avoided the worst of the winter by moving south to waters that are a little warmer but still in the Arctic. Then in spring they gathered in groups of hundreds, or even thousands, to return. Now they are moving northward with the ice-limit and will stay in Baffin Bay only until the water opens up even farther north and allows them to feed on the plentiful squid, fish and shrimps.

Generally the travelling narwhals mingle politely, observing the social hierarchy, but in June underwater fights are still frequent as the spring-into-summer breeding season nears its end and the males are jostling to climb a rung or two of the social ladder in their group. They do not battle to the death – a display of strength is the aim – but the ritual contests leave many a male injured. Snapped tusks are common. A narwhal may even carry the tip of an opponent's tusk embedded in its head. Older males are generally at the top of the ladder for as long as they can see off all challengers.

Female narwhals breed once in three years and are pregnant for 14-15 months. While the males compete for and mate with females whose calves are now two years old, those females who have recently given birth stay close to their calves. The 5ft (1.5m) long, dark grey babies are suckled for almost two years. Not until they are at least five years old will they be fully grown and ready to find their places in the social order. The males begin to grow a tusk when they are a year old. A few females also grow a tusk, and occasionally a male has two.

Even when fully grown a narwhal may fall prey to a polar bear or a killer whale – or a human, for Eskimos are still eager to trade them. If it escapes such predators, a narwhal may well live 20 years, or even up to 50 years.

NORTH AMERICA

Where sand tiger sharks give birth and mate

Cruising lazily to and fro, swimming close to the seabed, hundreds of sand tiger sharks have gathered at the bottom of the clear seas off Cape Hatteras, North Carolina, in the United States. The sleek grey sharks, each a little over 10ft (3m) long, have come to mate.

Often the cruising sharks are surrounded by shoals of smaller fish that would normally be in danger from their snapping jaws. But for now the sharks have other things on their minds, so the small fish gather round them for protection from other predators, such as barracudas.

A male sand tiger courting a female swims close alongside and nudges her with his snout and fins, often biting her on the back in front of her dorsal fin. When the female is ready to mate, the pair swim side by side with rear ends pressed together, moving as one. Many female fish lay their eggs in the water, where they drift at the mercy of myriad hungry fish. But the sand tiger shark keeps her dozen or so fertilised eggs within the protection of her womb.

LIFE BEFORE BIRTH

After about four months, the eggs hatch and the two dominant pups eat the others. The tiny shark pups, each about as long as a finger, swim about inside their mother and eat the infertile eggs that she carries on producing throughout her year-long pregnancy. Each one consumes hundreds of thousands, and grows to be almost one-third as long as its mother.

So active are the pups inside the female sand tiger that her heaving sides are plainly visible as she lies on the sandy seabed waiting to give birth in the June after mating. As she strains, the pups turn round inside her so that when they are expelled their sharp scales do not damage her soft tissues.

When the first pup comes out, it sinks for just a moment and then seems to jolt into life, swimming away from its mother into the blue water. It is soon followed by its twin. After so many months of protection inside their mother, the pups are independent within a few seconds of birth, and have to fend for themselves. They are born with a stomach full of yolk from all the eggs that they have eaten. However, within a few days, they must learn to feed.

Even when newborn, sand tiger sharks have an armoury of very sharp, inward-pointing teeth. Each time the shark feeds, the teeth are blunted or may fall out, but they are constantly replaced by new, sharper teeth.

The young sharks are in danger from other sharks, which will snap up baby sharks just as they would take any other fish. Even adult sand tiger sharks will eat the sand tiger babies when not preoccupied by mating. As the number of adult sand tigers builds up for another mating season, the youngsters migrate north from the danger area to the safety of the shallow waters of Chesapeake Bay. There they chase through shoals and seize small fish.

Nobody knows how long the youngsters may live, but they face pressure from fishermen and skin divers, as well as the hazards of water pollution, so many may not grow up to join their parents in the mating shoals of future years.

TELLTALE TEETH

In the 1980s a diver discovered that large numbers of sand tiger sharks gathered in June over wrecks off Cape Hatteras. Scientists wondered why. The sharks were of both sexes, in ones and twos and sometimes stacked four or five high.

A search of the sandy bottom gave the answer – it was littered with sharks' teeth. Courting sand tiger males bite their mates, and some of their teeth drop out. The divers had found a shark breeding site, and the sharks were queueing up to mate. Normally the teeth are buried in the sand by the movement of the current, but in the shelter of the wreck they remained exposed.

Out of danger *Thousands of sand tiger sharks gather to mate in June. Shoals of small fish gather round them, seeking safety from predators.*

Teeth for grasping *A sand tiger shark's jaws are lined with sharp, inward-pointing teeth for grasping and holding fish. Prey is swallowed whole, without chewing.*

The start of a wolf pup's life of teamwork

As the June sun warms the Canadian wilderness, five or six wolf pups frolic together and explore their surroundings. They were born six weeks ago, blind and helpless, in the nest chamber of a den tunnelled some 6ft (1.8m) into the earth of a sandy hill slope. Their mother has used the den for several years, and cleared it out for her new litter towards the end of her nine-week pregnancy.

The pups' eyes opened when they were about a week old, and at a month old they ventured outside for the first time. The mother will continue to suckle them until they are about ten weeks old, but even after weaning they will be too young to fend for themselves, and must be fed for some months on regurgitated meat brought to them by members of the wolf pack. By mating in winter and bearing pups in late spring, the wolves ensure their young will grow up while food is plentiful.

Wolves live in packs generally numbering around seven animals, although a pack may sometimes have as many as 36 wolves. All pack members are part of an extended family with a strict social order. The leaders are the dominant male and female, and all other animals, whether they are mature (over two years old) or immature, submit to them.

Normally, only the dominant male and female breed. At mating time, she suppresses the low-ranking females by repeated harassment. This disrupts their reproductive hormones and prevents them from breeding. The dominant

HUNTERS AS HERDERS

The wolf's natural cooperative hunting instincts are exploited by shepherds when training their sheepdogs to round up sheep. By directing the dog to lie down or to move, the shepherd can drive a flock of sheep in any direction he wants.

A good sheepdog has inherited the wolf's intelligence and its skilled responsiveness to its prey's behaviour, so can anticipate sheep movements and decide which way to go in order to drive them in the required direction or cut off their escape.

Sheepdogs treat the shepherd as just another member of the wolf pack – but the shepherd controls them and suppresses their instinct to race in for the kill.

Babysitter *Their mother, or one of the other adults in the pack, keeps constant watch on the month-old wolf pups when they first emerge from the den.*

male keeps other males away from her by displays of aggression. Most of the time, however, all the pack members are friendly and communicative, and greet each other with licking and tail-wagging when they have been apart, while hunting for example.

The subordinate members of the pack are the young from previous years' litters who have stayed on to help in the arduous task of raising the pups. If a pup licks a helper's face as it returns from hunting, it will be given regurgitated food. Helpers will also guard the young while the other adults go hunting.

Without the assistance of their helpers, the breeding pair would find it difficult to cope with so many cubs constantly in need of food and care. Unless they stay as helpers, the young leave when they are 1-2 years old to try to establish themselves in their own territories.

By the time they are 8-10 weeks old, the pups are strong enough to leave the den altogether. They live and play in the open, and the pack returns to the home area from hunting forays. The youngsters spend the days frolicking, wrestling together, and pouncing on small

creatures such as mice. But when the pups are about six months old, the pack returns to its normal nomadic lifestyle, and the pups learn how to hunt in earnest.

Like all large predators, wolves live in territories, ranging in size from about 25sq miles (65sq km) if prey is plentiful, to 20 times larger if prey is scarce. Territorial boundaries such as trees and boulders are scent-marked with urine, and the area is fiercely defended. Neighbouring wolf packs rarely trespass.

The wolves' eerie howling, audible to human ears up to 10 miles (16km) away, helps pack members to keep in touch and probably also plays a part in territorial defence, warning packs of one another's position and giving an exaggerated impression of pack size. Wolf packs sometimes sit in a group and howl together, in short bursts at about half-hour intervals.

SKILLED HUNTING PARTIES

Within its territory, the pack will travel up to 15 miles (24km) a day in search of food. An adult wolf, about the size of a German Shepherd dog, needs 5-6lb (2.5kg) of meat a day. Moving in single file, the pack searches out its prey among herds of deer, antelope, musk oxen or bison. The wolves can scent them more than 1 mile (1.6km) away, but only by cooperative hunting can an animal as large as a bull moose be brought down – the larger the animal, the more food for the pack. The wolves rarely attempt to take a fit animal but pick one that is old, young or weak and less able to fight or outrun them.

The pack splits to cut off the prey's escape routes and to drive the victim from the jaws of one wolf to those of another. They do not seem to follow a deliberate plan, but exploit opportunities that emerge as the hunt progresses. The success rate is generally about one kill in every ten attempts. When all else fails, the wolves make do with smaller prey such as mice, hares, birds, or even fish or berries.

Wolves were once widely distributed throughout the Northern Hemisphere, but their reputation as fearless killers hunting in packs has led to their extermination in many areas. Now they survive only in places where people find living conditions too difficult, such as the Arctic wastes of Canada and Russia, and the remote high deserts of central Asia.

The joy of living *The growing pups enjoy a carefree life playing and exploring in the home area. Howling in response to other members of the pack is all part of the fun of life, but also bonds them to the family team.*

California's ladybirds head for the hills

Glistening in the June sunlight, large red globes decorate some of the waterside plants in a Californian mountain creek. The globes are clusters of red, black-spotted beetles – convergent ladybirds gathering in groups before searching for patches of leaf litter where they can hide and doze away the summer. The ladybirds' name does not come from their habit of clustering, but from the two white lines that converge behind the head.

When the ladybirds changed from larvae to adults in May, they were 100 miles (160km) away in the fertile farmlands of California's Central Valley. By that time, the ladybirds' favourite food – aphids – was in short supply because they had already eaten most of the ample spring flush of aphids while they were still wingless larvae – each slate-blue and yellow-spotted, with six legs, strong jaws and huge appetites.

With the coming of June aphids were scarce, and the hot, dry days unlikely to produce a fresh supply. So the convergent ladybirds rose in their millions from the alfalfa fields and disappeared into the bright sky.

Making use of the calm weather and rising currents of warm air, the ladybirds flew straight up until they hit cold air. This made their flight muscles grow sluggish so they dropped down to warmer air again. Moving up and down in this way between 2000ft and 7000ft (610m and 2130m), the ladybirds made their way to the neighbouring mountains with the aid of air currents and following winds.

Once they have fed on pollen and built up their fat reserves, they gather in their clusters for the summer sleep, dozing until October, when autumn floods disturb them and they move to canyons just below the snow line to hibernate in sheltered places. There may be as many as 14 million ladybirds congregated in one place.

When spring warms the air again, it rouses the ladybirds. They spend several days in feverish mating, making the most of the hosts of available mates. Then they return to the Central Valley's crops, arriving just in time to catch the first spring aphids. This rich meal triggers the females to lay eggs, and start the life cycle again.

Beetle gathering Convergent ladybirds, well fed once more after their flight to the mountains, gather in clusters before finding a summer sleeping place. They will doze under leaf litter until the autumn rains.

Diving loons that wail in the wilderness

As the June twilight dims the barely ruffled surface of an Alaskan lake, the silence is suddenly broken by a spine-chilling wail as a dark, white-streaked shape bobs to the surface. A common loon is calling to her mate. She has been diving for small fish and larvae but now the light is too poor even for her large eyes to spot prey. She swims to their nest, a flattened mound of water weeds on the brink of the land. She adds a few strands of weed to it then presses her breast on the centre to hollow it out. In a few days, she will be ready to lay.

Returning to the water, the female loon again voices an eerie call, and this time her mate answers, swimming to her from the shadows fringing the shoreline. The two birds swim side by side and pretend to search for fish by gently nodding their heads and dipping their faces beneath the surface. This is a courtship ritual, and helps to sustain the bond between them, a bond that lasts as long as both are alive.

Suddenly, startled by a duck landing on the water, they both let out what sounds like a trembling laugh – their call of alarm. Next the male gives a long, yodelling cry as he swims to repel the intruder. The calls of the common loon are among the most piercing of any bird, and this yodel is the loon's most powerful call. It is used to declare ownership of its territory, an expanse of water and shore which may be about 1 mile (1.6km) long and 500yds (460m) wide. Loons do not usually tolerate other pairs in their territory and long chases and intense fights are common as territory holders drive off intruders.

The pair reunited on the lake in April after wintering separately at sea. After a month and more of courting and preparing the nest, the female lays her two brown-spotted, olive-coloured eggs. Both birds share the month-long incubation and care for the chicks, which are soon sailing, fluffy and grey-brown across the lake, sometimes riding on their parents' backs. The family stay together until autumn while the chicks learn the skills they need, especially in diving. The loon, known in Europe as the great northern diver, has a long, streamlined body with powerful, webbed feet set well back – a perfect design for swimming underwater but not for walking on land. Dives usually last about 45 seconds but may extend up to three minutes.

Waterside home The common loon – a clumsy mover on land – nests at the water's edge for easy access.

New outfit Bright and clean in her soft new shell, a female blue crab finally casts off her old shell. This female crab has been washed onto the beach.

Blue crabs slip out of their shells to mate

Swollen with eggs, a female blue crab is struggling to get out of her armour-like shell. She is more than 6ft (1.8m) down among the eel grass in the shallows, one of thousands of blue crabs, both male and female, gathered along the east coast of North America in June, their mating time. But before the crab can release her eggs, she has to moult her old shell.

The moult is set off when a male crab seizes a female in his powerful grip. It takes the female nearly three days to shed her old shell. While she does so, and until her new shell hardens, she is vulnerable to predators such as conger eels. She also gets breathless because her gills are disordered. The male, whose new shell is already hard, protects her in his embrace and also fans water over her to keep her supplied with oxygen. Eventually, the female releases her eggs into the water for the male to fertilise with his milt (sperm). The adults move on, leaving the eggs to hatch into larvae two weeks later.

But the male crab cannot protect his mate from one predator – man. North American Indians discovered the delicacy of freshly moulted blue crabs, with shells still soft, and taught early colonists to catch them. The crabs have been harvested ever since, and today, 300 years later, Chesapeake Bay on the US east coast is still the centre of a soft-shelled crab industry.

Life on the edge Kittiwakes find nesting sites safe from predators on inaccessible ledges high above the sea. Nests are cemented to the ledge with droppings.

Basking in the sun Razorbills (above) derive their name from their sharp-edged, hooked beaks. They are expert swimmers, and use their wings underwater.

....

Fancy-free flight Buoyant on the winds, a fulmar (right) glides stiff-winged near its home cliff. Although it looks like a gull, it belongs to the petrel family.

Life in a high-rise seabird colony

After spending the winter roaming at sea, most North Atlantic seabirds have gathered in their millions by June in various colonies on the precipitous cliffs skirting shores and islands. They are here to breed, and June is the time when their young hatch.

In each colony, the cliffs resound to the raucous cries of birds such as fulmars, gannets, puffins, kittiwakes, guillemots and razorbills, each with its own preferred level. Puffins, shearwaters and petrels nest in rock crevices or shallow burrows dug in the soft turf of the sloping cliff top. Gannets, with their 6ft (1.8m) wingspread, also favour the cliff top for their seaweed nests, for they like flat areas where they can land easily. Only a few dozen gannet colonies exist in the North Atlantic.

The upper heights of the cliff face belong mainly to gulls and sometimes to gull-like fulmars on the broader bare ledges. The middle levels are occupied mostly by guillemots, razorbills and kittiwakes. Guillemots crowd together on bare ledges, but razorbills form smaller groups in less-exposed crevices. Long, tapered guillemot eggs roll in tight circles if dislodged.

As the best site for a colony is as near as possible to rich feeding grounds out to sea, birds are often packed together in dense numbers.

Guillemots, for example, can cram three breeding birds onto an area the size of the open pages of this book. Such crowding produces a perpetual cacophony of screaming, wheeling birds flying to and from the sea to feed. Tensions arise when neighbours trespass on each other's space as they come and go. Fulmars are usually given a wide berth because they spit out foul-smelling stomach oil if disturbed.

The nearest feeding ground may be some distance away. Return journeys of 100 miles (160km) or more are common, so a foraging bird may be away for hours while its mate incubates the egg. Guillemots sometimes stay away for up to three days. Fishing gannets make spectacular dives from heights of about 100ft (30m), but many seabirds dive from the surface, and may stay submerged for up to a minute. Diving birds like razorbills and puffins have short, blunt wings that aid fast swimming underwater but make their flight ungainly. They get airborne by launching themselves off a high cliff or by frantic wing flapping as they run across the water.

Many seabirds carry fish back to their chick in their beaks. A puffin's large red and yellow beak can carry about ten small fish at once. Because guillemots are away from the nest for so long, they swallow the fish and then regurgitate it partly digested for their young. Each adult may eat about 11oz (300g) of fish a day, and a chick about two-thirds of that, so 2,500,000 guillemots nesting round the Arctic's Barents Sea alone probably consume about 70,000 tons of fish between them during the breeding season. Much of this is returned to the sea as droppings, providing a rich source of food for microscopic plankton. In turn, the increase in plankton leads to more fish in the area.

Because of the skill and energy needed to feed a chick, many seabirds can raise only one at a time. So the hen tends to lay a large egg to give the chick a good start in life. A fulmar egg, for example, is generally about one-seventh of the female's body weight – roughly equivalent to a 9 stone (57kg) woman producing an 18lb (8kg) baby. Most seabird eggs have plain shells, and birds know their own by the site and their mate. But guillemots and razorbills lay individually patterned eggs that the parents can recognise. And even in the hubbub of the colony, birds can pick out their chick by its call.

....

Seabird city Guillemots crowd onto every available ledge as they prepare to breed on the cliffs of the Isle of May off Scotland's east coast. Pairs usually return to the same spot year after year.

Free ride Young great crested grebes ride in comfort on either parent's back, sheltered between folded wings.

Caring for a family of great crested grebes

Boldly striped black-and-white chicks squeak shrilly as they ride on their mother's back between the reeds of a lake in south-west England on a June morning. They can see their father, a great crested grebe, approaching with a meal for them. Although the youngsters can swim as soon as they hatch, one of their parents often carries them on its back, between folded wings, while the other searches for food.

The foraging bird dives for small fish and feeds the chicks one at a time, presenting a whole fish head first so that its fins do not snag in the youngster's throat. Sometimes the meal may be an insect or a small water creature. Oddly, the grebes also give the chicks feathers to eat, and eat feathers themselves. This seems to be a way of getting rid of food debris from the stomach – the feathers help to form pellets that are regurgitated and spat out.

The parent grebes share all the work of raising a family. After their spectacular courtship displays of April and May, they spent about a week building the nest – a platform of vegetation about the size of a chair seat, hemmed in by reeds. The pair also took turns to incubate the four white, oval eggs for four weeks. If the sitting bird was disturbed and left the nest, it carefully covered the eggs with vegetation.

As the eggs were laid at 48-hour intervals, they hatched one at a time. When each chick broke free from its shell, one of the parents quickly collected the shell and dropped it in the lake some distance away from the nest, so that the chicks' presence was not betrayed to predators such as herons or gulls. As soon as all the chicks had hatched, the birds abandoned the nest.

Well fed by their parents, the grebe chicks will grow quickly during July and into August, and soon learn to dive like their parents. At any hint of danger, the parents dive with a splash, a signal for the youngsters to follow and seek safety underwater. At eight weeks old the grebe chicks can feed themselves, but they still clamour for food from their parents. By this time, one in ten pairs of parent birds will be preparing for a second brood as well as keeping an eye on the growing chicks.

Sometimes the adults favour one or two of their offspring, feeding them first and more often than the others. By 10-11 weeks old, the chicks will be fledged and can look after themselves, but sometimes the favourites are fed for five or six weeks longer.

Once the youngsters are independent, they may fly off to join other young grebes congregating at moulting grounds.

GETTING ACQUAINTED

When great crested grebes go courting in April and May, the water ripples beneath their graceful, ballet-like dance. This is how they establish a relationship.

Face to face The birds approach each other with crests pointing forwards and beaks held down. Both shake their heads from side to side.

Retire and return Suddenly, one of the pair dashes off across the water. Then it stops, its crest and wing feathers raised, and returns to its mate.

Heart to heart Both grebes dive, then they rise from the water with beaks full of weed. Their heads sway from side to side, and they thrash the water as they paddle breast to breast.

Hidden fawn *A newborn fallow deer relies on concealment for safety, and stays motionless in the grass waiting for its mother to return once or twice a day to suckle it.*

Life begins in hiding for a fallow deer fawn

Tucked away in the dappled shade of a European oak wood, a newborn fallow deer fawn lifts its head unsteadily in the still June afternoon and twitches its ears as its mother approaches to lick it. Its tawny, white-spotted mother found this quiet place in the long grass to end her eight-month pregnancy. The doe, slightly bigger than a goat and without antlers, glances about her nervously as she nuzzles her fawn and encourages it to stand.

After a few minutes the gangly newcomer totters onto splayed, shaky legs and seeks its mother's teats with outstretched nose and tongue. The doe gently pushes from behind to help, and the fawn is soon sucking eagerly, stimulated by its mother's licking as she cleans its spotted coat. Occasionally she turns away to snatch a few mouthfuls of grass for herself. Suddenly, she lifts her head and pricks her ears, her large nostrils twitching on the breeze. A noise has alerted her to possible danger, and she must leave the fawn for fear of betraying its presence. As yet, the newborn fawn cannot run and keep up with her, so it is best left hidden.

The doe moves off and the fawn curls up into a tight ball in the long grass. It will stay motionless for hours, however close danger comes – its life depends on it. If the tiny fawn should stir, it might give itself away to a predator such as a fox. For the first three days, the doe returns only once or twice a day to suckle her offspring, often under cover of darkness. Gradually the fawn's limbs strengthen and after three or four days it begins to follow its mother as she grazes or browses, usually at dawn and dusk, but it still rests for much of the day.

Soon it is gambolling with the other fawns, under the watchful eyes of their grazing mothers. The fawn gradually begins grazing, too, but is still suckled for up to seven months, long after it develops its grey-brown winter coat in October. Next spring, a young buck will begin to develop antlers. They are shed yearly, and are not fully formed until its fourth or fifth year. A young doe will bear her first fawn at about two years old, and then give birth every year of her 10-15 year life if she remains fit and well fed.

The first catch for a young grey heron

A long-legged grey heron steps from the still water of an English lake and stoops to lay its catch on some waterside rocks where it can peck at the plump carp. It could have gulped down many another fish whole, but this one is too big. It is June, and for the heron – about 2ft 6in (760mm) tall and not quite two months old – this is its first catch.

The young heron has been fishing in the lake after an unsuccessful attempt to catch an eel at the nearby seashore. After spotting the 1ft (300mm) long eel, it stabbed the water with its long yellow beak to come up with its wriggling prey. The captive wrapped itself round the heron's beak and after a wrestling match lasting several minutes twisted free and was gone.

The novice fisherman has only just left the nest high in a tree where its parents fed it, and its two nest mates, with regurgitated frogs, small mammals and birds. Occasionally they brought a goldfish from a garden pond. For now, food is plentiful and the young heron will not starve. But it must become a skilful hunter before winter, when seashore fish will be in hiding from storms, and ice may cover inland water.

Fisherman's fare A young heron comes ashore to make a meal of the fish it has caught. It would gulp down smaller fish on the spot, head first and whole.

Wasp nursery The spiky red growth on the stem of a wild rose (top), known as a robin's pincushion, is really a gall wasp's nest. It shelters the developing young (bottom) until they emerge as adults next spring.

What goes on inside a robin's pincushion

A mid the June tangle of leaves and stems on a wild rose in a British hedgerow, there is sometimes a round, deep red, spiky growth 1-2in (25-50mm) across. It stands out among the pink flowers, and is known as a 'robin's pincushion', 'rose king', 'sleepy apple' or 'rose bedeguar gall'. In May a female gall wasp, only a quarter the size of a common wasp, laid her eggs on a leaf bud of the rose. When the eggs hatched and the grubs chewed into the bud, its tissues began to swell as cells divided abnormally to form a gall (the robin's pincushion).

The pithy interior of the fully formed gall is divided into up to 60 sealed chambers. Within each is a single wasp grub that grows as it feeds on the gall tissue. Then it becomes a chrysalis (the transformation stage between larva and adult) and stays in its protective nursery all summer and winter. In the warmth of spring, all the new adults emerge from the dead cushion.

Usually they are all females; males are very rare. Unlike most gall wasp species, which must mate in alternate generations, these gall wasps lay eggs that can always develop without fertilisation, so males have become redundant.

A hawker dragonfly takes to the wing

M otionless apart from an occasional twitch, the larva, or immature form, of a dragonfly clings to a sedge stem beside a European mountain pool on a June morning. About the length of a little finger, the larva has climbed from the pool where it has lived for the last year or two, hunting insects and perhaps even tadpoles and small fish.

As it grew, the larva shed its skin several times to reveal another, more elastic skin underneath. Now it is time for the final change. Slowly its skin begins to split, and soon an adult southern hawker dragonfly struggles out through the narrow slit. It is a little longer than the larva, with large blue eyes and conspicuous green and blue markings on its slender black body.

The magnificent dragonfly rests for an hour or so while its crumpled wings swell and harden. It will spend the few weeks of its adult life flying over the nearby stream to feed on insects and search for a mate. After mating, the females return to pools or slow-flowing streams and lay their eggs among water plants.

Born again An ugly larva, newly emerged from a pool, rests on a stem (top). Its skin splits (bottom left) and from it (right) crawls a southern hawker dragonfly.

Stag beetles wrestle for a chance to mate

On an old tree stump in a garden in southern England, two male stag beetles are locked in conflict. Each of the 2in (50mm) long contestants holds the other with its huge, antler-shaped jaws. On this sultry June evening at the height of the mating season, one of the stag beetles raised his antlers to show off to a prospective mate. But he had a rival for her attentions, and the two engaged jaws.

Each pushes and shoves in an attempt to drive the other away. If this fails, one will try to wedge the other's body in his jaws and even lift him off the ground. But although the smaller female can give a powerful nip, the males' great jaws are too weak to bite hard. One will finally yield and wander off to find another female.

After mating, the female flies off to lay her eggs in the soft wood of a dead tree, preferably an oak. The month-long adult life of the stag beetles is now more or less over. The longest part of a stag beetle's life is spent as a grub. After hatching from the eggs, the grubs burrow into the rotten wood and spend up to three years munching through it. From time to time each grub moults its skin to allow room for growth. When fully grown, it makes itself a chamber in autumn and there spends the winter, changing into an adult beetle within a few weeks. But it does not emerge until the warmth of early summer.

Battle royal Two male stag beetles are locked in a struggle for a mate. Although they use their large, antler-like jaws, neither will be injured.

Night raid *Swooping on broad wings, a Blakiston's fish owl plunges its talons into the river shallows to grab a trout.*

An uncertain future for Blakiston's fish owls

At dusk on a June evening, a deep, resonant 'buu-bu' drifts across a forest in northern Japan. It is the call of a male Blakiston's fish owl, leaving his roost on powerful wings to hunt in the nearby river. A somewhat deeper 'bu' from his mate in their nest in a tree cavity follows so closely that it sounds like a single call. The spring flush of frogs has dwindled but the water still offers plenty of fish and crayfish. This time it is a trout that the owl takes back for his young in the nest. The family needs a large home, for these fish owls are among the biggest owls in the world, growing to 2ft 4in (710mm) tall.

The twin youngsters, nearing the end of their eight weeks as nestlings, peer out of the nest, hissing their demands for food. The female takes the trout and passes it to the noisiest youngster. Then both adults leave the nest, the male to hunt once more and the female to stretch and preen. She diligently incubated the eggs during the freezing March weather, and then guarded the chicks from predators such as martens. Now the youngsters are well grown and better able to defend themselves, but need more food, so their mother is able to leave them for longer and longer to help her mate hunt.

Once the youngsters are fledged and leave the nest, predators will no longer be a problem. But finding winter food and somewhere suitable to live will be; these problems have made the Blakiston's fish owl a rare bird. Being chiefly fish eaters, the owls must live near rivers and lakes, but in winter when much of the water freezes over they go hungry unless they can catch flying squirrels or birds.

And in modern forests few trees with cavities large enough for the owls are left, although in some places some of the world's largest nesting boxes have been set up for them. The owls take at least two years to mature, and few pairs seem to breed successfully every year. The present world population may be less than 1000 birds, of which 80-100 survive in north Japan and the rest in eastern Russia and possibly north-east China.

Mating chain Head to tail among the seaweed, sea hares mate in a line in warm, shallow water.

Sea hares perform a dual role when mating

As the sea warms up along the Atlantic coast of southern Europe in early summer, sea hares – a type of sea slug up to 12in (300mm) long – gather in shallow water to mate. They are named for the horn-shaped folds on their heads, which resemble a hare's ears.

Sea hares are hermaphrodites – creatures with both male and female sex organs – and their mating habits are highly unusual. They form a mating chain in which, apart from the front and rear animals, each sea hare's male organ fertilises the animal in front while its female part is fertilised by the sea hare behind. Mating sea hares may remain entangled for more than 24 hours before separating to lay their eggs. Each sea hare lays several million tiny, pale eggs in a string of jelly, which is often wrapped round the bottom of a seaweed frond. Most of the larvae that hatch will be eaten by fish, but a few will survive to reach adulthood.

A sea hare is a marine mollusc – a soft-bodied creature protected by a shell, such as a mussel or a limpet. But the sea hare's normal mollusc shell has been reduced to just a small horny plate on its back. The plate is covered by two body folds, which it uses for swimming. If startled, a sea hare will flap its folds and swim away looking rather like a butterfly on the wing. Or else it will secrete a foul-tasting substance thought to deter predators.

Most of a sea hare's life is spent crawling among seaweed, on which it grazes. Like other molluscs, it has a powerful serrated tongue which it uses to shred the seaweed gripped in its jaws. The food is then stored in an enormous sack, or crop, and digested slowly.

Why honey bees swarm and build new hives

Early summer in a honey bee colony is a time of intense activity. Workers (sterile females) are busy feeding larvae on nectar and pollen collected from flowers. These larvae are replacements for the many bees who died of cold or starvation during winter, and take about three weeks to develop from egg to adult. By May and June the colony is getting overcrowded.

A typical colony contains a queen, about 50,000 workers and 300 drones (males). Workers gather nectar and pollen from flowers and turn the nectar into honey. They also build the wax combs where eggs are laid and food is stored. After about a month they die exhausted and new workers take their places.

The queen bee is the sole egg-layer, and she is fed and tended by workers. As they clean her, they lick from her body a 'queen substance', which contains a chemical message preventing them from raising any more queens. As the colony expands during early summer, the amount of 'queen substance' available becomes insufficient for all, so some workers start to feed a number of the larvae on nothing but royal jelly, a nutritious secretion produced from glands in their mouths. These larvae will become queens.

Eventually, the existing queen, sensing the overcrowding, decides to leave. She flies off in the heat of midday, followed by a spectacular, zigzagging swarm of workers and a few drones. They alight on a low branch not much more than a stone's throw from the original hive, and cluster tightly round the queen to protect her while scout bees fly off to find a new home.

Once they have found somewhere suitable, such as a hollow tree or a chimney, the scouts pass on the location to the other bees in the swarm in the same way that foraging bees show the location of food, by means of a dance. They repeatedly indicate the direction to be taken in relation to the sun's position.

Back in the parent colony, the remaining workers know of the loss of the old queen within a few minutes because 'queen substance' is no longer available. They respond by feeding the larvae in the queen cells with more royal jelly, and soon new queens begin to emerge, usually one at a time. If two emerge at the same time, they may fight to the death with their stings.

If the colony is still quite large, some of these new queens will also leave the hive, but with a smaller swarm than the parent queen. These

Swarming workers After leaving their overcrowded colony to form a new one, a swarm of bees (top) clusters round the queen. Scout bees do a complicated dance (bottom) to show the direction of the new home.

flights are called 'casts'. In a good summer they may be successful in setting up new colonies, but their small numbers make them less likely to survive winter and bad weather.

The next young queen to be hatched in the parent colony will then be accepted by the workers, who will kill the other developing queens. This new queen will mate and take over the egg-laying, and by the end of the summer the colony will be big enough to have gathered enough honey and pollen to survive the coming winter. A new queen takes to the air at about five days old and usually mates on the wing with about ten drones. When she returns to the hive, the drones are denied entry and die. The sperm stored in the queen's abdomen will last her whole life, which she spends laying eggs.

The moth that never takes to the wing

A silken cocoon lies hidden in the bark of a hazel tree in a European hedgerow. As the June sun warms the trunk, a female vapourer moth emerges from the cocoon. She is covered with a fine, brownish-green down, but the most distinctive thing about her is that she appears to have no wings. Her wings are, in fact, reduced to tiny stubs, and are completely useless. Vapourer moths are just one of many species of moth that have wingless females, and which have therefore developed a specialised lifestyle.

The newly emerged female does not leave her cocoon. Instead, she sits on it and sets out to attract a mate. She emits a chemical known as a pheromone, which has a scent so powerful that, carried on the wind, it will be detected by a male vapourer up to 3 miles (5km) away. A vapourer male does have wings, and usually flies by day. He is also hairy, with slightly patterned chestnut wings bearing two white spots.

He detects the female's scent with his two large, feathery antennae. Once he has found her, the pair mate. Then the male flutters off to follow another scented message to a new mate.

Within a few hours, the female begins to lay about 300 brownish-white eggs in a crowded batch on the surface of her old cocoon. This done, she has completed her only task in life, and dies. Her brief life rarely exceeds two weeks. Eggs laid in spring or early summer hatch out as caterpillars within days.

In the warmer regions of Europe, the first male moths are on the wing in June and July, and there is time for two generations, with the

Butterfly or moth? One way to tell a moth from a butterfly is by the antennae, which are used to pick up scent. Most moths have feathery antennae, and males have larger feathering than females because they need to detect a female's sexual odour from afar. A butterfly's antennae are club-shaped at the tip.

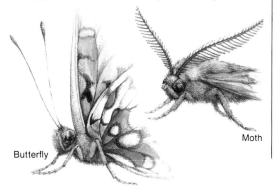

Butterfly   Moth

Stay-at-home female A male vapourer moth mates with a wingless female on the cocoon from which she hatched (top). Then she lays her eggs on the cocoon (below). Eggs laid in June will hatch within days.

second flight between August and October. Eggs laid in late summer will spend the winter on the surface of the cocoon and hatch the following spring. In cooler parts of Europe there is usually only one generation each year.

Like their parents, the caterpillars are very hairy. They are bright red, yellow and black with four tufts of stiff yellow hairs along their backs, and further tufts of longer silky hairs at each end. The hairs are tipped with strong irritant chemicals, which are a defence against birds and also a considerable discomfort to people who try to pick up the caterpillars.

In a good season, vapourer moth caterpillars may be found feeding on the foliage of limes, oaks, hawthorns and hazels. They will also eat the leaves of roses, fruit trees and many other cultivated plants, which can make them a pest, even in town gardens, all over Europe.

When a caterpillar is ready to pupate – start to change into an adult – it finds a safe crevice in the bark of a tree or in a wall and spins a cocoon, often incorporating some of the long hairs from its own body. About a month later, it will emerge as an adult moth, to begin the cycle again.

Nose for noise *Male hammerheaded bats make their loud love-calls with the aid of their inflatable nostrils with extendible flaps, and their large, bony larynxes.*

AFRICA

A courting bazaar for hammerheaded bats

Every evening in June, as the dry season gets under way, the tall trees lining the larger rivers of Central Africa are draped with rows of male hammerheaded fruit bats. With the occasional flutter of their leathery wings, the bats hang upside down, waiting expectantly.

A little while later, some female bats arrive. At once the males stretch out their 3ft (1m) wingspan, flap their wings energetically, and break into a cacophony of metallic-sounding calls. It is the mating season, and the male bats have formed a lek – a bazaar where they display their qualities as prospective mates. One by one, the females flutter along the rows, pausing momentarily here and there to inspect a particular male.

When a female has finally decided on a male, she returns to him again and again, eventually perching upside down beside him on his branch to mate. Then the female flies away and the male rejoins the lek, shouting out his qualities to attract more females.

The lion – king of beasts or a robber baron?

On the cracked, bare earth of a dried-up water hole on the Serengeti Plain in Tanzania, several lions lie stretched at length in the midday sun. Most of the pride of 10-15 animals are lionesses, who are related to one another, and their still-dependent youngsters. The three or four males who control the pride are probably brothers or half-brothers, but are not related to the lionesses.

It is June, the beginning of the four-month dry season – a time of dust and parched earth, and of hunger and thirst for the wildlife. Even the lions face a lean time, because the herds of wildebeest and zebra they prefer to feed on have drifted north-west to find better grazing, and stragglers from the migrating herds are increasingly hard to find. The few smaller animals remaining, such as warthogs and Thomson's gazelles, offer little sustenance for large cats.

As vultures begin to circle in the cloudless sky and then drop to earth close by, one of the dozing lionesses becomes suddenly alert. Vultures have sharp enough sight and smell to pick out dying animals or carcasses over a wide area – a lion must stumble across them by chance, or keep an eye on the vultures. The lioness gets up to investigate, and the rest of the pride follow. Soon they are squabbling over a young zebra that has died of thirst. The larger, heavier males feed first and take their pick, the lionesses eat next, and the youngsters feed last.

TERRIBLE TALONS

A lion's sharp, curved claws, like those of any member of the cat family, can be extended and retracted at will. The claws are controlled by elastic ligaments linked to muscles in the ankle.

Claws at rest *When retracted, the claw sits above the toe pad, its tip concealed between the lion's toes.*

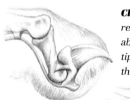

Claws in action
For an attack, the claws are thrust out about the length of a human thumb. The sharp points will slash and grip.

Fortunately there is enough for all in the zebra, but as times get leaner the youngsters can easily starve to death. Eight out of ten lion cubs are likely to die before they are two years old.

When the dry season strikes, the lions resort to robbing other predators. About 40 per cent of lions' meat is taken from hyenas, partly because hyenas are the commonest predators on the African grasslands, and probably also because few other predators hunt in groups big enough to bring down large prey such as wildebeest and zebra. Lions march in and take over about a quarter of hyena kills, driving the hyenas off before they have had time to demolish the carcass. The hyenas are luckier with smaller prey such as a gazelle, as they can usually eat most of it before the lions arrive.

THE HOME GROUND

An adult lion needs about 11lb (5kg) of meat a day. To stay alive, the average Serengeti lion needs to kill 32 animals a year, which might be, for example, seven wildebeest, five zebra, 16 Thomson's gazelles, one warthog, one buffalo and one or two other species ranging from giraffes to hares.

In the Serengeti's open grasslands, the scent-marked territory of a lion pride is typically about 77–155sq miles (200–400sq km). Because the Serengeti wildlife is partly nomadic, and migrates out of the area during the dry season, some lion prides follow their prey and become nomadic too. In better-watered places adjoining the plains to the south-east, such as Lake Manyara, more animals remain during the dry season so lion pride territories often cover only about 15sq miles (40sq km).

When lions defend their territory against intruders, their vibrant roars can be heard more than 1 mile (1.6km) away, reminding neighbours of their presence. Males are, of course, most concerned with keeping other males away from their mates, but their defence of the pride's territory also ensures that the stock of prey in the area is not depleted by strangers.

Apart from defending his females, a male lion leads a life of utter indolence. Male members of a pride seldom hunt – it is all done by the lionesses, although the males eat their fill first. The lionesses are the core of the pride, and usually stay together for many years. Adult males often have to fight fiercely to gain control,

Dry season *The bed of a dried-up water hole in the Ngorongoro Crater in Tanzania provides a warm spot for a pride of lions to bask in the sun.*

and can usually stay in charge for only a few years. The larger the group of related males, the longer they are able to hold sway.

When male lions take over a pride, they often kill all the cubs that are still being suckled. The females may resist but rarely win. The cubs are killed so that their mother will come into breeding condition straight away, and the males can begin siring their own cubs at once. Lions breed at any time of year. A female usually bears two or three cubs (whose coats are spotted at first), and mates once they are two years old.

HARD WORK FOR HUNTERS

Males not controlling prides live in bachelor groups or alone, and have to hunt for themselves. Hunting is hard work at the best of times, and only about one lion hunt in four ends in success. A pair of bachelor males hunting in the dry season have been known to go 26 days without managing a kill.

As most of the animals they feed on can easily outrun them, lions stalk their prey carefully, usually after sunset. A charging lion's top speed of about 43mph (70km/h) can match that of a zebra, if not that of a Thomson's gazelle, but the lion can keep it up for only about 110 yds (100m). Its prey, however, has the stamina to maintain speed for maybe 10 miles (16km) or more, so if the lion fails to catch its quarry straight away, it will lose it.

After stealthy stalking, the lion makes a final charge over about 50yds (46m), knocking down the prey before it has time to react, then taking it by the throat or muzzle to throttle it. Sometimes zebras and gazelles appear unconcerned when lions walk past them or rest close by – but only because they know that the lions they can see are unlikely to be hunting.

When lionesses hunt, they often work in a group. This way they can kill larger animals such as zebra and buffalo, which a lone lion

Heat exhaustion Oblivious of the flies that gather on its muzzle, a lion cub dozes in the heat of the day.

Shy but curious Lion cubs are nervous of strangers, but also inquisitive. Weaning begins at about three months old, the age when their spots start to fade.

finds too difficult to handle. Some of the lionesses circle round behind the herd and drive the animals into the jaws of the other lionesses waiting in hiding.

The 1500 or so lions on the Serengeti Plain, and a similar number in the Masai Mara Reserve that adjoins it to the north, consume nearly 10,000 prey animals a year. Although this seems a large number, it is only a tiny fraction of the several million animals that inhabit the area. Old and sick animals are most often the lions' victims, and this helps to keep the prey population healthy and fit to cope with the arduous life on the open plains.

The lions also play an important role in keeping down the numbers of the large grazing herds. When predators disappear from an area, their prey often increase rapidly and begin to damage their own habitat by overgrazing.

Within the last few hundred years, lions have been hunted to extinction in much of Africa and southern Asia – partly because of human fear of large predators, and partly because they also prey on domestic livestock.

Communal care Lionesses are unusually tolerant of young cubs, and will allow the cubs of any other female to nurse from them. Lionesses in a pride are usually related to each other, but not to the adult males.

A midsummer garden where sponges spawn

Beneath the clear, calm Caribbean Sea an underwater garden is flourishing. Already vivid with assorted plants and corals, it attracts a glittering array of animals. Angelfish flash brilliant blue, yellow and green between the reef's crooked branches. Sinuous anemones wave their fleshy arms, spiny lobsters scavenge and spider crabs drape themselves with seaweed shreds so that predators may mistake them for inedible debris.

Most striking of all in the midsummer water-world are the sponges – in a large variety of shapes, sizes and colours. The Caribbean lies between Central and South America and the chain of the West Indies – a huge expanse of about 1 million sq miles (2,700,000sq km). Sheltered, warm, and much of it shallow, it is a paradise for sponges. They form globes and tubes, stars and fans, cups and columns, smooth, furry or holed, and are of every colour from the coal-black lumps of the helmet sponge to the brilliant blood-red of the boring sponge.

Until 200 years ago, sponges were thought to be plants, but they are now known to be primitive animals lacking hearts, brains, lungs and nervous systems. There are more than 5000 known species, which have existed little changed for some 500 million years. Despite their variety, all share the same basic structure. Special cells inside the sponge suck in sea water through pores on its surface and sieve out food particles from it. The water is then discharged through round vents.

Just how sponges reproduce was a mystery until recently. Then one June afternoon and evening in the Palancar Reef near Mexico's Cozumel island, clouds of eggs and sperm were seen billowing from the vents of one sponge species. Though many eggs were eaten by lobsters, others were safely fertilised. What triggers off this mass spawning nobody knows. It could be the moon and tides, or something to do with the sea's temperature or saltiness.

....

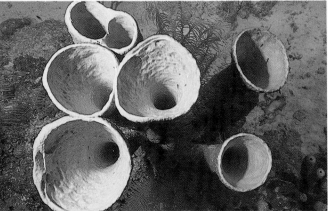

Clouds beneath the waters In a reef near Cozumel island off Mexico, all sponges of the same species spawn at the same time, releasing clouds of eggs and sperm (top). These float off and found new colonies. Sponges – including yellow and brown tube sponges (bottom) – also spread when small branches bud off.

A leatherback turtle sheds tears in the sand

On a sultry June night, a bulky shape slowly emerges from the Atlantic surf on a sandy beach in French Guiana. The 8ft (2.4m) long leatherback turtle wheezes and coughs as she hauls her 110 stone (700kg) body up the beach to where the sand is just right for digging. There she makes a hole 18in (460mm) deep in which she lays 100 or so round, white, soft-shelled eggs. Then she covers them and lumbers back to the sea. She will make about six nests in all, at ten-day intervals.

The leatherback is the largest sea turtle, named for its dark, oily skin. It has no visible shell, just bony ridges along the back and underside. When it moves on land, the weight of its body presses down on lungs and windpipe. Turtles lay their eggs on land because they are descended from land-living reptiles, and their eggs cannot hatch underwater.

Crying turtle Sticky tears ooze out to keep the turtle's eyes bathed with salt water (top) while she is out of the sea laying her eggs (bottom) on the beach.

Lookout A giant tortoise makes a convenient observation post for a Galápagos hawk scouring the island for prey.

The fearless hawk too tame for its own good

From the clear June sky, the Galapágos hawk sets its sights on the giant tortoise and dives to make a smooth landing on the domed shell more than 4ft (1.2m) long. The tortoise has nothing to fear from this bird of prey, which uses it merely as a substitute boulder, a handy vantage point for spying out food to take back to its mate. Settling in a hunched pose, the hawk is not disturbed even when the 'boulder' – weighing as much as about four men – rocks into motion and lumbers through the undergrowth.

Hitching a ride, the dark, handsome hunter takes a break from circling the skies. During June – the peak of the breeding season – he has more than himself to feed. In a sturdy nest of twigs built in a low tree and used year after year, his mate is sitting on one or two pale green eggs. The male brings her lizards, rats and other small prey; when the eggs hatch after about a month, he will help to care for the downy white offspring. He may be helped by other males, for the Galápagos hawk often has an unusual family life: up to four males may mate with the same female and all share paternal duties.

This is the only type of hawk in the Galápagos Islands and, like many Galápagos animals, it has developed in isolation for thousands of years. It is known to breed on only ten main islands of the rocky, volcanic chain scattered over about 3000sq miles (7800sq km) of the Pacific Ocean.

With no natural enemies, the birds are quite tame and in the last 100 years this unwary disregard of humans colonising the islands has allowed many to be killed. Their numbers also declined when new species of rat were introduced and ousted the native rat, an important part of the hawk's diet. But marine and land iguanas, insects and small lizards, doves, finches and mocking birds, and the young of sea birds, give the hawk a varied diet. It is also a scavenger, especially partial to the carcasses of feral goats descended from those brought by settlers, but now being killed because they are destroying the islands' vegetation.

Easy rider *A young koala travels on its mother's back when it becomes too big for her pouch. It will continue to ride there until it is about a year old.*

A young koala rides to eat gum leaves

As dusk falls on north-east Australia one June night, a koala stirs from her resting place on the forked branch of a eucalyptus (gum) tree. As she clambers upwards to feed, her teddy-bear-like six-month-old youngster clings to her back. When it was born the previous December and crawled into her pouch, it was no bigger than a grape. Now it is too big for the pouch. By the time it is two years old, it will be fully independent and she will give birth again.

Koalas feed almost entirely on the leaves of eucalyptus trees. A badger-sized adult eats about 1lb (450g) a day. Because the eucalyptus's tough leathery leaves are difficult to digest, the koala has a special offshoot from its gut that breaks them down. This offshoot, similar to a human appendix but longer, also produces pap on which the mother begins weaning her youngster when it is five months old. At about seven months old it starts to eat leaves itself.

A koala hardly ever descends to the ground. To help it to grip trunks and branches effectively, it has a second 'thumb' – an index finger that can oppose its other fingers. Koalas spend three-quarters of each day of their lives sleeping.

How a mallee fowl builds its own incubator

As the southern winter begins in June, there are already male mallee fowl preparing for spring. In the eucalyptus bushlands of southern Australia they are embarking on the long task of building an incubator for next season's eggs.

With backward flicks of its feet, a turkey-like male mallee fowl scrapes out a pit big enough to hold the equivalent of about 100 barrow loads of material. His lifelong mate may help a little with this, and with the laborious work of filling the pit with dead leaves and twigs collected in the sparse area. As the pile builds up and is wetted by the winter rain, it starts to rot. As it rots, it generates heat. The birds keep in the heat by covering the pile with a 20in (510mm) layer of sand, until the heap is more than 3ft (1m) high.

When spring comes in September, the female will lay up to 30 eggs over a period of weeks. They are pushed down into the vegetation and then covered with sand. The eggs incubate for two months in their hotbed, tended by the male. Every day he checks the temperature at regular intervals by taking a little of the fermenting pile into his mouth or touching it with his tongue. If it is too hot, he removes some sand. If it is too cold, he adds more. He manages the heap so well that its inner temperature is always within one degree of 33°C (91°F).

In summer, if the sun overheats the heap, the bird piles on more sand to protect it at midday, but removes it in the late afternoon as the sun's heat weakens. It is even said that a mallee fowl can anticipate weather changes and adjust the cover before a sudden change occurs.

When the chicks hatch, they have to break out of their eggs and then dig through the sandy covering. Once free, they vanish into the scrubland, never to know their own parents.

Hotbed *Mallee fowl eggs are laid in the top of vegetation that the male piles into a pit. The damp pile heats up as it rots and a cover of sand keeps in the heat.*

Pit stop *The female mallee approves the pit before the long task of filling it with leaves and twigs can be started.*

JULY

WHILE WALRUSES BASK IN THE NORTH AMERICAN SUN,
GRIZZLY BEARS CATCH SALMON. BATS AND BUTTERFLIES BREED IN THE
EUROPEAN SUMMER, JACKALS REAR THEIR YOUNG ON THE
AFRICAN PLAINS AND HUMPBACK WHALES COURT OFF AUSTRALIA'S COAST

Europe: Large white butterflies mate in a meadow

Icy leap *Even in high summer, sea ice still drifts in the inlets of Ellesmere Island in the Arctic. Bounding from one floating platform to another, a wolf crosses open sea.*

Life at the world's most northerly outpost

On Ellesmere Island in the Canadian Arctic, snow covers the ground throughout the year in many places, and the surrounding seas are never free of ice. Only 470 miles (756km) from the North Pole, the island rivals Greenland for the title of the world's northernmost land mass.

Yet this forbidding landscape, an area more than twice the size of Iceland, is far from being empty of life. Hardy lichens grow beneath the snow all year, and as July's high summer sun melts the snow in the more sheltered valleys, there is a flush of colour. The deep green of grass and moss contrasts with the purple and white flowers of heathers, the red and yellow of poppies, and the fluffy white of the cottongrass.

When the vast herds of caribou moved north from the plains of North America in the wake of the retreating ice about 10,000 years ago, those that found their way onto the Arctic islands became cut off by the rising sea. So they evolved features that adapted them to life in their snow-bound world, for they could no longer migrate south in winter, as do mainland herds.

Island caribou, like all caribou, have splayed, hollowed hooves that give them a better grip on icy surfaces. But they also have thicker, whiter coats and shorter legs to keep them warm. The shorter legs reduce the animal's total body surface in relation to its volume, so cut down heat loss.

In the brief northern summer, the island provides a rich profusion of herbs, marsh grasses and lichens. But the caribous' survival here in winter depends ultimately on their ability to find the rich supply of lichens, known as 'reindeer moss', growing under the snow, which they dig out with hooves and antlers. Caribou are said to be able to detect its pungent scent an arm's depth beneath the surface.

Grazing alongside the caribou are musk oxen, relatives of mountain goats and sheep, standing about 4ft 6in (1.4m) high at the shoulder and weighing up to 64 stone (400kg). A musk ox has dense woolly hair next to its skin, overlaid by an immense cape of thick matted hairs that sweeps the ground round its ankles and provides it with a warm quilt against the cold.

Faced by predators or bad weather, the musk oxen form a defensive circle with the young on the inside and the adults facing outwards, their curved horns providing a protective shield against all but the most aggressive wolves. When a blizzard descends on them, they can stand in their tightly bunched circle for days at a time, their shapes gradually becoming obscured by the snow heaping up around them. And in the calm that follows the storm, the column of warm air formed by their exhaled breath can be seen 5 miles (8km) away.

In July the musk oxen calves are two or three months old. When they were born in April or May, the youngsters weighed no more than 20lb (9kg), and their coats were so thin they had to nestle beneath their mothers' shaggy capes to survive the first few days of life. They will remain vulnerable to cold until their second summer, when they will finally begin to grow their own protective capes. Most calves are suckled for more than a year.

Among the smaller inhabitants of the lonely wastes of Ellesmere Island are the Arctic hares, with long silky coats of pure white to blend in with the snow. The hares produced their young – called leverets – in June, so there is a dramatic rise in the population during the summer. The hares cover the ground in great numbers as they nibble at the new grass, moving forwards in a dense flock. Arctic hares have unusually long muzzles with protruding teeth, and this helps them to search out creeping willows and saxifrages beneath the snow. They are said to break up the snow crust by stamping with their forefeet, and to remove chunks of frozen snow with their teeth as they forage.

The hares' main enemies are snowy owls, skilled, silent hunters who rely on a regular supply of lemmings and hares for survival. Although the owls breed almost as far north as there is land, they are rarely able to breed every year – their breeding success matches the population fluctuations of their prey.

Arctic wolves are the most successful predators of the north. Larger than their more southerly cousins, they can be some 6ft (1.8m) long from nose to tail and are greyish-white for camouflage against the snow. Not only do they hunt the caribou and musk oxen, they are also expert at scenting out the breathing holes where seals come up through the ice. On some parts of Ellesmere Island's coast, wolves have stalked seals so persistently over the years that the seals will no longer bask on the ice in the summer.

The wolves range over territories of 200sq miles (520sq km) or more, and hunt in small family packs of up to 12 animals – the two parents and their successive sets of offspring.

Summer exposure Of all the polar animals, the Arctic hare has the whitest fur. Caught against a summer landscape bare of snow, it stands out starkly.

A nose for survival Caribou survive on Ellesmere Island only because they can detect the pungent smell of lichens through the deep snow.

Hunter's camouflage The snowy owl's hunting success in the barren wastes of the Arctic depends on its ability to blend into the snow-covered landscape.

Moulting time Whistling and squeaking to each other, sociable belugas glide through shallow waters in summer.

White whales go to moult in shallow inlets

As the Arctic sea ice begins to break up in July, hundreds of belugas, or white whales, gather in the Arctic Ocean off Greenland's west coast and head north-west. At their journey's end, in the shallower inlets of Canada's Arctic islands, the 9-15ft (2.7-4.5m) long whales splash, scream, moo, whistle or belch in noisy abandon as they scratch and rub themselves on the bottom sand and gravel to shed their thick, rough skin. The surprising noises that the belugas make has earned them the nickname of sea canaries.

With the coming of autumn, the belugas head back east to the open ocean, ahead of the forming pack ice that would prevent them from reaching the surface to breathe.

Not all belugas are white. Newborn babies are dark grey, but they gradually get paler as they grow older. Some are fully white by five years old, others take longer, but all are white by the time they are 12 years old.

Mating time is in late winter or spring, and the 5ft (1.5m) babies are born 14 months later. Their mothers suckle them for 1½-2 years. The youngsters often stay with their mother for years, forming a family group of up to 15 animals. Female belugas mature at about five years old, and males, which are slightly larger than females, at about eight years old. Males often join up in groups.

Well insulated by their thick layer of blubber, the chubby belugas are at home in the sub-zero temperatures of the Arctic Ocean. They dive to depths of around 1000ft (300m) to feed mainly on fish, which they find by echolocation. Their chief predator is the killer whale.

A kangaroo rat with its own signature tune

Whiskers twitching, a young banner-tailed kangaroo rat leaves the burrow where it was born earlier in the month, and sets out in the July dusk to establish its own territory in the Arizona desert. Following a rainy winter, there are plenty of seeds available for food, and the youngster is one of the second litter its parents have bred this season. The Arizona desert is home to a wide range of animals, many of which hide from the searing heat of the day.

Using its strong back legs and big feet, the 4in (100mm) long rat jumps to a clump of grass and begins a meal of seeds. A banner-tailed rat has hearing four times better than a human's, so can detect the slightest sound of an enemy such as a snake, owl or coyote. Then its powerful legs help it to make a speedy getaway, its long tail serving as a rudder and brake.

To announce its occupancy of a particular patch, each banner-tail drums on the ground with its hind feet, beating a tattoo that is its own individual signature tune. This makes it the first vertebrate animal known to have its own calling card using movement rather than voice. The drumming is not only used as a warning. When the mating season comes round, males may drum their tune to attract females.

Desert dweller At dusk, the banner-tailed kangaroo rat emerges from its desert burrow to forage for seeds, which it can carry home in its cheek pouches.

Pink walruses sunbathe beside northern seas

A group of male walruses is basking in the midsummer sun on Round Island, off Alaska's south-west coast. Each animal's skin is blushed pink, gorged with blood to lose heat from the massive surface area of his body. Although the walruses were grey when they emerged from the cold sea, after half an hour in the sun they have turned lobster pink as they get rid of heat. Each of these huge sunbathers is about 9ft 6in (2.9m) long and weighs about a ton. Many of the older walruses are battered and scarred from seasons of fighting rivals when courting females.

While the males enjoy the midsummer sunshine, most of the females are much farther north where they gave birth to their pups on the receding ice of late spring. By July, the pups are about two months old and still dependent on their mothers. Each female spends much of the day suckling her one youngster, which is covered with fine red down and already weighs as much as a man. A pup is usually suckled for about 18 months, but begins to eat some solid food after six months.

When not feeding her pup, the mother dives in shallow water to feed herself. Walruses feel their way along the seabed with sensitive, bristly whiskers each nearly as thick as a drinking straw. They extract mussels, clams and cockles from the mud by either digging with their snouts or blowing water jets into the creatures' burrows to flush them out.

By autumn, as the ice advances again, the pups are ready to swim south with their mothers to rejoin the males for the winter. It is here, in January and February, that the male walruses use their great ivory tusks for their courtship battles. These may seem ferocious, but fatal wounds are uncommon. A walrus has skin more than 2in (50mm) thick round the neck and shoulders, where tusk wounds are usually inflicted. Beneath the skin, blubber a hand's-width thick provides more protection from injury, as well as from the biting cold of the winter sea. A female walrus gives birth about 16 months after mating, so can bear a pup only about once every two years.

Keeping cool Male walruses lazing on Round Island in Bristol Bay, Alaska, turn pink in the sun. The walrus's skin becomes engorged with blood in warm weather as it gives off heat to keep the animal cool.

When grizzly bears go fishing for salmon

It is July, and once again the sockeye salmon are beginning to surge up the rivers of Alaska and of British Columbia in Canada in their exhausting quest for the headwaters where they hatched. Attracted by the teeming numbers, brown bears gather at the rapids, where the fish are most visible and most vulnerable.

They wait patiently on midstream ledges or at the water's edge, ready to snatch at the fish in midair as they leap the rapids, or scoop them up with a paw from the shallows where they halt for a moment to rest.

Normally solitary creatures, the bears tolerate each other's company as long as the salmon are running and they can gorge themselves on fish. At other times a male bear will chase off intruders from its home range of about 10sq miles (25sq km).

American brown bears are also known as grizzly bears because in some areas their brown fur is grizzled with grey. Fully grown and on all fours, a grizzly can stand about 5ft (1.5m) high at the shoulder. Reared on its hind legs, a big male can tower a spectacular 10ft (3m) from head to toe. A good-sized adult male turns the scales at about 50 stone (318kg), and the Kodiak bears of southern Alaska can weigh twice as much. The heaviest ever recorded weighed 118 stone (750kg) when it was shot on Kodiak Island in the Gulf of Alaska in 1894.

Kodiak bears are by far the largest of the grizzlies. They compete with polar bears for the title of the largest bear. A grizzly's massive size gives it immense strength. A 56 stone (355kg) bear has been known to kill a 70 stone (445kg) bison and drag it a considerable distance.

In spite of the grizzly's clumsy appearance and shambling gait, it can charge at a speed of 28mph (45km/h) – an angry grizzly is all but unstoppable. The bear's curious, swaying gait results from the fact that instead of moving its left and right feet forward alternately, it moves both left or both right feet forward together.

Once brown bears were found throughout Europe, Asia and North America, but numbers have declined over the centuries. In all three continents, they are commonest in remote fir

Fisherman's paradise *Summer heralds the return of the salmon, fighting their way upstream to spawn. Grizzly bears gather at the rapids, where the fish can be easily caught, and make the most of the river's bounty.*

Midair catch *Standing in the swirling water, a young male grizzly snatches a sockeye salmon in its jaws as the fish leaps the rapids on its journey up the river.*

and spruce forests bordering the Arctic Circle. The European brown bear also survives in small numbers in coniferous forests in mountainous areas such as the Pyrenees.

An adult bear's ability to lay waste a cornfield did not endear it to farmers, and bears were trapped, poisoned and shot into extinction in many places. In North America, black bears were once common as far south as Mexico, but with 90 per cent of its range altered by man, it is now endangered in many southern states.

Although grizzly bears eat meat, they also eat a wide variety of fruits and vegetables, including roots and even grass – up to 30lb (14kg) a day. They also take honey from the nests of wild bees, and youngsters climb with remarkable agility to reach nests high in the trees. Their thick coats make them impervious to the bee stings. So agile are brown bears, they can stand balanced on their hind legs on a broad branch.

After summer's plenty, the bears begin to put on weight during the autumn. Then, as winter approaches, each hibernates alone in a rock hole or cave, or under the roots of a tree – a place sheltered from the worst of the weather. Their body functions slow down and they live off their fat reserves. As spring approaches, the females give birth to their two or three cubs. Although each cub is only a mere 1lb (450g) at birth, within its first year it increases to some 14 stone (89kg). For a human baby, that would be equivalent to increasing its weight from 7lb (3kg) to 98 stone (622kg) in its first year or so of life!

A silken tent for a moth caterpillar family

Early on a July morning in New York State, the sunlight falls on a tent-like web hanging among the twigs of a black cherry tree. It is not a spider's web, but the home of a family of eastern tent caterpillars. As the morning temperature rises, the caterpillars inside the tent begin to warm up and move about.

The hairy, black and yellow caterpillars are the larvae of a type of eggar moth that lays its eggs on cherry trees. Other types of eggar moth prefer apple, plum or even oak trees. Last summer, a mottled brown female moth with a fat, hairy body laid her bark-coloured eggs in a string round a pencil-sized twig on the tree.

Those eggs not eaten by birds hatched out in spring, and as soon as they emerged from the eggs, the tiny caterpillars spun their tent. They used spinnerets on their rear ends to produce the silk, and worked together until it was complete. At first they stayed within the safety of the tent, feeding on the discarded shells of their own eggs and on any buds or leaves close by.

Now, as they grow, the caterpillars need to search for food farther afield, and as the day warms up, they leave the tent and spread out along the branches of the cherry tree to feed on its leaves. Once they venture out of their tent, the stout, juicy caterpillars become vulnerable to attack from predators, particularly birds and carnivorous ants. At night they return to the tent for protection.

In addition to their intricate web, the caterpillars have another defence. As they feed, their internal organs extract highly poisonous cyanide compounds from the black cherry leaves – the caterpillars leave scent trails to the best leaves for providing the compound. The cyanide becomes concentrated into a liquid which the caterpillar regurgitates if it is grasped by an ant or bird. The fluid containing the cyanide tastes quite foul to the predator, which will then usually leave the caterpillar alone. Even if some caterpillars are killed, the majority of the family will survive and benefit, because the local predators soon learn to avoid anything that looks like a tent caterpillar.

When the caterpillars are fully grown, each spins a silk cocoon in which it pupates (changes into a moth). In summer, the moths emerge to mate and lay the eggs, preferably on black cherry trees, that will develop into next year's generation. In a good year for these eggar moths, there can be so many tent caterpillars that they strip fruit trees bare of their leaves. This prevents the trees from using sunlight to produce food, and ruins the fruit crop.

Double defences *Eastern tent caterpillars shelter in a silken tent at night. They can vomit cyanide if attacked.*

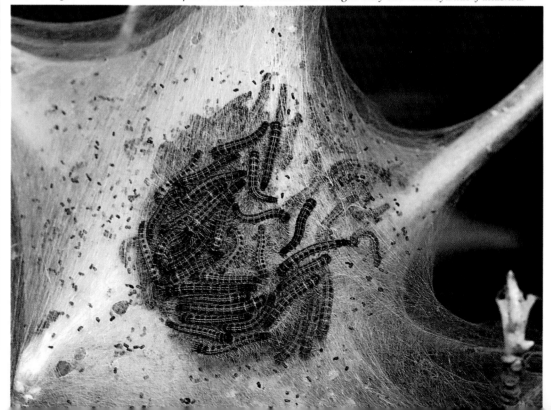

Filter feeding A whale's mouth breaks the surface, full of food and water. The upper jaw carries the baleen that filters the food. Scavenging birds sometimes get swallowed.

The humpback whale's room-sized mouth

Off the coast of Alaska, a huge creature looms through a sea teeming with life, for it is July – high summer. In one gulp it scoops up enough water to fill a room, and a whole shoal of fish disappears into the depths of its cavernous mouth. The monster's rounded black back and large, winglike flippers – which are nearly one-third the length of its body – identify it as a humpback whale. Although it weighs nearly 30 tons and is more than 40ft (12m) in length, this huge ocean mammal feeds on small fish such as herring and sardines, and also 2in (50mm) long, shrimp-like krill.

Microscopic plants (phytoplankton) thrive on the large amount of oxygen in the cold water. The smallest animals in the sea (zooplankton) eat the plants, and both types of plankton provide a rich food store for larger sea creatures. In summer, when sunlight encourages maximum plant growth, hundreds of species of fish and crustaceans (such as krill) thrive in the upper levels of the north Pacific. Northern Hemisphere humpback whales spend summer feasting in polar waters, and winters breeding in tropical waters, where there is little to eat.

To gather up the maximum amount of food, the humpback has about 30 pleats along its underside, running from chin to navel. With each gulp these pleats stretch to form a huge pelican-like pouch. It strains food from the water through a filter made up of several hundred horny (baleen) plates lining its upper jaw instead of teeth. Baleen, also misleadingly called whalebone, is a substance similar to human fingernails. Each plate ends in a bristly fringe that holds food when the water is forced out. Every day an adult humpback strains and eats a ton of food. One 45ft (14m) female was found to have 600 large herrings in her stomach.

A humpback sometimes engulfs its prey by soaring up from underneath to break through the water surface almost vertically. Prey is also corralled – the whale comes from below and slowly circles while releasing air bubbles. A chain of bubbles forms as it spirals, causing the prey to mill together. Then the whale bursts up through the bubble-net, mouth agape.

A mighty mouthful Pleats on the underside of the humpback whale allow it to open its mouth like a funnel as it rushes to engulf a school of fish or krill.

Blue streak The slender blue shark can reach speeds of around 40mph (64km/h). It has long pectoral (chest) fins.

Sharks on the move to warmer waters

In spring and early summer, the Atlantic Ocean warm-water belt shifts northwards as the sun's heat increases. With it moves a host of fast-swimming sea predators such as swordfish, sailfish and marlin. By July all have arrived to hunt and breed off North America's east coast.

Blue sharks, twice the length of a man, were the first to arrive in May, to mate off the New England coast. They moved ahead of the boundary between cold and warm water, taken as the 20°C (68°F) isotherm (a line joining places of equal temperature), so came into relatively cool seas. Like many sharks, they need to swim unceasingly to take in oxygen from the water passing through their gills. After mating, the male blue sharks have stayed in American waters, but the females are migrating across the ocean – following clockwise-flowing currents in the North Atlantic – to give birth in summer in the eastern Atlantic off Spain and Portugal.

During late June, short-fin mako sharks and swordfish – both about as long as the blue shark – arrived in the slightly warmer water behind the isotherm. Mako sharks have a heat-exchange system in the blood vessels supplying their swimming muscles. This keeps the muscles a few degrees warmer than the temperature of the surrounding water. As warm muscles are more efficient than cold, the mako can produce exceptional bursts of speed when chasing fast swimmers such as blue fish, squid, and the occasional swordfish.

A swordfish can sprint at about 40mph (64km/h) and has a heater behind each eye that keeps its eyes and brain warm. This makes it alert and quick to react whether hunting small fish or being hunted, and enables it to keep one jump ahead of marauding makos. The heater is a muscle filled with small blood vessels and packed in insulating fat. Blood carried between gills and brain goes through intricately plumbed arteries that transfer heat from the warm de-oxygenated blood that leaves the brain to the cold, oxygen-rich blood on the way from the gills, where oxygen is extracted from sea water.

In July, the largest and most dangerous of the sharks arrive – female great white sharks. These 20ft (6m) long monsters come north to give birth in the safety of deep-water coves and bays. They eat sea mammals and will attack humans, but here they feed mainly on whale carcasses.

Tiger sharks, up to 18ft (5.5m) long, follow in their wake. They have blunt snouts and are named for the faint blotches and vertical stripes on their backs, which become fainter with age. Tiger sharks eat almost anything – conches, crabs, lobsters, squid, bony fish, rays, dolphins, seals, sea turtles, seabirds, garbage, human remains, humans, and even other sharks. They come at a time of plenty, for many other sea creatures besides sharks breed, give birth or lay eggs along the American Atlantic coast between May and September. Nursery areas in bays and estuaries are comparatively safe from most big sharks, but not always from tiger sharks, which will swim in water as shallow as 7ft (2m). In autumn, predators and prey head south again as the warmer-water belt recedes southward.

Striped killer The powerful, thickset tiger shark is a voracious predator. Yet the remora, the small fish riding on its back, is tolerated by the shark.

Champion The fastest-known fish, a 12ft (3.7m) long sailfish can sprint at 68mph (110km/h) – faster than a cheetah.

Second set Large whites mating in July are from spring-laid eggs. Their eggs will be next spring's adults.

Courting complete After their elaborate dance, a pair of small skippers settle on a knapweed flower to mate.

Butterflies court in the summer sun

Two small skipper butterflies circle together in the warm July air over a European meadow, then rise and fall with their copper-coloured wings touching. The courting dance ends with the female's antennae stroking the male's wings, which makes him give out attractive scents. When she settles on a flower and raises her wings to expose her body, the male grasps the tip of her abdomen with claspers on his own tip. The pair mate like this, and fly clumsily while still coupled.

Afterwards the male leaves to court other females while the female darts about searching for long grasses such as Yorkshire fog and brome on which to lay her eggs. Over the next few days she will occasionally sip nectar, perhaps from a dandelion, but will spend most of her time laying batches of three to five eggs on blades of grass. Then her three or four weeks of life is over.

After three weeks, the eggs hatch into green caterpillars which do not feed, apart from eating their shells, but quickly spin silk cocoons in which to spend the winter. They do their feeding in spring, eating the grass chosen by the mother, before each makes a loose, tent-like cocoon of silk and grass in which it changes into an adult. All butterflies lay their eggs on or near the plants their caterpillars feed on. The large white, for example, cements its eggs on plants such as cabbages and hedge mustard, and the common blue lays its eggs on clover and other plants of the pea family.

WINGS BY DAY AND NIGHT

Food is probably the key to why, in the main, butterflies fly by day and moths by night. They fly when their own particular foodstuff is available, making the most of the food at hand by fitting into different niches. Butterflies feed from flowers that open by day, and night-flying moths from flowers that open at night. So the day fliers have colours that camouflage or are a warning to predators and rivals, but the night fliers are dull coloured and rely more on scent, so have elaborate scent organs.

Mating blues A male common blue shows off the violet upper sides of his wings to attract a mate. July adults are the second of two or three summer broods.

Fast and furious – the life of the shrew

Only slight upheavals in the thick July undergrowth covering the floor of an English woodland give the shrew away. Yet the little creature is perpetually scurrying hither and thither, for its life is an endless round of eating and searching for the next meal. It cannot even afford to sleep for long.

Food goes right through the shrew's system within three hours and the small creature carries little in the way of reserves in its finger-length body. It is on the go night and day between short naps, for it has to eat an amount equivalent to three-quarters of its own weight daily – mainly in earthworms and insects. Without food, it will die within 12 hours.

Despite their intense activity and great numbers, shrews are rarely seen because they lead their busy lives largely under cover. Rapidly tunnelling through dead leaves and grass, a shrew tracks down its prey with its acute hearing and smell, and the touch of the long ever-twitching whiskers on its pointed snout. Sharp teeth quickly tear victims apart.

Because of their constant need for food, shrews cannot afford to share a territory, so live alone. Every shrew vigorously defends its patch from other shrews, but if possible they avoid damaging physical combat, instead engaging in screaming matches with volleys of high-pitched squeaks. If neither gives way, one rears up to increase its stature, and only if this fails to impress do they come to blows.

Since both the sexes are equally aggressive, during the March-October breeding season a male shrew approaches a potential mate with caution – advancing, weaving, retreating. If not screamed at, he seizes his partner by the scruff of the neck. Females are receptive for less than 24 hours during each breeding cycle.

Between spring and late summer, when food is at its most plentiful, a female raises up to five litters in a nest of grass in her territory. The naked and helpless young, born after a pregnancy of 13-19 days, may be six to a litter. During the three weeks the mother suckles them, she has to eat twice as much as usual.

Young shrews feed themselves after weaning and have to survive winter before they breed in the following season. Their parents do not see a second winter; the hyperactive animals seldom live longer than 15 months. Most die of starvation in autumn because their much-used teeth are too worn down for them to eat. Shrews have few predators, apart from owls and foxes, because they are foul-tasting.

Throwing in the towel *In a fight over territory, one shrew concedes by flinging itself on its back. The other delivers a nip on the tail to underline its victory.*

Juicy morsel *Earthworms and insects are the favourite targets in the shrew's round-the-clock search for food.*

Launch pad *Once this young swift first takes off, it will be on the wing continuously for two years or more. It will feed, doze and, when mature, mate in the skies.*

Young swifts begin a flight lasting months

Leaving its nest for the first time, a young swift scans the blue July sky over Britain. High above, dark silhouettes are wheeling on long crescent wings, and their faint cries are the unmistakable screams of swifts, the most aerial of all birds. Within moments, the youngster will join the adults for its first flight.

It has spent many hours flexing its wings while peering out from the bowl-like nest under the eaves. The parent birds built the nest from feathers and leaves they caught as they flew, and pasted it together with saliva. Their two or three white eggs were laid in mid-May, and both parents shared in incubating them for three weeks. Then they both fed the youngsters constantly for seven or eight weeks.

Now, fully feathered and with astounding stamina, the young swifts are taking off to begin an independent life. Within hours of getting airborne, instinct leads them to embark on a journey of more than 6000 miles (9600km) to south-east Africa – and even then they will not touch down. They will be joined there by the adults, and all will winter in the warmth. The youngsters' first landing will be 22 months after leaving the nest – back in Europe where they may view possible nest sites for use when they are fully mature at three or four years old.

High summer huddle *Bats and their babies cluster in a soft, furry jumble on a roof timber in the nursery roost.*

Raising pipistrelle bats up in the roof

In the eerie light of the approaching July dawn, female pipistrelle bats flit back from their night of hunting insects. Their half-grown babies are waiting to be fed in the nursery – the roof-space of an English house. The bats, which are only about half as long as a little finger, neatly fold their wings and easily squeeze under a loose roof tile. They navigate in the gloom by echolocation – sending out high-frequency calls that bounce back from solid objects, warning the bats of obstructions. Although all the babies are huddled together, hanging with heads down from a beam, each mother identifies her own by its sound, and homes in to suckle it.

The young bats were born in the roof in late June. Birth is a tricky business for a mammal that spends most of its resting time hanging upside-down. Some female bats turn to hang tail down and cling to their roost with their wing claws so that gravity assists in labour. But most give birth while hanging upside-down, and catch the bald pink baby with their wings or in their tail membranes as it falls.

The tiny, blind creature is smaller than a walnut, but has strong claws on its feet and wings fully formed. Clinging on to its mother's fur with claws and milk teeth, the baby immediately clambers over her body until it reaches a nipple and clamps itself there until dusk. When the mother flies off to feed, the baby clings to the roost with all the other babies.

Within a week, the young bats can see and have grown greyish down. By two weeks they have their permanent teeth and at three weeks may take their first flight, following mother to the best feeding places. Male bats live separately and take no part in raising the babies. When they are five or six weeks old, the youngsters can catch insects for themselves, and find their way about by echolocation. They will not breed until they are at least two years old.

After raising a baby, the mother needs to regain lost weight and build up her fat reserves before the colder nights set in. She will mate in autumn when males and females gather in colonies together, but the sperm will remain dormant in her body throughout the three to four months of winter hibernation. Not until the bats begin to wake up in the warmth of spring will the female's egg (or occasionally a pair of eggs) be fertilised and pregnancy begin. It generally lasts from six to nine weeks, depending on the air temperature and the number of insects on the wing for the bats to eat. If the nights are cold and the daytime roost cool, the pregnancy is longer; if the female is warm and well fed, it is shorter. But next July the nursery will once again be brimming with baby bats.

A fishing marathon for puffin parents

With wings whirring rapidly, the sturdy, short-tailed puffin spreads its large orange feet to brake and lands on the cliff top of a remote European island. Its beak full of fish, it swivels its white-cheeked, clown-like face to check that all is safe, then waddles from the rock onto the grassy land behind and disappears underground to feed its waiting chick.

The breeding season began in April, with pairs of puffins working together to dig a burrow 3ft (1m) or more long. Some pairs saved themselves work by taking over an old rabbit burrow. Both parents took turns to incubate their single, purple and brown flecked white egg for about six weeks. Now in July the egg is hatched and the birds have barely six weeks of summer in which to fatten up their downy grey chick until it is the size of a plump partridge – seven times its present size and fatter than its parents.

All day long the puffins fly to and fro, bringing the chick sand eels, rockling and butterfish. To catch a meal, the birds sit on the water and dip their heads under to sight prey, then dive swiftly to catch it. The upper and lower rims of a puffin's open beak are parallel, so it can hold securely a row of small fish, carried crossways.

As its time in the nest nears an end, the chick is fed less often. By then it is very active, flapping its wings frequently to strengthen them. Eventually, one dark night, the youngster half flies, half tumbles down to the sea and launches itself into life as a seabird.

Singular catch *The plump sand eel in the puffin's heavy, handsome beak will make a satisfying meal, as good as half a dozen smaller fish, for the waiting chick.*

Water babies Two young otters play in the water – for which they are well adapted. They can see, hear and breathe with only part of the head above water.

Young otters learn to be expert swimmers

As the two otter kits roll and tumble in a secluded Scottish river on a sunny July morning, they are perfectly at home in the water. Now four months old, they are a far cry from the reluctant water babies that dog-paddled desperately on their first swim, in no way resembling the fluid movements of their mother keeping watch close by.

Baby river otters – blind, rat-sized and unable even to crawl – are born in spring in a well-hidden den, or holt. They learn to swim in summer, when their adult coats have grown, but are not eager. Their mother whistles and dives to encourage them, but sometimes has to push them in. After learning to swim, the alert, boisterous juveniles start to accompany their mother on her nightly hunting trips. The bulk of their food is fish, but otters pounce on frogs, ducks and other water birds, and will take small land mammals such as voles. Otters often dive beneath fish and grab them from below. They usually carry their catch ashore to eat it.

When not sleeping, hunting or grooming, the kits spend their time in play, chasing each other underwater and grappling together on dry land. In this way they learn the skills that will make them into fast and nimble predators. Once independent at about a year old, the otters will keep mostly to their own stretch of territory alongside the water. Male otters regularly mark their patch with strong-smelling oil, deposited with their droppings, to warn off other males, but females have less clear-cut home ranges.

Leaf-cutter bees build for the next generation

A small bee drones heavily across an English garden on a sunny July afternoon – apparently astride a sleek green vehicle. Its progress is slow and erratic, for the bee is carrying a piece of leaf. This female leaf-cutter bee, having sought out a male and mated, is beginning the task of building a nest in which to lay her eggs. With her strong, saw-edged jaws, she first shears an oval piece out of a supple new leaf – rose, lilac, willow and laburnum are especial favourites. A bush raided by several bees is riddled with holes and looks as if it has been peppered by gun fire.

After cutting, the bee folds the leaf section lengthwise, grips it in her jaws and lumbers off to the chosen nesting site. This is usually a tunnel left in an old tree stump where a beetle larva has emerged, or may be a hollow stem of cow parsley. The site must be dry and sheltered from the worst of the weather, as it will have to protect the developing offspring all winter.

The bee rolls the oval piece of leaf into a cylinder and pushes it into the tunnel as far as she can. Then she flies back to the same plant and cuts a round piece of leaf which she pushes into the cylinder to seal the bottom. Next she flies from flower to flower collecting pollen and nectar, then mixes it together until it is a syrup of pollen and honey and stuffs it into the chamber. With preparations complete, the bee lays a single egg in the chamber, which she closes with another round section of leaf cemented in place with juices from her mouth.

This process is repeated until the tunnel is filled with a line of egg chambers. Then the bee seeks another suitable place and does the same again. She lays unfertilised eggs, which become females, at the bottom of the tunnel and fertilised eggs, which will be males, at the top. The males will hatch first and fly off, lessening the chances of them mating with their sisters. In all, some 20 or 30 chambers are filled and sealed. Afterwards the exhausted bee dies.

When the eggs hatch, the tiny white grubs begin to feed on their private larders. By autumn, each grub is growing too big for its withering chamber and develops a hard protective case, a chrysalis, in which it spends winter inside the tunnel. If the mother has chosen her nest site well, the chrysalis will escape damp and the notice of birds, mice and predatory beetles, and survive until spring, when the adult bee that has developed within it will emerge.

Making a safe nest A female leaf-cutter bee cuts a piece of pliable rose leaf, then carries it to the nest site she has chosen – a narrow hole running into rotten wood. There she rolls the leaf and inserts it in the hole.

Sealing the larder The bee fills the leaf tube with nectar and pollen, lays an egg in it and closes the end with a piece of leaf. She continues making similar egg chambers until a line of them fills the nest hole.

The hunting skills of a web-footed fishing cat

After a drought lasting nearly eight months, the weather breaks. Heavy downpours quench the dried-up lakes and rivers of northern India as the monsoon season gets under way in late June. At a patch of protected marshland in Bharatpur in north-east Rajasthan, fresh shoots appear on the reeds and grasses that fringe the river, which is alive with fishes, frogs and crabs. Painted storks and sarus cranes go fishing in the shallows, and ibis and egrets look down from the trees.

The Bharatpur marsh is renowned for its birdlife, but the eyes that peer from between the reeds, fixed on the water, are not those of a bird. The animal lying patiently in wait is a cat. Timing its action just right, the cat suddenly hurls itself into the water with a loud splash. Moments later it surfaces with a flapping fish clamped between its jaws. Dripping wet from

Slippery catch A fishing cat grabs a writhing fish with its paw. This cat even swims underwater to capture a meal.

ANIMALS ON ALERT

An earthquake occurs when the friction and stress from deep underground movements builds up energy that is suddenly released at a weak spot in the earth's crust. Animals can often sense such things as tiny ground vibrations, changes in air pressure, and shifts in the earth's magnetic field up to 24 hours before an earthquake, and cats have been known to move their kittens from disturbed areas. Observers at Tianjin Zoo in China noted before the 1969 earthquake that tigers stopped pacing, a panda held its head and moaned and swans left the water. Scientists are now studying such reactions as aids to forecasting earthquakes.

head to foot, the cat, aptly named the fishing cat, clambers onto the riverbank, shakes itself, and settles in a secluded spot to demolish its meal.

Whether it dives in headfirst, swims underwater or paddles up to its neck, the solidly built fishing cat is completely at home in the water. It even has slightly webbed feet on its short, muscular legs and cannot entirely retract its claws. Its coat is waterproof, because the layer of dense fur next to its skin is kept dry by an outer layer of longer, coarser fur. Not only does the fishing cat hunt in deep water, it also crouches at the water's edge and scoops up a fish with one swipe of its paw.

Crabs, frogs and freshwater molluscs such as snails supplement its diet of fish, and any small creature that comes to drink at the water is also in danger. In times of drought a fishing cat has

to make do with mice, lizards and birds, and probably goes hungry – although it has a reputation for fearlessness and there are reports of fishing cats killing prey as large as young leopards, eagles, goats and dogs.

At first glance, a fishing cat could be mistaken for an outsize domestic tabby, for it has grey fur with darker stripes running over its head, and darker body spots and stripes. But its face is longer, its eyes closer together and its tail thicker and shorter, reaching only to the cat's heel when it is standing. A male is about 3ft (1m) long and can weigh more than 2 stone (13kg).

Fishing cats are elusive and uncommon, and are perhaps becoming more so as their habitat is being destroyed. They never stray far from water and keep to areas of the thickest vegetation amid marshes, mangrove swamps and forests.

AFRICA

Life on the rocks for a family of hyraxes

As the sun warms the rough boulders of a rocky outcrop on south-west Africa's arid plains on a July morning, the basking rock hyraxes stir themselves into action. Unlike most mammals they cannot control their body temperature very well, so before getting going in the morning they bask in the sun to warm up.

Three young hyraxes only a few days old scuttle playfully across the boulders. They are miniature versions of their furry, rabbit-sized parents. While the youngsters explore their barren surroundings, their mother keeps a watchful eye for black eagles, leopards, lions, jackals and snakes – all ready to make a meal of a hyrax, young or old.

With their blunt faces, plump bodies and stumpy tails, rock hyraxes look rather like guinea pigs and were once classed as belonging to the same order – rodents, or gnawing animals. Now they are known to be descended from primitive hoofed mammals, and their closest living relatives are the elephant, the aardvark (or ant-bear) and the sea cow. Hyraxes have rubbery pads on their toes and especially sweaty feet, which helps them to get a good grip on the rocky slopes of their home.

They live in family groups of one adult male, several adult females, and their offspring, and choose to live only among rocks where there are plenty of nooks and crannies in which to hide. They live on coarse, poor grass and leaves, and seldom need to drink. Groups feed by cropping a small patch of grass within easy reach of bolt holes, and one of them – usually the adult male – is always on lookout duty. All dash for cover if he utters a sharp cry of alarm.

The hyraxes' rocky refuge provides shelter as well as safety, and they spend a lot of time there. During the hottest hours they seek shady nooks where the surrounding temperature is fairly constant and they can keep a comfortable body heat. At night when the temperature drops, they huddle together in crannies to keep warm.

Separate family groups often live close together, but at mating time males defend their territories and sometimes fight fierce battles over females, who are receptive for only a few days each year. In south-west Africa mating is in December, before temperatures soar to 32°C (90°F) in January, so that after a pregnancy of about eight months the two or three babies are born in the cool of July. The youngsters are suckled for up to six months, and become sexually mature at 16 months old. Young females stay with the family, but males join the fringes of other groups, ready to take the place of a dominant male if the opportunity arises.

Sun worshippers *Rock hyraxes (also known as dassies) bask in the morning sun to raise their body temperatures for action. One of their closest relatives is the elephant.*

to return to the comparative safety of their den.

The den is no grand affair, but simply a hollow or tunnel abandoned by some other animal. After about two weeks' use, the mother often decides to move the family on to a similar shelter. When the pups are three months old, they no longer need a den and stay out in the brush with the rest of the family. By five months old they go with the foraging party and join in the feast direct – although as long as they stay with their parents they may occasionally have food regurgitated for them.

Rats, mice and fruits make up most of the silverbacked jackals' diet – fruit of the balanites tree is a particular favourite. Because the tree is in fruit, and because the rat numbers are at their annual peak, at the time when the young jackals are born between July and October, there are plenty of delicacies for nursing mothers and for pups when they are weaned. The jackals also eat insects, snakes, frogs, birds and smaller mammals such as hares and Thomson's gazelles, as well as a small amount of carrion.

FAMILY POWER

For jackals, keeping together as a family is the best way of ensuring the survival of their species. The family rests, eats, feeds, grooms and hunts together. The breeding male and female mate only with each other, and they remain mates for as long as they are able to defend their territory – which may even be for life.

Hunting together gives the jackals an advantage. Not only are they more likely to make a catch than a single jackal or a twosome, they are less likely to lose their kill to vultures. Together they can ward off marauders while they share an amicable meal.

Hunting jackals bound along enthusiastically, each of them slim, long-legged, about 3ft (1m) long in the body and 18in (460mm) high at the shoulder. Their large ears are pricked alertly forward, their dark, bushy tails are extended and the silver-flecked black saddles show prominently on their fine tan fur. Yelps and barks help them to keep in contact with one another.

The family forages over a territory of up to 1sq mile (2.6sq km), established by the breeding pair and held by them throughout the year. If it has a good food supply, the same territory may be used year after year. The male and female both scent-mark its boundaries with their urine, and ferociously drive out any intruding jackals. The 24lb (11kg) female fights off any females and the slightly heavier male tackles any males. They are clever combatants and agile in manoeuvre.

Family ties An older sister returning to the family den after foraging gets an eager welcome from one of the new litter of pups she is helping to care for.

for another month before it starts to eat the same food as the older jackals – brought back to the den and regurgitated for it by one of its parents or an older brother or sister.

This pup is a privileged one. The fourth of a litter of six, it has survived only because its mother has helpers – her home-bred au pairs. A male and a female from last year's offspring did not leave the family when they became sexually mature at 11 months old but stayed on for a year to assist their parents. They behave submissively to them, and also remain infertile until they leave to set up their own dens, because the breeding pair would not tolerate competitors.

If the mother and father had tried to rear the litter on their own, only one pup would have had a fair chance of survival. With one helper, three might have survived. With two helpers on hand, four of the litter are alive and doing well.

TASKS FOR MOTHER'S HELPERS

During the pups' first three weeks of life, their mother was with them in the den almost constantly. The helpers brought back enough food to keep her fit and ensure she had an ample milk supply for four pups. Now that the pups are out and about, the mother can go off hunting with her mate. She leaves the helpers to watch over the litter. If danger threatens, the elders bark a warning to the pups, telling them

Close bond *Mutual grooming helps to cement the long-lasting bond between a male and female jackal.*

The family firm shares in raising jackals

As the silverbacked jackal returns home from a foraging expedition in the dry brush of an East African woodland, she exchanges an affectionate nuzzling with a tiny pup pouncing and pawing around her. The homeward-bound hunter is not the pup's mother but its older sister, one of last year's litter.

The pup is one of this season's first litter, born at the beginning of July and just four weeks old. It made its first outing from the den only a week ago and goes back there frequently to rest and feed. Mother's milk will be its only nourishment

Haunting love songs for humpback whales

A haunting sound echoes from the sea off Australia's east coast in July. It is the eerie song of the humpback whales. After feeding on krill in the cold Antarctic seas, these huge 43ft (13m) mammals migrate to warmer waters where they breed and spend the winter.

Some gather off the southern tip of Australia's Great Barrier Reef. First to arrive at the breeding grounds are the solitary males. Only they sing, and mostly during the mating season. Their songs, which carry at least 18 miles (30km), are probably an invitation to females. They may also help to space out the males and reduce conflict.

Nevertheless, once the cows appear they are pursued by several suitors. A female keeps the same partner for only a day or two at a time. He stops singing while he is with her, but starts again once she has gone. Running through his repertoire morning, noon and night, he pauses only to surface for breath.

All the humpback whales of the same population sing the same set of songs and keep to the same basic themes, but each whale makes up individual variations. These may identify them to their rivals.

The songs the whales sing are the longest and most complicated of any animal, and can last up to 35 minutes. The sounds are not random; they are musical notes with low pulses and tones sweeping up and down the scale in an ordered sequence. Like birdsong, the sounds fall into a repeated pattern.

The whale songs, however, gradually change from one season to the next, with phrases rearranged and new ones added. All the whales change their songs to the current version, and memorise them from one year to the next, singing the themes in exactly the same way at the start of the next breeding season.

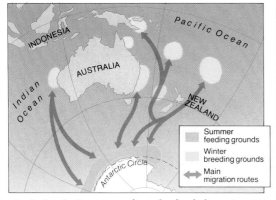

Back track *Every year, humpback whales return to the same areas to breed – off Australia's east or west coast or the south Pacific islands.*

Whale road *A humpback whale shepherds her calf as she migrates from Antarctica to winter off Australia.*

House husband *The male brown kiwi sits on the exceptionally large eggs of his mate for up to three months. He also digs out most of the nest burrow.*

Flightless kiwis nest in forest burrows

Hidden among tree roots in a forest in North Island, New Zealand, is what looks like a large rabbit burrow. Yet inside there are one or two large ivory-white eggs each weighing about 1lb (450g). This is the nest of a brown kiwi, a bird about the size of a domestic hen, which lays the biggest eggs in relation to its body size of any bird. Kiwis begin breeding in July. After laying her eggs, the female leaves the male to do all the incubating. He sits on the eggs for 9-12 weeks, which is one of the longest incubation periods of any bird.

Within a week of hatching, the young kiwis are accompanying their parents on foraging expeditions in the forest after dark. Kiwis cannot fly – they have stumpy, functionless wings concealed by feathers. The birds cut rather strange figures as they lope along at speed, their tailless, pear-shaped bodies covered in dark, shaggy, hair-like plumage.

But the heavy-footed kiwis are more likely to be heard than seen. The male announces his presence with shrill 'ki-wi' calls. Loud snorts also give the birds away as their long, curved beaks probe the dead leaves on the forest floor.

Unlike most other birds, the kiwi has an excellent sense of smell. The nostrils at the tip of its beak enable it to sniff out worms, slugs and insect larvae deep underground.

Dauntless fathers Hundreds of male emperor penguins incubate their eggs on the Antarctic sea ice. They cluster in a tight group to keep warm.

Emperor penguins hatch eggs on the ice

July finds the Antarctic in winter's grip, with an average temperature of −20°C (−4°F) and a constant icy wind – blizzards sometimes gust at up to 125mph (200km/h). Yet here on the sea ice, in some of the most extreme conditions on earth, hundreds of penguins are standing.

They are male emperor penguins, over 3ft (1m) tall. Each is a father incubating an egg balanced carefully on his feet under an insulating fold of belly skin. Huddled closely together to keep warm, the birds form a huge circular group called a 'tortue'. Each bird rests his beak on the bird in front, and the group slowly spirals as birds on the outside shuffle closer to the centre. The birds do not feed, and those in the middle use up only half as much of their body fat daily as those on the outside. During the six weeks of incubation, each bird will lose nearly half its body weight.

The penguins gathered in May, shuffling and tobogganing over the ice and snow on their bellies. In June, after a brief and noisy courtship and mating, each female presented her mate with a single egg. Then she left him to incubate it and returned to sea to feed. Diving after fish and squid is hard work. She needs to eat 6lb (2.7kg) of food a day just to survive, but may catch only one squid in every ten dives.

The chicks usually hatch just as the females return, and the mothers feed them a meal of regurgitated food. If the mother is late, the father can feed the chick for a few days with a protein-rich milk produced in his gullet. On her return, the mother takes over the task of caring for the chick for the next few weeks while the male goes to sea to feed and recover. After that, the large, fluffy, brown chick is fed by both parents. While both are away, the chicks gather into crèches to keep warm.

By December, the youngsters are ready to go to sea and fend for themselves. One chick in five will not survive its first year. Killer whales and leopard seals are the chief predators.

Snug chick A two-week-old penguin chick rests on its mother's feet, protected in a pouch-like fold of skin.

AUGUST

CARIBOU RUT IN THE NORTH AS TOOTH-BILLED CATBIRDS
SET THE STAGE FOR COURTING IN THE SOUTH. BRITISH HARVEST MICE WEAVE
NESTS, GREEK TIGER MOTHS SLEEP IN THE SUMMER HEAT
AND IN THE FLOODED AMAZON DOLPHINS SWIM AMONG TREE BRANCHES

North America: Killer whales trap a feast of salmon

THE ARCTIC

When caribous clash in the Arctic summer

As the Arctic summer draws to its close in August, male caribous, fattened on the varied fodder of far northern pastures, are ready for the most serious business of the year – the rut, when they fight for females.

The caribou herds arrived on the northern pastures – the tundra of Alaska and Arctic Canada – as it was unlocked from winter's snow in June. The newly emerged flowers and marsh grasses carpeting the ground in a rich profusion of colour offered a welcome change of food after a winter and spring spent in less snow-bound country to the south.

Soon the first snow will fall, and the caribous, close relatives of the European reindeer, will begin to drift south again. While the females wander in small groups searching out the most succulent grazing, the males carve out breeding territories for themselves. Females will mate only with males who are strong enough to command a territory, and with the chance to mate at stake, competition for territories among the males is intense.

A caribou male gallops to challenge a likely rival who follows a group of females onto the territory he is trying to establish. The two males pace up and down side by side, stiff-legged and with their 4ft (1.2m) spread of antlers tossing as they throw back their heads and give vent to harsh roars. The interloper is not easily intimidated, and matches the owner roar for roar while the pair assess each other's strength. Roaring is a surprisingly tiring activity, and only males with large reserves of stamina can keep it up for long. Weaker challengers quickly retreat.

If the challenger refuses to back down, the two will come to blows. Heads lowered, they lock their spreading but spindly antlers, which act as a springy cushion to push against. Twisting and shoving, the contestants strive to throw each other off balance. Although the main aim of the tussle is to discourage the rival by a show of strength, caribous are sometimes injured through a mistimed parry. Some males have as many as 40 tines (prongs) along the outer edges of their antlers, and these can inflict a lethal wound if they pierce an eye or puncture the skin over a vital organ. To reduce the risk, the males grow thicker skin and a mane of longer white fur over the neck and chest for this period of display and challenge.

Females wander at will across the territories of one male after another. Each male in turn will try to prevent them from leaving. The larger the territory a male can hold, the more females it will contain for him to mate with, and the greater his chances of fathering offspring. As there are far fewer territories than there are candidates for them, only the largest and most powerful males, those about 5ft (1.5m) high at the shoulder and weighing up to 50 stone (318kg), can withstand the onslaughts of eager rivals desperate to mate.

A territory holder must continue to evict intruding rivals throughout the breeding period, so has little time for feeding. Growing weaker by the day, he is eventually forced off by a stronger animal – if hunger does not make him leave of his own accord. Some males leave it too late. By the end of the mating season, many are too weak to survive the rigours of the following winter, by which time the herd will have migrated southwards to wooded areas. The surviving males band into bachelor herds. When the young are born on the tundra next June, their mothers will have sole care of the new arrivals, suckling them for two months before rejoining the herd.

Down to work *Frequent trials of strength with locked antlers exhaust the male caribous vying for a territory.*

THE MATING URGE

Spring sets in motion the yearly reproductive cycle of many animals, bringing a surge of sex hormones from the body's glands. This surge is timed by the pineal gland in the brain. The pea-sized gland contains pigments sensitive to light, which register changes from daylight to darkness and the seasonal changes in day length.

In caribous, when the gland registers that daylight exceeds darkness, it triggers the release of the hormones. They build up in both males and females over the following few months, and spur them to carry out the courting rituals that culminate in mating.

The cycle is timed so that the young are born in early summer, when the mothers can eat ample new grass and so produce plenty of milk for the newborn.

How musk oxen keep the wolves at bay

A herd of some 20 shaggy beasts rumble and belch contentedly as they graze peacefully on the brief summer plenty in the Canadian Arctic. They are musk oxen, standing about 4ft 6in (1.4m) high at the shoulder and weighing 55 stone (350kg) or more.

Suddenly the animals stiffen and swing round to face the late-setting August sun. Out of the haze, a wolf pack emerges, trotting resolutely against the wind towards the herd. A momentary veering of the breeze has carried their scent towards the musk oxen and at once the giant animals bunch together and form a defensive ring with heavy horned heads pointing outwards and narrow hips towards the centre. The calves cluster inside the ring, protected by the massive wall of muscle, bone and horn.

The wolves approach warily and circle carefully round, searching for weak points in the living stockade. As long as the musk oxen hold their formation, the wolves are powerless to do anything, for their intended prey have thick fur and horns big enough to thwart all but the most determined wolves. Only if they can provoke the musk oxen to break ranks and run will the wolves stand any chance of making a kill.

Suddenly one wolf races in and tries to snap at the muzzle of an old male in a bid to shift him. But the veteran swipes at the attacker with a lazy toss of his hooked horns and the wolf is lucky to get away without a nasty injury. Their first positive ploy having failed, the wolves settle for a prolonged test of nerves, stalking warily round the circle hoping that one of the giants will crack. Although musk oxen think nothing of standing immobile for days at a time during winter snowstorms, this time they are being harassed by snapping jaws all round. Eventually a defender breaks away and the wolves home in on a mother and calf.

Only after the killing is over and the wolves have receded into the haze do the musk oxen resume their endless search for grass. Despite their resemblance to cattle, they are related to sheep and goats and share the family habit of continuous feeding – no easy task in such poor country and with such a huge bulk to sustain.

....

Defensive circle *When wolves threaten, musk oxen form a circle (top), with weapons pointing out and calves guarded within. Only when panic breaks the ring (centre), can the wolves get a calf as victim (bottom).*

NORTH AMERICA

How killer whales hunt together as a team

Throughout the day on August 5 each year, fishing boats gather in Johnstone Strait, between Vancouver Island and the Canadian mainland. By evening there is a flotilla of about 300. They are waiting for 6pm, the start of the fishing season, when they can begin catching the summer run of millions of sockeye salmon returning unerringly from the Pacific Ocean to the river in which they hatched. Also in wait are the resident killer whales.

Killer whales, or orcas, are the largest of the dolphins. A bull, recognised by its tall, straight dorsal (back) fin, can be up to 32ft (9.8m) long and weigh 10½ tons. Cows are smaller.

There are 19 groups, or pods, of killer whales living all year round in Johnstone Strait and Puget Sound to the south. Each pod consists of 4-40 closely related animals, and each has its own home range where it hunts for squid and fish. Salmon make up their diet for much of the year – the spring salmon (or 'smileys') that run between spring and July, the sockeye salmon that arrive in summer, and the coho, humpback and chum salmon that come in autumn. Sometimes the chum arrive in winter.

To survive, each killer whale must eat the equivalent of one-twentieth of its body weight daily. So every day a bull killer whale needs about 75 salmon, each weighing 15lb (7kg). The key to the resident killer whales' successful survival is that each pod hunts cooperatively.

When searching for food, a pod swims close to the surface, each animal about 40yds (37m) from its neighbour. Among them are youngsters learning from their parents how to conduct the

Cooperating killers *A pod of killer whales traps a shoal of salmon (right and below). It is thought the killer whales may use high-intensity beams of sound to immobilise the fish, making them easier to catch.*

hunt. The pod members keep in touch with loud honks and screams as they slowly draw closer together. Then they stop calling and form a U-shaped phalanx round a shoal of salmon and drive them towards the shore. The trapped fish are then picked off one by one.

Eventually, a signal is given – probably by the pod's matriarch (bulls, despite their size, do not have the same social status as the older cows) – and the whales submerge and move off. They reappear some distance away and start to attack another shoal of salmon.

Occasionally, a killer whale pushes the upper one-third of its body vertically out of the water, behaviour known as 'spy-hopping'. In this way it can look round and see where fishing boats or flocks of gulls are located, both useful clues in helping to find another meal.

While the residents are hunting salmon, another type of killer whale – known as the 'transient' – is passing through the area. The 30 transient pods do not have particular home ranges but migrate up and down the coast in search of their prey. Unlike the resident pods, they will take prey such as seals and sea lions, and turn up at breeding colonies when the vulnerable youngsters are taking their first swim. The killer whales swim close to the shore and – although they communicate with squeaks and moans while they are travelling – home in on their victims in silence.

KILLER WHALE DIALECTS

The calls made by the young resident killer whales are learned from the older members of their own pod. Consequently, each pod has its own dialect. Research has shown that several pods have similar dialects and can be grouped together in 'clans'.

All the pods in the same clan are the descendants of a common ancestral group that grew and split several times. As time went on, each new pod developed separately from the others, so different dialects developed as the pods gradually drifted apart. Pods within the same clan share certain of their calls, whereas pods in different clans have few calls in common.

In the Johnstone Strait area there are four clans containing 19 pods – one clan of 10 pods, one of 4 pods, one of 3 pods, and one of 2 pods. The ancestral pod of the largest clan most likely arrived in the area before the smaller clans, so has had more time to divide and form more sub-groups.

Bat scramble *Millions of Mexican free-tailed bats emerge each evening from their summer nursery in Texas.*

Flying free-tailed bats ground an Air Force

At dusk on an August evening, bats by the million emerge from their nursery caves in Texas and New Mexico, and in a flurry of flimsy wings climb to 10,000ft (3000m) for a night's feeding. At Randolph US Air Force Base in Texas, the evening departure and morning return of these Mexican free-tailed bats show clearly on the radar screens, and air traffic controllers schedule flights to avoid them. The short tail extending beyond the edge of its rear membranes gives the bat the name free-tailed.

Each ½ oz (14g) bat eats half its weight in insects every night, so a population of 50 million eats about 127,000 tons of insects a year. The bats quickly eat up the local insects and may have to fly up to 40 miles (65km) a night to feed. Great horned owls keep down bat numbers at Carlsbad Caverns, New Mexico, snatching bats as they swarm from their caves each night.

After eating their fill during summer, the bats fly south some 800 miles (1300km) to Mexico, and feast on insects there through the winter.

Courting complete *Two queen butterflies mate after the male has soothed the female with his scent for hours.*

Skilled brushwork *Fine brushes extended from the abdomen of the male queen butterfly spread a scented aphrodisiac dust over the female to coax her to mate.*

Butterflies court with scented messages

Roadside verges still shimmer with wild flowers in late summer in the south-eastern United States, and wherever milkweeds grow, there are likely to be queen butterflies busily sipping the nectar, searching for mates or laying their eggs. In August, they are all the more noticeable for being in pairs, fluttering their rich brown wings that have bold black rims vividly spangled with white. They are absorbed in a courtship ritual that must be followed step by step if they are to mate successfully.

First the male and female find each other by scent and sight. The female gives out chemicals called pheromones that the male scents from a distance with his sensitive antennae.

The female recognises him by his appearance. However, as well as seeing him with the colours perceived by a human eye, she also sees an ultraviolet image that is invisible to humans.

Once the butterflies have found each other, the male hovers a little above and ahead of the female, then pushes out from his abdomen brush-like tufts known as hair pencils. Each fluffs out into 400 or so fine filaments covered with sticky, scented, pheromone-coated dust.

As he flies close above his partner, the male frequently dips to touch her, brushing her head and particularly her antennae with the sexually exciting dust, which sticks to her. Only if she is liberally anointed with this aphrodisiac will the female be encouraged to stay when the male approaches her to mate. Even so, it may take four or five hours before she is calm enough to settle on a flower or on the ground.

He lands between her wings and then they mate tip to tip, the female's wings partly cradling the male's and the male stroking her persistently. Afterwards, still locked with his mate, the male carries off the passive female to a secluded spot where they stay for several hours.

MALE IMAGE

The wings of many male pierid butterflies – those in the family of Whites and Yellows – are different from those of the females. Some of the tiny overlapping wing scales have ridges that reflect ultraviolet light, believed to be the means by which the females recognise the males. An ultraviolet-detecting camera can show a male pierid as his mate sees him.

Human view *Cream wings are edged with black.*

Mate's view *Centre reflects ultraviolet light.*

The dolphins' game of chase and catch

Smooth as a mirror, the dead calm waters of the Gulf of California lie under warm August air unstirred by any breath of wind. For hours the only sound has been the mournful chorus from distant Heermann's gulls circling idly. But now a sound like rushing water carries across the sea. As the noise comes closer, the surface of the water begins to seethe and soon a school of hundreds of dolphins passes by, leaping and plunging vigorously across the gulf.

The tan and grey bands on their black flanks show them to be common dolphins – slender, agile sea mammals up to 8ft 6in (2.6m) long. The dolphins are on the trail of a shoal of sardines.

The Gulf of California is a strip of water some 700 miles (1120km) long and only about 60 miles (100km) wide in parts. It lies between Mexico's mainland coast and the elongated western finger of land called Baja California. For the sardines and common dolphins the gulf is the arena for an eternal contest, with the silvery little fish and their sleek-backed pursuers moving to and fro across its waters, spurred by the seasonal pattern that the winds dictate.

The sardines spawn along the gulf's mainland coast in winter, when winds push the water away from the shore. An infill of cold water therefore wells up from the seabed alongside the coast and returns nutrients to the surface, encouraging the development of plankton.

This makes it a good time for the fish to spawn, as there will be ample food for the developing young. In spring, as the wind changes and the water warms, most of the adult and juvenile sardines move away from the mainland coast and are carried by the current across the narrow gulf.

Common dolphins are noisy creatures with a repertoire of clicks and whistles that can be clearly heard when a school passes. The echoes that bounce back help them to locate shoals of fish, and underwater mountains and canyons. Sometimes, however, they navigate in silence, especially when the sea is glassy and visibility good. Perhaps in good weather they navigate by the sun, and it is likely that the earth's magnetic field helps them.

The dolphins follow the movements of the sardines and by August they have congregated in the Canal de Ballenas, a narrow strait between Baja California and Angel de la Guarda, an island towards the north of the gulf. Here, strong currents have scoured a deep channel where the waters stay cool during summer.

To feed, the dolphins swim rapidly through a shoal of sardines, sending out a stream of high-frequency sound. The sound may confuse and panic the fish – it certainly makes them pack tightly together, as does the action of the dolphins as they leap in and out of the water. When densely packed, the fish are easier to catch. The dolphins snap up the slippery morsels in their beak-like mouths, which are lined with 180 sharply pointed teeth.

Groups of Bryde's whales may also follow the sardines. The whales feed by taking huge gulps of seawater and fish, then squeezing the water out again through the hair-like mesh called baleen in their mouths; the fish are left behind trapped in the baleen.

In late October, with the wind coming from offshore once more, the sardines, the dolphins and the whales begin moving eastwards to return to the mainland coast and complete their yearly journey round the gulf.

As well as hunting sardines at the surface, common dolphins regularly plunge to some 200ft (60m) at night to chase smelt and lantern fish. One dolphin has been recorded diving to 846ft (258m). A captive common dolphin holds the dolphin high-jump record at 21ft 6in (6.6m).

Dolphin circus Panicking a shoal of fish by leaping among them with high-frequency calls, a school of common dolphins crosses the Gulf of California. The dolphins are following sardines, a favourite food.

Common dolphins are among the speediest of dolphins, frequently reaching speeds of about 27mph (43km/h), and they are experts at riding along on the bow wave of a ship.

Among the most numerous of the dolphins, common dolphins are found in all the temperate and subtropical seas, sometimes in huge assemblies. Schools of several thousand have been seen catching anchovies and sprats in the Black Sea. Another school recorded off New Zealand was 32 miles (51km) long and ½ mile (800m) wide.

lengthways into eight or more strips with her sharp teeth. Then she weaves the strips, still attached to the stem at the base, into a framework, along with at least 20 more leaves split in the same way. Next, the mouse draws more blades through from inside, shredding and weaving them in until the nest is about the size of a tennis ball. Finally, she lines the plaited walls with layers of soft, finely chewed grass. The nest has no entrance. The mouse comes and goes through the walls, which are elastic enough to close up after her.

A litter may number up to eight babies, born blind, naked and only a tenth of their mother's weight. They start to grasp at two days old, and climb before they can walk. After nine days they can eat seeds, insects and other solid food. At 15-16 days old they are weaned and abandoned.

Young females can conceive at roughly six weeks old, and give birth some 18 days later. Harvest mice can live up to two years but few survive beyond six months old, being eaten by birds of prey and toads, or killed by stubble burning and combine harvesters. A surprising number escape the machinery by fleeing to the ground, and even nests can be caught up in the whirring blades and dropped again unscathed.

The mice are less resilient to changes in the weather – many are killed by heavy downpours or sharp drops in temperature. They thrive best when it is warm and dry. In winter, the mice live near the ground in flimsy nests under hedges or in thick tussocks of grass.

Thatched cradle Newborn harvest mice in a nest of woven grass are shown through a cutaway section. The mother pushes through the wall, which closes after her.

High endeavour A harvest mouse stands on the roof of her sturdy nest, suspended in a forest of wheat stems.

A castle in the air for a harvest mouse family

A tiny russet-coloured mouse stands upright among a forest of stalks and grass blades, hidden beneath a swaying canopy of wheat that is ripening in the August sun. Soon the mouse grabs hold of two tall stems with its long, flexible tail and strong hind feet, leaving its forefeet free to hold a leaf for chewing. A female harvest mouse is putting the final careful touches to another nest – her third this season.

The tiny mouse is only about 2½in (64mm) long and it weighs little more than a pencil, so it can easily swing on grain stalks. It is one of the world's smallest rodents, and its size and secrecy make it easily overlooked, but it is found all over Europe and northern Asia.

During the breeding season pregnant females build their sturdy, spherical nests hanging above ground among crops such as wheat, maize and oats, or among riverbank reeds, coarse grassy verges beside roads – indeed anywhere with plenty of tall, thick-stemmed vegetation. The males follow the females to the fields, verges and watersides, roving from one partner to another to mate.

By August, a female may be building a nest for her third litter. First she splits a leaf blade

Hot and cold slumbers for Jersey tiger moths

Each summer, clouds of Jersey tiger moths descend in a brilliant shimmer of wings on the 'valley of the butterflies' on the Greek island of Rhodes. By August, rocks and trees are encrusted with the moths, their cream-barred black wings resembling barbed arrowheads. There is an occasional flash of scarlet when a moth flutters and reveals its hind wings.

Millions of the moths have come to the valley to escape the searing heat. They remain in a death-like summer torpor (called aestivation) to conserve energy, and do not eat but live for weeks off fat reserves built up during the cooler spring. Evaporation from a stream in the valley bottom prevents the moths from dehydrating.

At the end of August, when the worst of the heat is over, the moths leave their retreat and spread out over the countryside again to breed.

After mating a female lays a batch of about 130 eggs on plants such as nettles and dandelions.

Two or three weeks later, the hairy caterpillars hatch and feed on the plants the eggs were laid on. When fully grown, they are black with cream spots and an orange stripe down the back. During winter they hibernate among roots, dead leaves or moss until the warmth of spring wakens them. Then they eat voraciously, always alert for predators such as birds. The tiger moth caterpillars can move much faster than most other caterpillars, and at the first sign of danger they scuttle for cover.

In June they weave a loosely spun silken cocoon inside which they change into adults, emerging three or four weeks later. They are not long on the wing before the heat drives them into retreat. By the time they die at the end of summer, they will have spent over half their lives in winter hibernation or summer slumber. The English name Jersey tiger is from the Channel Island where the moths are common.

Fleshy monster The giant puffball, the largest fungus in the world, thrives in moist soil rich in compost. It can grow to some 8ft (2.4m) in circumference.

From minute spore to mushrooming puffball

One would need both arms to encircle a fully grown giant puffball. At a distance it has even been mistaken for a reclining sheep. This colossal fungus appears in August in European pastures and meadows that are rich in manure or rotted vegetable matter.

The puffball is the fruiting body of a fungus whose main body, a network of tiny fibres known as mycelium, lies under the soil. The puffball begins as a tiny lump on this mesh of threads, and first emerges above ground as a small white knob. A few weeks later it has grown into a huge ball of firm, chalky white flesh lying on the grass. Only when a puffball is picked can you see its very short stem.

If picked while still young, the puffball is delicious to eat. As it continues to develop, the tasty white flesh begins to change. The outer skin, known as a veil, gradually splits to reveal the centre, called the glebe, which contains millions of microscopic spores packed in a dense mass intermingled with fine threads.

As the spores ripen, the puffball deepens from white to yellow. When fully ripe, the ball bursts open and the spores are released onto the breeze. Some will settle and produce mycelium on which, eventually, other puffballs will form.

Summer retreat Jersey tiger moths cover a tree trunk in the 'valley of the butterflies', on the Mediterranean island of Rhodes. They aestivate – rest immobile through the summer heat – and wake again to breed in August.

Sifting the secrets of a mighty whale shark

Massive whale sharks are known to be the largest fish in the sea. Yet although they can be 40ft (12m) long and weigh 12 tons, they are no threat to humans. Their mouths are wide but their teeth are tiny, and they feed by filtering in minute sea creatures and small fish. The whale shark's life-style has long been a mystery. Does it lay eggs or are its young born fully formed?

The sharks live in all the warmer waters of the world, and are regular but not common visitors to the Gulf of Oman, where sightings tend to increase from August to October. It is possible that they gather there from around the Indian Ocean to mate again after giving birth during August. It was in Matrah, Oman, in August 1989 that a fisheries scientist bought a baby whale shark in the fish market. It had been caught the previous night in a net about 5 miles (8km) off the coast. The arm-length baby was too small to have swum far, so must have been hatched or born in the Gulf.

Some scientists believe that whale sharks deposit large, leathery eggs and leave them to hatch on the seabed. In 1953, a giant egg containing a 14in (360mm) long whale shark embryo was found on the sea floor off the Texas coast in the Gulf of Mexico. But no one could be certain whether it had been deposited deliberately or aborted prematurely. The unusually thin egg case suggested a premature delivery.

Other scientists think that the whale shark's eggs stay inside the mother's body until the babies are well developed, giving the young a better chance of survival than in eggs left to drift at the sea bottom – a pregnant whale shark caught off Sri Lanka in the 1940s was found to be carrying 16 eggs. If the egg case breaks just before emergence, the young whale sharks would be launched as miniature versions of their parents – that is, born rather than hatched. This theory may well be correct, because the Oman baby had a scar rather like an umbilical scar, which suggests birth. Such a scar is left when a nourishing yolk-sac is finally reabsorbed. It disappears after a few weeks.

Mild monster The enormous whale shark dwarfs a human diver, who is in no danger from its tiny teeth. The shark itself is well-armoured against any attacker – its white-spotted skin is as thick as a man's arm.

River dolphin An 8ft (2.4m) long river dolphin (or boto) winds its way among the trees and vegetation submerged in the flooded Amazon rain forest at high water.

Where Amazon fish eat nuts among the trees

In the humid depths of the Amazon rain forest in August, when the river floods are at their height, the submerged trees are stirred not by birds but by passing fish and dolphins.

Following heavy rains earlier in the year, and the melting of the Andes snows, the Amazon and its tributaries overflow their banks and swamp a vast lowland area at least the size of Iceland. The flooding lasts for roughly three months – during June, July and August. In parts, known as the *várzeas*, the water is deep enough to submerge trees 30ft (9m) tall, but the vegetation survives this regular flooding. When the water recedes the silt left behind enriches the soil and brings lush growth.

The boto, a freshwater dolphin, swims slowly in and out of the submerged trees and scans for fish and crabs by echolocation, in the same way as its seagoing relatives. But botos have more flexible necks and a wider sound beam than other dolphins, and can pinpoint objects with such precision that they can detect the mesh of a net – although they do not always manage to avoid it. A boto has a ridge on its back instead of a dorsal fin, and it also has a long snout. Its flexible neck, together with its large side fins and tail fluke, helps the dolphin to manoeuvre through the tangle of vegetation.

Amazonia The vast rain forests of the Amazon cover an area half the size of Canada. The parts coloured dark green above are flooded for months every year.

Botos are not afraid of humans, and in some places will even respond to a special whistle or a paddle tapped on the side of a canoe. They drive fish into the shallows where fishermen can spear them, and are sometimes rewarded with fish. Usually, however, the botos make the most of the confusion caused by the fishermen to catch some of the fish for themselves.

There are plenty of fish to be had in the Amazon, some 2500-3000 species are found there. Some are flesh eaters and some eat the fruits and seeds of trees as they swim among the branches. Seed-eating piranhas wait for seeds, nuts or berries to drop from branches above water and attack them with gusto, crushing the nuts in their sharp teeth to remove the kernel.

Another seed-eating fish, the tambaqui, has crunching jaws about 2ft (610mm) long and can even crack the tough seeds of the rubber tree. The tambaqui listens for a seed to drop into the water, then homes in on it with its highly developed sense of smell. Throughout the Amazon, there are about 200 types of fish and trees that rely on each other for either food or seed dispersal.

Other fish that lie in wait beneath the trees are not hunting seeds or fruit. Arm-length, flat-sided arowhanas (or *aruañas*) leap man-high from the water to pluck large insects and hummingbirds from the branches. They have divided eyes that enable them to see above and below the water surface at the same time. The male also has a big mouth, not for gobbling more insects but for sheltering its young. They hatch in their father's mouth, where they have been carried as fertilised eggs, and live there for about a month. Every so often father opens his jaws and the tiny fry swim out to feed on algae and water fleas. If danger threatens, he opens his mouth and brings them home in one enormous gulp.

Strange birds of the flooded forest include the grouse-sized hoatzin and the crow-like umbrella bird. The hoatzin has a blue face and a spiky crest, and its young have wing claws with which to cling to branches. The umbrella bird has a mop-like crest that can be raised erect, and the male has a 10in (250mm) long wattle.

Monkeys are found where taller trees, such as the 130ft (40m) kapok, tower above the flood. Uakaris with bald, bright red faces, forage for seeds and flowers in groups of up to 50 spread out over a foraging range of about 2½ sq miles

Vegetarian fish Although related to the flesh-eating piranhas – said to strip a capybara of flesh in seconds – many Amazonian piranhas eat fruit and nuts.

Red-faced monkey The uakari looks rather human, so unlike other monkeys is rarely killed for the pot.

High jump An arowhana fish leaps from the water to grab an insect, a spider or even a small bird.

(6.5sq km). Its shaggy coat makes the hare-sized uakari look larger than it really is. Also living in the tree canopy are the smallest monkeys in the world – sparrow-sized pygmy marmosets that weigh about 6oz (170g). They hide below the leaves and in holes in the trees, searching for insects, and also use their sharp teeth to bite into tree branches and suck the sap.

Lurking in the more open, grassy areas of the flooded basin is one of the Amazon's largest animals – the crocodile-like black cayman that may grow to 15ft (4.6m) in length. This formidable predator hunts for capybaras beside ponds and lakes at night. Capybaras, which are about 2ft (610mm) high at the shoulder, are the largest rodents in the world.

In the low-water season the cayman eats fish, including the flesh-eating piranha. But the black cayman's young – the 50 or so hatchlings that emerge from each leafy nest after about six weeks of incubation during the low-water period – are at the mercy of the piranhas. These fish nibble the youngsters' toes, and while the water is low they cannot easily escape.

Even if the young caymans take temporary refuge on land (where they are at greater risk from predators such as snakes), they have to return to the water eventually. Usually they go into the bottom mud. When the floods come, the youngsters leave home for other areas, away from the fish. Not until they are bigger are the tables turned – then they can feed on the piranhas. For adult black caymans, man is the worst enemy, killing them for their skins. This may be why capybaras have increased to the extent that they are damaging crops.

Cane toads that changed from guests to pests

A huddle of giant cane toads crowds against a brick wall on a farm in west Queensland, Australia. They have come seeking shelter and food in the dry, dusty heat of August. The mottled, warty-skinned toads, some up to 9in (230mm) long and weighting about 3lb (1.4kg), find the food and water they need more easily around human settlements than in the wild.

The toads feed at night, each flicking out its long tongue to catch moths, then blinking its bulbous eyes to push down the roof of its mouth and force the food down its throat. Mostly they eat insects, but will also eat human food waste, reptiles, mammals, birds or even dung.

Cane toads were introduced to Queensland from Central and South America in 1935, in the hope that they would control a beetle destroying sugar-cane crops. But the cane fields offered few places for shelter during the day, so the toads moved into farms and gardens instead.

Now they have spread far afield, and threaten to wipe out fish, frogs and birds by consuming their food supply. The toads have no predators in Australia – they secrete poison from glands on their backs, and this puts off snakes and birds of prey – so they can spread unchecked.

Warty menace Cane toads cluster against a wall on a Queensland farm. Introduced to control beetle pests in sugar-cane fields, the toads invade human settlements in hordes, and have become a nuisance themselves.

Holding on Three-month-old eastern quolls – also called native cats – still cling to their mother whenever possible, even while she hunts. They are now too big to ride in her pouch.

Quolls, or native cats, prepare to be hunters

Scrambling from its den in a hollow log, a baby eastern quoll emerges into the fading light of a eucalyptus forest in north-eastern Tasmania. The bold white spots on its brown back gleam in the August twilight as it nestles up to its mother and clings on. She is about the size of a domestic cat – quolls are known as native cats – and is a night hunter with powerful claws and a lithe body.

The young quoll's five litter mates sit up and sniff the night air with large nostrils on pointed snouts. The smells are familiar, but the sights are new. The quolls were born in June, but their eyes have only just opened. Suddenly, one is startled as a litter mate pounces on its head. The young quoll twists round and nips the throat of its assailant. The two grapple, but the fight is only in play. Most of the youngsters' time is now spent biting, wrestling and chasing one another's tails, acquiring the skills they need to become efficient hunters. Soon all the young quolls begin to hug their mother. She usually goes hunting with the whole family, and they learn to hunt as they ride with her.

The mother carried her offspring with her in her pouch for the first two months of their lives, but they have now grown too bulky to be carried there. Originally, she gave birth to 30 tiny embryos, but only the first to attach themselves to her six teats were able to survive. In another two months, when spring provides plenty of insects to eat, the young will be weaned and will leave the den to fend for themselves.

During August, the coldest month of the Tasmanian winter when night temperatures fall to around freezing, quolls mostly make do with insects. But they are capable of killing birds, reptiles, mice and rats with one swift bite to the back of the neck.

Seldom seen, the eastern quoll is stealthy and solitary – and very rare. Disease, forest clearance and competition with introduced foxes, cats and dogs have brought it to the verge of extinction on the south-eastern mainland. The forests of Tasmania, where there are no foxes or dingoes, are its only sanctuary.

Body language The colours and patterns on the cuttlefish's skin change with its behaviour.

Bubble homes Tiny cuttlefish embryos are on view as they develop inside their grape-sized eggs.

Australian oddity The duck-billed platypus has a duck's beak, a frog's webbed feet and the fur of a mammal. Its young hatch from eggs, feed on mother's milk – and eventually hunt with a super-sharp tracking system.

Platypuses lay eggs and suckle their young

Ripples circle across a quiet river in eastern Australia as a sleek, brown-furred creature dog-paddles upstream on a night in late August. Its fully webbed front feet stroke the water firmly while its tail and partly webbed back feet act as rudder. Then it climbs out and waddles up to its burrow just above the waterline. This is a female duck-billed platypus returning to the nesting chamber she has prepared at the far end of a branching burrow almost 22yds (20m) long.

Since she mated at the beginning of the month, the platypus – about the size of a crouching cat – has changed remarkably. The milk glands on her underside have swelled from the size of a fingernail and now cover her belly. In September, a month after mating, this unusual mammal will lay two or three white eggs – a platypus does not bear live young, as most mammals do. She will incubate them for about a week by curling her tail round them.

When the eggs hatch, the youngsters will suck milk from her fur. It oozes out from two patches on her underside, for she has no teats.

During the three months that she feeds her babies in the nest chamber, the platypus will hunt regularly, blocking the entrance each time she goes out to stop snakes and rats from getting in and eating the babies. One summer's night, the youngsters will emerge from the nest to spend a couple of weeks with mother in the outside world before they fend for themselves.

Young platypuses have small teeth at first, but as time goes by these are replaced by grinding pads in the snout. The new generation will hunt like their parents, with eyes closed and heads thrust down to the stream bed. With ears and nostrils sealed, the platypuses use their broad snouts to scrabble in the darkness among the mud and pebbles. Even so, they come up with cheek pouches filled with small fish and crustaceans such as crayfish. This seemingly primitive mammal has electroreceptors in its beak-like snout – a sensitive tracking system that detects the minute electrical impulses given out by the muscles of its prey.

The many-coloured coat of a giant cuttlefish

Bevies of squat, squid-like creatures drift and roll in the shallows off Australia's east coast. They are giant cuttlefish, which come inshore during August to lay their eggs in warmer waters. But many of the cuttlefish, which are up to 5ft (1.5m) long, are picked off by snapper fish and albatrosses. They eat the soft parts and leave the hard internal shells, like miniature surfboards, to wash ashore.

Before long the survivors return to deeper waters. On its rubbery body each has eight arms and two tentacles, and as these move the cuttlefish continually changes shape from expansive spread to concentrated dart. Its colour also constantly shifts as blotches and stripes pass along its body, for pigment cells in the skin make it instantly lighter or darker in response to the animal's perceptions. This may be the way they 'talk' to one another. The range of patterns and subtle colour blends suggest a language as rich as spoken English.

Shark in the shallows *The female Port Jackson shark comes to a shallow, sheltered bay each year to lay and place her eggs. The shark, a pig-faced member of the bullhead family, is about 5ft (1.5m) long.*

A shark that screws its eggs into the rocks

In a sheltered Australian bay where a shallow sea is lapping the rocks, a blunt-snouted, marble-patterned shark is hard at work. Swimming powerfully, it pushes persistently against a rock, apparently driving a hand-length brown screw into a small crack. It takes almost two hours of the August day for this Port Jackson shark to wedge a pair of the pliable 'screws' firmly in position. They are in fact leathery egg cases that the shark is securing.

The nest site, which has been used year after year, is shared by several females and will eventually hold about 16 eggs. Before September is out, each female will have laid 10-16 eggs in pairs. Some eggs settle safely into the rocks, but the shark has to take others in her mouth and push them in. Each egg case holds a large yolk sac on which the young shark feeds during the 10-12 months it takes to develop – the length of time is affected by the water temperature.

The shark's heavy jowl, extravagantly curling nostrils and the ear-like crests above its eyes, have won it the name 'pig shark'. It has a sharp spine on each dorsal (back) fin which deters enemies and is useful for forcing a way under rocks to reach prey. Outside the breeding season, the shark lives in deeper waters – down to 500ft (150m) – where it sniffs out oysters, clams, crabs and sea urchins, which it demolishes with back teeth adapted for crushing. Its front teeth are used to catch fish.

Threaded egg *The egg case of the Port Jackson shark is unique among sharks' eggs. It has raised screw-like flanges that help to keep it in place in its rocky niche.*

How a catbird sets the stage for courtship

Busily tossing aside twigs and dead leaves from a patch of forest floor, a cock tooth-billed catbird is preparing a mating arena. It is August, and there is a lot of debris on the floor of Australia's east coast forests. Now and then, the thrush-like bird raises his head to utter a mewing wail, warning others off the territory he is claiming. When the round patch, a stride or two in width, is clear he flies to a nearby tree and cuts off a leaf with his saw-like beak. Each leaf stalk may take 15 minutes to saw through.

The catbird lays the leaf down on the cleared ground, not in a haphazard fashion but with the paler underside uppermost so that it shows in the forest gloom. Most catbirds gather about 20 large leaves, although some enthusiasts have collected as many as 200 small ones for their arena. Some birds take leaves from only one species of tree, and others collect at random. As the leaves wither, the catbird spruces the arena each morning with new ones.

With the stage now set – the locals call the bird a stage-maker – the catbird sits on a branch above it and sings a loud and complicated song that carries far into the forest. He may sing for two hours or more at a time. A female enticed to accept the male stays only for mating, then flies off to the nest she has prepared elsewhere. The male will never know his offspring. He prepares his stage again to lure another mate – indeed a succession of mates until January.

Stage craft *The tooth-billed catbird cock decorates a mating arena with leaves. Then he sings loud and long to advertise his availability to the hen birds.*

SEPTEMBER

STORKS FLY SOUTH FROM EUROPE, YAKS RUT ON TIBETAN
MOUNTAINS AND AFRICAN WILDEBEESTS BEGIN THE LONG TREK TOWARDS
GREENER GRASS. BABY GREEN TURTLES RUN THE GAUNTLET
ON SOUTH AMERICAN BEACHES AND POLAR BEARS FORAGE BY HUDSON BAY

Africa: Wildebeests and zebras brave a swollen river for pastures new

NORTH AMERICA

When polar bears pick up a meal in town

Cats and dogs, pigeons and rats, are familiar scavengers in many towns. In Churchill, one of Canada's most northerly towns, the scavengers are polar bears. Churchill lies on the western shore of Hudson Bay, and as the bears travel north in September from their summer feeding grounds along the Nelson river, the town's rubbish dumps offer them food with none of the effort it normally takes to hunt seals.

The annual invasion attracts many tourists to the town, although the bears are a nuisance to local people. Particularly aggressive bears are marked with dye so that people know to keep well away from them, and some are tranquillised and transported out of town. Some bears have fallen victim to poisons picked up from the refuse they eat.

As the bears loom on the outskirts of town, winter is already setting in. Sea ice is forming around the edge of Hudson Bay, and when the water freezes over the bears will move out to sea in search of seals. Around 500 bears spend the winter in the bay, forming one of the largest concentrations of polar bears in the world.

Camouflaged against the snow by their creamy-white fur, polar bears hunt by stealth, often lying in wait beside blowholes in the ice for seals to come up for breath. As well as patience, the bears have an acute sense of smell, and are said to be able to sniff out seal pups hidden in dens 3ft (1m) beneath the snow.

A polar bear occasionally hunts on land, perhaps taking a young musk ox. Its movements on land are surprisingly swift and agile. On flat ice it can run at 25mph (40km/h), and at speed can jump over snow hummocks as high as a man's shoulder and leap across distances twice that measure. A polar bear pursued by hunters has been known to take a flying leap of more than 50ft (15m) into the sea from the top of an iceberg. Unlike other bears, polar bears have fur on the soles of their paws and this helps them to move over slippery ice. Their powerful claws allow them to grip so effectively on hard-packed ice that they can climb steep ice walls.

Cooling down On the outskirts of Churchill, a polar bear travelling north to winter on Hudson Bay cools off after a scavenging spree. Polar bears overheat easily, and lie still and pant to lose heat.

Beached jellyfish Stranded Portuguese men-of-war lie in their thousands on a Virginia beach. Winds and currents have swept them to their deaths.

Men-of-war jellyfish lose their stunning sting

From the water's edge to the high tide mark, a beach on the USA's Virginia coast is littered with shimmering turquoise balloons. Each sits on a tangle of tentacles, shrivelling in the September sun. Not long ago, this was a shoal of Portuguese men-of-war. Now a stiff breeze has blown them ashore to their deaths.

Each man-of-war is not truly a jellyfish but a colony of animals known as polyps. One of the colony, the gas-filled balloon, keeps the rest afloat and is topped with a crest that acts as a sail. Beneath the balloon hang many tube-like polyps, each with a mouth and a trailing tentacle about 70ft (21m) long. The tentacles are armed with stinging cells that can paralyse fish brushing against them. The polyps draw the stunned fish up to their mouths, and once digested it is shared with the rest of the colony through connecting tubes. Yet one fish, the finger-length man-of-war fish, feeds unscathed among the constantly growing tentacles.

Blown around the world's warmer oceans, Portuguese men-of-war are sometimes carried by summer and autumn winds and currents to North American and European coasts. Apart from the wind and loggerhead turtles, they have few enemies and may live for ten years. Swimmers who encounter the jellyfish may suffer severe stings.

Antlered monarch A red deer stag bellows his challenge to rivals as he guards his harem. His roar may put off all but an evenly matched contender.

EUROPE AND NORTH ASIA

Roaring time for red deer in a Highland glen

A deep bellow echoes round a heather-clad valley in the Scottish Highlands. It is late September, and for the next month the red deer stags will be rutting – vying with each other as they try to gather harems of hinds to mate with. To show their strength, rivals roar loudly, parade alongside each other and thrash at branches with their antlers. Stags avoid fighting if possible, and a rival may be vanquished by a superior display of strength. Evenly matched rivals may lock antlers in bruising tussles. During the confusion of challenge and battle, large harems are often split into smaller groups, so a hind may mate several times.

In spring, the stags cast their antlers and grow new ones which, in a mature eight year old, have many points (tines). Except during the rut, stags live together in hilltop herds. The herds of hinds and their single calves – born in June – feed on the richer lower slopes. In Britain, the felling of forests has driven these forest-dwelling animals onto open moors and hills. With the first autumn frosts, the stags will move down to join the hinds, and the rut will begin again.

A jay stores autumn acorns for winter

The rustling of leaves in a northern European oak wood in late September is not just the sound of a falling acorn, or the breeze stirring the leaves. In the heart of the wood, lit up by mellow shafts of sunlight piercing the leaf canopy, a bird is busy burying an acorn.

The bird is a Eurasian jay, a handsome member of the crow family with reddish-brown plumage, a speckled black and white crown that can stand up as a crest, bright blue patches on each wing, and a black tail. Acorns are a favourite food, and the jay's instinctive response to their abundance in autumn is to bury some of the surplus, usually one nut in each spot.

Very much at home in deciduous woodland, including parks, orchards and large wooded gardens, jays feed on a variety of nuts and berries, insects, small mammals, eggs and young birds. The jay's harsh, squawking call is one of the characteristic sounds of an oak wood, but the bird itself is shy and not often seen.

In winter and early spring, food can be in short supply. This is when the jay will return to its cached acorns. Jays are good at finding their stores again. They do not seem to find them purely by luck, but either remember precisely where they buried their supplies or – perhaps more likely – store food in a particular type of

As winter approaches, the shorter hours of daylight and the drop in temperature trigger off the growth of winter coats in animals, and encourage animals that hibernate to seek suitable shelters.

But winter food storage is probably no more than an inborn response to autumn's fruitfulness. There is no evidence to suggest that animals are capable of the foresight needed to lay food aside deliberately. Whenever there is an over-abundant food supply, many animals will bury the excess. A fox raiding a chicken coop, for example, will try to bury what it has killed but cannot eat immediately. And animals probably develop winter fat because they feast on the abundant food available in autumn, not as a deliberate strategy to survive winter. Animals that bred in summer may fatten up in autumn because they are no longer having to share vital resources with their offspring.

place. Then they search out similar spots in winter in the hope of finding a hidden hoard.

Not all the stored acorns are found. Those that are overlooked and remain buried throughout the winter frosts may germinate in spring into oak seedlings. In time, some of the seedlings may grow into massive oaks, and provide later generations of jays with an autumn harvest and winter store.

Hidden asset A well-fed jay buries an acorn for winter food. The acorn may be forgotten and grow into an oak.

Aerial rush-hour In September, up to 12,000 storks have been counted soaring across the Strait of Gibraltar in one day. They are often joined by migrating hawks and eagles.

Wings over the straits as white storks migrate

A mass of 200 or more dark shapes fills the September sky above north-east Turkey. The silhouettes are unmistakable – broad wings with long necks stretched forward and long legs trailing. The birds soar effortlessly, wings scarcely moving, carried by rising warm air currents (thermals) above the last piece of land before the 2 mile (3.2km) strait of the Bosporus.

The birds are white storks migrating from their breeding grounds in Europe to winter quarters south of the Equator in Africa. In summer the breeding places provided insects, frogs and reptiles in abundance. Supplies will dwindle during the northern winter, but there will be ample food south of the Equator.

At the western end of the Mediterranean, the scene is similar as other flocks cross the Strait of Gibraltar. The storks – along with hosts of other migrating birds, especially birds of prey such as honey buzzards – avoid long sea crossings because only land produces the thermals that

lift them so effortlessly. Over a long stretch of water they could tire, lose height and drown. So they funnel into the two migration routes that allow the shortest sea crossings.

Western breeding storks move through Spain, across the Strait of Gibraltar and then over the baking Sahara – where thermals are particularly strong – and through West Africa. Birds breeding farther east move south past Turkey, across the Bosporus, round the Levant coast and through East Africa. Some birds, particularly birds of prey, will cross the water only when there is enough sun to ensure thermals, and no wind to beat them back as they glide across.

Because storks have declined in Western Europe as a result of pesticide use and land development, there are far more of them on the eastern route, where they provide one of the world's great birdwatching spectaculars. Flocks of up to 11,000 have been seen over the Bosporus, and 30,000 were once counted nearby in 1½ hours. In autumn 1971, 339,000 birds followed this migration route south. The return migration in spring is spread over a longer period, so is less impressive.

Flight paths Birds migrating between Europe and Africa south of the Equator take the two routes that involve the shortest sea crossings – across the Strait of Gibraltar in the west and the Bosporus in the east.

189

Food on hand A red ant prepares to grip the swollen end of a large blue butterfly caterpillar (top), with body raised in readiness. In the ants' nest (bottom), the caterpillar eats ant larvae and gives honeydew.

A butterfly becomes the paying guest of ants

Curious alliances are struck on the chalky downlands of continental Europe during September – alliances between red ants and the caterpillars of large blue butterflies, from which the caterpillars derive the most benefit. When it hatches from an egg at the end of July, the butterfly larva starts life in the same way as any other caterpillar, spending its first weeks eating the plant on which the eggs were laid – in this case the flowers of wild thyme.

About September, after it has moulted three

Finding thyme The large blue butterfly lays its eggs only on big, budding flower heads of wild thyme.

times and grown to the size of a grain of rice, the grey-pink caterpillar drops down from the seed-head of the thyme flower early one evening, crawls under cover and waits for a red ant to find it. If this does not happen within a day or two, the caterpillar will die of starvation.

When a red ant arrives on the scene, it circles the caterpillar and strokes it with its antennae. This makes the caterpillar produce small droplets of sweet liquid from a gland on its body. The ant drinks this honeydew and continues 'milking' until the caterpillar swells the first three segments of its body and raises them from the ground. At this signal the ant straddles the caterpillar, clamps its jaws round the swollen segments and hauls it off to the ant nest.

There the caterpillar, safely tucked away from predators, feeds on ant larvae and in return regularly produces honeydew – rich in nutrients and so highly prized by the ants that they sacrifice some of their offspring to have it on tap. The caterpillar feeds in the ant nest all winter, then in May, still in the nest, becomes a pale chrysalis in which it changes into an adult.

Sometimes the red ants bring home too many caterpillars. When this happens, all the ant eggs and larvae are eaten and the ant colony dies out.

Then the caterpillars die of starvation. Sometimes, also, if the ant colony produces a lot of queens, the workers kill the caterpillars.

In June or early July the adult butterfly emerges one morning, damp and bedraggled, from the chrysalis. The ants escort the butterfly to the surface, and as it sits on a plant near the nest to dry its wings, ants mill around below and ward off any predators. Then the butterfly, now a shimmering, black-spangled blue with wings about 2in (50mm) across, flies away.

PLEASING ONE'S HOST
Once a large blue butterfly caterpillar is taken into a red ants' nest, it uses various ploys to make itself less of an alien and so prevent the ants from killing it, as they do most intruders. Apart from giving the ants honeydew, it also talks their language.

Ants communicate through smell, taste and sound. The honeydew has an ant-like scent, and the caterpillar also emits an ant-like sound. Once it becomes a chrysalis, it scrapes its abdomen against its case to produce a rasping noise like the sound ants make by rubbing the head against the body.

Will to win *A moose thrusts hard with his huge antlers to drive an intruder away from his domain and his mate.*

Moose clash crowned heads in the forest

Disturbed from his browsing, the large bull moose (also known in Europe as an elk) turns slowly into the wind with head erect and sniffs. It is the rutting season, the time when males fight over females, and he has caught the scent of an approaching rival. As he swivels, jaws still chewing beneath his overhanging, bulbous nose, the bell of skin and hair hanging from his throat swings gently. His crown of massive antlers, with 18-20 points spread like many-fingered hands, glints in the September sun.

The moose, about 6ft (1.8m) high at the shoulder, reaches forward and rubs his head against a branch to mark it with scent from a large gland in front of his eye. This reaffirms possession of his domain bordering a lake in a Siberian forest. Then he walks into a clearing, spreading the ground with scent from glands between his huge, splayed hooves. The waiting challenger snorts, bellows and presents his flank as the resident moose stalks towards him.

Side by side the two pace across the grass, humped shoulders stiff with aggression. Sud-denly the resident male swings round with head lowered, and the two hurl their solid, three-quarter-ton bodies at each other. Antlers lock together with a sharp snap, and each male pushes with all his might, his hind hooves sinking into the ground. Then, the first assault complete, the contestants back off and prepare for another round. The battle lasts just a few minutes and ends with the resident triumphant.

For him, a well-tried veteran, it has proved easier than his earlier, closer-matched contests which went on for hours. Today's challenger not only looked less impressive but was missing two points on his antlers, which robbed him of some crucial pushing power. Rutting moose some-times suffer injuries – most often a broken antler. However, antlers are shed and regrown annually. Each male sheds them in December and has an impressive new set by next August.

The victor returns to his mate, who is feeding chest-deep in the lake on water lilies, horsetails and bladderworts. She is smaller than he is, and has no antlers. Within a few weeks she will come into season and the pair will mate. Next May, a single calf (or twins) will be born. The bull may stay with the cow until the calf is about ten days old, then spend the summer alone.

Farewell to the swallows as they fly south

On warm September evenings, telephone wires all over Europe are decorated with strings of swallows preening and chattering as they gather for their autumn journey. The summer's new generation and their parents must fly south, chasing the sun before the chill of autumn makes their food too scarce. The birds have grown fat on the midges, gnats and mosquitoes that swarmed in the summer air, but now need to find fresh feasts in another summer in Africa south of the Sahara.

The journey of around 6000 miles (9600km) will take the birds 6-8 weeks. Flying by day, they use the route across the Mediterranean and the Sahara, guided by the sun and the earth's magnetic field. The knowledge of where to go is programmed into the young birds before they hatch. Some of the youngsters may find the marathon flight too exhausting, but despite the losses, a good number of first-timers will survive the journey. Next April they will fly north again to the European summer.

Sign of autumn *Clusters of twittering swallows, along with house martins, congregate for a mass exodus to Africa, where food will be in ample supply.*

The shrinking world of the giant panda

On a mist-shrouded mountain in Sichuan, central China, a giant panda sits upright with arms reaching forward, looking for all the world like a cuddly toy. Munching doggedly at a bamboo shoot, it sits alone among the dense, damp undergrowth beneath tall trees, its dark eye patches giving it a doleful look. This female giant panda is having a final meal before she retires to give birth in a cave.

It is September, and the two cubs conceived in April will be born any day now – blind, smaller than hamsters and scantily covered with white fur. The mother will rear only one, leaving the other to die. The lucky one will be up and about at three months, weaned at six months and fully independent at a year old.

Growing to a thickset 5ft 6in (1.7m) from nose to rump, a panda ambles along with a pigeon-toed gait. Because the bamboo shoots it relies on are fibrous and largely indigestible, giving little nourishment, it devotes much of its solitary life to eating. Its jaws are powerfully developed to manage all this chewing. Sugar cane, reeds, bulbs, a few insects and the odd bamboo rat may supplement the panda's diet, but despite the apparent plenty, its numbers have shrunk to less than 1500. Much of its original range has been lost to farming and housing, and what remains is in separate pockets cutting off groups of pandas from one another. This limits the chances of females in season meeting a mate.

The panda's place in evolution is hotly debated. In its build and walk the giant panda resembles a bear, but the much smaller red panda looks very like a raccoon.

Family resemblance? *The bear-like giant panda (above) does not look much like the red panda (below). But they share the same home area, and both have an enlarged pad on the palm for gripping the shoots they eat.*

FLOWER PERIL
A fully grown panda needs 33-44lb (15-20kg) of bamboo a day to maintain its hefty 16-24 stone (100-150kg) body. Usually the supply is ample, but sometimes all the plants of the same type flower together – and then die. This happens unpredictably, perhaps after 15, 30, 60, even 120 years, and brings famine to the pandas until the flower seeds produce new plants. After such a bamboo blossoming in 1983, some 200 pandas died of starvation. A flush of plant hormones is thought to cause the mass flowering.

A plumed egret stalks among the lily pads

Slowly, on long, thin legs, an intermediate egret stealthily walks through the shallows fringing a lake. Monsoon rains pour down from September skies onto the lakes, rivers and marshes of northern India bringing new growth. Fresh green reeds and grasses and the lilies that spread over the lakes are the most noticeable signs. The small creatures that dwell among them – such as fish, frogs, shrimps, snakes and insects – are less eye-catching but are sought by hungry predators such as the egret.

Tempting victims are gulped down whole. With ample food for the taking, it is the time for egrets to raise their families. Hundreds nest together, always near water, and often with some ibises, spoonbills and other water birds.

Each male egret lays claim to a patch of territory and drives off other males by flaunting the long black plumes that develop on his back at this time of year. Although normally silent, he now emits hoarse, buzzing calls to assert his dominance. With his territory secured and a mate won, the egret collects twigs and reeds for her to make a nest. For three weeks the partners share the incubation of the three or four pale green eggs. Egrets can now sit on their eggs in comparative safety, but in Victorian times they were the victims of fashion; millions were killed on their nests so their cravat of silky, snow-white breeding plumage could adorn ladies' hats.

Ready to strike The cruelly sharp beak of the intermediate egret is swift to kill fish, frogs, and any other small creature that lives on or under the lilies.

Coming to a head Two male yaks clash their massive horns as they challenge each other over a female.

Grunting yaks on the top of the world

Huge shaggy yaks roam the mountainsides of Tibet, their loud snorts echoing among the barren slopes. They are among the highest-dwelling animals in the world, roaming slopes at 13,000-20,000ft (4000-6000m). In September especially, the males live up to their more descriptive name – the grunting oxen. It is the time of their rut, when bulls vie for the supremacy that will win them a female.

During most of the year, the bulls live peaceably enough in groups of ten or twelve young bachelors plus one or two older bulls. When September comes, they separate to attach themselves to the female herds. These number anything from 20 to 200 cows of breeding age, with young females and young bulls not yet three years old mixed among them.

A cow comes into season only once every two years – in the alternate years she is still suckling her single calf. For several hours before she is ready to mate, she is attractive to the bull. He sniffs her urine and genital region, using behaviour called displaying the flehmen, in which he stretches his neck, curls back his upper lip and works his tongue up and down to direct the scent to his sensitive detector – the Jacobson's organ above the palate. When the scent tells him the cow is ready, he tries to stop other bulls from coming near her.

Mostly, these massive half-wild cattle – which weigh about half a ton and stand as tall as a man – avoid open combat. But if threats, snorts and an aggressive stance of humped shoulders and lowered head fails to outface an opponent, a fight is likely. When yaks clash heads and lock their huge curved horns – which span 2ft 6in (760mm) – they can inflict serious injuries.

But what preoccupies yaks for most of the year is the battle against the elements. The sparse mountain grazing barely keeps starvation at bay, and exposure claims some lives in winter. Yaks are adapted to cope with the cold. Their coarse, black-brown coat has an under layer of dense fur, and their digestive system doubles as in-built central heating, for they digest food by fermenting it at 40°C (104°F). Indeed, they suffer as much from the heat, and in summer retreat to cooler spots higher up the mountain.

Wildebeests follow the rain to fresh pastures

In the still, dry air of a September morning, the choking dust rises in swirls from the plains of northern Tanzania, stirred by the hooves of countless wildebeests, also known as gnus.

The animals move wearily through the scattered trees north of the Mara river with heads down, searching among the parched grasses for palatable food. The long dry season has taxed their strength, making them lean and hungry, with hips and ribs prominent beneath dry, lustreless coats.

At last comes the welcome sign of a break in the weather. Thick banks of cloud billow on the northern horizon for the first time since May. Here and there dark shafts beneath them show where rain is already falling. Within a few days the slow-rolling clouds will be overhead and sudden downpours will transform the plains overnight from a desiccated off-white into fresh green. The subtle scent of wet soil will fill the air, and the landscape will sparkle once more, washed clean of the endless dust.

THE LONG TRAIL

As the belt of rain keeps moving south at the rate of about 12 miles (19km) a day, the animals begin to follow it, drawn on by the green shoots springing up everywhere. Long files of wildebeests converge, the trickle building to a stream and the stream to a flood until finally a million wildebeests are on the move, preparing to leave the Mara for several months. As far as the eye can see, columns of animals that look like scrawny, long-faced, long-legged cattle move inexorably on, jostling for space.

Scattered in small groups among them are 200,000 zebras. Built like sturdy ponies, they move with heavy-footed determination, their striped flanks flickering between the trees. Later, diminutive Thomson's gazelles will follow this assembly; some 600,000 of them will trot along sedately with heads high, the back-swept horns of the males nodding as they go.

Before long their way is barred by the mighty Mara river, which cuts across the dusty plain.

Dangerous crossing Travelling south to feed on lusher grasses, huge herds of wildebeests and zebras find their path blocked by the Mara river. Thousands of the migrants die in the surging swollen waters.

Unseen assailant In a flurry of spray, a crocodile charges through the shallows in an attempt to catch a zebra from a group dawdling at the water's edge.

Although the river gives life, it also harbours dangers. It conceals lurking crocodiles, waiting to feed on animals that come to drink. And now the river waters are swollen, not just by the local downpours but by rains that have fallen on the Rift Valley mountains far to the north-east. To cross the river, the migrating animals must swim the strong, surging flood.

Urged on towards their pastures by an instinctive drive, the wildebeests and zebras jump and slither down the steep banks into the water. Struggling against the flow of the river, they swim awkwardly, edging their way with much pushing and shoving towards the southern shore. Many thousands are carried away and drown, to be beached farther downstream where their bodies are picked over by vultures and crocodiles in competition with jackals and other scavengers. Even the wildebeests and zebras that reach the far bank may still fall prey to crocodiles.

Nor is the river crossing the only danger along their trail. The very presence of such a throng of potential prey attracts familiar predators – lions,

Caught unawares Slowed by the water, a heavy-footed zebra has fallen prey to a lioness, one of many predators that lurk in the bushes along the river bank.

wild dogs and hyenas – which scout and skulk along the route. Lions often lie in wait in the cover of thick bush ready to launch a surprise attack. Gangling wild dogs, distant relatives of the wolf and jackal, course the more open plains in packs of ten or more, pursuing their prey with loping strides until the victim falls exhausted.

Although many of the migrants succumb to

the hazards of the trail, so vast are their numbers that hundreds of thousands more survive and stream on through October and into November across the open Serengeti Plain towards the southern limit of the yearly trek – the slopes beneath the long-extinct Ngorongoro volcano, lying some 120 miles (193km) south-east of the Mara as the crow flies. This is the time of year when the region does not merit its local Masai name – Serengeti means 'white grass', for the rains have brought tender green shoots up over the fertile volcanic soils.

From about November to May the herds stay on the rich grasslands, where the young conceived last May are born in January and February. Although the southern Serengeti soils are fertile, they are porous and quick to drain. The lush covering of fast-growing grasses, so swift to appear during a rainy season, dies back just as quickly as the rain belt moves away south. Once again the green plain becomes the region of white grass.

This is the trigger for the herds to move west towards the margins of Lake Victoria. There, with higher rainfall, water-retaining soils and several large rivers flowing to the lake, the grass stays fresh longer. But by July, even these grasslands begin to dry up and the animals make their way back to the area north of the Mara river. Coarser and less juicy the long-stemmed Mara grasses may be, but they are welcome enough to the returning herd, which will see out the dry season on this tough fare.

Serengeti roundabout The shifting lure of good grazing, which is determined by the rainfall pattern, draws vast herds of wildebeests, zebras and gazelles on their yearly migration cycle round the East African plains. The herds move along well-defined trails, chiefly between three main areas – the region north of the Mara river, the southern Serengeti Plain to the north-west of the Ngorongoro Crater and the eastern margins of Lake Victoria.

Sifakas – the groaning ghosts of Madagascar

Arms widespread and body upright, what appears to be a monkey with a neat, dog-like face bounds energetically across an open stretch in the dry, deciduous forest of western Madagascar. It is a sifaka, one of the largest of the lemurs, and unlike smaller lemurs it is active by day. On this pleasant September morning, the sifaka is on a rare excursion to the ground – its usual haunts are the higher tree trunks, where its movements are spectacularly powerful, graceful and efficient.

In September the sifakas are at their liveliest, for their food – leaves and fruit – is relatively plentiful and the temperature is friendly. The comparatively cool dry season is almost over and the torrid humidity of the rainy season will not start until November. By now, infants born in July cling to their mothers' back instead of her belly fur, and begin to venture away to play.

The excitement of the mating season interrupted the daily round of eating and sleeping for a few weeks from January to March. But at that time of year it was so hot that the animals also spent as much as five hours each day dozing in the shade. In contrast, during the cooler days of June and July the sifakas became sun worshippers, climbing to the treetops to bask with heads and arms thrown back to catch the sun. When thoroughly warmed, they turned over to feel the sun on their backs.

Soft little grunts and grumbles carry the normal communications of family life but if danger comes, from birds of prey or humans, the group gives out an intimidating chorus of curious bubbling groans. When the first humans arrived on Madagascar some 2000 years ago, the eerie wails and howls from the forests convinced them that the island was inhabited by ghosts. Those ghosts turned out to be the sifaka and the indri, another member of the lemur family (named from the Latin *lemures*, 'spirits of the dead'). Lemurs are found only in Madagascar; their ancestors must have arrived from the African mainland more than 20 million years ago (probably crossing on floating collections of plant debris), and they have evolved in isolation from the rest of Africa's mammals.

Southern spring The sifaka's long, strong hind legs, designed for powerful leaps from one tree trunk to another, make it difficult for the animal to walk on all fours. On the ground it bounces along in great bounds.

Cantankerous rhinos with coveted horns

Two black rhinos stand side by side in the September sunshine of southern Africa. The male parades stiff-legged beside the female and nudges her. She, irritated by his pushiness, keeps rounding on him fiercely. The brief, crotchety encounter between these two heavyweights – he more than 5ft (1.5m) high at the shoulder and about a ton in weight, she only slightly smaller – ends with mating; it may occur at any time of year, but there is a peak of activity in September.

The sturdy, 6 stone (40kg) calves born of September matings are fortunate. They arrive some 15 months later when there is rainy weather ahead to bring on new growth and their well-fed mothers will produce ample milk. The calf will trot behind its ill-tempered mother until the next calf is due in another 2-4 years. The pair browse in wooded country or scrubby grassland in the early morning and late afternoon, resting in the shade during the heat of the day. They use the finger-like point of the top lip for tugging off twigs and shoots to eat. Except for mother and youngster pairings, black rhinos are solitary and likely to charge any other rhino they meet.

For such heavy animals, rhinos are fast and manoeuvrable, but they are shortsighted and can scarcely see beyond 25yds (23m). They just head wildly at whatever their keen hearing and sense of smell detect as a threat. If they make contact with a foe, they can rapidly inflict cruel damage with their horns of compressed hair; the front horn of the two can grow to 4ft (1.2m).

Its horns have made the rhino the victim of hunters who sell horn for prized dagger handles in the Yemen and for traditional medicines in the Far East. Despite efforts at protection, there are now only about 3000 black rhinos left. Protection has been far more successful for the related white rhino, which is a grazer and crops great mouthfuls of grass with wide, square lips. Its long head hangs low to be near the grass and is supported by a hump of muscle between the shoulders. The white rhino is bigger than the black rhino – up to 6ft (1.8m) at the shoulder and weighing more than two tons – but it is an amiable, mild-tempered animal.

Black and white Rhinos are named for the colour they take on from the soil and mud they roll in. Solitary black rhinos (top) meet only to mate. A white rhino mother (bottom) always nudges her calf ahead of her.

Secretary birds that hunt on the ground

Zigzagging its way through the long grass of a tree-scattered plain in Kenya early on a dry September morning, a long-legged bird is searching for prey. Back in its nest it has three seven-week-old chicks to feed, and its eyes are trained on the ground to spot insects, lizards, small mammals or snakes. The secretary bird is over 3ft (1m) tall, and the grass reaches just to its breast. Grey-bodied but with black trousers down to its knees, the bird is named for the quill-like plumes trailing from its head and neck, which are said to resemble the pens tucked behind the ear of a 19th-century clerk.

The secretary bird takes small prey such as grasshoppers with its sharp, hooked beak, but suddenly it jumps forward with both feet – it has spotted a snake. The bird batters its prey to death by kicking accurately with its strong feet and sharp claws, often leaping into the air and stamping furiously in the grass. The snake is venomous, but the bird's long legs, well feathered against the snake's fangs, put its vulnerable body out of reach, and it also shields itself with one wing. As the snake turns to defend itself, the bird thrashes the grass with its other wing and draws the snake in the direction it wants. Once the snake is dead, the bird swallows it whole.

Taking to the air on its black-tipped wings, each as long as a man's arm, the bird flies with long legs outstretched to its nest. The large platform of sticks, grass and plants is about 20ft (6m) above the ground in the fork of a flat-topped acacia tree. The three chicks are very demanding. Both parents have to search for food throughout the day to satisfy them. The parent bird regurgitates the snake, and the chicks strip it into bite-sized pieces. Small prey such as lizards or grasshoppers are presented to a chick whole.

The chicks hatched in July from eggs laid six weeks earlier. They will leave the nest when they are 11-12 weeks old, and will then have to learn how to hunt, following their parents through the grass of their territory with measured steps and heads moving from side to side. In the heat of midday they may rest in the shade or refresh themselves with a dust bath. Secretary birds spend most of their time on the ground, but every day the parent birds soar into the air to establish their territory and warn off intruders.

Spring fever A pronking springbok leaps nearly 7ft (2m) high in the air, its hairy white back crest erect. At courting time, males pronk to attract females.

A springbok spectacular at courting time

With great energy and dash, a springbok leaps stiff-legged into the air with all four feet off the ground. His arched back and lowered head show off to advantage the crest of bright white hairs erect along his back. This spectacular display – known as pronking – is interspersed with bouts of mad galloping, and is done to attract females. It is September, and with the summer rains approaching Namibia's arid plains, the springboks are courting.

Springboks, about 2ft 6in (760mm) high at the shoulder, are one of southern Africa's most numerous small antelopes. They usually breed during the rains, so courting time varies in different places. Males mark their territory by rubbing scent from glands in front of the eyes on grass stems and twigs, and also with droppings and urine. They spend a lot of time defending the area from rivals and displaying to gather a harem of females. A female produces a single youngster about six months after mating.

Springboks of both sexes also pronk in play or in alarm. Pronking while in full flight may be a way of confusing predators or a show of fitness to deter a predator. Observations suggest that pronking animals may be attacked less often.

Feeding time Three young secretary birds peck at their mother's beak to encourage her to regurgitate food.

Risky journey Before it is even an hour old, the tiny turtle hatchling must dig its way out of its nest and run the gauntlet of voracious predators as it crawls to the sea.

Ready for ambush Half under the sand, a ghost crab raises its eyes on stalks to watch for turtle hatchlings.

Raider on the wing Without even having to land, a frigate bird swoops low and, with perfect judgment, snatches in its beak a victim from the vulnerable procession of scrabbling baby turtles.

CENTRAL AND SOUTH AMERICA

A dangerous journey for baby green turtles

Sand heaves and quivers on a small patch of Costa Rican beach. Underneath there are tiny green turtle hatchlings, warmed by the September sun, struggling to break free from the nest. About ten weeks ago their mother dragged herself up the beach and laid about 100 eggs in a hole in the sand – one of several nestfuls she has laid this year, and one of hundreds laid the same night by a host of turtles.

Some of the hatchlings, each only half as long as a thumb, scrape away the ceiling of their nest and others undercut the walls. Those at the bottom compact the sand from above so that the floor rises as the ceiling collapses. Released, they all head unerringly towards the sea – probably guided by the sound of the waves and brighter light over the water. Few of them reach it.

The first danger is from black vultures. They gather round a nest, trampling the edges until it collapses and the trapped hatchlings are easy pickings. Dinosaur-like land iguanas swagger across the beach to grab turtles and crush them between powerful jaws. Nearer the water, ghost crabs dart from their holes, seize hatchlings by the flipper and drag them underground to devour. And just as the turtles are almost home, they are snatched by aerobatic frigate birds.

Once on wet sand, surviving turtles make swimming movements with their flippers and when a wave sweeps over them, swim away. They stay about 8in (200mm) below the surface, bobbing up for air every ten seconds. Now they have at least one form of escape – if a frigate bird flies over, they crash-dive to 10ft (3m).

Avoiding patrolling sharks offshore, the turtles search for a safe haven – a raft of floating sargassum weed. They may have to swim 50 miles (80km) to find it, but they will drift safely with it for the first 12 months of their lives.

At about five years old, when about 3ft (1m) long, the turtles will return to their birthplace to mate in the nearby water. Males never leave the sea, but the following year, surviving females will crawl up the same beach that saw their first risky journey to the sea and lay their first eggs.

Right whales mate in a cold southern sea

The wind is generally blowing hard where Peninsula Valdés juts out from the exposed Patagonian coast of Argentina into the Atlantic. Early September brings no exception. As the wind increases, massive 50ft (15m) southern right whales in the two gulfs formed by the peninsula get more and more boisterous. They roll and tumble in groups, and make sonorous 'burps' and 'moans' underwater.

The whales arrived here in June ready for the breeding season, which peaks in September. Six or seven competing bulls surround a receptive cow and, as she circles and dives, her train of suitors follows her. As heads bump together in the confusion, they are scarred by the hard white growths (callosities) each whale bears. Eventually, a couple come together, one perhaps placing a flipper over the other's back. They bring their undersides together and mate.

Females breed once every two to four years, so each year less than half the cows are ready to conceive. The females that mated last spring are giving birth in the more sheltered bays. Each cow bears a single calf about 18ft (5.5m) long, which usually arrives headfirst. It must be pushed to the surface immediately to take its first vital breath. Within a few hours it has learned to swim properly and can dive down under its mother to receive squirts of her milk.

After three weeks the calf will be making short forays away from its mother. By the time it is an adolescent, it will have learned to breach (leap from the water) and lobtail (slap its tail fluke on the surface). It will also have learned the art of 'head standing' – hanging upright in the water, with flukes above the surface. The youngster remains in the bay until it is four months old, and then all the whales swim slowly off to their summer feeding grounds far to the south in the Southern Ocean. There the youngsters are weaned, but will stay with their mother until they are 14 months old.

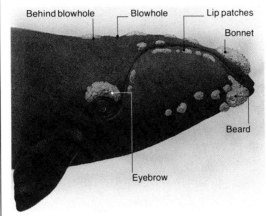

Head patterns Right whales have callosities – hard growths of horny skin on their heads. Each individual has its own pattern of growths.

Bill of fare The whimbrel uses its 4in (100mm) long down-curved beak to probe for marine worms and shellfish in the sand and mud of the shallows.

Whimbrels spend winter on balmy shores

A scattering of large wading birds is feeding on a sandy shore of the Galápagos Islands in the Pacific Ocean, each probing the sand with its beak. Most numerous are the whimbrels, which are just arriving in late September from their summer breeding grounds in the far north of Alaska and Canada. Before early autumn's icy winds brought the first snowfall, millions of waders left the Arctic, where they reared their young on the rich flush of food produced in the short summer.

The whimbrels flew in large, fast-moving flocks, keeping in contact with frequent snickering 'titti-titti-titti' calls. Some followed the American west coast and could have settled anywhere from Oregon in the north to Tierra del Fuego at the southern tip of South America. Many have been tempted by the Galápagos Islands, set on the Equator west of Ecuador and bathed by the cold waters of the Humboldt Current swirling northward from the Antarctic. The chill brings a particular richness to the food supply available on the shore for overwintering waders.

The mottled brown, curlew-like whimbrels, distinguished by a striped crown, will stay until March, sharing their winter feast with other waders from the Arctic as well as from South America. In March the whimbrels will forsake the balmy Galápagos and whirr away on the long journey north for another frantic breeding season in the short Arctic summer.

Heavy petting Each right whale in this courting group places its flipper on the back of the whale beside it.

Spring outing In Australia's eastern mountains, a short-nosed echidna emerges from its winter sleep.

AUSTRALASIA

A spiny anteater sleeps the winter away

In September, the spring sunshine falls on a north slope of Australia's Great Dividing Range where it straddles the border of Victoria and New South Wales. Suddenly a ball of bristly spines erupts from a hollow log – a short-nosed echidna is leaving the place where it has spent most of the winter in hibernation, waking up to forage for a few hours once every three weeks.

The rabbit-sized creature with stumpy legs shuffles along with its tubular nose against the ground. Also known as a spiny anteater, the echidna roots around for ants and termites, and digs into nests with its sharp claws. Then it mops the insects up with the sticky tongue, 7in (180mm) long, that flicks out of the tiny mouth at the end of its snout. Provided there is food, the short-nosed echidna is equally at home in cold highlands and arid deserts.

Like the duckbilled platypus, the echidna is an egg-laying mammal that suckles its young, but its method of temperature control is something like that of a reptile. Mammals, whatever the weather, maintain their body temperature at about 36°C (97°F). Reptiles, however, have the same temperature as the air around them, and need to bask in the sun to warm up and get their muscles working. The average temperature of the echidna is 31°C (88°F), but it varies with the weather. The echidna adjusts its activities accordingly. It comes out at midday in cold weather but in summer avoids the midday heat; in very hot spells it does not come out until night.

To survive in snow the echidna must hibernate, and must control its own temperature to some extent. Like other hibernating mammals, it eats well to put on weight, takes cover and then slows down its body functions, dropping its temperature by more than 20°C (36°F) to that of the surrounding air. Movement and basking will warm it up quickly again when it wakes. Not all echidnas go through this routine, for across most of Australia winter is warm. Only echidnas in the eastern mountains hibernate.

When the dunnart's fat tail is thin and empty

Warmer September weather is not the only sign that spring is starting in southern Australia. The open woodlands, heaths and grassy plains are once more alive with the clicking of grasshoppers and the churring of beetles, sounds that are soon picked up by the large, sensitive ears of a mouse-sized creature like a miniature wallaby – a fat-tailed dunnart.

Since June, when winter began, the dunnart has passed the lean months huddled under logs and rocks, living off the fat stored in its swollen tail – a built-in larder. Now its tail is thin and the dunnart is ready for a meal of insects.

Fat-tailed dunnarts have benefited from the spread of farmland, where there is plenty of the food they like. They prefer to hunt at night, and in one night a dunnart can get through enough insects to equal its own weight of about ½ oz (14g). Dainty and delicate but with powerful hind legs, it hops along kangaroo-fashion. An adult female is hindered at this time of the year by the four or five youngsters riding on her back. Her family is only half its original size. Up to ten babies were born in July and carried in her pouch at first, then later deposited in a nest of grass. The weaker ones died in their first weeks.

Now the ten-week-old survivors are nearly ready for weaning. This will coincide with the spring abundance of insects. The youngsters will be breeding themselves next season, and their mother may produce another litter in summer. Their lifespan is about 18 months.

Piggyback Carrying five youngsters, a female fat-tailed dunnart embarks on a night's insect hunting. The young are weaned in spring, when there is ample food.

OCTOBER

SNOW GEESE FLY SOUTH FROM THE ARCTIC WINTER,
MOUNTAIN GORILLAS FEAST ON BAMBOO IN AN AFRICAN FOREST, WASPS IN
EUROPE SEEK WINTER SHELTER, OCELOT LOVE-WAILS STIR
PARAGUAYAN FORESTS AND ALBATROSSES COURT IN SOUTHERN SEAS

Antarctica: Adélie penguins journey south to breed

A dazzle of geese *Thousands of lesser snow geese going south for winter break their journey on the California/Oregon border. They fly, feed and rest together in vast flocks.*

Migrant snow geese break their journey

Harsh quacks, wheezy whistles, honks and hisses sound across the Klamath Basin as millions of water birds break their long migratory journey here in October. They are on the way to warmer wintering grounds in Mexico and California, and the shallow lakes and flat, open fields of the basin, on the California/Oregon border, make a perfect stopping place.

Every so often hosts of lesser snow geese arrive. The whirr of thousands of wings beating the air in unison drowns even the din of this noisy haven. And with shrill, incessant barking calls of recognition, they snake across the sky in wavy lines like banners unfurling, and settle to the ground in a stunning spread of birds. Most are snowy white, relieved only by black wingtips, but there are also some coloured pale blue-grey.

Each autumn, as the days shorten, the snow geese leave western Canada, Alaska and eastern Siberia, where they nested in colonies of up to 1000 pairs, and head south. They always follow the same migration route west of the Rocky Mountains, known as the Pacific Flyway and up to 3000 miles (4800km) long, and touch down in the Klamath Basin in October as regular as clockwork. Other lesser snow geese from northern Canada fly a central route along the Mississippi Flyway to winter in Texas, Mississippi and Louisiana along the Gulf of Mexico.

But draining of the Klamath marshes to create farmland has drastically reduced the birds' haven. They squeeze into what remains, the ducks – mallard, gadwall, pintail, shoveller, teal – to feed on plants and tiny animals skimmed from the water surface, the geese to eat the marshland grasses and bulrushes. And to the farmers' dismay, the geese are also quite happy to eat their grain crops.

THE TIME TO MOVE

Animals migrate – undertake long, seasonal or periodic, two-way journeys – to ensure the best chance of survival and reproduction by securing a better food supply or escaping from hot or cold weather. Their movements may be triggered by variation in day length. A crucial amount of light affects part of the animal's brain and causes the release of hormones – chemical messengers in the blood – that affect behaviour.

Sallow moths that fly during the winter

Early morning sunlight strikes the fallen autumn leaves in an American wood as one small leaf seems to separate itself and quiver into life. The inconspicuous, pale-patterned triangle is indeed a live creature – a moth that has just emerged from its pupa (chrysalis).

In October, the time when most adult moths are dying, some species of sallow moth in the north-eastern United States – such as the spotted sallow and sidus sallow – are just becoming active. They will soon mate and lay their eggs, and the caterpillars that hatch from them will become pupae and change to adults in late winter. This second generation of 'winter' sallow moths will lay eggs that hatch before spring.

Winter temperatures may drop far below zero, yet the moths survive by hiding in the relative warmth under loose leaf litter. They can remain under cover for weeks, but then have to search for sugary tree sap to replenish their energy reserves. To warm themselves up for flight, the moths shiver for about 25 minutes. Their vibrating muscles raise the body temperature to about 30°C (86°F), suitable for flying.

Several body features help them to withstand the cold. The thorax (the part where the wings are attached) is covered with fine hairs that trap an insulating blanket of air. Between the thorax and the abdomen there are air sacs that prevent cold from the abdomen spreading to the thorax. In addition, the main blood vessels in the thorax are arranged so that their heat is retained.

Cold-weather moth Some species of sallow moth are active during the winter. They shelter in leaf litter and feed on the sap of damaged trees.

Journey's end *Monarch butterflies cover a tree in California after travelling the length of the USA.*

Monarch butterflies fly to find the sun

Huge clouds of butterflies billow through the October air to settle in their thousands on trees in California. So thick is this living cloak that the tree trunks and branches are invisible. The orange-brown monarch butterflies have arrived to sleep through the winter, stirring only on sunny days. Some trees are used year after year. They are known as 'butterfly trees', and are protected by law.

Hatched during early summer in southern Canada and the northern United States, the monarch butterflies – with a wingspan of 3-4in (75-100mm) – began the journey southwards in July. They slept by night and flew by day, generally covering about 80 miles (130km) in a day's flying, although some marked butterflies have been recorded as clocking up nearly 1200 miles (1900km) in less than a week. They stop to eat the nectar of many different flowers on the way, but also draw on stocks of body fat.

In spring the butterflies head north again in ones and twos. Many die on the way, but as the females lay eggs along the route, their offspring complete the journey north. The eggs are laid on the underside of milkweed leaves, the caterpillars' food plant, and hatch in a few days. The thumb-length caterpillars are banded with black, white and yellow – a warning to birds that they are poisonous. The poison is derived from the milkweed plants, and is passed on to the adult monarch butterfly.

Although the butterfly is easily seen against most backgrounds, any bird that takes it soon releases its victim and flies off with a bad taste in its mouth. Not only is the butterfly poisonous, its body is tough and leathery. It needs to be, to survive the incredible journey of around 2000 miles (3200km) it makes every year. The monarch is the only butterfly in North America that migrates such a long way along the same route generation after generation. Some get blown off course and end up in southern Britain. Others cross the Atlantic by hitching rides on ships. The butterfly is nicknamed 'The Wanderer'.

Shared feast *Whooper and Bewick's swans jostle amicably for winter food at low tide on salt marshes. Even a few dark coots, dwarfed by the swans, are allowed to join in.*

Migrating swans that trumpet their arrival

A distant bugling call penetrates the chill October mists that shroud an estuary in northern Britain. Six shapes emerge from the mist, flying lazily on massive wings. They drop to the water and make a rather undignified landing, their large webbed feet stretched out in front of them like water skis. The first whooper swans of the winter have returned.

These swans have just flown nonstop from Iceland – a distance of more than 850 miles (1360km) – and following close behind them are some 16,000 more. Only a few have remained in Iceland to see the winter through there.

The travellers cruised along at altitudes of up to 28,000ft (8500m) – as airline pilots can confirm – taking advantage of the strong winds at these heights to speed their journey. In this first

family to arrive at the wintering ground there are four cygnets – grey-brown youngsters with pinkish beaks. They hatched during the summer breeding season in Iceland. Their parents have crisp white plumage and graceful, elongated heads with yellow and black beaks. The family is tolerant of the other whoopers that are arriving, joining them in loose flocks that can number 100 birds or more.

The whoopers are tolerant, too, of other species. Some of the swans among the flock on the estuary are smaller than the whoopers, with thicker necks and shorter beaks that have more black on them. These are Bewick's swans, the rarest and smallest European swans, which have come from their breeding grounds in northern Russia before the freezing grip of winter. They are named after the celebrated illustrator of birds Thomas Bewick (1753-1828).

Sometimes squabbles erupt on the estuary and the whoopers break into loud bugling calls – not the sociable call made in flight, but a resonant threat. Now it becomes clear how the

whoopers got their name, for they have one of the loudest calls of the swan family. The musical hoots and honks of the Bewick's swans, noisy enough on their own, are no match.

The swans spend many days on the estuary shore, feeding on the short salt-marsh grasses, but as the winter goes by they spend more time on nearby farmland in search of grain among the stubble, or of potatoes and swedes and – to the irritation of farmers – newly sown seed.

As soon as the first longer, warmer days of spring arrive, the whoopers and the Bewick's hurry back home to their distant and widely separate breeding areas, where food is once again available. The days of peaceable mingling are over for another year. The young swans fly back north with their parents. This helps them to learn the migration routes and the feeding sites in both summer and winter quarters. Then their parents chase them away. Breeding pairs are just as firm in driving away other birds from their territory, for now they are intent on rearing another generation.

A queen wasp seeks a home for the winter

Hovering and buzzing, the large wasp investigates every nook it comes across on a pleasant October afternoon. This is a young queen common wasp, almost as long as a finger joint and nearly as thick as a pencil, and boldly marked with yellow and black.

She searches log piles, garden sheds, attics and hollow trees, looking for somewhere dark and sheltered where she can sleep through the winter. At last the queen chooses a small cavity under a hedge and settles on a root. All over Europe and north Asia, other queen wasps are on similar quests now that autumn is here.

The queen is one of a batch of queens that hatched in a hedgerow in late summer, in a papery nest the size of a football. Male wasps, almost as big as the queens but with longer antennae, hatched at the same time. They all left the nest together, three to six weeks after hatching, and shortly afterwards they mated.

In the nest they vacated, their mother, the old queen, has now stopped laying eggs and her female workers (which are only two-thirds the size of queens), have gone in search of rotting fruit to feed on. Some find their way into houses and cause panic, but they are not intent on attack. They will sting only if trapped or attacked, injecting a painful mixture of poisons

Royal rest A queen wasp, recently mated, spends the winter in a hole in a bank, clamping herself to a root with her jaws. In spring she will start a new wasp colony.

and the irritant histamine. Only females have stings, which are modified egg-laying tubes used to kill insects and caterpillars to feed to the larvae. Soon the old queen, the workers and the males will die, leaving only the young queens alive, hibernating in their dark corners.

Next spring, the young queen will emerge from hibernation, feed on energy-giving nectar from flowers, then set about finding a site for a nest. She may choose a deserted mouse burrow, a hollow low down in a hedgerow or the rafters of a loft. There she will chew up wood shaved from rotting stumps or fence posts, mix it with saliva and use this papier mâché to build a small nest consisting of a cluster of six-sided cells. In each cell the queen will lay a single egg.

When the eggs hatch, she will feed the larvae on partly chewed insects. The larvae grow quickly and develop into infertile females which become the workers of the wasp colony. The queen, free now of all the chores, can devote herself to laying more eggs. The workers enlarge the nest, adding more horizontal tiers of cells, until the nest eventually has accommodation for some 2000 wasps. Foraging workers feed on aphids, flies and caterpillars, and on returning to the nest regurgitate digested food for the queen, the workers on duty in the nest, and the larvae. The larvae give out a sweet liquid that supplements the wasps' diet.

As autumn approaches, the queen will lay a batch of eggs that will hatch into males and fertile females – the next generation of queens. Then her daughters will seek their own dark corners for the winter.

AVOIDING THE HARD LIFE

All earth's living species have survived by developing ways of dealing with unfavourable conditions. Birds may cope by migrating. Plants may change form and survive as seeds. Many mammals go into hibernation by slowing down their body systems. Insects may survive as eggs, larvae or chrysalises, or hibernate as adults.

The survival technique may be set off by different triggers. The commonest are temperature changes and daylight length, but others may include a shortage of the right food or of water. A queen wasp may have an extra spur to make her start laying the eggs that become males and fertile females instead of the usual workers. Perhaps the sperm she received when mating the previous autumn is almost used up.

Hints of the past in Chillingham cattle

A herd of small white cattle is grazing in English parkland on an October day. A bull among them bellows his dominance over the area he roams and grazes – his home range. The cattle belong to a herd that has ranged free in ½ sq mile (130ha) of parkland at Chillingham in Northumberland since the 13th century.

The bellowing bull shares his range with two subordinate bulls, sometimes sparring with them but generally tolerating them. Now and again they challenge him with glares, but soon turn aside and make a show of grazing to appease their overlord. The home ranges of similar groups of bulls overlap, but the groups seldom meet. The cows, calves and bullocks move all over the park in a loose group. Newborn calves are hidden in the bracken for a week or so before being introduced to the herd, each cow sniffing at a calf until it is accepted.

Now the weather is colder, the cattle are growing a warmer coat – but it may not be warm enough. Only 13 animals survived the hard winter of 1947. The herd now numbers over 50. Although the Chillingham cattle give a glimpse of how cattle once lived in the wild, they are not truly wild. They have no predators and no fixed breeding time – and if times are hard, a tractor will bring them a load of fodder.

Life almost in the wild Chillingham's wild white cattle have a hooting call. They are survivors of an ancient breed kept by the Celts 2000 years ago.

Wood clearers Ink-cap fungi (left) grow in dense clusters on dead wood. The sickener (right), which grows on the floor of a pine wood, looks similar to some edible mushrooms but has a peppery taste that can be nauseating.

Curious shapes Crinkled cups of orange-peel fungus (left) grow on the bare soil of woods and paths. The common earth-ball (right), a fungus of birch and pine woods, releases its black spores when its rough cap splits open.

Leaf eaters When it reaches maturity, the fruiting body of the shaggy parasol mushroom (left) amply fulfils its name – as does the amethyst deceiver (above). Both are fungi of the woodland floor which digest the plentiful leaf litter, producing food for themselves and a surplus that enriches the soil.

Mushrooms – the third kingdom of life

A lmost overnight, the floors of European woodlands are taken over by myriad mysterious shapes. Cups and parasols, balls and crumpled sheets, layered plates and overlapping shingles, muted and gaudy, they seem to appear from nowhere, thrusting up among the fallen October leaves or encrusting dead wood.

These newcomers can be classified as belonging to the third kingdom of life – not animals or plants but fungi, which burst into view only when their fruits form. Some of them are familiar to us as mushrooms and toadstools, but other fungi are truffles, yeasts, mildews, white and grey moulds, rusts and puffballs.

Fungi have none of the green chlorophyll which enables plants to make food, using light, carbon dioxide and water. Instead, fungi feed on animals and plants. Some fungi are parasites on living things – for example, rusts feed on growing plants. Most fungi, however, feed on dead matter. The vast majority grow in woodland or grassland where their food is abundant.

Although fungi seem to appear suddenly, they are growing throughout the year. The real body of the fungus – the equivalent of the trunk and roots of a tree – is a network of minute threads called hyphae. A mat of hyphae gives one group of fungi, the moulds, their characteristic cotton-

Rain burst The outer wall of the earth-star fungus peels back to reveal a bag inflated like a balloon. The pressure of raindrops on the bag is enough to force out a puff of spores that are carried off on the wind.

wool appearance. The flesh of the mushrooms we eat is made up of denser packs of hyphae.

A network of hyphae, known as the mycelium, spreads through the material on which the fungus is growing, seeking nourishment. A hypha breaks the material down into nutrients with digestive juices (enzymes) released from behind its tip. A fungus absorbs comparatively little of the nutrients it liberates, most going into the soil and enriching it, benefiting trees and other plants. Most trees have fungi growing within their roots, an arrangement that ensures a plentiful supply of nutrients for the tree and gives the fungus a protected place to grow.

The network of mycelium enables a fungus to grow outwards on its existing site at up to 12in (300mm) a year. For spreading to new sites, fungi have another system – the dispersal of spores. In the familiar field or button mushroom, for example, the rounded top that is the fruiting body swells and slowly opens outwards from the stalk like an umbrella, to form a cap. Fertilisation takes place internally, without the need for another fungus, and the narrow gills that radiate under the cap produce spores.

When the cap opens out, the spores are freed. Smaller than grains of dust, these spores are produced in vast quantities – perhaps as many as 16 thousand million from a mushroom cap 4in (100mm) across. Each one, borne off on the wind, has the chance to put out its own threads and form a new fungus.

Feast before fast *Late nectar from the ivy flowers is a boon for the comma butterfly feeding up for hibernation.*

THE TIME TO FLOWER

When it was found in 1920 that the time at which plants flower is linked to daylight length, plants were classified as long-day (henbane, peppermint, for example) or short-day (soya bean, tobacco). Later work showed that night-length rather than day-length is critical. In darkness, leaves produce a chemical, still not identified, that starts off bud development.

If a short period of artificial light interrupts the darkness, plants that need short nights (the long-day group) respond by flowering, but those needing long nights (the short-day group) do not flower. Commercial growers use these responses to produce out-of-season flowers.

In a mushroom, and other fungi, the forming of the spore-bearing caps is not triggered by light, but by a particular alternation of dry and wet conditions, coupled with the right temperature.

Ivy – the last filling station for insects

Neat, glossy and undemanding, ivy clothes walls, tree trunks and embankments with its profuse, dark-green growth. And when early autumn brings a late burst of warmth to western Europe – as it often does – ivy becomes the magnet for a flurry of activity. Its tiny, unobtrusive, greenish-yellow flowers are the attraction. Nestling discreetly among the leaves from September to November, they are one of the year's last sources of nectar (apart from garden flowers introduced from other continents).

Because the ivy flowers open only in bright sunshine, the precious nectar is preserved for the time when late bees, flies, butterflies and moths are most likely to be active. For the late warmth of an Indian summer brings out insects once more, offering those that hibernate as adults through the winter a last chance to stock up on food. With the bulk of the summer flowers well over, the ivy is a rare treat.

For most insects, however, adult life is little more than a brief flight in search of a mate. But for this they need energy-giving sugars, which they find in flower nectar. For them, too, the ivy is a boon, as it may mean the difference between the success and failure of a late brood.

An incidental reward for the plant is that visiting insects transfer pollen from the male to the female parts of flowers, fertilising them so that they set seed. There is certainly no shortage of pollinating insects for the ivy. In most years it produces an abundant crop of seed-bearing berries, which remain green through the winter and ripen to a shiny black in late spring. They are a nutritious food for blackbirds, thrushes, robins and other woodland and garden birds.

Ivy gives good value in other ways too. Small tortoiseshell butterflies stock up with its nectar and then crawl into the protection of the dense foliage to hibernate. Mice may also shelter there, and when spring comes birds nest among the leaves. In summer butterflies visit it again – this time the holly blue which lays its eggs among the ivy so that its autumn generation of caterpillars will hatch amid a plentiful store of their favourite food – ivy buds.

The start of something big *A Masai giraffe tends her newborn calf. Within hours it will master its gangly legs and enormous neck and be able to run with its mother.*

A giraffe returns to her home calving ground

In the light of an October dawn in the Masai Mara National Reserve in southern Kenya, a female giraffe nuzzles her newborn calf. She has been pregnant for 15 months, wandering the vast area of the Mara's scrubby grasslands. But during the past few weeks, as the time of her calf's birth approached, she migrated back to her calving ground – the place where many mothers return year after year to give birth, even if it is a long distance from their home range.

Their journey is worth the effort, for the return of other mothers-to-be ensures that several calves arrive on the calving ground at roughly the same time. This means that, after the first few vulnerable days have passed, each mother will be able to steal away for a few hours. She will go in search of food during the heat of the day, when most predators are asleep, leaving her calf in the relative safety of the group.

The giraffe is the tallest animal in the world, and those found on the Masai Mara are the largest. A female Masai giraffe is about 15ft (4.6m) high, a male up to 17ft (5m) high. Because the mother does not lie down when she gives birth, a calf's first experience in life is to be launched head first from a height of about 7ft (2m).

The newborn calf, which is about 6ft (1.8m) tall and weighs 15 stone (95kg), has difficulty at first in keeping its huge neck under control. After the mother has gently cleaned and nuzzled the calf, she quickly encourages it to get up. Mastering those long legs is also a struggle, but within an hour or so the calf is able to totter about and even run for short stretches.

It is vital that the mother closely supervises these first hours. A lion, the giraffe's chief predator, can easily pounce on the vulnerable baby if it is not protected, and leopards, hyenas or wild dogs may take a small calf. However, the giraffe is an excellent mother. If her calf bleats in alarm, she will kick out defensively with her soup-plate-sized hoofs, and drive off any predator that approaches. She will suckle the calf until it is 10-17 months old.

In the Masai Mara, births peak in October in

time for the November-December rainy season, which will bring lush vegetation for the mothers to convert into milk for their offspring. But in a land governed so strictly by seasons, giraffes are unusual – their feeding habits allow them to breed at any time of the year. This is because they browse on shoots and leaves, particularly acacia, using their long necks to stretch up into the trees. So when the plains dry out and

animals reliant on grass have to migrate in search of fresh pastures, giraffes can still find food on the trees growing along the wooded banks of rivers and streams.

This means that female giraffes stay in good condition throughout the dry season and can manage to rear their calves successfully in all but the driest conditions. However, most mothers take advantage of the arrival of the

life-giving rain and produce their calves in October, for then the calf has the best chance of being well-fed, strong and healthy and growing up to join its parents as they browse quietly in their lofty world.

Race from danger *Startled by an approaching lion, two female giraffes lead their young calves to safety at full tilt. They can sprint at 32mph (52km/h).*

Bright eyes *Large, saucer-like eyes glint in the dark as two bush babies prepare to set off for a night's feeding.*

Bush babies hunt moths in the African night

As darkness falls on the tree-scattered grass-land of East Africa, two furry, pale-grey heads poke out from a hollow in a tree and sniff the night air. They belong to lesser bush babies, rat-sized primates (of the same order as man) with long, slim tails. It is October – a good time for bush babies, for the rains have brought them food in plenty – insects and soft fruit.

The animals peer about with their huge eyes and listen intently with bat-like ears pricked. So sensitive are their ears that they can hear the erratic flight of approaching moths. They grip the branch with their hind feet, and as the moths flutter within reach, stretch up and grab one with a clapping motion of their hands. This was an easy catch, but bush babies can be swift and agile when leaping in pursuit of more difficult prey. They make repeated, plaintive cries to keep in touch in the dark.

Near by a mother bush baby reaches into her nest hole and lifts out, in her jaws, her tiny, week-old baby, for the young are born at this time of plenty. She carries it to a chosen feeding place and puts it on a tree branch where she can keep an eye on it while she eats. The baby clings to the branch with a strong instinctive grip. When she moves on, the mother carries the baby to another branch, keeping a sharp lookout for predators such as snakes, owls and small cats.

As yet, the baby is still breastfed. Mother and baby will continue to forage like this for a few weeks before taking up their more usual social life with a group of female relatives. Youngsters are weaned at 8-11 weeks old, and at about eight or nine months old the young males leave the family group to live alone or with a few other young males. Once a female has weaned her youngster, she will often mate again, and about four months later give birth to a second brood of one, two, or three babies, making the most of the March-May rainy season.

All bush babies have their own territory, which is marked by scent. They urinate into special pouches in their hands and feet, then walk about leaving scent marks as they go. Females share their territory with their female offspring, so building up a small group. Older, dominant males may range over the area of several female groups, and mate with them for as long as they can fight off rivals.

In the drier months from June to September, when few insects are about, the bush babies' diet includes tree gum. Their comb-like front teeth are useful for scraping away tree bark and getting at the liquid gum below. Another fleshy comb on the underside of the tongue helps them to clean their teeth. Bush babies also use their front teeth for grooming their thick fur, and have a special claw on each second toe of the hind feet for combing the head and neck. They often groom each other.

NIGHT LIFE
Like most animals that sleep by day and feed at night, bush babies rely most on their hearing in order to hunt and find their way about. They can turn their heads a full half circle, and their large ears, with fleshy ridges that help to channel sounds, can be moved in the direction of a sound. They can also fold their ears flat – one or both at a time – when sleeping, or as a protection if they are threatened.

Their very large eyes let in an exceptional amount of light, but are more useful at short range than long range, and their vision is rather blurred and not accurate in detail. Bush babies rely more on picking up scent than do other primates.

Cutting a dash A male ostrich sinks to the ground as he dances to woo a mate. During the breeding season he entices several females to lay eggs in his nest.

Communal clutch When his courting is done, the ostrich is left with a clutch of about 25 eggs in his nest – a scrape in the ground. They hatch in six weeks.

Baby minder Ostrich chicks gather round their guardian's feet as the tall bird scans the plains for danger. An ostrich has exceptionally good eyesight.

Fathering a family of ostrich chicks

The ostrich mating season is at its peak on the treeless borders of Africa's Namib Desert, in readiness for the December rains that will bring fresh growth for the new generation. In the dry, dusty October heat, flocks of male ostriches dash about excitedly when groups of female ostriches approach. The spectacular males – the world's biggest birds – are as heavy as a big man and at least a head taller. They hiss and snort as they raise their wings and tails, showing off their soft, loose, black and white plumes to attract the drab brown females.

It is the older males who succeed in attracting the most females. A female approaches the male of her choice and walks stiffly around him, signalling her approval. He escorts her to his nesting territory, where he shows off even more, repeatedly dropping to the ground, tail and wing feathers extended, as he sways his body and weaves his head and neck to and fro. When the female is ready, the pair mate.

The male scrapes out a shallow nest in the sandy soil, and the female lays 4–8 shiny, cream-coloured eggs in it. Then the male courts several other females, who also lay their eggs in his nest. Each hen lays every other day until there is a clutch of about 25 eggs, each 6in (150mm) long and 5in (125mm) across. Nest duties are shared by the male and the most dominant female. She incubates the eggs by day, he takes over at night. After about six weeks the chicks are ready to hatch, and call from within the thick-shelled eggs. From now on, the parents will know them by their calls. Sometimes the adults help to release the struggling youngsters. Only about half the eggs hatch.

Ostrich chicks can feed themselves on seeds and vegetation as soon as they hatch, but are in danger from predators such as foxes and jackals. The male and the dominant female gather the chicks into a crèche and watch over them constantly. If they are threatened, one bird may attempt to distract and draw off the hunter. By the following breeding season, the youngsters are big enough to fend for themselves, but they do not breed until they are about four years old.

Adult ostriches have little to fear from predators. Their height and their long, flexible necks give them an excellent view of their surroundings. Although they are far too heavy to fly, they can run as fast as a racehorse on their long, powerful legs as thick as a man's thigh.

Dreaded pests Flightless young desert locusts eat a leaf. Locusts have powerful jaws; an average swarm of 50 thousand million can eat 3000 tons of greenery a day.

Desert locusts strip the countryside bare

Wingless young desert locusts, called hoppers, seethe in a bright, munching mass across the North-east African grassland. After years of drought, September rains have encouraged females to lay more eggs than usual in the damp sandy soil – each laying ten batches of up to 100 – and in the warmth and humidity most have developed to hatch after two or three weeks. In many years breeding conditions are unfavourable and the number of hoppers is low, but this October the population has exploded, forcing the hoppers to travel in search of food.

Soon they will undergo a final moult and emerge with wings. Taking to the air, they will swarm across the countryside, stripping it of crops and greenery. A swarm may easily number 50 thousand million locusts. They are carried westwards by the prevailing winds. If the weather is humid and food abundant, they will lay eggs and begin a new swarm. If not, they will eventually starve. Occasionally they are blown out to sea, where they drown.

Airborne During plagues, swarms of locusts migrate in search of food, the winged adults carried on the winds and succeeded in the swarms by their offspring.

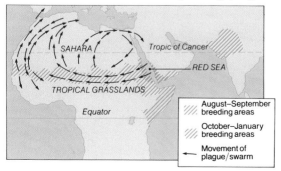

Gentle gorillas belie their fearsome looks

Nine mountain gorillas loll on the forest floor, the chewed remains of their two-hour meal of leaves and stems strewn around them. Having eaten their fill, the adults doze in the midday sun, eyes closed under their heavy brows. But even in the heat, the four youngsters in the group find it difficult to sit still and soon get a game going. With open-mouthed smiles, they rampage through the undergrowth and across the chests of tolerant grown-ups, who hardly bat an eye, even if their hair is pulled.

Clouds bring the siesta to an end. It is October, and from now until April there will be heavy rain every day for hours. The ground is permanently sodden, the leaves constantly drip and thick mists cling to the Virunga Mountains between Rwanda, Uganda and Zaire, the part of Africa where the gorillas live. They hate to get wet, and shelter under the trees. For most of the year the gorillas roam the rugged high slopes where rain forests provide plenty of leaves, shoots and stems for them to eat – they are solely vegetarian. The lower slopes below 10,000ft (3000m) usually have little to offer, but the rain has encouraged growth in the bamboo forests there, which are now sprouting high-protein fresh greens – a feast too good to miss. So the gorillas move down the mountain to feed.

The black, broad-backed animals walk leisurely on all fours, following their leader, a 16-year-old male. When he stands upright, the leader is about shoulder high to a man, but may well weigh more than 30 stone (190kg). His silvery back clearly identifies him as a mature male – known as a silverback. The three adult females in the group are all over ten years old and the youngsters that troop after them are between two and seven years old – and all born at different times of the year, for there is no particular breeding season. A young adult male brings up the rear. Young males are not driven out of the group, but may choose to wander alone until they can win mates.

In the bamboo forest, the gorillas make their presence felt. Their trails crisscross between the pole-like stems that rise as high as a two-storey house. Strong hands break young stems and dig

....

Fresh greens *A male mountain gorilla feasts on new, succulent bamboo shoots. Hunting and the destruction of their forest homelands have brought these gorillas to the edge of extinction. Less than 1000 remain.*

up shoots, and massive jaws rip them open to get at the pith. The gorillas often take only one bite from each piece – with such plenty they are spoilt for choice and wasteful. But they might as well make the most of the bounty, for within weeks the new bamboo will turn woody and unpalatable, and the gorillas will move up the mountain to feed on plants that have regrown during their absence.

The quiet of the forest is broken only by snapping branches, smacking lips, grunts and belches. Wherever the gorillas are ranging, the silverback sets the pace and pattern of their days, but their stomachs dictate their activities. An adult male eats about 66lb (30kg) of vegetation every day – all of it collected at ground level, for a full-grown male is too heavy to climb trees. The youngsters and females sometimes

climb into the trees to sleep as well as to feed.

Finding, eating and resting to digest food takes up most of the group's days. In their placid lives, the only aggression occurs when a young male challenges the status of the silverback. Then the opponents try to intimidate each other by roaring, tearing at vegetation, running sideways and beating their chests. Such clashes are largely bluff and are settled without injury.

Patient playmate *A boisterous infant tugs the massive forearm of this silverback gorilla. He weighs more than two men, but is gentle when pestered by youngsters.*

In safe custody *A male hornbill brings clay and mud to the nest hole for the female to narrow the entrance (left). They leave a small slit as wide as two fingers through which the male passes food, such as a lizard (centre), to the female inside. When the chicks are big enough, the female breaks out (right), and the chicks seal themselves in again.*

A hornbill holes up with her crowd of chicks

A handsome black and white bird with a large red beak flies to a narrow, vertical slit in a tree trunk and grips the bark with his splayed toes. Like a human posting a letter, the magpie-sized red-billed hornbill pops a large beetle into the slit. A glimpse of another red beak is the only sign that his mate is incarcerated in the tree with their three-week-old nestlings. The male hornbill departs, and a moment later some small white packages are pushed from the hole as the female throws out the chicks' droppings.

It is October, two or three months since the pair began nesting in a patch of forest amid the scrub and grassland of Kenya. The tree hole they selected is some 12ft (3.7m) above the ground, and big enough for the female and several large youngsters. There is also a dark recess leading upwards, where the birds can crawl if a snake should look in, searching for tasty morsels.

With the male's assistance, the female sealed off the entrance from outside with mud and clay until the slit was just big enough for her to squeeze through. Then she went in to begin

about two months of confinement. With her help, the male completed the wall, leaving a slit large enough for his beak to reach in with food, and through this he passed her leaves and bark for lining the nest, as well as snail shells for her to eat to provide extra calcium for egg production. While in the nest, the female moults.

A few days after this secure maternity ward was completed, the female hornbill began to lay her white, rather pock-marked eggs. For five days she laid a single egg daily, beginning to incubate immediately so that hatching occurred at roughly daily intervals. The first blind and naked chick appeared after 24 days, the others

soon after. Now, three weeks on, the five chicks are at their hungriest and the male is constantly on the go, bringing food to the nest. He turns over wood and lumps of earth to find beetles or grubs, or he follows the herds of big game on the plains for insects stirred up by their feet.

Soon the female will break her way out of the nest and share the feeding duties with him. The chicks will immediately re-seal the nest with their droppings. It will be another three or four weeks before they emerge, fully fledged and ready to fly. But the parent hornbills will continue to feed them for six more weeks, and the family will stay together until about March.

MAKING LIGHT WORK OF A BIG ATTRACTION

Although the red-billed hornbill's down-curving reddish beak is as big as its head, the bird is adept at using it for the delicate task of passing insects through a small slit into the nest. Such a large beak is not the impossible burden it might seem for a flying bird. The beak is hollow, strengthened by thin, bony struts, and is surprisingly light.

The red-billed hornbill is one of about 50 species of hornbill, some of them as big as

eagles. Half of the hornbill species live in Africa, the rest in the Far East or Australasia. All have massive beaks, often brightly coloured, and many species also have a hard growth – a casque – on top of the beak.

The beaks and casques probably help to attract mates, although southern Asian rhinoceros hornbills may also use their casques as weapons. Male hornbills often have bigger and more colourful beaks than females.

Booby chicks are killers while still in the nest

Their blue faces framed with fluffy down, two masked booby chicks waddle around their smaller mother. It is October and they are almost fully grown. Soon they will be leaving their crowded nest colony among the scrub to dive into the sea round their Galápagos island home – Genovesa (Tower Island) just north of the Equator – to search for squid and flying fish.

It is unusual to find two chicks together. The first bird to hatch usually kills its nest-mate. This probably ensures the survival of one well-fed, strong bird rather than two weak ones. But the second chick is likely to be killed even when there is plenty of food. Perhaps the second egg is an insurance for the parents in case the first is stolen or the chick dies.

South of the Equator, the masked boobies on Española (Hood Island) are just preparing for courtship. Why boobies on different islands in the Galápagos breed at different times is not known. It may be that the Humboldt Current, which shifts north and south with the seasons, brings fish to the islands at varying times.

Courtship is noisy and complicated. During the performance the birds call to one another and throw back their heads, wings open. The female trumpets loudly, but the male can only summon up a feeble, high-pitched whistle.

The parents incubate their eggs by covering them gently with their large webbed feet before settling with their breast feathers over them. Blood vessels in the webbing between the toes keeps the eggs warm. When it is too hot, a parent bird will stand like a sunshade to shield the eggs or chicks from the sun.

The masked, or blue-faced, booby is the largest of the tropical gannets. It is about the size of a goose and has a wingspan of up to 6ft (1.8m). It fishes by plunge-diving almost vertically into the sea. Sometimes 1000 birds together will make a spectacular plunge. Air sacs on a booby's throat and breast help soften the impact when it hits the water, and its eyes are in padded sockets. The nostrils have no opening on the outside; when not diving the bird breathes through air passages inside its beak.

Happy family It is rare for a mother to raise two masked booby chicks – the first to hatch usually kills the other.

Looks can kill Thousands of ocelots are killed for their beautiful dark-spotted coats. During courtship in October they make far more noise than at other times.

Noisy courtship for the shy, beautiful ocelot

Deep in the heart of a forest in Paraguay, an ear-splitting caterwauling rends the spring night. The loud yowling comes from an ocelot, a distant cousin of the domestic cat but about twice its size. Prowling the forests and scrub-lands from Mexico to northern Argentina, these skilled hunters, climbers and swimmers are normally shy and retiring. But October is mating time for the southern populations, and the males court with midnight serenades.

Ocelots usually communicate in other ways. A male has a territory that overlaps the ranges of up to three females. The animals live alone, but keep in touch by leaving scent marks of urine and droppings, and by rubbing against trees or rocks to release scent from body glands. A receptive female leaves a special odour, and the male gives voice when they mate at night.

The kittens – usually one or two – are born three months later and are destined for lives of secrecy and stealth. They will sleep away their days in hollow trees, and spend their nights stalking small mammals, birds and snakes.

High-flying possums in a warm, wet world

G limmering in the October twilight a creamy-furred possum hunches on a branch in the high Australian rain forest of northern Queensland. Reaching out a small pink hand, it snaps off a twig then quietly chews its way through its fistful of leaves until a slight threat – perhaps an approaching snake or bird of prey – sends it flying through the trees.

At once the stillness is broken by hissing squeaks. Panic has seized the possum's baby, temporarily left alone as its mother flees to draw the predator away. Just two months old, the young possum has only recently emerged from its mother's pouch, where it has been kept safe since its birth in August.

The mother, built like a small domestic cat with an overgrown tail, leaps 6ft (1.8m) or more at a time from branch to branch, with limbs spreadeagled and tail flailing. She can also run swiftly along the branches, and has thumbs on both hands and feet that allow her to grasp branches securely as thumb and fingers meet.

This striking gingery-white possum is found nowhere else in the world. It was once thought to be a separate species but now it is known to be a variant form of the dark-coated lemuroid possum, named for its likeness to the lemurs of Madagascar. About a quarter of lemuroid possums are gingery-white. Young born to white mothers may be white or dark, and dark couples sometimes have white offspring.

Lemuroid possums live only on the Atherton Tableland and the densely forested mountain peaks near Cairns, at altitudes over 3500ft (1100m). Seldom descending to the ground in this humid home, they spend the day curled up in tree hollows and feed at night on a variety of leaves, plus some fruit and flowers. Being more sociable than other possums, several animals eat together. At breeding time couples nest together – unusual behaviour for pouched mammals – and some fathers even stay with the family. Sadly, tree-felling is reducing the already small home region of these attractive creatures and threatening their survival.

Light in the night *Beautiful cream-furred lemuroid possums live in only one patch of Australian rain forest. Their bare-tipped tails act as extra hands to grip the branches as they leap and run in the trees by night.*

Nightbird *Nesting short-tailed shearwaters spend their days on land in burrows, and come out only at night.*

Shearwaters stop globe-trotting to breed

As the October dusk falls, spine-chilling shrieks rise from the earth on the desolate islands between Australia and Tasmania. It is the southern spring, and these are the courting calls of the short-tailed shearwaters, pigeon-sized birds that have gathered in huge and noisy flocks to breed in burrows. The globe-trotting shearwaters have spent the winter at sea feeding on squid, krill and fish.

Yearly round *Shearwaters make a five-month, 18,000 mile (29,000km) tour of the Pacific, following food. They breed on Australia's south-east coasts and islands.*

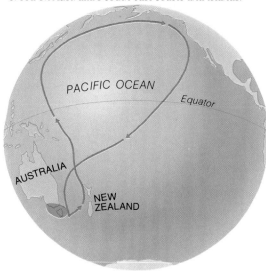

Colonies may number more than 100,000 pairs and the burrow entrances are only an arm span apart. A few pairs may have to dig new burrows, but most reclaim existing burrows. The nesting birds spend the day underground, coming above ground to feed only at night.

After mating in their burrows at the end of October, the birds go back to sea for three weeks to feed and build up their strength – needed for the female to lay a large white egg and for the male to survive the first two weeks of incubating, which he does alone. After that, both take turns at sitting on the egg for another six weeks. They call to each other enthusiastically when one arrives to relieve the other. Once the chick is hatched, it is fed huge meals of partly digested food by both parents once every few days – or even once a fortnight if food supplies are poor.

In late April or May, all the chicks spend about ten nights exercising their wings at the burrow entrances. Then they are ready to leave on the annual winter tour. Most of them will not return until their third summer and they will not breed until five years old if female, or six if male.

Although superbly graceful in flight, the shearwaters are awkward on land and are easy prey for cats and rats, so do not breed on islands where there are such predators. Elsewhere their chief enemies are gulls and ravens. The 19th-century settlers on the islands called the shearwaters mutton birds because they were a welcome addition to the usual meat – mutton. The fat of the very plump young birds, which may weigh about 2lb (1kg) a few weeks before they leave their burrows, also provided fuel.

Easy living for possums in a land of honey

In springtime the heathland bordering the arid centre of Western Australia bursts into a blaze of red and yellow blossoms. Although the soil is meagre and sandy, a huge variety of plants thrives there. Lured by the bright colours and strong scents, bees, beetles and flies alight on the blooms, sip the nectar and accidentally spread pollen as they go. Birds such as honey eaters and lorikeets also take their fill of nectar.

There is a night shift, too – the mouse-sized honey possum, one of the few mammals in the world to feed exclusively on nectar and pollen. With its tail wound round a eucalyptus shoot and its brown fur speckled with pollen, a honey possum pokes its long snout into a flower and sticks out its tongue, which is long and bristly at the tip, to pick up more nectar. Unlike all other possums, of which it is only a distant relative, it has toes instead of claws.

The honey possum can breed at any time of year but most litters of two or three young are born at the end of summer. They stay in their mother's pouch for about eight weeks, by which time each weighs a bit less than a sugar cube – little enough but a colossal gain since birth, when each weighed less than a grain of rice. The mother suckles them in the nest for 11 weeks during winter. So most young honey possums are weaned in time to benefit from the spring feast of nectar as they venture off alone to raid the flowers under cover of darkness.

Sweet store *Clinging to a stalk with tail, hands and feet, a tiny honey possum nuzzles into a coral gum flower and licks up nectar with its long tongue.*

ANTARCTICA

Adélie penguins march on short rations

In late October, Adélie penguins gather in noisy troops and trek southwards across the icy Antarctic wasteland to breed. They nest inland on exposed, rocky plains least liable to be smothered with snowdrifts and flooded in the summer thaw, and some birds have an arduous trek of 60 miles (100km) or more to reach their rookery (breeding ground). If their chicks are to get the full benefit of the summer supply of fish and krill, the penguins must breed as soon as possible in spring, so cannot wait for the warmer weather of November to melt the ice at the mainland edges and shorten their journey.

The longest journey takes nearly a week, for the penguins are a little over 2ft (610mm) tall, and can stride only 4in (100mm). When the ice and snow get smooth, they slide along on their bulky stomachs, paddling with their feet and flippers. They have a layer of fat under the skin to help keep out the cold, and their woolly down and overlapping feathers trap a layer of air that holds in body heat. The body fat is also a built-in larder, necessary because while a penguin is away from the sea there is nothing for it to eat.

After a week or so of courting at the rookery, with much braying, bowing and flapping of flippers, each couple builds a nest of pebbles high enough to keep the eggs above water as the ice melts. Once a hen has laid her two white eggs in early November, she leaves her mate to incubate them and returns to sea to eat. With the ice melted, the walk is much shorter, but if she does not come back within three weeks, he will have to go to feed as well, leaving the eggs to the skuas and the pebbles to the neighbours.

If all goes well, however, in the five weeks the eggs take to hatch, each partner does two shifts of incubating. Then both are kept busy feeding the chicks. When the chicks are about a month old, they huddle together in crèches, their numbers a protection against predatory skuas. Their parents feed them in the crèche, recognising their own chick by its call. At two months old the chicks go to sea, but the parents stay on land longer to moult.

Penguin parade Thousands of Adélie penguins march across the ice to their breeding grounds inland. They race against time to nest and raise their young before returning to the sea in autumn.

A wandering albatross comes home to breed

For nearly a year the wandering albatross has been constantly at sea, gliding effortlessly over great distances on her huge wings and now and then dropping to the water to seize fish and squid. But as the spring days lengthen, she is returning to the tussocky slopes and cliff tops of her home on Bird Island off South Georgia in the southern Atlantic to breed.

Spring is not a kindly season in this part of the world. Buffeted by the October gales, the swan-sized female albatross crash lands and almost overbalances on the muddy turf. Awkwardly she folds her wings – they span 11ft (3.4m), the greatest wingspan of any living bird – and waddles off on her large, webbed feet.

On a gentle but windswept slope, the female finds the nest she and her mate have used for many years – a mound of mud and vegetation cupped at the top. Her mate, who returned to the island a week ago, has been busy refurbishing the nest. The birds pair for life. Only death or several years of failing to produce a chick will separate them.

Reunited after their long separation, the albatrosses begin to court each other. Elaborate courtship is essential for renewing their bond, even if they are partners of many years' standing. The pair face each other with their wings outstretched, and bow and dip their heads elegantly in waving movements as they vibrate their beaks and groan and croak in unison. Then they throw back their heads in turn, pointing their pale pink beaks skywards before using them to fence with each other as they stand close together. The whiteness of their heads, necks and underparts is offset by the dark brown of their wingtips.

Other pairs of wandering albatrosses are reuniting around them, forming a loose colony of several thousand couples spread thinly over the hillside.

On the edge of this colony, small groups of immature birds display themselves to one another in a stilted version of the adult dance. The albatrosses do not breed until they are five or even ten years old, and may spend several breeding seasons displaying to a number of different birds before perfecting their courtship technique and choosing a permanent partner. They breed only once every two years, because it takes just over a year to incubate an egg and raise a chick until it is fully fledged.

A few hours after mating, the female albatross takes to the air again and is soon a white speck in the distance. She will not lay her single egg until December or January.

Before then she will visit her mate at the nest perhaps twice, but will spend the rest of the time at sea, eating as much food as she can to fuel the egg and give the chick a good start in life. Also, having spent several years choosing her partner, she wants to avoid the attentions of

Courting couple A pair of wandering albatrosses throw back their heads in a courtship dance, a ritual that helps to renew their bond after a long separation.

other males who might want to mate with her.

Once the egg is laid, the two birds will take turns in sitting on it and searching for food out to sea. The foraging bird often covers 9500 miles (15,200km) in just over a month, and each time it returns it is rewarded with an ecstatic display by its mate. Without this strong bond, the sitting bird could well be forced off the nest by its need

Atlantic neighbours On an island south of the Falklands, these two-month-old black-browed albatross chicks hatched in October while the wandering albatrosses were still courting.

for food. The chick does not hatch until March.

At first one parent stays with the chick while the other collects food for it, feeding it by regurgitation. But when the chick is about 7lb (3kg) and big enough to repulse most predators, both parents go in search of food. In the depths of winter the adults go to sea, returning very occasionally to feed the huge, bloated, fluffy youngster, which lives mainly off its fat reserves. When spring comes again, the parents return more often to feed the chick, now about six months old. At about 11 months of age, the youngster is fully fledged. The adults leave, and soon afterwards the chick also flies out to sea to wander alone until it is old enough to breed.

These magnificent birds have been known to journey across the southern oceans for some 20,000 miles (32,000km), taking advantage of the prevailing westerlies. Never once resting on dry land, they glide on the wind and fish in the sea until the breeding season comes round again.

223

Sunbathers *Young crabeater seals not yet old enough to breed rest on an ice floe as spring breaks up the Antarctic ice. Mature crabeater seals breed on the ice floes.*

Short family encounters for crabeater seals

Crabeater seals are probably more numerous than any other sea mammal. There are up to 35 million of them wandering the Antarctic and southern oceans – more than the human population of Australia and New Zealand combined. Early October is the peak time for crabeater births – the time of the southern spring when the edge of the Antarctic ice is breaking up into ice floes.

Pairs of crabeater seals haul themselves onto the smaller floes. The larger of each pair is the female, who is about to give birth. The smaller male is keeping her company in the hope of mating with her once her pup is weaned. On some of the larger floes there are bigger groups of crabeaters which are still too young to breed. Females can breed when they are about three years old and males when they are about four.

Soon the pairs on the smaller floes become trios. Each pale, coffee-coloured pup huddles close to its pale grey mother, feeding on her rich milk and growing fast. She will not leave the pup for a month or more, not even to feed, relying for nourishment on her fat reserves. And the males do not leave their females because another male could quickly take over.

A waiting male fights off challengers for his female, and is fiercely aggressive to the female

---

LIFE SUPPORT

Without shrimp-like krill, whales, seals, penguins, fish and squid could not survive. Some eat krill direct; others eat the creatures that feed on krill. Shoals of the 2in (50mm) long krill can stretch for some 650yds (600m), colouring the water red by day and blue-green by night. Krill themselves feed on plankton, caught in a sieve formed by their front six pairs of legs while they paddle with the rear five.

When threatened by a small fish, a krill will literally jump out of its skin, leaving its flimsy outer skeleton as a decoy. But the krill have no defence against crabeater seals, which gulp down dozens at a time.

---

herself as he presses her to mate with him. Yet the scars borne by most adult crabeaters are not inflicted by rivals or mates. The scars, which are usually parallel scoring, are almost certainly made by the teeth of the seals' chief predator, the leopard seal, during attacks when the crabeaters were pups.

By early November, the female seal has lost half her body weight providing milk for the now well-grown pup. As she comes into season she no longer resists the male. Once his long wait has been rewarded, the male crabeater seal leaves the female, and she takes to the water to feed and renew her layer of blubber. Hunger soon drives the pup into the sea.

There the youngster will either quickly become a meal for a leopard seal or a killer whale, or it will grow in wisdom and agility as it feeds at night on the summer swarms of krill. The seal's many-lobed teeth mesh together to form a perfect sieve for separating the krill from the water. In spite of their name, crabeater seals do not eat crabs. They are the only seals to feed almost entirely on krill, which are the most plentiful food in the sea.

NOVEMBER

SALMON LEAP UP EUROPEAN RIVERS AS WEDDELL SEALS SING
IN SOUTHERN SEAS. TERMITES SWARM AND CHEETAHS RAISE FAMILIES IN THE
AFRICAN GRASSLANDS. GANNETS CONGREGATE IN NEW
ZEALAND TO BREED AND TASMANIAN DEVILS SCREAM OVER CARRION

NORTH AMERICA

Where bald eagles feast before winter comes

With the approach of another winter in November, cold, harsh weeks stretch ahead for animals in the mountains and forests of southern Alaska. Soon after dawn, bald eagles cluster in their hundreds in the Ponderosa pines flanking the Chilkat river. The powdery snow falling on them makes their brownish-black bodies almost as white as their white-feathered heads and tails. Suddenly one of the birds, scanning with its superb vision, sights a salmon in the river below and launches itself into the air on a slow, cruising circle.

The eagle, 3ft (1m) long with a wingspan about twice this measure, floats with wings stretched flat and spread like fingers at the tips, where each flight feather is more than 12in (300mm) long. Turning its head slightly for a better view of the prey, the eagle swoops low over the water to grip the salmon with long, strong talons. The prey may weigh more than the predator but there is no contest. The eagle lifts it with very little effort and rises again to its perch.

Grasping the fish with one foot, the successful hunter tears off a meal with its huge, hooked, yellow beak. Well fed, it dozes off until hunger stirs it again. Like its companions, it huddles with feathers fluffed out to trap a blanket of air that retains its body heat. Its legs, too, have a protective covering of feathers. Despite its name (earned by its appearance from a distance), it is the bird's feet rather than its head that are naked and vulnerable to the cold; so it sits with one foot tucked into its belly feathers and crouches slightly to make its feathers cover all but one toe of the perching foot.

The eagles have assembled over the river ready for their migration south to spend winter in warmer states such as Idaho and Utah. Before they leave they are making the most of an annual bonanza. The autumn run of salmon to their shallow upriver spawning ground is just over, and the waters teem with the thrashing bodies of huge fish too exhausted to return to the sea. They make a feast not just for the diving adult eagles – less experienced young birds wade in up to their bellies to grab a passing fish. Bears, raccoons and foxes also take their fill. In a few short weeks, the salmon have either been eaten or have begun to rot and, with the weather becoming more wintry, the eagles fly south.

THE EAGLE'S EYE
Predatory birds such as eagles must have accurate vision in order to spot small prey in glinting water or among ground cover, often from a great height. Eagles have enormous eyes that face forward, narrowing the field of vision but giving sharper focus and better judgment of distance. The retinas at the back of their eyes are thick and crammed with light-sensitive cells – about ten times as many as in humans – making eagles' eyes unusually sensitive to fine detail and colour differences.

Sharp eyes Arctic hares are seen in sharp detail by a golden eagle's eyes.

Early bird In the chilly Alaskan dawn, a bald eagle snatches a dying salmon struggling in the gravel-bedded shallows; it makes a welcome easy meal as winter nears.

Upward bound *Atlantic salmon leap their way upstream to spawn in the place where they were born.*

Atlantic salmon conquer the rapids to spawn

In November, Atlantic salmon return to the European rivers of their birth to spawn. The salmon are spread widely in the northern Atlantic, and some swim more than 1000 miles (1600km), taking about six weeks. They may find their way by the earth's magnetic field, currents and stars; in coastal waters, the chemical make-up of the water may be their guide.

Only when rivers are swollen by autumn rains do the salmon surge upstream. Struggling through torrents, leaping rapids and falls, they head towards the gravel-bedded shallows far upstream, where the clear and fast-flowing water is loaded with oxygen. They do not even stop to eat. During the journey, males develop a sharp display hook, called a kype, on the tip of their lower jaw, and both sexes gradually change from a silvery colour to a pinkish-brown.

The females are heavy with thousands of eggs (or roe). On arrival at the spawning grounds, the males swim close alongside the females, nuzzling them with their head and flanks. Each female scrapes out a nest, called a redd, in the gravel bottom with powerful thrashes of her tail. Together, male and female swim repeatedly over the nest, depositing sperm and eggs. The eggs, about ¼ in (6mm) across, are fertilised as they drop. Scattered among the pebbles they are hidden from predators, but to make sure the female uses her tail to cover them with gravel.

Unlike some salmon species, which all die after spawning, some Atlantic salmon are fit enough to return to the sea. After one or two years fattening in the ocean, they will be ready to run the river and spawn again. The eggs they leave behind will hatch in the warmth of spring, and a year later the offspring will still be only half as long as a finger. Three years later they will have grown to a hand's length, feeding in the river on insect larvae, worms and other small water creatures, and will be ready for the ocean. Adults can be up to 5ft (1.5m) long.

The cosy dormant world of the dormouse

Curled cosily into a ball, a common (or hazel) dormouse is sleeping soundly in the damp chill of a European November. It lies on its back in its snug nest, eyes shut and nose pressed towards its tail. Sometimes, it clasps its hind legs with its fore feet, making the ball even tighter.

The dormouse made its hibernation nest – a ball of neatly woven, dried grass – in October among dead leaves at the base of a hazel bush. It will sleep out the winter there until April.

During November the dormouse enters the deepest period of its hibernation. It is cold and seemingly dead, and rarely makes the slightest stir, especially if the weather is cold. Later in the winter it will become more restless and from time to time will wheeze and whistle into wakefulness. This restlessness begins as its body releases hormones into its bloodstream as spring and the breeding season approach.

A dormouse looks like a plump, gingery-coloured mouse, but its hairy tail, its agility and its liking for the treetops give it some likeness to a squirrel. It especially loves thickets where oak, hazel and other berry and nut-producing trees are intertwined with a tangle of honeysuckle, bramble and dense undergrowth. Dormice feed at night, in spring and summer on insects and flowers such as catkins. In autumn they grow plump on nuts, fruits and berries – laying on fat to sustain them through hibernation.

Death-like sleep *The common, or hazel, dormouse hibernates for six or seven months of the year, curled up in a grassy nest under a bush or in leaf litter.*

Dawn raid A pine marten crouches intent over the water at first light, seeking a trout on its way upstream to spawn. This late-autumn delicacy is too good to miss, and the hunter braves daylight and water to catch it.

Winter velvet The new antlers that a roe buck grows during winter are clad in a nourishing velvety skin.

Hunting, fishing and climbing pine martens

Peering into an upland stream winding across wild Scottish moorland, a pine marten is intent on catching itself a rare treat. The trout returning to the stream in November to spawn are timely meals for the pine marten, which must fatten itself up before the winter makes food hard to find. Weak from their journey upstream, the trout fall easy prey.

Roughly the size of a cat but with a more elongated body, the pine marten has the wedge-shaped head, small ears and long bushy

Nimble hunter Perfectly at home in trees, a pine marten is quick enough to seize birds and can even outchase a red squirrel through the branches.

tail of the weasel family to which it belongs. It is not a natural swimmer, and to catch fish with confidence it has to change its hunting hours from night-time to dawn or early evening.

An agile climber, the marten often hunts among the branches of coniferous woods, chasing squirrels, tits, wrens and treecreepers. It pounces on them with both front paws outstretched. Insects and berries make a winter meal for the marten if fleshy prey fails.

During spring and summer, when the grass is long, the marten hunts mostly on the ground. Mice, frogs, snakes, lizards and the eggs and chicks of ground-nesting birds give it an extremely varied diet. In autumn, fruits, nuts and fungi provide plenty of fattening fare.

Martens are solitary, territorial animals that mark out their hunting areas with scent from their anal glands. Territories can range from a small wood to an area as extensive as a large town. Within this area, the martens roam on established routes and travel prodigious distances. They may cover 40 miles (64km) in one night, but all that people are likely to see of them are their rounded, cat-like footprints after winter's snow covering has arrived.

A roe buck grows new antlers in winter

November is the time when roe bucks shed their antlers, which drop off to lie amid the leaf litter in European woodland glades. Roe bucks, about 2ft (610mm) high at the shoulder, are the only deer that grow new antlers in winter – most deer shed them in spring and grow new ones in spring and summer.

During the summer breeding season, the roe buck's short antlers – up to 9in (230mm) long – played a vital part. He thrashed the ground and branches with them to display his strength and entice a female to mate. He also used them to drive rival males from his territory.

After mating, as the sex hormones in the buck's blood waned, the antlers were shed. New ones began growing once the scars had dried. Each has a thick velvety skin with a rich blood supply to nourish growth. In spring, the blood supply will cease and the velvet will fall off. The roe buck may rub his antlers against branches to aid its removal, and they will be bare and hard in readiness for the mating season next summer.

A tide of red land crabs returns to the sea

With flailing legs and pincers, a host of red crabs tumbles down a patio on Christmas Island, in the Indian Ocean. Urged on by the start of the heavy November rains, 120 million of them are making their annual migration to the coast to breed. The crabs clamber across anything in their way – roads, railways, patios, gardens – and traffic halts to avoid punctures from the sharp shells. Even so, many crabs are run over by cars, trucks and trains.

Christmas Island, mostly humid rain forest, covers 55sq miles (142sq km) and lies more than 250 miles (400km) south of western Java. It is overrun with 14 species of crab – there is one crab for every four or five paces of forest floor.

Red crabs are land crabs and spend most of the year sweeping the forest floor bare, feeding on fallen leaves, flowers and fruit. When they return to the sea to mate, the crabs face not only traffic, but also heat exhaustion. Marching during the cooler parts of the day helps, but about a million still die on the journey, which takes 8-18 days. The rest reach the shore at precisely the same time each year – in November within three days of the moon's last quarter.

Large, old male crabs lead the way, followed by the females. On arrival they immerse themselves in the damp sand, and bathe or drink in rock pools, lifting water droplets to their mouths

Red army *Millions of tiny red crabs crawl from the Indian Ocean after they have hatched, and journey inland.*

with their pincers. Refreshed, the males move to sandy terraces above the shore and fight for the best burrowing sites. Weaker crabs may die from overheating during the fights, which can last ten minutes or more. Once the burrows are dug, the males are joined by the females, and after mating the males return to the forest.

The female crabs shelter for 12 days while their eggs develop. Each has many thousands of eggs in the brood pouch under her tail. When ready, the crabs sit upright at the water's edge,

usually at night, and shake out their eggs. Some of the crabs are swept away, but survivors head back to the forest, the water behind them red with millions of minute crab larvae.

Twenty-five days later, the young crabs, no wider than $\frac{1}{4}$ in (6mm), emerge from the water in their millions and make their way inland, running the gauntlet of predators such as giant robber crabs, reef herons and island thrushes. Then they forage in the forest litter until it is their turn to go on the great trek to the sea.

Crab plague *Hordes of forest-dwelling red crabs on Christmas Island trundle to the sea each year to breed. Islanders shut their doors against the red tide.*

AFRICA

Wildebeests arrive for the Serengeti feast

Beckoned onward by the luscious grass that sprouts after the rains, a multitude of wildebeests is moving across the Serengeti Plain. Now, in November, they have reached the southern end of the 120 mile (192km) trek that started in September from their dry-season retreat north of the Mara river. During their six-month stay here near the extinct volcano Ngorongoro, the million wildebeests will devour almost three million tons of grass.

The 200,000 zebras that travel with the wildebeests are the first to feed at any new grazing area. Their preferred food is the tallest, coarsest grass, and as they eat it, the softer middle layer of growth becomes available for the wildebeests. When the wildebeests move on after eating this layer, the way is clear for Thomson's gazelles to feed on the shortest grass. The heavy grazing of the wildebeests encourages the grass to grow, in the same way that mowing encourages new growth on a lawn, and ensures that even more food is available for the half million or more gazelles when they arrive on the plain later.

NEWCOMERS AT THE FEAST

The wildebeests mated during May, before the migration began. And in January and February, about eight months later, nearly half a million miniature wildebeests are born within a two-week period. Each is immediately licked clean by its mother, who stands anxiously over it. Within a minute of birth, the calf will stagger to its feet, balance precariously on its long matchstick legs and then, a few minutes later, totter to join the herd.

Speed is essential for safety. The light tan calves are easy to spot and an easy catch for the many predators that live on the plain. The wildebeest mothers do their best to drive off attackers, whether small jackals or hefty lions. But a single wildebeest, although the size of a pony and weighing some 40 stone (255kg), can do little to foil enemies that hunt in packs, such as hyenas and wild dogs. *Continued on p. 232.*

Continued on p. 232.

....

Teeming plain *Thousands of wildebeests and zebras graze in harmony on the southern Serengeti Plain, on the new grass that springs up after the rains. They each crop the grass at different heights.*

One of the pack comes at the mother to keep her occupied as the rest close in on the calf. While the mother is putting up a desperate defence, the thousands of other wildebeests close by are apparently oblivious of the combat. If they were to unite, they could drive the predators away and save the calves.

But nature has taken a different course. Because all the calves are born at much the same time, the predators are swamped with potential prey. However much they gorge themselves, hundreds of thousands of calves will survive. The number of predators living on the plain is limited by the food available to them at the leanest times of year, so they never become numerous enough to eat all this glut of calves. And with the calves such easy prey, they do not often attempt to bring down adults – a more difficult task.

HUNTERS OF THE PLAIN

The predators themselves are a star cast with dovetailed habits that allow them all their turn on centre stage. Lions hunt mostly in the cool of the early morning and late afternoon, lying up during the heat of the day on the rocky outcrops that dot the plains. Cheetahs, the fastest of all living mammals, course the plains by day.

GEARED FOR GRAZING

The eyes, feet, teeth and digestive systems of grazing antelopes, related to cattle, have adapted to improve their chances of survival. Grassland offers little cover, so eyes positioned on the side of the head enable them to keep watch all round for predators.

For quick flight from a predator, each foot has only two large toes with a few thick bones, and is extended so that the animal stands on tiptoe, which lengthens its stride. The toes also have tough hooves to withstand pounding during running.

To break down the grass they eat, the animals have ridged rather than sharp-pointed teeth, and the lower jaw moves from side to side. Of the four stomachs needed to digest the grass, the first can return the food to the mouth for a second grinding session, called chewing the cud.

Hunter's ploys *A lioness lies in wait (top) watching the wildebeests pass by. Her legs are tucked beneath her flattened body ready to spring. Once she has selected a victim she attacks (centre). The wildebeests scatter but she reaches the victim, and grips its neck (bottom) to pull it to the ground for the kill.*

Caught out alone *As evening falls, a newborn wildebeest calf and its mother, isolated in the open away from the herd, are the target for a marauding pair of hyenas.*

Leopards stalk the wooded fringes with methodical grace by night, and drape their prey on branches beyond the reach of scavenging jackals and hyenas. Sometimes hyenas wait to feed on the lions' leavings. More often the lions take over the hyenas' kill for themselves, especially at times when food is harder to find.

The pack-hunters, too, work different hours. Hyenas often hunt at night, the pack exchanging eerie whoops across the moonlit grasslands as they keep in touch during the search for a victim. Wild dogs are active by day, gambolling through the grass and calling to one another with excited whimpers.

But once they have chosen a victim, the wild dogs transform without warning into formidable, organised hunters that take turns to lead the chase. In this way they run down their prey with ease, bringing down the exhausted victim by snapping at its heels and soft underbelly.

When the predators have taken their fill, the vultures descend to feast on the remains. Nothing is wasted in nature, and the vultures play one of the key roles in ensuring that the grasslands are not polluted by rotting carcasses. They are fast and efficient cleaners.

Among the most numerous of the vultures in the area are Rüppell's griffon vultures. These large birds nest in their hundreds high on the mountains beside the plain. To forage, they launch themselves on the updraughts of warm air rising from off the grasslands in the heat of the morning sun. Circling lazily upwards on broad wings that span about 8ft (2.4m), they gradually spread out and drift across the plain, peering down with keen eyes to spot dead or dying animals. One descending vulture soon attracts the eager attention of others, and from far and wide they gather to feast. Their long, flexible necks enable them to reach well inside a carcass, and as their necks are downy but unfeathered, they do not get badly fouled.

Another cleaning service is provided by dung beetles. With well over a million animals consuming several thousand tons of grass a day, their droppings would leave the plain knee-deep in dung by the end of their stay. The dung beetles roll the dung into marble-sized balls and then take them to their nest sites, moving backwards as they push the balls with their rear

Scavengers' work *Attracted by a wildebeest carcass, Rüppell's griffon vultures (left), a pack of hyenas, and a silverbacked jackal (front) squabble for the pickings.*

legs. There they bury the dung balls, each with one egg laid in it. When the eggs hatch, each larva has its own food store.

Meanwhile the lottery of life and death continues on the plain above. The wildebeest calves grow and are no longer so vulnerable to predators. By the end of May, there will be little grass left near Ngorongoro, and the great herds will move north-west to find better grazing on the damper region near Lake Victoria at the western side of the Serengeti.

Noon watch *Camouflaged in the dappled shade of a thorn bush, a family of cheetahs sit at their favourite viewpoint and scan the horizon for suitable prey.*

Cheetahs – fleet-footed hunters of the plains

A small herd of Thomson's gazelles moves slowly across the grassy East African plain, pausing at intervals to feed on the short grass. As the November sun gathers strength, ears and tails are set flickering against the flies that continually buzz round them. Unseen by the gazelles, two white-tipped ears are twitching beside an anthill about 55yds (50m) away. They belong to a female cheetah, watching patiently as the gazelles move unwittingly nearer. Beside the cheetah, her four half-grown cubs are

motionless, copying their mother. Lying on their sides with only their eyes and ears raised above the grass, the cheetahs are all but invisible.

As the gazelles draw level with the anthill, the female rolls quietly onto her front and gathers herself to hurtle the width of a football pitch across the plain, sprinting at about 63mph (100km/h). Her aim is to startle her prey into flight, single out one animal from the group, and rapidly overhaul it before it can get into its stride. Then she may either trip it up from behind with a deft flick of her forepaw, or bowl it over with a shoulder charge. Alternatively, if the gazelle is not moving very fast, she may pull it to the ground with one paw on its shoulder.

Cheetahs are easily dissuaded from pressing home an attack, however, especially if their victims refuse to stampede. A captive cheetah given to King George III of England for hunting in the 18th century refused to hunt red deer after it had been tossed by a stag that stood its ground. (The stag was given a gold collar.)

Cheetah cubs are half grown at six months old. These cubs were born in May, and by November they are finally weaned and ready to learn the hunting skills on which their survival depends. Alongside their mother, they begin, warily, to attempt stalking and killing for themselves. But it will be another year before they are fully independent. In the meantime, their mother continues to kill regularly to make sure they get enough to eat.

A female with cubs must make a kill almost every day, for many of her kills will be quite small, providing only about 10lb (5kg) of meat at a time. On the Serengeti Plain in East Africa, more than half the cheetah's victims are gazelles, and of those, two-thirds are immature animals. A lone cheetah cannot kill prey larger than itself. By no means every hunt is successful. A cheetah may succeed in catching only about a third of the adult gazelles it goes after, but will usually have a two-thirds success rate when hunting young animals.

Cheetahs are among the more social of the big cats, and groups of four or more often rest or hunt together. Normally, such a group is a mother and her almost fully grown cubs, or a number of adult males. Cheetahs hunting in groups can bring down prey as large as a young giraffe or young buffalo. Although they never cooperate in hunting in the same way as wolf packs, they coordinate their movements across the plain with low-pitched explosive yelps that can be heard up to 1 mile (1.6km) away. Four cheetahs together have been known to consume a 110lb (50kg) impala in just 15 minutes, leaving only the skin and bones.

Like most carnivores, cheetahs range over large territories, commonly around 30sq miles (80sq km). They are most active during the early morning and late afternoon, and spend the hottest part of the day stretched out on a favourite vantage point such as a termite mound or a clump of rocks, preferably in the shade of some thorn bushes. Such sites are commonly marked with urine-sprays and droppings to establish ownership. The cheetahs' spotted coats provide effective camouflage in the dappled light and shadow cast by the bushes as

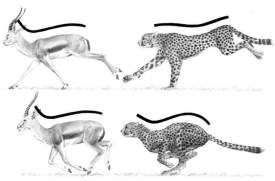

Striding out *An animal's speed depends on the length of its stride. An impala owes its long stride to its long legs. A cheetah's spine is so flexible that it can stretch its legs over the maximum possible distance.*

they watch for prey on the plains around them.

Cheetahs reach sexual maturity at two or three years old. Females then bear cubs at intervals of about 18 months. In East Africa, mating takes place between January and August, and the females give birth about 13 weeks later. There are usually four or five cubs in a litter, kept in a rough nest in long grass or beneath a thorn bush at first. They are blind at birth, about 12in (300mm) long and their fur is off-white.

When the cubs are about six weeks old and can move about on their own, they start to accompany their mother on her hunting expeditions, although they do not yet hunt. If their mother falls ill or is killed, they are likely to starve. The cubs' fur changes to adult colours after about three months, but until they are eight months old they have white fur on the top of the neck and the back.

Intimate moment *A male cheetah, in relaxed mood, rolls contentedly on his back in the sunshine beside his mate.*

Easy hunting *A gazelle fawn, flushed from its hiding place among tall grass, has little chance of escape if it is unfortunate enough to be discovered by a cheetah.*

Coup de grâce *A female cheetah finishes off her victim, a Thomson's gazelle, by strangulation, her jaws clamped round its neck in a well-practised grip.*

Termite towers with stores and gardens

Raindrops drumming against their mounds in November are the signal for swarms of termites in western Zimbabwe to take to the air to found a new colony. During the rains the soil is wet and easy to dig and there are plenty of rotting plants to eat, so the winged sexually developed termites – which are known as reproductives – leave home through holes bored in the mound by the colony workers. This exodus occurs once a year, at the same time in different mounds in the same locality.

As the termites take to the air above the tree-scattered grassland, insect-eating birds such as goshawks and bee-eaters have a field day, snapping up a feast from the fluttering cloud. During their brief flight, male and female termites pair off in the air. On landing they shed their wings and search the ground for suitable plots to build on. Termites live where there is plenty of dead wood for building, such as the feeding grounds of elephant herds. On the ground many of the searchers fall prey to toads, lizards, ants, spiders, shrews and even vultures. Only one in a thousand survives.

To start a new colony, the termite pair, who will stay together in their new home all their lives, find an earth crevice in which to mate. They begin to build walls of chewed wood and soil mixed with saliva and droppings, and the female starts to lay eggs. The first larvae to hatch are workers, who take over the building. In time, the mound will be more than 30ft (9m) tall.

The female grows from the size of an ant to a sausage shape about 6in (150mm) long, and when fully mature lays more than 30,000 eggs a day. The workers tend the eggs and the founding pair – the king and queen – whom they feed with regurgitated dead plant material. They also feed the soldiers, strong-jawed termites reared to defend the growing colony from enemies – particularly their arch-enemies, ants. Winged reproductives are reared once the colony becomes well populated.

The mound is a masterpiece of engineering, with nurseries for eggs, a food store for wood and leaves, and even a garden where leaves mixed with droppings are broken down by fungi to make them more palatable. With food fermenting and several million busy termites, a well-established colony needs ventilation. Air-conditioning designs vary, but all mounds have fresh air constantly circulating through them.

Termite city Towering, concrete-hard termite mounds are common in the tree-scattered African grassland.

Air conditioning All termite mounds have ducts to circulate fresh air. Some ducts exchange air through porous walls, as above. Others are open chimneys.

New life A winged termite (top) takes off to found a colony. A huge queen (bottom) mothers millions.

Hello world *A mother bat-eared fox looks on as two of her eight-week-old cubs emerge from the underground den for a first sight of sunlight.*

Big-eared foxes that listen for insects

In the cool of an early November morning on the Masai Mara National Reserve in Kenya, a bat-eared fox emerges from her den. She sniffs the air carefully and twitches her enormous ears, alert to the slightest sound. Stretching, she shakes her long, silver coat and licks her black legs and feet. Her belly fur has become thin during the past weeks, and her well-used teats are clearly visible. Eight weeks ago, some 8-11 weeks after mating, she gave birth to a litter of cubs in the safety of an underground den. At first they were covered in a silvery down and

were blind and helpless. Now they are furred, boisterous and ready to come above ground.

The fox turns to the mouth of the burrow and utters a soft, whickering call. Cautiously, the first of her cubs follows her out into the sunshine and sits bewildered at its first view of the world. Its father, returning from a night's foraging, trots over and licks the small cub, which is soon joined by his four litter brothers and sisters. In total, the family group numbers twelve, the adult pair – life-long mates – five of their offspring from two previous litters, and now the new family. At first, the playful cubs will not venture far from the den, and are at risk from hawks, eagles and hyenas.

Bat-eared foxes are slightly smaller than red

foxes. They live near herds of large hoofed animals, such as zebras and wildebeests, and feed mainly on the insects that live around these grazers, but occasionally take lizards or small mammals. Termites, which feed on fresh grass stems that sprout after the older leaves have been grazed away, are their favourite prey, along with scorpions and dung beetles.

As there is little chance of scenting a dung beetle in the middle of a pile of dung, the cubs will learn from their parents to locate beetles by listening with their huge, sensitive ears, and then be shown how to scratch them out with claws and teeth. By about five months old the cubs will be fully grown and may stay with the family to help rear the next generation.

Stealthy leopards that pounce in the night

Pale moonlight casts dusky shadows across the African woodland where a small antelope, a duiker, is browsing on greenery refreshed by the November rains. It is unaware of the stealthy, soft-padded leopard in the shadows above, lurking among the branches of a small tree and ready to pounce. With her three-month-old cubs just weaned, the leopard needs all her skill to feed herself and three other hungry mouths that daily grow more demanding. Like a spring released, she launches herself from the tree onto the unsuspecting duiker and sinks her teeth in its neck, then kills it with a twist of her powerful shoulders. She hauls the meat into the tree and drapes it over a branch.

As yet the cubs are still in the rocky den where they were born in August, blind, helpless, and each no heavier than 1lb 4oz (570g). Now the youngsters weigh 7lb (3kg) and will soon begin to venture out after their mother. She will keep guard during the cubs' outings, and at a low growl from her they will crouch and freeze. They are at risk from birds of prey or from hyenas nosing around for easy pickings.

At first they will only watch their mother's hunting forays, but within a year they will have

Stocking the larder *Leopards often store their prey in the fork of a tree, where it is safe from scavengers. They return to feed on the carcass for several nights.*

begun to hunt successfully for themselves. First they must learn the necessary skills, not only by watching but also by finishing off live victims their mother has caught, then loosed for them to catch again. Because of their stealth and agility, leopards are fearsome hunters. They are more heavily built than cheetahs, but not as big as lions, and can climb into trees with grace and

speed, using their tails – as long as a man's arm – to help them keep their balance.

The roar of a leopard at night strikes terror into a colony of monkeys, for leopards will chase them in the trees – the one place where the monkeys can normally take refuge from predators. Baboons, too, will break into a cacophony of panic-stricken calls until a marauding leopard has passed out of earshot. Leopards can move soundlessly through the forest in search of an unsuspecting victim. They have been known to take dogs, and even humans, from dwellings without waking the other occupants of a room.

Because they are economical hunters and store their food, leopards rarely kill more than once a week – twice a week for females killing meat for cubs. Kills are cached in trees, draped over the fork of a branch about 13ft (4m) above the ground, and the leopard returns to the carcass each night. The larder is relatively safe from pilferers and anything that does attempt to steal a meal gets short shrift: leopards have been known to kill jackals, hyenas, cheetahs, serval cats and even storks that they have caught tampering with a carcass. Other leopards, too, are chased away, and many leopards have scarred faces as a result of such encounters.

SELF-SUFFICIENT LIVES

Except at mating time, leopards are generally solitary hunters, although occasionally they are seen in pairs. Yet they clearly know the other leopards that live close by, and keep in contact with a loud, rasping call that has been described as sounding something like a hand saw cutting through a log.

Each leopard tends to remain within its own territory, which rarely covers more than 8sq miles (20sq km). The boundaries are marked by scratches on trees and by a scented secretion from the anal glands, which the leopard sprays out with its urine. Within this small area, a leopard often travels a long way in search of food, doubling back to visit parts of its range every few days. It will travel 16 miles (25km) in one night, or three times as far if disturbed. It is constantly on the move, and seldom spends more than two nights in one place.

Leopards are found throughout most of Africa and in southern Asia – in India and as far as the east and north of China. Although they mostly

Safe at home *Two five-month-old leopard cubs first learn about the world by watching from the den mouth. Leopards prefer well-protected dens such as caves.*

Surveying their kingdom From their command post on a rocky outcrop, a mother and her 14-month-old daughter keep watch for likely prey on the plains below.

prefer wooded country, they will live in almost any kind of country as long as there are suitable places in which to hide cubs – such as a hollow tree, a cave, a rock tunnel or an abandoned aardvark hole. Their numbers are on the increase in Africa, but severely reduced in northern Asia because of human encroachment on their habitats. Leopards have been widely hunted for their beautifully patterned skins, which range from pale fawn to orange-russet, and are covered with brownish spots – generally rosettes with a dark surround and lighter centre. The spots are smallest on the head and largest on the legs and belly. Leopard skins have often

been used as symbols of office. Among the Baganda people of East Africa, a leopard skin was a symbol of kingship, and only the head of the royal family was allowed to sit on one.

Young leopards stay with their mother until they are nearly two years of age and are confident enough to survive alone. Then they leave to find a territory of their own. Youngsters become sexually mature at about three years old, and in most of the animals' range mating takes place at any time of the year. A fully grown male leopard turns the scales at around 9 stone (60kg) and stands about the same height as a Labrador dog at the shoulder.

First taste A young cub dances around its mother as she carries an antelope to a secluded spot. There the leopards will feed, secure from intruding scavengers.

Morbid vigil When they spot a dying animal, lappet-faced vultures will perch in nearby trees, or even gather round the unfortunate beast, waiting for it to die.

Vultures have a busy month as undertakers

Perched on a treetop vantage point, two lappet-faced vultures survey the East African plain below. They take off to circle effortlessly on the warm air currents rising as the ground heats up on a November morning. Beneath their outstretched wings, the vultures swivel their snake-like heads to scan the ground for dead and dying animals. So acute is their vision that they can spot a dying animal just over a mile (1.6km) away, but at present the tree-scattered plain is littered with carcasses, as frail newborn antelope calves and other animals die of natural causes or are killed by predators such as lions.

Landing with an ungainly beat of wings, the vultures stalk warily towards a dead antelope calf. With powerful, hooked beaks they tear off chunks of skin and tendon, preferring the coarse tissue to more tender meat. This time of plenty is the natural time for the vultures to breed and soon, tearing off more meat, the two vultures fly to their treetop nest to feed their ravenous chick. Then they go on watch once more.

Lappet-faced vultures, named for the loose flaps – lappets – of skin hanging from their red heads, are the largest and among the rarest of vultures. They stand more than 3ft (1m) tall and have an 8ft 6in (2.6m) wingspan. Vultures may be despised for their ugliness, and the lappet-faced is perhaps the ugliest of them all. Yet, like its smaller cousins, it is invaluable in disposing of carcasses before they rot and breed disease.

Joining the happy family of a wild dog pack

A tangle of wild dog pups shoves and pushes as the assertive youngsters emerge into the sunlight from their den on the plains of northern Kenya. The litter was born three weeks ago, and now that their eyes have opened they can follow their mother about above ground in the vicinity of the den – an abandoned aardvark burrow. Sometimes the den is simply a shelter amid dense grass.

The November rains have brought a flush of new growth to the parched African plains and the grass provides the Thomson's and Grant's gazelles with plenty of food for rearing their fawns. In turn, the fawns ensure a good food supply for the wild dogs to rear their pups, which begin to eat regurgitated meat when they are two weeks old, although their mothers continue to suckle them until they are 10-12 weeks old. Once the pups reach about three months of age, they follow the pack and do not need a home base any longer. They still have their food provided by the adults of the pack and will be about 14 months old before they can fend for themselves.

Wild dogs live in family groups, and despite their savage reputation live in harmony and show affection towards one another. As they have litters of up to 12 pups their packs commonly number 15-20, although packs of 40 are not unusual. Only the dominant male and female of a pack normally breed. The other members, usually males from the breeding couple's previous litters, help to rear each new litter of pups by guarding them, bringing back food for them and letting the youngsters feed first when they eventually run with the pack. By the time the young dogs are two and a half years old, females will normally have left to join other packs, but the males generally stay in their original pack for life.

Before the wild dog pack sets off on the hunt, the members greet one another with high-pitched whimpers and kisses on the muzzle. Having worked themselves into a state of excitement, the dogs lope off determinedly across the plain – a formidable sight that strikes terror into the grazing animals of the grasslands.

Unlike most other carnivores, wild dogs do not hunt by stealth. They pursue their prey until it is exhausted. Chases of a mile (1.6km) are typical, with each dog taking its turn in the lead where it harries the prey and snaps at its heels while the rest of the pack eases off or takes a short cut. When the quarry drops, the dogs fall upon it. A pack can reduce an 8 stone (50kg) impala to a heap of bones in just ten minutes.

Riotous feast With up to 12 hungry pups in a litter, a wild dog mother needs great patience every feeding time.

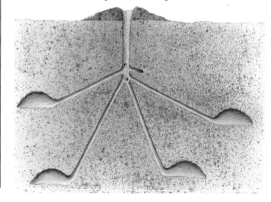

Bursting point The body of this honeypot ant has swelled to the size of a large pea from the honeydew it has been force-fed by its fellow ants.

The crowded family life of a flying fox bat

By day, the trees lining the north Australian coast are home to one of the largest bats in the world – a fruit-eating bat known as the black flying fox because of its fox-like face. Hundreds of thousands of these 10in (250mm) long creatures roost there together. Hanging upside-down from the branches, they fold their black, leathery looking wings round their bodies and sleep. Most of them cluster in the thick of the trees, but old males stay on the outskirts, keeping an eye out for intruders and raising the alarm if a snake, for example, should approach.

In November a different kind of disturbance is likely, for it is spring – the time when the females that mated in autumn some six months ago each give birth to a single baby. The first sign of life is the baby's head popping out from its mother's womb-opening as she hangs upside-down. Often the baby rests there for a while before emerging fully and crawling down to one of its mother's armpits to find a teat.

The baby's world for its first two weeks is the short, black fur of its mother's chest. Its claws and milk teeth help it to hold tight. Although well developed, the baby cannot fly – it clings to its mother wherever she goes. Later she will park it on a branch when she goes foraging, and by midsummer it will make its first solo flight.

At dusk the air is filled with the cries of waking bats, but once they launch themselves into flight the only sound from them is the flapping of their wings. Although their flight appears laboured, these bats have been known to clock up speeds of 32mph (51km/h) while they are streaming as far as 30 miles (48km) inland.

Flying foxes do not hunt by echolocation, as insect-eating bats do. They smell out flowers and fruit with their long snouts, and their large round eyes help them to see well in the near dark. As night falls they settle on trees such as eucalyptus and paperbark, and eat the blossom. As they crawl from flower to flower using their claws and hind feet, the bats help to pollinate the flowers. They also eat soft fruits and berries, mashing them up with ridges on the roof of the mouth; their droppings help to disperse seeds.

Hanging loose Wrapped in its wings, a flying fox (top left) wakens from its day's sleep. A baby's head emerges (bottom left) as its mother gives birth.

Honeypot ants store food in a living larder

By November, the flush of flowers that followed earlier rains has faded from the arid landscape of Western Australia. But deep in their underground nest, the honeypot ants have a plentiful supply of food cached away. The storage containers are their fellow ants – a caste whose sole purpose in life is to store food.

While the plants and flowers were in abundance, the worker ants busily stroked aphids that fed on plant sap. This made the aphids secrete a sticky honeydew. After drinking their fill, the workers took the sticky liquid in their mouths back to the nest for their 'honeypots'.

These living larders look like normal ants at first, but as they are force-fed they swell up like balloons, becoming so bloated that they cannot even walk. Once full to the brim, they are hung from the ceiling of nest galleries by their forelegs. When fresh food runs out in the long drought, the ants queue up to drink from them, stroking their abdomens to force out drips.

Low life Honeypot ants live in a nest of tunnels and galleries up to 14in (360mm) long which branch from a 1in (25mm) wide shaft and end in fist-sized chambers.

Young Tasmanian devils ride with mother

Basking in the late sun of a spring evening, two young Tasmanian devils sprawl over their mother's back. This November outing in the Tasmanian forest is the first time they have seen the world beyond their den under tree roots. Soon, when dusk closes in, their mother will be off on a foraging trip and they will ride with her, clinging to her back. Next time they will amble close behind her sturdy, corgi-sized form, all three black with a narrow white band on throat and flanks. After a few more months of hunting together, they will split up to lead solitary lives, each in a den of their own.

Adults mate in March or April, and about a month later the female produces naked, blind, thumbnail-length babies – two the first time, four in subsequent years. They scramble from the birth canal into their mother's pouch, a short journey as her pouch opening is at the rear, and spend almost four months being suckled there. Then they are big enough to leave the cosy nursery, but only for the den – it is winter and too cold for them outside. They stay in the den for another four months, gradually learning to cope with the meat their mother brings before they start to fend for themselves.

When the three go foraging by night, high-pitched squeals and grunts keep them in contact. But these are nothing to the mother's volley of screams when she has found food. Tonight it is the carcass of a rat-sized bandicoot, and another Tasmanian devil is already tearing at it with strong claws and sharp, pointed teeth. Without a second's hesitation, the hungry mother flies at the rival. Face close to face, the two scream ferociously at each other. The noise rather than the brief scuffle decides the contest and soon mother and young can feed, crunching the carcass between powerful jaws. Insects, reptiles and a few birds may be caught and killed, but Tasmanian devils are not skilful hunters, so much of their food is carrion.

Springtime A colourful boxfish couple keep close as the female (right) releases eggs for the male to fertilise in the warm waters above the Great Barrier Reef.

A chubby fish boxed in by its own defences

Gleaming in the clear water at dusk, a male boxfish swims stiffly among the crevices of the Great Barrier Reef off Australia's north-east coast. November has brought the springtime urge to spawn, and he is searching for mates. When he finds a likely one, he dashes round her to captivate her with his bright colours. Once she is interested, the pair make for the surface, where the male hums to her while they swim close beside each other, and as she releases her eggs he quickly fertilises them.

Although the boxfishes spawn some distance from the reef and its hungry inhabitants, most of their eggs are eaten by other fish. But some survive to settle unharmed on the seabed and hatch into tiny independent replicas of their parents. The adult is a handspan in length and has a rotund body with a long, tapering snout permanently puckered at the tip into a round mouth. With this the boxfish sucks in algae, coral polyps, worms, snails and other delicacies of the reef. The horn-like ridges above its bulging eyes earn it the alternative name of cowfish.

The name boxfish comes from its tough, protective covering of fused scales. These form a shell so rigid that the fish cannot flex its body to swim. It steers and paddles with its fins, and ripples its triangular tail for an occasional sprint. It can ooze a poisonous slimy coating that makes it distasteful to some predators – but it is still snapped up by larger fish.

First impressions Young Tasmanian devils cling to their mother's back for their first outing from the den.

Lizards that use their frills to frighten

As the dry winter months give way to monsoon rains across northern Australia in early November, female frilled lizards are busy scooping out holes for their eggs. Startled by a noise as she digs into the damp woodland soil, one female rises on her hind legs and streaks off to a high spot, a handy termite mound. There the slender, greyish-mottled creature, just under 3ft (1m) long, swells into a fearsome beast.

She rears up tall, swaying from side to side, and opens her huge mouth to display the gaudy interior and utter a fierce hiss. Rods of cartilage attached to her tongue stiffen and raise a great ruff about 12in (300mm) across, densely spotted with gold or orange. No wonder the would-be predator, such as a hawk, dingo or monitor lizard, turns tail. When the danger is past, the frill subsides into a cape round the lizard's shoulders and she returns to her task.

Since she mated about a month ago, eggs have been maturing in her body. Now she lays ten eggs in the hole, covers them with soil, and abandons them. They are soft-shelled, white and fragile. If the nest becomes too damp, they rot; if it is too cool, they do not develop; if it is too dry or warm, they bake. But they have a survival trick – when it rains they absorb water from the soil to see them through dry spells.

After four to six weeks, depending on the weather, the eggs hatch into miniature frilled lizards, which scuttle off into the bush to lead the same life as the adults. They are at home on trees or on the ground and hunt insects, small rats, mice and possums, or raid birds' nests for chicks and eggs. Such prey is at its most plentiful in the wet season when the young lizards hatch, and there is usually enough water for them too, unless they have the misfortune to arrive during one of Australia's droughts.

The baby lizards are complete with frills and from the start can stage small-scale displays. Like the adults, they also use the frill to control temperature. When they are cold, they spread it to the sun. Its thin skin is gorged with blood vessels that soak up warmth and transfer it to the bloodstream. When the lizard is too hot, it spreads its frill to a cooling breeze to lose heat.

....

Fierce reply Leaping to the top of a termite mound, a threatened frilled lizard appears to double in size as its mouth gapes wide and a spectacular frill of spotted skin unfolds umbrella-like round its neck.

Tightly packed *Australasian gannets nest on the cliff tops at Cape Kidnappers, New Zealand. Each nest is sited so that a sitting bird is just out of range of a neighbour's peck.*

Gannets congregate for successful breeding

A crowded colony of Australasian gannets is spread like a thick white, gold-flecked carpet on the flat, open cliff top. Here and there small upheavals erupt as some birds stretch and fly off – but not before a mate has come to replace them on the nest. Harsh voices resound as pairs make their greetings and watchful neighbours jealously guard their own small circles of territory.

It is early November and for a month now the gannets have been at Cape Kidnappers on the east coast of New Zealand's North Island. They arrived in formation, flying in Vs with sometimes as many as 80 birds in a flock, and wasted little time in pairing and nest-building. Gannets probably gain several advantages from all breeding at the same time in vast colonies. Many pale, sharp eyes are vigilant for danger, and many vicious blue beaks are available to mob a skua, rat or other predator and drive it away. Even if a predator does eat its fill, numerous chicks will still survive. The colony also acts as an information centre. Birds returning from rich feeding grounds are quickly noticed and followed on their next sortie. And with many birds scouring a large area of sea, it is more likely that good food sources will be found.

Within the colony itself, however, cooperation is unknown. Sleek golden-topped heads thrust forward aggressively as neighbours peck at each other, steal nest material and attack straying chicks. A gannet that overshoots on landing has a very painful struggle back to its nest site. Each nest is a small mound of seaweed, plants, earth and guano (droppings). Both parents incubate the single egg in turn for just over six weeks. The youngster is as noisy as its parents – even in the egg it yaps like a puppy. Black and naked when hatched, it is white and fluffy after a month and speckled brown and white after three months.

Both parents catch fish for the chick, making low-angle dives or sometimes spectacular plunges from about 100ft (30m) in the air – cushioned from injury as they hit the water by air sacs in the throat and breast. The youngster is about 15 weeks old before it flies. It will spend its first few years at sea off Australia's southern and eastern coasts. Not until it is four or five years old will the young gannet return to the colony. It will not breed until it is about five years old.

The peril facing the great white shark

With snout raised, jaws extended and mouth agape, a huge but cautious killer approaches its prey from below and behind. It slams razor-sharp triangular teeth into the victim's underside, and slices away a huge chunk of flesh. After this first mouthful the hunter, a great white shark, stands off and waits for the prey, a seal, to bleed to death. In this way it avoids being damaged by the seal's powerful claws during a prolonged struggle. Now that it is November and spring is in full swing, the seals have come to breed in the Dangerous Reef area south of Port Lincoln, South Australia.

The shark must eat as much as it can in one sitting, for its next meal may be many weeks or even months away. Its stomach temperature is raised by as much as 6°C (10°F) after feeding. This speeds up digestion and ensures that the shark's stomach is empty and ready if another opportunity to feed comes along soon.

Great white sharks are the largest predatory fish in the sea, found in all except the colder oceans. Females are larger than males, and are commonly about 20ft (6m) long, but can grow up to about 26ft (8m) and weigh 236 stone (1500kg). Such a large flesh eater will attack a man as easily as a seal, but is seldom found near coasts.

Sadly, the great white's reputed ferocity has led to its downfall. Females do not breed until they are 15-20 years old and may have only one baby at a time. Since the 1975 film *Jaws* particularly, the great white has become the ultimate prize of sporting fishermen. Many of the large, breeding females have been taken, and it is possible that the South Australian great white shark population could soon be extinct.

The real Jaws Rows of razor-sharp teeth approach from below as a great white shark makes towards its prey.

Swinging bait The bolas spider is an angler with a trick on its line. It swings a strand scented with moth sex pheromones to lure a nightly meal of male moths.

How spiders angle for courting moths

As balmy evenings in late spring bring out moths to breed, the bolas spider of eastern Australia sets out to make a meal of them. It rudely interrupts the courting insects and tricks them into its clutches.

Male moths find the females by scent – the females release sex pheromones, chemicals whose smell attracts the male. The spider takes advantage of this. It spins a long thread with a ball at the end, like the bolas a South American ranch hand uses to catch cattle. But the ball is no ordinary blob of spider web; it is coated with the same pheromone that the female moth produces to entice a male. Then the spider lets the bolas dangle beneath its perch on a branch or twig – and waits.

When moths flutter by, the spider swings its bolas slowly round with one leg to waft the pheromone into the air. The smell immediately attracts any male moths in the vicinity, and they close in on it. Once within range of the whirling thread, a would-be suitor is caught fast on the sticky bolas and hauled in for the spider to feast on. As many as eight moths may be fooled, trapped and eaten in a single night.

The thread itself is remarkable. Made from protein formed like rubber, it is stronger than man-made nylon and twice as stretchy, and can extend by more than a third of its original length without snapping. A strand of spider silk more than 250 times finer than a human hair has twice the strength of a similar strand of steel. Not even a large moth will break the bolas spider's thread.

Night landing *After riding ashore on the surf, fairy penguins gather for their nightly journey up the beach to their breeding burrows where their mates and chicks are waiting.*

Fairy penguins parade to change the guard

A distant braying floats on the air as the summer dusk falls on Phillip Island, off Australia's south-east coast. It heralds the nightly parade of fairy penguins, also known as little or blue penguins. The braying is the contact call that keeps the penguin flocks together at sea. Then, under cover of darkness, the penguins – each about 15in (380mm) tall – begin to emerge from the pounding surf and make the journey up the beach to their nests in the dunes, where their mates and chicks are hidden. They waddle with flippers outstretched looking rather like corpulent humans.

Fairy penguins have been parading this way every summer for thousands of years, but now they have to find their way up a narrow fenced corridor between rows of staring people, for their seemingly comical appearance has made them a tourist attraction. Their breeding area is surrounded by protective barbed wire, and floodlights play on the entire scene. Although intrusive, these measures do at least ensure that the penguins can continue their traditional breeding ritual without serious disturbance from human beings, and their numbers have increased in recent years.

In November, the breeding colony is at its busiest. Some birds have yet to lay their eggs, some are sitting on two chalky white eggs and others have two almost-fledged chicks covered in grey down. The nest is underground at the end of a burrow as long as a man's arm. At this stage, one parent stays at the nest throughout the day, an occasional low purring from below ground being the only sign it is there. The other parent spends the day at sea and joins the nightly journey ashore to feed the chicks and change shifts on the nest.

When the returning bird reaches the nest, the pair greet with a long moaning wail. Early in the season this is often followed by a mating display and sometimes by mating. Once the chicks have hatched such displays are cut short, for the first hungry chick plunges its head into its parent's open mouth to take regurgitated squid and fish.

By the turn of the year, most of the nestlings are more than three weeks old and large enough to leave their burrows. Then both parents go to sea, often for several days, and their return is greeted with great enthusiasm by the hungry youngsters standing expectantly at the burrow entrance. Five weeks later the youngsters will be ready to go to sea. By April the beach will be deserted and a winter calm will descend once more on Phillip Island.

The fairy penguin, smallest of the penguins, breeds on offshore islands round the coasts of southern Australia, Tasmania, and New Zealand from June or July to February. The alternative name, blue penguin, refers to its slaty blue back. Despite their small size, fairy penguins are fast and agile underwater. They sometimes work together to round up shoals of small fish then dive into the centre of the shoal to feed. Many also take small squid. Although some die in the winter storms that thrash the Tasman Sea, the penguins' main enemy has been fishermen, who used to cut them up as bait to catch crayfish.

A courting bowerbird paints and decorates

For weeks now, the satin bowerbird has been busily at work in the forest, perfecting his bower. It is November, late spring in eastern Australia, and the breeding season is in full swing. With elaborate care, the jackdaw-like bird dabs with his beak at the fenced platform he has constructed from twigs and grass, decorating it with paint made from berries or charred wood (the remains of a forest fire) mixed with his saliva. He dabs the paint on with a twig – being one of the few birds to use a tool.

At one end of the 16in (400mm) high construction, which is fenced on two sides but open at each end, the bowerbird has flattened a display ground. This he also decorates with brightly coloured feathers, pebbles, shells, leaves, and a few bottle tops from houses not far away. Most of his trinkets are in shades of blue, setting off his own shining black plumage, its lilac-blue sheen shimmering like satin in the sunlight. Other male bowerbirds that venture too close

LABOURS OF LOVE

Bowerbirds of different species build widely different bowers, but there are two main types – conical maypoles round a sapling, and avenues with parallel fences of sticks.

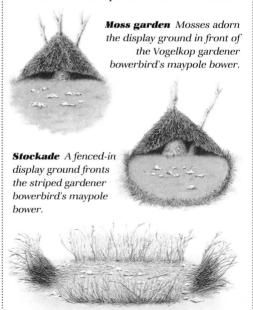

Moss garden *Mosses adorn the display ground in front of the Vogelkop gardener bowerbird's maypole bower.*

Stockade *A fenced-in display ground fronts the striped gardener bowerbird's maypole bower.*

Elaborate avenue *The Lauterbach's bowerbird makes an avenue bower the size of a bathmat. The four walls of sticks lean slightly outwards.*

Artist and audience *A female satin bowerbird admires a male's colourful display, which includes blue pegs.*

will be chased off aggressively. They might be rivals for the females he hopes to attract, or thieves come to steal some of his decorations – such pilfering is common.

His masterpiece refurbished, the bird is ready to display his bower and his charms. He announces his readiness to females – and warns off other males – with a loud, bell-like call. When a female appears, he encourages her into the platform of his bower, between the two fences, and begins an intricate display. Picking up a feather, shell, or flower from his collection, he stretches his neck, fans his tail and makes a throaty, growling sound. Then he struts around bowing and flapping his wings, and occasionally hopping stiff-legged into the air.

As the female watches this display, which goes on for about half a minute, she sometimes rearranges a twig or two in the bower. Then the pair mate, either in the bower or just beside it. Their pairing is short-lived. Mating over, the female goes off to build by herself a flimsy, cup-shaped nest high in a tree. There, on her own, she incubates her eggs – usually two – and

when the chicks hatch three weeks later, she feeds them on fruit and insects during their three weeks in the nest. As for the male, he continues his attempts to lure a succession of females into his bower, mating with each one.

The bowerbird chicks are fledged and ready to fend for themselves at two months old. Young males are the same colour as females, and become sexually mature before they develop full adult plumage at six years of age. The delay in acquiring adult colours perhaps reflects the time it takes for the young bowerbirds to perfect their bower-building skills. Their first attempts are just small piles of twigs with a few flowers, shells or feathers among them. In species where one male mates with several females in a single breeding season, males are often slow to mature.

Satin bowerbirds are the best known of all bowerbirds, but there are 17 other species – six others in Australia, nine in New Guinea, and two common to both areas. Their bowers vary in complexity, but generally the male bowerbirds that have the dullest plumage are the ones that build the most elaborate bowers.

Cold dip *A mother Weddell seal takes her pup on its first dip into an icy sea. The seals keep the breathing hole between floes clear by gnawing the edge of the ice.*

Weddell seals sing loudly to warn off rivals

As the icy Antarctic blizzards abate in the southern spring, seals begin to appear on the untidy icescape that surrounds the frozen continent. They are small-headed, 9ft (2.7m) long Weddell seals, rarely seen out of the water except in October and November, when the females haul themselves out onto ice floes to give birth. Often about 20 mothers with youngsters are spaced along the edge of a floe.

The females emerged from the sea through long cracks in the ice used as breathing holes. Below the crack, a male seal patrols his underwater territory while he waits for his females to wean their pups and be ready to mate. As he swims, the male sings a loud song of buzzes, trills and whistles to warn off other males. The song is learned from older seals, and the song sung by Weddell seals on one side of the Antarctic is different from the one sung by those on the other side. If the rival ignores the warning, the two bulky males fight underwater, manoeuvring with speed and agility.

Males have to wait up to eight weeks in the water below the nursery before the females will mate. A female Weddell seal will not leave her pup until it is ready to fend for itself. She coaxes it to swim before it is six weeks old, while it is still in its fluffy baby coat. When the pup is

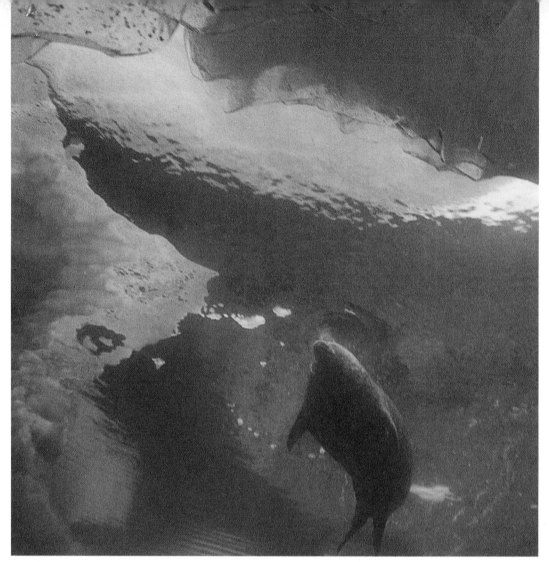

Singing patrol *A male Weddell seal patrolling his territory under the ice, sings a song learned from his elders.*

weaned at about seven weeks old, it will have moulted its baby fur. By this time, the female must take to the sea to feed and restore the body fat she has lost while suckling her youngster. A few days after the pup is weaned, she comes on heat, and mating takes place in the water.

Weddells are among the deepest diving seals. They usually dive no deeper than 330ft (100m) but may plunge to 1600ft (490m) or more beneath the ice, perhaps to catch Antarctic cod. The seals are insulated against the sub-zero temperatures by their thick layers of blubber.

HOW DEEP DIVERS SAVE THEIR BREATH

Seals, like humans, are air-breathing mammals, yet they can dive long and deep under the water – Weddell seals for up to 70 minutes – without coming up for air. And they can surface rapidly without suffering the bends – decompression sickness caused by nitrogen bubbles forming in the blood as pressure is reduced.

A diving seal stores twice as much oxygen as a diving human, mainly in its blood and muscles – and has twice as much blood for its weight as humans, with a higher proportion of oxygen-carrying red cells. As soon as a seal puts its head underwater, its body functions, including its heartbeat, slow down so its oxygen consumption is lower. Also, less blood flows to the organs not needed while diving, such as the kidneys.

Diving seals keep only a very small amount of oxygen in their lungs. To prevent bends, they breathe out when they dive, and at great depths what air remains in the lungs is squeezed into the windpipe, where nitrogen absorption is less of a risk.

DECEMBER

AFRICAN ELEPHANTS SEARCH FOR FRESH PASTURES,
EUROPEAN SQUIRRELS LIVE OFF FOOD CACHED FOR THE WINTER, ASIAN SNOW
LEOPARDS MOVE TO MILDER AREAS AND IN AUSTRALIA'S
SCORCHING SUMMER CORALS SPAWN AND KANGAROO BABIES LEAVE THE POUCH

Africa: Elephants migrate to new feeding grounds

Fighting on the beaches Two male northern elephant seals utter resounding threats as they square up for a fight. The victor wins the right to mate with scores of females.

Elephant seals fill their trunks for success

Loud bellows compete with the roar of winter surf pounding the American shore as two huge, ungainly creatures hurl guttural threats at each other. The male elephant seals rear up and inflate their long, trunk-like noses to amplify their roars and impress their rivals. Then they clash – butting heads, thumping noses and biting each other. Although their thick-skinned chests and necks bear the brunt, mouths and faces are gored and slashed.

December is the start of the mating season, for which these northern elephant seals have come south from their North Pacific feeding grounds to islands such as Ano Nuevo off the south-west US coast. The bulls – up to 20ft (6m) long and weighing up to 2½ tons – arrive first and haul their bulky bodies onto the beach. Then they fight for supremacy and the right to a harem of cows. Few fights continue to the death; most combatants retire hurt or exhausted.

The much smaller females arrive on the beaches in late December. They do not see one another as rivals, but seek one another's company so that up to 1000 may be close packed on the sand. Most of the cows are heavily pregnant from the previous year's mating and within a month or so each gives birth to a single black-coated pup. Not until its pup is weaned a month later will a cow be ready to mate.

But the males do not wait. Even before the pups are born they force themselves upon the cows, which are only about a third of their weight so can do little to resist. This aggressive mating not only harms the pregnant cows; it kills one in ten of the newly born pups. Some are lost in the turmoil and others are squashed to death by the huge bulls.

When the cows do become receptive, the dominant bulls each mate with up to 100 females. Mated females try to return to the sea, but lower-ranking males still desperate to mate bar the way. Some seals die in the ensuing scramble, but not enough to endanger the survival of the species. Slaughtered for the oil in their blubber, the seals had been reduced to only 100-200 worldwide by 1892. They are now protected by law, and on Ano Nuevo alone about 1500 pups are born every year.

Feathered invasion Huge flocks of red-winged blackbirds steal winter crops in the south-eastern United States.

The poorwill, America's hibernating bird

In a sheltered spot amid the sagebrush of Arizona, a brown and grey speckled bird is sleeping heavily through the bleak winter. Called *holchko*, 'sleeping one', by the Indians of Arizona, the common poorwill is the only bird in the world known to hibernate.

As in the dormouse and other small mammal hibernators, its heartbeat and breathing slow down and its temperature drops – by some 22°C from a norm of 41°C (106°F). Only a few poorwills have been found in this state, but they stayed in it for four days or longer. The birds' temperature can probably drop even more and they can possibly remain in torpor for up to 100 days.

Even when it is awake, the poorwill is rarely seen but more often heard repeatedly calling its name. When hunting, it flits silently through the night on soft-fringed wings to catch insects as they fly. Its large head and wide round eyes emphasise the smallness of its beak, which makes up in width what it lacks in length. When its beak is open the bird's whole face seems to split into a gaping trap.

The common poorwill is one of the nightjar family, most of which either live in tropical regions where food is always plentiful, or migrate to where insects are in season. But the poorwill stays all year in the temperate scrublands and prairies of the western United States and sleeps through the lean times of winter.

Deep sleep The poorwill survives the winter with hardly any food by hibernating in a sheltered place. Its bodily systems slow down, and it is in a state of torpor.

Where the blackbirds are black-listed

Throngs of dusky birds almost blot out the sky as a December evening descends on the farmlands of the south-eastern United States. Returning to their roosts are thousands of red-winged blackbirds, the most numerous land bird in North America.

In winter the birds move en masse from all over the country to the plentiful food supplies of the south-east. In Arkansas, 30 roosting places accommodate some 50 million birds, and Kentucky and Tennessee between them are host to 80 million birds.

The flickering, chattering mass of birds is not made up entirely of red-winged blackbirds – the jet-black males with their scarlet wing patches and the brown, thrush-like females. With them are other dark birds such as black grackles and brown-headed cowbirds.

At night the birds settle thickly on trees, huddled together for warmth. By day the invaders descend on the fields, their varied diet including the autumn-sown seeds of wheat and soya beans. With a comparatively small flock of 3000 tucking away 100lb (45kg) of food a day, the birds are regarded as major pests, to be shot and poisoned. Both their eating habits and noise are disliked, and they are suspected of passing disease to people and to cattle in their droppings. Unfortunately, the bird numbers increase with the amount of food available, so the more land there is under cultivation, the more birds there are to steal the crops.

Power play *With a flash of its fanned wings and tail, a magpie leaps to intimidate a young visitor, forcing it to abandon its morsel of food in the scuffled snow.*

Handsome magpies that act like gangsters

By December, the year's new generation of magpies have almost the same plumage as their parents. They are a delight to watch, swooping and cruising in their formal black and white suits with long, iridescent tails streaming. The same bold, domineering extroverts as the adults, they cackle with hoarse, football-rattle voices as they swagger among other birds to commandeer whatever food is going.

When they first left their parents, the young magpies – five to eight in each family – found life easy. In the farmland and gardens, insects, grain, berries, fruits, nestling birds, small mammals and carrion were plentiful. Now, however, winter has Europe in its grip and food is scarce. Not yet having mates or established territories, the young try to improve their chances by foraging in gangs of up to 100.

On their daily scouting of the frost-covered countryside the youngsters cross the territories of many established pairs of adult magpies, who jealously guard their patch. A resident bird soon harasses any intruder, rails at it raucously and threatens it with spread wings and tail. If the newcomer does not take the hint, the resident makes a full-scale attack with hefty beak and feet. Usually the younger bird gives in to avoid injury. This winter it is a loser, but by next winter it may have a territory of its own and will deal just as roughly with unwelcome visitors.

Grey squirrels prosper as red ones decline

On the upper branches of a tree, a red squirrel sits alert for a moment in the cold December dawn. It has just emerged from its snug, moss-lined nest of twigs in an ancient deciduous wood on the Isle of Wight in southern England. After a stretch and a scratch the squirrel takes off with its long, powerful hind legs, making tremendous leaps – some of 20ft (6m) or more. Its fluffy tail acts as a rudder, and its sharp, curved claws allow it to race up and down vertical trunks with impressive agility.

When it reaches an old oak tree with dead branches, the squirrel moves carefully along one of them, sniffing as it goes. Then it stops and reaches over to the underside of the branch, firmly anchored by its splayed hind feet. Its sharp nose has led it to a favourite winter food – a patch of *Vuilleminia* fungus growing beneath the dead bark. With tongue and sharp rodent teeth, the squirrel scrapes out the fungus. Then, after munching the tasty snack and a quick groom on the top of the branch, it bounds off again to find the next patch.

Not far away in mainland England, the ancient woods of the New Forest are filled with grey squirrels. Since it was introduced from North America at the turn of the century, the grey squirrel has multiplied enormously. This larger, heavier relative of the red squirrel spends the winter mornings foraging on the woodland floor, its silver-grey coat providing excellent camouflage against the frosted dead leaves. The squirrel hops about sniffing the ground for any hint of a buried acorn or hazel nut. When it finds one, it sometimes eats the morsel straight away, but occasionally it will cache the nut for later.

Both red and grey squirrels eat a variety of foods – in spring and summer catkins, shoots,

High liver *Most at home in the tree tops, a red squirrel relishes a morsel of fungus from beneath the bark.*

buds, flowers and insects, in autumn and winter fungi and, especially, tree seeds. They choose nuts for eating and caching by weight, turning them over and over in their front paws to assess whether they are heavy (containing a good nut) or light (containing a withered kernel).

Grey squirrels evolved in the deciduous forests of North America where they learned to make the most of a single fall of tree seeds, mostly acorns, in the autumn. Their digestive systems can cope with the poisonous tannins in acorns, and they prefer deciduous woods.

Red squirrels evolved in the conifer forests that covered Europe and northern Asia before the last Ice Age, and conifer seeds are their favourite food. When the ice retreated about 10,000 years ago, a few conifers had survived in Britain, but they were mostly replaced by birch, then hazel, and finally oaks. Red squirrels recolonised Britain about 9000 years ago, and adapted to eat hazel nuts but have not had time to evolve a digestive system to cope with acorns. Their preferred food is pine seeds, and they do not live in purely deciduous woods if conifers are available close by.

Wherever red and grey squirrels share an area, the greys will eat everything the reds enjoy and can still go on to a feast of acorns. The well-fed greys breed better, and quickly become numerous enough to eat their red cousins out of house and home.

In addition, red squirrel numbers fluctuate, both from year to year and over longer periods, without interference from grey squirrels. The main cause of death is starvation when the pine crop fails.

Predators, disease and parasite infestations also take their toll. And sadly, the coniferous woods they prefer are rapidly shrinking because of man's activities. All these reasons help to explain why grey squirrels have replaced reds over much of Britain.

Food to the fiercest *With talons to the fore, a hungry buzzard drives another from its food. On harsh winter days, they may fight to the death for a grub or a worm.*

Hungry buzzards can be deadly fighters

When frosts whiten Europe's hillsides and forests, a hungry female buzzard wheels slowly through the cold December air in search of scarce prey. Rabbits, voles and mice keep under cover more, and surviving small birds are wary of predators. Insect grubs and worms are mostly tucked well away. If there is a dead rabbit about, the buzzard will settle for carrion.

When her keen eye spots a young male eating grubs in a rotting tree stump, she swoops down to threaten him with shrill cries and flapping wings. The youngster is reluctant to give up his food and spreads his wings over it, but she puffs out her body feathers and raises her head and nape feathers. Then she drops back on her spread wings and tail, freeing her feet to strike. She is prepared to fight him, perhaps to the death. He submits to the appreciably larger and more experienced female, and escapes when she begins to feed. He has lost this meal, but at least he can fly away unharmed to find another.

Submission *The young male buzzard rolls onto his side with feet up and free wing spread to show that he is yielding his food to the intruding female.*

Ground-floor dweller *A grey squirrel carefully hides an acorn in leaf litter to sniff out and dig up later.*

253

A snow leopard that dies for its beauty

In a high alpine valley in the Himalayas, the half light of a December dawn spreads slowly across a remote, grassy slope where a slate-grey bharal, or blue sheep, is grazing. Suddenly a creamy-grey shape sprints from the shadow of a rock some 25ft (7.5m) away and springs on its victim. A snow leopard is making its kill.

Snow leopards, also called ounces, are seldom seen. The chances of spotting one are greater in December when they leave the alpine meadows above the tree line, about 12,000ft (3600m) up, to follow their prey down to valleys below 6000ft (1800m) for the harsh winter.

At dawn and dusk, the leopards hunt for prey such as sheep, mountain goats, deer and marmots, and in winter add wild boar, Tibetan gazelles and pikas – which are rat-sized, round-eared hare-like animals – to their menu. A snow leopard has a cushion of hair on the underside of its paws which not only keeps its feet warm, but also spreads its weight and helps it to run across snow without sinking in too deeply, enabling it to outrun its prey. Because of the scarcity of prey, snow leopards hunt in territories up to 40sq miles (about 100sq km) in area.

Herds of domestic sheep and goats range the highest pastures in summer. These flocks are ousting the leopards' normal prey, and the reduction in food supply is causing a rapid decline in the leopards' numbers. Its survival is even more threatened by illegal fur trappers. Snow leopard pelts are highly prized by the mountain people for their long, thick, beautifully marked fur. Tribesmen set poisoned snares, and snow leopard pelts can still be found on sale illegally in some places.

Lovely leopard *One of the most beautiful of the big cats, the snow leopard has long, thick fur to protect it from the harsh weather of its remote mountain home.*

Rare deer Barasingha stags have wide-spreading antlers. Some have brow prongs at right angles to the main beam.

A grassy sanctuary for endangered deer

In the Kanha National Park in central India, the barasinghas, or swamp deer, are restless. It is December, the beginning of their rut – mating displays – and the mating season lasts only two months. This is so that the young will be born in June or July, when the monsoon has brought new growth and tender green shoots for the deer to feed on. In the short mating season, each adult barasingha stag must quickly establish his dominance and win mates from the herds of hinds (females).

Stags and hinds are both yellowy-brown with fine hair that is almost like wool, but during the rut the stags become slightly reddish along their backs. Stags stand about 4ft (1.2m) high at the shoulder and have long manes. Their antlers are up to 3ft 5in (1.1m) long.

In the Kanha sanctuary, the barasinghas feed on the tall grasses that border open, grassy areas amid slopes covered with rain forest. Another race of barasingha in Assam in north-east India lives in marshland and swamps – hence the animal's name – and these animals have splayed feet to prevent them sinking into the ground.

Grazing domestic livestock have so seriously diminished the barasinghas' living space that they are in danger of extinction. The southern race is confined to the Kanha National Park, an area marginally smaller than Luxembourg, which it shares with gaur (Indian bison), tigers and packs of ferocious red dogs. Only three types of grass are available there during the dry season from November to May, and the deer make the best of the available foods by migrating between areas, though these may be only about 4 miles (6.5km) apart. The animals forage in the early morning and evening, preferring to hide and ruminate in the long grass from mid-morning to dusk, the hottest part of the day.

Numbers in the Kanha Sanctuary had dwindled alarmingly, from 3000 in 1938 to a mere 66 in 1969. However, since new conservation measures were introduced in 1978, numbers have increased to 283 and are still rising. The park management discovered that their regular grass-burning was affecting the barasinghas' breeding cycle, so they changed their methods to save the deer.

Male horned toads risk all to find a mate

Torrential rain falls from a sky heavy with clouds onto the tropical rain forest of Sarawak in East Malaysia. It is the rainiest time of a very rainy year, and by December the forest is sodden. Huge rain drops splash onto the forest floor, flipping over leaves and twigs and making the damp, brown-and-yellow-mottled leaf litter seem to be almost alive.

Suddenly a leaf seems to stir on its own and emits a squeak. It is not a leaf at all but a tiny Malaysian horned toad. A master of disguise, the toad is camouflaged to resemble the fallen leaves among which it hides. For most of the year the toads are silent, but at mating time, during the wettest time of year, the males sit in puddles and shallow streams of rainwater and call with a loud 'ching'. If they did not take the risk of calling and making themselves conspicuous, the females would never find them.

Malaysian horned toads are one of 76 species of horned toad found in South-east Asia. The Malaysian form has three pointed flaps, or 'horns' – one over each eye and one on the tip of its snout. Its skin is the same colour as the fallen leaves and is ribbed to look like a dead leaf. This disguise not only protects the toad from predators such as herons, cats, birds of prey and snakes, but also hides it from the creatures it preys on. With its large mouth, it will snap up any living morsel that passes by – including smaller versions of its own kind.

In hiding A Malaysian horned toad resembles a dead leaf. This conceals it from predators and prey, but male toads give themselves away when they call to females.

AFRICA

The roving life of an African elephant

In a forest in Zimbabwe, the temperature on a December day is around 24°C (75°F). The elephants raise their heads impatiently, flap their fan-like ears to cool themselves, and look at their leader. She is the oldest cow in this typical family group of 14 females and offspring, and at 40 years old is the mother of five and the grandmother of four.

Fully aware of the herd's restlessness, she lifts her trunk with its sensitive nostrils and sniffs the air to sense the weather and smell any danger. With the showers of recent weeks turning into a steady downpour, the five-month rainy season is under way, and the elephants are eager to leave the forest for new pastures.

During the May-November dry season they have stayed in the forest, usually near water, plucking the shoots of trees such as acacia with the two finger-like lips on their trunks. They have also used their trunks to uproot whole trees to reach the topmost shoots, and have eaten the bark, ripped off with their tusks, as well as dug up and eaten roots. The onset of the rains, when the elephants turn their backs on the mangled remains of many a meal, gives the forest a much-needed respite. Grass, which springs up as the heavy rains hammer Botswana's open plains some 100 miles (160km) to the south, is the food they like best. The matriarch signals the 'go-ahead' with a soft rumbling in her throat, and they all sally forth.

Not all elephants migrate if there is enough food to go round, but a 4-5 ton adult cow eats 500lb (228kg) of food a day and drinks about 40 gallons (182 litres) of water. The animals spend three-quarters of every day eating, and a herd needs to range over an area of some 300sq miles (780sq km) or more in search of food and water. In the confines of a national park, where numbers tend to increase, elephants sometimes destroy their own food supply, devouring trees and shrubs before they have time to regenerate.

The migrating elephants travel in single file at the same pace as a man. They keep together, often touching each other with their trunks or

December migration *Lured by the prospect of fresh grass at the start of the rainy season, African elephants make their way southwards from the forests of Zimbabwe towards the open plains of Botswana.*

Head-on collision *Two young bull elephants struggle for supremacy. The victor will be dominant for life.*

nudging stray infants back into line. Only the unruly adolescent males shove and push their elders. When they are 12 years old, they will be thrown out of the group to join other males of their age, or live alone.

By the time the elephants reach the plains, they have been joined by relatives, and their ranks have swelled to 40. Family herds link or split up according to the food available. Adult males migrate too. Most babies are conceived during the rains, when plenty of good food stimulates fertility.

The swampy plains, fed by the rising rivers, are a sea of green, and the elephants are soon tucking-in to the grass. Occasionally they take a cooling wallow in the water or mud, or a shower with water sucked up in their trunks.

One night, one of the females fails to settle, and just before daybreak, gives birth to an 18 stone (115kg) baby, unwrapping him from his foetal sac with her trunk. Half an hour later, the mother hoists her 3ft (1m) high calf to his feet with her trunk, and he stays upright for two minutes. Several attempts later he manages to stand, and uses his floppy trunk to feel his way to the two teats behind his mother's front legs. After one or two hours he can walk, sheltered under his mother's belly.

The other females of the group help to look after the baby and protect him. If anything happens to his mother, one of them will adopt him. At six years old, he will weigh nearly a ton.

Female elephants have their first calf when they are about 13 years old, after a pregnancy of

22 months, and youngsters are suckled for up to three years. During their long childhood they must learn what to eat and where to find it, and how to behave in company. Elephants use touch, gesture, scent and sound – snorts, growls and rumbles – to communicate.

Young males indulge in playful head-butting, a test of each other's dominance. As adult bulls they will roam a wider area than the females, and dominance will accord roughly with age and size. Elephants grow throughout their lives,

Bringing up baby *An elephant calf is protected and taught by all the females of its family herd. It has to learn how to pluck and grasp with its trunk.*

and an old bull may stand 11ft (3.4m) at the shoulder and have tusks 8ft (2.4m) long.

From the age of 15, each male spends two or three months of the year in pursuit of females to mate with, advertising himself as a healthy suitor by discharging from his temple glands, dribbling urine, and being aggressive towards the other bulls. This sexually excited state is known as musth or must (from an Urdu word meaning 'drunk').

Not all bull elephants are in musth at the same time. Bulls not in musth can mate, but give way to those who are. A musth male fends off rivals for as long as the female is on heat – a receptive female is worth staying with because pregnancy and suckling take up so much time that cows are on heat for only a few days every three or five years. But no male can keep up the searching and fighting for females, with little chance to eat, for long.

African elephant *Larger than the Asian elephant, the African has bigger ears for its size and two lips at the tip of its trunk. It has four toenails on each front foot, three on each back foot.*

Asian elephant *The trunk has only one lip. The back is more curved than in the African elephant, and the ears smaller. There are five toenails on each front foot, four on each back foot.*

Vanishing antelopes of the open plains

Amid the tall, yellowy-brown grass of the southern African plains, a female oribi is resting after giving birth. December and January are the best time for small antelopes to rear their young because the summer rains ensure good flushes of tender new grass.

The female is motionless, and her newborn fawn is nowhere to be seen. It is hidden in the grass some distance away, for she does not want to betray its presence to predators such as lions. The youngster lies flattened behind a clump of coarse grass. Not even an eyelid flickers, and its yellowish-brown coat blends into its surroundings. Oribi fawns remain immobile for hours at a stretch, and predators walk past unaware of their presence. Hiding in the grass is the young oribi's only means of protection.

The fawn's father, not much bigger than a whippet, is feeding, also some distance away. The parents are not often seen together because one normally feeds in the open while the other rests. Only in the morning and evening does the mother go to the youngster to suckle it. Then, for a few minutes, the fawn stretches its limbs gambolling around its mother's legs. Fawns stay hidden until they are three or four months old and can graze with their parents.

Although most antelopes are browsers – feeding on leaves and occasionally fruits – oribis feed only on grass, however dry and brittle it gets in the hot sun. They spend two-thirds of their day resting, chewing the cud, or simply hiding from predators by vanishing amid the tall grass, where they are well camouflaged.

Like most small antelopes, pairs of oribi have their own territory. Occasionally a male has more than one female and there may be up to five adults to each territory. On average, oribis range over a territory of about ⅛ sq mile (35 hectares), an area five times bigger than the territory of a small, forest-living antelope such as a duiker. The reason is that the oribi need the larger area to find sufficient grass of the type they can digest easily. Forest-living antelopes can find all the food they need in a smaller area.

To mark their territory, both male and female oribis have small scent glands, one just in front of each eye. They mark twigs and grass stems on the boundary by positioning the gland so that the tip of the twig or stem enters it. Then they move their heads to wipe the twig or stem round inside the gland, which exudes a sticky brown fluid. Successive coatings form dark brown beads as hard as glass. Both male and female mark and defend the territory, but as he alone has horns, the male most often chases intruders away. When young oribis are mature, they leave their parents' territory to find, mark and defend territories of their own.

Still life A female oribi sits erect and motionless amid the grass of the southern African plains. Her stillness and colouring help her to escape the notice of predators.

Babysitter In a grey meerkat colony, all adults sharing a burrow share the minding – and teaching – of youngsters.

How young meerkats learn their skills

The Kalahari is one of the most inhospitable deserts on earth. But in December, meagre occasional rains cause the tough desert plants to flourish and bloom briefly, bringing out the insects that feed on them. So this is the time when insect-eating meerkats raise their young.

The grey or slender-tailed meerkat is a type of mongoose, a bit bigger than a squirrel. Each meerkat shares its burrow with 10-15 others, and everyone takes turns to babysit. Litters of usually four youngsters are two weeks old when they first venture above ground, and their guardians have their work cut out to keep them from straying and to guard them from predators.

When meerkats are out and about, one of them stands upright on a rock or tree to watch for foxes, jackals or eagles. Unwary babies are easy prey, but they soon learn to vanish underground when a sentinel calls the alarm. At six weeks old the youngsters join group expeditions. A gang of meerkats will bite at a jackal's heels to drive it off, and will even mob a cobra.

The meerkats work hard for a living in their harsh home. The insects, small reptiles and scorpions they feed on hide underground from predators and the 40°C (104°F) sun. In one morning, a meerkat can dig 400 holes and shift 50 times its own weight of sand.

Although all adults share the teaching of young meerkats, each pupil becomes the apprentice of just one tutor. Digging for insect grubs is nothing but hard work, but catching geckos – small lizards – needs wit and practice. The teacher grabs the reptile with the mouth and drops it at the baby's feet. The baby pounces but misses, and time and again the adult retrieves the prey until the youngster catches its wriggly meal itself.

A gecko can do a meerkat no harm, but some food does. Light-footed meerkat veterans do not get nipped when stealing cocoons from a nest of biting ants, but trainees end up covered with the insects. Meerkats skilfully claw a scorpion out of its retreat under roots or rocks, or in a crevice, then gingerly disarm it by snipping off its stinging tail with their sharp teeth. Youngsters presented with intact scorpions learn the hard way. The sting hurts but does not kill them.

Warming up Desert nights can be bitterly cold, and grey meerkats often emerge at sunrise to stand with backs to the sun – all but one who acts as lookout.

Deadly efficiency A male osprey returns home with a plump fish for his growing family firmly clamped in his talons. The fish's head is pointing forwards for streamlining.

A handsome osprey fishes from the air

With slow beats of his powerful wings, an osprey, or fish hawk, circles above the food-rich waters of the Red Sea on a hot December day. He has a mate and two three-week-old chicks to feed, waiting in a bulky nest of sticks on top of a mangrove tree. The same weight as a herring gull but with a wingspan of 5ft (1.5m), he slices effortlessly through the air, scanning the sea with yellow, owl-like eyes.

Suddenly he stops, hovering in midair. He has spotted a likely prey and takes aim. Sweeping back his wings, the osprey plummets 100ft (30m) headlong towards the water. At the last moment he throws his legs forwards, smashes feet first into the sea – and disappears. Seconds later water flies in all directions as he re-emerges.

As the osprey gains height, his glistening quarry is revealed. The slithery fish gripped in his sharp talons set in spiky feet has little chance of escape. He carries it with its head pointing forwards, like a torpedo, to reduce air resistance. Hijackers such as the African fish eagle are waiting to harass the osprey to make him drop his catch, but this time he wins through.

The ospreys returned to the mangrove swamp by the sea three months ago and spent a few weeks repairing their eyrie. And since their blotchy, oval eggs were laid, they have divided their labour – the female staying at home while her mate hunts. Now that the chicks have hatched after five weeks of incubation, the male has stepped up his fishing trips to provide food for himself, his mate and the growing chicks.

When he takes his catch to the nest, the female rips it into manageable chunks with her hooked beak to feed the chicks. She feeds them for at least six weeks, during which time they change from helpless, downy babies into feathered juveniles, flapping their wings and able to dismember for themselves the fish brought by both parents. They do not actually fly until eight to ten weeks old. By the time they leave their parents in April they are well able to fish, and spend their first year near their birthplace.

CENTRAL AND SOUTH AMERICA

Web-footed water pigs in muddy havens

Wallowing in the muddy water of a shrinking pool, a group of capybaras escapes the searing noon heat of December on the Venezuelan plains. Frequent dips build up a layer of cooling mud on their bristly coats. Sometimes a capybara disappears underwater for up to five minutes to nibble submerged grasses. Water-loving and web-footed, capybaras are also known as water pigs, but are the world's largest rodents, related to guinea pigs. Females, larger than males, may be 2ft (610mm) at the shoulder.

The animals live in a family group with one dominant male, his blunt, oblong head bearing a distinctive black scent gland above the nose. Three adult females, his mates, are with him, and their offspring born about four months ago in the rainy season. The male keeps chivvying away a pair of young males from last year's litters, but the family shows no aggression towards other groups using the same pool. Many rivers and pools shrink and disappear as the dry season advances, and herds of 100 or so of the giant rodents collect at permanent water. They are so peaceable that a jacana bird, or lily trotter, can feed alongside them undisturbed.

In the cooler air of the late afternoon, the capybaras will leave the water to graze on the surrounding plain, but never far from the water. Vultures, dogs and foxes all prey on them, and at the first sight of one, the family rushes into the water. Yet even there they may meet disaster in the jaws of a crocodile-like cayman, although they often escape by their powerful swimming.

Like all rodents, capybaras have long, sharp incisor teeth that grow continuously to replace those worn down by gnawing their fibrous diet, mainly of grasses. Their teeth enable them to nibble the very short grass remaining towards the end of the December-April dry season.

When the rains begin to swell the rivers again in May, the herds of capybaras split up into family units and the breeding season begins. Mating takes place in the water but the young, about four to a litter, are born on land. Some will fall prey to hungry hunters, but enough will survive to ensure that when the next dry season comes round, the water hole herds are swelled by a new generation of vegetarian water pigs.

Marking time *The large gland on a dominant male capybara's face oozes sticky liquid that he uses to scent twigs and grass stems in his territory at mating time.*

Midday mudbath *A group of capybaras takes refuge from the burning Venezuelan sun in a muddy pool. They will graze on land in the cool of the late afternoon.*

Hungry brood *A mother fungus beetle shepherds her newly hatched offspring (top) towards a feast of fresh fungi. After two or three days (bottom) the grubs have grown large and are ready to begin changing into adults.*

Fungus beetle offspring grow fat on fungi

Rain splashes noisily on a tangle of leaves and ferns in dense rain forest on the island of Trinidad, off Venezuela. The heavy December rains promote a rash of fungi on damp, rotting timber, and bring the female fungus beetle out from her hiding place in rotting wood under bark. She mated soon after emerging from her cocoon, and now she must lay her eggs.

The beetle zigzags across the rotten stump of a fallen forest giant, sensing her way with busy antennae, looking for fresh fungi. A bracket fungus can sprout in an hour and disappear almost as fast, but the beetle can detect one at a very early stage of development. As soon as a small fungus is ready, she deposits about 100 tiny eggs on the underside and waits close by.

Within about an hour they hatch into black-and-white-striped larvae and begin to feed on the fungus. Then the mother is kept busy scouting for fresh fungi of the right size, for the hungry grubs grow at an incredible rate, and need bigger and bigger fungi to satisfy them. She herds them in groups from one patch to the next. The grubs are slow movers, so she gathers them within her legs for protection.

In just two or three days, the beetle grubs have grown large and fat, and are ready to pupate – transform into adults inside a cocoon. In a few more days they will emerge as beetles and set off into the forest to find mates.

Flesh-eating piranha fish meet their match

Piranhas glide among the submerged tree trunks of southern Guyana's flooded forests. They spread there with the rising waters that flood the river basins from March to September each year. But now, in December, the water is receding. In the area around the upper reaches of the Essequibo river, the piranhas are isolated in a string of pools. At first this was to their advantage because food was more concentrated. But now they are isolated and short of a meal. Suddenly a sleek, powerful 4ft (1.2m) long giant otter snatches a black piranha and crushes it with its strong teeth. The otters find piranhas easy prey to catch in the dwindling water.

There are many types of piranha in the Amazon basin. Some are largely fruit and seed eaters, the largest up to 2ft (610mm) long. Others are flesh eaters 4-16in (100-400mm) long, including the black piranha and the voracious red-bellied piranha. They generally eat other fish, but occasionally hunt in large groups and will tackle animals such as capybaras. With their razor-sharp triangular teeth, they shave out small semicircular chunks of flesh, which they shred and swallow. They are said to strip a victim to the bone in minutes.

The biter bit *A giant otter eats a piranha held firmly in its forepaws. The otter is one of the few creatures that preys on these fish with the fearsome reputation.*

Loving embrace Two deadly taipans entwine in mating. Each can produce a cupful of strong poison at a time – enough to kill thousands of small animals.

A shy but deadly snake goes courting

Amid the tussocky grass, dead wood and boulders of a southern Queensland forest, various hunters are at work in the warm, humid air of a December night. Spiders set invisible snares for flies, a praying mantis polishes off an ant and a taipan, one of Australia's most poisonous snakes, lies in wait for the next rat, mouse or bandicoot to come its way. Taipans come out in the cooler night in very hot weather, but usually hunt in early morning and late afternoon, being better than most snakes at coping with the heat of the day.

The taipan's ridged, 10ft (3m) long brown body blends into the surrounding leaf litter of the forest floor. Although motionless, the snake is more alert than it appears. Its forked tongue is constantly on the move, flicking in and out through a notch in its upper lip as it picks up tiny particles of scent from the air. Snakes do not hear well, and although many have good eyesight they all use their tongues to gain information about their surroundings.

A rat-like bandicoot is searching for insects, its long snout snuffling through the dead leaves. Before long it stops in its tracks, sniffs deeply and digs into the gravelly soil to expose juicy morsels of beetle larvae. The taipan scents the bandicoot with its tongue and prepares to rear up and sink its hollow, ½ in (13mm) long fangs into its victim. The venom that shoots through them will kill its prey within minutes.

Every so often the nervous bandicoot checks for signs of danger. It pays to be alert. On this occasion it is fate, not vigilance, that preserves the bandicoot's life. The taipan has picked up another scent as well – one powerfully designed to attract it. Female snakes let it be known they are ready to mate by leaving a trail of scent for males to follow, and this male taipan has picked up the scent of a female. He abandons the hunt and goes in pursuit of her.

When they meet, the male rubs his rough chin over his partner's lower back and moves up her body until the two of them are twisted together. After mating, the taipan couple split up, the male taking no further interest in becoming a father. The female, however, looks for a place to lay her eggs. It must be warm and well away from marauders – a place such as a rotting log, decaying vegetation, or a hollow in the ground.

She may search for several weeks, during

Drumbeat A palm cockatoo uses a drumstick he has made himself to beat against a tree trunk. He drums during courting and to proclaim his territory.

LETHAL WEAPONS

The taipan is one of the world's most poisonous snakes, ranking with the cobras of India and the mambas of Africa, to which it is related. Like them, it has poison glands behind each eye, and when it bites the glands compress, shooting poison down through the hollow fangs into the prey. As their fangs are at the front of the mouth these snakes stab and inject in one go, like a hypodermic needle. This is true of many venomous snakes. Others, however, have fangs farther back in the mouth and must first seize their prey then inject it with venom. Most of these species are not very dangerous, although there are exceptions, such as the African boomslang.

Snake venom is a cocktail of substances, including enzymes, and the strength of the poison varies between species. The tiger snake vies with the taipan for the title of most dangerous snake in Australia. But the taipan's poison is as potent as the tiger snake's, and it delivers up to five times more of it. It strikes repeatedly, and its longer fangs sink in deeper.

The venom courses through the victim's bloodstream and attacks the nervous system, causing nausea and paralysis. It can kill a human in 15-60 minutes. As for most snake poisons, antiserum is available.

Snakes have predators, too, including wild dogs, wild cats, raccoons, mongooses, serpent eagles, secretary birds and other snakes. Although few snakes go out of their way to attack people, they will bite in self-defence if stepped on. So snakes are most dangerous if they live in open country where many people work on the land, often with bare feet. In West Africa, for instance, carpet vipers account for most of the 17,000 snake-bite deaths a year.

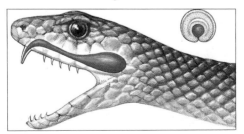

Jaws of death The taipan's hollow fangs, near the front of its mouth, receive poison from a gland behind the eye (shown in cross-section).

which time she does not eat. Finally, some time in January, she finds a suitable spot and lays 15 soft-shelled eggs, about the same size as hen eggs. From now on they are on their own. Their mother will do no more for them, and she goes off to look for food.

The eggs swell as the embryos develop. When they hatch in ten weeks' time, they will have doubled in size. The newborn taipans will be about 18in (460mm) long, fully armed with poison, and hungry.

Australia has more than 110 different types of snake, and is the only part of the world where venomous species outnumber non-venomous ones. The taipan is feared because it is the biggest of the venomous species, but taipans live only in the thinly populated north, and are shy and retiring. Most of the deaths from snake bite (under ten) that occur in Australia each year are from tiger snake or brown snake bites.

The cockatoo that beats a drum at dawn

The quiet of the December night is almost over. Soon the soft scratchings of tree rats, marsupial mice and possums will give way to a raucous dawn chorus punctuated by harsh screeches and shrill whistles, revealing the many birds that live in this rain forest in Cape York peninsula in northern Australia.

By day, courting and nest-building birds fill the trees with their impressive displays and loud songs. Now and again a drumming sound can be heard. The drummer is a bird – a male palm cockatoo hitting the hollow trunk of a eucalyptus tree with a small stick held in his foot. Some animals use tools to crack nuts or poke out insects, but the drumstick is one of the most superior tools in the animal kingdom. The cockatoo makes it himself, breaking off a small branch with his strong beak, snipping it to length and removing any leaves.

As he drums, the cockatoo pirouettes, watched by his female companion. Then, dropping the stick, he strokes her neck with his beak. When courting and nesting, cockatoos drum frequently. If two males dispute over a nest site in a tree hollow, the victor drums regularly to proclaim ownership. The female incubates the one egg, which hatches in about a month, and the chick spends just over three months in the nest, fed on nuts, berries and seeds – especially the seeds of the palm-like pandanus.

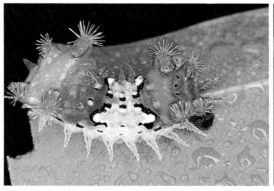

A stinging defence *The tufted cup moth caterpillar (left) has stinging hairs on its head and tail. The adult dries and expands its wings after emerging from its cup-shaped cocoon (right).*

Hairy and furry *These hairy caterpillars feed together side by side and move together head to tail. They eventually turn into furry white-tufted moths, here looking like miniature owls.*

Spiky caterpillars that change to sleek moths

During December, a slug-like caterpillar with the appearance of a Chinese junk is often seen on bushes in Australian gardens. It is the caterpillar of the cup moth, and the large tufts of hair protruding at the front and rear of its colourful body look like sails. If touched, these hairs give a painful sting and can cause swelling.

Australia has some of the most bizarre, the most beautiful and the biggest caterpillars in the world. A caterpillar is the feeding stage in the life cycle of a moth or butterfly – an elongated eating machine that munches its way through so much foliage that it outgrows its skin about four times and has to moult.

The eggs from which caterpillars develop are laid on or near a plant that will provide them with suitable food. On this plant a caterpillar is exposed and vulnerable to predators, so many types have developed defences such as camouflage, an unpleasant taste, or bright warning colours to deter attackers. In summer, each caterpillar changes into a chrysalis, spinning a cocoon in which it transforms into an adult. The cup moth gets its name from its cup-shaped cocoon, which has a removable lid through which the adult eventually emerges.

The Hercules moth of the rain forests of Australia and New Guinea carries out the change from caterpillar to adult on a grand scale. Before it is ready to spin its pear-sized cocoon, the spiky caterpillar eats and grows rapidly and can reach a length of more than 5in (125mm) – a giant among caterpillars.

The adult Hercules moth – one of the largest in the world – can have a wingspan of up to 14in (360mm). The male has two large feathery antennae, each equipped with more than 60,000 sensory hairs which he uses to pick up sexual odours the female releases by raising her tail. It is the only way they can find each other in their dense forest home. Downwind – even 2-3 miles (3-5km) away – the male moth can detect a single molecule of the female's scent, but needs about 200 to strike his antennae before he changes direction and zigzags towards the source until he reaches her.

Gargantuan moth *The spiky giant caterpillar of the Hercules moth (top) has just completed a moult. Eventually it will turn into an adult moth with a 14in (360mm) wingspan (centre and bottom).*

THE TIME TO GROW
Just when plants begin to put out new leaves, there are caterpillars ready to eat them. The caterpillars develop from eggs laid on the plant by the parent moth or butterfly. The signal for the overwintering parents or caterpillars to emerge is the same signal that causes the plant to grow – light intensity. Changes in the amount of light activate chemicals that affect growth. In temperate latitudes, day and night length and the intensity of daylight reach critical points in spring and autumn, triggering growth or dormancy.

A living cradle for a kangaroo joey

In the shady, wooded grasslands of eastern Australia, an eastern grey kangaroo pauses in the cool of the evening, her 11-month-old youngster, called a joey, peering from her pouch. Born last January, the youngster will shortly be leaving the pouch for good – unceremoniously tipped out to make way for a younger brother or sister already waiting to be born.

Over the last few months, the joey has been hopping in and out of the pouch while its mother grazed. Her joey's excursions are an anxious time for the kangaroo, as the youngster has little appreciation of danger such as lurking dingoes, and is not good at recognising her unless she calls to it. If the joey calls loudly to her, she will go to it. A kangaroo leans slightly forwards for her joey to re-enter the pouch. It gets in head first, then curls round.

Even when it is out of the pouch for good, the joey continues to feed on its mother's milk for another six months or so. So does the youngster it is making way for, but with different milk from a different teat. The female kangaroo mated several weeks ago, but the fertilised egg implants in the womb only when her pouch is vacated. The new joey is born 37 days after that, in January. Then the tiny, blind, naked creature, barely the length of a thumbnail, emerges from its mother's birth canal and, guided by smell, crawls up over her stomach and into the safety of her pouch – the journey takes about three minutes. Once there, it latches onto a teat, which swells to fill its mouth, so preventing it from falling off. There it stays for six months or so, until it is a miniature version of its mother.

Youngsters become fully independent at about 18 months old. Young males wander off to find a new range, but females settle down in a range near their mother. By two years old, the young kangaroos are sexually mature. Adult eastern grey males can be 7ft (2m) or more from head to tail tip, but females are generally no more than 6ft (1.8m). A big, dominant male, known as a boomer, usually has a harem of several females, and fights off challengers by boxing with his forefeet. Grazing kangaroos can cover around 6ft (1.8m) in one hop, and if alarmed can leap up to five times that distance.

Easy rider *A young kangaroo spends much of its first year in the safety and comfort of its mother's pouch. It first ventures out when about seven months old.*

Fertile female A saltwater crocodile lays her 50 eggs into a chamber in a large mound of sticks and plants.

Solitary watch The careful mother guards the precious clutch alone for up to three months until the young hatch.

A saltwater crocodile makes a good mother

As the December rainy season descends on the hot, sprawling wetlands of northern Australia, a female saltwater crocodile is patiently guarding her nest. She searched out a good nesting spot by nuzzling the ground with her lips, which have temperature receptors in their skin. For the developing eggs, the temperature is vital.

The nest is a mound of sticks and plants about two paces across and an arm-length deep. The crocodile has laid about 50 oval white eggs, each about the size of a tennis ball, in a chamber she hollowed out in the centre of the mound. Then she covered them.

Now they are developing in a fairly steady temperature, insulated by the air trapped in the mound round their chamber. With the start of four months of rain in December, the billabongs (stagnant backwaters) near the nest will fill with fresh water and spring into life. Small fish, insects and tiny frogs will abound – perfect food for a nursery of young crocodiles to grow fast and fat on when they hatch in March.

The female saltwater crocodile is a devoted mother, making careful preparations for the next generation. If the nest is in a damp, cool spot – maybe on a raft of weeds in a billabong, or beside a marsh – then the eggs will develop at a temperature of about 30°C (86°F). If it is on a bank in the sun, or away from water, it will be warmer, about 32°C (90°F). This tiny difference in temperature will have a crucial effect.

All the eggs developed at the cooler temperature hatch into females. All those developed in the warmer nest hatch into males. Any nests where the temperature is between these crucial figures produce a mixture of males and females, but usually with a majority of females. So influential is temperature that a nest built with one half at the water's edge and the other in the hot sun may produce females from the cooler part and males from the warmer.

The mother crocodile guards her nest ferociously, but many eggs are still lost to predators. These include monitor lizards, pigs, and even men – those willing to risk life and limb for a delicacy, for saltwater crocodiles are sometimes man-eaters. However, eggs are most often lost when a nest is unexpectedly flooded by the rains. A proven safe nesting place is used year after year by the same female, perhaps for all of her 40 or 50 fertile years.

Despite large losses of eggs, enough hatch successfully to maintain the population. During March the females answer the piping calls of their young, who are ready to be dug free of their nest. A mother picks up her babies delicately in her fearsome jaws and carries them to the nearest water in the pouch beneath her tongue, formed by the floor of her mouth. Once she puts them out they will fend for themselves in the maze of brackish pools and channels of their wetlands home.

The youngsters will not begin breeding until they are 6-10 years old. Then they will head upstream from the brackish coastal waters. There may be as many as eight females for every male. The sexes are attracted to one another by smells spread into the water from scent glands, which develop round the lips, and on females near their vents, at the beginning of the mating season – about November, as the hotter season approaches once more.

Mating takes place in the water, where buoyancy helps to support the creatures' huge bulk. The largest crocodiles can weigh more than ten men and be about 20ft (6m) long. A male may mate with many females. He leaves after mating, and from this point care of the next generation becomes a task for mothers only.

Moonlight and magic as the corals spawn

On a moonlit December night, the shallow, crystal clear waters off Australia's north-east coast turn into a thick, rainbow soup as they suddenly teem with millions of brightly coloured specks shooting upwards like a gigantic firework display. The corals have spawned.

Below the waters stretch the sheer cliffs, gullies and vast flat-topped mountains of the 1250 mile (2000km) long Great Barrier Reef, made up of several thousand individual coral reefs. Millions of tiny corals build a coral reef. Each coral is made up of one or more polyps, soft-bodied animals rather like sea anemones except that they secrete a hard limestone base for themselves. This base is a protective chamber that acts like a skeleton, and comes in many shapes and sizes. Under the sea the reef bristles with the soft, brightly coloured bodies of the animals that produce it – the living top layer on a mass of dead skeletons below. Corals feed by extracting nutrients from the sea water.

The corals (some 350 different species) jostle to reach the sunlight, for within each polyp live microscopic algae – plants that make their food from sunlight and the polyp's waste products.

In return for the safe home it offers the algae, the polyp gains a biological vacuum cleaner.

Coral polyps multiply in two ways. They can simply divide; a large coral may be a huge colony of related polyps which has grown by repeated division. They can also reproduce sexually, allowing their offspring to scatter and begin new colonies. Polyps have male or female sex organs, sometimes both. As the sea warms in summer, these organs produce eggs and sperm that mature in hundreds of packages differing in colour and shape according to the species.

When the packages are ready and the mid-summer sea is warm enough, all the polyps along the Barrier Reef release their packages together. This often occurs four or five nights after the December full moon, and sometimes in just one hour on a particular night. The multicoloured packages shoot out and burst, and eggs and sperm from the same species bump into one another. Within 24 hours they fuse, and minute larvae form and float away on the tides. Fish, crabs and other egg-eating predators have a field day, but the mass spawning ensures that they will soon be sated, so a fair proportion of the larvae will survive. They settle in 5-14 days and develop into polyps, founding new colonies that will one day add their own spawn to the strange marine orgy.

Jewelled sea Blue packages of eggs and sperm bubble up from a coral colony as it spawns into the warm sea.

Mountain hideaway Thousands of Bogong moths shelter from the scorching summer sun. Once they provided Aboriginal peoples with a summer feast.

Bogong moths swarm south for summer

Fierce December sunlight bakes the earth and toasts the grass in Australia's high summer. In the south-east, more than 6500ft (2000m) up among the Bogong Mountains, the cool caves and shady cracks are encrusted with moths hiding from the sun. They may fly at night, but only to feed.

The moths hatched as caterpillars over 600 miles (1000km) north in New South Wales and south Queensland, and fattened during winter on grassland plants and cereal crops (they chew through the stems and fell the plants, so are known as cutworms). In the spring warmth they became pupae and changed to moths in the soil. When they emerged, the moths migrated south to escape the intolerable heat, flying at night and sheltering by day. The southward stream provided a feast for birds, amphibians and other insects, but even so, huge swarms of moths arrived to sit out the summer until the cooler winds of April help them fly back north to breed.

Cooler circle The route of migrating Bogong moths takes them south to escape the extreme summer heat and north again for winter breeding among the crops.

QUEENSLAND

Winter feeding grounds

NEW SOUTH WALES

• Sydney

BOGONG MOUNTAINS

• Canberra

Mt. Buffalo

VICTORIA
Melbourne •

Mt. Bogong

Summer shelter

Blue-green algae tinge the Pacific Ocean 'red'

December's strong sun beats down on the azure waters off Australia's east coast, but the seas around the Great Barrier Reef have taken on a new hue. A dark, reddish tide, carried by currents, lies like a huge oil slick on the surface. The colour comes from dead blue-green algae, casualties of a population explosion.

In spring, when stronger sunlight penetrated the clear shallows over the reef, it spurred into activity the myriad speck-like living particles called plankton in the water. Some of them are animals, or zooplankton, and some, including algae, are plants, or phytoplankton. The blue-green algae are thought to be very primitive organisms – perhaps among the first types of life on earth – that may have floated in the oceans for more than two billion years.

Each blue-green alga is a single cell, and has its own minute air bladder that absorbs oxygen from the water as the temperature rises in spring and summer. With its bladder swelling, a cell becomes more buoyant and rises up towards the sun. Once floating a few feet below the surface, the cell begins to feed, taking in water, phosphates, nitrates and carbon dioxide from the sea and using energy from the sunlight to convert them into the proteins and sugars it needs for growth. Millions of other cells are doing the same, and when conditions are favourable, they 'bloom' – divide rapidly, feeding and multiplying until they form congested sheaves of slender, slippery filaments.

At first, the blooms provide a bonanza for the creatures, such as the zooplankton, that feed on them. But eventually there are so many blue-green algae in the sheaves that those nearer the surface shut out the light from those lower down, and the shaded algae die. Their tiny air bladders burst, releasing a slimy substance that coats the sea surface, and as they decay they give off a rotting smell and turn brownish-red.

These naturally occurring red tides are not poisonous and do no harm. But pollution can cause subtle changes in the chemistry of sea water and trigger off unnatural algae blooms. These may occur out of season, involve different kinds of algae and be poisonous, destroying the delicate balance that sustains the oceans' life.

Dark death Reddish sheets of dead algae float around Heron Island, on Australia's Great Barrier Reef, victims of a population explosion that shaded out their light.

BREAKING THE PATTERN OF THE SEASONS

ARMY ANTS REPRODUCE IN 35-DAY CYCLES AND NAKED MOLE
RATS EVERY 80 DAYS. NORTH AMERICAN CICADAS BREED EVERY 17TH YEAR AND
DESERTS MAY BURST INTO FLOWER BUT ONCE IN 20 YEARS.
ANDEAN CONDORS AND BANDED STILTS BREED ONLY WHEN CONDITIONS ALLOW

Aerial predator *Short-eared owls are dependent on lemmings and voles as food for their young. When populations crash, owls cannot breed successfully.*

Burrowing prey *Lemmings live in shallow burrows in summer, and feed on grasses, sedges, roots and bark.*

Arctic hunter *An Arctic fox scours the snow for signs of lemmings or voles, which live in burrows and tunnels beneath about 3ft (1m) of snow in winter, and feed underground on mosses.*

THE ARCTIC

Rich and lean lemming years in the Arctic

Nose to the ground, an Arctic fox sniffs in the snow for signs of lemmings, a favourite food. But the lemming population – which rises and falls in cycles – has crashed. Norway lemmings are scarce in the Scandinavian Arctic for the moment, and the fox is hungry.

Lemmings are 5in (125mm) long, short-tailed, guinea-pig-like rodents. Every four years or so, they undergo a population explosion. When they do, their predators, such as Arctic foxes and owls, enjoy a food bonanza and also increase in numbers. While lemming numbers are increasing, not only are females having bigger litters but the breeding season also lasts longer and females start to breed at an earlier age.

Normally lemmings have their young in the brief Arctic summer, between June and August. But in a favourable year – when food is plentiful, predators few and the covering of snow deep enough to keep their burrows warm – a female can become sexually mature at only 20 days old. Then she can have six litters, each of up to 13 babies, before her first birthday.

When the lemming numbers are at their height, there is not enough room or food for them all, so huge numbers – mostly immature males – leave home to find new pastures. Many die, but they do not, as is often believed, commit suicide. Although lemmings swim well, they will not enter the water unless they can see the far shore. But sometimes so many lemmings reach the water's edge that the sheer weight of numbers and the constant pushing and shoving force some to take to the water. If they do not find a landfall, they eventually drown.

Snowy and short-eared owls gorge themselves when lemmings are plentiful. Unlike many owls they hunt by day, and in the Arctic the summer days are long, with a peak spell of perpetual daylight. Arctic foxes breed in 'lemming years' – when lemmings are abundant – so do not breed every year. Their young are born in May, and are able to hunt for themselves by summer, when there is a glut of lemmings.

When lemming numbers reach their peak, the reproductive pattern goes into reverse. The breeding season gets shorter, fewer babies are born, youngsters take longer to reach sexual maturity and more young lemmings die – perhaps because of the shortage of food and the stress caused by overcrowding. In this time of social unrest, each lemming turns from breeding to fighting. Males fight over females, and successful males kill any small babies sired by another male so that the mother will quickly be ready to breed again. Females fight to defend themselves and their families from intruders, sometimes killing wayward juveniles.

Then the population crashes. Deprived of the lemmings as a food supply, some predators, such as snowy owls, migrate south in search of other food, so their numbers in the Arctic also decline. Arctic foxes turn to other sources of food, ranging from chicks to berries. Because of the food shortage their breeding is less successful and their numbers, too, decline.

Winter home *Voles and lemmings both dig extensive runways below the snow in winter. When the snow melts, the pattern of tunnels can be seen on the ground.*

NORTH AMERICA

The ups and downs of the snowshoe hare

Just one jump ahead of a lynx, a snowshoe hare races for its life through a forest in northern Canada. The hare gets its name from its 'snowshoes' – long hairs on the soles of its feet that help it to run on the snow surface. The long-legged lynx has furred pads, too. It can match the hare's speed of about 30mph (50km/h), but only for a short distance. It relies on a stealthy approach and then a quick dash to capture its prey.

Snowshoe hares undergo huge fluctuations in numbers over ten-year cycles. The regular rise and fall in the population has been plotted from the records of furs sold to the Hudson's Bay

Prey on the run A Canadian lynx chases a snowshoe hare through the snow. There is a better than even chance that the hare will escape.

Company by trappers since the mid-19th century. In 1866, for example, about 140,000 hare pelts were traded. Three years later the figure was almost nil, but in 1876 it was back to about 100,000. As the hares decline, so do their predators – lynx, red fox, coyote, eagle and other birds of prey. Creatures such as the sharp-tailed grouse are also affected, because when hares are scarce the predators prey on them.

The numbers of the snowshoe hare dictate the extent of a lynx's home range. In good times, a male lynx will patrol about 19sq miles (50sq km) and drive other males from the area. When hare numbers crash, the lynx enlarges its home range to cover some 95sq miles (246sq km), and this overlaps with the ranges of other males.

The population cycles of the snowshoe hare seem to depend on the amount of food available in winter. The hares feed on the bark and woody stems of aspen and white spruce trees. When the population is large all the food is soon consumed, many hares die of starvation and fewer youngsters are born the following spring. As the population drops, predators begin to

Winter tidemark *The bark on these aspen trees has been eaten away by snowshoe hares in the winter, when thick snow enables them to reach high up the trunk.*

outnumber the surviving hares, so in spring and summer hare numbers drop even further.

When the predators themselves run out of food, they also start to die off and the cycle reaches its lowest point. The surviving hares now have fewer predators and the winter food supply is shared by far fewer mouths. So more hares survive, numbers increase to reach another peak and the cycle begins again.

Sharks that gather by underwater volcanoes

A slowly meandering column of dark, sinister shapes glides through the water in the Gulf of California. They are 7ft (2m) long scalloped hammerhead sharks, which gather each day in huge numbers over seamounts (which are dormant underwater volcanoes) in the sea between the Baja California peninsula and the mainland of Mexico.

Until recently, this underwater spectacle was a complete mystery. Now it has been discovered that each seamount is a home base, a place where the sharks spend the day resting – neither feeding nor even searching for food. The school swims up and down the edge of the seamount, all heading in the same direction and spaced evenly in the water. If they pass through a shoal of prey fish, they ignore them.

Only late in the day or at dusk does the school break up into foraging parties, each with two or three sharks, and head off into deeper water. There they feed at night on squid and fish such as stingrays. In the morning they return once more to the seamount, where they begin cruising again – behaviour known as 'refuging'. This is thought to be a way of conserving energy while remaining close to the main feeding areas. Staying in a large group also provides a defence against predators such as killer whales and other species of shark.

Surprisingly, the schools, which may consist of between 20 and 100 sharks, are exclusively female. Large (older) females swim at the bottom of the school and smaller ones stay at the top. The older a female becomes, the less likely she is to get on with her neighbours, and the more likely to snap at them aggressively. The males live alone, gathering food along the shorelines.

Occasionally, a shark in the cruising school will shake its head or shift dramatically to one side – a movement called a 'shimmy dance'. Or it may perform a 'corkscrew'. In less than a second, the shark accelerates in a tight circle and twists through 360 degrees. Sometimes the movement ends with the performer butting the shark below it. Why the cruising female hammerheads should act in this way still remains a mystery.

....

Shark siesta *Scalloped hammerhead sharks, which have peculiar side branches to their heads, make an eerie spectacle as they cruise at the El Bajo Espíritu Santo seamount in the Gulf of California near La Paz.*

Sea animals that come up to graze at night

There are deep-sided underwater canyons off the eastern coast of the USA, including one that plunges about 1¼ miles (2km) deep into the north Atlantic off New York. Living there are millions of the world's tiniest animals, some too small for the naked eye to see. And every night these creatures – various species known collectively as zooplankton – rise from the ocean depths to near the surface, then sink back again.

This up and down migration of deep-sea and mid-water dwellers is common here and elsewhere in the world's oceans. The zooplankton do not just float idly about in the ocean currents, they actively rise at night to graze. Their food is surface-dwelling phytoplankton, the floating microscopic plant-life of the sea that uses sunlight to turn carbon dioxide and water into nutrients. By day the zooplankton (creatures such as copepods, crab larvae and comb jellies) sink to the depths again. The droppings these creatures release upon sinking move carbon

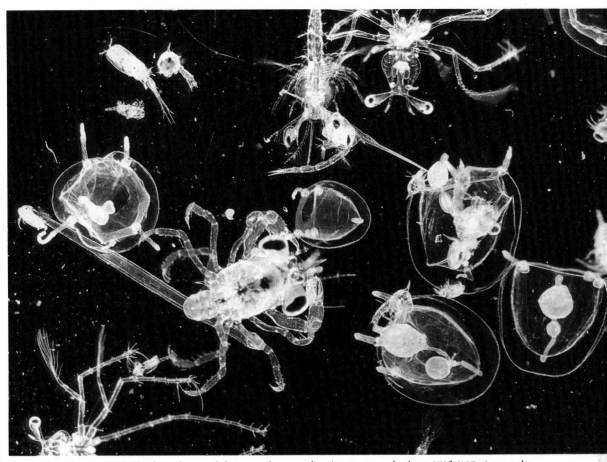

Living jewels *Tiny sea animals such as crab larvae and copepods migrate upwards about 350ft (105m) every day.*

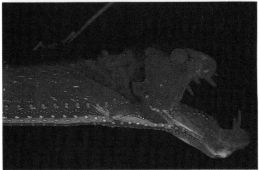

Glowing and ferocious *The viper fish is covered with coloured light organs that glow in the ocean twilight zones and reduce its silhouette as seen by predators from below. A viper fish seen in daylight (top) is drab compared with its appearance underwater (bottom).*

from near the water surface to the ocean depths.

Copepods, each no bigger than a matchhead, are minute hard-shelled animals with oar-like legs. They live about 350ft (105m) down during the day and at night come towards the surface in their millions. But they do not all move together. As dusk approaches an adventurous few make the first move upwards, then as darkness descends the rest follow. Larger deep-sea prawns travel even greater distances, some rising 1200ft (370m) before returning to the depths at dawn. Broadly speaking, it is either the light or the absence of it that seems to govern when and where the zooplankton go. On moonlit nights, when the light intensity is higher, there are fewer of them at the surface.

Small fish and squid – the predators of the deep – follow the zooplankton on their journeys. Some of the commonest fish to make this vertical migration are the lantern fish. These are small fish of varying size – some no longer than a little finger, others a handspan long. At least one species climbs from a depth of 5900ft (1800m).

Each of the 170 or so known species has its own battery of lights set along its body. These light organs, like pearl buttons, glow dimly in the perpetual gloom. Some species have headlights to illuminate their prey. On their tails, lantern fish have other light organs that flash a more visible light which is probably used when mating. At night their numbers can be staggering. A British weather ship returning to its base in Glasgow once encountered a shoal that it took five hours to pass through.

Another deep-water fish that exploits the nightly abundance of food at the surface is the viper fish. This voracious predator has enormous fang-like teeth set in a cavernous mouth, and jaws activated by powerful muscles that allow the fish to slash, bite and grasp its wriggling prey. A viper fish has a long, luminous, whip-like lure attached to the end of its dorsal (back) fin. The fish dangles the lure in front of its mouth to attract a meal to within striking distance of its deadly maw. Lantern fish are often on the menu.

A brief life After spending 17 years below ground as a nymph, the periodical cicada lives only a few days to mate.

The cicada population booms every 17 years

No other insect in the world takes as long to develop from egg to adult as the North American periodical cicada. Female cicadas lay their eggs in holes bored in twigs, often oak, apple or hickory, in spring. The nymphs – young wingless insects – hatch a few weeks later, drop to the ground and burrow into the soil.

There, for the next 17 years, each nymph lives on juices from plant or tree roots before boring a tunnel in which it splits its skin. Then it crawls up the rest of the tunnel to emerge above ground as an orange-winged adult. Within a month or so, the cicada mates, lays its eggs (if it is a female) then dies. In most years only a handful of adult cicadas emerge in a given area, because the cycles of the great majority are synchronised and all emerge in the same year. In such bumper years there can be as many as 960 million cicadas to 1sq mile (2.6sq km).

In the more southerly parts of the United States, where the climate is warmer, the insects take only 13 years to reach adulthood. In the State of Tennessee the two types – the southern 13-year and the northern 17-year cicadas – overlap. Once every 221 years their cycles coincide, and they produce a double crop. The last time was in 1868, so the next plague will be in 2089.

With so many of the insects emerging together, predators such as birds, small mammals and lizards are swamped with food, and during the short time the cicadas are alive cannot eat more than a small proportion of the population. As a result, more cicadas survive to breed. The long development cycle also prevents predators from increasing their own population in step with that of the prey.

Cicadas are also remarkable for possessing the most complex sound-producing organs of any insect. Only the males emit a deafening call, loud enough to be heard about 500yds (460m) away. The sound, a click like a tin lid being pressed in, is made by moving semi-rigid plates on the abdomen. The cicada's muscles can contract about 400 times a second, and each contraction produces a click that is greatly amplified by cavities inside the abdomen, behind the plates. When it is making its mating call, the male cicada 'switches off' its hearing organs, which are near the sound cavities – presumably to protect itself from its own song.

A sea horse father gives birth to his young

A sea horse bobs gently in the swell near the seabed, its tail wrapped round a clump of sea grass to hold it in place against the buffeting currents. In a day or so it will give birth to several miniature versions of itself. Yet it is a male.

Sea horses, named for their horse-like heads, are curious relatives of the familiar stickleback fish, and range from about 1½in (38mm) to 12in (300mm) long, depending on the species. They do not leave their eggs to fend for themselves in the open sea, as many sea creatures do, but give birth to live young. This characteristic is shared with a number of other fish species – quite a few sharks, for example, among them the lemon shark. But the sea horse differs from them all in that the male bears the young.

The female lays her eggs into a brood pouch under the male's belly. There he fertilises them and they develop in safety from the many predators that normally eat fishes' eggs. Up to seven weeks later, around the time of the full moon, the male expels the fully formed young with a series of contortions of his body.

A sea horse's life is a short one. From birth, it takes only about four months to mature and begin breeding. It is usually dead within a year.

Expectant father A pregnant male sea horse waits patiently for his new arrivals at the next full moon. He has incubated the female's eggs in his belly pouch.

Living thorns These thumbnail-sized thorn bugs have thorn-like spines rising above their heads. The spines protect them from predators while they feed.

Curious treehoppers with prickly defences

Sharp spikes sprout from the branches of a hibiscus in a Florida garden, making it look well equipped to deter any attackers. But every so often some of the shiny green spikes move, for they are in fact treehoppers that are sucking the plant's sap. Known as thorn bugs, these particular treehoppers are elaborately disguised as thorns to avoid being picked off by birds. Each has a sharp, thorn-shaped spine along its back, rising to a point above its head.

Most thorn bugs are found in Central and South America. Florida is just warm enough to have a race of its own, but whole populations can be wiped out by a cold spell. Dead bugs littering the ground can inflict severe cuts if trodden on with soft shoes or bare feet. Living bugs sometimes collect on cars and cover them with the sticky honeydew they secrete on plants for ants, which guard them from insect predators. Some ants stroke the bugs to encourage honeydew secretion, but it is not known whether this occurs with Florida thorn bugs.

Sunshine probably stimulates the thorn bugs to mate and lay eggs twice a year or more. The females lay their eggs in grooves made in the plant tissue, and stay with them for 10-12 days until they hatch. The young thorn bugs become spined, winged adults six weeks after hatching.

Fiddler on the beach Two male fiddler crabs meeting on a Florida beach stop to weigh each other up.

The tiny fiddler crab with the mighty claw

Out on the mudflats of a Florida shore, a tiny male fiddler crab, with a shell less than 1in (25mm) across, is feeding fastidiously. He sifts through the mud with dainty movements of his small claw, searching for the tiny animals and plant and animal debris that make up his diet. He does not feed with his other, much larger, claw. Suddenly the feeding crab pauses. He has sensed another fiddler crab close by, approaching warily. Slowly the crab moves towards the newcomer, another male, then stops, rears on his legs and lifts his large claw above his head.

In 1705 the Dutch naturalist Rumphius said of the fiddler crab: 'it waves its larger claw strenuously and continuously, as though it wanted to call people'. The crab also became known as the 'calling crab'. But this crab's wave is not friendly – it is a threat to the intruder.

The two male crabs face each other a little apart, their large claws waving in delicate circles. For a moment they touch claws, pushing gently against each other. Then the intruder, recognising a larger male by the strength of his push, sinks to a crouch and scuttles away. Fights rarely develop into genuine combat, but when they do males grip each other with their claws. The big claw, accounting for 40 per cent of the crab's total weight, can flip an opponent onto his back or crush his leg. For a human being, it would be the equivalent of trying to fight with a 66lb (30kg) sword in one hand.

Fiddler crabs are among the busiest members of the seashore community. They live life mostly at a run – a life dictated by the comings and goings of the tide, for they feed only when the tide is out. During high tide they stay in their burrows in the mud. The crabs are most active in the morning and at sunset – tides permitting – and scuttle for their burrows if disturbed. Shore birds such as the yellow-crowned night heron feed on them.

Only the males have an enlarged claw, with about half of them being right-handed and half left-handed. Apart from its use as a weapon, the claw also plays a part in courtship. A male waves it invitingly to attract a passing female, and may also stamp with his legs. Sometimes at night a courting male will vibrate his legs against parts of his shell, or tap the shell with a claw, adding a faint clacking to the night sounds of the shore.

Elephants that go to find salts underground

Every night, a string of African elephants emerges from the forest and makes its way to Mount Elgon, a dormant volcano on the Kenya/Uganda border. The elephants are on their way to spend the night in the salt mines.

Mount Elgon is near the Great Rift Valley, which is an enormous tear in the earth's crust that slices through East Africa from the Red Sea in the north to Mozambique in the south. The valley has a history of massive earth movements over millions of years, and volcanoes are scattered over the landscape.

Wind and rain have eroded Mount Elgon to leave its crater 6 miles (10km) wide and surrounded by a ring of small mountains. In the valleys between the peaks, large cave systems run into the mountain sides. One of these systems, Kitum, is the elephants' destination.

BURIED ESSENTIALS

In the mountain areas rainfall is heavy and many mineral salts are washed from the soil. So the plants on which the elephants feed are devoid of the salts essential for a healthy life. The elephants therefore obtain their salts from the cave's enormous 'salt licks', formed from hardened ash when the volcano was active.

After arriving at the wide, low entrance to Kitum, the elephants pass by a waterfall then gingerly pick their way in the darkness across a floor strewn with fallen rocks and crisscrossed by deep crevasses. The huge animals move slowly and deliberately, one behind another. One false move could be their last – the skeletons of several baby elephants lie in the bottom of a deep crevasse. Youngsters are reassured by the guiding trunk of an older female as they move carefully to avoid the dangerous drop.

When they reach the back of the cave, the elephants sniff the air with their trunks to locate the best mineral sites. Their tusks and trunks prevent them from getting their mouths close enough to actually lick the rock, so they prise off chunks of mineral-rich rock with their tusks.

Back to daylight *After spending part of the night underground in a cave digging out salts, elephants return to the surface at dawn. This extraordinary night shift is becoming increasingly rare because the elephants are being slaughtered for their ivory tusks.*

Then each beast picks up a piece of rock with its delicate trunk tip and delivers it to its mouth to crunch with its enormous molar teeth. Elephants that are the most frequent visitors to Kitum have short, stumpy tusks – the ivory has been worn away by many nights of digging.

The elephants remain in the caves for about four or five hours each night. They do not dig out salt all the time, but crunch away for about half an hour, and then sleep. Outside the caves the night temperature drops considerably, usually to about 8°C (46°F) and sometimes to below freezing. The caves, however, stay at a comfortable 14°C (57°F), with high humidity.

The large matriarch who usually guides the elephant herd into the caves leads them out again. In the morning, her loud, bellowing 'reveille' reverberates round the cave and warns the group that it is time to leave.

Often the elephants are not alone in the caves. Swallows and swifts nest in hollowed-out fossil logs, the remains of ancient forests felled when the volcano erupted violently ten million years ago. These ancient trees can be seen in the cave roof, with roosting bats hanging from their petrified branches.

Buffaloes, antelopes such as bushbuck, waterbuck and duiker, as well as troops of monkeys and baboons, all take part in the search for vital minerals. They lick the crystals in the cave walls, or gather up the tiny scraps of debris left behind by the elephants. Within the caves they are safe from marauding predators.

ELEPHANTS IN DANGER

The survival of the Kitum elephants has been seriously threatened by poachers armed with automatic weapons, the legacy of years of wars in Africa. Greedy to reap profits from the multimillion-dollar ivory trade, poachers shot the elephants, hacked out their tusks and left the carcasses to rot. The ivory was smuggled out of Kenya to be shipped to workshops in the Far East. Rangers of the Mount Elgon National Park patrol have had a dangerous job trying to protect the elephants, but through increases in government support, poaching has recently been brought under control.

The Kitum caves may not be a natural feature. It is possible that the elephants themselves have excavated them by mining the salts – generations of them digging over a period of 100,000 years. Yet in the space of two decades, because of the senseless slaughter of the elephants by ivory hunters, the incredible excavations have come precariously close to an end.

Precarious hold Fairy terns have extra long claws for gripping bare surfaces. An adult (top) incubates its egg on bare rock. A chick (bottom) clings to a tree branch as it calls for its parents.

The fairy tern's life in a watery world

The wide open spaces of its home in the tropical oceans give the fairy (or white) tern little land on which to nest. So at breeding time these dainty birds about 12in (300mm) long flock in their thousands to the handful of scattered coral and volcanic islands such as the Seychelles (in the western Indian Ocean), where they may breed about once every ten months.

A pair of courting terns perform elaborate aerial displays, diving, gliding and wheeling in harmony through the windswept skies, their white wings seeming translucent against the tropical sunlight. The birds' black beaks, black eyes and black legs stand out in stark contrast to their pure white plumage.

The sparse vegetation of so many of the islands offers the terns little opportunity for building a nest, so the female lays her single egg on the bare branch of a tree or in a tiny hollow on a coral boulder or sea cliff. Both parents take turns in sitting on their one egg while the other feeds at sea. The egg hatches after five weeks, and the chick does not fly until it is about two months old. Like its parents, the young tern has unusually long claws on its toes, and these help it to grip securely on a bare surface.

Queen's privilege A naked mole rat 'queen' walks across a huddle of her workers. A mole rat's lips fold behind its digging teeth to keep out soil.

The desert kingdom of the naked mole rat

The red soil of the Kenyan desert trembles and parts, and a small, hairless, wrinkled head bearing two immense teeth appears for a moment – a naked mole rat. This strange rodent, also known as the sand puppy, is only about 3in (75mm) long. It spends all its life underground, using its large front teeth to burrow an extensive tunnel system about 8in (200mm) or more down where it forages for roots and plant material.

Naked mole rats live in colonies where only a single 'queen' female actually breeds – once every 80 days. The rest of the colony of 30-100 are mainly her offspring. They are not sterile, but the queen puts out pheromones (chemical messengers) that stop them from breeding. She can produce as many as four litters of 3-11 a year. Successive litters act as workers, helping to dig or repair tunnels, defend them against intruders such as snakes, and tend the young.

Each task is carried out by a group of workers of the same size – the smallest and youngest being the tunnel diggers and the largest and oldest the defenders. The very largest animals form a caste of non-workers – the males that breed with the 'queen' and a few very large females who will eventually take over breeding when the queen dies or the colony splits.

Because of its underground life, a naked mole rat's eyes are small and it finds its way by feel and smell. As well as losing its fur, it has almost lost the ability to control its body temperature, which generally stays at the same constant temperature as the tunnels. If mole rats do get cold they huddle together for warmth.

A plant that lures beetles to carry its pollen

Growing visibly by the minute, a small red flower forces itself through the hard-baked soil of an arid plain in southern Africa. Four fleshy, petal-like red sepals join at the base to form a small tube that rests in the ground, and the inner face of each has a white, spongy surface that gives off a smell uncannily like that of rotting meat.

Attracted by the smell, carrion beetles enter the flower and begin to eat the spongy material. When they emerge, they are covered in pollen from within the flower, and when they enter a similar flower nearby, the pollen is scraped off onto its stigma (female part) so that fertilisation can take place. This red flower has come to be known as the beetle-trap flower.

Only once every few years does the beetle-trap plant send out its solitary flower. Most of its life is spent underground as a creeping stem that feeds on the roots of euphorbia plants. Once the beetles have fertilised the stigma, it grows into a starchy fruit that is eaten by animals such as jackals and baboons. The plant's seeds are distributed in their droppings.

So the beetle-trap flower relies on another plant to sustain it and passing mammals to disperse its seed. And to achieve pollination it makes use of the carrion beetles' preference for feeding on the carcasses of dead animals. But the beetle and the mammals get a satisfactory meal and the flower solves the problem of reproducing itself.

A helping hand By offering an evil-smelling titbit, the beetle-trap flower induces carrion beetles to enter its flower tube. Coated in pollen when they leave, the beetles pollinate other beetle-trap flowers they enter.

A sandgrouse flies with water for its chicks

Every day of the year, as dawn breaks over the desert areas of southern Africa, flocks of Namaqua sandgrouse begin to leave their nests and head for water. With a diet based entirely on moistureless seeds, daily drinking is essential in their hot, dry homeland. They may have to fly 50 miles (80km) to find a waterhole. On arrival, the birds first collect some distance away, then go to drink in a group so that there are many pairs of eyes to spot predators such as falcons or jackals.

Sandgrouse can breed only during a wet season, because at breeding time the birds have to take water home to their two or three chicks. This is only possible when more waterholes are available less far afield. Although the youngsters can feed themselves on seeds as soon as they are hatched, they need water brought to them for about two months until they can fly well.

The water-carrying is usually done by the male – the female does it only if he dies or cannot carry enough. The way sandgrouse carry water is unique in the animal kingdom. While he drinks, the male dips his belly feathers into the water, and special filaments on their undersides soak up water like a sponge. Then he flies back to the nesting area and the chicks drink from his feathers. His return has to be as fast as possible because the water soon evaporates in the heat. The distance a bird can carry a significant amount of water is about 20 miles (32km).

Experts in survival In the deserts of southern Africa, sources of life-giving water are few. Gathered round a waterhole (right), Namaqua sandgrouse drink their fill in the early morning. When they have chicks, the males submerge their belly feathers and carry the water the long miles home for the chicks to drink (below).

Midnight feast Hippos graze for five or six hours a night, after wallowing by day in water or mud. Oxpeckers, birds of the starling family, feed on ticks on the hippos' hides.

Heavyweight hippos graze in the night

Deep grunts of satisfaction stir the night air on an East African plain. Two lumbering hippopotamuses are grazing in the cool of the night, plucking the short grass with their broad lips. The hippos spent the sun-scorched day submerged in a river, only the tops of their massive heads and their ears, eyes and nostrils above the water surface. Now they have left the water in ones and twos to trek along their traditional pathways to the open plain. Crushed vegetation and distinctive four-toed footprints mark their path.

Hippos can spend only a few hours out of water or mud before their skin dries and they dehydrate. They are well adapted to their watery abode, because they can stay submerged for up to five minutes, swimming or walking on the lake or river bottom. One advantage of this way of life is that, because they spend all day lazing, hippos eat only about half as much food for their size as other animals.

In the water, hippos congregate in groups, usually 10-15 cows and their offspring led by an adult male, who is up to 13ft (4m) long and about 2½ tons in weight. He defends the stretch of water, marking his territory by flicking his short tail and spraying his dung around. The animals may mate at any time of year, but tend to do so

in a dry season, when they are concentrated in shrunken pools. So most calves are born in the rainy seasons – in East Africa April-May and October-November – when the grass grows best.

A calf weighs in at about 6 stone (38kg), and can walk, run and swim within five minutes. It is in danger from crocodiles and lions and stays close to its mother, who repels attackers with her sharp canine teeth. Hippos are most dangerous when protecting young, and lone and breeding males are also aggressive and often scarred from fights. Hippos harm more people than any other animal, including lions and snakes. Their barrel-like bodies bulldoze anyone who happens to be in their way, and boats that get too close are capsized.

A fleeting paradise of desert flowers

Once in a while – maybe only once in 20 years – the dull landscape of Namaqualand flares into a riot of colour. Plants bloom in their thousands – white, red and orange daisies, blue flax, purple cineraria, dark orange gazania and the yellows, pinks and purples of mesembryanthemums among the many. No one can tell when this brilliant patchwork will appear, but when it does, people flock to view it.

A coastal stretch of stone, sand and rugged, flat-topped mountains, Namaqualand, straddling the South Africa/Namibia border, is three times the size of England. Scant rain falls irregularly – a good year may bring about 6in (150mm) – but there may be none for years. Sun-scorched, wind-whipped and frozen by fierce frosts, it yet supports 4000 different plant species, many of them found nowhere else.

To survive, the plants must store water. Some hold it in swollen stems and have strange names such as elephant's trunk and baboon's fingers. Others store it in fleshy leaves, such as those of lithops – which look like pebbles on the ground – and protect themselves from the heat of the sun by keeping all but their leaves and flowers underground – as do the plants that store water in bulbs or tubers. The window plant has a leaf-tip window that stops the sun's heat but filters through light for growth.

Small splashes of colour occur when plants bloom after winter showers. But only when the conditions are just right – when enough rain occurs at the right time and the wind relaxes its harshness – does the land sparkle with a profusion of flowers from mid-July to mid-September. The flowers last for just two or three weeks and

Keeping an eye on things *A chameleon's eyes can swivel independently to look in two directions at once. To catch insects it darts out its long tongue.*

Quiver tree *Bushmen used to make quivers for their arrows from the tree's fibrous core.*

Tap dance *Tok tokkie beetles tap a courtship call on the ground before they mate.*

then die, and no one has yet found out exactly how some of them reproduce. The elephant's trunk unfurls a girdle of leaves after rain, but scientists have never seen it flower and do not know how it is pollinated. The wind plays its part in pollination, as do the bees, flies and beetles of the desert, some of which have life cycles linked to the flowers they pollinate. The insects in turn attract insect-eating birds and lizards, such as the Namaqua chameleon.

Real trees cannot survive in Namaqualand, but birds make their homes in tall succulents (water-storing plants) such as aloes. One, the kokerboom or quiver tree, attracts birds such as the Cape weaver to nest on its spiky crown.

Blaze of colour *Mesembryanthemums (above) and pebble plants (below) bloom only every 10-20 years.*

Dangerous stingrays dance with divers

Giant stingrays gather daily on the north coast of Grand Cayman, the largest of the Cayman Islands in the Caribbean Sea. The rays swim round in the shallow, crystal-clear waters expectantly, waiting for people to caress them and to hand-feed them with squid and small fish. Their favourite handout is 'ballyhoo' or halfbeaks, which are silvery fish with a curiously extended lower jaw and the habit of behaving like flying fish.

Yet these southern stingrays, up to 5ft (1.5m) across, are dangerous and powerful. On the top of its whiplike tail, each ray has a needle-sharp sting that can deliver venom which affects the victim's heart and respiratory system, causing sickness, a drop in blood pressure and intense pain. The sting can produce a gash a handspan in length, and bacteria on the sting may infect the wound, which can occasionally be fatal.

DEADLY DEFENCE

Usually, the stingrays spend their time buried in the sand on the bottom of North Sound in Grand Cayman. A careless bather who steps on a ray may trigger a reflex action that brings the tail slashing upwards, thrusting the sting into the victim's foot, leg or thigh.

The movement is so strong that stings have been found embedded in the sides of boats. There have even been two freak cases in Australia where stingrays drove their spines right into the victims' hearts. The bathers had been swimming in shallow water, and had startled the rays by swimming directly over them. But stingrays are not known to attack humans – they use their venomous spines purely for defence.

Normally the rays at North Sound are spread widely across the sands, each ray rigorously defending its own patch against all intruders. But when the first tourist boat appears, the rays leave their territories, and seem not to swim but to fly majestically through the water like dark shadows, moving along with gentle undulations of their broad, bat-like 'wings' – really fins.

They do not rush. Unlike their relatives, the

Underwater ballet *Wispy white clouds in a tropical blue sky form a backdrop for southern stingrays as they dance on their underwater stage in the Caribbean.*

Stingray experience *For the prize of a fish, dangerous stingrays permit a diver to swim among them.*

Marauding army ants scour the forest floor

A huge column of ants makes its way through the Brazilian rain forest. It numbers half a million or more, and forms a front some 30ft (9m) across. The large, pincer-jawed soldiers in the lead feel their way methodically with their antennae, and the ants behind – workers in the centre and more soldiers guarding the flanks – follow the scent of those in front.

Anything in the army's path that cannot escape is captured, no matter the size. Even a large scorpion will be attacked, overwhelmed and dismembered, then methodically transported back through the lines by the workers to help feed the whole colony. A column moving forward at a constant 45ft (14m) an hour can take 30,000 insects, spiders and scorpions a day.

MARCHING AND CAMPING

Army ants live in huge colonies, each behaving as one gigantic organism. Together, the ants are among the most fearsome predators of the rain forest, killing every living creature in their path. The day-to-day life of the colony is not regulated by winter or summer, rainy season or dry. Instead it alternates between a period of travelling and a period of staying in one place.

After travelling through the forest for 15 days, the ant colony comes to a halt and makes a semi-permanent camp. The ants stay in this one spot for 20 days while the queen lays between 50,000 and 100,000 eggs. During this time, the workers forage for themselves and the queen. They explore the surrounding forest according to a fixed pattern like the spokes of a wheel. On the first day they all head off in one direction to track down a meal.

The next day the direction they choose for their raid is 123 degrees different from that of the previous day. The ants change their direction by the same degrees each day, and in this way do not comb the same piece of forest twice. A raiding party of 200,000 ants can travel more than 200yds (180m) in a day.

The eggs soon develop into larvae that can be carried on the next march. While the army is camped, larvae from previous layings spin cocoons in which they change to adults. When these young ants emerge from their cocoons, there are many more mouths to feed and the colony must once more be on the march in order to find sufficient food. So at dawn an advance party of soldiers and workers streams

sharks, the stingrays exhibit no frenzy at the prospect of food. Territorial aggression is forgotten, they swim along together and gather close to the diving tenders, where wet-suited tourists with aqualungs and facemasks join them in the water.

With such an abundance of food, the rays not only tolerate each other but also allow underwater tourists to touch and even hug them. Some scuba divers experience a stingray 'kiss' – the ray seizes the pink-coloured regulator valve from the diver's mouth, mistaking it for a piece of squid.

When the weather is good, up to 200 people a day visit 'Stingray City' – at the risk of occasional injuries. If the weather is bad and divers are unable to bring the rays their free meal, the creatures become aggressive with the next divers to arrive, and unpredictable.

Rays were first attracted to boats many years ago, congregating for food when local fishermen cleaned their day's catch in the quiet waters behind the reef. An enterprising tourist guide then encouraged the rays to take food from the hand – an experience that has now become one of Grand Cayman's main attractions.

Normally, a stingray feeds on bottom-dwelling animals such as worms, flatfish and shellfish. Instead of having a large number of individual teeth, all its teeth are fused into a broad plate in each jaw, and with these it can crush the shells of mussels and clams.

The ray cannot see the food it eats because its eyes are on the top of its head and its mouth is underneath. It finds its food by a combination of smell, touch and electro-reception. Tiny pits in its snout can detect minute electric currents, such as those produced when muscles contract. In this way, the ray can even find a worm or shellfish that has burrowed about 12in (300mm) deep in the sand.

To catch its prey, the ray flattens its body on the sand then raises itself slightly to create a vacuum that sucks the prey to the surface. Then it squirts water from its mouth to flush away the sand. It eats only the soft parts of its prey – the fragments of crushed shell are discarded.

Stingrays themselves sometimes fall prey to sharks, although they gain some protection from their camouflage colouring – dark above and light below – and their habit of burying themselves in the sand.

NEWBORN STINGRAY

Caribbean rays are born in the warm tropical waters around the islands. A female retains the eggs in her body until the babies are ready to hatch. Each newborn ray, from a brood of about ten, shoots out of the opening at the base of its mother's tail and heads straight for the safety of the sandy bottom, where it feeds on worms and small shellfish. It may live for 25 years.

With the superabundance of food handed out each day by tourist divers, marine biologists are expecting some of the North Sound stingrays to grow eventually to world record sizes.

Pulling together *A team of army ants transports a captured katydid (long-horned grasshopper).*

Ant groupies *The white-browed antbird is one of the many birds that follow an ant column and seize the insects fleeing from its path.*

Poisonous beauties *Sweet Oil and Olive Transparent butterflies follow the marauding ants to feed on the droppings of the antbirds.*

out from the camp, leaving behind the queen and the workers caring for the larvae.

The ants maintain a constant compass heading, changing direction only if they encounter the scent trail of another colony of ants. They are not interested in getting involved in unnecessary battles with their own kind. Faced with a stream, some of the workers interlock legs and form a living bridge over which the rest of the colony can safely travel.

The queen and the rest of the colony, carrying the larvae, follow the same path at night. They travel for about eight hours under the cloak of darkness, then form themselves into a ball before dawn. Temperature in the ball is maintained at a steady 28.3°C (83°F) even though the surrounding air temperature can vary sharply during the day and night.

The behaviour of the ants is regulated by pheromones – chemical messages that pass between individual ants or are laid on the ground as a trail for others to follow. This method of communication enables the ants to coordinate their activities for the greater good of the colony – a kind of collective intelligence.

In some places in the South American rain forest, this great procession led by army ants following their 35-day cycle is welcomed, not feared, by humans. Villagers in the path of a column leave their homes temporarily and allow the ants to pass through. The ants, in return, remove all the pests from the house.

FORTUNATE FOLLOWERS

Like all armies, the ants have their followers. Flitting through the trees and bushes alongside and ahead of the advancing column are parasitic flies and antbirds that prey not on the ants but on any small creatures that the ants flush out. And there is order here too. Some antbirds are dominant in the pecking order and occupy the best positions just ahead of the ants. Others follow along behind and do not feed so well.

In the trees above, still more birds join the procession. Large flocks of insect-eaters, fruit-eaters and seed-eaters do not depend on the ants, but rely on the antbirds to act as sentinels against birds of prey. If a predatory hawk should swoop through the forest canopy to seize a small bird, the antbirds all utter warning cries.

So the other, less alert birds can feed in safety.

But one species of antbird has taken advantage of this position, and cheats. If an insect, such as a grasshopper, escapes from the ant column and a rival bird is about to catch it, the antbird gives a false alarm. The rival is momentarily startled and starts to take evasive action. In a split second the grasshopper is caught instead by the deceiving antbird.

The parade of hangers-on does not end there, for following the antbirds are ant butterflies. They feed on the droppings of the birds, locating the ant columns by the odours given off by the ants themselves. The birds do not eat the butterflies, which contain poisonous substances. During their caterpillar stage, the butterflies feed on plants containing noxious chemicals and these are retained in the body of the adult.

Periodic breeders Condors roost on high crags in the Andean foothills, and breed when carrion is plentiful.

Condors – giant birds that thrive on disaster

A high mountain ledge amid the steep crags of the Peruvian Andes is home to the condor. One of the world's biggest birds, it has the lowest natural breeding rate of any bird. This is partly because each pair has only one egg at a time and takes two years to raise the chick. It is also because, for many, their food supply fluctuates considerably.

Condors are vultures, feeding on carrion. As they glide and soar on air currents, they can spot a corpse or a dying animal a long distance away. Under normal conditions the condors living in the hot, dry Andean foothills in the north of Peru have a fairly meagre existence, and few breed. But every five years or so the devastation caused by storms along the South American Pacific coast as a result of El Niño (see right) enormously increases their food supply.

Wildlife and farm animals suffer disease caused by a sudden proliferation of flies, mosquitoes and parasites. Weak and ageing animals do not survive the bad weather. The glut of corpses brings a time of plenty for the condors – a time when all the breeding pairs may raise young. A year after the 1982-3 El Niño storms, the ledges were packed with year-old birds. In the years between the storms, most birds do not breed.

Their lengthy breeding cycle means that condors are at great risk, especially those inland in the High Andes. They cannot recover their numbers after poisoning by ranchers or if there is no El Niño for several years. Condors in the coastal mountains feed on seabird chicks and eggs and are less dependent on the periodic gluts of carrion after storms.

Giant vulture The world's largest bird of prey, the Andean condor has a wingspan of about 10ft 6in (3.2m). Most condors feed mainly on carrion.

How El Niño upsets the weather and wildlife

When El Niño struck the Pacific Ocean in 1982-3, fish disappeared to deep waters, so seabirds on Christmas Island and along South American coasts had to abandon their nests and fly far out to sea to find food. Many died. On Anacapa Island in southern California, brown pelican chicks that had almost fledged were left to die, and elephant seal pups were washed off beaches and drowned in tumultuous seas. Under the sea, corals died. What brought about this state of affairs?

Every year, warm waters termed El Niño invade the normally cold currents that bathe the Pacific coast of South America north of Chile. This upset in ocean circulation is caused by changes that take place farther west in the Pacific, and is known as El Niño, meaning 'The (Christ) Child', because it occurs at about Christmas time.

In most years El Niño's effects on the weather are negligible or mild, but sometimes, in periods ranging from every five to every 16 years, it brings serious disruption to parts of the Southern Hemisphere and badly affects weather and wildlife. These are termed El Niño years.

The 1982-3 El Niño was one of the severest on record, affecting not only the Southern Hemisphere but the Northern Hemisphere too. The weather deteriorated across much of the world south of the Equator, and in parts of the north. Drought in southern Australia caused unchecked bush fires to destroy forests and homes. Red dust storms smothered cities. Cyclones cut a swathe through Hawaii, and also through Tahiti – which is not normally affected by them. In Ecuador, rain was so heavy that landslides buried villages. Storms along the west coast of the USA eroded coastlines.

DISRUPTIVE INFLUENCES

Normally, an area of low atmospheric pressure is centred over Indonesia. Towards it blow the south-east trade winds from the 'South Pacific High' – an area of high pressure stretching over Tahiti and Easter Island. But at the start of the 1982-3 El Niño, the low-pressure area was not as low as usual and moved eastwards. And the high-pressure area was not as high, and moved south-eastwards.

Over much of the tropical Pacific, the trade winds weakened, and in the western ocean even reversed. This caused warm water that is normally built up in the western Pacific by the winds to start flowing east. The sea level at Guadalcanal in the western Pacific dropped by 6in (150mm), and at Christmas Island in the central Pacific it rose by the same amount. A surge of warm water headed for the Galápagos Islands and the South American continent.

The warm water overrode the cold, northward-flowing Humboldt Current and the upwellings of cold, nutrient-rich bottom waters that occur along the South American Pacific coast. The productive waters off Chile and Peru – and many parts of the equatorial Pacific from the Galápagos Islands to the central Pacific – became an ecological disaster area as essential nutrients ceased to be available to fish living near the surface. A similar state of affairs occurred in the northern Pacific, where the eastward flow of warm water disrupted the cool, south-flowing California Current and the upwellings of cool water off California.

El Niño results from the turbulence and instability inherent in the fluid nature of the atmosphere and the sea. It is not known which particular interactions are the cause, and various theories have been put forward.

Drastic changes *In normal years (top) cool water wells up off east Pacific coasts near the Equator. In El Niño years (below) warm easterly currents suppress it.*

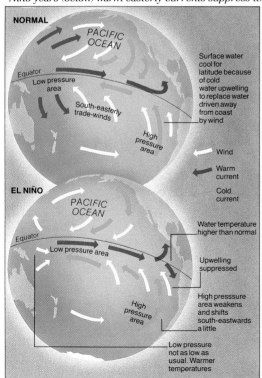

Rock-pool monster *The marine iguana thrives in the cold waters of the Galápagos, but must surface to breathe.*

Where marine iguanas feed on sea lettuce

A prehistoric-looking lizard hauls itself from the water of a rocky inlet and blows a shower of salty water vapour out through its nostrils. It is a rare marine iguana, about 4ft (1.2m) long, found only in the Galápagos Islands, which are in the Pacific west of Ecuador.

Marine iguanas are the only lizards to feed in the sea. They bask on the shore to warm up their bodies and then, propelling themselves with their flattened tails, swim down 50ft (15m) or more to feed on seaweeds such as sea lettuce growing on the rocks on the sea floor. While they are underwater they cannot breathe, but they conserve oxygen by slowing down their heart rate, so reducing their blood flow. When they come up to breathe, they also expel excess salt taken in while eating underwater. They have glands in their nostrils for excreting the salt.

For marine iguanas, El Niño (see left) is likely to bring famine. During the 1982-3 event, when the Pacific waters warmed and the sea level rose, some of their usual grazing places were too deep to reach. And their main food plants died

because of the changes in water temperature and salinity – heavy rains diluted the water. Many of the iguanas could not digest the new plants that grew in their place. On some of the islands, half the marine iguanas died and many of the survivors were dangerously underweight.

While the marine iguanas suffered, their land relatives were thriving. The normally dry and dusty islands suddenly bloomed with lush plant life, and land iguanas were presented with a superabundance of food.

Underwater feeder *A rare marine iguana grazes on seaweed. It is related to the land iguana, and they probably had a common plant-eating ancestor.*

Sleeping sharks *White-tip reef sharks rest during the day on the floor of a South Pacific coral reef, and ventilate their gills by opening their mouths from time to time. They hunt at night, keeping to the reef.*

Rare giant *The spectacular silversword is found only on two Hawaiian islands, in volcanic craters.*

PACIFIC ISLANDS

Reef sharks home in on a fish's heartbeat

Each night when it hunts among Pacific coral reefs, the white-tip reef shark uses a sixth sense that all sharks possess – electromagnetic detection. On its head and snout it has tiny, jelly-filled pits that can pick up electromagnetic signals emanating from its prey's muscle activity, including its heartbeat. So even a flatfish or ray buried beneath the sand cannot elude this fearsome hunter. The heartbeat that keeps the fish alive can unwittingly invite its death.

A white-tip is named after the white tips on the first fin on its back and on its tail fin. The rest of the shark's 5ft (1.5m) long body is blue-grey. Although it is slender and flexible, the shark is slow and rather clumsy in manoeuvring through the canyons and caverns of its hunting ground among the coral reefs surrounding tropical Pacific islands.

White-tips swim mostly in water 16-130ft (5-40m) deep, rarely in the shallows or over the coral flats. They tend to occupy the same stretch of reef for many years, feeding on a variety of sea creatures including reef fishes, octopuses, crabs, lobsters and sea snails. Like most other sharks, the white-tip uses all its senses to find prey. Apart from electromagnetic detection, it can detect low rumbling noises caused by tiny disturbances in the water, such as those coming from an injured fish. It can also follow a smell back to its source, and it has good eyesight.

By day the sharks rest, often in small groups, hugging the sea floor in crevices or caves, or beneath overhanging rock or coral. They face upstream with mouths agape, so that water currents will help to ventilate their gills. Oceanic sharks, unlike the reef sharks, have to swim continuously to ventilate their gills.

White-tip reef sharks may sometimes attack humans. They are unlikely to do so for food, but may slash at a swimmer rather than take a bite, as a warning to keep clear. The sharks are intelligent and able to learn, and some have been taught by humans to take food from the hand without harming their trainers.

A towering plant takes ten years to bloom

Only at the end of its 10-15 years of life does the silversword bloom amid the ash and cinders of a volcanic crater. Its striking flower spike is as tall as a man and bears a succession of some 500 maroon florets, each about 2in (50mm) across. The plant grows only on the two Hawaiian islands of Maui and Hawaii, and only in volcanic craters such as Haleakala.

Named from its long and narrow silver leaves, which are covered with tiny hairs that reflect the sunlight, the silversword starts life as a short brown stem from which the leaves radiate. Not only do the leaves store water, they form a rosette that protects the plant's growing point from extremes of temperature, for in a crater 10,000ft (3000m) above sea level it is scorching hot by day and freezing cold at night. The flower spike appears when the leaf rosette is about 2ft (610mm) across. After flowering, when the black fruits have formed and the seeds set, the plant dies, leaving a bleached skeleton in the sun.

How spinner dolphins wind up for the hunt

As the mid-afternoon sun glints on the softly lapping waters of a Hawaiian bay, the dolphins who live there begin to build up a chorus of clicking sounds and occasional whistles. As the noise and excitement increase, the whistles outnumber the clicks. When the sounds reach a crescendo, a slim grey form shoots up from the water and twists lengthwise high in the air before dropping, sometimes slapping down hard on the water with head and tail. Other dolphins follow suit, while some roll over and round each other in the water.

These are 6ft (1.8m) long spinner dolphins, named for their acrobatic leaps, and they are getting in tune for the night's hunting ahead. Many animals that hunt in groups, such as wolves and wild dogs, behave similarly before setting off. A successful hunt depends on cooperation, so the group's activities have to be coordinated in some way.

Gradually, each of the dolphins swims in zigzag fashion to and from the mouth of the bay, and by late afternoon, all are spinning or zigzag swimming. Dolphins leap from the water and slap down again, and whistles and clicks merge into one confused cacophony. When all of them call and swim to the mouth of the bay together, the group is ready to leave.

In the open sea, the group may join with other groups to form a large hunting school, sometimes numbering thousands. In an ever-changing formation, and sometimes swimming in lines abreast, the dolphins spread out over a large area. They may hunt as deep as 330ft (100m) but rise to the surface to blow (breathe) every three or four minutes. As they swim, they scan the sea ahead of them for shoals of fish or squid. They do not scan with their eyes, which

Afternoon spin A spinner dophin leaps from the water and twists its 6ft (1.8m) long body lengthwise in midair. It is warming up for a night's hunting.

would be useless in the dark, but with an echolocation system based on clicking sounds.

These sounds are produced by air taken in through the blowhole in the top of the dolphin's head and passed over flaps and valves in tubes below the blowhole. The sounds are probably directed forward through an oil-filled 'melon' in the forehead which focuses the sound waves into a beam that the dolphin can direct. Echoes of the sounds bouncing back from an object are received by the dolphin on its lower jaw, and are transferred to its ears along a fatty channel in each side of the jaw.

In this way, the dolphin 'sees with sound'. It can detect a large shoal of perhaps 4000 fish when 330ft (100m) away, but the prey it finds is usually less than 165ft (50m) away. The nearer the object the dolphin is scanning, the faster the echo returns and the more frequent the clicks emitted. Dolphins are not thought to make use of one another's signals, but are aware of them and switch off their own to avoid interference when passing in front of one another. The dolphins sometimes cooperate in herding fish into a tight shoal, allowing them all easier catches. At dawn, after a busy night of hunting and feeding, the dolphin school breaks up as the smaller groups return to their home bays to spend the daytime resting and playing.

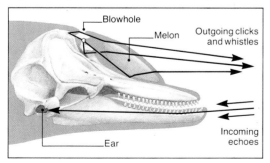

Scanning system This cross-section drawing of a dolphin's head shows the probable echolocation signal flow – out from the forehead and back via the lower jaw.

Blowhole
Melon
Outgoing clicks and whistles
Incoming echoes
Ear

Off to hunt In late afternoon, groups of spinner dolphins leave the shallow bays of Hawaii to hunt at sea.

Beached whales *An error of navigation may have led this group of long-finned pilot whales to become helplessly stranded in the shallows of a Tasmanian bay.*

Why do pilot whales navigate to disaster?

Confused and alarmed, a group of whales thrashes in the shallows of a Tasmanian bay, gradually stranding themselves on the sandy beach as the tide goes out. The huge creatures are helpless on land and their internal organs are in danger of being crushed by the unfamiliar weight of their own 1 or 2 ton bodies when unsupported by the sea. These are long-finned pilot whales, facing certain death unless they are rescued by teams of naturalists.

The phenomenon of stranded whales has excited curiosity for centuries. The Greek philosopher Aristotle commented on it as early as the 4th century BC. Since 1920, many hundreds of whales have been recorded as being stranded on British beaches alone, and similar occurrences have been documented all over the world. The stranded whales are quite often pilot whales – the short-finned pilot whales of the tropics as well as the long-finned species.

What puzzles observers is why the whales seem so determined to swim onto the beaches, even when well-meaning humans try to drive them away or carry them back into the water. Many explanations have been suggested, such as mass suicide, water pollution, confusion of the whales' echolocation mechanism, brain diseases or viruses that disorientate the animals in some way. It has even been suggested that the strandings result from a primitive instinct to flee onto land in moments of panic, a half-forgotten leftover from the time 60 million years ago when the whales' ancestors were land animals.

None of these explanations can account for all the strandings that occur, however. So scientists are now exploring a new suggestion – that whales become stranded in unfamiliar waters as a result of a navigation error of a rather unexpected kind. It has been observed that the species of whale that tend to get stranded are those that live out at sea – those that live near the shore rarely do.

What has attracted scientists' curiosity is the observation that beaches where strandings are common tend to have the contours of the earth's geomagnetic field running at right angles to the shore line rather than parallel with it. The earth's magnetic field is what makes a compass needle point to the north, but differences in the magnetic properties of rocks distort the north-south orientation of the field to produce bends and kinks. In addition, these local magnetic 'hot spots' cause the strength of the magnetic field to vary from place to place.

Whales may use the tiny differences in the magnetic field to maintain a fixed course by swimming along magnetic contours, just as walkers try to keep to the height contours when going round a mountain side. Whales possibly learn the local characteristics of the magnetic field over a wide area during their wanderings in search of food. But they may run into trouble when, while following lines of equal geomagnetic strength, they are led into unfamiliar shallow waters near land. If there is a local 'hot spot', they may not be aware of the problem, and so become trapped in a bay or near a beach with their echolocation system confused. Pilot whales travel long distances following the erratic migrations of their favourite prey, squid, and this may take them into unfamiliar waters more often than other whales.

Local people have learned that whale groups (or 'pods') are likely to venture near shore in search of food in particular areas, and have exploited this by driving whales inshore to catch them for oil and meat. The best known of these whale drives is the annual killing of pilot whales in the Faeroe Islands, in the North Atlantic. The Faeroese use lines of boats to shepherd the whales into the shallows. Written records document the custom as far back as 1584. On the British and Irish coasts, whale driving was a regular form of fishery from at least 1602, but had died out in most places by the beginning of the 20th century as oil and other whale products became less important.

There is some evidence to suggest that the size of pilot whale populations around the Faeroes may be subject to natural cycles over periods as long as 110 years. Surprisingly, the heavy hunting over the past few centuries does not seem to have reduced their numbers severely, unlike the near-extinction of the giant blue and right whales. But – as with all animals – too much hunting can easily force the population below the number from which it can recover. Extinction then looms rapidly.

A plague of starfish destroys coral reefs

Coral reefs are living organisms made up of tiny creatures known as polyps. The reefs have built up over the centuries by the accumulation of limestone secretions from the polyps, which are rather like sea anemones and live in partnership with microscopic plants. But by 1980, the coral reefs of the Pacific Ocean had come under serious threat. They were being steadily eaten by crown-of-thorns starfish in numbers reaching plague proportions.

This starfish grows up to 2ft (610mm) across and can have up to 21 arms, each covered with the poison-tipped spines that give the creature its name. It eats by extruding its stomach through its mouth and enveloping the coral. Strong digestive juices then dissolve the soft-bodied polyps.

In 1969, in just two weeks, 13,847 starfish were collected from a reef off Western Samoa. And in 1980, at the height of the plague, the coral round just one island of the Great Barrier Reef, off Australia's north-east coast, had been invaded by 1½ million starfish. The effect was devastating – a 24 mile (39km) stretch of reef was almost totally destroyed in two and a half years.

The reason for such a dramatic explosion in the starfish numbers remains uncertain. One suggestion was that the predators of the starfish – such as tritons (marine snails) and large fish – had been killed off by water pollution or excessive fishing. Another suggestion was that nutrients washed into the seas during unusually wet years foster a large amount of plankton – microscopic plants and animals. This allowed more starfish larvae, which graze on minute plants, to survive than usual. Fossil records show that a boom in starfish numbers can occur at irregular intervals, possibly with periods as long as 1000 years between.

Although protected by its spines, the crown-of-thorns starfish is eaten by the triton, a giant snail with a shell up to 16in (400mm) high. In one study, 15 tritons ate 125 starfish in three months. Larger starfish are sometimes only partly eaten, and may regrow the lost parts. So a decline in predators alone may not account for any dramatic increase in starfish numbers.

By 1992 the plague of crown-of-thorns starfish seemed to have subsided. The decrease in numbers on the Great Barrier Reef may have been caused by a parasite that destroys the starfish from the inside. Scientists are not sure.

Deadly embrace *On the Great Barrier Reef, a crown-of-thorns starfish wraps itself round the branches of a coral colony and digests the soft parts.*

Trail of destruction *Round white patches of dead coral lie behind a crown-of-thorns starfish as it feeds on a reef. It can destroy 7sq yds (5.8sq m) of coral in a year.*

Formidable foe *Despite the protection of its poison-tipped spines, the starfish is a favourite prey of the giant triton, which is one of the largest sea snails.*

Stinging embrace *A young clownfish, which is both male and female, seeks safety among an anemone's tentacles.*

Double chance *All fairy basslets begin life as females (bottom). But if the shoal's dominant male (top) dies, the largest female changes sex and takes his place.*

Fish that change sex as needs demand

A brightly hued clownfish swims through the clear water off Australia's north-east coast, among the corals and other softly coloured growths. Life here on the Great Barrier Reef seems idyllic. Yet as for most of the teeming creatures of the reef, the fish's life is a never-ending struggle – locked in the rhythms of day and night, high tide and low tide.

The clear sea carries little food, so predators abound and only the most adaptive species survive. Because so many fish are lost to predators, and because food supplies are limited, reef fish must ensure that enough members of each sex survive to continue breeding. So some species have developed the ability to change sex when the need arises, making the most of their chances of survival.

The thumb-length clownfish – an eyecatching orange clown anemone fish with white, black-edged bands round its body – dodges predators amid the tentacles of poisonous stinging anemones. Most fishes would be stunned and killed by the anemone, but the clownfish is immune to its stings and has developed a special relationship with it. In return for the anemone's protection, the clownfish provides it with leftovers and droppings from its meals of plankton (microscopic plants and animals).

All clownfishes live in family groups dominated by an adult female. She does not mate with other males of the family, but with roving males that have dispersed from other families, so avoiding inbreeding. Her offspring begin life as potentially both male and female (hermaphrodites) but develop into males, some of which swim away from the family to find mates elsewhere. If the female dies or is eaten, then the most dominant male of the family assumes her role and turns into a breeding female.

The fairy basslet (or jewelfish) – a finger-length plankton eater – is another sex-changing species. All fairy basslets start life as females. They live in shoals dominated by one or two males of a different colour who continually display with their huge dorsal (back) fins erect. While there is a male around, the females mate with him and breed normally.

But if the male dies, or is eaten by a bigger fish (as often happens), then the largest dominant female in the shoal starts to behave like a male, and within a few days has irreversibly changed sex. And if the new male is eaten straight away, another female takes his place. This means that every fish has two chances to reproduce, first as a female and then as a male.

Banded stilts – wading birds from nowhere

Once in a while, Lake Torrens in southern Australia becomes a breeding ground for thousands of wading birds, their nests closely packed on sandy islands. They are long-legged banded stilts, which breed in huge flocks on lakes formed when salt flats are flooded.

But rain is rare in the vast, hot plains of southern Australia. If it rains at all, the water soon evaporates from the parched earth. The shallow beds of salt there – themselves the scant remnants of former lakes – may be transformed into real but temporary salt lakes. But this happens to Lake Eyre only every 10-20 years, and to the more southerly Lake Torrens usually only about once in a century. How the banded stilts survive, and where they are able to breed for the rest of the time, is still a mystery.

The first breeding colony was recorded in 1939 on Lake Torrens. Then in 1989, just a few days of heavy rain in April turned Lake Torrens into a shimmering sheet of water – an oasis nearly twice the size of Majorca. This gave scientists an excellent opportunity to study the animals and plants that had managed to exploit such a fleeting home.

One of their most exciting discoveries was a colony of banded stilts – white, black-winged birds with chestnut-coloured V-shaped chest bands. They flew in from the surrounding wilderness to nest. Nobody knew how far they had travelled or where they had all come from, but they gathered together, jostling on a small sandy island in the middle of the lake.

VAST NURSERY

Each pair in the colony laid a clutch of up to four large, speckled eggs in a shallow nest scraped out of the sand – nests with five eggs probably resulted from more than one female laying there. By May there were 100,000 nests, in places crammed together with less than a hand-width between them. While the parents carefully incubated their clutch, flocks of marauding silver gulls, which had followed the stilts to the island, circled overhead waiting for a chance to steal an egg or a small chick.

When the fluffy chicks were hatched, they could walk about almost at once, and fed with

Hatching ground When Lake Torrens sprang briefly to life for only the second time this century, thousands of banded stilts crammed their nests on a sandy island.

their parents. Later, they gathered together in crèches of up to a thousand. Each crèche was guarded by a number of adults while the breeding females tried to hatch a second clutch before the lake began to dry out. The crèche guards shepherded their charges on a ¼ mile (400m) walk to the island shore, then across the water to the lake edge 65 miles (104km) away. Some chicks swam the distance in only six days, bobbing along in untidy rafts. Some died on the way, or were plucked from the lake by the ever-present silver gulls.

Once they reached the lake shore, the chicks wandered about on their long pink legs, probing the mud with their slim beaks in search of brine shrimps or other small creatures that had quickly colonised this temporary lake.

As the chicks grew, they moulted into smarter plumage by July, and then left the crèches to feed alone. As Lake Torrens slowly dried out, the banded stilts flew off across the saltbushes to disappear into the wilderness once again.

Proud parent A banded stilt settles down to incubate its eggs in a scrape of soil on a temporary island. Before they fly, the chicks swim in groups to the lake shore.

HOW ANIMALS SPEND THE YEAR

RHYTHMS OF LIFE SET BY THE SUN AND THE SEASONS

The animals and plants are listed by the name generally used, such as *barn owl*, *snowy owl*, but *gorilla, mountain*. Both forms are given in the index. The measurements shown are for mature animals. Where there is only one figure it indicates the average. In some entries, the seasonal activities given do not cover the animal's entire range. Where activities cannot be described in four seasonal columns, the entry is spread over wider columns.
★ Denotes that the animal is becoming rare. ★★ Marks animals in danger of extinction.

	March/April/May	June/July/August	Sept/Oct/Nov	Dec/Jan/Feb
ADDER (COMMON VIPER) **Where found** Europe except Ireland and the south; also across Siberia to the Pacific Ocean. Moors, heaths, hedges and pasture, open woodland and gardens. **Length** Up to 2ft (610mm); female sometimes longer. **Lifespan** 10-25 years.	Males emerge from hibernation 2 weeks before females and perform combat dances to establish dominance. Males shed their skins. Emerging females are often courted by males waiting by their burrows. Mating peaks in April, and adders then go to summer feeding areas.	Females shed their skins. In late August they are heavily pregnant and return to their burrows to give birth. Eggs hatch as they leave the female's body, and 5-12 young, each about 6in (150mm) long, emerge and disperse to lead independent lives.	Some late births may occur in September. As the temperature falls in autumn, adders return to hibernation sites. The young born that year are the last to hibernate, and nearly half of them do not survive until spring.	The adders hibernate through the winter. They use existing burrows or natural crevices underground that are cool and dry. In a good, roomy place they hibernate in groups. Main entry p. 73.
 **ADÉLIE PENGUIN** **Where found** Fringes of Antarctica and nearby islands. **Height** 2ft 4in (710mm). **Weight** About 2lb (1kg). **Lifespan** Probably at least 10 years.	Adult birds are land-locked for 2-4 weeks while they moult all their feathers and grow a new set. Loss of feathers destroys their insulation and waterproofing so that they cannot swim. They take to the open sea once their new feathers have grown.	Winter is spent out at sea, their thick blubber protecting the penguins from the cold. They feed on krill and small fish, often far from land. Dives last only a few minutes. The penguins' chief predator is the leopard seal.	The birds return to land and trek across the ice to their breeding grounds inland. Some journeys may take nearly a week. A female lays 2 eggs in November, by which time melting ice has opened up fresh feeding places. After laying, the female goes to sea to feed.	The male stays on the eggs for 2-3 weeks until the female returns. Both then incubate the eggs in turn. Chicks hatch in December, when food is plentiful. Both parents feed the young. Juveniles fledge late January-early February and go to sea. Main entry p. 221.
 **ALBATROSS, BLACK-BROWED** **Where found** Southern oceans. Breeds on sub-Antarctic islands. Sometimes seen in North Atlantic. **Length** About 3ft (1m). **Wingspan** 7ft 2in-8ft 2in (2.2-2.5m). **Lifespan** More than 30 years.	Different populations of birds migrate north to their wintering areas. A few reach the North Atlantic, but most go no farther north than Peru and West Africa and search for food in the Humboldt and Benguela Currents. As their main food, krill, is plentiful, birds can breed yearly.	In late August, the adults begin to head for Isla de los Estados (Staten I), South Georgia, Kerguelen, Heard I, Macquarie I, Campbell I and the Falkland and Antipodes Islands to breed in the southern spring. The similar grey-headed albatross often nests beside the black-browed.	Courting displays, in which the tail is fanned, wings outstretched and head thrown back, are accompanied by loud braying. Nests are made of compacted earth and vegetation, and are usually 5ft (1.5m) apart. A female lays a single egg, which is incubated for just under 10 weeks.	Adults forage up to 55 miles (90km) for nutritious krill for the chick. It fledges at 4 months. The grey-headed albatross feeds on less nutritious squid and takes longer to raise a chick, so can breed only once every 2 years. No main entry, see p. 223.
 **ALBATROSS, WANDERING** **Where found** Breeds on islands in the southern oceans and off Antarctica. **Length** Up to 4ft 6in (1.4m). **Wingspan** Up to 11ft (3.4m). **Weight** Up to 27lb (12kg). **Lifespan** At least 40 years, and possibly up to 80 years.	Youngsters hatched February-April stay on the nest throughout their first summer and are fed through the southern winter. They may not fledge for 10-12 months. As a result, adults can breed in alternate years only. Pairs mate for life.	Wandering albatrosses fly great distances. Some winter 8000 miles (13,000km) from their nest site. Birds may wander 300 miles (500km) a day in search of fish and squid, which they pluck from the sea surface. They soar using the upcurrents from waves for lift.	After a year flying round Antarctica, birds of Bird Island (part of South Georgia in the southern Atlantic, and a main breeding ground) return to breed in October. Pairs go to the same nest of mud and vegetation, often in boggy moorland, and mate after an elaborate courtship.	Single white eggs laid December-January are incubated for more than 2 months. Both parents feed the chick up to 4lb (1.8kg) of squid or fish at a time. Birds hatched last season fledge from December to February, then go to sea. Main entry p. 222.

	March/April/May	June/July/August	Sept/Oct/Nov	Dec/Jan/Feb

ARCTIC FOX

Where found Land bordering Arctic seas.

Head-and-body length 20-33in (500-840mm); tail 10-17in (250-430mm). **Shoulder height** 11in (280mm).

Weight 7-18lb (3-8kg).

Lifespan 15 years in captivity.

March/April/May: Arctic foxes breed every 3 or 4 years when lemmings are plentiful. A dog fox mates with up to three vixens, starting as early as March. Each vixen digs a den – in a hillside for example – soon afterwards. Litters of 5-10 (but sometimes up to 13) cubs are born in May or June.

June/July/August: The cubs stay near the den until early autumn, but the home range can cover 3-7sq miles (8-18sq km). Adults give a warning bark if there is danger near the den. Breeding pairs stay together for the season, but the vixens usually forage in separate parts of the range.

Sept/Oct/Nov: The foxes' coats thicken to provide insulation. Foxes that patrol shorelines and hunt on the ebb and flow of the tide have browny-grey coats all year. Those that live inland and in mountains moult their summer coat for a white one, which gives them camouflage in the snow.

Dec/Jan/Feb: Arctic foxes do not hibernate, for with their thicker winter coats they can tolerate temperatures down to −70°C (−94°F) before they shiver to keep warm. They sometimes follow polar bears and feed on any carrion they leave.

No main entry, see p. 272.

ARCTIC HARE (BLUE or MOUNTAIN HARE)

Where found Alaska, Canada, Greenland; North Eurasia; Alps; Central Asian mountains. Open country, tundra.

Length 19-26½in (480-670mm).

Weight Up to 12lb (5.5kg).

Lifespan 4-5 years.

March/April/May: Mating begins in April, and the large groups disperse as males take up breeding territories. In the north, the hares then moult their long white winter coats. The short summer coats are also white, but camouflage the hares effectively against the stony landscape.

June/July/August: In June, females bear 2-5 young (leverets) and rear them until they are independent, at about 3 weeks old. Males often abandon females after the young are born and join groups of unmated hares. Leverets hide in hollows under stones if alarmed. They often feed in the cool of night.

Sept/Oct/Nov: In some areas, females may produce a second litter in September. Litters often remain together and congregate in autumn. By the onset of winter, juveniles are full adult size, and disperse with the adults. They feed on mosses and plants where wind has blown off the snow.

Dec/Jan/Feb: In the worst winter weather hares shelter in rock crevices or hollows under boulders. Coats grow longer, and hares are more or less invisible against the snow. They often stay motionless in full view of a predator, such as an Arctic fox.

No main entry, see p. 149.

ARCTIC TERN

Where found Breeds in Arctic and sub-Arctic, and on northern temperate coasts. Winters in the southern oceans.

Length 14in (360mm). **Wingspan** 2ft 8in (810mm).

Weight About 4oz (113g).

Lifespan Up to 30 years.

March/April/May: In May adults arrive in the north from southern oceans. Migration routes include the Pacific coast of the Americas and the Atlantic coasts of Africa and Europe. Terns that come from the farthest south breed the farthest north. Birds mate for life and join their partners at the nesting site.

June/July/August: The 2-3 eggs laid May-June hatch in 3 weeks. The fluffy chicks are mottled for camouflage. It is thought they study the skies to learn the signs that will help them to find their way back to the site when older. They fly at 4 weeks and seek geographical clues about the nest site.

Sept/Oct/Nov: Adults and juveniles fly south to the Southern Hemisphere. Birds from eastern Canada and Greenland ride on the winds across the Atlantic Ocean and join birds from Europe flying down the west coast of Africa.

Dec/Jan/Feb: Most birds moult at the end of their journey. Some birds circumnavigate Antarctica, feeding in the southern oceans, before going north to breed. Juveniles do not go north until their third year, but some 2-year-olds fly part of the way.

Main entry p. 102.

ARMADILLO, NINE-BANDED (COMMON LONG-NOSED ARMADILLO)

Where found Southern USA southwards to Argentina. Semi-deserts and grasslands.

Length 15-17in (380-430mm).

Weight 9-18lb (4-8kg).

Lifespan About 4 years.

March/April/May: In Central America identical quadruplets are born in a burrow in March and suckled for 2 months. Armadillos are mainly nocturnal, and avoid the heat of the day by staying in deep burrows. They eat mostly insects and spiders, but occasionally take small reptiles and amphibians.

June/July/August: Central American armadillos mate, the female lying on her back. The implantation of the fertilised egg is delayed for a while. Armadillos are often noisy when foraging. When alarmed by a predator they can roll into a ball and are protected by their armour-plated skin.

Sept/Oct/Nov: The fertilised egg implants in the female's womb in November, and pregnancy begins. In the southern part of their range, the armadillos dig into ant or termite nests with their strong claws, and mop up the occupants with their long tongues.

Dec/Jan/Feb: Armadillos are quite social creatures. A burrow may be shared by as many as four animals, who are always the same sex.

Main entry p. 97.

ARMY ANT

Where found Tropical Africa and South and Central America. Rain forest.

Length Up to ¼in (6mm).

Colony size 170,000-700,000 ants.

Lifespan Queen 6 years.

Colonies alternate 20-day stationary phases based at a bivouac, when the queen lays her eggs, with 15-day nomadic phases, when the colony hunts for food. Each colony has four castes: (1) majors or soldiers that defend the colony; (2) submajors that lead the foraging teams, carry large prey items back to the bivouac, and carry the smallest workers during the nomadic phase; (3) workers, who forage, and carry and tend the queen; (4) minims that care for the growing brood. At the onset of the dry season, large colonies stop producing workers and rear six new queens and 4000 males. When the queens are ready, workers form two raiding groups that head off in opposite directions. The six queens run along each of the columns, but only two gather workers to form new colonies; the four losers are left to die. The males, still in cocoons, are shared between the two new groups. They emerge winged, and fly to another colony to mate with a queen, fooling her workers and soldiers by emitting a queen-like scent. In their lifetime, fertilised queens travel up to 40 miles (64km) and lay some 6,000,000 eggs.

Main entry p. 286.

	March/April/May	June/July/August	Sept/Oct/Nov	Dec/Jan/Feb

ARUM, HAIRY DRAGON

Where found Mediterranean: Corsica, Sardinia, Balearic Islands. Scrubland and grassy places near the sea.

Height Up to 3ft (1m).

Flower diameter Up to about 9in (230mm).

Lifespan Several years.

In April, tiny flowers develop on a spike with only its tip projecting from a wrapped purple leaf. Flies drawn by a carrion-like smell, and perhaps carrying pollen, crawl in and are trapped by down-pointing hairs. If pollen brushes the female flowers at the base, it fertilises them.

The male flowers on the upper part of the spike open after 3 days. The pollen dusts the flies, which carry it to the next flower when the trap of hairs withers and lets them out. Female flowers develop into orange-red berries. Birds eat them and expel the seeds with droppings.

Only the stout, lobed leaves, often purple-blotched, are still visible. After a dry summer they are often withered and tattered. Food and water have been stored in the plant's tuber, a swollen underground stem.

When the weather is cool and damp during February, new leaves begin to grow from the tuber. Seeds expelled by birds the previous summer may germinate where they have fallen and begin to grow into new plants.

Main entry p. 88.

AVOCET

Where found Breeds Europe and northern Asia. Winters mainly Africa; Middle East. Coasts and wetlands.

Length 17in (430mm).

Wingspan About 2ft 7in (790mm).

Weight 7-14oz (200-400g).

Lifespan Up to 24 years.

Most birds fly north from their wintering grounds to breed. They nest in colonies. After an elaborate courtship females lay 3-4 blotched, buff-coloured eggs in shallow scrapes on open ground or in short vegetation. Parents share incubation and eggs hatch after 3-4 weeks.

Both parents tend the sooty-brown and grey chicks, which follow them about and feed themselves as soon as they hatch. Chicks fledge after 5 weeks and in late summer or early autumn moult into immature plumage (black and white with mottled head and grey on the nape).

The adults complete the moult from breeding to non-breeding plumage (similar to the immature plumage). Most birds migrate for winter, and gather in small flocks, usually 6-30, to fly south, mainly to Africa and the Middle East.

Birds winter on mud flats and marshes, feeding on shrimps, worms and other small water creatures. In February they moult from winter plumage into black and white breeding plumage, losing their grey feathers and mottling.

Main entry p. 116.

AYE-AYE★★

Where found Madagascar. Rain forests on the east coast.

Head-and-body length 16in (400mm); tail 16in (400mm).

Weight 4½lb (2kg).

Lifespan 9 years in captivity.

Little is known about the life of the aye-aye, which is a relative of the lemurs. It is a nocturnal animal that feeds on fruit, seeds, insects and wood-boring grubs. Food may be short during the drier months, but aye-ayes can scratch grubs from deep inside rotten tree trunks with their specialised long, thin, third digit, and probably gain water from this source too. They are generally solitary, and come together only at mating time.

The aye-ayes mate between September and November, just before the wetter time of the year. The period of pregnancy in other lemurs varies between 2 and 4½ months, and for aye-ayes the period is probably similar.

Single young are born. The mother carries her youngster on her back while she forages for food. She may suckle it for more than a year.

Main entry p. 55.

BADGER

Where found Europe and Central Asia. Forests, woods and grassland.

Length 2ft 6in (760mm); female slightly less.

Weight About 26lb (11.8kg); female slightly less.

Lifespan 11 years; 19 years in captivity.

Insects begin to supplement the earthworm diet. This year's cubs are weaned, and mating peaks soon after. The fertilised egg stays in the female's reproductive tract until December. Most of last year's cubs leave the parental sett (den) to find their own territories.

Badgers are active at night but, with the short nights of summer, they spend less time outside their dens. They feed heavily on cereals in late summer, as crops ripen for harvesting.

Setts are repaired and new tunnels dug ready for winter. Communities usually number about 15 (adult boars and sows and one or two litters). The autumn fruits of many shrubs make an important contribution to the diet. A few of this year's cubs leave to find their own territories.

The fertilised egg usually implants in the womb in early December. Litters of 2-3 cubs are born mostly in February, but maybe late December-May. As vegetable food is scarce, badgers depend on earthworms and often lose weight.

Main entry p. 71.

BALD EAGLE

Where found Aleutian I; Alaska and Canada (not the far north); USA; Baja California (Mexico). Near water.

Length About 3ft (1m).
Wingspan Up to 8ft (2.4m).

Weight 7-14lb (3-6.4kg); female larger than male.

Lifespan Up to 14 years.

This fish eagle is the US national bird. Those birds that migrate go north in spring – many Floridan youngsters disperse along the Atlantic coast and into the Great Lakes, perhaps to avoid summer heat. In south British Columbia eggs are laid March-April, in Alaska in May.

Females lay 1-3 eggs, (usually 2), which take about 5 weeks to hatch, so eggs are hatching in Alaska in early summer. Chicks start to feather at 3 weeks and leave the nest at 10-11 weeks. Some do not attain adult plumage until their fifth summer, when most start to breed.

Migrating birds go south. Populations in Florida begin courtship – pairs, who mate for life, lock talons and wheel down through the air. They repair their stick nests, which can be 12ft (3.7m) thick and 150ft (46m) up in a tree, and females lay November-January.

Floridan parents share incubation and feed the chicks – the first chicks hatch in December. They eat mainly fish, but also waterfowl and small mammals. The eagles usually roost singly at night, but immature birds may roost together.

Main entry p. 226.

	March/April/May	June/July/August	Sept/Oct/Nov	Dec/Jan/Feb
BANDED STILT **Where found** Australia. Shallow and temporary lakes and salt marshes. **Height** 16in (400mm). **Wingspan** 2ft 1in–2ft 7in (635–790mm). **Weight** 7oz (200g). 	Banded stilts are irregular breeders. Few records of their breeding are available. In April 1939, birds nested in a large colony on islands in Lake Torrens in South Australia, mudflats that became a temporary lake after rains. Females lay clutches of up to 4 eggs in scrapes in the ground.	The eggs hatch after probably 2 weeks. The downy chicks are fed on shrimps by both parents for a few weeks, and are then minded in large crèches by adults. Chicks and minders then swim to feeding grounds on lake shores. Females stay to raise second broods.	The birds probably migrate within Australia, but the routes and destinations are unclear.	The feeding and moulting grounds at this time of year seem to be generally at coastal saltpans. Main entry p. 295.
BARN OWL **Where found** North and South America; Europe; Africa; Central Asia; Australasia. In open lowland. **Length** 13–14in (330–360mm). **Wingspan** 2ft 6in (760mm). **Weight** 8–12oz (230–340g). **Lifespan** Up to 21 years. 	In the Northern Hemisphere barn owls begin nesting in March, in holes in trees, buildings, cliffs and similar places. The birds usually use traditional nest sites. Females lay 4–7 eggs at intervals of 2–3 days, and incubate them for about 4 weeks. Most youngsters hatch in May.	The chicks are cared for and fed by both parents. They fledge after 8 weeks, and 3–5 weeks later are independent. In years of good weather and ample food, a few parents may rear a second brood.	Chicks in late second broods are dependent on their parents until late October. Young birds disperse from their home areas and try to establish their own territories.	Pairs hold their territory throughout the winter, feeding on mice, voles, rats and other small mammals. Many young birds die – only one in three survives for more than a year. Main entry p. 110.
BARNACLE GOOSE **Where found** Breeds within the Arctic Circle. Winters in Western Europe. **Length** 23–27in (580–690mm). **Wingspan** 4ft 8in (1.4m). **Weight** 4–5½lb (1.8–2.5kg). **Lifespan** Up to 25 years. 	The geese migrate to their breeding grounds in Greenland, Svalbard (Norway) and Novaya Zemlya (Russia). They arrive by the end of May, already paired, and build nests of lichen and down on cliff ledges. The females lay and incubate 4–6 white eggs.	The eggs hatch 3–4 weeks after laying, in late June or early July, when summer comes to the Arctic. Each gosling weighs about 2oz (57g) on hatching, but within 5 weeks is adult size. In the long summer days birds feed on sedges and mosses for up to 24 hours a day.	Both parents tend the goslings. At nearly 8 weeks old, the youngsters accompany their parents on the long flight to wintering grounds in western Scotland, Ireland, the Netherlands or northern Germany.	Coastal grasslands that are periodically flooded by high tides provide the geese with rich grazing during winter. In some areas, the birds also feed on farm land. Main entry p. 124.
BAT-EARED FOX **Where found** East Africa southwards from Ethiopia; South Africa. Grassland and scrub. **Head-and-body length** 18–23in (460–580mm); tail 9½–13in (240–330mm). **Weight** 6½–11lb (3–5kg). **Lifespan** Perhaps 6 years. 	In East Africa, some young foxes, now about 5 months old, leave the group and either hunt alone for a season or pair straight away. Other youngsters stay with their parents. The family group may number up to 12 foxes.	It is the dry season, when life-long pairs of adult foxes mate. Females are pregnant for 8–11 weeks. The foxes forage mainly for insects and have extra molars and specialised large jaw muscles that enable them to chew their prey rapidly.	Litters of 4–6 pups are born in an underground burrow and suckled for up to 8 weeks. They emerge from the burrow November–December. Those young foxes from previous litters that have stayed on help to tend the pups.	New pups begin to hunt with their parents. It is the wet season, and foxes feast on termites, digging up mounds with their forepaws, and rapidly chewing the insects. Main entry p. 237.
BEAVER **Where found** North American beaver: Alaska, Canada, USA. European beaver: France eastwards to Mongolia. **Head-and-body length** 2ft 6in–3ft 6in (760–1065mm); tail 10–20in (250–510mm). **Weight** 24–66lb (11–30kg). **Lifespan** 15–21 years. 	Beavers emerge from their lodges and begin essential repairs to lodges and dams. They feed on fresh vegetation. Females give birth to 1–9 kits in April, and suckle them for 2–4 months (sometimes up to 9). The family carry vegetation back to the nest for the kits to chew.	Kits emerge from the lodge for the first time, and are minded by other members of the family group. Water levels may drop in high summer, and the beavers' lodge becomes vulnerable to predators such as pumas, bears, lynxes, wolverines and coyotes.	All members of the family gather sticks, logs and trunks of aspen and birch, as well as waterside plants, and store them underwater in piles round the main lodge. Dam-building is also done in readiness for winter. In November, last year's kits leave home.	As the water ices over, the beavers are confined to the chamber within their lodge. They feed all winter on the material stored under water and now below the ice. They mate in January, and females are pregnant for 15 weeks. Main entry p. 84.

	March/April/May	June/July/August	Sept/Oct/Nov	Dec/Jan/Feb

BEETLE-TRAP FLOWER

Where found Tropical and southern Africa and Madagascar. Arid plains.

Height 6in (150mm)

Flower diameter 3-4in (75-100mm).

Fruit diameter 1½-2in (38-50mm).

For most of the time, this curious plant is completely hidden underground. It is a parasite living on the roots of euphorbia plants. The plant is leafless and rootless, pushing out thick, creeping underground 'stems'. Every few years or so, it sends up a large, solitary, pinkish-red flower that has pollen-bearing anthers and a pollen-receiving stigma enclosed within petal-like sepals which join to form its trumpet – it has no true petals. The inside is covered with spongy material smelling of rotting meat. Carrion beetles, attracted by the scent, feed on the material and become dusted with pollen. The beetles transfer the pollen to the stigma – a button-like protrusion on the underground ovary – of another beetle-trap plant. Once fertilised, the ovary grows into a starchy fruit containing hundreds of minute seeds. Jackals, porcupines and baboons dig up the fruits and feast upon them. The seeds pass out with the animals' droppings and are dispersed to produce new plants.

Main entry p. 280.

BELUGA (WHITE WHALE)★

Where found Arctic Ocean and adjacent seas.

Length Up to 16ft (5m).

Weight 2425lb (1100kg); female 25 per cent smaller than male.

Lifespan 30 years.

Adult belugas mate at sea in ice-filled water. When the warmer weather melts the ice, the whales migrate northwards to new feeding grounds. Females are pregnant for about 14 months.

Females give birth to single calves. Young are suckled for 1½-2 years, so the females give birth only once every 3 years. Groups of up to 2000 belugas gather in estuaries and spend the last weeks of summer moulting their skin in the shallow water there.

The whales head southwards to their winter quarters at the limit of the ice. They are generally rather slow swimmers, and spend a lot of time near the water surface.

Winter is spent out at sea. Belugas are toothed whales, and feed on fish and crustaceans such as shrimps. Young males reach sexual maturity at about 8 years old, young females at 5 years old.

Main entry p. 150.

BISON, AMERICAN

Where found North America. Prairies and Yellowstone National Park.

Length 12ft 6in (3.8m).
Shoulder height About 6ft (1.8m).

Weight Male 1800lb (820kg); female 1200lb (545kg).

Lifespan Up to 40 years.

Births start in April. Each pregnant cow leaves the herd to bear one calf after a 9-10 month pregnancy. She rejoins the herd after 3-4 days, and for its first 2-3 weeks the calf follows close on its mother's heels as she grazes with the herd.

Births continue into June. Mating takes place July-September, with rival bulls bellowing and head-butting. Bull calves begin to grow horns 2 months after birth, and yearling bull calves now have a beard and thick woolly hair on the shoulders. Bison mature at about 3 years old.

Calves may be weaned at 7 months old, but if the grazing is good, cows produce enough milk to suckle their calves well into the winter. The calves moult their reddish fur, which is replaced by a chocolate-brown coat.

Protected by their thick winter coats, bison can face into a blizzard. They clear snow with their heads to reach grass beneath. In Yellowstone National Park (USA), bison gather near warm springs and geysers in the worst weather.

Main entry p. 12.

BLACK BEAR, AMERICAN

Where found Alaska; Canada; USA: Rockies, north-west, Appalachians, Florida. Woods and forests.

Length 4-6ft (1.2-1.8m).

Weight Male 253-595lb (115-270kg); female 203-309lb (92-140kg).

Lifespan Up to 32 years.

Cubs stay in the winter den with their mother until April or May, and remain with her for up to 2 years. Mother and cubs roam a home range of up to 36sq miles (93sq km). Adults need around 15lb (7kg) of food a day, mostly plants but also insects, fish, rodents and carrion.

Adults mate May-July. Cubs are weaned July-September. Bears in the north mature at the age of 8-10 years, those in southern coastal areas at 4-6 years. The bears climb well, and the cubs will take to the trees if they are alarmed.

Bears living farthest north may hibernate from October to May, bears farther south for shorter periods; those in the southern USA may not do so at all. During hibernation, body temperature drops from 38 to 31°C (100-88°F). The bear may emerge briefly to forage on warm days.

In January or February, 1-5 (but usually 2 or 3) cubs are born in the den. They are blind, almost naked, and weigh up to 2lb (900g) each.

No main entry, see p. 13.

BLACK GROUSE

Where found Europe and Siberia. Woods and heaths.

Height 16-21in (400-530mm).
Wingspan 2ft-2ft 8in (610-810mm).

Weight Up to 2¾lb (1.3kg); female much lighter than male.

Lifespan Up to 5½ years.

Males gather at the lek (courtship display area) and females come to select a mate. After mating, the female lays 6-11 buff-coloured eggs, and incubates them for 3-4 weeks.

When the young hatch, they follow their mother immediately, feeding on small insects, especially ants and spiders. As they grow, they gradually change to a more adult diet of vegetation – shoots, buds, flowers, roots and leaves. They can make their first flight when 2-3 weeks old.

The chicks become independent when they are 3 months old. The birds fatten for the winter on berries and fruits.

Food may be scarce in winter, and the weaker youngsters often die. Experienced adults scrape beneath the snow for shoots, roots and tubers. Catkins may be available in January and February.

Main entry p. 112.

	March/April/May	June/July/August	Sept/Oct/Nov	Dec/Jan/Feb

BLACK SKIMMER

Where found North, Central and South America, from Massachusetts south to the Strait of Magellan. Coasts and waterways.

Length About 18in (460mm).
Wingspan 3ft 6in-4ft 2in (1.1-1.3m).

Weight 4-7oz (110-200g).

North American birds lay May-July. The female incubates the 1-2 eggs, and hatchlings leave the nest once their down is dry. Chicks lie still if threatened, camouflaged by their mottled brown upper parts, or take to water. Adults may feign injury to lure a predator from a chick.

Hatchlings soon scrabble about for food such as shrimps and insects. Once they are fledged, their lower beak grows rapidly and they start to 'skim' – fly with their longer, lower beak shearing the water.

Some Amazon skimmers migrate south to the Mato Grosso area in September and birds breed on seasonal sand banks at low water. Colonies number about 4000, and nests are shallow scrapes in the soil. Some North American birds move to the Carolina and Gulf coasts.

Some North American birds winter on the Pacific coast south from San Diego and on the Atlantic coast south from Florida. Amazon birds breed in January before the water rises.

No main entry, see p. 25.

BLACK SWAN

Where found Australia (not the north-east and the central deserts); Tasmania; New Zealand (introduced 1864).

Length About 4ft (1.2m).
Wingspan 6ft 8in (2m).

Weight Male 13½lb (6.2kg); female 11lb (5kg).

Lifespan 33 years in captivity.

In the north it is the main breeding season, following the onset of the rains; adults moult until the end of June while incubating their eggs and guarding their cygnets. The previous year's cygnets leave to join flocks of unpaired birds. Southern birds are in their winter ranges.

Northern populations disperse to winter ranges on more permanent coastal waters, with cygnets accompanying their parents. Southern populations in Tasmania begin breeding. From July females lay 4-6 pale green eggs which hatch 5-6 weeks later.

One-year-old southern cygnets begin to leave their families and join flocks of unpaired birds. Most will not pair up until their third year. In the south, incubation ends in October and adults start to moult.

Northern populations return to their breeding grounds and build nests – heaps of vegetation 3ft (1m) across near shallow water. Egg-laying begins in February.

Main entry p. 100.

BLAKISTON'S FISH OWL★

Where found Eastern Russia; Japan (Hokkaido); perhaps north-east China. In riverside forest.

Length About 2ft 4in (710mm).

Weight 5½-7½lb (2.5-3.4kg).

Lifespan Possibly several decades.

Nesting begins in mid-March. Females lay 1 or 2 eggs in a large tree cavity. Incubation takes about 37 days, and the chicks fledge after 8 weeks. After the snow melts in early spring, the birds feed heavily on frogs.

By now the birds have switched to their main diet of trout, char and salmon. The young leave the nest in June, but are still fed on fish by their parents all through the summer.

The family remains together throughout the autumn in its year-round territory. The birds call all through the year, but increase in autumn, reaching a peak in winter just before breeding.

Many rivers freeze, so the birds feed on small rodents, especially voles, flying squirrels, and birds. Parents may again feed the young in severe weather. Courtship feeding and mating begin in February, the coldest, snowiest month.

Main entry p. 137.

BLUE CRAB

Where found Caribbean; east coast of the Americas from Nova Scotia south to Uruguay. Shallow and brackish waters.

Width of carapace (shell) About 9in (230mm).

Lifespan About 3 years.

Breeding begins in spring. In the Northern Hemisphere, females start spawning on low-salinity coasts in early spring, but on coasts with the saltiest waters not until May. In Chesapeake Bay, which has both types of water and is the largest and safest spawning area for blue crabs on the US coast, spawning peaks June-August. In Florida, breeding is from February to October. In the Southern Hemisphere breeding begins in September. Spawning takes place in water 6-10ft (1.8-3m) deep. A female swollen with eggs must moult her hard shell before she can release them. She exudes a substance that

attracts a mate, who cradles her to protect her until her new shell hardens. The male fertilises her eggs – up to 2 million of them – as they are released. The eggs hatch after 2 weeks. Young crabs migrate to tributaries, tidal marshes and patches of eel grass when their shells are ½-2in (13-50mm) across. Adults moult every 3-7 weeks, but young crabs every 1-2 weeks, so by the time they reach adult size at 15 months, they have moulted about 20 times. They first spawn at 27 months.

Main entry p. 131.

BLUE SHARK

Where found All seas except polar seas. In the open ocean, and in coastal waters where the continental shelf is narrow.

Length Up to 12ft (3.7m); average 6-8ft (1.8-2.4m).

Weight 65-114lb (30-52kg).

In the northern Atlantic in late spring and early summer, males and females converge on the north-east coast of the USA, where mating takes place. The male holds the female by biting the thickened skin on her back, and inserts his clasper into her genital opening.

In the recently mated females the sperm is stored and will not fertilise eggs for a year or more; birth is a year after that. On the eastern side of the North Atlantic, females that mated about 2 years earlier on the western side come inshore to bear 16in (400mm) long babies.

On the western side of the North Atlantic, sharks move south and into deeper water in the autumn. Where the eastern females go is a mystery, but some eventually return to the western side.

On moonless winter nights, blue sharks of the northern Pacific gather off the California coast to feed on swarms of millions of mating opalescent squid (often called California market squid).

No main entry, see p. 156.

		March/April/May	June/July/August	Sept/Oct/Nov	Dec/Jan/Feb

BOGONG MOTH

Where found South-east Australia. Mountains and grasslands.

Length Adult about 1in (25mm); larva 1½in (38mm). **Wingspan** About 2in (50mm).

Lifespan Adult 9-10 months; larva about 7 weeks.

The moths' colour pales before swarms of them fly north in April from south-east Australia to drier parts in south-west Queensland and north-west New South Wales. Strong west winds may blow some off course to die in the Tasman Sea. Survivors arrive May-June, disperse and mate.

Females lay their eggs in the soil in early winter, and all the adults die. The eggs hatch, and the larvae (which are known as cutworms) feed on plants. They are a serious pest on winter crops, especially cereals.

In early spring the larvae pupate, changing into adults in the soil. When they emerge, the air temperature is rising and their plant food is dying off, so the moths head south, flying by night and resting by day. Billions reach the cool heights of the south-east mountains in November.

The moths shelter in crevices and caves in the Bogong Mountains, which are in the Great Dividing Range about 140 miles (225km) south-west of Canberra. They scarcely breathe or feed all summer. Many are eaten by mice.

Main entry p. 269.

BOTO (AMAZON RIVER DOLPHIN)★★

Where found Amazon and Orinoco river systems of northern South America.

Length Male up to 8ft 6in (2.6m); female 6ft 6in (2m).

Weight Male up to 353lb (160kg); female 328lb (150kg).

Lifespan Up to 30 years.

The dolphins generally live a solitary life feeding on fishes and crabs, especially bottom-living fish. They prefer silt-laden and turbid waters and swim slowly, cruising at about 2½mph (4km/h) and finding their way by echolocation. The colour of the dolphins' skin varies with the clarity of the water. Muddy water contains pink-skinned botos, but in clear water the dolphins have darker, grey skins. They hardly ever dive for longer than 90 seconds. As the rivers rise from December to June, the dolphins spread from the river channels into the flooded rain forests and grasslands (várzeas). At low water in January, the

botos are confined to the main channels or trapped in stagnant pools, where they live well off the catfish and other fish also trapped there. Females are pregnant 10-11 months, and most youngsters are probably born at high water, June-August. They are about 2ft 7in (790mm) long at birth, and weigh 15-17½lb (7-8kg). Females may become pregnant again while still suckling their youngster. Males can begin to breed by the time they are about 6ft 6in (2m) long, and females when a little shorter.

No main entry, see p. 180.

BOXFISH

Where found Shallow tropical and subtropical seas and coral reefs worldwide.

Length Up to 19in (480mm); average, 6-12in (150-300mm).

This family of brightly patterned fish, also known as trunkfish, have an outside skeleton of fused bony plates. The only holes in this protective shell are for the eyes, mouth, fins, gills and vent. The armour plating makes the fish's body inflexible, and it swims slowly by whirling its side fins, like the wheels of a paddle steamer, using its tail only occasionally to give extra thrust. Boxfish also secrete a toxic mucus to deter predators. This makes them difficult to keep in aquariums because they poison the other fish and themselves. Some boxfish, known as cowfish, have horn-like projections over their eyes. The fish feed on

worms, snails and other small invertebrates of the seabed, flushing them out with jets of water from the mouth. Some also eat plants. In some species, males and females have different colouring. Despite its armour and poison, the small thornback cowfish of Australia's Great Barrier Reef is eaten by large fish whose strong stomachs can take it, toxin and all. Another Reef species has an unusual springtime mating procedure: at dusk a male darts round a chosen female and 'hums' to her before spawning.

Main entry p. 242.

BROWN BEAR

Where found North America (known as grizzly); Europe; Asia. In forests.

Length Grizzly 6-10ft (1.8-3m); Eurasian 6-7ft (1.8-2.1m).

Weight Grizzly 500-1200lb (227-545kg); Eurasian up to 700lb (320kg).

Lifespan 30 years.

In spring, as late as April in the north, brown bears leave the dens where they have spent winter, and feast on roots and fungi. Cubs in their second spring start to become independent.

Canadian bears prey extensively on salmon running up rivers in July. Elsewhere bears feed on the rich variety of forest fruits in summer, and on small mammals, birds, insects and wild honey. The summer mating season peaks in July. Weaning of cubs begins.

Bears put on weight in preparation for their winter sleep. Some northern bears begin to settle down in caves or tree hollows as early as October. Autumn adds a rich variety of rosehips, berries, beechmast, acorns and chestnuts to the diet.

Females give birth January-February to usually 2 cubs, during the winter sleep. Most bears sleep all winter, living off stored fat. They may emerge briefly on warm, sunny days.

Main entries: Eurasian p. 68 Grizzly bear p. 153.

BROWN PELICAN

Where found USA; Caribbean; Pacific coast of South America. Coastal waters.

Length 3ft 9in (1.1m) including beak 13in (330mm).

Weight 8lb (3.6kg).

Lifespan Probably up to 15 years.

This is the main breeding period in the USA, where large colonies form for mating and nesting. Females lay 2-3 eggs that hatch after 4-5 weeks. The chicks' eyes open on the second day. They fly after 9-10 weeks. In more tropical areas the breeding season is longer.

In USA populations, parents feed their nestlings. In tropical populations, which may breed all year round, breeding is less common during this period.

USA breeding birds disperse to coasts and islands. Juvenile birds undergo their first moult into winter plumage. The more northerly populations (in New England and near the Canadian border) migrate southwards to avoid severe winter weather.

Birds in the USA break up into smaller flocks of about 50, and fish in shallow coastal waters, mainly for pinfish, menhaden (also known as oldwives), minnows and other small fish.

Main entry p. 83.

	March/April/May	June/July/August	Sept/Oct/Nov	Dec/Jan/Feb

BROWN (NORWAY) RAT

Where found Near human habitations worldwide, except polar regions and low-lying inland towns in the tropics.

Head-and-body length Up to 11in (280mm); tail up to 12in (300mm).

Weight About 17½oz (500g).

Lifespan 1-2 years.

Urban rats show little seasonal variation in behaviour, and often breed all year round if food is abundant. In the Northern Hemisphere, rural rats stay near buildings in spring, but in late March youngsters from last year's litters leave home as adults begin mating.

Rural rats move out into fields to feed on cereals, root crops, seeds and invertebrates such as earthworms. The rural populations start to produce litters of usually 7-8 babies, which are weaned at 3 weeks old. Adults immediately mate again and the next litter is born 3-4 weeks later.

Rural breeding continues. Females can bear their first litters at 11 weeks. The young may be forced out of the colony by aggressive breeding adults. Most youngsters die before they reach maturity, but population growth is rapid, and the total peaks in autumn.

Rural populations find shelter in buildings. Rats may do considerable damage to grain stores on farms. Many rats die in winter, and some 90 per cent of the adult population dies every year.

Main entry p. 70.

BUMBLE BEE

Where found Most temperate and subtropical lands.

Length Worker up to ⅝in (16mm); queen about 1in (25mm).

Weight Up to 0.02oz (0.6g).

Lifespan Queen up to 18 months.

In the Northern Hemisphere from March onwards, queens (mated females) may emerge from hibernation on warm days to feed on nectar. Once nectar is plentiful, queens build nests and lay eggs; these hatch into larvae that develop into workers (unmated females).

The colony expands as the queen lays more eggs, which are tended by the workers until they have developed into adults. Other workers fly from the nest to gather nectar, which they store as honey to feed the developing larvae.

In August or September, the queens lay unfertilised eggs, whose larvae become males. Larvae from fertilised eggs are given extra food and grow into queens. Males and young queens leave and mate with partners from this or other nests. Males die, and queens seek hibernation sites.

In Australia and New Zealand, where the bees were introduced, colonies are expanding during summer. In the Northern Hemisphere, all bees are dead except the young queens hibernating in places such as under bark.

Main entry p. 90.

BUSH BABY, LESSER

Where found Tropical Africa. Forests and tree-scattered grasslands.

Head-and-body length 6½in (165mm); tail 9in (230mm).

Weight 7-10oz (200-285g).

Lifespan 12-15 years.

In East Africa, young male bush babies leave their mother's territory to set up their own. Female youngsters stay with their mother's group. Females who mated again after weaning youngsters about last January give birth to another brood of 1-3 babies.

Dominant adult males (whose territories spread over those of several female groups) seek out females that are on heat and mate with them. Females are pregnant for about 16 weeks. During these dry months, bush babies eat a lot of liquid tree gum as well as their favourite insect prey.

Babies are born as the rains start. They remain alone with their mother for several weeks before both join their group of related adult females and their young.

The youngsters are weaned when they are 8-11 weeks old. Some females may mate again, and produce a second brood 4 months later.

Main entry p. 212.

BUZZARD

Where found Europe, including Poland and central Scandinavia. In open, wooded country.

Length 20-22in (510-560mm). **Wingspan** About 4ft (1.2m).

Weight Male 1lb 13oz (820g); female 2lb 3oz (1kg).

Lifespan 5-6 years.

In the south breeding begins March-April, in the north as late as May or June. The female lays 2-5 white eggs with red or brown markings in a large tree nest. Each pair uses one of up to 15 nest sites yearly. Incubation is mostly by the female. The eggs start to hatch after 4-5 weeks.

The chicks are tended by the female for the first week, and then by both parents – but mainly by the female – for up to 8 weeks, when they fledge. The parents continue to feed and supervise the young until they are independent about 7 weeks later.

Buzzards living in the far north fatten, moult and migrate south for the winter. Those in the south fatten on young and inexperienced birds and small mammals such as rabbits, voles and mice, before the colder winter months.

Food is in short supply, and some of the young hatched in the spring die of starvation. Those birds that migrated return north to breed between February and April, depending on the weather conditions.

Main entry p. 253.

CANE TOAD (GIANT or MARINE TOAD)

Where found Native to South and Central America; introduced to north-east Australia.

Length 4-9in (100-230mm).

Weight Up to 3lb (1.4kg).

Giant toads were introduced in Queensland and northern New South Wales in 1935 to control a beetle pest in the cane-sugar fields, and became known as cane toads. They multiplied to become a pest and have spread to Cape York and the Northern Territory. The toads are active all the year, and spawn and spread in flood seasons. A female can produce up to 35,000 eggs a year. Dry intervals are spent in ponds, billabongs (stagnant river backwaters) and farm dams. Cane toads have skin glands that secrete a potent poison; this can kill predators such as wild birds, reptiles and carnivorous mammals. The toads

feed at night and shelter by day, often in farms and gardens. In places such as Darwin, at the height of the dry season in August, hordes of the toads invade swimming pools, rainwater tanks, lavatories and similar places. Their usual diet consists of flying and crawling insects, but because of their bulk they find food easier to come by in places such as gardens rather than in thick vegetation, and have adapted to eating waste food from dustbins as well as dung.

Main entry p. 182.

	March/April/May	June/July/August	Sept/Oct/Nov	Dec/Jan/Feb

CAPE BUFFALO

Where found Africa south of the Sahara. Woodland and grassland.

Length Up to 8ft (2.4m).
Shoulder height 5ft (1.5m).

Weight Male 1870lb (850kg); female 1210lb (550kg).

Lifespan Up to 20 years.

Large herds in the west disperse in the dry season as grazing deteriorates. Many newly weaned calves die, and lions take more. Herds go to water in the morning and evening, and avoid the noon heat in dense undergrowth. The bulls are more solitary than the cows.

The herds roam over their clearly defined home ranges, grazing on the grass mostly at night. Sometimes they will browse on trees and shrubs. In the far south, grazing conditions improve with the higher rainfall of the southern winter.

The larger herds form again as the grazing improves. Cows are in the later stages of pregnancy, which lasts just under 12 months.

Except in the far south, most calves are born in January, when the summer rains bring a flush of new grass. Cows are on heat from February to March. Adult bulls fight to establish dominance. Only bigger, dominant bulls mate.

Main entry p. 53.

CAPYBARA

Where found South America. Near water in open grassland and tropical rain forests.

Length 3ft 6in-4ft 5in (1.1-1.3m).
Shoulder height 2ft (610mm).

Weight 60-174lb (27-79kg); male slightly smaller.

Lifespan 12 years.

In the northern grasslands it is the end of the dry season, and the capybaras survive by cropping the very short grass with their long front teeth. Mating (in water) can occur at any time of year, but peaks in May as the rains arrive. The herds split into smaller family units.

The first litters of up to 8 (but usually 4) babies are born on land after a pregnancy of about 4 months. Mothers feed the babies and then return to the water. The youngsters follow after 3-4 days, and once in the group form a crèche with other babies.

The youngsters can eat grass within a week, but continue to take milk from any nursing female until 16 weeks old. They become sexually mature at 15 months. Births continue throughout the rainy season, and the capybaras grow fat on lush vegetation growing beside and in the water.

It is the dry season in the grassland and some forests. As pools and wallows dry out, capybaras gather in herds at the best water holes. Herds may number up to 65 animals. Many fall prey to foxes, caymans and vultures.

Main entry p. 262.

CARIBOU (REINDEER)

Where found North American Arctic; Arctic Europe and Siberia. Woodland, tundra.

Length Up to 7ft 3in (2.2m).
Shoulder height 5ft (1.5m).

Weight Male up to 700lb (318kg); female 275lb (125kg).

Lifespan 15 years.

Canadian caribou migrate north into the tundra as it becomes snow-free and plants begin to bloom in May and June. This spring migration is slower and more wandering than the autumn trek south. The caribous eat mainly grasses, sedges, and birch and willow leaves.

Females give birth in the summer plenty. Calves can walk within 2 hours of birth, and are weaned at 2 months old. The bulls fatten up ready for the rut, which begins in late August as the first snow falls and the mainland caribous start to move south to avoid the Arctic winter.

The main rut takes place, with the males fighting fiercely among themselves for the right to mate with females. Mainland caribous, on the move southward, travel about 100 miles (160km) a day along traditional migration routes.

The animals often have to paw away snow to reach their main foods, mosses and lichens. Most grow a whiter winter coat. Males cast their antlers in December, females in February; new ones begin growing about a month later.

Main entry p. 168.

CARMINE BEE-EATER

Where found West, Central and southern Africa. Tree-scattered grasslands.

Head-and-body length About 10in (250mm); tail streamers about 5in (125mm).

Weight About 2oz (57g).

Lifespan Up to 7 years.

Breeding usually occurs in the rainy season, and for most birds of the northern race it is under way by April. The females lay 3-5 eggs in burrows in sandy cliffs, often by rivers, at 2-day intervals. The eggs hatch after about 3 weeks, and the young leave the nest when 4 weeks old.

The northern birds disperse from their breeding grounds in search of food such as grasshoppers, ants, bees and other insects caught on the wing. Bee-eaters soar on updraughts of warm air after their prey, often reaching heights of 330ft (100m).

It is the main breeding season for the southern race of bee-eaters in Zambia and Zimbabwe. They nest in burrows in river banks. There may be 100-1000 burrows in one colony. Egg-laying may span a period of up to 3 weeks.

Birds of the southern race quit their breeding colonies and disperse widely, north or south, in search of food. Some northern bee-eaters follow migrating locust hordes as they move in search of water, eating vast numbers of insects.

Main entry p. 22.

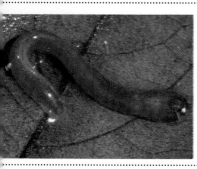

CATFISH (TARUMAZINHO)

Where found South America. In the Amazon basin, in banks of leaf litter along one of the tributaries of the Rio Negro.

Length About ½in (13mm).

Catfish are named for the whisker-like barbels on their jaws, although not all catfish have them. The barbels have chemical sense organs, used for navigation and probably for finding food in the dark waters where the fish live. The tarumazinho, only recently discovered, is one of the most curious of catfish. It is blind, looks like a small red worm, and lives in leaf litter above water level when the rivers are at their lowest around January. When put in the water, it climbs out using its whiskers. Where it goes when the rivers flood once more is a mystery. There are some 2500 catfish species worldwide, most living in fresh water. They include banjo catfish, walking catfish and glass catfish, and range in size from the huge wels of places such as the Baltic, 660lb (300kg) and 10-15ft (3-4.6m) long, to the tiny tarumazinho. Catfish do not have scales – they have either thick skins, like the tarumazinho, or bony armour. South America has more types of catfish than anywhere else. They include the cuiu-cuiu, about 4ft (1.2m) long and armoured with spined, bony plates, and the 1in (25mm) long candirú – a parasite on other fishes.

No main entry, see p. 26.

	March/April/May	June/July/August	Sept/Oct/Nov	Dec/Jan/Feb

CAVE (NEST) SWIFTLET, EDIBLE

Where found South-east Asia. Limestone caves in tropical forests.

Length 4in (100mm).
Wingspan 12in (300mm).

Weight About ⅓oz (9g).

With their first nests destroyed, the birds build second, thinner nests that are taken by collectors for the highly prized oriental bird's-nest soup. The birds then build third nests and lay 2 eggs that hatch after 3-4 weeks. Chicks are fed insects from outside the cave.

If chicks fall from the nest they are torn apart by crickets, cockroaches and crabs living in the swiftlet and bat dung on the cave floor. Survivors fledge at 6-7 weeks, and must learn to fly in total darkness to reach the cave entrance. Racer snakes on the cave walls take swiftlets and bats.

The swiftlets roost by night and forage in the forest by day. At dawn and dusk they find their way through the cave entrance by echoloca-tion – as the bats, which hunt by night and roost by day, fly the opposite way. Forest predators include eagles that may eat six birds in an hour.

Breeding begins. First nests, as high as 490ft (150m) in the cave roof, are cups of solidified saliva and moss 2in (50mm) wide. Each weighs about ⅓oz (9g). Collectors destroy the first nests and take the second, of pure saliva.

Main entry p. 18.

CAYMAN, SPECTACLED (COMMON CAYMAN)★

Where found South America from Venezuela to the southern Amazon basin. Slow rivers and streams; lakes, swamps.

Length Up to 8ft (2.4m).

Lifespan Possibly up to 100 years.

As the waters begin to rise in April, the cay-mans feed on fish, snails, frogs, small deer, pigs, and large toads whose skin toxins poison other predators. The caymans 'herd' fish by curving their body and tail to the shore. They are successful in about one attack out of six.

Caymans breed in most years, after high water in August and through until April, to avoid nest flooding. A male displays with his tail before the pair mate in the water. On the bank a female builds a nest of foliage and mud, about 3ft (1m) across and 18in (460mm) high, and lays 25-30 white eggs 1-2in (25-50mm) long. After 10-13 weeks, one of the parents digs out the eggs, cracks them with its teeth, and carries the 6in (150mm) long babies to water. The youngsters eat mainly water beetles, often lie along a parent's back, and may stay with the adults until they reach 2ft (610mm) long. At low water, caymans lie in pools, wallow in mud or hide in the forest to avoid overheating. They eat mainly armoured catfish and carrion, but may also take young caymans up to 20in (510mm) long.

No main entry, see p. 27.

CHAMOIS★★

Where found Central, eastern and southern Europe; Turkey. Mountain areas.

Length About 4ft (1.2m).
Shoulder height 2ft 6in (760mm).

Weight Male 88lb (40kg); female 73lb (33kg).

Lifespan Up to 20 years.

Females and young animals congregate in mountain woodlands. As the weather improves, they move out onto the alpine meadows. The adult males remain solitary. Births begin in May after a 5½-month pregnancy.

Births continue in June. Pregnant females separate from the herd and go to secluded spots to bear their kids (usually 1-3). A kid begins grazing almost from birth, but is also suckled for some months.

The mating season begins in October. On the alpine meadows, the adult males of about 8 years or more chase away subordinate males and defend harems of females. A courting male follows a female about and nudges and kicks her before they mate.

The flocks split up as the grass gets sparse. Most chamois spend winter in woodland on the lower mountain slopes. Young males are now ready to leave their mother and lead a nomadic life.

Main entry p. 115.

CHEETAH★★

Where found Africa south of Sahara; Iran. Grass and scrub.

Head-and-body length 4ft (1.2m); tail 2ft 6in (760mm).
Shoulder height 2ft 6in (760mm).

Weight Male 117lb (53kg); female 106lb (48kg).

Lifespan 15-16 years.

Cubs may be born at any time, but in East Africa births peak in the March-May rains that bring an increase in prey. The cubs are hidden in a 'form' in deep grass. Their eyes open within 10 days, and by 6 weeks old they accompany their mother when she goes hunting.

Births continue during June and July. Litters, born after a 13-week pregnancy, average 3 cubs but may number 1-8. At 2 months old the cubs start to develop adult colouring with a spotted coat. They will not be sexually mature until almost 2 years old.

Cubs born earlier in the year are weaned by November. In East Africa, they benefit from an increase of prey coinciding with the November rains. Cubs born the previous year leave their mothers to take up their own territories.

Mating takes place during the early months of the year and may continue into August. On the Serengeti Plain, cheetahs move north following the migration of herds of Thomson's gazelles, which are their main prey.

Main entry p. 234.

CHILLINGHAM CATTLE

Where found England: Chillingham Park, Northumberland.

Length About 9ft (2.7m).
Shoulder height About 3ft 6in (1.1m).

Weight Male 1760lb (800kg); female 780lb (350kg).

Lifespan Up to 18 years.

Most calves are born in spring, but the cattle can breed at any time of the year. Cows bear single calves after a pregnancy of 10 months. They give birth among tall bracken in secluded parts of the park and keep their calves away from the herd for 7-10 days.

Breeding continues. Calves stay with their mother for up to a year. Youngsters do not breed until they are 3 years old, so the numbers in the herd increase only very slowly.

The cattle grow thicker coats to protect them against the winter cold. Mature bulls remain in groups of two or three, each with a dominant bull and a home range. The cows, calves and bullocks remain in their herds and are free to wander through the bulls' ranges.

Some cattle may die during the cold winter months. The herd is fed meadow hay to cut down losses. Some calves are born at this time of year, but the mothers often lack enough milk to feed them, and they die.

Main entry p. 207.

	March/April/May	June/July/August	Sept/Oct/Nov	Dec/Jan/Feb

CICADA, PERIODICAL (17-YEAR CICADA)

Where found South-east Canada and eastern USA. Woods, brush, gardens and deserts.

Length Adult 1¼in (32mm). **Wingspan** 3in (75mm).

Lifespan Adult about a month; larva up to 17 years.

The cicadas' life cycle is timed for hordes of the insects to emerge at once, so that finding a mate is easy. Males make a clicking call to attract females, especially in bright sunlight. After mating, females lay eggs in woody stems. The eggs hatch after a week or two, and the larvae fall to the ground and burrow into the soil with their greatly enlarged forelegs. There, with mouth-parts well adapted for piercing and sucking, they feed on the sap of roots. This is poor, watery food and in the north it takes the larvae nearly 17 years to reach adult size – after moulting 7 times. A fully grown larva excavates a tunnel to the surface, sheds its last coat in the tunnel and emerges (usually at night) as an adult, well camouflaged with smoky orange-veined wings. By dawn the cicada has dried and hardened and can fly. In the southern states, the larvae take only 13 years to grow into adults. Although a cicada brood takes such a long time to develop – as far as is known, longer than the larvae of any other insect – a different brood emerges somewhere in North America every year.

Main entry p. 276

CLOWN ANEMONE FISH

Where found West and central Pacific Ocean. Among coral reefs.

Length 2½in (64mm).

Weight A few grams.

Lifespan More than 5 years.

There are about 300 types of small, colourful fish in the clownfish or damselfish family, spread world wide. Those of the genus *Amphiprion* are known as 'clown anemone fish', or simply 'anemone fish', because they live in close association with large sea anemones – as on Australia's Great Barrier Reef. The anemones eat small fish, which they trap and kill with their stinging tentacles. The anemone's sting cells are set off by an amino acid, glutathione, in the victim's skin mucus. Anemone fish lack this substance, so are able to live within the anemone's protection and probably provide it with crumbs of food. Clownfish swim in groups and feed by day on plankton (minute plants and animals) at the surface. At the time of hatching, clownfish are potentially male or female. They develop into males and some go off to join other groups. The leader of a group is the breeding female, who mates with roving males but not males of her own group. However, if she is taken by a predator or dies, the group's dominant male changes into a female to take her place, and breeds with roving males. And so the group goes on.

Main entry p. 294.

COD, ATLANTIC

Where found North Atlantic Ocean, down to about 2000ft (600m).

Length Up to 5ft (1.5m).

Weight Up to about 100lb (45kg).

Lifespan About 20 years.

Cod spawn in sea temperatures of 4-6°C (39-43°F). Depending on her size, a female releases up to 5 million tiny eggs, and the male fertilises them as the sexes come together in the open sea. The eggs hatch 2-4 weeks later into young fish not quite ¼in (6mm) long.

The young fish feed on zooplankton (minute animals). After 3-5 months, when they are 1¼-2½in (32-64mm) long, they move to the sea bottom. In spring and early summer, immature cod in the Barents Sea hunt capelin (a smaller fish), coming close to the northern Norway coast.

Mature cod living in the Barents Sea begin their south-westwards migration to their breeding grounds round the Lofoten Islands off the Norwegian coast. Cod become sexually mature at 6-15 years old.

The cod arrive at the Lofoten Islands during January and February and stay until April. When their spawning is finished, they return to the Barents Sea. Other populations of cod undertake similar migrations.

Main entry p. 36

COMMON POORWILL

Where found The western half of the USA. In scrublands, arid bush country, dry prairies and rocky slopes.

Length 7-8½in (180-215mm).

Weight About 1⅜oz (40g).

Lifespan Possibly 5 years.

Spring is a time of plenty for the poorwills, which belong to the nightjar family. They hunt beetles, grasshoppers and moths at night. A poorwill is rarely seen, but more often heard. Its call is a mellow 'poor-will' – hence the name.

Female poorwills lay 2 white or cream eggs in a shallow depression in gravel or bare rock. Both parents take turns at incubating the eggs, which hatch into downy chicks. The period of incubation is unknown.

The youngsters probably become independent in the autumn.

When insects are few in winter, poorwills can hibernate to survive – the only birds known to do so. A bird shelters in a rock niche in a state of torpor, with its body temperature lowered by up to 22°C (40°F), for 4-100 days.

Main entry p. 251.

CONDOR, ANDEAN

Where found South America south from Colombia. Andes mountains and Pacific coasts.

Length 3ft 6in (1.1m). **Wingspan** 10ft 6in (3.2m).

Weight Male up to 31lb (14kg); female smaller.

Lifespan More than 50 years in captivity.

Condors are a species of vulture, and their broad wings with feathers forming slots at the tip enable them to soar up to 15,000ft (4570m), using rising currents of warm air and updraughts to gain height. They spot their food, carrion, as they soar high in the air. Condors show little seasonal variation in behaviour. Peruvian birds migrate to the coast from December to February to feed on dead sea lions. A vulture with a fully distended crop has probably gorged on about 3lb (1.4kg) of meat. In Colombia breeding is in July, but in Chile eggs are laid September-October. There is no nest – a female lays one white egg on a mountain ledge or in a cave on a steep cliff. Pairs, who stay together for several years, share nest duties. They incubate the egg for about 2 months, and feed the nestling for 6 months on regurgitated carrion. Chicks remain dependent on their parents for much longer, so condors can breed only once every 2 years, and even then successful breeding depends on a good food supply. Females are sexually mature at 8 years old, males at 6 years.

Main entry p. 288.

	March/April/May	June/July/August	Sept/Oct/Nov	Dec/Jan/Feb

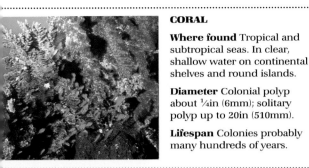

CORAL

Where found Tropical and subtropical seas. In clear, shallow water on continental shelves and round islands.

Diameter Colonial polyp about ¼in (6mm); solitary polyp up to 20in (510mm).

Lifespan Colonies probably many hundreds of years.

Individual polyps in a colony usually grow upward at a rate of up to ⅝in (16mm) a year. Each polyp has eight tentacles which it uses to catch microscopic animals carried in water currents. Most corals also use microscopic single-celled plants found in their soft tissues to supply them with essential nutrients. While the water is clear and warm, at 20-30°C (68-86°F), coral polyps divide by budding – producing small, identical versions of the parent. In this way the existing colony spreads. When the water is cool – but above 17°C (63°F) – and food is in shorter supply, the polyps may not bud as often. Corals also reproduce

sexually. Polyps release packages of mature eggs and sperm into the sea when the conditions are right and the water temperature suitable. The packages burst and the eggs and sperm fuse to form tiny mobile larvae. These are carried by currents and eventually settle on the seabed, where they transform into small versions of their parents and found a new colony. Spawning has been observed (often 4-5 nights after a full moon) off Australia's north-east coast December-January and off the north-west coast in March.

Main entry p. 269.

COSTA'S HUMMINGBIRD

Where found South-west USA and Mexico. Arid scrub areas.

Length 3in (75mm).

Weight 0.07oz (2g).

Lifespan Possibly up to 10 years.

The hummingbirds migrate northwards from Mexico to the Colorado Desert to feed on the nectar of desert flowers. Nests of leaves, plant down and lichen are built on bush limbs or yucca stems. A female lays 2 eggs that hatch after 2-3 weeks.

The mother regurgitates food for the nestlings. They are fledged at 3-4 weeks old. Even when temperatures rise above 38°C (100°F), the hummingbirds stay in the desert. Costa's is the only hummingbird species known to be able to survive without water.

The birds return south, to take advantage of the new growth of flowers there. They seem to like the nectar of red flowers best. The birds also take some small insects when feeding on flowers.

The hummingbirds spend the winter in their southern ranges. They have green and white plumage, but the male is distinguished by his iridescent violet crown and throat patches.

Main entry p. 65.

COYOTE (PRAIRIE WOLF)

Where found North America (except east); Central America. Prairies and open forest.

Head-and-body length 2ft 9in (840mm); tail 14in (360mm). **Shoulder height** 20in (510mm).

Weight 25-33lb (11.5-15kg).

Lifespan Up to 14½ years.

Females bear the first pups of the year in April, after a pregnancy of 9 weeks. Litters of 5-10 (but usually 6) pups are born blind and helpless in the den, and are suckled for 5-7 weeks. At first the male brings the female food, but later both parents hunt to feed the pups.

Successful at adapting to new conditions, coyotes have spread to deserts and suburbs. They eat almost anything, but most of their food is small mammals, such as rabbits, and carrion. They also eat snakes, insects, fruit, fish, frogs and garbage.

The first pups of the season, now 6-7 months old, leave their parents, and may wander up to 100 miles (160km) before taking up their own vigorously defended territories. They will be able to breed in the coming season.

Mating time is January-March. As pairs unite and mark territories with urine, the eerie call of high-pitched yelps and a long wail is heard more often. Coyotes usually hunt alone, but pursue prey such as deer in packs of 3-8.

No main entry, see p. 13.

CRABEATER SEAL

Where found Antarctic ice and nearby sea; occasionally off Australia, New Zealand, South Africa and South America.

Length Up to 8ft 6in (2.6m); male slightly smaller.

Weight Up to 500lb (225kg).

Lifespan 15 years.

Shrimp-like krill are the seals' main food. They also take small fish. Krill are caught mostly at night when near the surface. The seals suck in water and strain them out with their sieve-like cheek teeth. Seals fall prey to leopard seals, and often bear scars left by leopard seal teeth.

In the southern winter, the seals move north-wards as the pack ice expands. They stay mainly along the edge of the ice, and are rarely seen on land, although they are probably the most numerous of Antarctic seals. Males can breed at 4 years, females at 3 years.

The seal pups are born in September or early October, about 5ft (1.5m) long. They are suckled for about 4 weeks and a male waits nearby until the female is ready to mate again. She bites him on the head if she is not ready. Mating occurs on the ice in late spring.

The pack ice has shrunk, and from January to March, seals gather in the Ross Sea and west of Graham Land in their thousands. Adults moult in January, but still swim and feed. The coat tends to fade to off-white and is replaced by darker fur.

Main entry p. 224.

CROSSBILL, COMMON

Where found Europe; Asia; North America; North Africa. In coniferous woods.

Length 6½in (165mm).

Weight 2oz (57g).

Crossbills eat conifer seeds such as spruce, larch and pine, which grow inside cones that form in late summer. Their breeding season varies according to the seeds available and is longest in spruce forests, where they can breed as early as August and through to May. In pine forests the breeding season is usually December-April. Males defend breeding territories. After courtship and mating, a nest of twigs, grass and moss is built in which the female lays 3-4 eggs. She incubates them while the male brings her seeds. The eggs hatch after about two weeks, and the male is then hard pressed to feed all the family – a large

chick may need 3500 partially digested seeds a day. Young crossbills stay about 3 weeks in the nest, fed by both parents after the first week. They can extract seeds for themselves when 6-7 weeks old, but most are helped by their parents for some time after. By June nests are usually abandoned and the birds disperse. If the cone crop fails in an area, the crossbills are forced to make mass movements, called irruptions, to a better area, sometimes travelling long distances.

Main entry p. 16.

	March/April/May	June/July/August	Sept/Oct/Nov	Dec/Jan/Feb

CROWN-OF-THORNS STARFISH

Where found Indian and western Pacific oceans, from the East African coast to Hawaii. Coral reefs.

Diameter Average 12in (300mm); maximum 2ft (610mm).

Lifespan 8 years.

Starfish behaviour has little seasonal variation. The population size may vary in long-term cycles. When a starfish is ready to spawn, it produces several thousand tiny eggs each no bigger than the point of a pin. While the embryos are developing inside them, the eggs float free close to the sea surface. The larvae hatch from the eggs after about 4 days, and grow rapidly over the next 2-3 weeks. They then attach themselves to a firm surface on the seabed and develop into juveniles, each with five arms. The juveniles are 10 times larger than the eggs, but are still no bigger than a pinhead. During the next

5-6 months the juveniles graze on algae and other encrustations on the rock or coral on which they have settled. They develop 12 extra arms and grow to about ⅜in (10mm) long. After this they grow rapidly, attaining adult size and up to 4 more arms in the next 18-20 months. As adults they feed on coral polyps. At the age of 2 years, they are mature enough to breed, and the cycle begins anew.

Main entry p. 293.

CROWNED EAGLE

Where found Africa south of the Sahara. Among forests and wooded rocky hills.

Wingspan Male 7ft (2m); female 7ft 6in (2.3m).

Weight 7-8lb (3.2-3.6kg); female generally heaviest.

Lifespan About 14 years.

Crowned eagles spend much of the day soaring above the trees. They usually kill on the ground, but may snatch monkeys from forest trees with their great talons. In more open areas they feed mainly on hyraxes and small antelopes. Prey is eaten on the perch.

Most females lay July-October – up to a year after mating, which takes place on the nest after noisy aerobatic displays by the male. Pairs build or repair a nest of sticks and leaves high in a tree. They use the same nest from season to season, and it can become 10ft (3m) thick. The female lays 1-2 eggs and does most of the 7 weeks of incubation; her mate brings her food. The snow-white downy chicks are tended mostly by the hen but fed by both parents. If there are twin chicks, the larger chick kills the smaller one. A chick first flies at about 4 months, but is fed for another 9-11 months until it can hunt successfully.

Some East African eagles lay eggs in December or January. The eagles can normally breed only once every 2 years. Youngsters first breed at 4 years old, when their double crest has grown. A pair hunts over 4-10sq miles (10-25sq km).

Main entry p. 53.

DAMSELFLY, COMMON BLUE

Where found Temperate Eurasia and North America. Near water. One of 5000 species of dragon/damselfly.

Length 1¼in (32mm). **Wingspan** 1½in (38mm).

Lifespan Larva (nymph) 2-4 years; adult up to 1 year.

In spring, 2-4-year-old nymphs climb out of the water along plants and then cast their last larval skin to emerge as adults. They hunt midges and other small insects. In May, males chase after females and mate. Females lay eggs in plant tissue just below the water surface.

The eggs hatch and tiny wingless larvae burst from the tissue. They live in the water and hunt other small water creatures. As they grow they moult 15 times during 2 or 3 summers. They take larger prey such as tadpoles as they get bigger.

As the water cools in autumn, the larvae spend more time in the warm mud and among the roots of water plants at the bottom of rivers and ponds.

The larvae are less active in winter. During very cold weather they may remain buried in bottom sediment.

Main entry p. 109.

DESERT LOCUST

Where found Africa north of the central forests; Middle East; Indian subcontinent (except the far south); southern Spain; Portugal; southern Russia; central Asia.

Length Male about 2in (50mm); female up to 2½in (64mm).

During dry seasons, locusts are solitary and remain camouflaged in the dried grass. They do not eat much vegetation, surviving off fatty tissue which they stored during the last wet season. Eggs are laid in rainy seasons, when the soil is damp. They hatch after a period ranging from 10 days to 10 weeks, depending on temperature and humidity. Wingless nymphs, called hoppers, emerge from the eggs and continue to develop, moulting five times – the last time into solitary, camouflaged winged adults; it may be weeks or months before they can breed. In this solitary phase, the locusts are not particularly

evident. But if there is enough rain to provide plenty of fresh vegetation they breed quickly, and as numbers increase their behaviour changes. They start to congregate, and the emerging hoppers become brightly coloured. Swarms of winged adults and hordes of hoppers migrate in search of food, the adults breeding as they go. Adult swarms are carried by the prevailing winds – some may be carried out to sea and drowned, but others reach favourable feeding grounds. They do immense damage to crops.

Main entry p. 213.

DOLPHIN, COMMON

Where found Warm and temperate seas. Inshore and offshore waters.

Length Male up to 8ft 6in (2.6m); female up to 7ft 6in (2.3m).

Weight 165lb (75kg).

Lifespan Probably up to 50 years.

Although the common dolphin is one of the most widespread and numerous of dolphins, little is known about its life in the wild. The dolphins live in schools (herds) which may vary in size at different times of year according to the food available. They feed on squid and fish, especially fish that gather in shoals, such as sardines, which they follow. Dolphins in the Gulf of California follow sardine schools to the Baja California coast in late spring, and by August the dolphins have congregated in the cooler waters of the Canal de Ballenas there. Off Gibraltar in the western Mediterranean in summer, huge dolphin

schools follow migrating tunny through the Strait into the Atlantic. In late October, when the sardines are spawning off the mainland coast of the Gulf of California, the dolphins follow and feed on them. Dolphins probably breed all year round, with peaks in spring and summer. Females are pregnant for 10-11 months, and babies, about 2ft 9in (840mm) long at birth, are suckled for about 18 months. Youngsters are generally ready to breed once they are around 6ft (1.8m) long and about 6 years old or more.

Main entry p. 174.

	March/April/May	June/July/August	Sept/Oct/Nov	Dec/Jan/Feb

DORMOUSE, COMMON

Where found Europe (not Ireland, Denmark, Iberia) Russia; Asia Minor. Coarse vegetation and hedgerows.

Head-and-bodylength 3-3½in (75-90mm); tail 2½in (64mm).

Weight ½-1½oz (14-43g).

Lifespan 4-6 years.

As spring temperatures rise, dormice come out of hibernation and begin to feed at night on insects, catkins, buds and flowers. In cold years they may not emerge until late spring. Mating begins in late April, and litters of 2-7 babies are born 3-4 weeks later.

Youngsters stay in the nest for a month. It is made of woven grasses in tangled vegetation among bushes or trees, or in a hollow tree trunk or branch. Only the female tends the young. They are independent at 6-8 weeks old. In a good summer some females produce a second litter.

Last litters are born in October. Dormice fatten on hazel nuts, fruit, hips, haws and seeds. They make hibernation nests of thickly woven grass, usually at the base of a bush such as a hazel, or among tree roots. As temperatures begin to fall, the dormice hibernate.

The dormice hibernate throughout the winter. The first phase of their hibernation is usually the deepest. They may waken on warm days, but quickly hibernate again when they can find nothing to eat.

Main entry p. 227.

DRAGONFLY, SOUTHERN HAWKER

Where found Europe; North Africa; northern Asia. Near water. One of 5000 species of dragonfly/damselfly.

Length 2-2¾in (50-70mm).

Wingspan 4in (100mm)

Lifespan Larva 2 years; adult 2-3 months.

About April, larvae (or nymphs) hatch from eggs laid last summer on water plants in stagnant pools or slow-moving streams. The larvae live in the water, where there are also larvae that hatched the previous spring. They hunt small water insects, pond snails and shrimps.

In June, larvae in their second summer climb from the water and hang on a plant while their skin splits. From this an adult emerges and flies off, to hunt for insect prey. Adults return to the waterside in July to mate, then females lay eggs on water plants, just below the surface.

In October the last adults die, but the larvae live on in the water. Nearly 2in (50mm) long, they are greenish-brown with six legs, and they obtain oxygen by drawing water through gills in the body. They can shoot away fast from danger by rapidly ejecting jets of water.

The larvae continue to hunt during the winter, sheltering among water plants or on the bottom of the pond or stream. They capture their prey with two hooked fangs that shoot forward on a hinged mask from the lower lip.

Main entry p. 136.

DUCK-BILLED PLATYPUS

Where found Eastern Australia; Kangaroo Island (South Australia); Tasmania. In quiet waterways.

Head-and-body length 20in (510mm); tail 5in (125mm).

Weight Male 2-5lb (1-2.3kg); female half as heavy.

Lifespan More than 10 years.

The platypuses feed on bottom-dwelling water creatures such as crayfish, freshwater shrimps and insect larvae. In Tasmania, young platypuses emerge from their nest burrows about 2 months later than those on the mainland.

The breeding season starts in August. Mating takes place in water. The female's mammary glands grow until they cover her belly. She prepares a river-bank nest at the end of a long burrow, lining it with leaves or grass she drags there in the crook of her curled tail.

In September the female lays 2-3 eggs in the nest and incubates them for about a week, curling her tail round them. Her milk begins to flow when the eggs hatch, maybe 10 days later. The ½in (13mm) babies suck it from her fur. They stay in the burrow while she forages for food.

By late January-March the youngsters are almost full grown. They are let out of the burrow 14 weeks after hatching, and stay with their mother for 2 weeks until they are fully weaned. Then they are able to fend for themselves.

Main entry p. 183.

DUGONG★★

Where found Indian Ocean; Persian Gulf; western Pacific Ocean. In shallow coastal waters.

Length 8-13ft (2.4-4m).

Weight 550-770lb (250-350kg).

Lifespan Up to 70 years.

One known seasonal activity of dugongs occurs in Shark Bay, Western Australia, in March. As the southern autumn begins, the dugongs there move some 100 miles (160km) from their summer feeding grounds on the east side of the bay to winter in the west. Dugongs graze on marine grasses, which grow prolifically all year in their tropical habitats. With such a constant supply of good food, the numbers of dugong populations are believed to remain fairly constant throughout the year. Females give birth to calves at any time of year, after a pregnancy lasting 13 months. Calves are suckled for up to 18 months, but from 4 months old start to take increasing amounts of grass. They stay with their mother for at least 2 years. Females generally calve at intervals of 3-7 years. In Australia, most calves are born September-December. At birth they are 3-4ft (1-1.2m) long and weigh 44-77lb (20-35kg).

Main entry p. 80.

EASTERN (AMERICAN) TENT CATERPILLAR

Where found South-east Canada; eastern USA. Mainly on cherry trees.

Length Caterpillar up to 2¼in (57mm); moth 1½in (38mm).

Wingspan 1-1½in (25-38mm).

Lifespan Caterpillar about 3 months; moth about a week.

Caterpillars hatch from batches of eggs laid on twigs and then spin a communal 'tent' in which to hide. They eat their egg cases and later leave the tent by day to feed on leaves. Some are taken by ants and birds, despite their bristly hairs, warning colour, and repellent vomit.

The caterpillars are fully grown by early summer, and in July they pupate, each spinning an oval silk cocoon in which to turn into an adult moth. Adults emerge and mate. In late July, female moths lay bands of 300-400 eggs round cherry twigs. All the adults soon die.

The eggs of the tent moth overwinter on the twigs. Although the band round the twig is bark coloured for camouflage, many eggs are eaten by birds.

Tent moths belong to the species *Malacosoma* (of the eggar family). They are yellow or reddish-brown and have plump, furry bodies, short – often scalloped – wings, and only rudimentary mouthparts, so cannot feed. Their eyesight is also poor.

Main entry p. 154.

	March/April/May	June/July/August	Sept/Oct/Nov	Dec/Jan/Feb

ECHIDNA, SHORT-NOSED or COMMON (SPINY ANTEATER)

Where found Australia; central and south New Guinea. Most habitats from deserts to permanent snows.

Length 12-21in (300-530mm).

Weight 5½-13lb (2.5-6kg).

Lifespan More than 50 years.

Adult echidnas spend their time on their own. At dawn and dusk they forage for ants and termites, but in cold weather may come out at midday, or in hot weather at night. When not feeding they shelter in places such as thick vegetation, crevices or hollow logs.

The breeding season is the only time that adult echidnas can be found together. Up to six males may pursue one female, and 9-27 days after mating, a female lays 1 egg into her pouch. The baby hatches after 10 days and stays in the pouch. In snowy areas, echidnas hibernate.

A mother echidna pushes her baby out of her pouch when she feels its developing spines start to prickle. She leaves it hidden in a burrow. The youngsters born the previous year become independent. With the coming of spring, hibernating echidnas emerge.

The infant echidna feeds on its mother's milk for 3 months, and stays with her throughout the first year of its life.

Main entry p. 202.

EGRET, INTERMEDIATE

Where found Asia from India to Japan; Australia; Africa except north and south-west. Near fresh water.

Length 2ft 2in-2ft 4in (660-710mm).

Weight About 2lb (0.9kg).

Lifespan Possibly 20 years.

Breeding can be at any time of year, typically towards the end of the rains, when prey is plentiful. In Sri Lanka, breeding is well under way in April. The birds nest in trees (often with other water birds), in colonies of up to 1000 flimsy nests of twigs lined with grass.

In northern India, breeding time is July-September. Females lay 3-4 smooth, pale green eggs. Both parent birds incubate them for 3-4 weeks. Youngsters leave the nest after 3 weeks, but are not fully fledged for another 2 weeks.

In southern India, courting displays are under way. Nesting begins in November. Males defend a small territory and display the long black tail fan that is part of their breeding plumage. They also flap their wings, clatter or snap with their long beaks and shake twigs.

In the dry season, egrets disperse or migrate to find water. They often form small flocks of up to 50, and feed by day on prey such as fish, frogs, insects and shrimps, taken in shallow water or on nearby pastures after patient stalking.

Main entry p. 193.

ELEPHANT, AFRICAN★

Where found Africa south of the Sahara. Forest, grassland.

Length Male 20ft-24ft 6in (6-7.5m); female smaller.

Shoulder height Male 10-11ft (3-3.4m)

Weight Male 6 tons; female 4 tons.

Lifespan 55-60 years.

During the rainy season, elephants feed in the open grassland. Most females conceive during this time of plenty, and bulls compete with each other to mate with receptive females – who are in heat for only a few days every 3-5 years. The wet season occurs at different times throughout the elephant's range. In the north the rains are generally April-October and in the south October-April. Near the Equator there are two wet seasons each year (for example, on the Serengeti Plain March-May and October-December). Females have one of the longest pregnancies of any land mammal – 22 months. They bear single calves

weighing about 250lb (115kg), and suckle them for about 3 years – often into their next pregnancy. Elephants are now largely confined to national parks and reserves. They live in herds of 4-16, comprising mothers, calves and immature animals of both sexes. Mature bulls are mainly solitary, travelling from herd to herd after receptive females at mating time. Young bulls join bachelor herds at about 12 years old. In the dry season, elephants move to wooded areas to feed on trees. In the heat of the day they rest in the shade.

Main entry p. 257.

ELEPHANT SEAL, NORTHERN

Where found Eastern side of northern Pacific Ocean.

Length Male up to 20ft (6m); female averages 10ft (3m).

Weight Male up to 2¼ tons; female up to ⅞ ton.

Lifespan 14 years.

The seals rest on land and shed their winter coats. Then they make their way out to sea to feed on squid. They travel north as far as the south of Alaska.

Most of the time the seals are far out at sea. Females and youngsters sometimes come ashore to rest. Bulls rarely do. Elephant seals are the deepest diving of all seal species. They commonly feed on fish and squid living at a depth of about 1320ft (400m), but sometimes go as deep as 4920ft (1500m).

The seals come ashore to breed and moult on islands off the coast of California/Mexico. Males fight for dominance. Females give birth to calves conceived 10-11 months earlier, and are ready to mate after 4 weeks of suckling them.

Main entry p. 250.

EMPEROR PENGUIN

Where found Antarctic seas. Breeds on the sea ice around Antarctica.

Height 2ft 8in-3ft 9in (810-1140mm).

Weight Up to 90lb (40kg).

Lifespan May reach 20 years.

The penguins leave the sea and migrate across the sea ice, sometimes for long distances – up to 60 miles (97km) – to their breeding sites, generally sheltered by an ice cliff. They congregate for a brief period of courtship, and mating follows.

In June, the female lays a single egg. The male balances it on his feet and incubates it for 6 weeks in temperatures of −20°C (−4°F) while the female goes to sea to feed. She returns as the chick hatches and the male goes to sea. He returns after 6 weeks to feed the chick.

In October the chicks gather in crèches while both parents bring back food. In November, the chicks begin migrating to the edge of the ice, and wait in groups for it to break up with the approach of summer. Chicks and adults all moult as they drift northwards on ice floes.

By December, the ice floes have melted and moulting is complete. The young penguins take to the water and fend for themselves. The birds can dive to depths of up to 870ft (265m) to catch squid and fish.

Main entry p. 166.

	March/April/May	June/July/August	Sept/Oct/Nov	Dec/Jan/Feb

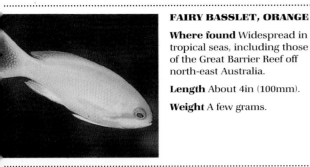

FAIRY BASSLET, ORANGE

Where found Widespread in tropical seas, including those of the Great Barrier Reef off north-east Australia.

Length About 4in (100mm).

Weight A few grams.

On the Great Barrier Reef, the basslets live on the outer slopes where the water is clear and there are currents flowing. They also live around the heads of corals on the landward side of the reef. Basslets live in shoals and feed on plankton (minute sea animals and plants). In each shoal there are only one or two males – the other basslets are all females. If the shoal's males are eaten by larger fish, or the shoal gets too large, the dominant female changes into a male. At other times the male basslets continually harass the oldest females to stop them from changing sex. Spawning time is in November and December. At dusk, the males court the females, displaying with dorsal (back) fins erect and pushing their snouts against a female's abdomen. When a pair is ready to spawn, they swim to the surface and away from the reef. The female secretes a substance that stimulates the male to produce milt (sperm), then releases thousands of eggs as the male releases his milt. The pair dive back to the safety of the reef and the eggs drift in open water, away from the reef's many predators. The eggs hatch into females.

Main entry p. 294.

FAIRY PENGUIN (LITTLE/ BLUE PENGUIN)

Where found Southern Australia and New Zealand. In inshore waters.

Height 15in (380mm).

Weight 2-4lb (0.9-1.8kg).

Lifespan 11 years or more.

In March a few late-breeding birds are still at their nests on offshore islands, but by April all the penguins are at sea, feeding on small fish and small squid.

The first breeding birds come ashore in June in New Zealand and July in Australia. They nest in shallow burrows below tussocks or rocks, or occasionally under houses. A month later each female lays 2 eggs, and these hatch after 6 weeks.

The first chicks hatch in September, and remain in the nest for about 8 weeks. Both parents feed them in shifts. Older chicks wait at the burrow mouth to be fed. In November the first chicks leave for the sea, but some late-breeding females may only just be laying their eggs.

Some females lay second clutches as late as February, and the chicks hatched from them do not leave the nest until April. At this time the breeding season is all but over and the adults and young go to sea.

Main entry p. 246.

FAIRY TERN (WHITE TERN)

Where found All oceans and islands throughout the tropics.

Length 12-13in (300-330mm).

Weight 4-5oz (113-140g).

Except when breeding, fairy terns remain at sea feeding on fish, squid and crustaceans such as shrimps and crabs. They breed on isolated islands where there are few predators, but in the Seychelles many fall prey to barn owls – introduced in the 1950s to reduce the rat population. Birds may breed every 10 months, and somewhere within their range, fairy terns are breeding during every month of the year. They probably pair for life. Pairs mate after elaborate, noisy displays. The female lays a single egg, coloured to blend with its surroundings, in a slight hollow on a tree branch, coral boulder or coral cliff ledge. Both parents incubate the egg in turns for 5 weeks. The chick has strong feet and claws to enable it to cling to its precarious perch. Its down and first plumage are speckled to provide camouflage. The parents bring small fish for the chick to eat. It fledges after about 2 months, but the parents continue to tend it for several more weeks. It may be more than 4 years old before it breeds.

Main entry p. 280.

FALLOW DEER

Where found Europe; introduced to Africa, Australia, North and South America. Open woodland.

Length 4ft 6in (1.4m).

Shoulder height Male 3ft (1m); female 2ft 7in (790mm).

Weight Up to 227lb (103kg).

Lifespan 10-15 years.

European males cast their antlers and begin to grow new ones that are covered with velvety skin. They tend to live in separate herds from the females. Most of the females are 5-7 months pregnant. The deer feed mainly on sweet grasses, rushes and foliage from bushes and trees.

Males shed the velvet on their antlers, which are fully grown by August. All deer have summer coats by mid-June. Single fawns, maybe twins, are born June-November. For a few days they stay hidden in long grass or bracken, then follow their mother to the female herd.

Males aggressively defend their territory during the rut in October and November. They mate with as many females as possible. Young males may rejoin female groups to avoid the aggression. The deer fatten on acorns and other seeds and fruits.

The deer have darker, thicker winter coats, which started to grow in late September or October. The mature males are usually in poor condition after the rut, and the weaker ones die in severe winters.

Main entry p. 135.

FAT-TAILED DUNNART

Where found Southern Australia. In open woodland, shrubland and grassland.

Head-and-body length 4-6in (100-150mm); tail 8in (200mm).

Weight ½oz (14g).

Lifespan 18 months.

Dunnarts are normally solitary, but during autumn groups huddle together to keep warm. When food is scarce they live off fat stored in their long tails.

June – mid-winter – is the start of the breeding season. Females are pregnant for about two weeks. The newborn young (usually 6-10) attach themselves to teats in their mother's pouch. Generally only 5 youngsters survive, and are weaned at about 10 weeks old.

The youngsters from the first litter become independent. Females often have a second litter in late spring or early summer – after October.

During high summer there are plenty of grasshoppers and other insects for the newly independent youngsters to eat. They are able to breed at 6 months old, but do not usually do so until winter.

Main entry p. 202.

	March/April/May	June/July/August	Sept/Oct/Nov	Dec/Jan/Feb

FIDDLER CRAB

Where found Widely distributed on shores and in coastal waters.

Width of carapace (shell) ⅝-⅞in (16-22mm).

Weight ¼-½oz (7-14g).

Lifespan Probably 3-5 years.

Fiddler crabs (there are 62 species) belong to the ghost crab family. The males have one exceptionally large claw, used for signalling or in ritual combat. The life of the fiddler crab has daily and monthly rather than seasonal rhythms, largely due to the tides. It is generally active around dawn and dusk, and most active at those times of the month when the highest and lowest tides coincide with dawn and dusk. The crab is solitary, feeding on organic debris in the mud exposed at low tide. At high tide, or when the temperature is too high, it retreats to a deep burrow in the mud above the tide line. Most species

are darker in colour by day and lighter at night. Fiddler crabs are preyed on by shore birds such as the yellow-crowned night heron. The crabs mate at the mouth of the female's burrow or inside the male's burrow. When the fertilised eggs have developed, the female shakes them from her body into the water where they hatch (some immediately) into minute larvae. They spend the early part of their lives as zooplankton (minute sea animals), moulting several times before they change into adult form.

Main entry p. 277.

FISH EAGLE, AFRICAN

Where found Africa south of the Sahara. Near coasts or inland water.

Length 2ft 8in (810mm).
Wingspan Male 6ft 3in (1.9m); female 7ft 9in (2.3m).

Weight Male 5lb (2.3kg); female 7lb (3.2kg).

Lifespan 10-15 years.

The fish eagles are common near many African waterways, although pollution from pesticides is reducing their numbers. Pairs often stay together outside the breeding season, but are usually well dispersed. Where food is plentiful, each pair has a relatively small territory centred on a suitable nest site in tall trees near the water, with lookout posts close to their preferred fishing grounds. Fish eagles rarely settle on the ground. They feed mostly on fish, but may also take small rodents, amphibians and birds. The breeding season varies in different parts of Africa. North of the tropics breeding is generally in

October and November, but on the Equator it is from June to September. Just to the south of the Equator the birds generally breed in May and June, but the season extends from March to September farther south. Female African fish eagles lay 1-3 white eggs, which hatch after 6-7 weeks. Youngsters fly at 9-11 weeks. There are few signs of seasonal migration, but some birds in the drier areas close to the Sahara may extend their range into the desert during the rains, when the gullies become full of water.

Main entry p. 120.

FISHING CAT

Where found Indian subcontinent; South-east Asia. Among forest swamps and marshes.

Head-and-body length 2ft 4in-3ft 3in (710-990mm); tail 12in (300mm).

Weight Up to 33lb (15kg).

Little is known about the life and habits of the elusive fishing cat. The animals probably live alone or in pairs. Females give birth after a pregnancy of 9 weeks, a litter of 1-4 kittens being born probably in a lair beaten out among long, dense grass or reeds. Births probably occur at the beginning of the wet season, when food is most plentiful, but the wet season occurs at different times throughout the animal's range. In some parts, however, it is wet all the year round – in Sumatra and Java, for example. The cats are opportunist hunters, and despite their name do not feed entirely on fish. They also take small

mammals (such as mice), lizards, birds, insects, and freshwater molluscs (such as snails), but in a dry season may often go hungry. A fishing cat uses its partially webbed forefeet to scoop prey from the water as it crouches on a rock or overhanging bank, or stands at the water's edge. It does not mind entering the water, and is a good swimmer.

Main entry p. 162.

FLAMINGO, LESSER

Where found Africa. Chiefly in the soda lakes of the Great Rift Valley.

Length 3ft 2in (970mm).
Wingspan 3ft-3ft 3in (910-990mm).

Weight About 4½lb (2kg).

Lifespan Up to 25 years.

Chicks in crèches have already fledged (at 9-13 weeks), and have grey plumage. They stay in the crèche until 3 or 4 months old, then join the vast numbers of flamingos that, each night at dusk, migrate to and from different lakes to find good feeding grounds.

All year round, flamingos feed on tiny water plants such as algae, and also on tiny fly larvae and shrimps. Food is filtered from the water through the flamingo's beak. Young flamingos do not develop pink plumage until at least 2-3 years old – about the age that they start to breed.

Breeding may occur at any time of year, but peaks after rains. Many birds start breeding displays in October or November. After mating they build mud nests in huge colonies on shores and mud banks of soda lakes. Nests are mounds some 12in (300mm) high, to be clear of the water.

Both parents incubate the 1 egg (rarely 2) for 1 month. Chicks stay in the nest 1 week; both parents feed them red 'milk' regurgitated from the crop. When the chicks leave the nest, they gather in crèches of tens of thousands.

Main entry p. 50.

FLYING FOX, BLACK

Where found North and north-east Australian coast; Sulawesi (formerly Celebes) in Indonesia; New Guinea. In rain forests.

Length 10in (250mm).
Wingspan Up to 4ft 4in (1.3m).

Weight Up to 1½lb (700g).

Males establish their territories at the start of the mating season. They occupy one part of a tree and see off rivals. Before they mate, the bats spend a lot of time grooming and displaying themselves to attract the attention of females. Mating peaks in April.

Throughout the year, the bats roost by day in large colonies on trees in coastal rain forests, especially dense mangroves. At night they fly up to 30 miles (50km) inland to feed. Their favourite food is eucalypt blossom, but they also eat soft fruit.

Females give birth to one baby about 6 months after mating. Births peak in October. A baby bat is well developed at birth, but cannot fly. At first it is carried all the time by its mother, then left to roost on a branch. The youngsters from the previous year become sexually mature.

Young bats make their first flight when they are about 3 months old. In Australia it is summer, and there is plenty of food for them in the form of blossom and fruit.

Main entry p. 241.

	March/April/May	June/July/August	Sept/Oct/Nov	Dec/Jan/Feb

FOWLER'S TOAD

Where found Eastern USA.

Length 2-5in (50-125mm); male smaller than female.

Weight About ½oz (14g).

Lifespan Up to 15 years.

Toads gather in shallow ditches, creeks, and pools to mate, especially on wet nights. Males clasp females, fertilising the eggs as they are laid in tangled strings of up to 25,000 eggs. Within a week, the eggs hatch into dark olive tadpoles that feed on green algae on the rocks and mud.

When the tadpoles are about 1in (25mm) long, they transform into toadlets. By June most have left the pond to live in damp vegetation close by. Many toadlets are eaten by herons and garter snakes.

By now, the adult toads are living well away from their breeding ponds in grassland, scrub, woods or farmland. They come out at night to catch flying insects, spiders, centipedes and even scorpions on their long tongues. In towns, some feed on insects attracted by street lights.

In warmer areas, the first males return to breeding ponds in February, and begin calling to attract females. Females select a mate by the depth and rapidity of the calls, which can also scare off competing males – fights are rare.

Main entry p. 87.

FRIGATE BIRD, MAGNIFICENT

Where found Tropical and subtropical oceans, coasts and islands.

Length 3ft-3ft 8in (1-1.1m).
Wingspan 6ft 4in-7ft 4in (1.9-2.2m).

Weight Male up to 2¼lb (1kg); female 25 per cent larger.

These large, acrobatic seabirds live near coasts, but rarely alight on the water because their plumage soon gets waterlogged. The birds have the largest wing area for their weight of any bird, and soar magnificently. They snatch prey from the ground or water surface while on the wing, taking flying fish, squid, fish, green turtle hatchlings and chicks (even untended frigate bird chicks). Frigate birds are also known as man-of-war birds – pirates – because they chase other birds, particularly boobies, and force them to regurgitate food, which they snatch as it falls. Frigate birds breed only once every two years,

but may breed at any time of year. At mating time males develop a bright red throat sac which they inflate to the size of a man's head to attract a mate. A mating pair raise their beaks, spread their wings, and gurgle to each other. The male's sac does not deflate and fade until the hen lays her single white egg in a rough nest of twigs in a tree. The pair incubate the egg for 6-9 weeks. Both feed the chick on regurgitated food for about 7 weeks. The chick flies at 5 months old, but is fed at times for a few weeks more.

No main entry, see p. 200.

FRILLED LIZARD

Where found Northern Australia and New Guinea. Open woods and forests.

Length About 3ft (1m); frill almost 12in (300mm) across.

Lifespan Probably 50 years.

As the hot, wet summer ends, frilled lizards may take longer to warm up in the mornings, so they extend their neck frill, which is well supplied with blood vessels, to soak up heat.

During the dry winter, frilled lizards may be inactive for long periods to conserve energy and moisture. At this time they need little food.

In spring the lizards mate, and a month later the females lay 6-10 soft-shelled eggs in a hole dug in damp soil. The eggs may increase in weight as water is taken in through the shell, and lose weight in dry conditions. Independent youngsters hatch 4-6 weeks later.

It is the hot, wet season, when frilled lizards are most active, feeding on insects and small mammals such as mice and possums as well as on chicks and eggs.

Main entry p. 243.

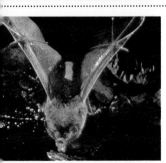

FRINGE-LIPPED BAT

Where found The Americas from southern Mexico to Brazil, including Trinidad. Tropical rain forests.

Length 3-3½in (75-90mm).
Wingspan About 9in (230mm).

Weight 1¼oz (35g).

Throughout the year the bats, named for their wart-studded lips, hunt small mudpuddle frogs, which average only 1¼in (32mm) long. Hunting activity peaks at the start of the rains – in April in Panama, for example. The bats home in on the frogs' calls, ignoring the calls of nearby poisonous toads. On a moonless night, when the frogs cannot see the flying bats, the bats catch about 6 frogs an hour. Fringe-lipped bats have hearing especially sensitive to two sound frequencies – the ultrasonic frequency into which their own echolocation system is tuned, and the lower frequency of the frogs' calls. As well as

eating mudpuddle frogs, the bats also eat small animals such as lizards, and possibly a small amount of fruit. When not hunting, they roost in hollows low down in large tree trunks and in caves. The breeding season probably varies in different parts of the bats' range. Pregnant females and mothers with young have been found in different places from February to December.

No main entry, see p. 99.

FROG, COMMON

Where found Europe from northern Scandinavia to northern Spain; Siberia. Damp places not far from water.

Length 3½-4in (90-100mm).

Lifespan Up to 10 years; 12 years in captivity.

In early spring frogs gather in water to mate and spawn. Females lay masses of floating, jelly-covered eggs. Tadpoles hatch 2-3 weeks later, and feed on algae and debris filtered from the water. Adult frogs leave the water in about April. By 7 weeks old, the tadpoles have hind legs.

Tadpoles develop front legs, absorb their tails and leave their ponds as tiny froglets. Together with the adults, they often live in long, wet grass and feed on prey such as tiny insects, spiders and snails.

Females begin to develop their eggs in autumn. As the weather gets colder, the frogs hibernate. Males often return to their ponds to hibernate in the bottom mud, but females and froglets hibernate on land in hollows and under stones or logs.

The frogs remain in hibernation throughout the winter. In February, or when the weather is warm enough, females (and any males that hibernated on land) return to the water to breed. Frogs first breed at about 2-3 years old.

Main entry p. 44.

		March/April/May	June/July/August	Sept/Oct/Nov	Dec/Jan/Feb

FULMAR

Where found North Atlantic and north Pacific Oceans, except polar areas. Breeds on coasts.

Length 17-20in (430-510mm).

Weight 2½lb (1.1kg).

Lifespan Up to 25 years.

March/April/May: Coastal breeding colonies peak in size, with up to 80,000 birds in some. Courting pairs make cackling calls. In May, just before the eggs are laid, many birds desert the colony and go to sea for a while to feed. The female lays 1 egg on a bare cliff ledge or in a slight hollow.

June/July/August: Egg-laying continues. Male and female take turns to incubate the large white egg in shifts of 4-5 days while the other feeds out at sea. The egg hatches after 8 weeks, and the chick is fed on regurgitated, half-digested fish once a day by either parent for up to 7 weeks.

Sept/Oct/Nov: After breeding, the birds disperse to spend their time at sea. They are solitary and rarely come to land. However, large numbers may gather at fishing vessels to feed on offal. Young birds fend for themselves, and do not breed until they are 6 years old or more.

Dec/Jan/Feb: The birds begin to gather at the coastal breeding sites in late winter, their numbers building up gradually into the spring. Activity is 'low-key', with much visiting of neighbours and displaying.

No main entry, see p. 132.

GALÁPAGOS GIANT TORTOISE★★

Where found Galápagos Islands, Pacific Ocean; there are about 10 different races.

Length of carapace (shell) Male 4ft (1.2m) or more.

Weight Male up to 600lb (272kg); female 300lb (136kg).

Lifespan Probably 100 years.

March/April/May: On some islands, the tortoises are courting and mating. This takes place from January to August, depending on the race. The tortoises may wallow and mate in mud pools.

June/July/August: Egg-laying is from June to December, depending on the race. A female seeks a dry, lowland area and digs a shallow pit in which she lays 6-11 eggs, each about 2in (50mm) across, and covers them. She often lays in the same place each year. Females on Santa Cruz may lay twice in a year.

Sept/Oct/Nov: Galápagos tortoises sleep for about 16 hours in 24 throughout the year. They forage by day on vegetation. Those with dome-shaped shells feed on low-growing grass and shrubs, and those with saddle-shaped shells and long necks browse on taller plants.

Dec/Jan/Feb: Eggs hatch 6 months after they were laid. The hatchlings have to break out of the hard covering of dried mud on top of the nest. Eggs or young may fall prey to rats, cats and pigs, all introduced by man. As a result, the species is endangered.

Main entry p. 56.

GALÁPAGOS HAWK★

Where found Galápagos Islands, Pacific Ocean. In the arid coastal lowlands especially.

Length About 22in (560mm).
Wingspan Up to 4ft (1.2m).

Weight 1½-2¼lb (0.7-1kg).

Lifespan Possibly up to 25 years.

March/April/May: Except in drought years, courting and mating begins once the January-May rainy period has brought a flush of food to the islands' arid coastal regions. The hawks hover or glide in search of food such as young birds, lizards (especially iguanas), rats, centipedes and carrion.

June/July/August: A female may mate with up to 4 males, who often help to raise the young. Courting birds scream noisily. The female lays 1-2 eggs in a large nest of sticks (used year after year) on a tree or rocky outcrop. About 4 weeks after laying, downy white chicks hatch from the eggs.

Sept/Oct/Nov: Adults guarding a nest are strongly territorial, diving at intruding humans or predators and screaming loudly. Nevertheless, some chicks fall prey to feral cats. The youngsters leave the nest at about 8 weeks old.

Dec/Jan/Feb: During the hotter season from February to April, some birds may still be breeding. Young birds wander in search of mates, but pairs and family groupings of a female with two or more males stay together throughout the year.

Main entry p. 145.

GANG GANG COCKATOO

Where found South-east Australia. In mountain forests and heavily wooded lowlands.

Length About 14in (360mm).

Lifespan Possibly 30 years.

March/April/May: In the southern autumn, flocks of up to 100 birds gather to feed on nuts and berries. In May, late autumn, the cockatoos begin to come down from the mountains to search for food in the warmer lower valleys, coastal regions and gardens.

June/July/August: During winter, the cockatoos stay in the lower, warmer regions feeding on nuts, berries and other fruit.

Sept/Oct/Nov: In spring birds return to the mountains to breed. Females lay 2 or 3 eggs in holes in eucalypt trees, and both parents incubate them for 4-5 weeks.

Dec/Jan/Feb: The chicks leave the nest 7 weeks after hatching, but are fed by their parents for another 4-6 weeks.

Main entry p. 121.

GANNET, AUSTRALASIAN

Where found Southern oceans. Breeds on small islands off Tasmania, Victoria (Australia) and New Zealand, and at Cape Kidnappers on New Zealand's North Island.

Length 3ft (1m).

Wingspan Up to 6ft 6in (2m).

Weight About 5½lb (2.5kg).

March/April/May: Newly fledged birds from New Zealand fly across the Tasman Sea to the coasts of southern and eastern Australia, where they stay until ready to breed at about 5 years of age. Adult birds remain in the seas around New Zealand.

June/July/August: Gannets catch fish by diving into the water at a shallow angle, or by plunge-diving from 100ft (30m). The birds moult. Immature speckled brown birds 3-5 years old acquire new white feathers during the moult. Breeding adults have white plumage.

Sept/Oct/Nov: The birds nest in huge colonies. A female lays 1 egg during October or November. Both parents take turns to incubate the egg for 6-7 weeks, and both then feed the youngster, which is black-skinned and has fluffy white down by a month old.

Dec/Jan/Feb: The young gannets are able to fly after 15 weeks. They explore the area around their nesting grounds, picking up geographical clues to the site to help in their return 4 or 5 years later.

Main entry p. 244.

		March/April/May	June/July/August	Sept/Oct/Nov	Dec/Jan/Feb

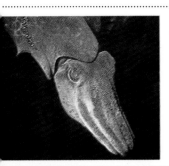

GIANT CUTTLEFISH

Where found Australian coasts.

Length Up to 5ft (1.5m) (from tip of body to tip of outstretched tentacle).

Male and female cuttlefish court and mate. Rival males raise two arms in front in an aggressive display. When mating, male and female entangle arms and the male uses a tentacle to pass a sperm package to his mate. Waves of changing colour pass along their bodies.

In August, the female cuttlefish move inshore from deeper water to spawn. Each female lays 100-300 white, grape-sized eggs among soft coral or seaweed. The eggs are covered with a protective camouflage of ink and guarded for a few hours.

The hatchlings are just ½in (13mm) long and miniature replicas of their parents. They drift with the zooplankton (tiny animals) for a short time and then are able to jet around. Cuttlefish feed on prey such as crabs, prawns and fish, and are preyed on by sharks and dolphins.

Cuttlefish move by jet propulsion, squirting water from a built-in siphon that can be swivelled to change direction and dilated or closed to control speed. They can move slowly by flapping the 'skirt' of skin round the body.

Main entry p. 183.

GIANT (BRAZILIAN) OTTER★★

Where found Northern and central South America. Slow streams and shallow creeks.

Head-and-body length 3ft-4ft (1-1.2m); tail 17-26in (430-660mm).

Weight Up to 66lb (30kg).

Lifespan Up to 12 years.

These large otters spend less time on land than other otters; their large, flat feet make them poor walkers. They usually live in family groups of 3-8 – a breeding pair and 1 or 2 litters. The pair have several small, waterside territories, which they clear of vegetation and mark with scent, urine and dung. Active by day, the otters mostly hunt fish, especially small piranhas 4-16in (100-400mm) long and small catfish. Like all otters, they catch fish with their powerful jaws and hold them between their forepaws to eat. Their life is governed by the rise and fall of the water. At high water in the Amazon Basin (April-September),

the otters fish in the flooded forests. As the waters recede, the animals may form groups of 10-20 to feast on the abundant fish concentrated in the dwindling waters. The females are pregnant for 10 weeks, and annual litters of 1-5 (but usually 2) kits are born in river-bank dens, which often have underwater entrances. Breeding seems to occur at any time of year, but mating and births may be timed to coincide with the annual time of plenty – low water.

No main entry, see p. 263.

GIRAFFE

Where found Africa south of the Sahara. Grassland and open woodlands.

Head-and-body length Male up to 15ft 6in (4.7m); tail 3ft (1m). **Overall height** Male up to 17ft (5m); female 15ft (4.6m).

Weight Male up to 1.7 tons.

Lifespan About 25 years.

Giraffes browse mainly at dawn and dusk on the leaves and shoots of trees such as acacia and mimosa. Their long necks – nearly half of their total height – allow them to reach high into the trees. Because of their different heights, males and females browse at different levels, so do not compete for food. In a dry season giraffes can still find food among high foliage beside rivers and streams, so are able to breed at any time of the year. But mating tends to be timed so that females will give birth just before the onset of a rainy season. The mother will then be able to find plenty of food and produce rich milk for the calf. The

times of rainy seasons vary throughout the giraffe's range. In the Masai Mara Reserve and the Serengeti Plain in southern Kenya and northern Tanzania the wet seasons are March-May and October-December. Females give birth at traditional calving grounds after a 15-month pregnancy. Giraffes are sexually mature at 3-5 years old, and females can give birth every 17-20 months. Giraffes have few predators apart from man, but may be caught by lions when they spread their forelegs to drink.

Main entry p. 210.

GOLDEN TOAD★★

Where found North-west Costa Rica. In the Monteverde cloud forest among the Tilaran Mountains.

Length Up to 1in (25mm).

Lifespan A few years.

The start of a month or so of rains in April or May triggers the toads to gather at small breeding pools for mating. The golden males arrive first and are shortly followed by the yellow, black and red females. The males cling to the females to fertilise the spawn as it is produced.

The tiny tadpoles, which hatched from the eggs a few days after spawning, stay in the pools until they develop into toadlets after about 5 weeks. By August, the pools are deserted.

Golden toads are thought to live in springs and cavities underground, or to stay hidden among dead leaves. It is not known what they feed on there. The toads will not be seen again until they return to breeding pools during the next April-June rains.

The toads may still be underground. None have been seen at breeding sites since 1988. It is feared that the adults may have been killed by parasites or by a major change in the physical environment.

Main entry p. 97.

GORILLA, MOUNTAIN★★

Where found Zaire, Rwanda and Uganda. On forested mountain slopes.

Height upright Up to 6ft (1.8m).

Armspan Up to 9ft (2.7m).

Weight Male 310-450lb (140-205kg); female 200lb (90kg).

Lifespan Up to 35 years.

Gorillas show little seasonal variation in behaviour. They roam the rain forest in family groups of usually 5-10, comprising a dominant male, females and their young. Some sleep at night in nests of branches, others, including older males too heavy to climb, sleep at the foot of a tree. They feed on bamboo, fruit and succulent plants. The gorillas generally live above 10,000ft (3000m), but during the season of heavy rains from September to April they may be tempted to the lower slopes to feed on new bamboo shoots. Mating is at any time of year. A female bears one baby weighing about 4lb (1.8kg) after a 9-month

pregnancy, and suckles the infant for 2½-3 years. The youngsters start to walk at 4-6 months old. Females are sexually mature at 7 years old and can give birth every 3½-4½ years, but usually raise a baby to maturity only once in 7 years; disease, climbing accidents and leopards take a heavy toll of the youngsters. Males mature later, and because of the competition for mates do not usually breed until they are 15. When a new male takes over a group, he kills suckling infants so that the females will soon be ready to mate again.

Main entry p. 214.

	March/April/May	June/July/August	Sept/Oct/Nov	Dec/Jan/Feb

GREAT BUSTARD★

Where found Southern Europe and central Asia. Grassy plains.

Length About 3ft (1m).
Wingspan Up to 8ft 6in (2.6m).

Weight Male up to 40lb (18kg); female 12lb (5kg).

Lifespan Maybe 10-15 years.

In March males perform spectacular displays on the large communal breeding grounds to attract females, and may mate with 3-5. After mating, a female makes a shallow, unlined scrape in the ground and lays 2 or 3 glossy eggs. She alone incubates the eggs for 3-4 weeks.

The chicks hatch and leave the nest almost at once. They are buff-coloured with brown markings. The female feeds them beak-to-beak at first, but they soon learn to peck at food for themselves. They fledge at 5 weeks, but stay near their mother until they are a year old.

After breeding, adults moult (June-September). As winter approaches, bustards gather in huge flocks or droves on open grassland. Within the flocks, distinct groups are still evident – either mature males or females with youngsters.

Many birds migrate, particularly to escape very cold weather or lack of food (insects and vegetation). In late winter the birds return to their traditional breeding grounds and males moult into their breeding plumage.

Main entry p. 72.

GREAT CRESTED GREBE

Where found Europe, Asia, Africa, Australia and New Zealand. Breeds by freshwater lakes; winters on coasts.

Length 19in (480mm).
Wingspan Up to 3ft (1m).

Weight Up to 3lb (1.4kg).

Lifespan Up to 10 years.

In Britain, birds migrate from their wintering grounds on large lakes or south-west coasts to freshwater breeding lakes or rivers that have plenty of vegetation at the water's edge. Courtship displays and mating may begin as early as January but peak April-May.

Females lay 3-6 (usually 4) eggs in cupped piles of waterside vegetation in a secluded spot at the water's edge. Both birds incubate the eggs, which hatch in 3-4 weeks. Late hatchings occur in June and July. Both parents feed and tend the striped chicks, and let them ride on their backs.

The chicks can fly and are independent at 10-11 weeks old, but may stay with their parents for a while longer. Grebes feed by diving under the water for 10-40 seconds for food such as insects and shrimps. The birds fly to wintering grounds and adults moult into drab winter plumage.

Large congregations of adult and juvenile birds may build up at the favoured wintering grounds. Early in the year, the adults begin to grow their colourful breeding plumage. Australian birds breed November-January.

Main entry p. 134.

GREAT GREY SHRIKE

Where found Across Eurasia; also North America and North Africa. In open woodland and at forest edges.

Length 9½in (240mm).

Weight About 2oz (57g).

Lifespan Up to 7 years.

Birds begin breeding from late April in the south of their range, and from June in the north. They make bulky cup-shaped nests of grass, moss and twigs in thorn bushes or high in trees. The female lays 5-7 eggs, and incubates them for 15 days while the male feeds her.

The chicks hatch naked, and are tended by both parents, who bring them food such as small birds, mice and insects; food may be stored on a thorn. The young leave the nest at about 3 weeks old and are independent at about 5 weeks old (mid-June to late July).

With the approach of winter, the great grey shrike populations in the northernmost areas of their range move south.

Southern birds remain in pairs and guard their breeding territory against intruders. Even birds in their wintering areas, far from the breeding sites, will defend their territory against intruders.

Main entry p. 111.

GREAT WHITE SHARK

Where found All tropical, subtropical and temperate seas, both coastal waters and open ocean.

Length Male 14-16ft (4.2-5m); female up to 26ft (8m).

Weight Up to 1½ tons.

Off Victoria, south-east Australia, sports fishermen catch most great white sharks in April and July; no one knows why – the sharks may be following prey or breeding. Females bear up to 9 (usually 1-3) young about 3ft (1m) long. Pregnancy lasts possibly 22 months.

In June, catches of the sharks peak off Queensland (north-east Australia). In the USA, great whites appear off the New England coast, probably coming from the pupping areas to the north, as young sharks have been seen there. Females can breed once they are 14ft (4.2m) long.

In November, sharks in Californian waters arrive where there are colonies of elephant seals and feed on seals arriving there to breed. The sharks attack mainly where the sea bottom is rocky, as their slate-grey back colour makes them hard to see against the rocky bottom.

In November great white sharks start arriving off South Australia; arrivals peak in January. The sharks take young sea lions from breeding grounds on offshore islands, for example at Dangerous Reef south of Port Lincoln.

Main entry p. 245.

GREEK TORTOISE★★

Where found North-east Greece; Turkey; southern Spain; round the eastern and southern Mediterranean. Woods and meadows.

Length of shell 8in (200mm).

Weight 2lb (900g).

Lifespan Perhaps more than 100 years.

The tortoises come out of hibernation and begin to feed on a variety of plants, especially those with soft leaves or orange flowers, or both. As the temperature rises, the tortoises become more active; the males start to court females by nipping their legs and battering at their shells.

Mating occurs after a long courtship. Females dig nests with their hind feet and lay about 12 eggs. Incubation time varies with temperature, but often lasts 3-4 months. Temperature may determine the sex of the young – warmer nests produce females, cooler ones males.

Many tortoise hatchlings are taken by predators such as foxes and birds. Some youngsters manage to scuttle into the undergrowth where they feed on vegetation and put on weight before the winter sets in. As the temperature falls, the tortoises retire into hibernation.

The tortoises hibernate throughout the winter in underground cavities or rock crevices.

Main entry p. 115.

	March/April/May	June/July/August	Sept/Oct/Nov	Dec/Jan/Feb

GREEN TREE PYTHON

Where found New Guinea and north-east Australia. In tropical rain forests.

Length Up to 7ft (2.1m).

Lifespan 20-30 years in captivity.

The snakes lead solitary lives high in the trees; they have tails that can easily grasp branches, and greatly enlarged front teeth excellent for grasping prey such as birds, lizards and rodents. The pythons kill by suffocating prey in their coils. They have no venom. Active by night, they can locate prey up to 4ft (1.2m) away in pitch darkness, having lip cavities on either side of the snout that can detect differences in temperature of less than 0.001°C (0.002°F). Most spend the day sleeping, curled on or round a branch, or sometimes shelter in houses. About every 6 weeks, they slough off their old skin.

As the rains arrive in November the snakes moult, and females with mature eggs inside them give off a scent that attracts males to fertilise them. A few weeks after mating, the female lays about 15 soft-shelled eggs on a high branch, and curls round them to protect them.

In January, bright orange, 12in (300mm) long babies are hatched. The female leaves to find her first meal in 2 months or more. In the next 2 weeks the young snakes take on adult colours of leaf green with white back spots.

Main entry p. 31.

GREEN TURTLE★★

Where found In seas and oceans between latitudes 35°N and 35°S.

Length of carapace (shell) 3ft-3ft 9in (1-1.1m).

Weight 200-300lb (90-137kg).

Lifespan Perhaps more than 50 years.

In Florida the turtles breed April-July and in Bermuda April-June. They mate offshore, the male hooked onto the female's back by his flippers. Males stay in the water, but after mating females lay eggs (those fertilised the year before) on the beach where they hatched.

Costa Rican turtles nest from July to September in every third year. The females haul themselves to the top of the beach, and each digs a hole in which she lays her eggs. In all, each female lays more than 400 eggs in four batches at 12½-day intervals.

Eggs hatch after about 10 weeks, beginning in September for Costa Rican turtles. Nests take about 48 hours to clear. East-coast hatchlings head for the Atlantic to spend a year among floating sargassum weed. On the Great Barrier Reef off Australia, turtles lay on Heron I in November.

In January, turtles from Brazil that hatched on Ascension Island in the mid-Atlantic, start their 6-7 week swim to the island to breed. Young female turtles come ashore to lay eggs for the first time when they are 4-6 years old.

Main entries pp. 29, 200.

GREY HERON

Where found Throughout most of Europe, Asia and North Africa. On shores and marshes.

Length About 3ft (1m).

Weight 2¼-4½lb (1-2kg).

Lifespan Up to 25 years.

Breeding began in February, and nests already contain 3-5 eggs of greeny-blue. Platform nests of twigs are on the tops of tall trees, usually close to water. Both parents incubate the eggs, which hatch after 3-4 weeks, and both feed the downy nestlings on regurgitated food.

Young herons grow quickly. They stay in the nest for 7-8 weeks and exercise their wings regularly, ready to leave the nest by midsummer and start hunting for prey such as fish and frogs. Parents that bred early may lay a second clutch in June.

Birds from central and eastern Europe begin moving south to the Mediterranean for the winter. West European birds stay near the nest site, although in severe weather they may move to the seashore, where there is more chance of finding food than in fresh water.

By February, herons have returned to their nest sites, usually in colonies on high trees but in the far north on scrub or cliff ledges. They tidy and add new twigs to old nests, and some begin laying eggs in late February.

Main entry p. 136.

GREY (SLENDER-TAILED) MEERKAT

Where found Southern Africa. In arid, open areas.

Head-and-body length 11in (280mm); tail 7½in (190mm).

Weight 1½-2lb (624-964g).

Lifespan Up to 12 years.

Young 3-month-old meerkats become fully independent within their colony, and can now forage on their own. Some stay in the home burrow shared by 10-15 animals, some may move to other burrows.

In many parts it is the dry season and food is scarce. The meerkats spend much of their time digging for insect larvae or searching for prey such as lizards, spiders, scorpions and small mammals. If food runs out in the area, the meerkats move on and dig new homes.

Dominant animals in the colony usually mate at this time of year. Females are probably pregnant for about 8-9 weeks.

Where summer rains bring out insect food, litters of 2-5 babies are born in shallow burrows. They emerge at 2 weeks old, and from 6 weeks old join the colony's adults and learn how to forage. They are weaned at 7-9 weeks.

Main entry p. 260.

GREY SQUIRREL

Where found Eastern North America; Britain (south, Midlands, parts of north). Deciduous and mixed woodland.

Head-and-body length 10in (250mm); tail 8in (200mm).

Weight 12-25oz (340-709g).

Lifespan 5-6 years.

Most spring litters are born March-April in nests (dreys) of twigs and leaves in treetops or tree holes. The young (1-6 but usually 3) are fully furred and making trips out of the nest at 6-8 weeks, and weaned at 10. At this time, their food is mainly catkins, shoots, buds, flowers.

By now squirrels have brownish summer coats. Most summer litters are born in July, some of them second litters. Squirrels forage all day, but snooze at midday. At this time, before autumn fruits and seeds become plentiful, they strip the bark from deciduous trees to get at the sap.

As young squirrels become independent, the population swells. Nuts, acorns, and beech mast are plentiful and squirrels are active for most of the day without rest. They start to moult into silvery winter coats, fatten up for winter, and bury or cache food.

The squirrels are active all through the winter. They begin courting during November and December, and the first frenzied mating chases can be seen in the leafless treetops. Females give birth 6 weeks after mating.

Main entry p. 252.

		March/April/May	June/July/August	Sept/Oct/Nov	Dec/Jan/Feb

GREY TREE FROG

Where found East Africa and southern Africa. In hot, arid regions.

Length 3in (75mm); female larger than male.

The grey tree frog is one of 184 species of Old World tree frog. Once a frog leaves the pool where it developed from a 2in (50mm) long tadpole into a froglet, it never lives in the water again. Most of the frog's life is spent high and dry in the trees, feeding on insects. Large discs on its toes act as suckers and help the frog to climb smooth tree trunks and branches.

In southern Africa the temperature is climbing towards the hottest time of the year (in February). If it rises above 40.5°C (105°F), the frogs cool themselves by sending up little fountains of liquid. This evaporates on the skin and cools them in the way perspiration cools people.

The frogs mate after periods of rain. Above a rain pool, the pair whip up liquid excreted by the female to make a foam nest, into which she lays up to 150 eggs. Tadpoles hatch after 3-4 days, and 2 days later drop into the water.

Main entry p. 21.

GREY WHALE

Where found North Pacific. Breeds off California (USA), Baja California (Mexico) and South Korea.

Length Up to 49ft (15m).

Weight Up to 35 tons.

Lifespan 40-60 years.

Whales migrate north from breeding grounds off Baja California to feeding grounds in the Arctic. The orderly procession is led by the newly pregnant cows. Adult bulls, non-breeding cows and juveniles follow, with mothers and their new-born calves in the rear.

The whales reach their Arctic feeding grounds in the Bering Sea and Chukchi Sea. There they feed on shrimp-like crustaceans, worms and molluscs, which they scoop from the sea bottom. After 7 months of being suckled, the calves are weaned during August.

In October, the whales begin to head south again. The procession is led by cows nearing the end of their 13½-month pregnancy. They are followed by immature females and adult males, with immature males at the rear. The young become sexually mature at about 8 years old.

The migration south continues. Mating takes place during the journey, peaking on December 5, and continues off Baja California. Females give birth in the lagoons of Baja California. Calving peaks on January 10.

Main entry p. 40.

GROUND SQUIRREL, CALIFORNIAN

Where found Western North America from Washington to Baja California. Short grass.

Head-and-body length 7-11½in (180-290mm); tail 5½-10in (140-250mm).

Weight 1-1¾lb (500-800g).

Lifespan 6-8 years.

Single litters of 3-15 (usually 7) are born March-August. The young, helpless at birth, leave the nest at about 8 weeks, and are able to breed the next year. The squirrels live in family groups in burrows or under rocks on rocky or wooded hillsides up to about 10,000ft (3000m).

In late May-July, adult males aestivate (go into a dormant state as it becomes too hot), as there is little vegetation. Females and youngsters are active day and night. Youngsters especially fall prey to weasels, bobcats and coyotes.

Males emerge in late August or September. All the squirrels feast on seeds, nuts, acorns, green vegetation, cereals. They carry food back to their burrows in cheek pouches. North of San Francisco, adults begin hibernating in October or November to avoid cold and food scarcity.

The squirrels that hibernated start to emerge in January. Mating begins in February, and females are pregnant for about a month. The animals may eat insects and carrion until new growth is available.

Main entry p. 15.

GRUNION

Where found Southern California (USA) and northern Baja California (Mexico). Inshore waters.

Length 6-7½in (150-190mm).

Lifespan 3 years.

From March, when the highest (spring) tides are at night, grunion spawn on beaches. The fish ride on waves to the top of the beach, where the females thrust their tails into the sand and lay their eggs, making a squeaking sound. Males gather and shed their milt, fertilising the eggs.

Spawning continues on nights with spring tides, just as the tide starts to ebb. The fertilised eggs are left high and dry on the beach, out of reach of sea predators. The eggs take 8 days to develop, but the young do not emerge until the next spring tide, which washes them out to sea.

The 6-month breeding season has now ended. Every 2 weeks during the season, each mature female grunion will have deposited up to 3000 eggs in the sand. Sea birds take some of the grunion eggs.

For the rest of the year, grunion live within 1 mile (1.6km) of the shore. As their breeding time approaches, the mature fish stop growing and each channels its energy into the development of eggs or sperm.

Main entry p. 63.

GUILLEMOT

Where found North Atlantic and north Pacific Oceans. Coastal waters.

Length 16½in (420mm).

Weight 1½-2¼lb (680-1000g); female slightly larger than the male.

Adults congregate in breeding colonies, some numbering 100,000 or more, on rocky offshore islands. They crowd close together on rock ledges. A female lays 1 egg on bare rock from mid-May to early June. Both parents incubate it, changing shifts several times a day.

The chick hatches after 4-5 weeks, and stays on the ledge for 3-5 weeks. Then it flutters off the ledge into the sea where it is looked after by an adult as it swims along. It is not fully fledged until 6-8 weeks old.

Most of the chicks are now independent, and breeding adults have completed their moult. Many birds are now feeding well out to sea, and others are offshore where there are good supplies of small fish, shellfish and worms.

The birds are widely dispersed – especially young birds, which stay at sea for their first year. But many adults stay near their breeding sites, even in the Arctic. In February they begin to congregate at the breeding sites.

No main entry, see p. 132.

	March/April/May	June/July/August	Sept/Oct/Nov	Dec/Jan/Feb

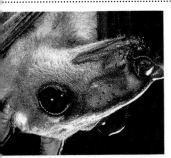

HAMMERHEADED BAT

Where found West Africa and Central Africa eastwards to Uganda. In forests beside large rivers.

Length 10-12in (250-300mm). **Wingspan** Male 3ft (1m).

Weight Female about 15oz (425g); male heavier.

All year round, individuals generally roost alone or in small groups on tree branches among foliage, or very occasionally in caves. Every evening, the bats leave the roost to fly in search of food – ripe forest fruits.

It is mating time. In the early evening, males gather in groups on trees that overhang rivers – away from the daytime roosts. Many females have just given birth and have their babies with them, but are ready to mate again. Females are attracted by the males' loud croaks.

When fruit trees such as mangoes and bananas, are in fruit, the bats often raid gardens.

Babies are born about 6 months after mating. Females produce their first baby when they are about 1 year old. After giving birth, many females mate again. Mating is brief, with no lasting bonding.

Main entry p. 140.

HARE, BROWN

Where found Europe and Asia eastwards to China. Introduced to New Zealand, Chile and parts of the USA. On open grasslands.

Length Female 22in (560mm); male slightly smaller.

Weight About 8lb (3.6kg).

Lifespan Up to 12 years.

In the Northern Hemisphere breeding occurs mainly January-August, tending to peak in spring. Females bear litters of usually 2-4 fully furred young after a 6-week pregnancy. Each baby is in a separate 'form' beaten out in long grass; the mother visits each one to suckle it.

The babies (leverets) are independent at 1 month old. A female may have several litters a year. The hares generally rest by day, flattened among vegetation. They feed mostly in the evening, mainly on cereals and grasses, and may forage up to 1 mile (1.6km) from their daytime shelter.

The hares become largely nocturnal in their habits, and are more solitary than during the breeding season. Young hares are ready to breed when about 1 year old.

During winter the hares feed mostly on root crops, bulbs and the bark of young trees.

Main entry p. 70.

HARLEQUIN-PATTERNED TREE FROG

Where found Costa Rican rain forests.

Length Up to 1½in (38mm).

Weight About ¾oz (21g).

The frogs are explosive breeders, gathering to mate in large numbers on nights when the heavy rains begin in late April or early May. Males sit on leaves and call to attract a mate. A male fertilises his mate's eggs as she deposits them on the leaves of the marsh plant *Spathiphyllum* in the open, safe from most predators except leaf-climbing snakes. Meanwhile, the water level on the ground below begins to rise. When the tadpoles are ready to emerge from the eggs, they drop down, still encased in jelly, into the flood waters that can eventually be waist deep to a man. There they swim away and eventually develop into

froglets. In the marsh areas inhabited by the frogs, there are large, venomous spiders that sit on grass stalks and blades and are dangerous predators. They catch frogs, and are particularly successful at night during the frog breeding season. Although harlequin-patterned tree frogs appear strongly coloured during the day, like many other tree frogs they take on paler hues at night. No one knows why.

Main entry p. 98.

HARP SEAL

Where found Northernmost reaches of the Atlantic Ocean and nearby Arctic Ocean.

Length 6-7ft (1.8-2.1m).

Weight Male 295lb (135kg); female a little less.

Lifespan At least 30 years.

It is the peak season for births in the south of the seals' range. A female bears a single pup on floating ice, and about 2 weeks later goes to sea to feed and mate. After moulting on the ice floes, the adult harp seals begin to migrate north to their summer feeding grounds.

The females become pregnant in late July, 4½ months after mating, when the fertilised egg finally implants in the womb. The seals spend much of the summer feeding on fish in the rich hunting grounds that are provided by the ice-free sectors of the Arctic Ocean.

Canadian seals begin to move south as the Arctic Ocean freezes, and reach Newfoundland and the Gulf of St Lawrence by late December. However, European seals stay in Arctic waters longer, because a warm current (the North Atlantic Drift) keeps the Russian coast ice-free into December.

European seals finally begin a rapid migration southwards, arriving in the White Sea, an inlet of the northern Russian coast, by mid-January. White Sea populations begin pupping in January.

Main entry p. 66.

HARVEST MOUSE, EUROPEAN

Where found Across Europe and northern Asia. In grassland and hedgerows.

Head-and-body length 2½in (64mm); tail 2½in (64mm).

Weight ¼-½oz (7-14g).

Lifespan About 6 months.

As soon as the grass begins to grow in spring, harvest mice climb up stems seeking suitable nest sites. The breeding season begins, and the females build spherical grass nests well above the ground, attached to stems. A female bears a litter of 3-8 babies after a pregnancy of 17-19 days.

By midsummer, a female may already have raised two litters. She can be pregnant with one litter while still suckling the previous one. Young-sters, which have grey-brown coats, are weaned at 15-16 days old, then abandoned. Young females can breed at 6 weeks old.

The breeding season ends in autumn. As the grass dies back, the mice seek cover among low vegetation or maybe occasionally in barns. They moult their reddish-brown summer coats and grow darker winter coats.

During winter, some mice shelter in rough winter nests on the ground in grass tussocks and hedgerows. Many of the mice die from cold or starvation, because their normal diet of seeds, grain and insects is scarce.

Main entry p. 176.

	March/April/May	June/July/August	Sept/Oct/Nov	Dec/Jan/Feb

HERCULES MOTH

Where found Northern Australia and New Guinea. In tropical rain forests.

Wingspan 6½ -14in (165-360mm).

Wing area Up to 47sq in (30,300sq mm), one of the largest of any moth.

Lifespan A few months.

With food and warmth always available in the rain forest, the moths are active all year. They feed mainly at night on the nectar of sweet-scented flowers high in the forest canopy. The huge adults have sickle-shaped forewings and long 'tails' on their hind wings, and look almost like birds on the wing. The moths probably breed throughout the year, with more than one generation in a year. Females lay oval, rust-red eggs on the leaves of various rain-forest trees, such as the bleeding-heart tree. The eggs, which are glued to the leaves, eventually hatch into bluish-green caterpillars with red spots. The caterpillars are armed with yellow spines along their backs. They grow rapidly over several months, moulting regularly, until they reach a length of more than 5in (125mm) and are as thick as sausages. Then they pupate – spin 4in (100mm) long, spindle-shaped cocoons of silk around themselves in which to change into adults. The cocoons, which are suspended from leaves in the tree canopy, look like large fruits hanging in the trees. Adult moths eventually emerge from their cocoons, and fly off to find mates.

Main entry p. 266.

HIPPOPOTAMUS

Where found Africa: central, eastern and southern. Areas with short grass near water.

Length Up to 13ft (4m).
Shoulder height 4ft 10in (1.4m).

Weight Male up to about 3 tons; female 1⅓ tons.

Lifespan About 45 years.

Hippopotamuses spend the day submerged in pools or mud hollows to keep cool. At dusk they leave the water to graze, treading set pathways. An adult can eat 395lb (180kg) of grass in one night. Usually the hippos live in groups of 10-15 animals, but some are occasionally solitary. Groups are mostly made up of a bull with his females and their offspring, but there are some bachelor groups. Breeding males defend territories on land, and drive off intruders fiercely – fights between males can end in injury or death. Mating tends to occur during a dry season, when the hippos are in groups of up to 150 in shrunken pools. A bull mates with several females. Most calves are born in a rainy season when new grass is plentiful. Females are pregnant for 8 months, and leave the herd to give birth to a single calf on land or in shallow water. If it is born underwater, the baby paddles to the surface for its first breath. The mother rejoins the herd after 10-14 days, and suckles the calf for about 8 months. Males are generally sexually mature at 7 years old, females at 9 years.

Main entry p. 282.

HOATZIN

Where found South America. In the Amazon Basin beside rain-forest rivers.

Length 2ft (610mm).

Weight 1¾lb (800g).

As rivers rise in April, foraging flocks of hoatzins split into smaller breeding groups of parents and juveniles from the previous breeding season. Each group sets up a territory and builds a simple nest platform of twigs in which 2-4 eggs are laid. The group members share the 4-week incubation and feed the chicks, which begin to feed themselves after about 2 weeks. If danger threatens, the chicks – which can swim but not fly – jump into the flood water below the nest. When the danger has passed, they haul themselves back into the nest using beak and claws, including an extra pair of claws on each wing. When not breeding, the hoatzins forage in flocks of 20-30, feeding on the leaves, flowers and fruit of tough marsh plants such as arum and white mangrove. To help digest this food, the birds have a digestive system similar to that of a cow. Aromatic oils in their food give hoatzins a distinctive smell. Villagers call them 'stink birds' and avoid them, but the aroma can attract capuchin monkeys, which eat the chicks. Hoatzins keep in touch with loud croaking and hissing calls, and their name may be derived from the noise they make.

Main entry p. 98.

HONEY BEE, WESTERN

Where found Europe; North African coast. Nests in tree, rock and wall cavities.

Length Queen ⅞in (22mm); male ¾in (19mm); worker (sterile female) ⅝in (16mm).

Lifespan Queen up to 5 years; male (or drone) and worker about 1 month.

In April the queen resumes egg-laying and workers forage and tend the queen and larvae. Fertilised eggs produce more workers and unfertilised eggs produce drones. The queen puts out a substance that inhibits workers from feeding larvae on royal jelly to produce queens.

As the hive gets full, not all workers receive the 'queen substance', so produce royal jelly and rear new queens. Between May and July the old queen leaves with a swarm of workers to found a new colony. New queens leave to mate (with drones), and one takes over the hive.

The other queens found new colonies, and the drones, their sole task done, are refused entry to the hive and die. As the weather gets colder most workers die, but some spend the winter in the hive with their queen. The hive may be in a hollow tree, cavity wall, chimney, man-made hive or similar place. The bees survive winter by feeding on honey (sugary nectar), water and protein-rich pollen stored in the honeycomb, which is made of wax secreted from the bees' wax glands.

Main entry p. 138.

HONEY POSSUM

Where found South-west Australia. On heathlands.

Head-and-body length 2½ -3½in(64-90mm);tail2½ -4in (64-100mm).

Weight Male ⅜oz (10g); female ½oz (14g).

Lifespan 1 or 2 years.

Babies are carried in their mother's pouch until they are about 8 weeks old and too bulky for it. They are then placed in a nest such as a tree hole or an abandoned bird's nest, and suckled until about 11 weeks old. At about 3 months old they are independent.

The winter months are generally the wettest part of the year. The agile youngsters climb plants, often hanging by their tails, and use their long snouts to reach nectar from winter flowers. The possums are sexually mature at about 6 months old.

Spring brings a flush of flowers and insects for the possums to feed on. Mating can occur at any time of the year, but the fertilised egg may lie dormant in the female's womb. Births are usually timed so that the babies will be weaned at a time when nectar becomes plentiful.

Once an embryo starts to develop, pregnancy lasts about a month. Most litters of 2-3 young are produced in January or February. The babies are extremely tiny, and remain in their mother's pouch, which has four teats inside.

Main entry p. 219.

	March/April/May	June/July/August	Sept/Oct/Nov	Dec/Jan/Feb

HOODED SEAL

Where found Arctic and sub-Arctic waters of the northern Atlantic Ocean.

Length Male 8ft (2.4m); female 6ft 6in (1.9m).

Weight Male 420-770lb (190-350kg); female slightly smaller.

Lifespan Up to 35 years.

Seals arrive to breed at whelping grounds on pack ice off Greenland and Canada. A female bears one pup, which grows rapidly on her rich milk. Mating takes place 2 weeks after pupping, but pregnancy is delayed. The adults fast most of the time, living on stored blubber.

Many adults are now in poor condition. The seals migrate to their moulting grounds on drift ice off south-east Greenland to grow new coats. Immature seals keep away from the large moulting congregations. A female's fertilised egg implants in her womb 4 months after mating.

Populations disperse throughout the northern reaches of the Atlantic. They feed on squid and fish in order to build up stores of blubber for the winter ahead.

The seals spend the winter at feeding grounds on the Grand Banks off Newfoundland, near Labrador, or around south-east Greenland. They start to migrate to their whelping grounds in January.

Main entry p. 82.

HORNED TOAD

Where found Thailand; Malaysia; Indonesia; Borneo; Philippines. In rain forests. (76 species.)

Length Female 4¾in (120mm); male smaller.

Weight 1¾oz (50g).

Lifespan Up to 10 years in captivity.

In still inlets off rain-forest riverlets in East Malaysia, free-swimming horned toad tadpoles are developing rapidly. Some species have tiny teeth radiating from a funnel-like mouth, kept half in the water to trap air and so aid buoyancy. Eventually the tadpoles develop into toadlets.

The well-camouflaged toadlets and adults hide in leaf litter. They are coloured in browns, greens, yellows and greys, and even have diverging lines on their backs to simulate leaf veins. They sit in wait to grab passing insects or other tiny creatures with their long tongues.

The toad's sensitive 'horns' (one on its snout and one over each eye) are not only part of its camouflage but probably help it to avoid rubbing against objects such as twigs. In East Malaysia the rains increase from October to February, and this is when the horned toads breed.

At breeding time, male toads make themselves conspicuous by calling with loud 'chings', and females are attracted to males with the loudest calls. When mating, a male grabs and holds a female and fertilises her eggs as they are laid.

Main entry p. 255.

HORSESHOE (KING) CRAB★

Where found East coast of North America from Nova Scotia to the Gulf of Mexico; western Pacific Ocean. On sandy and muddy coasts.

Length Up to 2ft (610mm); male smaller than female.

In early spring, Atlantic horseshoe crabs begin to move towards the sandy beaches of New Jersey and Delaware, especially Delaware Bay. In late May they emerge from the sea, males first. Females emerge at high tide. Males fight to fertilise batches of eggs laid in holes in the sand.

By early June the crabs have returned to deeper water, and many of the millions of pinpoint-sized eggs that were laid at each high tide are eaten by thousands of migrating birds on their way north. Embryos begin to grow inside the surviving eggs.

The developing eggs may be devoured by predators such as waders, seabirds, sparrows, starlings, foxes, raccoons, moles and worms. After several weeks, larvae about ⅜in (10mm) long hatch from the surviving eggs, and float off on the tide.

The larvae moult several times before returning as adults 3 years later to breed where they hatched. Horseshoe crabs are not true crabs. They resemble woodlice and are in fact arthropods (belonging to the same group as spiders).

Main entry p. 106.

HOUSE MARTIN

Where found Breeds in Europe (including northern Scandinavia) and Russia; probably winters in Africa. Buildings, ledges or cliffs.

Length 5in (125mm).

Weight ½-¾oz (14-21g).

Lifespan 7-15 years.

The birds migrate north from wintering grounds in Africa to temperate regions of Europe. They have come to breed, taking advantage of the plentiful seasonal supplies of insects to eat. The birds mate and pairs build cup nests of mud, usually under the eaves of a building.

Females lay 4-5 white eggs, which hatch after 2-3 weeks. Both parents catch insects for the chicks, which fledge at about 3 weeks old and fly straight from the nest. The parents continue to look after them for a while but also rear another brood, or possibly two more.

The birds feed as much as they can to gather strength for their migration south. They leave in September and complete the journey in a few weeks, feeding or sleeping on the wing for much of the time. Some birds die crossing the barren Sahara.

European house martins are thought to spend the winter flying high over Africa south of the Sahara. Exactly where they go is still something of a mystery.

Main entry p. 108.

HUMPBACK WHALE★★

Where found All oceans from the Arctic to the Antarctic, to the edge of the ice. In summer in cold-water feeding grounds, in winter in warmer breeding grounds.

Length About 43ft (13m).

Weight 25-30 tons.

Lifespan Up to 48 years.

Humpbacks in the Northern Hemisphere migrate north to spend summer in their feeding grounds in the cold waters of the north Pacific Ocean and the Atlantic Ocean.

In summer, the cold waters offer northern whales plenty of food such as fish and krill. Humpbacks in the Southern Hemisphere spend the winter in warm waters – off the coasts of Australia, for example, where the females give birth and mating takes place.

At the onset of the northern winter, the food supply dwindles and the whales move south to warmer waters. On the way, the males sing long, melancholy songs as a prelude to mating. Whales in the Southern Hemisphere begin to migrate south to their feeding grounds.

Northern whales spend the winter in the warmer waters of the north Pacific and Atlantic. There the females give birth to single calves after a pregnancy of just under a year. Calves born the previous year are weaned.

Main entry p. 155.

	March/April/May	June/July/August	Sept/Oct/Nov	Dec/Jan/Feb

HYENA, SPOTTED

Where found Africa south of the Sahara. In grassland and open, flat terrain.

Length 4ft-4ft 7in (1.2-1.4m). **Shoulder height** 2ft 6in (760mm).

Weight 110-176lb (50-80kg); female heavier than male.

Lifespan 25 years.

In the north of their range, most hyenas are born in April. Mothers leave the clan and give birth in a separate den. The litter of 2-3 young, born with woolly brown coats, is the sole responsibility of the female. She suckles them for 12 months or more.

By now, mothers with cubs have rejoined the clan. The youngsters stay close to their mother. In the north it is the dry season, and the hyenas spend a lot of time foraging. They eat almost any flesh, including fish, tortoises and carrion. Hyenas hunt alone or in groups.

Young hyenas born in April are starting to develop spots. Those born the previous year are now nearly full grown and fully weaned. They will not breed until they are 2 or 3 years old. In the south of the hyenas' range, it is mating time.

In the north, most mating takes place at this time of year. In the south, females are giving birth after a pregnancy of about 4 months. The rainy season south of the Equator provides plenty of food such as newborn wildebeests.

Main entry p. 20.

IMPALA

Where found East Africa and southern Africa as far south as Zimbabwe and Mozambique. Open woods, bush and grassland.

Length 5ft-8ft 6in (1.5-2.6m). **Shoulder height** 3ft (1m).

Weight 143-198lb (65-90kg).

Lifespan 10-12 years.

In the south of the impalas' range it is the main mating season, with males fighting many battles to hold a territory. In the north it is the main birth season, which coincides with the March-May rains on the East African plains.

In the north during the East Africa dry season, females abandon their small wet-season ranges and move up to 6 miles (10km) in large herds in search of better grazing and browsing. Impalas range through lightly wooded grassland.

In East Africa it is the main mating season, and impala males taking up their territories drive out juvenile males; the youngsters join bachelor herds. In the south it is the start of the birth season. Females bear a single calf after a 7-month pregnancy.

In the south births continue, the summer rains bringing plenty of fresh vegetation for the nursing mothers. The youngsters are hidden in the grass until strong enough to join the herd. Many fall prey to predators such as hyenas.

Main entry p. 118.

IVY

Where found From western Europe to western Asia. In woods and hedges and on rocks, walls and buildings.

Height Up to 100ft (30m).

Lifespan 100 years or more.

Last winter's berries turn black and ripen. They are eaten by blackbirds, thrushes and other birds. The ivy's dense, climbing foliage offers nesting places for creatures such as wrens, blackbirds, garden warblers and mice.

In July and August, the year's second generation of holly blue butterflies lay their eggs on ivy plants. When the eggs hatch, the pale green holly blue caterpillars feed on the ivy's flower buds.

The yellowish-green five-petalled ivy flowers open in the sunshine from September until early November. They provide a late feast of nectar for many late-flying insects. In September the holly blue caterpillars pupate and transform into adults under ivy leaves.

Ivy berries develop, and stay green through the winter. Ivy leaves also remain on the plant all winter, although severe frosts can kill tender shoots. The leaves provide shelter for wrens and hibernating small tortoiseshell butterflies.

Main entry p. 209.

JACKAL, SILVERBACKED (BLACKBACKED)

Where found Africa (eastern, southern). In woods, brush.

Head-and-body length 3ft (1m); tail 16in (400mm). **Shoulder height** 18in (460mm).

Weight 15-33lb (7-15kg).

Lifespan 8-9 years.

On Tanzania's Serengeti Plain, the jackals start mating during May, as a rainy season is ending. Females are pregnant for 8-10 weeks. Breeding pairs maintain their territory, and some young from last year's litters live with their parents in a family group of maybe 4 or 5.

The first of last year's pups become mature at 11 months old. Some leave; the others help to raise new pups. From July, when food such as rodents and balanites tree fruits are plentiful, litters of about 6 pups are born in a den. On the Serengeti Plain mating ends in August.

Litters are born into October. Newborn pups are suckled for 8 weeks, and for the first 3 weeks their mother is fed by the group and rarely leaves them. After that parents and helpers feed them with regurgitated food. In Transvaal mating is in October, at the end of a dry season.

Leopards or other predators take many pups; others starve for lack of enough helpers to feed them. Pups stop using the den at 3 months old, and by 5 months are not fed. The last new pups cease to be fed in January.

Main entry p. 164.

JAMAICAN BROMELIAD CRAB

Where found Western Jamaica, in the hilly karst (limestone) regions. In rainwater pools formed at the centre of bromeliad plants.

Width of carapace (shell) ¾in (19mm).

Crab eggs deposited in bromeliad plant pools take 10-12 weeks to develop. The minute larvae that emerge from the eggs take 9-10 days to change into young crabs. Female crabs keep their ponds clean and safe by removing debris such as the larvae of predatory damselflies.

The mother crabs catch millipedes and insects and feed them to the young crabs. They also protect the youngsters from predatory lizards and spiders.

The baby crabs disperse from the ponds to find their own bromeliad plant ponds. Each lives in a separate plant. The young crabs are sexually mature when they are ½in (13mm) long.

Mature crabs mate during the 4 weeks from mid-January to mid-February. A male leaves his bromeliad plant to join a female. She carries 100 eggs attached to her abdomen. After the male has fertilised them, he returns to his own pond.

Main entry p. 56.

	March/April/May	June/July/August	Sept/Oct/Nov	Dec/Jan/Feb

JAPANESE (MANCHURIAN, RED-CROWNED) CRANE★★

Where found Breeds Manchuria, nearby Russia, Hokkaido (Japan). Winters east China, Korea, east Hokkaido.

Length 4ft 7in (1.4m).
Wingspan 7ft 10in (2.4m).

Weight Up to 33lb (15kg).

Lifespan 30-50 years.

From mid-March, pairs disperse or migrate from wintering areas to breeding sites in extensive marshes and reed beds. From late March to late April females lay 2 eggs in a nest-mound of reeds. Both birds share incubation for a month. Juveniles leave wintering areas in April or May.

All through summer the new families wander in their territories, with the parents helping their young to find food such as roots, tubers, grasses, sedges, shoots, buds, insects and fish. Non-breeding birds spend the summer alone or in small groups at large lakes and marshes.

Families gradually leave their nesting territories, and gather at favoured wintering areas. Birds on the Asian mainland move south, and those in Japan remain in east Hokkaido. When the ground begins to freeze, the birds congregate in large numbers.

During the coldest months, with the ground frozen and a lot of snow, the cranes gather at safe winter roosts. They forage along ice-free rivers and streams and on farmland. Cranes in Hokkaido begin courting in February.

Main entry p. 41.

JAPANESE MACAQUE

Where found Throughout the islands of Japan, except for Hokkaido. In forests.

Length 20in (510mm).

Weight Male 26lb (11.8kg); female 20lb (9kg).

Lifespan Female up to 25 years; male less.

Spring brings a greater supply of food as bushes and trees produce new crops of leaves. In the warmer southern areas, the birth season begins. Females bear a single baby weighing about 1lb (450g) after a pregnancy of 5-6 months.

In the cooler north it is the main birth season. Last year's infants are weaned, but still depend on mother for comfort and security and for some transport. Older infants increasingly join groups of juveniles. Unless food is abundant, females give birth only in alternate years.

The animals forage more extensively on autumn fruits. They live in groups of 30-40, made up of 5 or 6 males and about 10 related females and their offspring. In the more southerly areas, the mating season begins in September.

It is the main mating season in most areas. In the far north, some macaques move down to the more sheltered valleys to avoid the winter snows. Some groups use natural hot springs to keep warm when snowed in.

Main entry p. 42.

JAY, EURASIAN

Where found Europe; Asia; North Africa. In deciduous and mixed woodland.

Length 13½in (340mm).

Weight 5-7oz (140-200g).

Lifespan Up to 16 years.

In early spring jays feed mainly on berries and acorns. Courting birds often chase each other, calling noisily. From April, pairs build twig nests lined with hair, often in a tree fork. In May, the female lays 5-7 green or buff eggs. She alone does most of the incubating for 2-3 weeks.

At first the male feeds the chicks while the female stays on the nest. After that both parents feed the chicks with regurgitated food such as caterpillars and insects. The youngsters fly after about 3 weeks, usually by mid-June. The jays do not raise a second brood.

The birds feed on nuts, acorns, berries, insects, small mammals, young birds and eggs. In years when many youngsters are produced or when food is short, jays may irrupt into new areas, but such invasions are usually short-lived. Jays bury excess supplies of acorns to eat later.

With food in short supply, the birds are reliant on buried acorns, and search likely sites for caches. To eat an acorn, a jay holds it in one of its claws and tears at it with its beak.

Main entry p. 188.

JERSEY TIGER MOTH

Where found Britain (south Devon, Channel Isles only); central and south Europe; west Asia. Scrub, open woods.

Wingspan 2½in (64mm).

Colour variations Hind wings usually red, may be yellow or rarely terracotta. Black on forewings may vary.

The caterpillars emerge from hibernation and feed on dandelion, white deadnettle, nettle, ground ivy, groundsel, plantain and other plants. Fully grown caterpillars are black and hairy, and have an orange stripe down their backs and cream spots on their sides.

The caterpillars spin web-like cocoons among fallen leaves and change into adults, emerging after 3-4 weeks. In southern Europe the moths aestivate (remain torpid during the worst heat) on trees. Moths fly in search of mates at night. Females lay about 130 eggs, and adults die.

The next generation of caterpillars hatches 2 weeks later. The small caterpillars feed for a while, and then go into hibernation among plant roots.

The caterpillars hibernate through the winter months.

Main entry p. 177.

KANGAROO, EASTERN GREY

Where found Tasmania and eastern Australia. On grassland.

Head-and-body length Up to 5ft 3in (1.6m); tail 3ft (1m).

Weight Male 50-155lb (23-70kg); female 30lb (14kg).

Lifespan 23 years.

The kangaroos are dispersed in small groups, with numbers concentrated wherever rainfall provides good grazing. Males and females are usually in separate groups, but breeding may occur at any time of the year. Youngsters of 16 months become independent.

For the peak mating season in winter, males join the female groups. There may be a lot of fighting among the large males, who try to hold together groups of females to mate with as they come on heat. Joeys (infants) leave the pouch for the first time at about 6 months old.

In the north and west of the kangaroos' range, births often peak with the advent of summer rains from October to January. Females may mate again straight after giving birth, but the fertilised egg does not implant in the womb for 11 months.

In most areas, the peak time for births is ending. Last year's joey leaves the pouch for good to make way for the new baby, born 5-6 weeks after the fertilised egg implants in the mother's womb. The new joey crawls into the pouch.

Main entry p. 267.

	March/April/May	June/July/August	Sept/Oct/Nov	Dec/Jan/Feb

KANGAROO RAT, BANNER-TAILED

Where found South-west USA; north Mexico. Scrub-covered desert slopes.

Head-and-body length 4-8in (100-200mm); tail 4-8½in (100-215mm).

Weight 1¼-6¼oz (35-175g).

Lifespan Up to 9 years.

In most years, rain storms cause the desert to bloom, providing the rats with plenty of seeds and leaves to eat. They carry some food back to their burrows in cheek pouches, and store it for times of drought. Mating is at its peak. To attract females, males drum with their hind feet.

Females produce 1-8 (usually 2) babies 4 weeks after mating, and in a good year may bear 3 litters. The babies stay in the burrow for 6 weeks. The rats survive the long dry season by feeding at night. They seldom drink, getting the water they need from their plant food.

Breeding continues. Youngsters are able to breed at 2-3 months old. Each adult rat lives in a separate burrow system which has up to 12 openings and is within a territory of 485sq yds (405sq m). Both sexes drum with their hind feet to proclaim their territory.

In the colder time in the desert uplands, there is very little breeding. When temperatures drop down close to freezing, the rats may not emerge for nights on end, living off their stores of food.

Main entry p. 150.

KILLER WHALE (ORCA)

Where found All oceans and seas, from the Equator to the poles.

Length Male 26ft (8m); female 20ft (6m).

Weight Male 6 tons; female 3 tons.

Lifespan Male 30 years, female 50 years.

From spring to July, resident pods (groups) of north-east Pacific killer whales hunt 'smileys' (spring salmon) at river mouths on the Washington and Oregon coasts (USA). Off Península Valdés (Argentina), whales grab sea lions at the water's edge on the shingle beaches.

In June, Antarctic whales go north to avoid the worst of the winter. In August, north-east Pacific whales gather in Johnstone Strait (British Columbia) to take sock-eye salmon returning to their hatchery rivers. In the same area, nomadic pods hunt sea lions in their breeding colonies.

In autumn, north-east Pacific resident pods hunt salmon – coho (silver), humpback (pink) and chum (dog). Mating occurs, mainly between related animals in a pod, but sometimes between whales from different pods. In November, the Antarctic whales return to the far south.

In the north-east Pacific females give birth October-March after a pregnancy of 16 months. At birth, calves are up to 8ft 3in (2.5m) long. A female calves every 5-6 years on average, bearing 5 or 6 calves in her lifetime.

Main entry p. 170.

KING PENGUIN

Where found Antarctic and sub-Antarctic seas. Breeds on islands, but not on the Antarctic mainland.

Height 3ft (1m).

Weight 30-40lb (14-18kg).

Lifespan About 20 years.

Females who mated late in the season lay a single egg between February and April. By the end of May, chicks hatched last December have reached 80 per cent of their adult weight. They need the fat to survive the winter. Parents almost abandon their chicks, which huddle in crèches.

Many chicks die, but those hatched May-June from March-April eggs have the least chance of survival. At the end of August or in September, parents begin to return after the winter, and feed the surviving chicks regularly once more.

Penguins breeding early court and mate in October, and lay their single egg in November. Both birds incubate the egg in 5-day shifts for 7-8 weeks. At the end of November, chicks hatched last December are now ready to leave for the sea and fend for themselves.

When the egg hatches, both parents feed the chick. Late chicks hatched in May fledge January-February; their parents will breed again next November. Adults whose chick has just left moult for 6 weeks and mate January-February.

Main entry p. 122.

KINGFISHER

Where found Europe and Asia east to China; north-west Africa. Breeds by slow-flowing rivers and streams.

Length 6½in (165mm).
Wingspan About 10in (250mm).

Weight About 1½oz (43g).

Lifespan Up to 15 years.

Birds that migrated for the winter return to their breeding grounds. A breeding pair excavates a burrow in a waterside bank and the female lays 4-7 glossy white eggs in a nest chamber at the end. Both parents incubate the eggs, which hatch after about 3 weeks.

Both parents are busy feeding the first brood. The chicks fledge when less than a month old. By that time, the parents have probably mated again and the female is sitting on her second brood. The youngsters become independent a few weeks after fledging.

Adults may continue to raise chicks until the end of September. Chicks are fed fish head first so they can swallow them easily. As the weather gets colder and small streams ice over, the kingfishers travel to larger rivers or the coast. Those in the north of the range may move south.

Many kingfishers spend the winter fishing in coastal pools which do not freeze. But they have to wash off salt regularly in fresh water to keep their plumage in good condition. Many in-experienced youngsters die during hard winters.

Main entry p. 113.

KITTIWAKE

Where found North Atlantic and North Pacific oceans. Breeds on coastal cliffs.

Length 15-16in (380-400mm).

Weight 15oz (425g).

Lifespan 21 years.

Kittiwakes return to their breeding colony, the same one each year, to find their lifelong mate. They nest on narrow cliff ledges, or maybe on windowsills of tall seaside buildings. The cup nest of grass, mud and seaweed is cemented to the ledge with droppings.

Females usually lay 2 eggs, and both parents incubate them for about 4 weeks. Both feed the chicks, spending maybe half the day finding food out at sea. The chicks fledge at 5-6 weeks old. In August, the immature birds disperse into mid-ocean and the adult birds moult.

Adults disperse from the breeding colony out to sea, but rarely move far unless blown by gales. Immature birds stay at sea until ready to breed at 3-5 years old and may travel up to 1600 miles (2600km).

Adult birds are usually in ones or twos at this time, and rarely come to land. Kittiwakes feed mainly on fish and shellfish, scooped from the water while swimming or diving.

No main entry, see p. 132.

	March/April/May	June/July/August	Sept/Oct/Nov	Dec/Jan/Feb

KIWI, BROWN (COMMON)★

Where found New Zealand (North, South and Stewart islands). In forests and scrub.

Length Male up to 18in (460mm); female 22in (560mm).

Weight Male 6¼lb (2.8kg); female up to 7¾lb (3.5kg).

Lifespan 10 years or more.

The flightless kiwis forage by night, pairs calling to keep in touch in thick forest. They rest by day in burrows or under spreading tree roots (except on Stewart Island, where they are active by day). Kiwis probably mature at 2 years old, pairing for life. They breed once a year.

The main breeding season begins. After pairs have courted and mated, the female lays 1 large white egg (or possibly 2) weighing up to 1lb (450g) in July (midwinter). The male incubates it for 9-12 weeks. Pairs maintain breeding territories.

The breeding season continues. A kiwi chick emerges from its nesting burrow to feed within a week of hatching. Kiwis have nostrils in their beak tips, and probe soil and dead leaves with their long beaks to scent and feed on spiders, worms, beetles, insect larvae, seeds and fruit.

Egg-laying ends in February. Because much of their habitat has been cleared for farming, kiwi numbers have declined They are now protected and some are living on farmland. Kiwis are preyed on by dogs, cats, stoats and opossums.

Main entry p. 165.

KOALA

Where found Eastern Australia. In eucalyptus forests.

Length 21-33in (530-840mm). Largest in south of range.

Weight Male 14-26½lb (6-12kg); female 11-24lb (5-11kg).

Lifespan 20 years.

Koala babies spend the southern autumn inside their mother's pouch, attached to a teat. They were only 1in (25mm) long at birth and are not yet big enough to move about on their own. Adults sleep by day and feed between dusk and midnight, mainly on eucalypt leaves.

At 5 months old the babies' eyes open and they begin to peer out of the pouch. They are weaned onto pap the mother produces from digested leaves and excretes at intervals instead of her normal droppings. Infants first leave the pouch when they are 6-7 months old.

Newly emerged infants can move about on their own, but are carried by the mother, usually on her back, when she travels any distance. Infants nibble leaves, but are not fully weaned until 11-12 months old. In the north mating peaks in November.

Mating peaks in December in the south. Males, fully mature at 5 years old, compete noisily and scent-mark trees with oil from a chest gland. A female bears a single baby 5 weeks after mating. It crawls into her pouch.

Main entry p. 146.

KOMODO DRAGON (ORA)★

Where found Indonesia, on the Lesser Sunda Islands of Komodo, Rintja, Padar, Gili Mota, Owadi Sami and Flores. Scrubland.

Length About 10ft (3m).

Weight About 365lb (166kg).

Lifespan 20-30 years, perhaps even 50.

In March the dragons take advantage of the mallee fowl breeding season, digging up and eating their eggs. The dragons' eggs hatch after the rainy season, about 9 months after laying. The emerging hatchlings are about 12in (300mm) long. They disperse to fend for themselves.

May-June is the dragons' main breeding season. Courtship and mating take place when several dragons are attracted to carrion. Females lay about 30 eggs in the dry season, 2-4 weeks after mating. They bury them 2ft (610mm) deep in a pit on the grassy lower slopes of an island.

The komodo dragon is the largest of the monitor lizards. In the islands where the dragon lives, there are no carnivorous mammals – it fills the niche they would normally occupy. A komodo dragon feeds by day, taking feral goats, wild pigs and deer as well as carrion, and swallows some prey whole – it can swallow a small pig in 15 minutes, drawing it slowly in by movements of its jaws. Large prey is torn into chunks with teeth and claws. The dragon has a long forked tongue with which it scents its prey.

Main entry p. 76.

LADYBIRD, CONVERGENT

Where found California, USA (where it is known as a ladybug or ladybeetle). In all but the driest parts.

Length Adult ¼-⅜in (6-10mm); larva ½in (13mm).

Lifespan Adult rarely more than a year; larva 3-4 weeks.

The ladybirds fly from the mountains to the valleys to feed on aphids. Females lay batches of about 50 oval, yellow eggs on the undersides of leaves. These hatch in a few days into blue-grey larvae, which also feed on aphids, and change into adults in May.

To transform, each larva attached itself to a twig or grass stem where it split its skin to reveal a brown pupal coat from which it emerged as an adult a few days later. By June it had flown into the coastal hills or Sierra Nevada mountains to escape the parched lowland vegetation.

The new adults (and older adults that have escaped hunting birds) feed to build up fat reserves, then doze through the summer clustered on plants. In the cool of autumn they seek sheltered places in caves, canyons or tree trunks and hibernate in tens of thousands.

On warm February days, the ladybirds begin to emerge. They mate, then fly to the lowlands of the Central Valley. They are the commonest of 125 species of Californian ladybird, and are useful in controlling aphids on valuable crops.

Main entry p. 130.

LANGUR, COMMON (GREY)

Where found Indian sub-continent, including Sri Lanka. Forest and scrubland.

Length Up to 2ft 6in (760mm).

Weight Male 40lb (18kg); female 24lb (11kg).

Lifespan 20 years or more.

In most areas it is the main birth season. In the north, the spring's new leaves give an improved diet, and females can produce more milk for their newborn. The first of last year's infants are weaned after suckling for 10-15 months. Group takeovers by new males reach their peak.

New group leaders may kill the unweaned infants to bring the females on heat again, and the social life of the groups is disrupted. High summer temperatures force the langurs to seek shade in the middle of the day. All last year's infants are weaned by August.

It is the main mating season, especially in the more seasonal areas of the north. Females are pregnant for 6 months. They give birth only once every 2 years. The langurs now feed mainly on leaves as fruit becomes less available.

In southern areas, which are less strictly seasonal, the birth season begins. In the far north, in the Himalayan foothills, winter forces the langurs to travel farther afield in search of food such as leaves, tree bark and roots.

Main entry p. 49.

		March/April/May	June/July/August	Sept/Oct/Nov	Dec/Jan/Feb
	**LARGE BLUE BUTTERFLY** **Where found** Europe, only where wild thyme grows. In Britain became extinct in 1979. Heaths, dunes, hillsides. **Length** Caterpillar about ⅝in (16mm). **Wingspan** 1½-2in (38-50mm). **Lifespan** Adult a few weeks; caterpillar about 9 months.	In red ant nests, hibernating caterpillars wake up and resume eating ant eggs and grubs. A few weeks later, in May, each caterpillar hangs from the nest roof by its hind legs and turns into a chrysalis, inside which it spends 3 weeks transforming into an adult.	In June or early July, an adult butterfly emerges from each chrysalis, leaves the ant nest and finds a mate. Females lay eggs on wild thyme buds. At the end of July the caterpillars hatch and feed only on the buds and flowers of the wild thyme plant.	When about ⅛in (3mm) long, each caterpillar drops off the plant onto the ground and waits to be picked up by a red ant, which carries it to the ant nest. The ants stroke the caterpillar, which then secretes honeydew, on which they feed. The caterpillar eats ant eggs and larvae.	The caterpillars spend the winter hibernating in the red ant nest, which is often under a wild thyme plant. Main entry p. 190.
	**LEAF-CUTTER BEE** **Where found** Throughout Eurasia; USA (introduced in imported leaf stalks). Grassland and open woods. **Length** ½in (13mm). **Lifespan** Adult 3-4 months.	The bees emerge as adults from their pupal cases in tunnels in tree trunks or hollow stems, and begin to feed on nectar gathered from open flowers. They lead solitary lives, and therefore have no need to collect nectar to store as honey in a communal nest or hive.	Bees seek partners and mate. In July, females cut out oval pieces from leaves and make 20-30 leaf nests; each contains honey and an egg and is sealed with a piece of cut leaf. Nests are tucked into hollow stems or old boreholes in rotten wood. The larvae hatch after a few weeks.	Male bees have died after mating, and the females die after egg-laying. In their nest chambers, the larvae hatched from the eggs feed and grow until they turn into pupae (develop protective cases in which they change into adults). The leaf nests disintegrate.	The pupae remain within their pupal cases inside the stalk or bore-hole throughout the winter. Some may be eaten by birds or destroyed by damp. Main entry p. 161.
	**LEATHERBACK TURTLE★★** **Where found** Tropical waters; sometimes temperate and even subpolar seas. Breeds on beaches. **Length of carapace** (shell) 8ft (2.4m) or more. **Weight** About 1900lb (860kg). **Lifespan** Possibly 50 years.	In South Africa, leather-backs nest on Natal beaches, laying about 100 eggs 2in (50mm) in diameter in holes in the sand. Each female fills about 6 nests at 10-day intervals. Incubation time varies with the temperature, and may take 4 months or more.	In French Guiana, 300 leatherbacks (one of the largest nesting groups) mate off Silebache Beach before the females go ashore to lay the eggs fertilised last year. Each hatchling is 2¾in (70mm) long, weighs 2oz (57g) and has white marks on its back. They disappear when it is 5ft (1.5m) long.	North Atlantic leather-backs regularly enter temperate waters as they follow jellyfish drifting on the Gulf Stream. They sometimes mistake plas-tic bags for jellyfish and choke to death. The larg-est leatherback found was washed up at Har-lech, Wales, in 1989; it weighed 2014lb (914kg).	All year, leatherbacks feed mainly on jellyfish. Little is known of their lives, as they are difficult to keep in captivity. Their rubbery shells are ridged, and their front flippers, spanning about 9ft (2.7m), are longer than in other turtles. Main entry p. 145.
	**LEMMING, NORWAY** **Where found** Scandinavia. In regions of low-growing vegetation on permanently frozen subsoil (tundra). **Length** 4-5in (100-125mm). **Weight** 1½-4oz (43-113g). **Lifespan** 1-2 years.	Breeding starts early in the year if food such as moss, roots and lichen is in good supply and the population numbers are low. Also if there is sufficient snow cover above burrows, and no flooding. Females are pregnant for about 3 weeks and bear 1-13 (usually 5 or 6) young.	It is the main breeding season, when food is at its most abundant. The lemmings' globe nests of grasses, lichens and mosses are sited under fallen trees and stones. The youngsters are weaned at 14-16 days old, and are able to breed at 4-5 weeks old.	When populations increase to very high numbers, breeding is reduced and youngsters take longer to mature. Many young adults are forced to find new pastures, and go on large-scale migrations to search for new territory. Many die in the attempt.	Lemmings do not hiber-nate, but are active under the snow, feeding on mosses and moving about in crisscross systems of snow tunnels. Main entry p. 272.
	**LEMON SHARK** **Where found** West Atlantic from New Jersey to Brazil; east Pacific from Gulf of California to Ecuador. Inshore waters. **Length** Up to 10ft 6in (3.2m). **Weight** Over 265lb (120kg). **Lifespan** Probably over 50 years.	In early spring, sharks gather in shallow bays, such as Florida Bay (by Florida Keys), to mate. The embryos take a year to develop within the female's body. Females arrive at their pupping grounds, such as Bimini atoll (Bahamas), in May. They bear up to 19 pups, but usually 11.	Pups disperse at birth and establish territories (for example, among mangrove roots). They stay there a year feeding on small sea creatures. When 2ft 6in-3ft 4in (760-1015mm) long, they tend to eat octopuses. In their 2nd year the pups move farther afield, and then go to sea.	Lemon sharks are a common species, named for the yellow tinge on their skin. They feed at night on bony fish and rays in saltwater creeks and around docks and wharves. During the day they head for deeper water. They are slow and sluggish, and can tolerate warm water temperatures and low oxygen levels. The young, 2ft (610mm) long at birth, grow at an average rate of 6in (150mm) and 8lb (3.6kg) a year. They are not sexually mature until at least 12 years old, when about 7ft 8in (2.3m) long and 250lb (114kg) in weight. Main entry p. 107.	

	March/April/May	June/July/August	Sept/Oct/Nov	Dec/Jan/Feb

LEMUROID POSSUM

Where found Australia. A small area of upland rain forest in north Queensland.

Head-and-body length 12-16in (300-400mm); tail 10½-13in (265-330mm).

Weight 1½-2¼lb (700-1020g).

Lifespan 4-5 years.

Young possums 8-10 months old begin to leave their parents to establish their own territories. Where there are plenty of leaves, fruit and flowers for them to eat, small groups of possums forage together in the trees at night.

In August, females give birth to single babies; the length of pregnancy may be 2-7 weeks, as far as is known. Each tiny youngster, at birth only about half the weight of a sugar cube, hangs on to a teat in its mother's pouch. Females born the previous year are now sexually mature.

Young possums leave their mother's pouch at 2 months old and ride on her back. The father may help to look after the baby. The possums are very agile and leap from tree to tree using hands, feet and tails. The long tail has a patch of bare, roughened skin at the tip to help it grip.

The youngsters are weaned when they are 6-7 months old, but do not yet leave their mothers to live independently.

Main entry p. 218.

LEOPARD★

Where found Africa (mainly south of the Sahara); Asia (mainly south). Forest, scrub.

Head-and-body length About 5ft (1.5m); tail 3ft (1m).
Shoulder height 2ft (610mm).

Weight Male 132lb (60kg); female 120lb (55kg).

Lifespan Up to 20 years.

Leopards, unlike other large cats such as lions and cheetahs, prefer to live in woods and forests, so their eating habits are less seasonal. They will eat any animal they can catch – small antelopes, rodents, monkeys, fish, birds, snakes, domestic animals – and will also take carrion. They are good, fast climbers and swimmers. Generally, leopards are solitary hunters and tend to hunt by night. Any leftovers from a kill are cached in a tree. Leopards defend their territory all year round, marking the boundaries with urine and scrapes on tree trunks. Pairs come together only for mating, which occurs in winter in temperate areas – northern Asia, North Africa, and the far south of Africa – but elsewhere at any time of the year. Litters of 1-3 cubs are born about 14 weeks after mating. They are hidden in thickets or rocky outcrops until weaned at about 3 months, then start to accompany their mother on hunting forays. At 22 months, they leave to find their own territory. Females rarely manage to rear more than one cub of a litter, because of the scarcity of food and because of predators such as tigers, hyenas and wild dogs.

Main entry p. 238.

LEOPARD SEAL

Where found Antarctica, and occasionally beyond. Round the fringes of the ice pack and islands.

Length 9-12ft (2.7-3.7m).

Weight 605-990lb (275-450kg).

Lifespan About 25 years.

Female seals become pregnant as the embryos inside them (fertilised in November or December) implant in the womb. Pups will be born 8 months later. The seals hunt alone, generally around islands and the edge of the ice. They feed mainly on penguins and other seal species.

In midwinter, when the pack ice is at its thickest and greatest extent, the seals may swim long distances to find food, perhaps more than 1550 miles (2500km). They sometimes travel as far as southern Australia and South Africa.

In November, the first births of the season occur on the loose pack ice or small islands. Females suckle their single pups for about a month, then abandon them and mate with males that have hauled out onto the ice. Then they return to sea.

Births and mating continue in December. After mating, the implantation of the fertilised egg into the womb is delayed. Newly independent pups catch small fish and krill at first.

Main entry p. 32.

LION, AFRICAN

Where found Africa: not north or west/central forests. Grassland and scrub.

Head-and-body length Male 9ft 6in (2.9m); female 8ft 6in (2.6m); tail 3ft (1m). **Shoulder height** 3ft 9in (1.1m).

Weight 290-410lb (130-190kg).

Lifespan Up to 30 years.

In East Africa, mating peaks April-May, in the rainy season, when the lions prey heavily on wildebeest. Lions can breed all year round, but mating peaks at different times in different places. A female mates again when her cubs are 2 years old. Lions are able to breed at 3-4 years old.

Lions on Serengeti Plain (northern Tanzania) are short of food because their prey has migrated to better grazing. Many cubs under 2 years old starve. In East Africa, births peak August-September. Females bear litters of 1-5 cubs (usually 2-3) after a 15-week pregnancy.

Births peak in the south. While they hunt, females keep their cubs secluded in cover, away from the pride. This is to protect the cubs from predators such as hyenas, and also from adult male lions – outsiders that may kill them when they attempt to take over the pride.

In East Africa, newborn zebras, wildebeest and gazelles provide the lions' main food as the November-December rains produce abundant new grass. Cubs are weaned at 3-6 months old. They can hunt for themselves at 1 year old.

Main entry p. 140.

LOON, COMMON (GREAT NORTHERN DIVER)

Where found Breeds on lakes in Alaska, Canada, Iceland, Greenland. Winters on North American coasts.

Length 2ft 6in-2ft 9in (760-840mm).

Wingspan 4ft 6in (1.4m).

Weight 6-8lb (2.7-3.6kg).

From mid-March, birds wintering in the Gulf of Mexico head north and arrive on inland lakes as the ice breaks up. Birds reach Alaska singly, in pairs or in small flocks from late April to early May. Pairs establish a territory in 2 weeks and prepare a nest by the waterside.

Egg-laying begins in late May or June. A female normally lays 2 eggs, which both parents incubate for 4 weeks. Once the chicks hatch the nest is abandoned. Chicks can dive at 2-3 days, and may ride on a parent's back until 3 weeks old. The territory is kept until August.

Chicks can feed themselves at 6 weeks old, and can fly at 3 months old. Northern birds head south in September. In eastern North America, flocks of 700-800 gather on the Great Lakes, before heading south. In October, the first birds arrive in the Gulf and Baja California.

Loons winter along the west coast from south Alaska to Baja California, and along the east coast from Maryland to the Gulf of Mexico. They spend most time on the water, feeding by day on fish, crustaceans such as small crabs, and insects.

Main entry p. 131.

		March/April/May	June/July/August	Sept/Oct/Nov	Dec/Jan/Feb

LYNX

Where found Alaska; Canada; north USA; Eurasia. Northern and alpine coniferous forests.

Length 2ft 6in-4ft 3in (760-1300mm).
Shoulder height 22in (560mm).

Weight 40-55lb (18-25kg).

Lifespan 12-15 years.

March/April/May: Mating takes place in March or April. Males utter carrying calls to deter other males, and rivals may fight. Females are pregnant for 8-11 weeks, and in May or June bear 1-4 young in a den such as an old badger sett or among tree roots. Kittens' eyes open at 9-10 days old.

June/July/August: At 6 weeks old the kittens can catch very small prey, and they are weaned at 8 weeks old but stay with their mother until the following spring. Lynxes hunt mainly at night. Their prey is mostly snowshoe and Arctic hares, young deer or chamois, lemmings and ground birds.

Sept/Oct/Nov: In good years, prey such as hares is still plentiful. Lynxes are mainly solitary and defend a home territory, defined by scent marks. North American lynxes have more extensive home ranges during bad years – when snowshoe hares are scarce.

Dec/Jan/Feb: Youngsters usually spend the winter with their mother, and leave to find their own ranges in spring. They can breed at 1 year old. In most of Europe, loss of their habitat has made lynxes rare.

No main entry, see pp. 103 and 273.

MACARONI PENGUIN

Where found Sub-Antarctic seas. Breeds on islands such as the South Shetland Islands and South Georgia.

Height 2ft 4in (710mm).

Weight 9lb (4kg).

Lifespan 10 or more years.

March/April/May: Adult penguins moult for 3-4 weeks; they do not feed but live on fat reserves. In April, adults and youngsters abandon the breeding colonies for the sea. Young penguins do not return to land to breed until they are at least 5 years old.

June/July/August: At sea as on land, the penguins lead a sociable life. They feed mostly on krill, and also take fish and squid. Their chief predators are leopard seals and killer whales.

Sept/Oct/Nov: In October, the birds return to breeding areas. Colonies can number 5 million birds. A male establishes a territory round the nest site, and usually mates with last year's partner. A female lays 1 small and 1 large egg, but only 1 chick is raised. Parents share the 4-5 weeks of incubation.

Dec/Jan/Feb: Chicks are at risk from seabirds such as skuas. A male fasts while he guards his chick for 2-3 weeks and the female feeds it. Then the chicks form small crèches and are fed by their parents for 8-9 weeks. Adults fatten up for the moult.

No main entry, see p. 34.

MAGELLANIC PENGUIN

Where found South America. Breeds on coasts southward from about Valparaiso (Chile) and Buenos Aires (Argentina).

Height 2ft 4in (710mm).

Weight 9lb (4kg).

Lifespan 10 or more years.

March/April/May: All birds complete the moult and then go to sea to feed on fish and squid. Atlantic birds fish in the cold Falklands Current along South America's east coast, and Pacific birds in the cold Humboldt current along the west coast.

June/July/August: Most prey is found near the surface, and the penguins do not dive more than about 16-32ft (5-10m) when feeding. Some birds come ashore coated in oil from ballast water illegally dumped by oil tankers. In August the males begin to arrive at breeding areas to claim nest sites.

Sept/Oct/Nov: Females arrive in mid-September to join last year's mate. New breeders pair and dig shallow burrows up to 3ft (1m) long with their feet. Egg-laying begins in October, a female laying 2 eggs in the burrow. At first she incubates while the male feeds at sea. The eggs hatch after 4 weeks.

Dec/Jan/Feb: Pairs are still tending late chicks, but leave them for short periods to fish. Juvenile birds, which arrived in late November, go inland to practise courtship. The chicks gather in crèches and fledge in January. Juveniles begin to moult.

Main entry p. 57.

MAGPIE

Where found Eurasia, western Canada and western USA. In most areas (except in the far north and in coniferous forests).

Length 18in (460mm), including tail 8-10in (200-250mm) long.

Weight About 9oz (260g).

March/April/May: In late March or April, pairs build large, domed nests of sticks. The female lays 5-8 bluish-green eggs, which she alone incubates. They hatch in 2-3 weeks. The chicks are fed by both parents and fledge after 3-4 weeks.

June/July/August: The young magpies stay within their parents' territory during the summer, learning to search out their own food – such as insects, carrion, fruit, the eggs and nestlings of other birds, frogs, snails and small mammals. Their parents may continue to feed them for some time.

Sept/Oct/Nov: The youngsters leave their parents and often join up in large, noisy groups as they search the countryside for food. Some try to establish territories of their own, and may be attacked if they encroach on the territory of an established pair.

Dec/Jan/Feb: In hard winters, magpies may squabble over food. In urban areas they have been quick to exploit the food people put out for other birds, and their harsh, chattering call has become common.

Main entry p. 252.

MALLEE FOWL

Where found Southern Australia, except the east coast. In dry eucalyptus scrubland.

Length 2ft (610mm).

Weight About 4lb (1.8kg).

Lifespan Up to 25 years in captivity.

March/April/May: In suitably damp conditions the breeding season may continue through to the end of April, but in dry years it ends earlier. Mallee fowl feed mainly on insects, seeds, buds, fruit and small animals.

June/July/August: Although rarely seen together, mallee fowl pair for life. In winter, pairs begin preparing a mound in which to lay their eggs in spring. They scrape out a huge pit and then gradually fill it with sand and leaf litter from a wide area round about until it is more than 3ft (1m) high.

Sept/Oct/Nov: The male regulates the mound temperature by opening or covering it. He allows the female to lay eggs only when the conditions are right. She lays 15-30 eggs into the top of the mound at 1-14 day intervals, depending on her own condition and the rainfall, as the leaves need to be moist.

Dec/Jan/Feb: Egg-laying continues through the southern summer in the wetter habitats. Eggs hatch after about 8 weeks and the chicks dig their way out of the mound. They take to the scrub to live independently, and can fly when 1 day old.

Main entry p. 146.

	March/April/May	June/July/August	Sept/Oct/Nov	Dec/Jan/Feb

MANATEE, WEST INDIAN (CARIBBEAN)★★

Where found West Atlantic coast from North Carolina (USA) to central Brazil. Warm waters – coastal shallows, estuaries, rivers.

Length 8-15ft (2.4-4.6m).

Weight 880lb (400kg).

Lifespan Maybe 28 years.

A manatee (a type of sea cow) has a stocky body, one pair of flippers and a rounded tail. Though active at any time, manatees browse mainly at night on underwater plants, in sea or fresh water. They need a lot of food to keep their huge bodies going, and to digest it have intestines more than 150ft (46m) long. A 15ft (4.6m) long manatee kept in captivity ate 60-99lb (27-45kg) of food daily. A manatee's molars, needed to grind the tough food, are replaced throughout its life. To find food, manatees rely on touch – with their bristly snouts – and possibly smell, and sometimes take up food in their flippers. They usually surface to breathe every 3-5 minutes, but can stay submerged for 20 minutes. Although mating may occur at any time, in some areas it takes place seasonally – at times of plentiful food. After a year's pregnancy, a female bears a single calf about 3ft (1m) long, weighing 40-60lb (18-27kg), and born underwater. The calf is suckled for 12-18 months. It stays with its mother for 1-2 years, and is sexually mature at 3-10 years. Manatees shun water cooler than 20°C (68°F), so in autumn US manatees migrate to warmer water.

Main entry p. 39.

MARINE IGUANA★

Where found Galápagos Islands (Pacific), on coasts of some islands only.

Length Up to 5ft (1.5m).

Weight 7½lb (3.4kg).

The only sea-going lizards, marine iguanas spend much of their time on traditional roosting rocks, basking in the sun to raise their body temperature before swimming. Every 3-5 days, at low water, they make 20-minute-long dives to 15ft (4.6m), sometimes 50ft (15m), to feed on seaweeds. Breeding takes place from January to March, during the rainy season in the arid lowlands where the iguanas live. On different islands, males are different colours – dark grey, red or green. A male may hold a territory containing several females. Rival males are challenged with a bout of head nodding, followed by a fight if the warning is ignored. After mating, a female digs a burrow, using both fore and hind feet, in the soft grey lava sand. Then she turns round with just her head protruding from the entrance so that she can lay her eggs deep in the burrow; she lays 2 oval, soft-shelled eggs with an 8-minute interval between them. After laying, the burrow is filled, carefully disguised and left. The eggs hatch after about 16 weeks (May-July). The 12in (300mm) babies emerge and fend for themselves. Feral dogs are the chief predator.

Main entry p. 289.

MASKED (BLUE-FACED) BOOBY

Where found Tropical islands and coasts, including the Galápagos Islands (Pacific Ocean).

Length 2ft 6in (760mm).

Wingspan Up to 6ft (1.8m).

Weight About 5lb (2.3kg).

Lifespan Up to 23 years.

April is the peak breeding time on the tropical islands and coral islets of the Australian coast. Booby populations breed in loose colonies at the same time each year, but populations in different localities breed at different times, even in the same island group.

On Genovesa (Tower Island in the Galápagos group) the birds lay August-November, on the bare ground. The females lay 2 chalky white eggs, which are incubated on the birds' webbed feet. The eggs hatch after 6-8 weeks.

On Española (Hood Island in the Galápagos group) adult boobies are courting as the new generation of Genovesa chicks are close to fledging. Youngsters start to breed at 2-6 years old.

Boobies on Española lay their eggs November-February. If both eggs hatch, the older chick will usually kill the younger one eventually. Laying 2 eggs is probably an insurance against loss of the first chick.

Main entry p. 217.

MAYFLY, GREEN DRAKE

Where found Europe. Near fresh water. (One of 2000 species worldwide).

Length Adult 2-3in (50-75mm) including tail; larva (nymph) up to 1in (25mm).

Wingspan 1½in (38mm).

Lifespan Adult 2-3 days; nymph up to 3 years.

Fully grown nymphs climb out of the water onto plant stalks to moult into winged sub-adults each with a ⅝in (16mm) wingspan. Sub-adults moult into black and gold adults. The adults do not feed, but fly for a day or so, and mate in the air. Females lay eggs into the water.

The eggs hatch below the surface of the water almost at once. The nymphs burrow into the bottom mud using their forelegs and tusks on their jaws. They breathe through gills and feed mainly on algae. Some mayfly species emerge, fly and mate in June.

Nymphs moult maybe 20 times or more as they develop. Like the winged adults, they have three long, jointed tails. Some species of nymph feed on algae as they cling to stones in fast-running water. As the weather gets colder, nymphs may become less active.

Many nymphs seek refuge in the warmer depths of rivers and streams, often below a layer of ice.

Main entry p. 114.

MESEMBRYANTHEMUM

Where found North and southern Africa; South America. In desert and semi-desert areas.

Height Up to 12in (300mm).

Diameter of flower 1-4in (25-100mm).

Lifespan A few weeks.

Mesembryanthemums flower at the start of the wet season, and release their seeds in wet weather, which is when they germinate best. In the driest areas of southern Africa, sporadic rains – perhaps once every 20 years – cause buried seeds to germinate. The plants grow quickly, producing masses of white, yellow, pink or purple daisy-like flowers. These are pollinated by the many insects that appear after the rains. Within 2 or 3 weeks, the flowers develop into fruiting capsules, which split, releasing seeds that fall into the dry soil. The plants die, but their seeds survive until the next rains. In less arid areas, many mesembryanthemums survive a dry season by storing water in their fleshy leaves. The plants are well adapted to desert life, for they breathe in carbon dioxide (used in food production) at night and store it for photosynthesis (using sunlight to trigger food production) by day. Thus they can close their breathing pores by day, reducing water loss by up to 90 per cent. There are about 2000 species, including the ice plant *Cryophytum*, a native of southern Africa often grown in European gardens.

Main entry p. 283.

	March/April/May	June/July/August	Sept/Oct/Nov	Dec/Jan/Feb

MEXICAN FREE-TAILED BAT

Where found Mexico and southern USA. Roosts in caves or buildings.

Head-and-body length 1¾-4¾in (44-120mm).
Wingspan 10in (250mm).

Weight ⅜-½oz (10-14g).

Lifespan At least 8 years.

In spring, millions of bats arrive in New Mexico (USA) and roost in caves. At Carlsbad Caverns in south-east New Mexico from May to October, the outpouring of 500,000 bats at dusk every evening is a tourist attraction. From a distance the bats look like a smoke plume.

Births occur in June and July after a pregnancy of about 3 months. Infants of mothers out hunting for night-flying moths and beetles are sometimes suckled by other mothers. Young bats are weaned and can fly at 3-4 weeks old. By July some join the nightly exodus from the caves.

Bats may have to travel 40 miles (65km) from the caves to find food. At the peak of the evening exodus, they may fly out at a rate of 5000 a minute for an hour before a cave is empty. In November, the bats head south into Mexico, some travelling as far as 995 miles (1600km).

The migrating bats fly high and fast, averaging 25mph (40km/h). Some may hibernate for short periods. Mating is in late winter or early spring at traditional breeding sites in Mexico, before the bats migrate north. Some males do not migrate.

Main entry p. 172.

MINK

Where found North America; Europe; Russia; central Asia. Near rivers and lakes.

Head-and-body length Male 16in (400mm), tail 5in (125mm); female usually smaller.

Weight 1-3lb (450-1370g).

Lifespan About 10 years.

During March and April, males mate with several females. In some of the females, the fertilised egg does not implant in the womb immediately. Births may be anything from 5 to 11 weeks after mating. Litters, one each year, usually number 5 or 6 kits, although 17 have been recorded.

The young are born blind and naked in a den such as an old burrow or a crevice among tree roots or stones. They are tended by their mother alone, and are weaned at 8 weeks old. Then they join their mother in hunting for voles, frogs and other small animals.

Mink swim well, and catch slower-moving prey such as crayfish. In September, youngsters begin to search for territories of their own. They are mostly solitary, and defend waterside or marsh territories marked by scent and droppings. Youngsters can breed at about 1 year old.

Many young mink die in winter, when food is scarce. In late February, mature males start to wander widely in search of females to mate with.

Main entry p. 91.

MIRROR ORCHID

Where found Mediterranean area. In undisturbed grassland and woods.

Height 4-12in (100-300mm).

Lifespan Several years.

In March and April, the orchid produces flowers that have a lower lip with a shiny blue centre and a hairy, reddish fringe. The shape and scent resemble the female of a hairy wasp species. Newly emerged male wasps try to mate with the flower, and in doing so pollinate it.

By July, about 40 per cent of the orchid flowers will have been fertilised by the wasps. The flowers produce dry, brown, cylindrical fruit capsules that contain many seeds. Eventually the capsules split to release the tiny winged seeds.

The broad, strap-shaped leaves of the mirror orchid wither away, but its round, underground root tubers store food and last through the winter. Some of the seeds settle in places suitable for germination.

Buds on the tubers develop into new shoots early in the year, ready to flower in March. Some of the seeds will have germinated, but the seedlings take several years to reach maturity and flower.

Main entry p. 88.

MONARCH BUTTERFLY

Where found Southern Canada; USA; northern Mexico; Caribbean. Fields and meadows where there are milkweed plants.

Wingspan 3-4in (75-100mm).

Lifespan Adult possibly up to 1 year; caterpillar 10-38 days.

The butterflies are in the south of their range, and begin the journey north. Some breed on the way, but most on arrival. Eggs are laid on milkweed and hatch after a few days. The caterpillars feed on the leaves, and after 1-6 weeks turn into chrysalises. Butterflies emerge after 9-15 days.

In July the monarch butterflies, mostly those hatched on the way or on arrival, gather in large numbers to begin the journey south to spend winter in California, Mexico, Florida and the Caribbean. On the way, they fly and feed on nectar by day and rest during the night.

During October the butterflies arrive in their wintering areas and get ready to hibernate on trees. As caterpillars they absorbed poisons from milkweed leaves, and the butterflies, like the caterpillars, have a bitter taste that deters most predators. But some are eaten by mice.

Trees in the wintering areas are covered with thousands of hibernating monarchs. On sunny days, they wake up and take short flights before settling down again. Some colonies in the far south neither hibernate nor migrate.

Main entry p. 205.

MOOSE (ELK)

Where found Eurasia; North America. Northern forests, often by lakes and marshes.

Length 8-10ft (2.4-3m).
Shoulder height 5ft 6in-7ft 6in (1.7-2.3m).

Weight Male up to 1765lb (800kg); female smaller.

Lifespan Possibly 20 years.

In May, after a pregnancy of nearly 9 months, females leave their groups to give birth to 1 or 2 calves. Calves stay hidden in undergrowth until about 10 days old, when they can follow their mother and join her group. Males start to grow their new antlers in spring.

The last calves of the year are born in early June. For long hours, the females feed on green plants and leaves, often wading into the water, to maintain good condition while they suckle calves. Males fatten up in readiness for the rut, and shed the velvet on their huge antlers.

Calves are weaned, but stay with their mother for 2 years. Females come on heat and males fight each other to mate with them. Most fights are won by older, more dominant males, which father the most calves. Males lose weight during the rut, and may also sustain injuries.

The males shed their antlers. Weak, thin or exhausted animals may die, or fall prey to wolves. In winter the moose browse mainly on trees and shrubs. Young females mature at 2-3 years old.

Main entry p. 191.

	March/April/May	June/July/August	Sept/Oct/Nov	Dec/Jan/Feb

MUGGER (MARSH) CROCODILE★★

Where found Indian sub-continent. In freshwater marshes, lakes and rivers.

Length Up to 14ft (4.2m).

Weight About 250lb (114kg).

Lifespan Maybe 40 years.

Egg-laying continues until May. The female guards the nest mound, which is 5-7ft (1.5-2.1m) across and up to 3ft (1m) high, for 7-11 weeks. Egg stealers include jackals, mongooses, monitor lizards, pigs and people. Warm nests (34°C, 93°F), produce mainly males, and cool nests females.

When the hatchlings start to call, one of the parents digs them out and carries them to the water in a pouch formed by the floor of its mouth. Each hatchling is 10in (250mm) long and weighs 2-3½oz (60-100g).

During their first 2 years, the youngsters grow at about 4in (100mm) a year. Many fall prey to predators such as wading birds. Females are sexually mature at 6 years old, males at 10 years old. The crocodiles feed mainly on fish, frogs, turtles, water birds and deer.

Mating begins in January. In February, the female lays 10-50 oval eggs 3¼-1¾in (82-44mm) in a hollow scooped out in sandy soil. She covers them with earth and stays on top of the nest for long periods.

Main entry p. 75.

MUSK OX

Where found Greenland; Canada. In Arctic tundra.

Length Up to 7ft 6in (2.3m). **Shoulder height** 4ft 6in (1.4m).

Weight Male 700-900lb (319-410kg); female smaller.

Lifespan About 20 years.

Calves are born in April or May; they can follow their mother at an hour old but rarely join the herd until 2-3 days old. In danger from wolves, the calves often travel beneath their mothers' trailing coats. In late spring oxen moult their undercoats, and feed on willow and pine shoots.

Mating occurs in August. Rutting males give off a strong scent. Young bulls from bachelor herds challenge the dominant males in charge of herds. Cows are old enough to breed at 5 years of age, and normally bear one calf every other year.

Calves born the previous year are weaned. When attacked by predators such as wolves, the herd forms a tight defensive circle with the calves in the centre. In autumn the oxen start to grow their winter undercoats, which lift the outer ones to give the animals a shaggy look.

Herds in the south of the animals' range may move to snow-free grass. Elsewhere, the oxen paw through snow to find grasses, lichens and mosses to eat. Oxen survive blizzards by standing in a tight circle, often buried by snow.

Main entry p. 169.

NAKED MOLE RAT

Where found East Africa. In arid grassland and deserts.

Head-and-body length 2½-3½in (60-90mm); tail 1in (25mm).

Weight About 1-3oz (28-85g).

Lifespan 5 years in captivity.

Mole rats live in colonies of 50-100 animals in a system of tunnels 8-36in (200-910mm) below ground. Because they live underground, the mole rats are unaffected by the seasonal changes. The temperature in the tunnels is more or less constant at about 30°C (86°F), and the animals have all but lost their ability to regulate their body temperature in the way that most mammals do. They tend to be slow-growing and have small appetites. Mole rats are vegetarian, living off the underground roots and tubers of hardy desert plants. Their tunnels give them access to this food at all times, so they need never surface. In each

colony, there is one breeding female, or 'queen'. A handful of large males mate with her, and she gives birth to maybe 4 litters of up to 11 pups a year. The youngsters are suckled for about 3 weeks. All the offspring have set jobs: the smallest dig new tunnels and carry food to the central nest, bigger ones patrol the tunnels to make repairs and watch for intruders such as snakes, and the largest animals see off any intruders. If the queen dies, a large female takes over her role.

Main entry p. 280.

NAMAQUA SANDGROUSE

Where found South-west Africa. Desert fringes.

Length 11-19in (280-480mm).

Weight 5-14oz (140-400g).

Sandgrouse are pigeon-like birds that feed on seeds picked up from the ground. Usually they feed at dawn and dusk, often in flocks of up to 100. The birds may live a long way from water, and flocks of thousands regularly fly to water holes once a day. They breed during the wet season, when small seeds offer plenty of food for the growing chicks, and water is less scarce. In the west (Namibia), the rains occur June-August, and in the east (north-east Namibia, Botswana and Transvaal) October-March. The nest is a simple scrape in the ground, in the open or under a bush. The female lays 2-3 eggs, which both parents

incubate for 3-5 weeks. Chicks can feed themselves at once, but need to have water brought to them. At water holes, males soak their belly feathers in water and carry it to their chicks. Chicks fly at 4-5 weeks old, but not well enough to reach a water hole for another 4 weeks. Sandgrouse have dense, downy plumage that protects their nostrils from dust, and feathers on their legs to protect them from temperature extremes. Both chicks and adults are taken by birds of prey, particularly falcons.

Main entry p. 281.

NANKEEN NIGHT HERON

Where found Australia; South-east Asia (Indonesia, New Guinea, Philippines). Swamps and offshore islands.

Length 21-25in (530-640mm).

Weight 1¼-1¾lb (570-800g).

Lifespan Possibly up to 21 years, as in other night herons.

Many birds are in breeding colonies of 250 or more nests, with well-grown youngsters in the nests. The chicks start to wander from the nest at 3-4 weeks old, but they cannot fly until 6 weeks old. They are not fully independent until they are 7-8 weeks old.

The herons disperse in search of suitable swampy feeding areas, with dense thickets close by in which they can roost by day. They feed at night, mainly on fish, shrimps, small birds, small mammals and insects, as well as baby sea turtles.

On Australia's Great Barrier Reef, the first birds return to the nesting colonies in October, and renovate their stick-built nests in trees or on the ground. In November, females begin laying clutches of 2-3 eggs (sometimes up to 7). Both parents incubate the eggs.

The eggs hatch after 3 weeks, and the downy nestlings are fed by both parents. On the Great Barrier Reef, breeding coincides with the mass hatching of green turtles, ensuring a plentiful food supply for the chicks.

Main entry p. 58.

	March/April/May	June/July/August	Sept/Oct/Nov	Dec/Jan/Feb

NARWHAL★

Where found Seas in the Arctic region.

Length 12-16ft (3.7-5m).

Weight ¾-1½ tons.

Lifespan 30-50 years.

The narwhals are in the southern part of their range. As the weather gets warmer and the pack ice begins to melt, herds of up to 3000 collect at the edges of the ice, waiting to move farther north. Most mating takes place during the spring and early summer.

The narwhals move into summer quarters, for example the north of Baffin Bay (Canada). In July and August, females that mated in spring the year before produce single calves after a 14½-month pregnancy. Calves, about 5ft (1.5m) long at birth, are suckled for about 20 months.

As the northern seas start to freeze over, the narwhal herds migrate south. Young females can breed at 5-8 years old, young males at 11-13. Females give birth once every 2-3 years.

Winter is spent in more southerly waters at the edge of the pack ice. Narwhals feed on squid, shrimps and fish such as cod and flounder. They can dive for up to 20 minutes before they need to surface to blow and breathe.

Main entry p. 125.

NASSAU GROUPER

Where found West Indies; Bahamas; Bermuda. Near reefs and rocks.

Length Up to 3ft (1m).

Weight Up to 55lb (25kg).

For most of the year, Nassau groupers are solitary fish that feed on other fish and vigorously guard a territory against rival groupers. They are one of several types of grouper, which belong to the bass family, and are probably named for their habit of 'grouping' during courtship. The fish come together only at their traditional spawning grounds – for example, 100ft (30m) down off the coral reefs along the coast of Belize. Here the groupers congregate just before the year's first full moon. Bermudan groupers spawn as late as July, coinciding with the full moon. During their courtship display, groupers swim about

erratically, assessing the relative numbers of males and females. If there are not enough males, some older females will change into males ready for the next season. About 3 nights after the full moon, groups of 30-40 fish dive to 120ft (37m), then surge upwards, releasing ripe eggs and milt (sperm) at about 80ft (24m). The eggs float out to sea with the tide and currents, and those that are not eaten will eventually hatch into tiny fishes that may survive long enough to find their way back to the reef.

Main entry p. 28.

NILE CROCODILE★★

Where found Tropical and southern Africa, from Egypt (Upper Nile) to Transvaal. Rivers and lakes.

Length 15ft (4.6m); maximum 18ft (5.5m).

Weight Up to 1 ton.

Lifespan Possibly more than 40 years.

Crocodiles a few weeks old gather in crèches, but hunt alone for prey such as spiders. They themselves may be taken by fish eagles. Adults sit in waterside lairs dug in the sand, and slide into the water to feed on fish. In North-east Africa females are laying eggs.

In much of East and southern Africa it is the dry season, and the adult crocodiles may feed on large prey such as antelope, forced to drink from main rivers and deep water holes. Young crocodiles that are now 6 months old are about 18-20in (460-510mm) long.

It is the mating season in much of East Africa. Adults court and then mate in the water. A female digs a nest in the sand not far from water and lays tiers of 20-80 eggs. She covers the nest with soil and guards it. Eggs may be taken by animals such as monitor lizards or mongooses.

The babies hatch after about 13 weeks. The mother carries them to water in her mouth, and looks after them for a few weeks, sometimes helped by the father. Egg-laying continues in East and southern Africa and starts in West Africa.

Main entry p. 54.

OCELOT★★

Where found Americas from Mexico to northern Argentina. Forests and brush.

Length 2-3ft (610-910mm).

Shoulder height 18-20in (460-510mm).

Weight 24-35lb (11-16kg).

Lifespan 12-15 years.

Ocelots are medium-sized cats with buff or grey coats marked with dark brown spots or blotches and dark stripes on the neck. They are extensively trapped or shot for their beautiful fur, but little is known about their lives. In the southern USA they are probably extinct. The cats live mostly in thick forests and spend much of their time in the trees – they are good climbers. They generally sleep by day and emerge at dusk to hunt for small animals, birds and reptiles. Their prey also includes some of the larger ground-living rodents such as pacas and agoutis, as well as monkeys and pig-like peccaries. Unlike most

cats, ocelots run down their prey rather than ambush it. There is some evidence that they live and hunt in pairs. In many areas, ocelots breed at any time of the year, but in the north and south of their range mating takes place in spring, when males can be heard calling to mates at the beginning of the season. Females are pregnant for 12-13 weeks and give birth to litters of 1-4 kittens – usually 1 or 2 – probably in a rock crevice or hollow tree.

Main entry p. 217.

ORANGE-BELLIED PARROT★★

Where found South-east Australia. Breeds in west Tasmania and winters in southern Victoria and South Australia. Grassland and forest.

Length 8in (200mm).

The parrots leave Tasmania in March, as winter approaches, because the wet weather does not suit them. They migrate across the Bass Strait to south-east Australia. The parrots are an endangered species, and perhaps fewer than 300 survive.

On the Australian mainland, the parrots generally frequent open areas with scattered bushes, such as coastal grasslands, flats and salt marshes. They feed mainly on seeds. Young birds probably remain with their parents until next breeding season.

As summer approaches, the parrots return across the waters of Bass Strait to Tasmania. After courting and mating they nest in tree holes, often in eucalypt trees in remote forests. Females lay probably 2-5 eggs.

The female incubates the eggs for about 3 weeks, and is brought food by her mate. The parrot chicks hatch in midsummer, and leave the nest when they are 4-5 weeks old. They are fully fledged by the autumn.

Main entry p. 30.

		March/April/May	June/July/August	Sept/Oct/Nov	Dec/Jan/Feb

ORIBI

Where found East and southern Africa. Open grasslands.

Length 20-26in (510-660mm).
Shoulder height 2ft (610mm).

Weight 31-46lb (14-21kg).

Lifespan 12 years.

Mating takes place as soon as last season's fawns are weaned. The youngsters begin to accompany their parents on their daily foraging round their territory. Oribis feed mainly on short grass.

This is generally the coolest time of year south of the Equator. Oribis on the high plateaus of southern Africa are often at their most active, seeking out sufficient food to allow them to keep up their body temperature.

Last year's fawns are now 9 months old or more and are fully independent. They leave their parents' territory in search of mates. From September to January, the next generation of fawns is born. In East Africa, the November rains bring a new flush of grass.

Summer rains in most parts of the south ensure plenty of grass, so there is ample food for the females to produce plenty of milk. Fawns stay in hiding for the 3-4 months during which their mothers suckle them.

Main entry p. 259.

OSPREY (FISH HAWK)

Where found Worldwide, except South America. Near fresh and salt water.

Length 20-23in (510-580mm).
Wingspan 5ft (1.5m).

Weight 3-4¼lb (1.4-1.9kg).

Lifespan 5-15 years.

In March, birds that breed in the north move there from southern wintering areas such as Africa and Paraguay. They arrive at breeding areas in April or May, often returning to the same nest. Some juvenile birds fly north in May, others wait until next year's migration.

Females lay 2-4 eggs in large stick nests on top of trees, bushes, rock pinnacles, or rarely on the ground. Incubation lasts about 5 weeks. The male brings fish (the birds' main food) to his mate, and to the chicks until they are 6 weeks old. They fly when they are 8-10 weeks old.

Northern breeders start migrating south in August and September. Some birds go only as far as the Mediterranean or the Caribbean. Red Sea birds re-occupy island nest sites in September; their chicks hatch late-November-December. In warmer areas, breeding birds do not migrate.

Breeding in the southern tropics coincides with the rains. Courting displays by male ospreys include soaring, swooping and diving from high in the air, sometimes carrying fish. Ospreys reach sexual maturity at 3 years old.

Main entry p. 261.

OSTRICH

Where found South Africa; East Africa; Sahara and adjacent Sahel region. In dry grasslands.

Height Male about 8ft (2.4m); female about 6ft (1.8m).

Weight 140-230lb (63-105kg).

Lifespan 30-68 years.

In South Africa, the adults and the growing chicks band together in larger groups and establish a pecking order. In different localities, ostriches breed at different times, but often before the onset of rains so that growing birds will have enough to eat.

Their long legs enable ostriches to forage over long distances to find food plants amid sparse vegetation. In East Africa, ostriches breed during the dry season. In South Africa, the sexes separate into different flocks ready for the courtship before they disperse into nesting territories.

In South Africa, breeding begins. A male mates with 3 or 4 females, and in the next 3 weeks each lays 4-8 eggs in one nest (a scrape in the soil) to give a clutch of about 25. The eggs are incubated for 6 weeks by the male and dominant female. About half hatch. Chicks feed themselves at once.

Chicks are tended by the male and the dominant female; they may try to distract predators such as jackals. They also shade the chicks from the sun, and lead them to food and water. Only about 1 chick in 10 survives to be 1 year old.

Main entry p. 213.

OTTER, EUROPEAN (EURASIAN) RIVER★★

Where found Europe and Asia south of tundra; North Africa. Quiet rivers, streams.

Head-and-body length Male up to 3ft (1m), tail 16in (400mm); female smaller.

Weight About 22lb (10kg).

Lifespan 15 years.

In spring, females give birth to up to 5 cubs (usually 2-3) after a 9-week pregnancy. They are born in a secluded den in a river bank and are suckled for about 7 weeks. Youngsters of 1 year old are now fully independent and begin to establish their own territories.

By midsummer the cubs are very active and spend much of their time playing. At 2-3 months old their fluffy baby coats change to waterproof adult coats and they take their first swim, learning from their mother how to catch food such as eels, crayfish and roach.

In the southern part of their range particularly, otters breed at any time of the year. Females come on heat for about two weeks every 30-40 days. Otters feed mostly at night – mainly on fish, which they carry ashore to eat. They groom their coats a lot to keep them sleek and waterproof.

Northern adult otters seek mates, finding each other by scent. The male mates with a number of females along a stretch of river, and plays little or no part in rearing the youngsters. Usually female otters have only one litter a year.

Main entry p. 161.

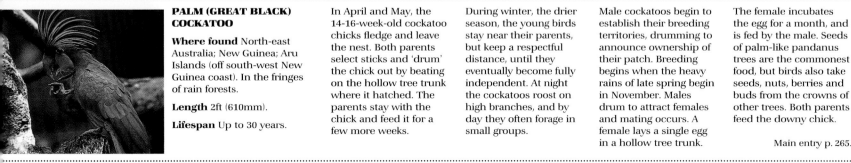

PALM (GREAT BLACK) COCKATOO

Where found North-east Australia; New Guinea; Aru Islands (off south-west New Guinea coast). In the fringes of rain forests.

Length 2ft (610mm).

Lifespan Up to 30 years.

In April and May, the 14-16-week-old cockatoo chicks fledge and leave the nest. Both parents select sticks and 'drum' the chick out by beating on the hollow tree trunk where it hatched. The parents stay with the chick and feed it for a few more weeks.

During winter, the drier season, the young birds stay near their parents, but keep a respectful distance, until they eventually become fully independent. At night the cockatoos roost on high branches, and by day they often forage in small groups.

Male cockatoos begin to establish their breeding territories, drumming to announce ownership of their patch. Breeding begins when the heavy rains of late spring begin in November. Males drum to attract females and mating occurs. A female lays a single egg in a hollow tree trunk.

The female incubates the egg for a month, and is fed by the male. Seeds of palm-like pandanus trees are the commonest food, but birds also take seeds, nuts, berries and buds from the crowns of other trees. Both parents feed the downy chick.

Main entry p. 265.

		March/April/May	June/July/August	Sept/Oct/Nov	Dec/Jan/Feb

PANDA, GIANT★

Where found Central and western China. In a few cool, damp, bamboo forest areas.

Length 5ft 6in (1.7m).
Shoulder height 2ft 6in (760mm).

Weight 220-330lb (100-150kg).

Lifespan 20 years.

In April or May, female pandas come on heat for a few days only. The pandas live in separate territories, and find mating partners by voice and scent. Females can breed when they are about 5 years old, males at about 7 years old.

After mating the partners split up and continue their solitary lives. They feed mainly on bamboo shoots, held in their forepaws. A female is pregnant for 4-5½ months. As the time of birth draws near she builds a nest of bamboo stalks in a cave or other sheltered den.

In October or November, the female gives birth to 1 or 2 cubs, but raises only one of them. The small, helpless baby weighs only about 5oz (140g) and is carried in its mother's mouth. Its eyes open when it is 6-8 weeks old.

A new cub begins to move about on its own at 3 months old. At 4 months old it weighs about 6½lb (3kg). It is weaned at 6 months old. Cubs are independent once they are about 1 year old, when they weigh about 60lb (27kg).

Main entry p. 192.

PEAFOWL

Where found India, Pakistan, Sri Lanka. Wooded areas, especially in foothills.

Length Male (without train) 3ft 3in-5ft 3in (1-1.6m); female 3ft (1m).

Weight Male 9-13lb (4-6kg); female 6-9lb (2.7-4kg).

In south India it is the main breeding season. Males defend territories and attract females by displaying their train in a fan-shape. A male may mate with 3 or 4 hens. After mating a female lays 4-6 eggs in a shallow scrape sometimes lined with grass, in the ground amid undergrowth.

It is the main breeding season in northern and central regions. After laying, females alone incubate the eggs for a month. Chicks leave the nest within hours and follow their mother. In high summer, the birds feed mainly at dawn and dusk, and shelter by day in dense cover.

All through the year peafowl (except for the females sitting on eggs) roost at night in tall trees to avoid predators such as mongooses and cats. By day the birds feed mainly on seeds, berries and plant shoots, and will also take insects, worms, reptiles and small animals.

It is the main breeding season in Sri Lanka. At any time of year, males call with ear-splitting shrieks. After breeding, a male usually moults his train. Young males attain full breeding plumage at 3-5 years old. Females probably mature earlier.

Main entry p. 48.

PETREL, SOUTHERN GIANT

Where found All southern oceans. Breeds on Antarctica and on sub-Antarctic islands.

Length 3ft (1m).
Wingspan Up to 6ft (1.8m).

Weight Up to 10½lb (4.8kg).

Lifespan 20 years.

Petrels are feeding their single chicks on the nest (a scrape, hollow or cliff niche) with regurgitated fish, squid, penguin eggs and young birds. Giant petrels also eat carrion, including dead seals. After 4½ months in the nest, a chick leaves in May or June to fend for itself.

During the southern winter the birds feed at sea, some as far north as South America or South Africa. Juveniles may circle Antarctica on the westerly winds several times before returning to their birthplace 5-8 years later to breed. Petrels breed only once every 2-3 years.

Adults arrive at the breeding colonies in September (in the north) and October (in the south). They usually find last year's partner and nest site. After mating, pairs go to sea to feast for the rigours ahead. On her return, the female lays 1 large egg in November or December.

Males take the first turn at incubating, which lasts 8-9 weeks. The downy chicks hatch January-February. Both parents share tending and feeding for about 3 weeks, repelling skuas. Last year's young moult juvenile plumage at sea.

Main entry p. 33.

PILOT WHALE, LONG-FINNED

Where found Southern oceans and north and south Atlantic outside the tropics.

Length Male 18ft 9in (5.7m); female 15ft (4.6m).

Weight Male 1¾ tons; female 1 ton.

Lifespan 30-50 years.

In the northern Atlantic mating peaks April-May. Young males become sexually mature when 12-20 years old and about 16ft (5m) long. Females mature at 6-10 years old, when about 12ft 6in (3.8m) long. Females produce a single calf only once every 3½ years.

Most northern Atlantic calves are born in July or August. After a pregnancy of 14½-15 months, females bear calves 6ft (1.8m) long weighing around 166lb (76kg). The calves are suckled until 20-22 months old, but take solid food before they are a year old.

In the Southern Hemisphere, mating probably peaks in October and November. The pilot whales live in pods (groups) of up to 100, but pods may merge at times. Adult females outnumber adult males by 3 to 1, and dominant males may mate with many females.

January-February is probably the peak birth time in the Southern Hemisphere. The whales feed mainly on squid, but also eat fish. Their dives normally last less than 10 minutes. Some travel long distances to areas of seasonal plenty.

Main entry p. 292.

PINE MARTEN

Where found Central and northern Europe; western Asia. Coniferous forests.

Head-and-body length Male 18in (460mm), tail 9in (230mm); female smaller.

Weight 1-3½lb (0.5-1.6kg).

Lifespan 2-3 years.

Pine martens are solitary, except at mating time. In March or April, females give birth after 8 or 9 weeks of pregnancy. Litters of about 3 blind, naked babies are born in a den among rocks or tree roots. The babies are furred by 3 weeks old, and weaned at 6-7 weeks old.

Youngsters emerge from the den at about 8 weeks old. Pine martens hunt mostly at night, preying on squirrels and other small animals. In July and August, adults mate. A female may mate with several males, but the fertilised egg does not implant in the womb until later.

Young martens leave home to find their own territories when about 6 months old. They may start to breed at 15-16 months old. The pine martens fatten up for the winter months, and supplement their diet with autumn berries, fruits, and maybe fish going upstream to breed.

Pine martens are active all winter. The fertilised egg implants in the female's womb in January, being triggered by the short winter days.

Main entry p. 228.

	March/April/May	June/July/August	Sept/Oct/Nov	Dec/Jan/Feb

PINE PROCESSIONARY MOTH

Where found Southern Europe. In pine woods.

Wingspan 1½-2in (38-50mm).

Lifespan Adult a few days; caterpillar several months.

Caterpillars hatch in May, and spin a flask-shaped nest between the twigs of a tree. They feed mostly at night on the needles of pine and other conifers, the family of maybe 100 travelling to their feeding grounds in a long nose-to-tail procession.

The growing caterpillars moult several times, then each forms a pupal case (underground or in the nest) inside which it turns into a moth. In late summer, the moths emerge and mate within a few days. Each female spins a cocoon on the bark of a pine, and in it lays up to 100 eggs.

The adult moths, which each have pale brown forewings and white hind wings, die shortly after mating and egg-laying. But the eggs laid by the females remain in the protective cocoon.

The eggs lie dormant within the cocoon throughout the winter. When the weather gets warm in spring, they will hatch into caterpillars.

Main entry p. 112.

PIPISTRELLE BAT

Where found Eurasia; the Americas (southern Canada to Honduras); Madagascar; Africa; Australia. Roosts in roofs, caves, tree holes.

Length 1⅜in (35mm).
Wingspan 8½in (215mm).

Weight ¼oz (7g).

Lifespan 11 years.

If the weather is warm and insects are on the wing, northern bats begin to come out of hibernation. By May they are fully active on most nights, and female bats become pregnant as stored sperm is released. Southern bats mate, and in colder places they hibernate for winter.

Northern females seek out nurseries, in the roof cavity of a house, for example. Each female bears one baby, usually in June. Mothers feed at dusk and roost and suckle the babies by day. The nursery is deserted when the youngsters become independent in July or August.

Northern bats mate in September, but the sperm is stored in the female, and the egg is not fertilised until spring. As the nights get colder, northern bats look for a good place to hibernate, such as a cool dry roof or cave. By November the bats are torpid for long periods.

Northern bats are hibernating, with males and females in the same roost. They sometimes wake and fly out during the day. During the southern summer, the female pipistrelles are rearing their youngsters in nursery roosts.

Main entry p. 160.

PIRANHA, RED-BELLIED

Where found South America, from Colombia to northern Argentina. In fresh water.

Length 10in (250mm).

Weight 4½lb (2kg).

Rivers and streams in the Amazon Basin begin to rise, and eventually burst their banks and flood the surrounding rain forest. Piranhas spread out into the new feeding grounds and mate and lay eggs. The tiny larvae develop among the prolific vegetation in the water.

Young piranhas grow fast, feeding on small fish, aquatic worms and insect larvae, and may be guarded by adults. The youngsters may take bites at larger fish with their very sharp, inward-pointing teeth, and are themselves eaten by large fish or crocodile-like caymans.

The rivers begin to fall, and many piranhas go back to the main rivers and channels. Some are trapped in isolated pools, which become overcrowded. They thrive at first on the abundant food.

The rivers and streams are approaching their lowest levels, and the piranhas are crowded even in the main channels. They often hunt in groups and may attack animals entering the water. Some fall prey to giant otters.

Main entry p. 263.

PIRARUCU

Where found South America. Tropical rivers and swamps.

Length Up to 10ft (3m).

Weight 440lb (200kg).

As Amazon waters rise in April, the fishes, now in bright red breeding colours, find partners. They make a nest hole up to 8in (200mm) deep and 20in (510mm) across among plants on the bottom in water less than 7ft (2.1m) deep. The female lays 50,000 eggs, which the male fertilises.

The pair guard the eggs, which hatch after 4-6 days. The larvae swim at 6-7 days, and at 9 days start rising to breathe air. The male escorts groups of them, their dark colour camouflaging them against his blackish head. Both eggs and larvae are taken by fish and other predators.

The young are abandoned when able to fend for themselves, and the adults change back to a pale grey colour. All pirarucus swim to the surface to breathe air with their modified swim bladder – adults normally every 10-15 minutes, and young fish every 4-7 minutes.

By January the rivers are low. Many fish are concentrated in small areas and are often torpid in the low-oxygen water, so are easy prey for the air-breathing pirarucus. They fatten up ready for breeding time, when prey will be dispersed.

No main entry, see p. 27.

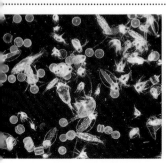

PLANKTON

Where found Oceans, lakes and rivers. In surface waters.

Size Generally microscopic.

As the days lengthen in spring in the Northern Hemisphere, the sun stimulates the growth of phytoplankton (minute plants) and they bloom, or reproduce, rapidly. Blooms are at their greatest from mid-May to mid-June.

Zooplankton (minute animals) feed on the glut of plant plankton and grow rapidly. The dead plankton falling to the sea floor provide food for many deep-sea creatures, which also reproduce. Live plankton are eaten by many kinds of sea creatures, such as krill and basking sharks.

Off Australia's east coast and in the Indian Ocean reddish streaks may be seen on the sea surface August-December. The streaks are caused by a blue-green alga (minute plant), *Trichodesium*. Its dead cells float to the surface to be blown into swirls, and they look like a rusty, oily sheen.

From October to December, cold water may well up off the central east coast of Australia, bringing to the surface phosphates and nitrates, which nourish plankton blooms. They include types that cause poisonous 'red tides'.

Main entry p. 275.

	March/April/May	June/July/August	Sept/Oct/Nov	Dec/Jan/Feb

POLAR BEAR★★

Where found Arctic; northern Canada adjoining Arctic. Icebound sea, coasts.

Length Male up to 10ft (3m); female 6ft (1.8m). **Shoulder height** Up to 5ft (1.5m).

Weight 900-2210lb (408-1002kg).

Lifespan 40 years in captivity.

Females with cubs emerge from winter dens in March. Bears head northwards to feed on ringed seal pups. Mating takes place in April or May, but egg implantation is delayed. Females with cubs do not mate; a mature female normally breeds every third year.

The bears continue their journey to the sea ice. Some may wander onto the ice-free mainland to eat berries and grass, but seals are the main food. By June the cubs are weaned. At 2 years old they will leave their mother to become solitary adults, first breeding at 4-5.

In September, the fertilised egg implants in a mated female's womb. The bears begin to migrate back to their wintering areas, and forage to put on fat for the winter. In November, pregnant females start to make themselves dens under the snow.

Pregnant females spend winter in their dens, bearing 1-3 cubs in December or January. The mother suckles them, living off her fat reserves. Males and females who are not breeding take to dens only in severe winters.

Main entries pp. 60, 187.

PORT JACKSON SHARK

Where found Australia and New Zealand. Coastal waters.

Length 5ft (1.5m).

Lifespan Probably 20-30 years.

The sharks mate. Mating has not been observed in the wild, but in captivity, a male shark seizes a female by the left pectoral (chest) fin and inserts his right clasper into her genital opening. Port Jackson sharks belong to the bullhead shark family, and have blunt snouts.

The females migrate inshore to particular breeding sites where they deposit their tough, pliable egg cases. A spiral flange round the outside of the case enables the shark to hold the case in her mouth and 'screw' it into a crack in the rocks.

Egg-laying continues until early October, by which time a female will have deposited 10-16 eggs. They harden, and cannot be removed without 'unscrewing' them. The eggs take 10-12 months to hatch, and the hatchlings may take 10 years or more to become mature adults.

The sharks are out to sea at depths of around 500ft (150m). They feed mainly on sea urchins and shellfish, detected by scent, and have two sets of teeth – a pointed front set for grasping prey and a flatter back set to grind it up.

Main entry p. 184.

PORTUGUESE MAN-OF-WAR

Where found Atlantic, Indian and Pacific oceans; Mediterranean Sea. Tropical and subtropical areas.

Length Float up to 12in (300mm); tentacles up to 100ft (30m).

Lifespan Up to 10 years.

These jellyfish-like creatures drift passively on the ocean surface with the wind or currents. Prolonged winds from one quarter can cast them onto shores in thousands. On both sides of the Atlantic, most strandings occur in summer and autumn. Each individual man-of-war is a colony of many small animals called polyps that live cooperatively and cannot survive alone. There are different types of polyp – one forms the float, which is filled with gas from special glands, and others have long, trailing tentacles armed with cells that inject a nerve poison almost as powerful as cobra venom into their small

fish prey. The fish is paralysed, and the tentacles then contract to draw it up into feeding polyps. Other polyps have the job of breeding. When they are mature – probably at any time of year in tropical and subtropical waters – they release masses of sperm and egg cells into the sea. These unite to form new individuals, which start life as tiny free-floating larvae. Each larva grows a tiny bladder, and then feeding and stinging polyps start to bud off from it. As the colony grows, breeding polyps bud off also.

Main entry p. 187.

PRAIRIE DOG, BLACK-TAILED

Where found USA and extreme north of Mexico. In the drier, western prairies.

Head-and-body length 12in (300mm); tail 3in (75mm).

Weight 1½-3lb (680-1370g).

Lifespan Up to 8 years.

It is breeding time, and the territory boundaries between neighbouring groups of prairie dogs (really a type of squirrel) are relaxed to allow males from one group to mate with females from other groups. After a pregnancy of 1 month, females give birth to litters of 2-10 pups.

The pups are born in a burrow in the colony's network of tunnels. They emerge above ground at under 5 weeks old, and are weaned at 4-6 weeks, at the start of summer, when the grass and plants they feed on by day are plentiful. Pups spend a lot of time at play; adults often join in.

Separate groups begin to re-establish their area boundaries. Groups may contain around 8 or 9 animals. If the home tunnels and burrows get too overcrowded with youngsters, the adults leave the home burrow to their offspring and dig new burrows.

Territories are well defended in winter. When danger threatens, the animals give sharp dog-like barks to warn others. The males chase away any intruders. In the severest winters, the animals may hibernate for short periods.

Main entry p. 64.

PUFFBALL FUNGUS, GIANT

Where found Throughout Europe.

Diameter 2-24in (50-610mm).

Lifespan Puffball (fruiting body) about 1 month from first emergence.

As the ground warms up in spring, the main part of the puffball – the underground network of tiny fibres called the mycelium – begins to grow and spread. It feeds by absorbing organic matter from the soil.

In August, the first small puffballs, which are fruiting bodies that grow from the fibre network, emerge above ground. Some continue to grow for several weeks and reach a massive size. Puffballs are good to eat only when they are still firm and white.

Puffballs continue growing during early autumn. The skin slowly splits and they change colour from white to yellow and then brown. They shed millions of microscopic brown spores. Later they break off from their tiny stalks and are blown round in the grass.

Spores that settle on fertile soil may establish a new network of fibres underground. This lies dormant during the coldest months of winter.

Main entry p. 177.

	March/April/May	June/July/August	Sept/Oct/Nov	Dec/Jan/Feb

PUFFIN

Where found Northern Europe, including Iceland and Spitsbergen; Greenland. Breeds on coastal cliffs.

Length 12in (300mm).
Wingspan 18½-24in (470-610mm).

Weight 14oz (400g).

Lifespan About 21 years.

Birds arrive from the sea to court and breed. They nest in burrows, safe from gulls and skuas, but in the far north where the ground is frozen they use cliff ledges. Puffins may dig burrows 3ft (1m) or more long with their beaks, or use abandoned rabbit or shearwater burrows.

In May or June a female lays 1 egg (rarely 2), which is incubated for 6 weeks. The chick is fed by both parents, and the survival rate is high. When the chick is about 7 weeks old, it leaves the burrow at night for the sea. It does not breed until it is 4-5 years old.

Adults and juveniles leave the breeding grounds for the ocean fishing grounds. They dive underwater to pursue and catch small fish. Adults moult into their non-breeding plumage and their beaks become smaller and less brightly coloured.

Puffins feed at sea as far north as the pack ice. In early spring, before going ashore, the adults moult into brighter breeding plumage, and develop brighter legs and feet and fuller, brighter beaks.

Main entry p. 160.

QUEEN BUTTERFLY

Where found South-east USA; West Indies. Fields, grasslands and gardens, usually on milkweed plants.

Length 1½in (38mm).
Wingspan 3in (75mm).

Lifespan Adult up to 1 year; caterpillar 1-6 weeks.

After spending the winter in a sheltered spot, the butterflies fly and mate in late March. The females lay their eggs on the leaves of milkweeds, oleanders and succulents such as *Stapelia*. The eggs hatch after 3-12 days, depending on temperature. The caterpillars are brownish-white with yellow cross-stripes, and have greenish stripes running the length of the body. They feed on the leaves of the plant the eggs were laid on, and some of the substances they absorb make them poisonous to birds and other predators. After 10-38 days, depending on temperature, the caterpillars pupate – develop an outer case inside which they

transform into adults. The gold-coloured pupal case hangs from a leaf vein, and after 9-15 days the butterfly emerges from it to feed on nectar from milkweed and other flowers, at the same time pollinating them. The butterflies, like the caterpillars, are poisonous to predators, and have an unpleasant smell. They mate, the females lay eggs and usually (except in autumn) both sexes soon die. There may be three generations of queen butterflies in one year, the autumn generation overwintering as butterflies.

Main entry p. 173.

QUELEA, RED-BILLED (A type of WEAVER BIRD)

Where found Africa south of the Sahara. In tree-scattered grasslands.

Length 4½in (115mm).

Weight ⅝oz (18g).

Lifespan About 1½ years.

Huge flocks of red-billed queleas move backwards and forwards across African grasslands with the seasonal rains and breed when they can. In Tanzania, for example, large flocks of birds arrive from the north towards the end of the March-May rains, when the new grass has seeded, and seeds and insects offer them abundant food and a chance to breed. About September-October, queleas are moving northwards to breed in Sudan and Ethiopia following the rains, and in December-January it is the main breeding season in southernmost areas as the queleas there migrate from the east coast to the west,

often rearing successive broods at different places on their route. The largest breeding colonies can cover more than 1sq mile (2.6sq km) and contain 10 million nests. Males weave globe-shaped grass nests attached to grass stems to entice females. After mating, the female lays 2-3 eggs that hatch 12 days later. Youngsters are independent at 3 weeks old, and may stay to feed on dry grass seeds when their parents move on. In dry seasons, quelea flocks may descend on irrigated ripening grain crops.

Main entry p. 23.

QUOLL, EASTERN (NATIVE CAT)

Where found Tasmania. Forests, heaths and farmland. May be extinct in Australia.

Head-and-body length 12-18in (300-460mm); tail 8½-12in (215-300mm).

Weight 2-4½lb (0.9-2kg).

Lifespan Up to 7 years.

In autumn, quolls add seasonal fruits to their diet of animals and insects. They are solitary and hunt at night. Young quolls just under 1 year old become sexually mature, and the mating season is in May, with much fighting between rival males. Females are pregnant for 3 weeks.

In June a female bears perhaps 30 babies, each about the size of a grain of rice. Only the first 6 to attach themselves to the teats in her pouch are reared. After 2 months, the babies are placed in a grass-lined den. By late winter they play outside the den and go with their mother to forage.

The young quolls are weaned when they are about 5 months old, just as spring provides plenty of food for them to eat. Quolls find prey mainly by scent and feed mostly on the ground, although they are quite good at climbing. By day they sleep in crevices in rocks or hollow trees.

By summer the young quolls are independent. They can fatten up on abundant food such as frogs, fish, small animals, ground-nesting birds and chicks, and prepare for the autumn mating season and the rigours of winter.

Main entry p. 182.

RATTLESNAKE, WESTERN DIAMOND-BACK

Where found South-west USA. Dry prairies, cactus deserts and rocky foothills.

Length 3-7ft (1-2.1m).

Lifespan More than 10 years.

Not long after emerging from hibernation, as the weather warms up, the rattlesnakes mate. The females may bask in the sun more often while their young are maturing inside them. The snakes hunt prey such as mice and rabbits, which they kill with venom injected through their fangs.

After 3-4 months the females give birth to 4-23 live young. As soon as they emerge, the young snakes slither away to find safe hiding places; there is no parental care. At a few days old, a youngster sheds its first skin and starts to grow a rattle from a horny knob at its tail tip.

Young rattlesnakes feed mainly on prey such as frogs and lizards. In November, as winter approaches, rattlesnakes seek out a place to hibernate. They often congregate in dozens in caves, crevices and animal burrows.

The rattlesnakes begin to emerge from hibernation in February, as the temperature begins to rise. They are thin, having not eaten since November, and are intent on catching small rodents such as mice or gophers to eat.

Main entry p. 38.

	March/April/May	June/July/August	Sept/Oct/Nov	Dec/Jan/Feb
RAZORBILL **Where found** North Atlantic Ocean. In coastal waters; breeds on cliffs. **Length** 15-16in (380-400mm). **Weight** About 1½lb (680g). **Lifespan** About 20 years. 	In breeding colonies on coastal cliffs or offshore islands, males vigorously defend nest sites under boulders or in crevices. Egg-laying starts in May. The 1 egg is laid on bare ground, maybe with a few plant scraps spread round. The pair incubate the egg in 12-hour shifts for 5 weeks.	Both parents bring the chick food such as fish and shrimps. In July the 2-week old chick leaves the colony. Not yet able to fly properly, it flutters into the sea, where it swims, still tended by its parents, as the birds· leave for the open ocean. Adults begin moulting as the chick leaves the nest.	The moult goes on into September. In their non-breeding plumage, the birds' throats become white instead of black. The birds spend most of their time at sea, often gathered in 'rafts'. They catch fish and shellfish by surface diving, usually to depths of 6-10ft (1.8-3m).	The adults begin to congregate at breeding colonies again in late winter, and moult into their breeding plumage. Young birds do not return to the breeding colony until they are 4-5 years old. No main entry, see p. 132.
RED CRAB **Where found** Christmas Island, in the Indian Ocean. Rain forest. **Width of carapace** (shell) Up to 4in (100mm). **Lifespan** More than 12 years. 	For most of the year red land crabs live on the forest floor, feeding on fallen leaves, flowers and fruit. The red crabs are not the only crabs living on Christmas Island; there are 14 species of freshwater and land crab, including the 13in (330mm) wide robber land crab.	The island has a wet, humid climate with high rainfall for most of the year. August is the driest season, and at this time the red crabs – more than 120 million of them – spend their time in moist burrows in the forest.	With the arrival of the heavy November rains, red crabs leave the forest by the million and trek to the shore, perhaps taking 18 days. They arrive there within 3 days of the moon's last quarter. Males fight for the best burrow sites, dig burrows and then the females join them.	After mating in the burrow, a female stays there for 12 days while her eggs ripen. Laying lasts 5-6 nights. She shakes up to 100,000 eggs into the sea, then returns to the forest. Hatchling crabs come ashore 25 days later. Main entry p. 229.
RED DEER **Where found** Europe; Asia (north and central). Forests, grassland and moors. **Length** Male 6ft (1.8m); female smaller. **Shoulder height** Male 4ft (1.2m). **Weight** Male 200-600lb (90-275kg). **Lifespan** 5-20 years. 	Many weaker deer die during or after a hard winter, when the grass and foliage they eat is scarce. In March and April, stags cast their antlers, which are often chewed by the pregnant hinds for the calcium they contain. Stags begin to grow new antlers.	In June, pregnant females leave the herd and find a secluded spot to give birth to a single calf. Mothers and calves rejoin the herd after 4 weeks. Stags rub off the velvet' (protective skin) on their new antlers, which can reach 3-4ft (1-1.2m) across, against trees and fences.	Stags come into breeding condition in September. Their necks thicken and they grow bristly manes. The rut (display and mating) begins. Mature stags about 8 years old are the most successful. In October the exhausted stags abandon the hinds for bachelor herds.	Stag and hind herds remain apart, the females choosing the richer grazing to help calf development. Hinds suckle last year's calves until February – or for longer if they fail to mate. Hinds first breed at about 2 years old Main entry p. 188.
RED FOX **Where found** Europe; North Africa. Woods, fields, gardens. **Head-and-body length** Male 2ft 2in (660mm); tail 17in (430mm); female smaller. **Shoulder height** 12in (300mm). **Weight** 11-13lb (5-6kg). **Lifespan** Up to 12 years. 	In March or April, females bear litters of 4-5 cubs after a 7-8 week pregnancy. The male provides meat and his mate suckles the pups in a den in a cavity or earth. Once cubs are 3-4 weeks old, both parents feed them. By May they are often seen above ground near the den.	By 2 months old the cubs' brown baby coats have changed to reddish brown, and their blue eyes to amber. They start to go with their parents on their nightly hunts. Worms and fruit feature prominently in the diet. Foxes eat all kinds of food – small animals, crabs, insects, scraps.	In September the cubs are about adult size, and are usually driven off their parents' territory to fend for themselves. Many are killed by cars. Young males begin to search for unoccupied territories, and there are often fights. Foxes are sexually mature at 9-10 months old.	It is the mating season, when the foxes are very active and vocal. Males compete for females to mate with, and also spend much time scent-marking the boundaries of their territories. Pairs may stay together for a season or longer. Main entry p. 16.
RED PANDA (LESSER PANDA)★ **Where found** Nepal; South-west China; western Burma. High-altitude bamboo forests. **Head-and-body length** 20-24in (510-610mm); tail 12-20in (300-510mm). **Weight** 7-11lb (3-5kg). **Lifespan** Up to 14 years. 	In spring, the pandas' preferred food, bamboo shoots, is plentiful. Red pandas usually sleep by day, curled up on a tree branch, and forage at night. From about mid-May, females give birth to usually 1 or 2 babies in a den such as a hollow tree. The mother alone cares for them.	The babies are furred but blind at birth, and their eyes open at 3-4 weeks. Red pandas can climb well, but usually feed on the ground. They have an extra 'thumb', an enlarged pad on each palm to help grip shoots. They also eat fruit, acorns, lichens, grass roots and eggs.	The young are weaned at 5 months old, but stay with their mother for up to a year. They do not become sexually mature until they are 18-20 months of age. Red pandas live in pairs or family groups. They are docile creatures, but when startled, stand on their hind legs and hiss.	In December, the mating season begins; females will give birth 3-5 months after mating. Red pandas have bushy, ringed tails and thick, rust-red coats to protect them from the sub-zero winter temperatures of their mountain home. No main entry, see p. 192.

	March/April/May	June/July/August	Sept/Oct/Nov	Dec/Jan/Feb

RED SQUIRREL

Where found Europe, including Scandinavia; northern Asia. Woods, especially coniferous woods.

Head-and-body length 8in (200mm); tail 7in (180mm).

Weight 8-13oz (227-365g).

Lifespan Up to 6 years.

Spring litters arrive January-March. The 1-6 babies (usually 3) are born blind and naked in a drey (nest) or tree hole. By 6-8 weeks they are furred and making trips from the nest, and at 10 weeks they are weaned. If cone seeds are short, squirrels eat catkins, buds, shoots, flowers.

Summer litters are born May-July, most of them a young female's first litter. The squirrels forage all day, resting at midday in the nest or snoozing on a branch. In midsummer, squirrels in deciduous woods may starve. Some survive by stripping bark from trees to get at the sweet sap.

As the youngsters become independent, the competition for food increases. The seeds of deciduous trees become available, and the squirrels are active for most of the day without rest. They fatten up and bury or cache seeds for the winter.

Squirrels are active all through winter. Breeding begins in November or December, when the first mating chases are seen in the treetops. Females mate on the one day that they are on heat; young are born 5-6 weeks later.

Main entry p. 252.

RED-BILLED HORNBILL

Where found Africa: Central, East and southern. Grassland, woods and thorn scrub.

Length 15-18in (380-460mm).

Weight 4-8oz (113-227g).

In the far north of Ethiopia, breeding is well under way, but in Kenya the hornbills are still in flocks where there is plenty of food such as insects, fruit and small animals. They take up their territories to begin nesting when the March-May rains arrive.

In Kenya, the peak of egg-laying occurs in July and August. Females are walled in with mud in tree-hole nests, where they lay clutches of 3-6 eggs. The male feeds the female through a slit in the mud barrier. The eggs hatch after about 3 weeks' incubation.

The female leaves the nest about 3 weeks after the eggs have hatched. The young are walled in by themselves, and are fed with insects and grubs through the slit by both parents. They emerge when 6-7 weeks old. In the Transvaal in southern Africa, nesting is just beginning.

Kenyan families stay together for the dry season and following rains. Flocks of 100 or more gather where food is abundant, especially around water holes. In north Ethiopia, the dry season is ending and breeding is beginning.

Main entry p. 216.

RED-SIDED GARTER SNAKE

Where found Southern Canada to Texas (USA), east of the Rocky Mountains. Pond and lake edges; damp meadows.

Length Up to 4ft (1.2m).

Lifespan Up to 6 years in captivity.

The snakes mate from mid-March to May. In April, Canadian snakes emerge from hibernation and mate at once as the summer is short. Males emerge first and wait at dens for females, which exude a substance that attracts them. Maybe 30 gather round 1 female but only 1 male mates.

After mating the snakes disperse to feed on prey such as frogs, fish, worms, insects, birds and small mammals. Garter snakes do not poison or constrict their prey; it is suffocated when they swallow it. Females give birth to often 12-18 live young from July to September.

During the year the garter snakes, like all snakes, shed their skins several times, hiding and not feeding beforehand. In the autumn, garter snakes in Canada desert their waterside hunting grounds and congregate in caves and crevices to hibernate during the harsh northern winter.

Hibernating garter snakes do not feed at all in winter. In the warmer south, the snakes do not need to hibernate. Garter snakes produce an evil-smelling substance as a defence against an attacker, such as a bobcat.

Main entry p. 86.

RED-WINGED BLACKBIRD

Where found USA; southern Canada; Mexico. Grasslands and marshes.

Length 7-9½in (180-240mm).

Weight 4½-7oz (125-200g).

As the weather warms up, males head north from wintering areas and claim territories. Females follow and mating occurs. Females build cup-shaped nests of grass in reeds or small bushes. Each lays 3-5 eggs and incubates them alone until they hatch after about 12 days.

Chicks leave the nest at 10-13 days old. Young males that have failed to mate gather in flocks to await the next season. After breeding, huge flocks of birds feed on cereal crops and cause much damage. In late summer, flocks hide in marshes while moulting their flight feathers.

When new flight feathers have grown, the birds begin to make ready for the winter. They feast on the last of the season's seeds, grain, insects and spiders. Some gather in huge flocks ready to move southwards to the warmer wintering areas.

Huge flocks arrive in the southern USA and Mexico to join birds that spend the year there. At night, over 1 million may roost together for warmth, sometimes with grackles and cowbirds. A pest here too, they eat winter-growing cereals.

Main entry p. 251.

RHINOCEROS, BLACK★★

Where found Africa: East and southern. Bush, grassland and woodland.

Length 11ft (3.4m).
Shoulder height 5ft 4in (1.6m).

Weight Male ¾-1 ton; female smaller.

Lifespan 45 years in captivity.

Black rhinos are the smaller of the two African rhinos. The white rhino of the open grasslands stands about 6ft (1.8m) at the shoulder and weighs about 2 tons. Neither species has a seasonal pattern of behaviour. Mating may occur at any time of year. Males can breed at 7 or 8 years old and females at 5-7 years. Females give birth to single calves after a pregnancy of 15 months in the black rhino and 16 months in the white. However, births tend to peak in November, when rains have brought fresh greenery. The calves can walk within 3 hours of birth, but are suckled until they are about 2 years old. Both black and white rhinos prefer country with dense thickets where they can rest during the day. They need to drink regularly, and often wallow in mud to cool their bodies and protect their hides from insects. Black rhinos are mainly browsers, eating the leaves and shoots of bushes. White rhinos are grazers, eating grasses. Both species have been hunted almost to extinction, mainly because their horns (formed from matted hairs) command very high prices as a traditional remedy in the Far East.

Main entry p. 198.

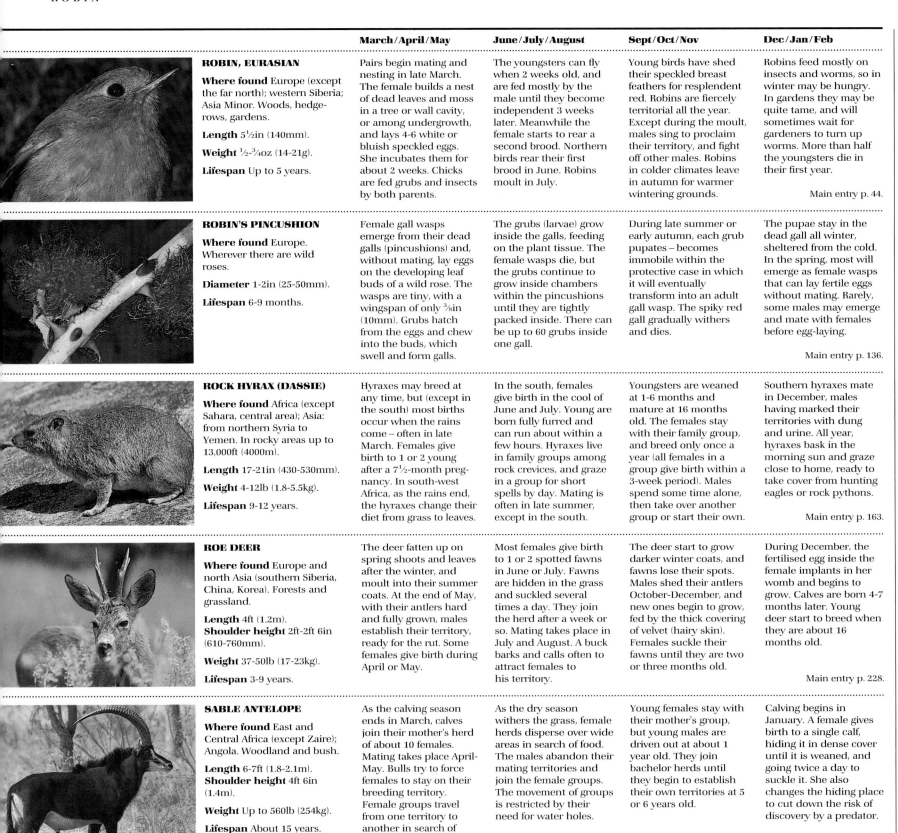

	March/April/May	June/July/August	Sept/Oct/Nov	Dec/Jan/Feb
ROBIN, EURASIAN **Where found** Europe (except the far north); western Siberia; Asia Minor. Woods, hedgerows, gardens. **Length** 5½in (140mm). **Weight** ½-¾oz (14-21g). **Lifespan** Up to 5 years.	Pairs begin mating and nesting in late March. The female builds a nest of dead leaves and moss in a tree or wall cavity, or among undergrowth, and lays 4-6 white or bluish speckled eggs. She incubates them for about 2 weeks. Chicks are fed grubs and insects by both parents.	The youngsters can fly when 2 weeks old, and are fed mostly by the male until they become independent 3 weeks later. Meanwhile the female starts to rear a second brood. Northern birds rear their first brood in June. Robins moult in July.	Young birds have shed their speckled breast feathers for resplendent red. Robins are fiercely territorial all the year. Except during the moult, males sing to proclaim their territory, and fight off other males. Robins in colder climates leave in autumn for warmer wintering grounds.	Robins feed mostly on insects and worms, so in winter may be hungry. In gardens they may be quite tame, and will sometimes wait for gardeners to turn up worms. More than half the youngsters die in their first year. Main entry p. 44.
ROBIN'S PINCUSHION **Where found** Europe. Wherever there are wild roses. **Diameter** 1-2in (25-50mm). **Lifespan** 6-9 months.	Female gall wasps emerge from their dead galls (pincushions) and, without mating, lay eggs on the developing leaf buds of a wild rose. The wasps are tiny, with a wingspan of only ⅜in (10mm). Grubs hatch from the eggs and chew into the buds, which swell and form galls.	The grubs (larvae) grow inside the galls, feeding on the plant tissue. The female wasps die, but the grubs continue to grow inside chambers within the pincushions until they are tightly packed inside. There can be up to 60 grubs inside one gall.	During late summer or early autumn, each grub pupates – becomes immobile within the protective case in which it will eventually transform into an adult gall wasp. The spiky red gall gradually withers and dies.	The pupae stay in the dead gall all winter, sheltered from the cold. In the spring, most will emerge as female wasps that can lay fertile eggs without mating. Rarely, some males may emerge and mate with females before egg-laying. Main entry p. 136.
ROCK HYRAX (DASSIE) **Where found** Africa (except Sahara, central area); Asia: from northern Syria to Yemen. In rocky areas up to 13,000ft (4000m). **Length** 17-21in (430-530mm). **Weight** 4-12lb (1.8-5.5kg). **Lifespan** 9-12 years.	Hyraxes may breed at any time, but (except in the south) most births occur when the rains come – often in late March. Females give birth to 1 or 2 young after a 7½-month pregnancy. In south-west Africa, as the rains end, the hyraxes change their diet from grass to leaves.	In the south, females give birth in the cool of June and July. Young are born fully furred and can run about within a few hours. Hyraxes live in family groups among rock crevices, and graze in a group for short spells by day. Mating is often in late summer, except in the south.	Youngsters are weaned at 1-6 months and mature at 16 months old. The females stay with their family group, and breed only once a year (all females in a group give birth within a 3-week period). Males spend some time alone, then take over another group or start their own.	Southern hyraxes mate in December, males having marked their territories with dung and urine. All year, hyraxes bask in the morning sun and graze close to home, ready to take cover from hunting eagles or rock pythons. Main entry p. 163.
ROE DEER **Where found** Europe and north Asia (southern Siberia, China, Korea). Forests and grassland. **Length** 4ft (1.2m). **Shoulder height** 2ft-2ft 6in (610-760mm). **Weight** 37-50lb (17-23kg). **Lifespan** 3-9 years.	The deer fatten up on spring shoots and leaves after the winter, and moult into their summer coats. At the end of May, with their antlers hard and fully grown, males establish their territory, ready for the rut. Some females give birth during April or May.	Most females give birth to 1 or 2 spotted fawns in June or July. Fawns are hidden in the grass and suckled several times a day. They join the herd after a week or so. Mating takes place in July and August. A buck barks and calls often to attract females to his territory.	The deer start to grow darker winter coats, and fawns lose their spots. Males shed their antlers October-December, and new ones begin to grow, fed by the thick covering of velvet (hairy skin). Females suckle their fawns until they are two or three months old.	During December, the fertilised egg inside the female implants in her womb and begins to grow. Calves are born 4-7 months later. Young deer start to breed when they are about 16 months old. Main entry p. 228.
SABLE ANTELOPE **Where found** East and Central Africa (except Zaire); Angola. Woodland and bush. **Length** 6-7ft (1.8-2.1m). **Shoulder height** 4ft 6in (1.4m). **Weight** Up to 560lb (254kg). **Lifespan** About 15 years.	As the calving season ends in March, calves join their mother's herd of about 10 females. Mating takes place April-May. Bulls try to force females to stay on their breeding territory. Female groups travel from one territory to another in search of better grazing.	As the dry season withers the grass, female herds disperse over wide areas in search of food. The males abandon their mating territories and join the female groups. The movement of groups is restricted by their need for water holes.	Young females stay with their mother's group, but young males are driven out at about 1 year old. They join bachelor herds until they begin to establish their own territories at 5 or 6 years old.	Calving begins in January. A female gives birth to a single calf, hiding it in dense cover until it is weaned, and going twice a day to suckle it. She also changes the hiding place to cut down the risk of discovery by a predator. Main entry p. 52.

	March/April/May	June/July/August	Sept/Oct/Nov	Dec/Jan/Feb

SAILFISH

Where found All tropical, subtropical and temperate seas.

Length Up to 12ft (3.7m).

Weight Up to 275lb (125kg).

The sailfish is named for its high, sail-like dorsal fin, which runs almost the length of its back. It has a long, sword-like beak like that of the swordfish (although not as long as the swordfish's) and a streamlined, torpedo-shaped body, and is the fastest known fish in the sea, able to sprint at 68mph (109km/h). It feeds on other fish and squid. Like the swordfish, the sailfish is a seasonal migrant, moving from the tropics when the warm-water belt extends during spring and summer and in autumn heading back to the tropics for the winter. Sailfish and swordfish are caught and tagged on the North

American east coast in summer – swordfish are found in inshore waters as far north as Nova Scotia (Canada), but sailfish not so far north. (A swordfish tagged in summer off the south of Nova Scotia was caught again 2 months later 1253 miles (2016km) miles to the south in the Caribbean, having travelled an average of 22 miles (35km) a day.) Sailfish belong to the same family as the blue marlin and striped marlin, also large, fast predatory fishes with sword-like beaks.

No main entry, see p. 156.

SALLOW MOTH

Where found North America. Deciduous forests.

Wingspan 1½in (38mm).

Lifespan Less than 1 year.

The moth caterpillars that hatch from winter-laid eggs feed on tree buds until the spring temperature rises. In May each caterpillar pupates – forms a case in which it transforms into a moth. The moths emerge and then stay dormant through much of the summer.

The sallow moths are active on warm summer nights. They mate and lay eggs, then die. Some eggs hatch and some are dormant through winter. The caterpillars from the hatched eggs may spend winter dormant as caterpillars or pupae.

Some of the caterpillars that pupate emerge in late autumn as the first batch of winter sallow moths. In Vermont, in north-east USA, they feed on nectar from witch hazel (the season's last flowering plant) and pollinate the flowers. They mate and lay eggs.

Another batch of moths emerges in late winter and feeds on the sap of damaged trees. They hide in leaf litter to keep warm, and have air sacs and a blood system that cut down heat loss. They mate and lay eggs that hatch before spring.

Main entry p. 205.

SALMON, ATLANTIC

Where found North Atlantic. Spawns in rivers in north-east USA and Canada, and in Europe from Spain to Arctic Russia.

Length Up to 5ft (1.5m).

Weight UK up to 62lb (28kg); Norway 86lb (39kg).

Lifespan Up to 10 years.

About 6 weeks after hatching, young fish leave the nest to take food such as insect larvae and worms. They are called parrs from the time they are about 4in (100mm) long until they go to sea usually 3 years (but up to 7 years) later. April-May sees the main seaward migration.

Salmon that are at sea travel north to the north Atlantic or Baltic feeding grounds. Here the fish fatten up and the parrs mature. The salmon eat small crustaceans such as shrimps and small fish such as sprats, herrings, capelin and sand eels.

In November, after 1-5 (but usually 2) years at sea, adults arrive in the rivers of their birth to spawn. Some leap 10ft (3m) up waterfalls on the way. When she arrives at the spawning ground, a female uses her tail to scoop a redd (nest) in the gravel and lays eggs which the male fertilises.

When spawning ends in December, many adults die, but some return to sea and come back to spawn again in 1 or 2 years. The eggs hatch after 3 months into ¾in (19mm) long larvae, which feed on the yolk attached to their egg sac.

Main entry p. 227.

SALTWATER (ESTUARINE) CROCODILE★★

Where found South-west India; Malaysia; Indonesia to north Australia; Philippines. Rivers, estuaries, marshes, mangrove swamps.

Length 12-20ft (3.7-6m).

Weight Up to 1300lb (590kg).

Lifespan Over 50 years.

Although the saltwater crocodile lives in brackish water, it breeds only by freshwater streams and marshes. Breeding is timed so that the eggs will hatch well into the wet season, when there is plenty of food such as aquatic insects, tadpoles, and tiny fish for the hatchlings to eat. The wet season in south-west India is May-October, and in north Australia November-March. In Sri Lanka and south Malaysia it is wet all year and breeding occurs at any time. Males must establish a territory before they can mate. Each female lays 30-90 eggs in a nest-mound, and guards them for the 13-week incubation. Floods

sweep away many eggs, and fish, waterfowl, other crocodiles and men take more. The female carries the 8in (200mm) hatchlings to water, and may watch over them for a while. They grow rapidly, eating birds, fish, frogs and lizards. When they are 6 or more years old and about 7-8ft (2.1-2.4m) long, they can breed and kill large animals such as cattle. Growth slows after this, and males may not be tough enough to claim a territory until 10 years old. They may swim far to find one – maybe from Australia to New Guinea.

Main entry p. 268.

SAMBAR DEER

Where found South China; Nepal; India; Sri Lanka; Burma; Malaysia; Indonesia; Philippines. Woodland.

Length 4ft 8in (1.4m).

Shoulder height 4ft 6in (1.4m).

Weight 600lb (274kg).

Lifespan 10 years.

In India, males begin to shed their antlers in March; in Nepal and Burma most do so May-July. The deer feed mainly at night on grass, leaves and fruit. Tigers prey on them, and are said to lure them by mimicking their calls. Crocodiles prey on deer that are drinking.

Females bear single calves after an 8½-month pregnancy, births peaking late May-June in India and June-July in Nepal, at the start of the rains. During July, most males are solitary and have antlers in velvet (hairy skin). Female groups of more than 6 are rare.

In India, mating takes place from September to April, depending on the region. In Sri Lankan hills, it starts in October. The sambar stags roam widely, but establish a small territory for the rut (display and mating). They roar loudly to attract 6-8 hinds instead of rounding them up.

In central India and Burma, the stags rut November-December. In Nepal, most stags have full, hard antlers by December or January, and rutting lasts into April. Antlers may be 2ft (610mm) or more long.

No main entry, see pp. 75-6, 93, 95.

	March/April/May	June/July/August	Sept/Oct/Nov	Dec/Jan/Feb

SAND TIGER SHARK

Where found All tropical and subtropical seas except those of the eastern Pacific Ocean. Coastal waters.

Length About 10ft (3m).

Lifespan Up to 10 years in captivity.

The sharks' year depends on the seas where they live. In cooler northern waters sand tiger sharks are more strongly seasonal in behaviour, and in late spring they migrate from warmer southern waters back to their traditional coastal feeding and breeding grounds.

In June, large shoals of sand tiger sharks gather in places such as the USA's North Carolina coastal waters to mate. The females do not mate every year. Those females that have been carrying their 1 or 2 pups for a year give birth.

The sharks are busy feeding, often 600-4000ft (180-1220m) down. They sometimes form large shoals, which may herd fish before they kill them. The sharks' prey includes cuttlefish, squid, lobsters, and small sharks and rays.

The sharks prefer water where the temperature is 10-21°C (50-70°F). Where the temperature falls, they may migrate to warmer waters for the winter. In South Africa the shark is called the the ragged-tooth and in Australia the grey nurse.

Main entry p. 127.

SATIN BOWERBIRD

Where found Eastern Australia and New Guinea. Rain forest.

Length 10½-13in (265-330mm).

Weight 3½-9oz (100-260g).

Lifespan Possibly up to 15 years.

Young bowerbirds fend for themselves at 2 months old. The birds are dispersed through the forest, feeding mainly on fruit, leaves and stems of succulent plants. They will also take insects, worms, spiders, small frogs and nestlings.

In winter, bowerbirds gather in flocks that can contain 100 or more birds. They may move from the forest to feed in orchards. By August, the males have returned to the forest to begin selecting sites for their mating bowers.

In Australia, from September onwards, the males begin to build fenced, decorated avenue bowers in which to display and attract a succession of mates. Breeding reaches a peak in November. Less is known of the breeding habits in New Guinea.

Breeding continues until February. The females nest 3-100ft (1-30m) up in a tree and lay up to 3 eggs, incubating them for about 3 weeks. The chicks stay in the nest for another 3 weeks, fed on fruit and insects by their mother.

Main entry p. 247.

SCALLOPED HAMMERHEAD SHARK

Where found Worldwide. Tropical inshore and coastal waters.

Length 7-12ft (2-3.7m).

Weight 95lb (43kg).

Lifespan Probably more than 25 years.

Scalloped hammerhead sharks live mainly in water warmer than 22°C (72°F), and probably migrate to waters of the right temperature. Little is known of their routes, but they tend to move towards the Equator in winter and towards the poles in summer. Why the hammerhead sharks have mallet-shaped heads is unknown, but the extensions do act as hydrofoils, giving them greater manoeuvrability. They also spread the shark's eyes farther apart and increase the area of its electro-receptive field, aiding the detection of prey buried under sandy sea floors. This may be why they are good at catching rays – a

hammerhead shark was once found with 54 stingray barbs in its mouth. The sharks frequent estuaries of the Gulf of Mexico in summer. In the Gulf of California, large shoals of females rest over seamounts during the day, and late in the day break up into small groups to hunt. Males live alone. In late summer, a female bears up to 31 live pups 16½-20in (420-510mm) long, but where the breeding grounds are is unknown. Pups are born head first, their head extensions folding back to ease their passage.

Main entry p. 274.

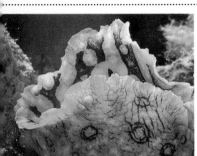

SEA HARE

Where found Worldwide except in the coldest Arctic and Antarctic seas. Shallow waters offshore.

Length Up to 12in (300mm).

Weight Up to 2lb (900g).

Lifespan 1 year.

In northern temperate seas, spawning occurs mostly March-June. The sea hares come inshore to mate as the sea temperature rises. They are hermaphrodite (both male and female), and often form long chains in which each fertilises one neighbour and is fertilised by the other.

The eggs are laid among seaweed, often in a long tangled chain of many thousands. They hatch 2-3 weeks later. Most sea hares die after spawning. Many of the tiny larvae are carried away by the tides, but some stay among the weeds, where they are safer from predators.

A pinkish-brown larva develops a small internal shell (a horny back plate covered by skin) early on, and then gradually grows darker and like its parents. Sea hares spend most of their time grazing seaweed with their tough, tooth-spiked tongue (radula).

Sea hares living where the water is colder in winter may be less active. When disturbed, an adult ejects a foul-tasting slimy fluid from its mantle (the thin covering over its back plate). This is thought to put off predators.

Main entry p. 138.

SEA HORSE

Where found North Atlantic Ocean; Mediterranean. Coastal waters.

Length 1½-12in (38-300mm), depending on species.

Lifespan Up to 1 year.

Sea horses are small fishes covered in bony plates. They prefer water of moderate depth – down to about 200ft (60m) – and a seabed with plenty of vegetation to provide cover. During storms and while resting, they wrap their tails round seaweeds and other plants in order to avoid being swept away. A sea horse swims upright, using the dorsal (back) fin to propel itself, and feeds on minute larvae with the tiny mouth at the end of its tube-like snout. The fish spawn in spring and summer – mainly June-August. A female lays 250-400 eggs, which she transfers in small batches to a male's brood pouch under his

belly. There he fertilises them and carries them while they incubate. The eggs hatch about 3-6 weeks later, but the youngsters are not ejected for another 10 days or so, when they are about ¼in (6mm) long. They largely fend for themselves, and are very vulnerable to fish predators while so small. Sea horses are able to reproduce when they are about 4 months old.

Main entry p. 276.

	March/April/May	June/July/August	Sept/Oct/Nov	Dec/Jan/Feb
SEA OTTER **Where found** North American and Russian Pacific coastal waters. **Head-and-body length** 4ft 6in (1.4m); tail 10in (250mm). **Weight** Male up to 120lb (54kg); female 80lb (36kg). **Lifespan** Up to 20 years.	The main birth season in the north is April-June. A female has usually only 1 pup, born furred with eyes open, and about 15in (380mm) long. She carries the pup on her chest as she swims on her back. The pup is suckled for about 1 year, but weaning begins at a few weeks old.	Pups are born throughout the year in much of the rest of the otter's range. Mating occurs in water, but the fertilised egg may not implant in the female's womb until several months later. Pups are born 8 months after implantation.	Sea otters live in water 10-30ft (3-9m) deep, mostly within 1 mile (1.6km) of the shore. Some individuals may stray briefly beyond their normal range, but the otters do not migrate, mainly because their chief food (shellfish such as clams and mussels) is abundant all year.	In California, most births tend to be in winter and spring. Otters first breed at about 3 years old, and females usually bear pups in alternate years. The otters rarely go ashore, sleeping at night on their backs in the water, often in kelp beds. Main entry p. 67.
SECRETARY BIRD **Where found** Africa south of the Sahara. Grassy plains. **Length** 3-5ft (1-1.5m); female slightly smaller than male. **Wingspan** Up to 6ft (1.8m). **Weight** 7½-9lb (3.4-4kg). **Lifespan** Probably over 10 years.	The birds breed at any time of year, depending on the food supply. In Kenya, the earliest egg-laying is in May and June. The platform nest of sticks, up to 6ft (1.8m) across, is in a low bush or tree. The female lays 2-3 eggs, which she incubates for 6-7 weeks.	Both parents feed the downy chicks, on partly digested food at first then on solids. The youngsters leave the nest after 11-12 weeks and join their parents as they hunt on foot, taking prey such as snakes, locusts and young birds. In the Sudan egg-laying is July-October.	In Cape Province, South Africa, eggs are laid in spring (October), and more egg-laying takes place in Kenya October-December. Pairs may mate for life, and they defend a huge territory in the breeding season. Courtship displays take place in the air.	All year, the birds roost by night on low trees and hunt by day, maybe walking more than 20 miles (32km) a day. They fly well, but rarely do so, and rest only at the hottest times, sheltering beneath a tree or in tall grass or undergrowth. Main entry p. 199.
SHEARWATER, SHORT-TAILED **Where found** Breeds Tasmania, south-east Australia, islands in the Bass Strait. Winters circling the Pacific Ocean. **Length** 14in (360mm). **Weight** 1¼lb (570g). **Lifespan** 20 years or more.	Chick rearing is in full swing in the breeding colonies on island shores. Every few days, a parent feeds its hungry chick in its burrow on partly digested seafood. In late April or May, the chicks (about 5 months old) leave their burrows at night, and all the birds fly off to sea.	The birds fly an 18,000 mile (29,000km) figure-of-eight trip round the Pacific. Some adults complete the first 5500 miles (8850km) in a month. The shearwaters spend June-August wintering in the far north of the Pacific. They return riding the trade winds and westerlies.	The adults reach the breeding colonies in October. Burrows are claimed, or dug some 9ft (2.7m) into the soil. Mates recognise each other by their calls. After mating, pairs feed at sea for 18 days. The female then lays 1 white egg in the burrow, mostly from November 24 to 26.	The male incubates the egg for the first 2 weeks, then both parents share the task for another 6 weeks. Both birds feed the blind, downy chick on regurgitated krill, fish and squid. The chick spits oil to defend itself against any intruders. Main entry p. 219.
SHREW, COMMON **Where found** Europe (except Ireland, some offshore islands and Mediterranean area); northern Asia. Woods, hedges, heaths, grasslands. **Head-and-body length** 3in (75mm); tail 1½in (38mm). **Weight** Up to ½oz (14g). **Lifespan** About 1 year.	Mating starts in March, when insect food begins to be abundant. About 2-3 weeks after mating, a female bears a litter of 6-7 babies, born in grass nests under cover of matted vegetation. The youngsters are suckled for about 3 weeks.	Females can be suckling youngsters and pregnant at the same time, so by midsummer a female may have already raised one litter, and be starting another. She may have 5 litters in the year. The young become fully independent when they are 1 month old.	By October, the end of the breeding season, all youngsters born during the year have become independent. Shrews live mainly solitary lives, both sexes defending their own territory – a tunnel system dug through leaf litter and soil, and covering up to 600sq yds (500sq m).	All year, shrews spend most of the time foraging for food such as worms and woodlice in their tunnels. They are active day and night, in spells of a few hours at a time. Most adults have starved by winter, their teeth so worn they could not eat. Main entry p. 159.
SIFAKA, VERRAUX'S★ **Where found** Western Madagascar. Deciduous forests. **Head-and-body length** 20in (510mm), tail 20in (510mm). **Weight** 11lb (5kg).	The mating season continues into March, interrupting the daily round of eating and sleeping, mostly high in the trees. Many forest trees are fruiting, so the vegetarian sifakas eat a lot of berries at this time of year, as well as leaves, flowers and bark.	June-July is the coolest, driest time of the year. Youngsters born last year are 1 year old and become independent, ceasing to ride on their mothers' backs. They will not be sexually mature until 3 years old. Females bear single infants in a 2-week period in mid-July.	Youngsters are suckled regularly, but begin to venture off on their own while their mothers rest. By November, they are carried on their mother's back instead of her belly. The weather is pleasant and the sifakas lively, but as the wettest season approaches, it brings misty mornings.	In December-January, in the hot and humid wet season, sifakas sleep in the trees until the mists have dispersed, and for much of the day doze in the shade. Youngsters are weaned at 6 months old. The mating season begins in January. Main entry p. 197.

	March/April/May	June/July/August	Sept/Oct/Nov	Dec/Jan/Feb

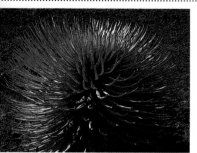

SILVERSWORD

Where found Hawaii and Maui, in the Pacific Ocean. Non-active volcanic craters on the islands.

Height 6ft (1.8m).

Diameter of rosette 2ft (610mm).

Lifespan 10-15 years.

The silversword plant, related to the sunflower, grows among volcanic rocks up to a height of 12,000ft (3600m) above sea level in the craters of the volcanoes Mauna Loa, Mauna Kea, Hualalai and Haleakala. It takes 10 years to grow, then dies after flowering. In the early stages of growth, narrow leaves form a rosette round the dark brown stem, which is 6in (150mm) tall. When the leaf-rosette has reached a diameter of about 2ft (610mm), usually between June and October, the flower spike grows to 5-6ft (1.5-1.8m) tall. A mass of about 500 yellow and maroon flowerlets, each 2in (50mm) across, bloom in succession round the stem. At the end of flowering, the silversword produces dry, black fruits about ½in (13mm) long, each containing one seed. When they are ripe, the hard fruits fall to the ground, and the seeds may germinate to produce other plants that will flower in about 10 years' time.

Main entry p. 290.

SKUA, SOUTH POLAR

Where found Breeds around Antarctica; goes north for the winter.

Length About 21in (530mm).

Weight 2-3¼lb (0.9-1.5kg); female slightly bigger and heavier than male.

Lifespan Probably up to 20 years.

By March (the end of the Antarctic summer), the skuas leave their nesting areas and fly north to avoid the cold, darkness and food scarcity of the coming Antarctic winter. Some go no farther than just beyond the pack ice; others travel far north into the Atlantic, Indian and Pacific oceans.

Some birds have been recorded as far north as Greenland by mid-July. Most are at sea in the southern oceans, catching fish or stealing them (they harass other birds until they drop their catch, then snatch it).

The birds begin returning south to Antarctica. Some are seen off the North American coast in October. Egg-laying starts in late November. A female lays 2 eggs in a scrape in the ground, the second 2-3 days after the first, and starts to incubate them.

The eggs hatch after 4 weeks. Some eggs and young chicks are taken by other skuas or killed by bad weather. The chicks are fed by both parents for 6 weeks, but the second chick will not survive unless food is plentiful.

Main entry p. 34.

SKUNK CABBAGE

Where found Eastern North America. Wet deciduous woods, meadows and swamps.

Height Up to 3ft 4in (1m); height of spathe (floral sheath), 3-6in (75-150mm).

Lifespan About 7 years.

The purple and green spathe enclosing the knob-like flower spike can go on growing well into April. In late spring, when the flowering has finished, the huge leaves unroll. The root of the skunk cabbage is really an underground stem that grows to about 12in (300mm) long.

The large veined and mottled seeds usually germinate close to the parent plant, but some are taken farther afield by squirrels. The plant also pushes out pencil-sized shoots from its underground stem. If damaged, the skunk cabbage has a foul smell, hence its name.

Germinating seeds grow roots that pull them deep into the soil. The underground stem that develops may grow ⅛in (3mm) each year. The plant does not flower until 6-7 years old, and its flowers are only ¼in (6mm) across.

About February, the plant pushes up its purple-green spathe. The flower spike inside heats up, and any snow round the plant melts. Warmth and the plant's odour attract flies and gnats, which take pollen from plant to plant.

Main entry p. 37.

SMALL SKIPPER BUTTERFLY

Where found Most of Europe; North Africa; Asia Minor. Long grass.

Wingspan 1¼in (32mm). **Length** Caterpillar 1in (25mm).

Lifespan Adult 3-4 weeks; caterpillar 9-10 months.

Caterpillars awake from hibernation in mid-April. Each eats its way out of its cocoon and then feeds on grass. Soon a caterpillar cobbles the edges of a blade together and feeds on grass while inside its tube (hidden from predators) by day and night. It moults its skin four times.

In June the caterpillar spins a cocoon round several grass blades. Inside it changes into an adult. The butterfly emerges 2 weeks later and darts (skips) from flower to flower, feeding on nectar. After mating, females lay batches of 3-5 eggs in curled blades on tall grasses.

The eggs hatch after 3-4 weeks in July or August, and the newly hatched caterpillars eat most of their egg case and then each spins itself a silken cocoon in the sheath of a grass blade. There it hibernates. By the end of August, all the butterflies are dead.

The caterpillars hibernate in their cocoons throughout the winter, amid the grass in the meadows, verges and woodland clearings where next season they will fly as butterflies and sip the nectar from scabious and thistles.

Main entry p. 158.

SNOW GOOSE, LESSER

Where found Breeds Alaska, eastern Siberia, western Canada, in tundra. Winters Californian and Mexican Pacific coasts, Gulf of Mexico, in marshes, fields, lagoons.

Length Up to 2ft 6in (760mm).

Weight 4-6½lb (1.8-3kg).

Lifespan Up to 20 years.

Birds reach their northern breeding areas to live in huge colonies of up to 100,000 pairs. After mating, a female lays 3-8 eggs in a hollow lined with greenery and down. The chicks hatch after 3-4 weeks and soon leave the nest, but stay with their parents until next spring.

The geese stay in the Arctic for the summer, feeding on marsh plants, sedges and grasses. The Arctic growing season is short, and often only those birds that started to breed before the tundra vegetation began to grow again in spring will be successful in raising their brood.

Large flocks head south in groups, each group following the same aerial routes year after year. In October, many birds that follow a course west of the Rockies stop to rest and feed at the Klamath Lakes on the Oregon/California border.

The birds reach their wintering grounds to feed in wetlands and cereal fields. Before they fly north in late winter, they feed to put on fat so that they can lay and incubate eggs before the Arctic vegetation starts to grow in the spring.

Main entry p. 204.

		March/April/May	June/July/August	Sept/Oct/Nov	Dec/Jan/Feb

SNOW LEOPARD (OUNCE)★★

Where found Central Asia. On mountains, in rocky scrub.

Head-and-body length 3ft-4ft 3in (1-1.3m); tail 3ft (1m).

Shoulder height 23in (580mm).

Weight 55-165lb (25-75kg).

Lifespan 16 years in captivity.

The mating season ends in May. From April, after a 3-4 month pregnancy, the female lines a den with her fur and gives birth to 1-5 cubs, each weighing about 1lb (450g). Their eyes open after 7-9 days. The male leopard probably takes little or no part in their upbringing.

By 2 months old the cubs are still being suckled but are eating some solid food. At 3 months they can follow their mother about. During summer, snow leopards roam alpine meadows up to about 20,000ft (6000m) above sea level.

Throughout their first autumn and winter, the leopard cubs hunt with their mother. Their prey includes rodents (such as marmots) and musk deer, pheasants, wild sheep and wild goats. The youngsters do not reach sexual maturity until about 3 years old.

During winter, the leopards follow their prey lower down the mountains to areas below about 5900ft (1800m). The leopards are usually solitary, but they hunt in pairs when the mating season begins in January.

Main entry p. 254.

SNOWSHOE HARE (VARYING HARE)

Where found Alaska; Canada (including Newfoundland); USA (mountain areas). Forest and brush country.

Length 16-27in (400-690mm).

Weight 3-15½lb (1.4-7kg).

Lifespan About 5 years.

Breeding begins in mid-March. A female bears a litter of usually 3-4 leverets after a 7-week pregnancy. Each leveret is hidden in a 'form' hollowed out amid vegetation. The young are born well furred and can soon move about. The hares' white coats turn brown for summer.

The hares may bear up to 4 litters a year. The mother visits the leverets every 2 days for just 5-10 minutes to suckle them. At 7 weeks old they are weaned, and feed on green plants. In summer, snowshoe hares create 'highways' of grazed vegetation through their forest homes.

The last litters are born in September. In a good year, some females may have had litters of up to 10 leverets. The hares' coats change to winter white, and they grow long hairs on their feet for grip on snow. When green plants become scarce, they feed on leaves, buds and shoots.

In winter, the hares pack down snow on regular routes to create snow 'highways', so making travel easier. When buds and leaves are scarce, the hares may cover up to 5 miles (8km) a day while foraging, and eat bark and woody stems.

Main entry p. 273.

SNOWY OWL

Where found Breeds in Arctic regions. May winter farther south. On tundra (low vegetation on frozen subsoil).

Length 19-25in (480-640mm).

Wingspan About 5ft (1.5m).

Weight 3-6½lb (1.4-3kg); female heavier than male.

Lifespan Up to 9 years.

In spring, snowy owls may be seen as far south as Alabama (USA), the Black Sea and northern India. They are lost migrants from a major movement south that occurs about every 4th autumn, when increased owl numbers coincide with a food shortage.

It is the breeding season. A female lays 5-8 eggs in a ground hollow, often on a raised hillock, and incubates them for 6-7 weeks, fed by the male. When lemmings, usually the owls' main food, are plentiful, there may be up to 11 eggs. In some parts, the owls eat mainly Arctic hares.

The downy hatchlings are fed by the female alone. Their eyes open 4-5 days after they hatch. The chicks can fly at 8-9 weeks old, and they disperse in preparation for the winter. About every 4th autumn many owls migrate south.

Some snowy owls may remain in the Arctic tundra in winter, but some move south. In North America snowy owls are often seen on the Canadian prairies.

No main entry, see pp. 149, 272.

SOOTY TERN

Where found Atlantic, Indian and Pacific oceans. In tropical and subtropical areas.

Length 16-17in (400-430mm).

Weight 7oz (200g).

Lifespan Probably up to 20 years.

In the Caribbean, the terns gather in their breeding colonies. A female lays 1 egg in a scrape on the ground. Both parents incubate the egg for 1 month, and feed the chick for 8 weeks. In May, Indian Ocean terns begin to congregate around their breeding colonies.

The Caribbean adults disperse into the Gulf of Mexico and southwards. Their youngsters cross the Atlantic towards the winter feeding grounds off West Africa. In the Indian Ocean, it is the main breeding season near the Seychelles. Terns breed for the first time in their 6th year.

The Indian Ocean terns begin moving south from the Seychelles breeding colonies, drifting on the trade winds. But as in all sooty tern colonies studied in detail, the adults stay close to the breeding area. The terns feed mainly on fish.

Caribbean youngsters return from West Africa. Immature birds (2-5 years old) may winter off northern South America. Indian Ocean terns are widely distributed, some as far as Australia. Some tropical colonies breed at any time of year.

Main entry p. 117.

SOUTH AMERICAN SEA LION

Where found South American coasts, south from Peru and Uruguay.

Length Male 7ft 6in (2.3m); female 6ft (1.8m).

Weight Male 550lb (250kg); female 265lb (120kg).

Lifespan Up to 15 years.

Pups are left in groups on the beaches while mothers make fishing trips. The pups are suckled for 6 months or more, sometimes until the next pup is born the following year. At Punte Norte in Argentina, killer whales pluck sea lions from crowded breeding beaches in March.

After the breeding colony has broken up, the sea lions feed well on squid and fish for half the year, preparing for the next breeding season in the southern summer. The bulls begin to show an interest in females as early as August.

In September, the sea lions sometimes patrol penguin colonies and feed on the penguins returning to their breeding sites in the southern spring. They take gentoo, rockhopper, and magellanic penguins.

Sea lions gather at the breeding beaches. Pups are born mid-December-early February, and mating is a week after pupping. Bulls without harems try to take cows from harems, so harem bulls have no food or rest for 8-9 weeks.

Main entry p. 78.

	March/April/May	June/July/August	Sept/Oct/Nov	Dec/Jan/Feb

SOUTHERN RIGHT WHALE ★★

Where found South Atlantic, Indian and Pacific oceans.

Length 50ft (15m); female slightly larger than male.

Weight Over 50 tons.

Lifespan Probably more than 30 years.

South American whales are feeding in the food-rich waters of the southern oceans. They begin their northward migration to breeding areas during April and May. Mothers gradually wean last year's calves, and will not be ready to mate again for another year or so.

The whales arrive in the bays of Peninsula Valdés, Argentina, in June and the first births occur. Females that mated last year produce single calves 18ft (5.5m) long, which swim well at a few hours old. Courting right whales gather in boisterous groups, and early mating occurs.

The last calves are born and mating ends about mid-November. Adults and youngsters leave for their summer feeding grounds. Calves keep close to their mothers. They grow at a rate of about 3ft (1m) a year; they will reach sexual maturity when they are about 45ft (13.7m) long.

The whales are in their summer feeding areas, and mothers feed for the first time since their calves were born. Right whales sieve krill from the surface and deeper waters. Adults may feed side by side, particularly when the krill is dense.

Main entry p. 201.

SPECKLED BUSH CRICKET

Where found Most of Europe and northern Asia. Trees and bushes.

Length Up to ⅝in (16mm).

Lifespan Adult 2-3 months; nymph (larva) 3 months.

Tiny insects that look like speckled greenflies hatch about May from the thin, papery eggs that have overwintered in a slit in a plant or tree bark. They are nymphs of the speckled bush cricket. They begin to feed on leaves, and grow and moult five times during the summer.

After 3 months, the nymphs moult for the sixth and last time, and emerge as adults during August or September. They become active in the late afternoon, and males 'sing' to attract females well into the night. They feed on leaves and also eat soft-bodied insects.

The adults cannot fly but can hop distances of 2ft (610mm) or so. The crickets mate, and the female lays her eggs singly in bark crevices, or in slits in plant stems. As the frosts begin, the crickets die.

The eggs lie dormant through the winter, safe from the cold. Bush crickets have antennae longer than their bodies, and they are also known as long-horned grass-hoppers. Speckled bush crickets are just one species of bush cricket.

Main entry p. 112.

SPERM WHALE

Where found All oceans.

Length Male 50ft (15m); female 36ft (11m).

Weight Male 45 tons; female 20 tons.

Lifespan Up to 60 years.

In the Northern Hemisphere, mating occurs in tropical and subtropical waters in spring. Males follow family groups of 10-20 females and their youngsters, and fight aggressively for the right to mate with the receptive females. The females usually mate every 4-6 years.

In the Northern Hemisphere calves from matings in the previous spring are born in late summer and autumn. They are about 12ft (3.7m) long at birth and are suckled for 1½-3½ years or more. Males leave the family groups and migrate to Arctic waters to feed.

In the Southern Hemisphere, mating is in spring and early summer in tropical waters. Bulls may not reach sexual maturity until they are about 18-21 years old and 36-39ft (11-12m) long, and may not be strong enough to gain a mate until 25 years old.

South of the Equator, calves are born January-April. Birth is 14-16 months after mating. Adult males migrate south to spend the summer feeding in Antarctic waters. Sperm whales eat mostly squid and octopus.

Main entry p. 77.

SPINNER DOLPHIN

Where found Tropical and subtropical seas.

Length 6ft 6in (2m).

Weight 110lb (50kg).

Lifespan 15-30 years.

North of the Equator, it is spring and baby spinner dolphins are born 10-11 months after their parents mated. The youngster is 2ft 6in (760mm) long at birth, and as soon as it is born, its mother nudges it to the surface to breathe. Youngsters are suckled for about 11 months.

In the Northern Hemisphere, spinner dolphins in the eastern Pacific Ocean mate in late spring and early summer. Males become sexually mature at 6-9 years old, and females at 4-6 years. Spinner dolphins live in schools that may number from a few to about 1000.

Spinner dolphins feed mainly at night on fish and squid. In pursuit of food they make limited migrations – those found near Pacific coasts have shown ranges of 185-435 miles (300-700km). The exceptions are the Pacific spinners around Hawaii, the Marquesas Islands, Christmas Island and Tahiti, which stay close to the islands all year. In the eastern Pacific, spinners are often found with spotted dolphins and tuna, and are netted by tuna fisher-men, who inadvertently catch dolphins with tuna.

Main entry p. 291.

SPONGE, YELLOW TUBE

Where found Caribbean Sea and off Florida (USA) and Brazilian coasts. On coral reefs.

Height 1⅛-19½in (28-500mm); tube diameter ⅜-3¼in (10-82mm).

Lifespan Many years.

This sponge lives on coral reefs at depths of 16-130ft (5-40m). It consists of a cluster of greenish-yellow tubes like hollow candles – tube sponges are some-times called candle sponges. Each tube is a colony of single cells living together, and has a network of tangled fibres that include whip-like threads on the inner walls. These draw water into the tubes, and the water is sucked into microscopic chambers in the walls. In these chambers, minute plants and animals and dead animal matter are sieved out as food. Periodically, the sponge releases clouds of sperm and eggs into the sea for up to 20 minutes at a time. The sponge is then said to 'smoke'. Sometimes whole colonies of tube sponges smoke together. In the water, sperm and eggs fuse to form larvae, which swim freely for several days and then settle onto coral reefs and turn into the typical tube shape. They grow slowly, budding off new tubes as they expand. A tube sponge is soft when fresh (like a natural bath sponge from the Mediterranean Sea) and releases a harmless purple dye if squeezed. When it dies, it turns hard as wood.

Main entry p. 144.

	March/April/May	June/July/August	Sept/Oct/Nov	Dec/Jan/Feb

SPRINGBOK

Where found Southern Africa. Arid western areas.

Length 3-4ft (1-1.2m); male smaller than female.
Shoulder height 2ft 6in (760mm).

Weight 55-99lb (25-45kg).

Springboks breed during the rains, which occur at different times throughout their range. The males mark their territory with urine and dung, which they leave in piles at the borders, and with scent from glands beneath their eyes, rubbed onto grass blades. They gather and guard groups of females until the females come on heat and can mate. Pregnancy lasts 6 months. As the rains approach, the springboks gather in large herds and move to new feeding grounds. The first births usually coincide with the arrival of the rains. Females bear single fawns, which are hidden amid grass for 2 weeks, until they can

follow their mothers. They are suckled for several months, but are independent at about 6 months old. Springboks feed on grass and leaves, sometimes digging for roots, and are active at dawn, dusk and during the night to avoid the heat of the day. They can exist on very little water. Once they roamed in herds numbering thousands, but were slaughtered because they destroyed crops. Now they are scarce in the wild, but some are farmed for meat and hides.

Main entry p. 199.

SQUID, OPALESCENT (MARKET SQUID)

Where found Pacific Ocean, off the west coast of North America.

Length 3-6in (75-150mm) including tentacles.

Lifespan 3 years.

Young opalescent squid hatch about 3 weeks after their parents mated. They are under ⅛in (3mm) long and still have a yolk sac attached. They swim to near the surface and away from the spawning ground. Creatures such as arrow worms, comb jellies and jellyfish prey on them.

As the squid grow, they gradually move deeper into the sea and become predators on other sea dwellers. They are voracious feeders, grabbing anything small enough for them to handle. Squid move by jet propulsion, and emit a jet of inky fluid as a defence mechanism.

Coastal currents disperse the squid, and they hunt from sea bed to sea surface. They take small fish, but about a quarter of their prey is fellow squid. The squid are themselves eaten by nearly every large predator. At 3 years old they are ready to mate.

On moonless nights from late November to April, opalescent squid gather in millions off southern California to mate. The females attach 10-20 egg capsules, each with 100-200 eggs, to sea-floor rocks or weeds. The adults then die.

Main entry p. 37.

STAG BEETLE

Where found Europe and northern Asia. Where there is decaying wood.

Length Male up to 2in (50mm); female 1¼in (32mm).

Lifespan Adult about 1 month; larva up to 3 years.

Inside rotting wood, such as in old trees, stag beetle grubs (larvae) are secure in tiny chambers, feeding on the wood. Some larvae that have been in the wood for 3 years are not feeding but have become pupae, and are inside pupal cases in which they are changing into adults.

Adults emerge from their pupal cases and fly off to find mates. They do not feed, but live on reserves built up as larvae. Males battle to win the right to mate with females. After mating, females burrow into suitable rotting wood, particularly that of oak and fruit trees, to lay their eggs.

The adults die after about a month. The eggs hatch, and the larvae, which are white with brown heads, begin to feed on the rotten wood. In autumn, larvae that are now 2 years old develop into pupae.

Larvae and pupae are protected from the winter weather within their home of rotting wood, such as old tree stumps, dead branches, rotting logs and fence posts.

Main entry p. 137.

STELLER'S SEA EAGLE★

Where found North-east Asia: northern Sea of Okhotsk. Also winters northern Japan. On rocky coasts, near forests.

Length Male 2ft 11in (890mm); female 3ft 4in (1m).
Wingspan Over 8ft (2.4m).

Weight Male 12lb (5.5kg); female 15-20lb (7-9kg).

Courtship displays begin in March, and in late March or April adults start migrating north to breeding grounds on the Siberian coast of the Sea of Okhotsk. They begin building and refurbishing nests. Mating and egg-laying occur early April-May. Females lay 1-3 eggs (usually 2).

Eggs are incubated for 5-6 weeks and hatch in early June. The parents work hard to feed the eaglets with fish. The youngsters stay in the huge nests of sticks in tall forest trees until they fledge in late July or early August.

Adults and young move slowly to the wintering grounds. Some stay in Russia, but others migrate up to 1120 miles (1800km) and gather in large numbers in places such as the Shiretoko Peninsula (Hokkaido). Smaller numbers of birds go south along the Sea of Japan coast.

The birds winter at large, sheltered, communal roosts, where they can be found in their hundreds. They forage during the day along the coast, the ice-edge and at sea, taking ducks and gulls and especially fish (Alaskan pollock).

Main entry p. 46.

STELLER'S SEA LION

Where found North Pacific from northern Japan round to southern California. Coastal waters.

Length Male 9ft 6in (2.9m); female 8ft (2.4m).

Weight Male 1 ton; female 600lb (275kg).

Lifespan At least 22 years.

Females begin moving to the pupping beaches in May. Pups are born about 3 days after the mother's arrival. She stays with the pup for 9 days, then starts a cycle of foraging at sea and returning to suckle the pup. The males establish their territories on the breeding beaches.

Births peak in June and early July, and mating takes place afterwards. Competition for females is intense; only males that hold territories mate. By July, most of the pups are swimming well and learning to dive and hunt. In August, males begin moving north to the Bering Sea.

In September, Californian females move north from the breeding grounds with the pups, which are generally suckled for 3-4 months, sometimes for 12. The young bulls are not sexually mature until they are 3-6 years old. Young females breed at 4-5 years old.

As winter sets in, the sea lions move southwards from Arctic waters into their winter feeding grounds off the coasts of eastern Russia and western North America. Herds of a thousand animals may gather to feed on squid and fish.

Main entry p. 105.

	March/April/May	June/July/August	Sept/Oct/Nov	Dec/Jan/Feb

STINGRAY, SOUTHERN

Where found West Atlantic coast from New Jersey (USA) to northern Brazil. Shallow waters down to 200ft (60m).

Width of body disc Up to 5ft (1.5m).

Weight 58lb (26kg) for 3ft (1m) width.

Lifespan Up to 25 years.

The stingray gets its name from the sharp spine near the base of its long, thin tail. This spine is used for defence (against predators such as sharks) and is linked to venom sacs, so can deliver poison to a wound inflicted by the stingray's lashing tail. Southern stingrays are the largest stingrays in North American waters. They live near the shore in bays and on sheltered reefs, and are often partly buried in the sand with eyes, spiracles (breathing holes) and tail exposed, but they can swim fast if need be in pursuit of prey. The stingrays feed on bottom-dwelling creatures such as worms, fish and shellfish, and can detect electrical activity in the muscles of prey buried in the sand. They crush their prey with their fused, flattened teeth. Normally, each stingray vigorously defends a territory. On the north coast of Grand Cayman island south of Cuba, rays congregate around tourist divers and are fed by hand. Their territorial aggression disappears with the abundance of food. Mated females retain their eggs inside the body and give birth to 3-5 live young, each about 7in (180mm) long, which are miniatures of their parents.

Main entry p. 285.

STORK, WHITE

Where found Breeds in Europe (except Scandinavia), north-west Africa, Asia. Winters in Africa. Woods, marshes.

Length 3ft 3in-3ft 9in (1-1.1m).

Weight 5-10lb (2.3-4.5kg).

Lifespan Up to 26 years.

The storks leave their wintering grounds in southern and central Africa, and return to the north by April. They mate on the nest. A week later, from mid-April to early May, females lay 3-4 (rarely up to 7) eggs at 1-2 day intervals. Both birds incubate the eggs for 4-5 weeks.

The eggs hatch by early June. Both parents feed the chicks for 8-9 weeks until they can fly. They regurgitate food such as fish, frogs, mice and insects onto the floor of the nest. The chicks remain near the nest until early August, when they set off on migration followed by the adults.

Early September is the peak time for migration across the Bosporus and Strait of Gibraltar. By late September, the storks have reached Africa, and continue their journey south. During their stay, many live near marshes and shallow pools, stalking prey through the water or long grass.

The storks remain in Africa, often concentrated in large groups. In February, they begin their journey north, the first birds returning to south-west Europe by the end of February or in March. Some get shot on the way.

Main entries pp. 91, 189.

SUPERB LYREBIRD

Where found Eastern Australia. In the temperate coastal and mountain forests to the east of the Great Dividing Range.

Length 2ft 7in-3ft 2in (790-970mm) including tail.

Lifespan 20-25 years.

Male lyrebirds start their spectacular courtship displays in the southern autumn. They scratch together mounds of earth and do a graceful dance on top of each one. They sing, often mimicking other birds, and thrust forward their lyre-shaped tail feathers, making them quiver.

A female visits more than one male. Mating takes place beneath the male's shimmering tail feathers, and afterwards the female builds a nest of sticks lined with moss. She lays a purple-brown egg, incubates it for 6-7 weeks, and tends the chick in the nest for a further 6-7 weeks.

It is the end of the breeding season, and the male birds moult their decorative tail feathers. Young birds stay with their mother for some months, maybe until winter. Superb lyrebirds are shy and rarely seen, living in the densest and most remote parts of the temperate rain forest.

The birds are normally solitary, but during summer they feed in groups of 4-5. They scratch up insects, grubs, spiders and worms from the soil of the forest floor. Adult males begin to grow a new set of tail feathers.

Main entry p. 121.

SWALLOW (BARN SWALLOW)

Where found Breeds North America, Europe, North Asia. Winters South America, southern Africa and Asia. Open country, farm buildings.

Length 7½in (190mm).

Weight ¾oz (21g).

Lifespan 5-6 years.

Birds begin arriving in their breeding areas in late March. Pairs build cup-shaped nests of mud pellets, sited under eaves, in barns, on beams or bridges, and (rarely) in caves. Females line the nests with feathers or grass. Mating occurs, and egg-laying begins in May.

A female lays 3-6 speckled white eggs, and usually incubates them alone for about 2 weeks. Both parents feed the chicks with insects in the nest for about 3 weeks until they fledge. The male feeds them for 10-11 days more while the female starts a second brood.

By now the swallows (youngsters and adults) have begun to gather in large flocks, in Europe often with martins. They leave for the wintering grounds in the Southern Hemisphere, European migrants travelling on a broad front southwards. Late leavers may be killed by bad weather.

Swallows spend the winter in tropical areas. As at all times of the year, they feed on day-flying insects, which they catch in flight. The birds roost in vast numbers, often in reed beds growing in water.

Main entries pp. 89, 191.

SWAMP DEER (BARASINGHA)★★

Where found Central and northern India; southern Nepal. Marshland or grassy plain.

Length 5-6ft (1.5-1.8m).
Shoulder height About 4ft (1.2m).

Weight 507-624lb (230-283kg).

North Indian and Nepal-ese deer live in or beside swamps; stags shed their antlers in March, and females give birth to usually 1 calf April-May. Central Indian deer live on the edge of grassy forest clearings; stags shed their antlers in May. The deer graze at dusk and early morning.

In central India the young are born June-July, when the monsoon rains bring a new growth of grass. Calves have amber to golden-brown coats with pale spots. By summer, the adults have moulted into paler golden-brown coats, females having paler coats than males.

As winter approaches the adults' coats darken. Stags brush their antlers, which may be about 3ft (1m) long, against shrubs and tall grass to remove the velvet (hairy skin). The deer rest in long grass from mid-morning to dusk. In the north the rut (mating display) peaks in November.

The rut peaks in January in central India. A large, dominant stag collects up to 30 females. Stag challenges stag by roars lasting about a minute. If this fails, they lock antlers and fight. After rutting, large males form bachelor groups of 6-8.

Main entry p. 255.

	March/April/May	June/July/August	Sept/Oct/Nov	Dec/Jan/Feb

SWIFT (COMMON SWIFT)

Where found Breeds Eurasia eastwards to central China, and in north-west Africa. Winters Africa south of the Equator. Open country and urban areas.

Length 6½in (165mm).

Weight 1½oz (43g).

Lifespan 10-15 years.

Swifts arrive back in Eurasia from late April, and breeding starts in mid-May. A pair usually mate for life. They build a cup-shaped nest of feathers, straw and grass cemented by saliva, in a roof or crevice. Courting displays and mating occur on the nest or in the air.

Both parents incubate the 2-3 eggs for about 3 weeks, and both feed the chicks. If food is scarce and the chicks are not fed for some days, their bodies 'shut down' until fed again, but they may then stay longer in the nest. They fly at 5-8 weeks old, and leave for wintering areas at once.

By now, all the birds have migrated – those in Britain leave in late July. Young birds often stay in Africa through the next summer, and may not breed until their 3rd or 4th year. Swifts eat insects, feeding in flight. They are able to store fat for times when insects are scarce.

The birds winter south of the Equator. They do not land, and sleep and feed on the wing, high in the air. They ride the rising warm air currents between bouts of wing-flapping to gain height.

Main entry p. 159.

TAIPAN

Where found New Guinea and north-east Australia. Dense tropical rain forest and dry grassland.

Length 6ft 6in-10ft (2-3m).

Lifespan More than 20 years.

Within days of emerging from their eggs, young taipans – 18in (460mm) long – make their first kill and embark on their solitary lives. By day the snakes hunt birds and small mammals, which they find by scent. Youngsters may fall prey to monitor lizards.

In the southern winter, taipans spend more of their time coiled up in sheltered dens, such as under fallen trees or branches. Taipans are venomous, injecting poison (that can be fatal to humans) through their fangs, but they are shy and rarely seen.

Warmer spring weather brings the snakes out to bask in the sun and then shed their skins. In the north of their range, the snakes mate early in spring and lay eggs in November, but in most areas, stormy, humid weather in November signals the beginning of the mating season.

In summer the snakes may hunt in the cool of the night. Egg-laying begins in January. A female lays 10-15 eggs (rarely, up to 20) in a hollow in soft soil or in a rotting log. She leaves them, and they take 2½-3½ months to hatch.

Main entry p. 264.

TASMANIAN DEVIL

Where found Tasmania. Open forests, coastal heaths, farms, bushy suburbs.

Head-and-body length About 2ft (610mm); tail 9-12in (230-300mm).

Weight 13-17½lb (6-8kg).

Lifespan 6 years.

Tasmanian devils are mostly solitary. In the March-April mating season, adults call to seek mates. A month after mating females bear 1-4 babies, each about ½in (13mm) long, which crawl into their mother's rear-facing pouch to suck milk.

In August or September the young leave the pouch for the first time at 15 weeks old, while their mother is resting in the den – which is in a hollow log or cave, or under the roots of a tree. Tasmanian devils feed mainly on carrion, but take some live prey, such as reptiles and insects.

Cubs are suckled in the den for 15 weeks more, being weaned gradually onto flesh. In November they leave the den for the first time but usually stay with their mother for a few weeks before making their own den. Youngsters, more agile than adults, will climb to take nesting birds.

Devils forage at night all year round, and if several claim the same carcass, there is likely to be a screeching match. Youngsters may be killed in disputes over food. They first breed at about 2 years old; first litters may have 1 or 2 babies.

Main entry p. 242.

TERMITES

Where found Worldwide in tropical, subtropical and warm temperate areas. In tree-scattered grassland.

Length Queen 3-6in (75-150mm) or more; others about ¼in (6mm).

Lifespan Queen and king at least 15 years.

Heavy rains trigger winged, reproductive termites (both male and female) to fly from the nest mound in swarms. In equatorial Africa, this occurs in April. When the termites land, their wings break off and they scurry about to find mates. Pairs seek a soil crevice in which to mate.

Above their crevice, a pair (a king and queen) begin building a mound of chewed wood, saliva and droppings, and the queen starts to lay eggs. In the mounds of older colonies, workers extend and renovate the nest mound, which can be 30ft (9m) tall and hold thousands of termites.

In Zimbabwe termites swarm in the November rainy season, which also triggers more swarms in equatorial Africa. Birds and other predators, such as lizards, feast on the swarms. But only the aardvark (ant bear) and hyena-like aardwolf can break into established termite mounds.

All year, workers emerge at night to feed on dead plant material, and take food to others in the mound. Soldiers repel ants and other mound intruders. In her chamber the queen constantly lays eggs which the king fertilises.

Main entry p. 236.

THOMSON'S GAZELLE

Where found Kenya; Tanzania; southern Sudan. Open, grassy plains.

Length 2ft 6in-4ft 6in (760-1370mm).

Shoulder height 2ft (610mm).

Weight 40-60lb (18-27kg); male larger than female.

Lifespan 10-12 years.

On the Serengeti Plain, vast herds of these small gazelles follow migrating herds of zebras and wildebeests. The gazelles graze the short grass in the wake of the wildebeests, and will cover 9 miles (15km) in a night to reach a new flush of vegetation. Where grazing is good, the gazelles can go a long time without water, but in dry conditions they drink each morning and evening. Adults are taken by cheetahs, wild dogs, lions, leopards and hyenas. When startled, they 'stot' – leap abruptly with stiff legs – and their white rump hairs flare to warn herd mates. Males establish territories up to 300yds (274m) across in which they mate. Rival males may lock horns, but injuries seldom result. Females give birth to a single fawn 6 months after mating, leaving the herd to find a suitable spot. The fawns may be born at any time of year, and a female may produce 2 a year, but births usually peak after the rains. In East Africa births tend to be in January, February or July. A fawn lies in deep cover until it can run with the herd, and jackals take many fawns. Survivors are independent at 9-15 months old.

No main entry, see pp. 140, 142, 164, 195, 230, 235, 240.

	March/April/May	June/July/August	Sept/Oct/Nov	Dec/Jan/Feb

THORN BUG, FLORIDA

Where found Florida, USA. On hibiscus, acacia, young jacaranda and young royal poinciana trees.

Length ⅛-½in (3-13mm).

Thorn bugs – treehoppers that resemble thorns – have piercing mouthparts that they use to suck the sap of the plant they live on. From late spring onwards, they mate and lay eggs. Sunshine is thought to trigger their breeding, and they may reproduce twice a year or more. A female makes a groove in a stem or twig of the plant, and lays her eggs in it. She protects the eggs for 10-12 days until they hatch. The larvae do not yet have spines or wings. They feed on the sap from the plant's leaves, and during the next six weeks moult their skins five times, finally emerging as adults. The thorn bugs exude honeydew onto the plant they live on; it is eaten by ants, which guard the bugs against predators such as spiders and beetles.

The very cold spells that occasionally hit Florida in winter may wipe out a whole population of thorn bugs. But any eggs that overwinter on a plant provide a new generation next spring.

Main entry p. 277.

TIGER★★

Where found India; Burma; Nepal; Bangladesh; Indonesia; China (south and Manchuria); Siberia. Forests.

Length About 10ft (3m).
Shoulder height 3ft (1m).

Weight Male up to 600lb (274kg); female smaller.

Lifespan 15 years.

Cubs about 3 months old go on hunts with their mother, but only to watch. The cubs are weaned in April or May. Tigers hunt at night for prey such as deer and antelope; only about one attack in ten succeeds. Cubs 15 months old are growing fast and getting too big to climb trees.

The tigers spend much of the day in deep shade to avoid the heat. Cubs born last December now begin learning to hunt, but will not be able to make a kill on their own until they are about 18 months old. Young tigers become independent at about 3 years old.

The mating season begins. The males mark their territories more often when the females are in season. Females are on heat for only a few days. A male mates with several females whose territories overlap with his own. Tigers can breed when they are about 3-4 years old.

Most births occur between now and May. Females bear litters of 3-4 cubs after a 3½ month pregnancy. The cubs are born in a den in a cave or thick undergrowth. Up to half die within 2 weeks of birth, mainly from malnutrition.

Main entry p. 92.

TIGER SALAMANDER★★

Where found Canada (southernmost prairies); USA (excluding much of the far west except California); north-east Mexico. Damp meadows, mountain forests and arid plains.

Length 3-9in (75-230mm).

Lifespan Possibly 20 years.

Lizard-like land salamanders are rarely seen above ground. They burrow into moist soil or leaf litter and usually emerge only when it is raining or during the breeding season, when they congregate in ponds and pools. The salamanders tend to mate and lay their eggs during the wettest time of the year – in winter and spring in the west, and spring and summer in the east. They lay eggs in masses in water. The eggs develop into tadpole-like larvae, which live in the water – some for two years or more – and feed on insects and other small creatures; second-year larvae also eat first-year larvae. They lose their gills and tail fins when they change into adults and leave the pond. Some larvae never develop beyond the tadpole-like state. On land the salamanders feed on small creatures such as worms, insects and slugs. They rarely return to water, except to breed, but in drier regions or during dry periods stay near water so that they can regularly douse themselves, for without moisture they die. In the northern and higher parts of their range, the salamanders hibernate through the coldest time of the year.

Main entry p. 65.

TIGER SHARK

Where found Tropical and warm temperate waters. Coasts and open ocean.

Length 11-18ft (3.4-5.5m).

Weight 850-2000lb (385-910kg).

Lifespan More than 12 years.

Tiger sharks in the western Atlantic leave deeper waters and begin to make their way north with the warm-water belt, moving closer inshore along the US coast. The sharks have a broad, blunt head and faint stripes and blotches on their backs (hence their name).

By July, sharks in the western Atlantic are as far north as Cape Cod; they feed well on new-born prey of many kinds. Off Hawaii in the Pacific, sharks gather to take albatross chicks from the sea surface. Southern Hemisphere tiger sharks move nearer the Equator for winter.

In the northern autumn, Northern Hemisphere sharks head towards the Equator for winter. Where and when the sharks mate or pup in the wild is unclear, but it is believed they reach sexual maturity when about 9ft 6in (2.9m) long. Females give birth about 1 year after mating.

A mated female retains the fertilised eggs inside her body and produces a milk-like substance that supplements the food each embryo receives from its yolk sac. She gives birth to 10-80 pups that are about 2ft (610mm) long.

No main entry, see p. 156.

TOOTH-BILLED CATBIRD

Where found North-east Queensland, Australia. Mountain rain forest.

Length 10in (250mm); male slightly larger than female.

Weight About 4oz (113g).

Outside the breeding season, the birds live unobtrusively in the forest canopy. Young tooth-billed catbirds are a darker brown on top than their parents, but their throat and breast feathers are paler.

All year, the catbirds feed mainly on leaves, which they snip off from the tree with their saw-edged beaks. They also eat fruit, and some insects. Mostly the birds are solitary, but they occasionally feed in mixed flocks along with spotted catbirds and bowerbirds.

In August, males begin to clear display areas in the forest and decorate them with leaves, which they place with their undersides uppermost. A male perches above his 'bower', calling with loud whistles and harsh notes to attract females. He mates with several during the season.

A female makes a shallow cup nest of plant tendrils and small twigs in thick vegetation. She lays 2 eggs, which she incubates for 3 weeks, then feeds the chicks for 3 weeks. Males leave their bowers by the end of January.

Main entry p. 184.

	March/April/May	June/July/August	Sept/Oct/Nov	Dec/Jan/Feb

TREECREEPER

Where found Europe (except Spain, western France). Coniferous and deciduous woodland.

Length 5in (125mm).

Weight ⅓oz (9g).

Pairs are busy with courtship and building a nest in a tree crevice. In April the female lays usually 6 eggs, which she alone incubates for 2 weeks. Both parents feed the chicks for 2 weeks, with food such as small caterpillars (which are plentiful in the spring), weevils and woodlice.

The youngsters are weak fliers at first, but can climb well to feed on tree insects. The parent birds may rear another brood in June. The birds spend summer feeding alone or in small flocks. They 'creep' up tree trunks looking for food in crevices, and may also seek food in stone walls.

Flocks of treecreepers often join flocks of tits during the winter, probably for mutual protection against predators such as sparrowhawks in the less leafy, more exposed woods. The treecreepers feed mainly on the eggs and pupae (chrysalises) of insects found in tree bark. Often the treecreeper adults keep to their own territory, simply 'hitching a ride' with the more mobile tits as they pass through. Many birds die in hard winters. Those that can find a snug roost in a tree crevice have a better chance of survival.

Main entry p. 17.

TURNSTONE, RUDDY

Where found Worldwide: breeds on Arctic tundra; winters on coasts as far south as Australia, South Africa, Argentina.

Length 9in (230mm).

Weight 3½-5¼oz (100-150g).

Lifespan Up to 18 years.

The turnstones move north from wintering areas to breed on the Arctic tundra. South American birds heading for the Canadian tundra may pause at Delaware Bay, on the US east coast, to feast on horse-shoe crabs' eggs as the crabs emerge to lay their eggs in the sand.

The birds nest late May-early August, usually in a small ground hollow lined with vegetation. The female lays 2-4 eggs, which both parents incubate for 3-4 weeks. The chicks fly after 3 weeks. The turnstones feed on sedge seeds, and before leaving fatten up on crowberries.

The turnstones fly south in loose flocks. Some North American birds head for Pacific islands, others go to South America. East Canadian and Greenland birds cross the Atlantic to Europe and north-west Africa. Siberian breeders go as far as the Indian Ocean and Australia.

Winter is spent feeding on coasts and mud flats. The birds use their strong necks and short, stout beaks to flick seaweed and stones sideways. Any small creature underneath will be eaten, sometimes after a chase.

No main entry, see p. 106.

UAKARI, WHITE/RED★★

Where found South America. In the rain forest of the Amazon Basin.

Head-and-body length 15-20in (380-510mm); tail 5½-7in (140-180mm).

Weight Up to 9lb (4kg).

Lifespan More than 20 years.

Little is known of the monkeys' breeding times in the wild, but captive troops in the Northern Hemisphere mate and give birth May-October. Males become sexually mature at 6 years old. Females first breed at 3-11 years, and have 1 baby every 2 years, 6 months after mating.

The Amazon rivers are at their highest, and the low-lying areas (the *várzeas*) are flooded. Uakaris forage in troops of 10-30 in the tops of tall trees, feeding mostly on fruit but also on leaves and insects. They have bare, red faces and hair that is reddish or pale (white).

The uakaris prefer to live along the banks of small forest rivers and lakes, and avoid the large rivers. They are active by day, moving smoothly through the trees on all fours, and can leap as far as 70ft (21m) or more from tree to tree. They are not as noisy as most other species of monkey.

With the rivers at their lowest, the *várzeas* dried out and fruit scarce, the uakaris may feed on seedlings – otherwise they rarely forage on the ground. They sleep on high, thin branches to avoid jaguars, eagles and other predators.

No main entry, see p. 181.

VAPOURER MOTH

Where found Europe; Asia (temperate); North Africa; North America. Trees and bushes.

Length Female ½in (13mm).

Wingspan Male 1½in (38mm).

Lifespan Caterpillar and male moth up to 4 weeks; female moth about 2 weeks.

In the warmth of spring, eggs laid last year hatch into brightly coloured caterpillars, which have yellow tufts and also black spiky hairs that cause a rash if touched. The caterpillars feed on leaves, and within a month each spins a cocoon inside which it changes into an adult.

Moths emerge from their cocoons in June: They are found on most trees and bushes, particularly on limes, oaks, fruit trees and heather, hawthorn, rose and hazel bushes. The females waft scents to attract males. Mating occurs, and each female lays about 300 eggs on her cocoon.

In southern parts a second generation of vapourer moths may have emerged to lay their eggs. Female vapourer moths are virtually wingless, and cannot fly. By the end of October, all the moths have died.

The brownish eggs stay dormant all winter on the female's abandoned cocoon. The cocoons may be in places such as crevices in tree bark, in fence niches and under the roof overhang of sheds or outhouses.

Main entry p. 139.

VULTURE, LAPPET-FACED

Where found Africa: East; southern; much of Sahel; south and west Sahara. Arid plains and thorn scrub.

Length 3ft 4in (1m).

Wingspan 8ft 6in (2.6m).

Weight 15lb (7kg).

Lifespan Probably 20 years.

At any time of year, the vultures are rarely active early or late in the day because they depend on updraughts of warm air for soaring. Their food is mostly carrion, found by searching from the air. They are one of the largest of the vultures, and others often give way to them at a kill.

Egg-laying occurs in Tanzania, Kenya and South Africa. A pair occupies a huge nest in a thorn tree or on a crag. The 1 egg (rarely 2) is incubated probably by both birds for 7-8 weeks. In the southern Sahara, some pairs separate during the rainy season (June-September).

Egg-laying begins in Uganda and Somalia. Both parents feed their chick on the nest and for several months after it fledges at 4-5 months old. The vultures probably do not breed every year, and when not breeding, pairs may have separate ranges.

The main breeding season in the north of the vultures' range. A pair often start to build and occupy a nest 6 months before the egg is laid. The nest of sticks is about 7-10ft (2-3m) across with a cup 3ft (1m) across.

Main entry p. 240.

	March/April/May	June/July/August	Sept/Oct/Nov	Dec/Jan/Feb

VULTURE, RÜPPELL'S GRIFFON

Where found Africa south of the Sahara as far as northern Tanzania. Arid and mountainous areas.

Length About 3ft (1m).
Wingspan About 8ft (2.4m).

Weight 15-20lb (7-9kg).

Lifespan Probably 20 years.

There may be some breeding at any time of year, but the birds tend to lay at the end of a rainy season. In Kenya egg-laying occurs May-June, after the long rainy season. The birds form large breeding colonies of up to 1000 pairs on cliffs. They feed on carrion.

A pair share the incubation of the 1 egg (rarely 2) for 6 weeks. The grey, downy chick weighs about 6oz (170g) on hatching in August. Once well grown it needs up to 1lb 12oz (800g) of food a day. When it fledges at about 4 months old it weighs about 15lb (7kg).

Egg-laying peaks in October in Ethiopia, and October-November in West Africa. Courting pairs soar together around the nest site. Both sexes build the stick nest on a ledge. The nest is about 2ft (610mm) across and 8in (200mm) deep, and lined with grass.

On the Serengeti Plain (northern Tanzania), breeding occurs again in January at the end of the short rainy season. Young vultures have brown down on their necks, which becomes white when they mature.

No main entry, see p. 233.

WALLABY, TAMMAR

Where found Southern Australia and its offshore islands. Arid thickets and scrubland.

Head-and-body length About 2ft (610mm); tail about 22in (560mm).

Weight 6½-11lb (3-5kg).

Lifespan 8 years.

As food becomes scarcer with the approach of winter, the wallabies space out to forage in larger areas of their arid homeland. They browse on shrub leaves. At this time, a mother often has a youngster (joey) following her around, one in the pouch, and an embryo in storage.

It is winter, and as at any time of year, the wallabies feed at night and hide in the scrub during the day. They can live for 8-9 months without a drink, feeding on plants that contain little moisture and even on very salty ones. The wallabies can also drink sea water.

In September, the joey that was born last summer vacates the pouch for the first time. It will still return there when danger threatens, until the pouch has another occupant. The youngster dives in head first and curls itself round to peer out.

After midsummer, the embryo conceived last summer develops and is born 1 month later in late January or early February. It crawls into its mother's pouch. The mother mates again, and a new embryo develops a little then is quiescent.

Main entry p. 30.

WALRUS

Where found Throughout Arctic and sub-Arctic seas.

Length 8ft-10ft 6in (2.4-3.2m); female slightly smaller than male. Tusks 14-22in (360-560mm).

Weight ¾-1¼ tons.

Lifespan Up to 40 years.

Females give birth to single calves on pack ice in May – 15-16 months after mating and after a pregnancy of about 11 months, because the fertilised egg does not implant in the womb until 4-5 months after mating. This means females can calve only once every 2 years.

In females that mated last winter, the fertilised egg implants in the womb in May or June. Females and males are usually in separate herds in summer. They feed at sea on molluscs such as clams, cockles and mussels, then haul ashore to rest. In the sun their thick skins go pink.

In autumn, females and their youngsters join the herds of bulls. Calves of 6 months or more start to follow their mothers in search of food, but they will not be weaned until about 18 months old. Young females usually begin to breed at 6-7 years old, males at about 15 years.

Mating occurs in the sea during the coldest months, each bull associating with a herd of up to 30 cows. He courts them, making a series of whistles, 'knocks' and bell-like sounds with an inflatable throat sac.

Main entry p. 151.

WASP, COMMON

Where found Europe; North Asia; North Africa.

Length Queen ¾in (19mm); male (drone) ⅝in (16mm); worker about ½in (13mm).

Lifespan Queen 1 year; drone 3-4 weeks; worker up to 6 months.

In late spring, queens emerge from hibernation and find a nest site such as a disused mouse or vole burrow. They chew wood from posts or logs to make papery pulp, and with it they build horizontal tiers of cells. Eggs laid in the cells hatch as larvae, which are fed on insects.

The larvae become worker wasps (unmated females), who take over the task of finding food and rearing the other larvae in the nest while the queen is egg-laying. Near the end of summer, both males and females (new queens) are reared. They mate, and the colony disperses.

With no more larvae to tend, the workers feast on fruit and other sweet things. In October, the new, mated queens look for a suitable hibernation site in a sheltered corner, perhaps inside a house or outbuilding. The males, workers and the old queen die as the weather turns colder.

The new queens hibernate all winter, ready to begin the cycle again next spring and found a colony of maybe 2000 wasps that will use their stings to kill food such as flies, caterpillars and aphids.

Main entry p. 207.

WEDDELL SEAL

Where found Coasts of Antarctica; occasionally near sub-Antarctic islands.

Length Male 8ft 3in (2.5m); female 8ft 6in (2.6m).

Weight 880-990lb (400-450kg).

Lifespan Up to 18 years.

For most of the year, Weddell seals hunt at depths down to about 330ft (100m), but may dive down to 1600ft (490m) to catch cod. They eat mostly fish and squid. Sometimes a seal brings a fish 5ft (1.5m) long and weighing 66lb (30kg) to the surface and eats it within 3 hours.

In the Antarctic winter, the seals spend most of their time in the water, and can be heard calling to each other under the ice. They keep breathing holes open by biting the ice with their canine teeth. These get worn down and become infected, leading to the seal's death.

By October, the first bulls and pregnant cows are at their breeding sites. Pups 5ft (1.5m) long are born on the sea ice October-November. Pups enter the water at 8-10 days old, with their woolly coats only partly moulted. When weaned at 6-8 weeks, they weigh 243lb (110kg).

Mating occurs at sea in December, but the fertilised egg implants in the womb January-February. Seals continue to arrive at the breeding sites until February, a few yearlings and juveniles among them. Females first mate at 3 years old.

Main entry p. 248.

	March/April/May	June/July/August	Sept/Oct/Nov	Dec/Jan/Feb

WESTERN GREBE

Where found Western North America as far south as Mexico. Prairie marshes, lakes and open bays.

Length 22–29in (560–740mm); male larger than female.

Weight 3lb (1.4kg).

Birds that migrated south for winter return north to breed in the US Midwest. Birds that wintered on the coast fly to summer breeding colonies on central lakes. By mid-May most birds are at their breeding sites, where they begin their graceful courtship dances.

By mid-June, females have laid clutches of 3-4 eggs. Both the parents incubate them, taking turns to go and feed. The eggs hatch after 3 weeks, and the chicks leave the nest soon afterwards. Both adults feed them with fish and insects, and carry them on their backs.

By November, most birds have left for their wintering areas on the Pacific coast or the Gulf of Mexico, including the youngsters, who are now independent; they will not breed until 1-2 years old. A few birds do not migrate, but remain inland throughout the winter months.

Flocks of up to 1500 birds assemble on coastal waters and feed on fish throughout the winter. Birds feeding at sea have been seen to take many herring and their relatives. Most of their food is caught by diving under water.

Main entry p. 105.

WHALE SHARK

Where found All tropical and warm temperate seas. Coasts and open ocean.

Length Up to 40ft (12m).

Weight Up to 12 tons.

Lifespan Probably more than 60 years.

The whale shark is the largest fish in the sea, but little is known about its behaviour. It is most often seen at the surface, where it feeds on shrimps, squid and small fish, extracting them from water filtered in through its broad mouth and expelled through its gills. Inside its mouth – which is like a gigantic letterbox – there are about 300 rows of 3000-5000 tiny backward-pointing teeth, each less than ⅛in (3mm) across. Sometimes several sharks are seen feeding together. They are slow swimmers, with a cruising speed of about 4mph (6km/h). Their tough skins, underlain with thick, hard muscle and covered with tiny tooth-like bumps, protect them from predators such as killer whales. When danger (such as a harpoon fisherman) threatens, the shark dives down into the deep sea. In the Gulf of Oman, between the Persian Gulf and Indian Ocean, sightings of whale sharks are more frequent in autumn; the sharks may congregate there either to mate or give birth, or both. It is thought the sharks give birth to 'live' young, but this is not certain and they may lay fertilised eggs in large 'mermaid's purses' – envelope-like containers.

Main entry p. 179.

WHIMBREL

Where found Breeds in the Arctic or far north; winters farther south, mostly in the Southern Hemisphere. Marshes and shores.

Length 15½–19in (390–480mm).

Weight 10½–21oz (300–600g).

Lifespan Up to 12 years.

In March the birds begin returning to their northern breeding sites. They often fly at night, males keeping in touch by calls. After mating in May or June, a female lays 3-5 eggs in a ground hollow on moorland or tundra. Both birds incubate the eggs for about 1 month.

The chicks leave the nest soon after hatching. Both parents feed them insects, worms, snails and berries. They can fly at 5-6 weeks old. The whimbrels migrate south after breeding, often in large flocks. They fly strongly, and tend to follow inland routes more than coasts.

Whimbrels arrive at their wintering grounds in September. They prefer rocky beaches, estuaries and exposed reefs, and like to eat crabs. They sometimes travel inland to golf courses. The birds feed singly or in small groups. Sometimes they defend feeding territories.

The adult birds moult as late as December. The moult is completed with the flight feathers, which regrow in mid-January. In winter, the whimbrel is the commonest wader to be seen in the Galápagos Islands in the eastern Pacific Ocean.

Main entry p. 201.

WHITE-TIP REEF SHARK

Where found Tropical and subtropical waters of the Indian Ocean, Red Sea and Pacific (mainly the western Pacific). Near reefs.

Length Up to 6ft (1.8m).

Weight 50–60lb (23–27kg).

Lifespan Up to 25 years.

Although it is a common shark, little is known about the life of the white-tip reef shark. It is active mainly at night, usually in waters 16-132ft (5-40m) deep where it hunts in a set territory covering maybe 2-3sq miles (5-8sq km) for fish, crabs, lobsters and octopuses. Some white-tips have been found at depths down to 1085ft (330m). The shark spends the day resting on the sea floor in caves or below overhanging rock or coral. An individual may occupy the same daytime spot for years. Although slender in body, the white-tip reef shark is a slow and clumsy swimmer, and is taken by tiger sharks. During mating, the male holds the female's pectoral (chest) fin with his mouth. The female keeps the fertilised eggs inside her body and gives birth to 1-5 live young, each around 2ft (610mm) long. The babies may fall prey to fish such as groupers and to other sharks. At first the youngsters grow about ½in (13mm) each month, but when they are 2ft 6in (760mm) long, the growth rate slows to around 1in (25mm) per year.

Main entry p. 290.

WHOOPER SWAN

Where found Breeds in the Arctic, Iceland, Scandinavia, Siberia; usually winters in Western Europe. In or near fresh water.

Length 5ft (1.5m).
Wingspan 6ft 6in (2m).

Weight About 25lb (11kg).

Lifespan Up to 30 years.

The swans leave their wintering grounds in Western Europe for the northern breeding areas, mostly arriving by late April. They begin to nest when the ice clears, probably in late May in the more southerly breeding areas, or in June farther north.

After courting and mating, a pair build a large nest of reeds and sedges on open, boggy moor, on an islet or beside a lake or pond. The female lays 3-5 eggs and incubates them for 5-6 weeks. Both parents feed the cygnets on water plants and small pond creatures.

The youngsters fly when they are about 2 months old. By September, the first of the birds that have not bred begin to move south. The adults with new youngsters follow them soon afterwards. The swans have a loud, trumpeting call, but are fairly quiet while in flight.

The swans feed by day in salt marshes and arable fields, the families staying together among large flocks throughout the winter. They return to roost at night on estuaries and lakes, but may feed all night long if there is moonlight.

Main entry p. 206.

		March/April/May	June/July/August	Sept/Oct/Nov	Dec/Jan/Feb

WILD BOAR

Where found South and central Europe; Asia; North America (introduced). Open woodlands and steppe.

Length 3-6ft (1-1.8m).
Shoulder height 3ft (1m).

Weight 110-440lb (50-200kg).

Lifespan Up to 20 years.

In spring, females leave their family group (one or more adult females and their offspring) to give birth (farrow) after a pregnancy of about 4½ months. A female builds a grass nest, where she has up to 12 striped piglets. They stay in the nest for 10 days, then join the group.

The piglets are suckled until they are 3 months old, when they moult their stripes for bristly, dark brown adult coats. The youngsters stay with their mother for up to a year, until she is ready to farrow again. They eat roots, nuts, fungi, fruit, greenstuff, larvae, worms and small animals.

Mating is in late autumn. The males, which are normally solitary, seek and court females. They 'chant', with much grunting, and nudge the females until one will mate. After mating, they go off to seek other females. In deciduous woods, the wild boars fatten up on tree seeds.

The wild boars grow their thick, bristly winter coats. They are active all winter, ranging in search of food and will root under the snow for tubers, bulbs and roots. The pigs may spend colder periods protected in sheltered dens.

Main entry p. 116.

WILD DOG (CAPE HUNTING DOG)★★

Where found Africa south of the Sahara. Open grassland.

Head-and-body length 3ft (1m); tail 14in (360mm).
Shoulder height 2ft (610mm).

Weight 35-60lb (16-27kg).

Lifespan 12-15 years.

In South Africa, females give birth March-July after a pregnancy of 9-11 weeks. Litters of 2-12 pups are born in a den such as an abandoned burrow. In East Africa, pups about 6 months old can now fend for themselves, and are beginning to learn how to hunt with the pack.

The dry season in East Africa brings hardship for the packs as prey gets scarcer. The death rate of both pups and adults rises sharply. Packs of 10-15 dogs are usually made up of a dominant pair, adults (mostly males) and pups. By 2½ years, most females have joined other packs.

In East Africa, mating occurs in September so that the young will be born about the time of the October-December rains, when there will be newborn gazelles to eat. Pups are suckled for about 3 months, and are gradually weaned on meat brought to the den by other pack members.

With up to 12 pups in a litter, a pack of 10-15 adults – a breeding pair and some of their last season's offspring – is fully occupied providing just one litter with meat. In South Africa, the mating season begins about January.

Main entry p. 240.

WILDEBEEST, BLUE (BRINDLED GNU)

Where found East and southern Africa (except the far south). Grassland.

Length 6-7ft (1.8-2m).
Shoulder height 4-5ft (1.2-1.5m).

Weight 350-580lb (160-260kg).

Lifespan 16-20 years.

Most animals are feeding in small herds where the best grazing is to be found, such as on the southern Serengeti Plain. Mating peaks May-June, with males holding territories often only about 33yds (30m) across near their female herds. As the grass dries up, herds move on.

At the height of the dry season in the southern Serengeti, the herds are moving north-westwards to Lake Victoria, where there is still grass because of the wetter soil. In July they move on again, north across the Mara river to where there is always grass, but of coarser quality.

As the rain belt moves southwards, bringing a wave of fresh grass, the herds cross the Mara river and trek south-eastwards towards the Ngorongoro Crater in the southern Serengeti. They will graze in the southern plain until next May, when the grass dries up.

In January or February, females who mated 8-9 months ago give birth to a single calf weighing about 48lb (22kg). Calves are suckled for 7-8 months, but start to eat grass much earlier. By 2 years old they will be independent.

Main entries pp. 195, 230.

WILLOW PTARMIGAN (WILLOW/RED GROUSE)

Where found North America; northern Eurasia. Mountain tundra, high moorland and forest clearings with brush.

Length 15-17in (380-430mm).

Weight 1lb-1lb 9oz (450-700g).

Lifespan Up to 7 or 8 years.

The birds begin to moult white winter plumage for brown breeding plumage (except the red grouse, which is brown all year). Red grouse begin nesting in April, but other races begin in early May in the south. A female lays 6-9 eggs in a nest in a ground hollow sheltered by vegetation.

In the far north, breeding begins in early June. The female alone incubates the eggs for about 3 weeks. The downy chicks leave the nest at once to feed on buds, leaves, catkins and insects. Both parents go with them. The chicks can fly when they are about 2 weeks old.

Pairs raise only 1 brood a year. Family groups stay together until late autumn, when they may join up to form flocks. In autumn northern birds moult their speckled brown plumage for winter white, giving them better camouflage in winter snow.

In winter, birds may feed together in large flocks. In very severe winters, many leave the tundra for the coniferous forests to the south. They are often taken by large birds of prey such as hawks, as well as by foxes and wolves.

Main entry p. 125.

WOLF, TIMBER/GREY★★

Where found North America; Eurasia. Arctic regions and some temperate forests.

Head-and-body length Up to 5ft (1.5m); tail 20in (510mm).
Shoulder height 2ft 8in (810mm).

Weight 85-95lb (40-45kg).

Lifespan About 12 years.

In the Arctic and more northerly areas it is the mating season. In the south it is the main birth season. Females give birth to 4-7 pups after a 9-week pregnancy. The pups' eyes open when they are about a week old, and about 3 weeks later they emerge from the den for the first time.

It is the birth season in the Arctic and more northerly areas. The den, perhaps a cave or rock crevice, is used until the pups are about 10 weeks old and are weaned. The pack members will feed them on regurgitated meat until they are big enough to travel and hunt with the pack.

At 6 months old the pups begin to hunt with the pack of 7 or more wolves – the breeding pair and offspring from previous litters. Food may include caribou, deer, hares, beavers and lemmings. Wolves from Arctic tundra areas migrate south following the caribou herds.

Food is short in the northern areas; Arctic wolves often attack adult musk oxen. The wolves hunt in large territories, and howl to muster the pack. In southern areas, mating begins in January or February.

Main entry p. 128; Arctic wolf, see pp. 149, 169.

	March/April/May	June/July/August	Sept/Oct/Nov	Dec/Jan/Feb

WOLVERINE (GLUTTON)★★

Where found North America; northern Eurasia. Tundra and coniferous forests.

Head-and-body length 2ft 6in (760mm); tail 8in (200mm). **Shoulder height** 15in (380mm).

Weight 20-55lb (9-25kg).

Lifespan Up to 13 years.

Young wolverines are born February-March. A female gives birth to 2-3 kits in a den in a rock crevice, snowdrift, or hollow tree. The young are blind at birth, but have thick, woolly fur. They are suckled for 9 weeks. Wolverines are the largest members of the weasel family.

Mating takes place April-August, but the fertilised egg does not implant in the female's womb until December. Females are sexually mature at 2 years old, and can then give birth every year. Wolverines scavenge for carrion but are powerful hunters. They also eat eggs, grubs and berries.

The youngsters stay in their mother's territory until autumn. The young females may stay longer (up to 2 years) until they are driven off to set up their own territories elsewhere. Wolverines are normally solitary. A male's territory may overlap those of a number of females.

The wolverines do not hibernate in winter. They scavenge carcasses from other animals, such as lynxes, or hunt prey such as deer. Their large feet spread out their body weight, and even in powdery snow they can outrun a reindeer.

No main entry, see p. 103.

WOMBAT, COMMON

Where found South-east Australia and Tasmania. Forested hills.

Length Up to 4ft (1.2m). **Shoulder height** 14in (360mm).

Weight 33-77lb (15-35kg).

Lifespan 26 years in captivity.

Cooler weather in April brings the wombats out of their burrows to feed in daylight, although they are usually active at night. Females bear a single baby between April and June. It crawls into its mother's pouch, which faces to the rear so that no dirt enters while she is burrowing.

Wombats feed on roots, fungi and grasses, and have incisor teeth that grow continuously (as in rats and mice). They range over large areas in search of food, and may travel 2 miles (3km) in a night. They are mainly solitary, except for females with young.

After about 6 months, a youngster emerges from the pouch and begins to forage with its mother. Infants who left the pouch the previous year now leave to fend for themselves. Wombats are powerful diggers and their burrow systems can have tunnels up to 22yds (20m) long.

In summer the wombats are wholly nocturnal, spending the day in a burrow system, often dug in a slope near the base of a tree. Burrows are used as casual accommodation by foraging wombats.

Main entry p. 100.

WOOD DUCK

Where found South-east Canada; USA (eastern States and west coast); Cuba. Forest pools, lakes and rivers.

Length 17-20in (430-510mm).

Weight Male about 1½lb (680g); female lighter.

Lifespan Up to 20 years.

In the north, mating displays are under way by March. A female lays 8-14 white eggs in a bed of down in a tree hole and she alone incubates them for 4-5 weeks. Within a day of hatching, the downy young jump from the nest to the water or ground below.

The ducklings fly when they are 8 or 9 weeks old. They stay with their parents for several weeks. The family tends to stay in the shadier areas of pools or rivers in summer. The adults put heads and necks under water to search for plants or sometimes small insects as food.

In southern areas, the birds may stay in small parties within their breeding area through the winter. Others may move south to warmer areas, including Mexico, in autumn. The ducks spend part of the day roosting in trees, holding on by their sharp claws.

Southern pairs begin their mating displays by January, and egg-laying starts in February. The ducks nest in tree holes such as old woodpecker nests, often using the same one for years. The nest may be up to 50ft (15m) above ground.

Main entry p. 87.

YAK (WILD)★★

Where found Tibet. Mountain tundra and ice fields at 13,000-20,000ft (4000-6000m) above sea level.

Length 10ft (3m). **Shoulder height** Up to 6ft 6in (2m).

Weight ½ ton.

Lifespan About 25 years.

In spring, herds of up to 200 yaks gather to eat the newly sprouting grass. In their mountain home (they are one of the highest-dwelling animals in the world) good grazing can be sparse. But during this time of plenty, last year's calves, now about 11 months old, are weaned.

In June, yaks shed their winter coats in patches. Females give birth to single calves after a pregnancy of about 9 months. The yaks roam the lower slopes of their range, feeding on grass and shrubs. When the weather gets too hot for them, they move back up to the higher reaches.

Except at mating time, males live in bachelor herds. The onset of colder weather is the start of the mating season. Males engage in head-to-head combat in fights over females, who breed every other year.

By now the yaks have grown new winter coats. With their thick, coarse, shaggy hair underlain by dense soft hair, they can stand temperatures below −40°C (−40°F). But some do die each winter of exposure and starvation.

Main entry p. 193.

ZEBRA, COMMON (PLAINS)

Where found East and southern Africa. Grassland.

Length Up to 8ft (2.4m). **Shoulder height** 4ft 2in (1.3m).

Weight 600lb (273kg).

Lifespan 25 years.

Zebra herds include family groups of 10-15, usually 1 male and the rest females and their foals, which are suckled for about 7 months. Females can breed at about 2 years old. By day, the herd grazes on the longest, coarsest grass, and visits a water hole regularly.

As the grass dries out, herds grazing on the southern Serengeti Plain go north-west towards Lake Victoria, ahead of the wildebeest herds, which eat shorter grass. They then cross the Mara river, and graze there. Elsewhere, the dry season forces herds to stay near water.

About September, as the rain belt moves southwards, the herds north of the Mara follow the wave of fresh grass into the southern parts of the Serengeti Plain. Many fall prey to lions on the way.

This is the main birth season. Females bear a single foal weighing about 66lb (30kg) after a pregnancy of 11½ months. Mating follows at once. Newborn foals often fall prey to big cats, hyenas and wild dogs.

No main entry, see pp. 140, 142, 195-6, 230.

INDEX

Page numbers given first in bold type, eg **278**, refer to main text entries; other references in the text are given in ordinary type, eg 190. Page numbers in italic type, eg *324*, refer to entries in the year chart beginning on page 296.

A

adder **73**; *296*
Adélie penguin **221**; 32-3, 34; *296*
aestivation 15; 177
African elephant **257-8**, **279**; *310*
African fish eagle **120**; *312*
African lion **140-3**; 196, 232, 233; *327*
albatross, black-browed 223; *296*
    grey-headed 296
    wandering **222-3**; *296*
algae, blue-green **270**; 13
Amazon **25-7**, **180-1**
American bison **12-13**; *300*
anaconda 27
Andean condor **288**; *306*
anemone fish 294
ant, army **286-7**; *297*
    communication 190
    honeypot **241**
    red 190
antbird 287
antelope, sable **52**; *340*
aphid 130, 241
Arctic fox 272; *297*
Arctic hare 149; *297*
Arctic tern **102**; *297*
Arctic (grey) wolf 148, 149, 169; *354*
armadillo, nine-banded **97**; *297*
army ant **286-7**; *297*
arowhana 181
arum, hairy dragon **88**; *298*
Asian elephant 258
Atlantic cod **36**; *306*

Atlantic salmon **227**; *341*
Australasian gannet **244**; *314*
avocet **116**; *298*
aye-aye **55**; *298*

B

badger **71-2**; *298*
balanites tree 164
bald eagle **226**; *298*
baleen 155, 175
bamboo 192, 214
banded stilt **295**; *299*
bandicoot 264
banner-tailed kangaroo rat **150**; *324*
barasingha (swamp deer) **255**; *348*
barnacle goose **124**; *299*
barn owl **110**; *299*
barn swallow *348*
basslet, fairy **294**; *311*
bat 18
    fringe-lipped 99; *313*
    fruit (flying fox) **241**; *312*
    hammerheaded **140**; *319*
    Mexican free-tailed **172**; *330*
    pipistrelle **14**, **160**; *335*
    wrinkle-lipped 19
bat-eared fox **237**; *299*
beaks, hornbills 216
bear, American black 13; *300*
    brown **68-9**, **153-4**; *302*
    grizzly (American brown) **153-4**; 13, 62, 69; *302*
    Kodiak 62, 153
    polar **60-2**, **187**; *336*
beaver **84-5**; *299*
bee, bumble (humble) **90**; *303*
    leaf-cutter **161**; *326*
    western honey **138-9**; *320*
bee-eater, carmine **22**; *304*
beetle, carrion 280
    dung 233
    fungus **263**
    ladybird **130**; *325*
    stag **137**; *347*
    tok tokkie 283
beetle-trap flower **280**; *300*
beluga **150**; *300*
Bewick's swan 206
bird's nest soup 18, 305
bison, American **12-13**; *300*
blackbacked (silverbacked) jackal **164**; 233; *322*
black bear, American 13; *300*
blackbird, red-winged **251**; *339*
black-browed albatross 223; *296*
black cayman 27, 181
black flying fox **241**; *312*
black grouse **112**; *300*
black rhinoceros **198**; *339*
black skimmer 25, 26; *301*
black swan **100**; *301*
black-tailed prairie dog **64**; *336*
Blakiston's fish owl **137**; *301*
blowfly 88
blue butterfly, common 158
blue crab **131**; *301*
blue damselfly, common *308*

blue-faced (masked) booby **217**; *329*
blue-green algae **270**; 13
blue penguin **246**; *311*
blue shark **156**; *301*
boar, wild **116**; *354*
body clocks 43
Bogong moth **269**; *302*
bolas spider **245**
booby, masked **217**; *329*
boto 180-1, *302*
bowerbird, bower types 247
    gardener 247
    Lauterbach's 247
    satin **247**; *342*
boxfish **242**; *302*
Brazilian otter *315*
brindled gnu (wildebeest) **195-6**, **230-3**; 140; *354*
brown bear **68-9**, **153-4**; *302*
brown hare **70**; *319*
brown (common) kiwi **165**; *325*
brown pelican **83**; *302*
brown rat **70**; *303*
brown skua 34
buffalo 279
    Cape **53**; *304*
bumble bee **90**; *303*
bush baby, lesser **212**; *303*
bustard, great **72**; *316*
butcher bird 111
butterfly, 26
    ant 287
    comma 209
    common blue 158
    day/night flying 158
    holly blue 209
    large blue **190**; *326*
    large white 158
    monarch **205**; *330*
    olive transparent 287
    pierid 173
    queen **173**; *337*
    small skipper **158**; *344*
    sodium salts intake 26
    sweet oil 287
    tortoiseshell 209
    ultraviolet light in sex recognition 173
buzzard **253**; *303*

C

cabbage, skunk **37**; *344*
cachalot whale 77
Californian ground squirrel **15**; *318*
Californian tiger salamander **65**; *350*
cane toad **182**; *303*
Cape buffalo **53**; *304*
capelin 36
capybara **262**; 181; *304*
caribou (reindeer) **168**; 103, 148; *304*
carmine bee-eater **22**; *304*
carpet viper 265
carrion beetle 280
catbird, tooth-billed **184**; *350*
caterpillar, ant communication 190
    eastern tent **154**; *309*
    emergence, timing of 266

caterpillar, life cycle 266
caterpillars, Australian 266
catfish 19, 26; *304*
cat, fishing **162**; *312*
    native **182**; *337*
cattle, Chillingham **207**; *305*
cave swiftlet, edible **18-19**; *305*
cayman, black 27, 181
    common or spectacled 25, 27; *305*
chameleon, Namaqua 283
chamois **115**; *305*
cheetah **234-5**; 232; *305*
Chillingham cattle **207**; *305*
cicada, periodical or 17-year **276**; *306*
clown anemone fish (clownfish) 294; *306*
cockatoo, gang gang **121**; *314*
    palm (great black) **265**; *333*
cod, Atlantic **36**; *306*
colour change, cuttlefish 183
common cayman 25, 27; *305*
common crossbill **16**; *307*
common dolphin **174-5**; *308*
common dormouse **227**; *309*
common frog **44-5**; *313*
common langur **49**; *325*
common loon **131**; *327*
common poorwill **251**; *306*
common shrew **159**; *343*
common swift **159**; *349*
common wasp **207**; *352*
common wombat **100**; *355*
common zebra *355*
condor, Andean **288**; *306*
convergent ladybird **130**; *325*
copepods 275
coral **269**; 43, 293; *307*
Costa's hummingbird **65**; *307*
cowfish 242
coyote 13; *307*

I J K

L

LONG JUMPERS		
	maximum	
	ft	*m*
Snow leopard	60	15.2
Red kangaroo	42	12.8
White-tailed deer	40	12.2
Racehorse	39	11.9
African lion (downhill)	39	11.8
Impala	35	10.6
Killer whale	30	9.1
African leopard	30	9.1
Siberian tiger	30	9.1
Domestic dog	30	9.1
Man	29.2	8.9
Chamois	25	7.7
Pine marten	11.5	3.5
Polar bear	13.1	4

M

N O

P Q

R

SPRINTERS ON LAND

	maximum	
	mph	km/h
Cheetah	63	101
Brown hare	45	72
Ostrich	45	72
Thomson's gazelle	44.7	72
Lion	43.5	70
Racehorse	43.3	69.6
Greyhound	41.7	67
Coyote	40.4	65
Grey kangaroo	40	64
Mountain zebra	40	64
Red fox	40	64
Polar bear	35	56
Black rhino	32	51.1
Giraffe	32	51.1
Wolf	28	45
Grizzly bear	28	45
Man	27.9	44.9
African elephant	24.5	39.4
Reindeer	20	32

WATER SPRINTERS

	maximum	
	mph	km/h
Sailfish	67.7	109
Bluefin tuna	64	103
Striped marlin	50	80
Swordfish	40.4	65
Killer whale	40	64
Mako shark	35	56
Common dolphin	27.6	44.4
Californian sea lion	25	40
Great barracuda	25	40
Leopard seal	24.2	39
Atlantic salmon	23	37
Leatherback turtle	22.4	36
Sperm whale	20	32
American manatee	19.9	32
Adélie penguin	17	27.2
Walrus	15	24
Sea otter	12	19.3
Beluga	11.5	18.5
Conger eel	7.5	12
Grey whale	7.5	12
Polar bear	6	9.6
Man	5.1	8.2

ACKNOWLEDGMENTS

The publishers acknowledge their indebtedness to the following people and organisations, books and journals, which were consulted for reference:
The Ranthambhore Society, Grantchester, Linden Gardens, Leatherhead, Surrey KT22 7HB (0372) 372026; Fateh Singh Rathore; The Zoological Society of London, Regent's Park, London NW1 4RY; Malcolm Walker.
Tigers: The Secret Life Valmik Thapar; photos by Fateh Singh Rathore (Elm Tree Books); *The Encyclopaedia of Mammals* edit Dr David Macdonald (Unwin Animal Library); *Mammals of the World* Ernest P Walker (The Johns Hopkins Press); *Field Guide to the Mammals of Southern Africa* Chris & Tilde Stuart (New Holland); *Amazon: the Flooded Forest* Michael Goulding (BBCL Books); *Whales and Dolphins* Dr Anthony Martin *et al* (Salamander Books); *A Dictionary of Birds* edit Bruce Campbell & Elizabeth Lack (T & A Poyser); *The Encyclopaedia of Birds* edit Dr Christopher M Perrins & Dr Alex L A Middleton (Unwin Animal LIbrary); *Eagles, Hawks and Falcons of the World* Leslie Brown & Dean Amadon (Country Life Books); *The Encyclopaedia of Reptiles and Amphibians* edit Dr Tim Halliday & Dr Kraig Adler (Unwin Animal Library); *The Encyclopaedia of Insects* edit Christopher O'Toole (Unwin Animal Library); *The Encyclopaedia of Underwater Life* edit Dr Keith Banister & Dr Andrew Campbell (Unwin Animal Library); *Wildlife Magazine* (BBC); *Sharks* edit John D Stevens (Merehurst Press); *The Book of Indian Animals* S H Prater (The Bombay Natural History Society; *The Library Atlas* edit Harold Fullard & H C Darby (George Philip); *Crocodiles* C A W Guggisberg (David & Charles).

Picture credits

The pictures in *The Wildlife Year* were supplied by the people listed below. Names given in *italics* refer to illustrations that are Reader's Digest copyright.
BCL=Bruce Coleman (UK); BCI=Bruce Coleman Inc (NY); OSF=Oxford Scientific Films; NP=Nature Photographers; PEP=Planet Earth Pictures; AA=Animals Animals; *T*=top; *C*=centre; *B*=bottom; *L*=left; *R*=right.
Front cover NP/Baron Hugo van Lawick, Artist *Malcolm Porter*. **Back cover** NP/Hugh Miles. **1** Dr Rüdiger Schmidt. **2-3** Imperial Press/M Iwago. **4** *TC* DRK/John Oerlach, *BL* Wolfgang Bayer Associates/Wolfgang Bayer. **5** *TL* Imperial Press/M Iwago, *BR* Dr Rüdiger Schmidt. **6** *TL* Photo Researchers Inc/Jo Di Stefano, *TR* Wolfgang Kaehler, *BC* BCL/John Cancalosi. **7** PEP/J R Bracegirdle. **8** *CL* BCL/Bill Wood, *TL* NHPA/S Krasemann, *TC* OSF/Frank Schneidermeyer, *BR* OSF/P K La Val. **9** *TL* OSF/John Downer, *CL* NHPA/Stephen J Krasemann, *C* NHPA/E Hanumantha Rao, *BC* NHPA/ANT, *BR* NHPA/C & S Pollitt/ANT. **10** Imperial Press/M Iwago. **11** PEP/Jonathan Scott. **12-13** Wolfgang Bayer. **13** *TC* BCL/Erwin & Peggy Bauer, *C* OSF/Stan Osolinski, *BC* BCL/Wayne Lankinen. **14** Merlin D Tuttle/Bat Conservation International, Artist *Gill Tomblin*. **15** *TR* NHPA/R J Erwin, *CR* NHPA/Brian Hawkes, *BR* BCI/Wolfgang Bayer. **16** Artist *Peter Barrett*, *TL* NP/Chris & Jo Knights, *BR* Frank Lane Picture Agency/D T Grewcock. **17** NP/Don Smith. **18** Eric Valli & Diane Summers from *Bird's Nest Gatherers of Tiger Cave*, Thames & Hudson 1990. **19** *TL* OSF/Alastair Shay, *TR* PEP/Philip Chapman, *CL* NP/S C Bisserot, *C & CR* PEP/Philip Chapman. **20-1** PEP/Jonathan Scott. **21** *TR* AA/Michael Fogden, *CR & BR* OSF/Michael Fogden. **22** BCL/Michael Fogden. **23** BCL/G Ziesler, Artist *Malcolm McGregor*. **24-5** Biofotos/Brian Rogers. **26** *TL* NHPA/Stephen Krasemann, *TR* Andrea Florence, *CL* NP/Paul Sterry. **27** Michael Goulding. **28** *TL* Doug Perrine *TR* AA/Carl Roessler. **29** Chris McFarling, Artist *Malcolm Porter*. **30** *TL* NHPA/Dave Watts, *BR* NHPA/Joe Blossom. **31** NHPA/Karl Switak. **32-3** BCI/Jen & Des Bartlett. **33** *TR* Minden Pictures/Frans Lanting, *BC* British Antarctic Survey/S Fraser. **34** *TL* OSF/Kim Westerskov, *BC* OSF/T S McCann. **35** BCL/Steven Kaufman. **36** OSF/Doug Allan, Artist *Colin Newman*. **37** *TR* OSF/Richard Kolar, *BL* PEP/Norbert Wu. **38** Wolfgang Bayer. **39** DRK/Doug Perrine. **40** Artist *Malcolm Porter*, *TL* BCL/Jeff Foott, *CL* Dr Craig R Smith, *BL* PEP/Robert Hessler. **41** *TL* NHPA/Orion Press, *BR* Mark Brazil. **42** BCL/Steven Kaufman. **43** *TR* AA/David C Fritts, *BR* Photo Researchers Inc/F Gohier. **44** *TL* NHPA/GDT-Silvestris (Robert Gross), *BR* NP/Paul Sterry. **45** OSF/Terry Heathcote. **46** Artist *Malcolm McGregor*, Mark Brazil. **47** Mark Brazil/Takuya Kanouchi. **48** DRK/D Cavagnaro. **49** BCL/Gunter Ziesler, Artist *Richard Bonson*. **50** *TL* OSF/Richard Packwood, *BL* BCL/Gunter Ziesler. **50-1** BCL/Peter Davey. **52** *TR* OSF/Carol Farneti/Partridge Films, *BL* BCL/Jane Burton. **53** *TL* Ardea/Alan Weaving, *BR* Gerald Cubitt. **54** *TL, TC & BL* Wolfgang Bayer. **55** Minden Pictures/Frans Lanting. **56** Rudolf Diesel, Artist *Richard Bonson*, *TL* BCL/Frans Lanting. **57** *TC* P Dee Boersma, *BR* BCL/Jen & Des Bartlett. **58** *TC* D Parer & E Parer-Cook, *BC* NHPA/Bill Wood. **59** Auscape/Ben Cropp. **60-1** The Image Bank/Co Rentmeester. **61** *TR* Colorific/Co Rentmeester, *CR & BR* Bryan & Cherry Alexander. **62** Artist *Malcolm McGregor*, *BL* PEP/Jim Brandenburg. **63** *TR* Survival Anglia/Jeff Foott, *BC* BCL/Jeff Foott, *BR* Survival Anglia/Jeff Foott. **64** DRK/Jim Brandenburg, Artist *Richard Bonson*. **65** *TR* Stan Osolinski, *BL* AA/Zig Leszczynski. **66** Bryan & Cherry Alexander. **67** *TR* Photo Researchers Inc/Pat & Tom Leeson, *C* BCL/Jeff Foott. **68** Francisco Marquez. **69** Artist *Malcolm Porter*, *TR & BR* Francisco Marquez. **70** *TL* NHPA/Stephen Dalton, *BR* NHPA/GDT-Silvestris. **71** Artist *Malcolm McGregor*, OSF/Alastair Shay. **72** *TR* NP/Kevin Carlson, *BL* BCL/Mark N Boulton. **73** NP/Owen Newman. **74-5** Gunter Ziesler. **76** *TR* Nigel Marven, *BL* PEP/Sue Earle. **77** Flip Nicklin, Artist *Richard Bonson*. **78** Martyn Colbeck. **78-9** BCL/Jen & Des Bartlett. **80** Auscape/Ben Cropp. **81** Valmik Thapar & Fateh Singh Rathore. **82** *BL* Photo Researchers Inc/Norman Lightfoot, *BR* Biofotos/J M Terhume. **83** Fulvio Eccardi. **84** *TC* NHPA/John Shaw, *BR* BCL/Jen & Des Bartlett. **85** *TL* OSF/Judd Cooney, *TR* Frank Lane Picture Agency/M Newman, *C* Ardea/Francois Gohier. **86** Ardea/Francois Gohier. **87** Artist *Malcolm McGregor*, *TR* BCL/S Nielsen, *BL* BCL/John M Burnley. **88** *TR* OSF/David Thompson, *BL* OSF/Sean Morris. **89** Melissa Wellbourn. **90** *TL, CL & BL* NHPA/J B Free. **91** Artist *Malcolm Porter*, *TR* NHPA/Manfred Danegger, *BL* BCL/Erwin & Peggy Bauer, *BR* BCL/Joy Langsbury. **92** Valmik Thapar & Fateh Singh Rathore/The Ranthambhore Trust; Artist *Sandra Pond*. **93, 94 & 95** Valmik Thapar & Fateh Singh Rathore. **96-7** DRK/Michael Fogden. **97** BCL/Jeff Foott. **98** *TL* Premaphotos/K G Preston-Mafham, *BR* Stuart D Strahl. **99** Merlin D Tuttle/Bat Conservation International, Artist *Malcolm McGregor*. **100** *TR* BCL/Frances Furlong, *BL* NHPA/Dave Watts/ANT. **101** Minden Pictures/Frans Lanting. **102** Artist *Trevor Boyer*, *BL* BCL/Norbert Rosing. **103** *TC* Frank Lane Picture Agency/Hannu Hautala, *C* Frank Lane Picture Agency/Rudolf Hofels/Silvestris, *CR* NHPA/Eero Murtomaki. **104-5** NHPA/Philippa Scott. **105** BCL/Charlie Ott. **106** *TL* Minden Pictures/Frans Lanting. **107** Doug Perrine. **108** Ardea/Ian Beames, Artist *Robert Morton*. **109** Premaphotos/K G Preston-Mafham. **110** *TL* PEP/P N Raven, *BR* BCL/George McCarthy. **111** Gunter Ziesler. **112** *TL* OSF/Larry Crowhurst, *TC* BCL/WWF/Fred Mercay, *BR* OSF/Paul Taylor. **113** Frank Lane Picture Agency/F Polking, Artist *Peter Barrett*. **114** OSF/G I Bernard. **115** *TL* Jacana/Frederic, *BR* BCL/Udo Hirsch. **116** *TL* BCL/Hans Reinhard, *BR* NHPA/N J Dennis. **117** NP/Jeff Watson. **118-9** Imperial Press/M Iwago. **119** *TR* NHPA/Nigel Dennis. **120** NHPA/Peter Johnson, Artist *Richard Bonson*. **121** *TR* Auscape/Jean-Paul Ferrero, *BL* Ardea/Hans & Judy Beste. **122** Minden Pictures/Frans Lanting. **123** Imperial Press/M Iwago. **124** NP/Hugh Miles. **125** *TR* Flip Nicklin, *BL* NHPA/John Shaw. **126-7** Helmut Horn. **127** Artist *Malcolm McGregor*. **128** Jim Brandenburg. **129** Art Wolfe. **130** Tom Stack & Assoc/Kevin Schafer. **131** Photo Researchers Inc/Tony Florio, *TR* BCL/Charlie Ott. **132** *TL* Premaphotos/R A Preston-Mafham, *BL* NHPA/Jim Bain, *BC* Ardea/Ian Beames. **133** OSF/David Wright. **134** Artist *Robert Gilmore*, *TL* Gunter Ziesler. **135** BCL/Andy Purcell. **136** Dragonfly sequence, PEP/Geoff du Feu, *TC* NHPA/Stephen Dalton, *C* OSF/Waina Cheng, *BL* P Munsterman. **137** *TR* Mark Brazil/Sumio Yamamoto, *BL* NP/Paul Sterry. **138** BCL/John Taylor. **139** Artist *Richard Bonson*, *TL* NHPA/Stephen Dalton, *TR* NHPA/L Hugh Newman, *CL* NHPA/Stephen Dalton, *CR* OSF/Bob Fredrick. **140** Artist *Richard Bonson*, Merlin D Tuttle/Bat Conservation International. **141, 142 & 143** Imperial Press/M Iwago. **144** *TL* PEP/Peter Scoones, *BL* Doug Perrine, *BC* Tom Stack & Assoc/Tom Stack. **145** *TR* Frank Lane Picture Agency/Fritz Polking/GDT, *CL & BL* NHPA/Jany Sauvanet. **146** Artist *Richard Bonson*, *TL* OSF/Kathie Atkinson, *BR* Ardea/Hans & Judy Beste. **147** Neville Fox-Davies. **148** Jim Brandenburg. **149** *TC* Jim Brandenburg, *TR* Tom Stack & Assoc/Joe Mcdonald, *BR* PEP/Jim Brandenburg. **150** *TL* DRK/Jeff Foott, *BR* DRK/C Allan Morgan. **151** NHPA/Stephen Krasemann. **152-3** BCL/John Shaw. **154** *TL* Biofotos/Brian Rogers, *BR* AA/Donald Specker. **155** Ardea/Francois Gohier, Artist *Richard Bonson*. **156** *TL* Marty Snyderman, *BR* Doug Perrine. **157** Doug Perrine. **158** *TL* Dr Robert E Stebbings, *BR* BCL/Gunter Ziesler. **159** Artist *Ann Savage*, *TL* NP/Hugh Miles, *TR* Premaphotos/K G Preston-Mafham, *CR* BCL/Kim Taylor, *BR* OSF/Tim Shepherd. **160** *TL* Neville Fox-Davies, *CL & BL* Premaphotos/K G Preston-Mafham. **161** Artist *Gill Tomblin*, *TR* NHPA/Melvin Grey, *BL* David Hosking. **162** *TR* DRK/Stanley Breeden, *TCR, TCL & C* DRK/Belinda Wright, *TL* DRK/Stanley Breeden. **163** OSF/Anthony Bannister. **164** *TL* OSF/Stan Osolinski, *CL* NP/W S Paton. **165** Artist *Malcolm Porter*, *TR* BCL/Frances Furlong, *BL* Auscape/Mike Osmond/Pacific Whale Foundation. **166** *TC* Dr Rudiger Schmidt, *BR* OSF/Doug Allan. **167** Leonard J Aube. **168** *BL* Thomas D Mangelsen. **169** *TR* Jim Brandenburg. **170** Artist *Richard Bonson*. **170-1** Leonard J Aube. **172** *TR* NHPA/Stephen J Krasemann. **173** Artist *Richard Bonson*, *TL* Photo Researchers Inc/Joe Distefano, *TR* Thomas Eisner. **174-5** Don Croll. **176** NP/Owen Newman, Artist *Sarah Fox-Davies*. **177** *TR* OSF/David Thompson, *BL* NP/Andrew Cleave. **178-9** Marty Snyderman. **180** Artist *Malcolm Porter*, Ardea/Andrea Florence. **181** *TC* Photo Researchers Inc/Tom McHugh, *C* OSF/Michael Goulding, *BR* OSF/Rodger Jackman. **182** *TR* Auscape/D Parer & E Parer-Cook, *BL* NHPA/Peter Krauss/ANT. **183** *TL* Auscape/D Parer & E Parer-Cook, *TR* AA/Carl Roessler, *CR* Ardea/Ron & Valerie Taylor. **184** Artist *Richard Bonson*, *TL* BCL/C B & D W Frith, *BR* Ardea/Ron & Valerie Taylor. **185** PEP/Jonathan Scott. **186-7** NHPA/John Shaw. **187** *BL* PEP/Flip Schulke. **188** *TL* PEP/Ron Perkins, *BR* NHPA/Stephen Dalton. **189** Artist *Malcolm Porter*, Ardea/G K Brown. **190** *TL* Biofotos/Jeremy Thomas. **191** *TL* NHPA/John Shaw, *BR* Roger Hosking. **192** *TL* Jacana/J P Ferrero, *BL* Ardea/Pat Morris. **193** *TL* BCL/Mark Boulton, *BR* NHPA/C & S Pollitt. **194-5** PEP/Jonathan Scott. **196** Artist *Malcolm Porter*, *TL & C* PEP/Jonathan Scott. **197** PEP/Nigel Tucker. **198** *TL* PEP/Jonathan Scott, *BL* NHPA/Peter Pickford. **199** *TR* BCL/Barrie Wilkins, *BL* Ardea/Peter Steyn. **200** *TC* PEP/Rod Salm, *CL* Photo Researchers Inc/Nick Bergkessel, *CR* Photo Researchers Inc/S E Cornelius. **201** Artist *Malcolm McGregor*, *TR* Minden Pictures/Frans Lanting, *BL* BCL/Jen & Des Bartlett. **202** *TL* OSF/Kathie Atkinson, *BR* NHPA/I R McCann/ANT. **203** NHPA/Jonathan Chester/ANT. **204** Minden Pictures/Frans Lanting. **205** *TR* OSF/M P L Fogden, *BL* DRK/D Cavagnaro. **206** BCL/Gordon Langsbury. **207** *BL* NHPA/G I Bernard, *BR* Stephen Hall. **208** Artist *Richard Bonson*, *TL* OSF/G I Bernard, *TC, CL, CR & BC* Premaphotos/K G Preston-Malham, *BL* Survival Anglia/John & Irene Palmer. **209** Premaphotos/K G Preston-Mafham. **210** *TL* PEP/Jonathan Scott. **210-11** Imperial Press/M Iwago. **212** Dr S K Bearder. **213** Artist *Malcolm Porter*, *TL* AA/Leonard Lee Rue III, *TR* Claude Nuridsany & Marie Perennou, *CL* BCL/Jen & Des Bartlett, *BL* NHPA/Nigel Dennis. **214 & 215** OSF/Andrew Plumptre. **216** *TL* BCL/Gunther Ziesler, *TC & TR* Survival Anglia/Alan Root. **217** *TR* PEP/Doug Perrine, *BL* OSF/Peter Ryley. **218** NHPA/Andrew Dennis/ANT. **219** Artist *Malcolm Porter*, *TL* Auscape/Jean-Paul Ferrero, *BR* OSF/G H Thompson. **220-1** NHPA/Jonathan Chester/ANT. **222** OSF/Ben Osborne. **222-3** Minden Pictures/Frans Lanting. **224** NHPA/Philippa Scott. **225** PEP/Jonathan Scott. **226** Artist *Malcolm McGregor*, OSF/Lon E Lauber. **227** *TL* BCL/Ronald Thompson/Frank Lane, *BR* BCL/George McCarthy. **228** Artist *Peter Barrett*, TL Richard Balharry, *TR* OSF/Press-Tige Pictures. **229** *TR & BC* NHPA/John Hicks/ANT. **230-1 & 232** Imperial Press/M Iwago. **233** *TC* Imperial Press/M Iwago, *BR* PEP/Jonathan Scott. **234** PEP/Anup & Manoj Shah. **235** Artist *Malcolm McGregor*, *TR* Swift Picture Library/Thomas Dressler, *CR* PEP/Jonathan Scott, *BR* Swift Picture Library/Thomas Dressler. **236** *TL* NHPA/Anthony Bannister, *C* Edward S Ross, *BC* Edward S Ross. **237** OSF/Stan Osolinski. **238** *TC* NHPA/Peter Pickford, *BL* PEP/Jonathan Scott. **239 & 240** PEP/Jonathan Scott. **241** Artist *Richard Bonson*, *TL* Auscape/Hans & Judy Beste, *TR* Derek Roff, *BL* Jan Aldenhoven. **242** *TR* Roger Steene, *BL* NHPA/Dave Watts/ANT. **243** NHPA/Klaus Uhlenhut/ANT. **244** Ardea/B L Sage. **245** *TR* Mantis Wildlife Films/Jim Frazier, *BL* Ardea/Ron & Valerie Taylor. **246** NHPA/Otto Rogge/ANT. **247** OSF/Kathie Atkinson, Artist *Malcolm McGregor*. **248** *TL* NP/E C G Lemon, *TR* PEP/David Rootes. **250** Survival Anglia/Jeff Foott. **251** *TL* BCL/Jeff Foott, *BR* BCL/John Shaw. **252** *TL* Mike Wilkes, *BR* Frank Lane Picture Agency/B S Turner. **253** Artist *Richard Bonson*, *TR* NHPA/Manfred Danegger, *BL* OSF/Dave Houghton. **254** AA/Michael Dick/OSF. **255** *TL* BCL/P Evans, *BR* BCL/M P L Fogden. **256-7** Herman Potgieter. **258** Artist *Malcolm McGregor*, *TL* Photo Researchers Inc/Mitch Reardon, *BC* Imperial Press/M Iwago. **259** NHPA/Peter Johnson. **260** *TL* OSF/David Macdonald, *BL* David Curl. **261** Yossi Eshbol. **262** Artist *Richard Bonson*, NHPA/Martin Wendler. **263** *TL & CL* Premaphotos/K G Preston-Mafham, *BR* Nick Gordon. **264-5** NHPA/Pavel German/ANT. **265** Artist *Richard Bonson*, NHPA/Klaus Uhlenhut/ANT. **266** *TL* NHPA/Otto Rogge/ANT, *TC* PEP/David Maitland, *TR, CL & C* OSF/Mantis Wildlife Films, *CR & BR* NHPA/Klaus Uhlenhut/ANT. **267** Auscape/Esther Beaton. **268** *TL* BCL/C B & D W Frith, *CL* NHPA/ANT. **269** Artist *Malcolm Porter*, *TR* NHPA/Roy Blakers/ANT, *BL* Peter Harrison. **270** NHPA/Ralph & Daphne Keller/ANT. **271** Imperial Press/M Iwago. **272** Artist *Malcolm McGregor*, *TL* PEP/Jim Brandenburg, *TR* NHPA/L Campbell, *CR* Naturfotograferna N/Janos Jurka. **273** *TR* BCL/Charlie Ott, *BC* Photo Researchers Inc/Alan Carey. **274** Marty Snyderman. **275** *TR* OSF/Peter Parks, *CL* Jacana/C Carre, *BL* Jacana/Jean-Marie Bassot. **276** *TL* Photo Researchers Inc/Michael Lustbader, *BR* Ardea/Pat Morris. **277** *TL* Ardea/Donald Burgess, *TR* Jacana/Chaumeton. **278** OSF/C & D Bromhall. **280** *TL* Ardea/B L Sage, *TC* AA/Raymond A Mendez, *CL* Biofotos/Heather Angel, *BR* BCL/Jane Burton. **281** *CR* BCL/M P Kahl, *BL* BCL/Jen & Des Bartlett. **282** Imperial Press/M Iwago. **283** Artist *Richard Bonson*, *TC* OSF/Michael Fogden, *TR & C* NHPA/Anthony Bannister, *BR* OSF/T C Middleton. **284-5 & 286** David & Anne Doubilet. **287** *TL* Edward S Ross, *TR* Ardea/John S Dunning, *CR* Premaphotos/K G Preston-Mafham. **288** *TL & BC* BCL/Gunter Ziesler. **289** Artist *Malcolm Porter*, *TR* Tom Stack & Assoc/Gerald & Buff Corsi, *BR* Paul Humann. **290** *TL* Marty Snyderman, *TR* BCL/William E Townsend. **291** Artist *Malcolm McGregor*, *TC* Bernd Wursig, *BR* AA/Tim Rock. **292** PEP/Anthony Joyce. **293** *TR* NHPA/Bill Wood, *CR* Tom Stack & Assoc/Tom Stack, *BR* OSF. **294** *TL* NHPA/Ashod Papazian, *TR & CR* Australasian Nature Transparencies/Mike Thomas. **295** *TR & BR* Dr Clive D T Minton.
Pictures in the chart on pages 296-355 are numbered from 1, from top to bottom on each page:
296 *1* BCL/George McCarthy, *2* BCL/Jen & Des Bartlett, *3* NHPA/Peter Johnson, *4* OSF/Ben Osborne. **297** *1* NHPA/Stephen J Krasemann, *2* OSF/A R Martin, *3* OSF/C M Perrins, *4* BCL/J Cancalosi, *5* BCL/David Houston. **298** *1* OSF/Sean Morris, *2* OSF/Ennio Boga, *3* BCL/Norman Myers, *4* NHPA/Nigel Dennis, *5* OSF/Kjell B Sandved. **299** *1* BCL/M P Kahl, *2* NHPA/Stephen Dalton, *3* NHPA/Philippa Scott, *4* BCL/Peter Davey, *5* BCL/Wayne Lankinen. **300** *1* BCL/Jane Burton, *2* OSF/Margot Conte, *3* OSF/Frank Schneidermeyer, *4* BCL/Leonard Lee Rue III, *5* BCL/Gunter Ziesler. **301** *1* OSF/Stan Osolinski, *2* BCL/WWF/Fred Mercay, *3* BCL/Steven Kaufman, *4* BCL/Leonard Lee Rue III, *5* OSF/Steve Earley. **302** *1* OSF/Mantis Wildlife Films, *2* Ardea/Andrea Florence, *3* BCL/Bill Wood, *4* BCL/Francisco Erize, *5* BCL/Jeff Foott. **303** *1* BCL/Hans Reinhard, *2* NHPA/M I Garwood, *3 & 4* BCL/Rod Williams, *5* BCL/C B & D W Frith. **304** *1* BCL/Halle Flygare, *2* NHPA/Jany Sauvanet, *3* OSF/Frank Huber, *4* BCL/A J Deane, *5* NP/Paul Sterry. **305** *1* BCL/Michael Freeman, *2* BCL/Gunter Ziesler, *3* NHPA/Manfred Danegger, *4* BCL/M P Kahl, *5* BCL/Jane Burton. **306** *1* OSF/William D Griffin, *2* NHPA/Bill Wood, *3* NHPA/Jeff Goodman, *4* Tom Stack & Assoc/Don & Esther Phillips, *5* NHPA/Haroldo Palo. **307** *1* NHPA/Kelvin Aitken/ANT, *2* BCL/B & C Calhoun, *3* BCL/Jeff Foott, *4* OSF/Doug Allan, *5* BCL/Wayne Lankinen. **308** *1* BCL/Bill Wood, *2* PEP/Keith Scholey, *3* NHPA/G J Cambridge, *4* BCL/John Markham, *5* BCL/Alain Compost. **309** *1* BCL/George McCarthy, *2* OSF/Alastair Shay, *3* NHPA/Dave Watts/ANT, *4* BCL/Allan Power, *5* OSF/James H Robertson. **310** *1* BCL/P Evans, *2* BCL/Gunter Ziesler, *3* NHPA/Stephen J Krasemann, *4* NHPA/Henry Ausloos, *5* NHPA/ANT. **311** *1* Australasian Nature Transparencies, *2* NHPA/Otto Rogge/ANT, *3* NHPA/Peter Johnson, *4* NHPA/E A Janes, *5* NHPA/I R McCann/Macdown Productions/ANT. **312** *1* NHPA/John Shaw, *2* NHPA/Roger Tidman, *3* DRK/Belinda Wright, *4* OSF/John Downer, *5* BCL/Leonard Lee Rue III. **313** *1* OSF/Mike Linley, *2* OSF/Kenneth Day, *3* BCL/John Cancalosi, *4* Merlin D Tuttle/Bat Conservation International, *5* NHPA/Stephen Dalton. **314** *1* BCL/N G Blake, *2 & 3* BCL/Frans Lanting, *4* BCL/Fritz Prenzel, *5* OSF/Richard Packwood. **315** *1* BCL/Neville Coleman, *2* NHPA/Martin Wendler, *3* NHPA/Stephen Krasemann, *4* OSF/P K La Val, *5* OSF/Andrew Plumptre. **316** *1* BCL/Konrad Wothe, *2* NHPA/Dave Watts/ANT, *3* OSF/Perry D Slocum, *4* NHPA/Kelvin Aitken/ANT, *5* BCL/Hans Reinhard. **317** *1* BCL/Gunter Ziesler, *2* BCL/Frans Lanting, *3* OSF/Richard Packwood, *4* BCL/Jill Sneesby, *5* OSF/Press-Tige Pictures. **318** *1* NHPA/S Robinson, *2* BCL/Jeff Foott, *3* BCL/Jeff Simon, *4* BCL/Jeff Foott, *5* NHPA/Laurie Campbell. **319** *1* Merlin D Tuttle/Bat Conservation International, *2* NHPA/Manfred Danegger, *3* BCL/Michael Fogden, *4* BCL, *5* OSF/G I Bernard. **320** *1* OSF/Mantis Wildlife Films, *2* BCL/G D Plage, *3* BCL/Francisco Erize, *4* BCL/H J Flugel, *5* OSF. **321** *1* BCL/Norman R Lightfoot, *2* BCL/M P L Fogden, *3* BCL/Mike Price, *4* OSF/Mark Hamblin, *5* BCL/Francisco Erize. **322** *1* NHPA/S Robinson, *2* OSF/Richard Packwood, *3* OSF/Michael Leach, *4* NHPA/Peter Pickford, *5* Rudolph Diesel. **323** *1* BCL/Orion Press, *2* BCL/Steven Kaufman, *3* OSF/Barry Walker, *4* BCL/Adrian Davies, *5* OSF/Kathie Atkinson. **324** *1* NHPA/E J Erwin, *2* NHPA/Henry Ausloos, *3* OSF/Kjell B Sandved, *4* BCL/John Markham, *5* OSF/Paul Taylor. **325** *1* BCL/Frances Furlong, *2* NHPA/C & S Pollitt/ANT, *3* BCL, *4* OSF/M A Chappell/AA, *5* BCL/Gunter Ziesler. **326** *1* BCL/Dennis Green, *2* BCL/Kim Taylor, *3* BCL/Frans Lanting, *4* BCL/Gordon Langsbury, *5* OSF/Miriam Austerman. **327** *1* NHPA/Andrew Dennis/ANT, *2* NHPA/Anthony Bannister, *3* OSF/Doug Allan, *4* OSF/Richard Packwood, *5* BCL/Wayne Lankinen. **328** *1* OSF/Tom Ulrich, *2* NHPA/Haroldo Palo, *3* BCL/Francisco Erize, *4* OSF/Barry Walker, *5* OSF/Babs & Bert Wells. **329** *1* NHPA/Henry Ausloos, *2* NHPA/Karl Switak, *3* OSF/W Pfunder, *4* BCL/Kim Taylor, *5* OSF/T C Middleton. **330** *1* NHPA/Stephen Dalton, *2* BCL/Jane Burton, *3* OSF/J A L Cooke, *4* BCL/Roger Wilmshurst, *5* BCL/Jeff Foott. **331** *1* BCL/Dieter & Mary Plage, *2* BCL/Erwin & Peggy Bauer, *3* OSF/Scott Camazine, *4* NHPA/Nigel Dennis, *5* OSF/Michael Fogden. **332** *1* Flip Nicklin, *2* OSF/Joe Dorsey, *3* OSF/Carol Farneti/Partridge Films Ltd, *4* PEP/Doug Perrine, *5* NHPA/Dave Watts/ANT. **333** *1* BCL/R I M Campbell, *2 & 3* BCL/Gordon Langsbury, *4* NHPA/Laurie Campbell, *5* NHPA/J Blossom. **334** *1* BCL/Steven C Kaufman, *2* OSF/Steve Littlewood, *3* BCL/Francisco Erize, *4* PEP/James D Watt, *5* OSF/Michael Leach. **335** *1* BCL/John Anthony, *2* BCL/Frank Greenaway, *3* BCL/H Rivarola, *4* Andrea Florence, *5* PEP/R Arnold. **336** *1* NHPA/S Krasemann, *2* Ardea/Ron & Valerie Taylor, *3* OSF/Laurence Gould, *4* NHPA/John Shaw, *5* OSF/David Wright. **337** *1* OSF/Richard Packwood, *2* OSF/Patti Murray, *3* BCL/M P L Fogden, *4* NHPA/Dave Watts/ANT, *5* BCL/R Carr. **338** *1* BCL/Roger Wilmshurst, *2* NHPA/John Hicks/ANT, *3* BCL/Gordon Langsbury, *4* OSF/John Downer, *5* BCL/Gerald Cubitt. **339** *1* NHPA/Laurie Campbell, *2* BCL/Peter Davey, *3* BCL/Rod Williams, *4* OSF/Patti Murray, *5* BCL/R I M Campbell. **340** *1* OSF/Terry Heathcote, *2* NHPA/E A Janes, *3* BCL/Halle Flygare, *4* BCL/Hans Reinhard, *5* BCL/Leonard Lee Rue III. **341** *1* Doug Perrine, *2* DRK/D Cavagnaro, *3* BCL/M Roggo, *4* BCL/Steven Kaufman, *5* BCL/Gerald Cubitt. **342** *1* BCL/N Tomalin, *2* OSF/Babs & Bert Wells, *3* BCL/Jack Stein Grove, *4* OSF/Peter Parks, 5 BCL/Jane Burton. **343** *1* NHPA/Stephen Krasemann, *2* NHPA/Anthony Bannister, *3* Auscape/Jean-Paul Ferrero, *4* BCL/Jane Burton, *5* OSF/Mark Pidgeon. **344** *1* OSF/Deni Bown, *2* OSF/Ben Osborne, *3* OSF/Stan Osolinski, *4* OSF/Bob Fredrick, *5* BCL/Jane Burton. **345** *1* BCL/Rod Williams, *2* OSF/Harry Engels, *3* BCL/Andy Purcell, *4* BCL/M P Kahl, *5* OSF/Doug Allan. **346** *1* OSF/Doug Allan, *2* OSF/Larry Crowhurst, *3* OSF/Godfrey Merlen, *4* Bernd Wursig, *5* OSF/Laurence Gould. **347** *1* NHPA/Nigel Dennis, *2* BCL/Jeff Foott, *3* OSF/Sinclair Stammers, *4* Mark Brazil, *5* OSF/Tom Ulrich. **348** *1* PEP/Doug Perrine, *2* BCL/N G Blake, *3* BCL, *4* BCL/Dennis Green, *5* OSF/Margot Conte. **349** *1* OSF/Derek Bromhall, *2* NHPA/Ken Griffiths, *3* BCL/J Cancalosi, *4* BCL/Jane Burton, *5* BCL/Frans Lanting. **350** *1* Ardea, *2* NHPA/E Hanumantha Rao, *3* OSF/M P L Fogden, *4* Doug Perrine, *5* BCL/C B & D W Frith. **351** *1* BCL/Roger Wilmshurst, *2* BCL/Bob & Clara Calhoun, *3* BCL/L C Marigo, *4* BCL/Andy Purcell, *5* OSF/P & W Ward. **352** *1* PEP/John Downer, *2* OSF/Sally Birch, *3* BCL/Francisco Erize, *4* BCL/Kim Taylor, *5* NHPA/Haroldo Palo. **353** *1* BCL/M P Kahl, *2* OSF/Pam & Willy Kemp, *3* BCL/Uwe Walz GDT, *4* BCL/Bill Wood, *5* BCL/Uwe Walz GDT. **354** *1* BCL/Hans Reinhard, *2* NHPA/Peter Pickford, *3* BCL/Barrie Wilkins, *4* BCL/John Shaw, *5* NHPA/Stephen Krasemann. **355** *1* BCL/Erwin & Peggy Bauer, *2* OSF/John Cooke, *3* BCL/John Cancalosi, *4* BCL/Dieter & Mary Plage, *5* NHPA.

40-269/2